# CONTENTS

# SCHAUM'S SOLVED PROBLEMS SERIES

## 2000 SOLVED PROBLEMS IN

# DISCRETE MATHEMATICS

by

**Seymour Lipschutz, Ph.D.**
Temple University

**Marc Lars Lipson, Ph.D.**
University of Georgia

## McGRAW-HILL

New York   San Francisco   Washington, D.C.   Auckland   Bogotá   Caracus   Lisbon
London   Madrid   Mexico City   Milan   Montreal   New Dehli
San Juan   Singapore   Sydney   Tokyo   Toronto

Seymour Lipschutz, Ph.D., *Professor of Mathematics at Temple University.*
Dr. Seymour Lipschutz, who is presently on the mathematics faculty of
Temple University, formerly taught at the Polytechnic Institute of Brooklyn
and was a visiting professor in the Computer Science Department of Brooklyn
College. He received his Ph.D. in 1960 at the Courant Institute of
Mathematical Sciences of New York University. Some of his other books in
the Schaum's Outline Series are *Discrete Mathematics,* and *Probability,* and
*Linear Algebra, 2/ed.*

Marc Lars Lipson, Ph. D.
Marc Lars Lipson is on the faculty of University of Georgia and formerly taught
at Northeastern University and Boston University. He received his Ph.D. in
finance in 1994 from the University of Michigan. He is also the coauthor of
*Schaum's Discrete Mathematics* (2nd edition) with Seymour Lipschutz.

2000 SOLVED PROBLEMS IN DISCRETE MATHEMATICS

**Library of Congress Cataloging-in-Publication Data**

Lipschutz, Seymour.
  2000 solved problems in discrete mathematics / by Seymour Lipschutz,
  Marc Lipson.
      p.     cm.—(Schaum's solved problems series)
  Includes index.
  ISBN 0-07-038031-7
    1. Mathematics—Problems, exercises, etc.   I. Lipson, Marc.
II. Title.   III. Title: Two thousand solved problems in discrete
mathematics.   IV. Series.
QA43.L66   1992
510'.76—dc20                                                      91-14108
                                                                      CIP

10 11 12 13 CUS/CUS 0 9 8 7 6

ISBN 0-07-038031-7

Sponsoring Editor: David Beckwith
Production Supervisor: Leroy Young
Editing Supervisors: Meg Tobin, Maureen Walker

# To The Student

This collection of thousands of solved problems covers almost every type of problem which may appear in any course in discrete mathematics. Moreover, our collection includes both computational problems and theoretical problems (which involve proofs).

Each section begins with very elementary problems and their difficulty usually increases as the section progresses. Furthermore, the theoretical problems involving proofs normally appear after the computational problems, which can thus preview the theory. (Most students have more difficulty with proofs.)

Normally, students will be assigned a textbook for their discrete mathematics course. The sequence of our chapters follows the customary order found in most textbooks (although there may be some discrepancies). However, whenever possible, our chapters and sections have been written so that their order can be changed without difficulty and without loss of continuity.

The solution to each problem immediately follows the statement of the problem. However, you may wish to try to solve the problem yourself before reading the given solution. In fact, even after reading the solution, you should try to resolve the problem without consulting the text. Used thus, *2000 Solved Problems in Discrete Mathematics* can serve as a supplement to any course in discrete mathematics, or even as an independent refresher course.

In this chapter capital letters $A, B, C, \ldots$ denote *sets* and lowercase letters $a, b, c, p, \ldots$ denote the *elements* or *members* in the sets. We also use the set notation:

$$p \in A \qquad p \text{ is an element of } A \text{ or } p \text{ belongs to } A;$$

$$A \subseteq B \text{ or } B \supseteq A \qquad A \text{ is a subset of } B \text{ or } B \text{ contains } A;$$

$$A \subset B \text{ or } B \supset A \qquad A \text{ is a proper subset of } B;$$

$$\varnothing \qquad \text{the empty set;}$$

$$\mathbf{U} \qquad \text{the universal set;}$$

Special symbols will also be used for the following sets:

$\mathbf{N}$ = the set of positive integers: $1, 2, 3, \ldots$      $\mathbf{Q}$ = the set of rational numbers

$\mathbf{Z}$ = the set of integers: $\ldots, -2, -1, 0, 1, 2, \ldots$      $\mathbf{R}$ = the set of real numbers

## 1.1 SETS, ELEMENTS, EQUALITY OF SETS

**1.1** Rewrite the following statements using set notation:
(*a*) The element 1 is not a member of $A$.
(*b*) The element 5 is a member of $B$.
(*c*) $A$ is a subset of $C$.
(*d*) $A$ is not a subset of $D$.
(*e*) $F$ contains all the elements of $G$.
(*f*) $E$ and $F$ contain the same elements.

▌ Use the above set notation and a slash through a symbol to denote negation of that symbol: (*a*) $1 \notin A$, (*b*) $5 \in B$, (*c*) $A \subseteq C$, (*d*) $A \nsubseteq D$, (*e*) $G \subseteq F$ or, equivalently, $F \supseteq G$, (*f*) $E = F$.

**1.2** Describe, with examples, the two basic ways to specify a particular set.

▌ One way, if it is possible, is to list its members. For example,

$$A = \{a, e, i, o, u\}$$

denotes the set $A$ whose elements are the letters $a, e, i, o, u$. Note that the elements are separated by commas and enclosed in braces $\{\ \}$. The second way is to state those properties which characterize the elements in the set. For example,

$$B = \{x : x \text{ is an integer}, x > 0\}$$

which reads "$B$ is the set of $x$ such that $x$ is an integer and $x$ is greater than 0", denotes the set $B$ whose elements are the positive integers. A letter, usually $x$, is used to denote a typical member of the set; the colon is read as "such that" and the comma as "and".

**1.3** State (*a*) the Principle of Extension (which formally states that a set is completely determined by its members), and (*b*) the Principle of Abstraction (which formally states that a set can be described in terms of a property).

▌ (*a*) **Principle of Extension:** Two sets $A$ and $B$ are equal if and only if they have the same members.
   (*b*) **Principle of Abstraction:** Given any set $U$ and any property $P$, there is a set $A$ such that the elements of $A$ are exactly those members of $U$ which have the property $P$.

**1.4** List the elements of the following sets; here $\mathbf{N} = \{1, 2, 3, \ldots\}$.
(*a*) $A = \{x : x \in \mathbf{N}, 3 < x < 12\}$
(*b*) $B = \{x : x \in \mathbf{N}, x \text{ is even}, x < 15\}$
(*c*) $C = \{x : x \in \mathbf{N}, 4 + x = 3\}$.

**▮** (*a*)   *A* consists of the positive integers between 3 and 12; hence

$$A = \{4, 5, 6, 7, 8, 9, 10, 11\}$$

(*b*)   *B* consists of the even positive integers less than 15; hence

$$B = \{2, 4, 6, 8, 10, 12, 14\}$$

(*c*)   No positive integer satisfies the condition $4 + x = 3$; hence *C* contains no elements. In other words, $C = \varnothing$, the empty set.

**1.5**    List the elements of the following sets:
(*a*)   $A = \{x: x \in \mathbf{N}, 3 < x < 9\}$
(*b*)   $B = \{x: x \in \mathbf{N}, x^2 + 1 = 10\}$
(*c*)   $C = \{x: x \in \mathbf{N}, x \text{ is odd}, -5 < x < 5\}$

**▮** (*a*)   *A* consists of all positive integers between 3 and 9; hence $A = \{4, 5, 6, 7, 8\}$.
(*b*)   *B* contains all positive integers satisfying the equation $x^2 + 1 = 10$; hence $B = \{3\}$.
(*c*)   *C* contains the positive odd integers between $-5$ and 5; hence $C = \{1, 3\}$.

**1.6**    List the elements of the following sets; here $\mathbf{Z} = \{\text{integers}\}$.
(*a*)   $A = \{x: x \in \mathbf{Z}, 3 < x < 9\}$
(*b*)   $B = \{x: x \in \mathbf{Z}, x^2 + 1 = 10\}$
(*c*)   $C = \{x: x \in \mathbf{Z}, x \text{ is odd}, -5 < x < 5\}$
(Compare with Problem 1.5.)

**▮** (*a*)   *A* consists of all integers between 3 and 9; hence $A = \{4, 5, 6, 7, 8\}$.
(*b*)   *B* contains all integers satisfying $x^2 + 1 = 10$; hence $B = \{-3, 3\}$.
(*c*)   *C* contains the odd integers between $-5$ and 5; hence $C = \{-3, -1, 1, 3\}$.

**1.7**    List the elements of the following sets:
(*a*)   $\{x: x \text{ is a vowel}, x \text{ is not ``}a\text{'' or ``}i\text{''}\}$
(*b*)   $\{x: x \text{ names a U.S. state}, x \text{ begins with the letter } A\}$

**▮** (*a*)   Omit "*a*" and "*i*" from the vowels *a, e, i, o, u* to obtain $\{e, o, u\}$.
(*b*)   There are exactly four such names: {Alabama, Alaska, Arizona, Arkansas}

**1.8**    Specify the following sets by listing their elements:
(*a*)   $A = \{x: x \in \mathbf{R}, -5 < x < 5\}$.
(*b*)   $B = \{x: x \in \mathbf{N}, x \text{ is a multiple of 3}\}$.
(*c*)   $C = \{x: x \text{ is a U.S. citizen}, x \text{ is a teenager}\}$.

**▮** (*a*)   Since *A* is infinite, we cannot list its elements; hence we refer to *A* by its properties as given.
(*b*)   Since *B* is infinite, we cannot actually list its elements although we frequently specify the set by writing

$$B = \{3, 6, 9, \ldots\}$$

where each element is 3 greater than the preceding element.
(*c*)   Although *C* is a finite set at any given time, it would be almost impossible to list its elements; hence we refer to the set *C* by its properties as given.

## Equality of Sets

**1.9**    Let $A = \{x: 3x = 6\}$. Does $A = 2$?

**▮** *A* is the set which consists of the single element 2, that is, $A = \{2\}$. The number 2 belongs to *A*; it does not equal *A*. There is a basic difference between an element *p* and the singleton set $\{p\}$.

**1.10**    Which of these sets are equal: $\{r, s, t\}$, $\{t, s, r\}$, $\{s, r, t\}$, $\{t, r, s\}$?

**▮** They are all equal. Order does not change a set.

**1.11**    Consider the following sets:

$$\{w\}, \{y, w, z\}, \{w, y, x\}, \{y, z, w\}, \{w, x, y, z\}, \{z, w\}$$

Which of them are equal to $A = \{w, y, z\}$?

▌ The sets $\{y, w, z\}$ and $\{y, z, w\}$ are identical to $A$; That is, they have the same three elements. The other sets are not equal to $A$ since they do not contain all the elements of $A$ or contain other elements.

**1.12**   Consider the sets:

$$\{4, 2\}, \qquad \{x: x^2 - 6x + 8 = 0\}, \qquad \{x: x \in \mathbf{N}, x \text{ is even}, 1 < x < 5\}$$

Which of them are equal to $B = \{2, 4\}$?

▌ All the sets are equal to $B$ since they all contain the elements 2 and 4 and no other elements.

### Empty Set Ø and Universal Set U

**1.13**   Determine which of the following sets are equal: Ø, $\{0\}$, $\{\text{Ø}\}$.

▌ Each is different from the other. The set $\{0\}$ contains one element, the number zero. The set Ø contains no elements; it is the empty set. The set $\{\text{Ø}\}$ also contains one element, the null set. (This third set is a set of sets.)

Problems 1.14–1.16 refer to the following sets:

$$X = \{x: x^2 = 9, 2x = 4\}, \qquad Y = \{x: x \neq x\}, \qquad Z = \{x: x + 8 = 8\}$$

**1.14**   Is $X$ the empty set?

▌ There is a no number which satisfies both $x^2 = 9$ and $2x = 4$; hence $X$ is empty, i.e., $X = \text{Ø}$.

**1.15**   Is $Y$ the empty set?

▌ We interpret "$=$" to mean "is identical with" and so $Y$ is also empty. In fact, some texts define the empty set as follows: $\text{Ø} \equiv \{x: x \neq x\}$.

**1.16**   Is $Z$ the empty set?

▌ The number zero satisfies $x + 8 = 8$; hence $Z = \{0\}$. Accordingly, $Z$ is not the empty set since it contains 0. That is, $Z \neq \text{Ø}$.

**1.17**   Consider the words (i) empty, (ii) void, (iii) zero, (iv) null. Which word is different from the others, and why?

▌ The first, second and fourth words refer to the set which contains no elements. The word zero refers to a specific number. Hence zero is different.

**1.18**   Define, with examples, the universal set **U**.

▌ In any application of the theory of sets, the members of all sets under investigation usually belong to some fixed large set called the *universal set* or *universe of discourse*. For example, in plane geometry, the universal set consists of all the points in the plane; and in human population studies the universal set consists of all the people in the world.

**1.19**   Given that $\mathbf{U} = \mathbf{N} = \{\text{positive integers}\}$, identify which of the following sets are identical to $\{2, 4\}$:

$$A = \{\text{even numbers less than 6}\}, \qquad B = \{x: x < 5\}, \qquad C = \{x: (x - 2)(x - 4)(x + 2) = 0\}$$

▌ Sets $A$ and $C$ are identical to $\{2, 4\}$. Set $A$ does not include negative even numbers or zero since they are not in the universe. Set $B$ includes both 1 and 3 which are not in the specified set. Set $C$ does not include $-2$ since it is not a positive integer.

**1.20**   Describe a situation where the universal set **U** may be empty.

▌ Suppose **U** is the set of music majors at a given college. It is conceivable that in a given year there are no such majors and hence $\mathbf{U} = \text{Ø}$.

## 1.2  SUBSETS

**1.21**   Explain the difference between $A \subseteq B$ and $A \subset B$.

▌ The statement $A \subseteq B$ (that $A$ is a *subset* of $B$) says that every element of $A$ also belongs to $B$, which includes the possibility that $A = B$. The statement $A \subset B$ (that $A$ is a *proper subset* of $B$) says that $A$ is a subset of $B$ but $A \neq B$; hence there is at least one element in $B$ which is not in $A$.

**1.22** Describe in words how you would prove each of the following:
(*a*) $A$ is equal to $B$.
(*b*) $A$ is a subset of $B$.
(*c*) $A$ is a proper subset of $B$.
(*d*) $A$ is not a subset of $B$.

▮ (*a*) Show that each element of $A$ belongs also to $B$ and each element of $B$ belongs also to $A$.
(*b*) Show that each element of $A$ belongs also to $B$.
(*c*) Show that each element of $A$ belongs also to $B$ and at least one element of $B$ is not in $A$. Note that it is not necessary to show that more than one element is not in $A$.
(*d*) Show that one element of $A$ is not in $B$.

**1.23** Show that $A = \{2, 3, 4, 5\}$ is not a subset of $B = \{x : x \in \mathbf{N}, x \text{ is even}\}$.

▮ It is necessary to show that at least one element in $A$ does not belong to $B$. Now $3 \in A$ and, since $B$ consists of even numbers, $3 \notin B$; hence $A$ is not a subset of $B$.

**1.24** Show that $A = \{2, 3, 4, 5\}$ is a proper subset of $C = \{1, 2, 3, \ldots, 8, 9\}$.

▮ Each element of $A$ belongs to $C$ so $A \subseteq C$. On the other hand, $1 \in C$ but $1 \notin A$. Hence $A \neq C$. Therefore $A$ is a proper subset of $C$.

**Theorem 1.1:** (i) For any set $A$, we have $\emptyset \subseteq A \subseteq \mathbf{U}$.　(iii) If $A \subseteq B$ and $B \subseteq C$, than $A \subseteq C$.
(ii) For any set $A$, we have $A \subseteq A$.　(iv) $A = B$ if and only if $A \subseteq B$ and $B \subseteq A$.

**1.25** Prove Theorem 1.1(i).

▮ Every set $A$ is a subset of the universal set $\mathbf{U}$ since, by definition, all the members of $A$ belong to $\mathbf{U}$. Also the empty set $\emptyset$ is a subset of $A$.

**1.26** Prove Theorem 1.1(ii).

▮ Every set $A$ is a subset of itself since, trivially, the elements of $A$ belong to $A$.

**1.27** Prove Theorem 1.1(iii).

▮ If every element of a set $A$ belongs to a set $B$, and every element of $B$ belongs to a set $C$, then clearly every element of $A$ belongs to $C$. In other words, if $A \subseteq B$ and $B \subseteq C$, then $A \subseteq C$.

**1.28** Prove Theorem 1.1(iv).

▮ If $A \subseteq B$ and $B \subseteq A$ then $A$ and $B$ have the same elements, i.e., $A = B$. Conversely, if $A = B$ then $A \subseteq B$ and $B \subseteq A$ since every set is a subset of itself.

**1.29** Show that $A = \{a, b, c\}$ is *not* a subset of $B = \{a, e, i, o, u\}$.

▮ It is necessary to show that at least one element of $A$ is not in $B$. Now $b \in A$ but $b \notin B$, hence $A$ is not a subset of $B$. Alternately, $c \in A$ but $c \notin B$; hence $A \not\subseteq B$. (It is not necessary to show that *both* $b$ and $c$ do not belong to $B$.)

**1.30** Consider the following sets:

$$A = \{a\}, \quad B = \{a, c, b\}, \quad C = \{c, a\}, \quad D = \{c, b, a\}, \quad E = \{b\}, \quad \emptyset$$

Which of them are subsets of $X = \{a, b, c\}$? Which are proper subsets of $X$?

▮ All the sets are subsets of $X$ since the elements of every set belong to $X$ (including the empty set $\emptyset$ which has no elements). In particular, $A$, $C$, $E$ and $\emptyset$ are proper subsets of $X$ since they are not equal to $X$.

**1.31**    Consider the following sets:

$$X = \{x : x \text{ is an integer, } x > 1\}$$
$$Y = \{y : y \text{ is a positive integer divisible by 2}\}$$
$$Z = \{z : z \text{ is an even number greater than 10}\}$$

Which of them are subsets of $W = \{2, 4, 6, \ldots\}$?

▌ Only $Y$ and $Z$ are subsets of $W$ since their elements belong to $W$. (In fact, $Y = W$.) $X$ is not a subset of $W$ since there are elements in $X$ which do not belong to $W$, e.g., $3 \in X$ but $3 \notin W$.

**1.32**    Let $A = \{x, y, z\}$. How many subsets does $A$ contain, and what are they?

▌ We list all the possible subsets of $A$. They are: $\{x, y, z\}$, $\{y, z\}$, $\{x, z\}$, $\{x, y\}$, $\{x\}$, $\{y\}$, $\{z\}$, and the null set $\emptyset$. There are eight subsets of $A$.

Problems 1.33–1.36 refer to the following sets:

$$\emptyset, \quad A = \{1\}, \quad B = \{1, 3\}, \quad C = \{1, 5, 9\}, \quad D = \{1, 2, 3, 4, 5\}, \quad E = \{1, 3, 5, 7, 9\}, \quad \mathbf{U} = \{1, 2, \ldots, 8, 9\}$$

**1.33**    Insert the correct symbol $\subseteq$ or $\nsubseteq$ between: (*a*) $\emptyset$, $A$; (*b*) $A$, $B$.

▌ (*a*)   $\emptyset \subseteq A$ because $\emptyset$ is a subset of every set.
(*b*)   $A \subseteq B$ because 1 is the only element of $A$ and it also belongs to $B$.

**1.34**    Insert the correct symbol $\subseteq$ or $\nsubseteq$ between: (*a*) $B$, $C$; (*b*) $B$, $E$.

▌ (*a*)   $B \nsubseteq C$ because $3 \in B$ but $3 \notin C$.
(*b*)   $B \subseteq E$ because the elements of $B$ also belong to $E$.

**1.35**    Insert the correct symbol $\subseteq$ or $\nsubseteq$ between: (*a*) $C$, $D$; (*b*) $C$, $E$.

▌ (*a*)   $C \nsubseteq D$ because $9 \in C$ but $9 \notin D$.
(*b*)   $C \subseteq E$ because the elements of $C$ also belong to $E$.

**1.36**    Insert the correct symbol $\subseteq$ or $\nsubseteq$ between: (*a*) $D$, $E$; (*b*) $D$, $\mathbf{U}$.

▌ (*a*)   $D \nsubseteq E$ because $2 \in D$ but $2 \notin E$.
(*b*)   $D \subseteq \mathbf{U}$ because the elements of $D$ also belong to $\mathbf{U}$.

Problems 1.37–1.40 refer to the following sets:

$$A = \{x, z\}, \quad B = \{y, z\}, \quad C = \{w, x, y, z\}, \quad D = \{v, w, z\}, \quad E = \{z, y\}$$

**1.37**    Insert the correct symbol $\subset$ or $\not\subset$ between: (*a*) $A$, $C$; (*b*) $A$, $D$.

▌ (*a*)   $A \subset C$ since $A$ is a subset of $C$ but $A \neq C$.
(*b*)   $A \not\subset D$ since $x \in A$ and $x \notin D$; that is, $A$ is not even a subset of $D$.

**1.38**    Insert the correct symbol $\subset$ or $\not\subset$ between: (*a*) $B$, $C$; (*b*) $B$, $E$.

▌ (*a*)   $B \subset C$ since $B$ is a subset of $C$ but $B \neq C$.
(*b*)   $B \not\subset E$. Although $B$ is a subset of $E$, we also have $B = E$.

**1.39**    Find the smallest set $X$ containing all the sets as subsets.

▌ Let $X$ consist of all the elements in the sets (excluding repetitions); hence, $X = \{v, w, x, y, z\}$.

**1.40**    Find the largest set $Y$ contained in all the sets.

▌ Let $Y$ consist of those elements common to all the sets; hence $Y = \{z\}$.

**1.41**    Let $X = \{1, 2, 3\}$, $Y = \{2, 3, 4\}$, and $Z = \{2\}$. Find the largest set $W$ that makes all the following statements true: $W \nsubseteq X$, $W \subseteq Y$, $Z \nsubseteq W$.

▌ Since $W \subseteq Y$, only 2, 3 and 4 can belong to $W$. Since $Z \nsubseteq W$, the element 2 does not belong to $W$. Thus

$W = \{3, 4\}$ satisfies the required conditions. The set $\{4\}$ also satisfies the required conditions but it is not the largest set.

**1.42**   Identify the smallest set $X$ containing the sets:

$$\{\text{dog, cat}\}, \{\text{fish, cat, ferret}\}, \{\text{dog, ferret}\}$$

▌ Let $X$ consist of all the elements in the sets:

$$X = \{\text{dog, cat, fish, ferret}\}$$

**1.43**   Let $X = \{1, 2, 3\}$ and $Z = \{1, 2, 3, 4, 5\}$. Find all possible sets $Y$ such that $X \subset Y$ and $Y \subset Z$, i.e., $X$ is a proper subset of $Y$ and $Y$ is a proper subset of $Z$.

▌ $Y$ must consist of the elements 1, 2, 3 in $X$ and at least one other element of $Z$, 4 or 5. Thus $Y = \{1, 2, 3, 4\}$ or $Y = \{1, 2, 3, 5\}$. Note $Y$ cannot contain both 4 and 5 since $Y$ must be a proper subset of $Z$.

**1.44**   Let $A$, $B$, $C$ be nonempty sets such that $A \subseteq B$, $B \subseteq C$ and $C \subseteq A$. What can be deduced about these sets?

▌ Since $B \subseteq C$ and $C \subseteq A$, we have $B \subseteq A$. This with $A \subseteq B$ yields $A = B$. Similarly, $B = C$. Thus all three sets are equal.

Problems 1.45–1.50 refer to an unknown set $X$ and the following five sets:

$$A = \{1, 2, 3, 4\}, \qquad B = \{2, 3, 4, 5, 6, 7\}, \qquad C = \{3, 4\}, \qquad D = \{4, 5, 6\}, \qquad E = \{3\}$$

**1.45**   Which of the five sets can equal $X$ if $X \subseteq A$ and $X \subseteq B$?

▌ $X$ can equal $C$ or $E$. Note that $B$ and $D$ are not subsets of $A$, and $A$ is not a subset of $B$.

**1.46**   Which of the five sets can equal $X$ if $X \nsubseteq D$ and $X \subseteq C$?

▌ $X$ can equal $C$ or $E$. Note that $A$, $B$, and $D$ are not subsets of $C$ and that $C$ is a subset of itself.

**1.47**   Which of the five sets can equal $X$ if $X \nsubseteq D$ and $X \nsubseteq B$?

▌ $X$ can equal $A$. Note that $B$, $C$, $D$, and $E$ are subsets of $B$.

**1.48**   Which of the five sets can equal $X$ if $X \nsubseteq E$ and $X \subseteq B$?

▌ $X$ can equal $B$, $C$ or $D$. $A$ is not a subset of $B$, and $E$ is a subset of itself.

**1.49**   Find the smallest set $M$ which contains all five sets.

▌ $M$ consists of all elements in any of the sets; hence $M = \{1, 2, 3, 4, 5, 6, 7\}$.

**1.50**   Find the largest set $N$ which is a subset of all five sets.

▌ $N$ consists of those elements common to all five sets. No such elements exist; hence $N = \varnothing$, the empty set.

**1.51**   Does every set have a proper subset?

▌ The null set $\varnothing$ does not have a proper subset. Every other set does have $\varnothing$ as a proper subset. Some books do not call the null set a proper subset; in such case, sets which contain only one element would not contain a proper subset.

**1.52**   Prove: If $A$ is a subset of the null set $\varnothing$, then $A = \varnothing$.

▌ The null set $\varnothing$ is a subset of every set; in particular $\varnothing \subseteq A$. By hypothesis, $A \subseteq \varnothing$. The two conditions imply $A = \varnothing$.

**1.53**   Suppose $A \subseteq B$ and $B \subseteq C$ and suppose $a \in A$, $b \in B$, $c \in C$. Which statements must be true? (1) $a \in C$, (2) $b \in A$, (3) $c \notin A$.

▌ (1)   By Theorem 1.1, $A$ is a subset of $C$. Then $a \in A$ implies $a \in C$, and the statement is always true.
  (2)   Since the element $b \in B$ need not be an element in $A$, the statement can be false.
  (3)   The element $c \in C$ could be an element in $A$; hence $c \notin A$ need not be true.

**1.54**   Suppose $A \subseteq B$ and $B \subseteq C$ and suppose $d \notin A$, $e \notin B$, $f \notin C$. Which statements must be true? (1) $d \in B$, (2) $e \notin A$, (3) $f \notin A$.

    ▮   (1)   The element $d$, which is not in $A$, need not be in $B$; hence the statement might not be true.
        (2)   Since $e \notin B$ and $A \subseteq B$, $e \notin A$ is always true.
        (3)   Since $f \notin C$ and $A \subseteq C$, $f \notin A$ is always true.

### Comparable, Noncomparable and Disjoint Sets, Venn Diagrams

**1.55**   Define: (*a*) comparable and noncomparable sets, (*b*) disjoint sets.

    ▮   (*a*)   Sets $A$ and $B$ are comparable if $A \subseteq B$ or $B \subseteq A$; hence $A$ and $B$ are noncomparable if $A \nsubseteq B$ and $B \nsubseteq A$.
        (*b*)   Sets $A$ and $B$ are disjoint if they have no elements in common, i.e., if no element of $A$ belongs to $B$ and no element of $B$ belongs to $A$.

**1.56**   Consider the following sets:

$$A = \{1, 2\}, \qquad B = \{1, 2, 3, 4\}, \qquad C = \{1, 5\}, \qquad D = \{3, 4, 5\}, \qquad E = \{4, 5\}$$

Which of the above sets are comparable?

    ▮   $A$ and $B$ are comparable since $A \subseteq B$, and $D$ and $E$ are comparable since $E \subseteq D$. Any other pair of distinct sets are noncomparable.

**1.57**   Which of the sets in Problem 1.56 are disjoint?

    ▮   Sets $A$ and $D$ and sets $A$ and $E$ are disjoint. Any other pair of sets have one or more elements in common.

**1.58**   Describe those sets which are comparable to: (*a*) the empty set $\varnothing$, the universal set **U**.

    ▮   Every set $A$ is comparable to $\varnothing$ since $\varnothing \subseteq A$, and every set $A$ is comparable to **U** since $A \subseteq$ **U**.

**1.59**   Describe a Venn diagram of sets.

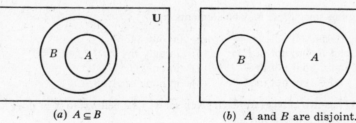

        (*a*)   $A \subseteq B$                 (*b*)   $A$ and $B$ are disjoint.             (*c*)

**Fig. 1-1**

    ▮   A Venn diagram is a pictorial representation of sets by sets of points in the plane. The universal set **U** is represented by the interior of a rectangle, and the other sets are represented by disks lying within the rectangle. If $A \subseteq B$, then the disk representing $A$ will be entirely within the disk representing $B$ as in Fig. 1-1(*a*). If $A$ and $B$ are disjoint, i.e., have no elements in common, then the disk representing $A$ will be separated from the disk representing $B$ as in Fig. 1-1(*b*).

        However, if $A$ and $B$ are two arbitrary sets, it is possible that some objects are in $A$ but not $B$, some are in $B$ but not $A$, some are in both $A$ and $B$, and some are in neither $A$ nor $B$; hence in general we represent $A$ and $B$ as in Fig. 1-1(*c*).

**1.60**   Draw a Venn diagram of sets $A$, $B$, $C$ where $A$ and $B$ have elements in common, $B$ and $C$ have elements in common, but $A$ and $C$ are disjoint.

    ▮   See Fig. 1-2(*a*).

**1.61**   Draw a Venn diagram of sets $A$, $B$, $C$ where $A \subseteq B$, sets $A$ and $C$ are disjoint, but $B$ and $C$ have elements in common.

    ▮   See Fig. 1-2(*b*).

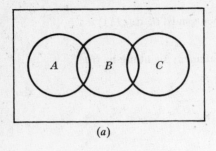 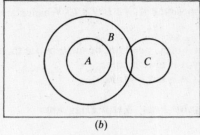 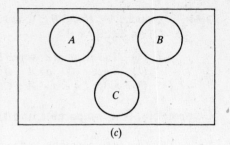

(a)         (b)         (c)

**Fig. 1-2**

**1.62** Draw a Venn diagram of sets $A$, $B$, $C$ where $A \subseteq B$, sets $B$ and $C$ are disjoint, but $A$ and $C$ have elements in common.

    ❚ No such Venn diagram exists. If $A$ and $C$ have an element in common, say $x$, and $A \subseteq B$; then $x$ must also belong to $B$. Thus $B$ and $C$ must also have an element in common.

**1.63** Draw a Venn diagram of sets $A$, $B$, $C$ where all three sets are disjoint from each other.

    ❚ See Fig. 1-2(c).

**1.64** Draw a Venn diagram of three arbitrary sets $A$, $B$, $C$ which will divide the universal set $\mathbf{U}$ into $2^3 = 8$ regions. Why are there eight regions?

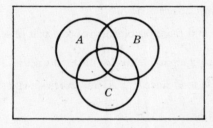

**Fig. 1-3**

    ❚ See Fig. 1-3. There are eight regions since there may be elements:

| | | |
|---|---|---|
| (1) in $A$, $B$, and $C$ | | (5) in only $A$ |
| (2) in $A$ and $B$, but not in $C$ | | (6) in only $B$ |
| (3) in $A$ and $C$, but not in $B$ | | (7) in only $C$ |
| (4) in $B$ and $C$, but not in $A$ | | (8) in none of $A$, $B$, $C$ |

In other words, each element $x$ of $\mathbf{U}$ has two choices for each given set $X$, i.e., belongs to $X$ or does not belong to $X$. Thus there are $2^3 = 8$ possibilities for three given sets.

**1.65** Consider a general Venn diagram of four sets $A_1$, $A_2$, $A_3$, $A_4$. Into how many regions will the universal set $\mathbf{U}$ be divided?

    ❚ The universal set $\mathbf{U}$ will be divided into $2^4 = 16$ regions.

## 1.3 SET OPERATIONS

**1.66** Define the set operations of: (a) union and (b) intersection.

    ❚ (a) The *union* of two sets $A$ and $B$, denoted by $A \cup B$, is the set of all elements which belong to $A$ or to $B$:

$$A \cup B = \{x : x \in A \text{ or } x \in B\}$$

    Here "or" is used in the sense of and/or.

    (b) The *intersection* of two sets $A$ and $B$, denoted by $A \cap B$, is the set of elements which belong to both $A$ and $B$:

$$A \cap B = \{x : x \in A \text{ and } x \in B\}$$

    (Note that $A \cap B = \varnothing$ means that $A$ and $B$ do not have any elements in common, i.e., that $A$ and $B$ are disjoint.)

**1.67** Using a Venn diagram of sets $A$ and $B$, shade the area representing: **(a)** $A \cup B$ and **(b)** $A \cap B$.

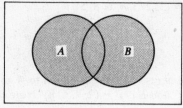

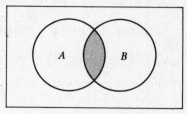

(a) $A \cup B$ is shaded.

(b) $A \cap B$ is shaded.

**Fig. 1-4**

┃ **(a)** See Fig. 1-4(a). **(b)** See Fig. 1-4(b).

**1.68** Define the set operations of: **(a)** absolute complement or, simply, complement of a set, **(b)** the relative complement or difference of two sets.

┃ **(a)** Recall that all sets under consideration at a particular time are subsets of a fixed universal set **U**. The *absolute complement* or, simply, *complement* of a set $A$, denoted by $A^c$, is the set of elements which belong to **U** but which do not belong to $A$:

$$A^c = \{x : x \in \mathbf{U}, x \notin A\}$$

Some texts denote the complement of $A$ by $A'$ or $\bar{A}$.

**(b)** The *relative complement* of a set $B$ with respect to a set $A$ or, simply, the *difference* of $A$ and $B$, denoted by $A \backslash B$, is the set of elements which belong to $A$ but which do not belong to $B$:

$$A \backslash B = \{x : x \in A, x \notin B\}$$

The set $A \backslash B$ is read "$A$ minus $B$". Many texts denote $A \backslash B$ by $A - B$ or $A \sim B$.

**1.69** Using Venn diagrams, shade the area representing: **(a)** $A^c$ and **(b)** $A \backslash B$.

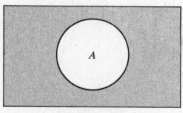

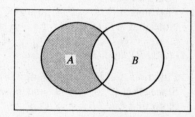

(a) $A^c$ is shaded.

(b) $A \backslash B$ is shaded.

**Fig. 1-5**

┃ **(a)** See Fig. 1-5(a). **(b)** See Fig. 1-5(b).

Problems 1.70–1.78 refer to the following sets:

$$\mathbf{U} = \{1, 2, 3, \ldots, 8, 9\}, \qquad A = \{1, 2, 3, 4\}, \qquad B = \{2, 4, 6, 8\}, \qquad C = \{3, 4, 5, 6\}$$

**1.70** Find **(a)** $A \cup B$, **(b)** $A \cup C$, **(c)** $B \cup C$, and **(d)** $B \cup B$.

┃ To form the union of $A$ and $B$ we put all the elements from $A$ together with all the elements from $B$. Accordingly,

$$A \cup B = \{1, 2, 3, 4, 6, 8\}$$

Similarly,

$$A \cup C = \{1, 2, 3, 4, 5, 6\}, \qquad B \cup C = \{2, 4, 6, 8, 3, 5\}, \qquad B \cup B = \{2, 4, 6, 8\}$$

Note that $B \cup B$ is precisely $B$.

**1.71** Find: **(a)** $(A \cup B) \cup C$ and **(b)** $A \cup (B \cup C)$.

┃ **(a)** We first find $(A \cup B) = \{1, 2, 3, 4, 6, 8\}$. Then the union of $(A \cup B)$ and $C$ is

$$(A \cup B) \cup C = \{1, 2, 3, 4, 6, 8, 5\}$$

(b)  We first find $(B \cup C) = \{2, 4, 6, 8, 3, 5\}$. Then the union of $A$ and $(B \cup C)$ is

$$A \cup (B \cup C) = \{1, 2, 3, 4, 6, 8, 5\}$$

Note that $(A \cup B) \cup C = A \cup (B \cup C)$.

**1.72**  Find: (a) $A \cap B$, (b) $A \cap C$, (c) $B \cap C$, and (d) $B \cap B$.

▌  To form the intersection of $A$ and $B$, we list all the elements which are common to $A$ and $B$; thus $A \cap B = \{2, 4\}$. Similarly, $A \cap C = \{3, 4\}$, $B \cap C = \{4, 6\}$, and $B \cap B = \{2, 4, 6, 8\}$. Note that $B \cap B$ is, in fact, $B$.

**1.73**  Find: (a) $(A \cap B) \cap C$, and (b) $A \cap (B \cap C)$.

▌  (a)  $A \cap B = \{2, 4\}$. Then the intersection of $\{2, 4\}$ with $C$ is $(A \cap B) \cap C = \{4\}$.
(b)  $B \cap C = \{4, 6\}$. The intersection of this set with $A$ is $\{4\}$, that is, $A \cap (B \cap C) = \{4\}$.
Note that $(A \cap B) \cap C = A \cap (B \cap C)$.

**1.74**  Find: (a) $A^c$, (b) $B^c$, and (c) $C^c$.

▌  $X^c$ consists of the elements in the universal set $\mathbf{U}$ which do not belong to $X$. Therefore,
(a) $A^c = \{5, 6, 7, 8, 9\}$, (b) $B^c = \{1, 3, 5, 7, 9\}$, (c) $C^c = \{1, 2, 7, 8, 9\}$.

**1.75**  Find: (a) $A\backslash B$, (b) $C\backslash A$, (c) $B\backslash C$, (d) $B\backslash A$, and (e) $B\backslash B$.

▌  (a)  The set $A\backslash B$ consists of the elements in $A$ which are not in $B$. Since $A = \{1, 2, 3, 4\}$ and $2, 4 \in B$, then $A\backslash B = \{1, 3\}$.
(b)  The only elements in $C$ which are not in $A$ are 5 and 6; hence $C\backslash A = \{5, 6\}$.
(c)  $B\backslash C = \{2, 8\}$    (d)  $B\backslash A = \{6, 8\}$    (e)  $B\backslash B = \varnothing$.

**1.76**  Find: (a) $A \cap (B \cup C)$ and (b) $(A \cap B) \cup (A \cap C)$.

▌  (a)  First find $B \cup C = \{2, 3, 4, 5, 6, 8\}$; then $A \cap (B \cup C) = \{2, 3, 4\}$.
(b)  First find $A \cap B = \{2, 4\}$ and $A \cap C = \{3, 4\}$; then $(A \cap B) \cup (A \cap C) = \{2, 3, 4\}$.
Note that $A \cap (B \cup C) = (A \cap B) \cup (A \cap C)$.

**1.77**  Find: (a) $(A \cup B)^c$ and (b) $A^c \cap B^c$.

▌  (a)  First find $A \cup B = \{1, 2, 3, 4, 6, 8\}$; then $(A \cup B)^c = \{5, 7, 9\}$.
(b)  Since $A^c = \{5, 6, 7, 8, 9\}$ and $B^c = \{1, 3, 5, 7, 9\}$, we have $A^c \cap B^c = \{5, 7, 9\}$.
Note that $(A \cup B)^c = A^c \cap B^c$.

**1.78**  Find: (a) $(A \cap B)\backslash C$ and (b) $(A\backslash B)^c$.

▌  (a)  $A \cap B = \{2, 4\}$. Note that $4 \in C$, but $2 \notin C$; hence $(A \cap B)\backslash C = \{2\}$.
(b)  $A\backslash B = \{1, 3\}$; hence $(A\backslash B)^c = \{2, 4, 5, 6, 7, 8, 9\}$.

**1.79**  Prove: $(A \cap B) \subseteq A \subseteq (A \cup B)$ and $(A \cap B) \subseteq B \subseteq (A \cup B)$.

▌  Since every element in $A \cap B$ is in both $A$ and $B$, it is certainly true that if $x \in (A \cap B)$ then $x \in A$; hence $(A \cap B) \subseteq A$. Furthermore, if $x \in A$, then $x \in (A \cup B)$ (by the definition of $A \cup B$), so $A \subseteq (A \cup B)$. Putting these together gives $(A \cap B) \subseteq A \subseteq (A \cup B)$. Similarly, $(A \cap B) \subseteq B \subseteq (A \cup B)$.

**Theorem 1.2:**  The following are equivalent: $A \subseteq B$, $A \cap B = A$, and $A \cup B = B$.

**1.80**  Prove Theorem 1.2.

▌  Suppose $A \subseteq B$ and let $x \in A$. Then $x \in B$, hence $x \in A \cap B$ and $A \subseteq A \cap B$. By Problem 1.79, $(A \cap B) \subseteq A$. Therefore $A \cap B = A$. On the other hand, suppose $A \cap B = A$ and let $x \in A$. Then $x \in (A \cap B)$, hence $x \in A$ and $x \in B$. Therefore, $A \subseteq B$. Both results show that $A \subseteq B$ is equivalent to $A \cap B = A$.

Suppose again that $A \subseteq B$. Let $x \in (A \cup B)$. Then $x \in A$ or $x \in B$. If $x \in A$, then $x \in B$ because $A \subseteq B$. In either case, $x \in B$. Therefore $A \cup B \subseteq B$. By Problem 1.79, $B \subseteq A \cup B$. Therefore $A \cup B = B$. Now suppose $A \cup B = B$ and let $x \in A$. Then $x \in A \cup B$ by definition of union of sets. Hence $x \in B = A \cup B$. Therefore $A \subseteq B$. Both results show that $A \subseteq B$ is equivalent to $A \cup B = B$.

Thus $A \subseteq B$, $A \cap B = A$ and $A \cup B = B$ are equivalent.

Problems 1.81–1.88 refer to the following sets:

$$A = \{M, W, F, S\}, \qquad B = \{S, SU\}, \qquad C = \{M, T, W, TH, F\}, \qquad D = \{W, TH, F, S\}$$

where $\mathbf{U} = \{M \text{ (Mon)}, T \text{ (Tues.)}, W \text{ (Wed.)}, TH \text{ (Thurs.)}, F \text{ (Fri.)}, S \text{ (Sat.)}, SU \text{ (Sun.)}\}$

**1.81** Describe in words the sets $B$ and $C$.

▌ Set $B$ consists of the weekend days, Sat. and Sun.; and set $C$ consists of the weekdays, Mon. through Fri.

**1.82** Identify the sets: (*a*) $A \cup B$, (*b*) $A \cup C$, (*c*) $B \cup C$, and (*d*) $B \cup D$.

▌ The union $X \cup Y$ consists of those elements in either $X$ or $Y$ (or both); hence
(*a*) $A \cup B = \{M, W, F, S, SU\}$     (*c*) $B \cup C = \{M, T, W, TH, F, S, SU\} = \mathbf{U}$
(*b*) $A \cup C = \{M, T, W, TH, F, S\}$     (*d*) $B \cup D = \{W, TH, F, S, SU\}$

**1.83** Identify the sets: (*a*) $A \cap B$, (*b*) $A \cap C$, (*c*) $B \cap C$, and (*d*) $B \cap D$.

▌ The intersection $X \cap Y$ consists of those elements in both $X$ and $Y$; hence

(*a*) $A \cap B = \{S\}$,     (*b*) $A \cap C = \{M, W, F\}$,     (*c*) $B \cap C = \emptyset$,     (*d*) $B \cap D = \{S\}$

**1.84** Find: (*a*) $A^c$, (*b*) $B^c$, (*c*) $C^c$, and (*d*) $D^c$.

▌ The complement $X^c$ consists of the elements in $\mathbf{U}$ but not in $X$. Thus
(*a*) $A^c = \{T, TH, SU\}$     (*c*) $C^c = \{S, SU\} = B$
(*b*) $B^c = \{M, T, W, TH, F\} = C$     (*d*) $D^c = \{M, T, SU\}$

**1.85** Identify the sets: (*a*) $\mathbf{U} \backslash A$, (*b*) $A \backslash C$, (*c*) $C \backslash B$, and (*d*) $D \backslash A$.

▌ The relative complement $X \backslash Y$ consists of those elements in $X$ which do not belong to $Y$. Thus
(*a*) $\mathbf{U} \backslash A = \{T, TH, SU\} = A^c$     (*c*) $C \backslash B = \{M, T, W, TH, F\} = C$
(*b*) $A \backslash C = \{S\}$     (*d*) $D \backslash A = \{TH\}$

**1.86** Find: (*a*) $(A \cup D)^c$ and (*b*) $(A \backslash B)^c$.

▌ (*a*) First find $A \cup D = \{M, W, TH, F, S\}$; then $(A \cup B)^c = \{T, SU\}$.
(*b*) Here $A \backslash B = \{M, W, F\}$; hence $(A \backslash B)^c = \{T, TH, S, SU\}$.

**1.87** Find: (*a*) $(A \cup B) \backslash D$ and (*b*) $(A \cap C) \backslash D$.

▌ (*a*) First find $A \cup B = \{M, W, F, S, SU\}$ and then omit the elements of $D$ to obtain $(A \cup B) \backslash D = \{M, SU\}$.
(*b*) First find $A \cap C = \{M, W, F\}$; then $(A \cap B) \backslash D = \{M\}$.

**1.88** Find: (*a*) $(A \backslash B) \cap D$ and (*b*) $(C \cap D) \backslash A$.

▌ (*a*) First find $A \backslash B = \{M, W, F\}$; then $(A \backslash B) \cap D = \{W, F\}$.
(*b*) First find $C \cap D = \{W, TH, F\}$, then $(C \cap D) \backslash A = \emptyset$.

**1.89** Show that we can have $A \cap B = A \cap C$ without $B = C$.

▌ Let $A = \{1, 2\}$, $B = \{2, 3\}$, and $C = \{2, 4\}$. Then $A \cap B = \{2\}$ and $A \cap C = \{2\}$. Thus $A \cap B = A \cap C$ but $B \neq C$.

**1.90** Show we can have $A \cup B = A \cup C$ without $B = C$.

▌ Let $A = \{1, 2\}$, $B = \{1, 3\}$ and $C = \{2, 3\}$. Then $A \cup B = A \cup C = \{1, 2, 3\}$ but $B \neq C$.

Problems 1.91–1.94 refer to the following sets:

$$A = \{\text{coat, hat, umbrella}\} \qquad C = \{\text{sweater, hat, mittens, scarf}\}$$
$$B = \{\text{boots, coat, mittens, scarf}\} \qquad D = \{\text{coat, boots}\}$$

**1.91** Find: (*a*) $A \cup B$ and (*b*) $B \cap C$.

**▮ (a)** Combining the elements of $A$ and $B$ yields

$$A \cup B = \{\text{boots, coat, hat, mittens, scarf, umbrella}\}$$

**(b)** The elements in both $B$ and $C$ yield $B \cap C = \{\text{mittens, scarf}\}$.

**1.92**   Find: **(a)** $C \backslash B$ and **(b)** $A^c$.

**▮ (a)** Omitting the elements of $C$ which also belong to $B$ yields $C \backslash B = \{\text{sweater, hat}\}$.
**(b)** Since no universal set $\mathbf{U}$ is given, one cannot specify $A^c$ except to say that $A^c$ consists of all elements except "coat", "hat" and "umbrella".

**1.93**   Find $(A \cup C) \cap (B \backslash C)$.

**▮** First find

$$A \cup C = \{\text{coat, hat, umbrella, sweater, mittens, scarf}\} \quad \text{and} \quad B \backslash C = \{\text{boots, coat}\}$$

Then $(A \cup C) \cap (B \backslash C) = \{\text{coat}\}$.

**1.94**   Find $B \backslash (A \cap D)$.

**▮** First find $A \cap D = \{\text{coat}\}$; then $B \backslash \{\text{coat}\} = \{\text{boots, mittens, scarf}\}$.

Problems 1.95–1.102 refer to the following sets:

$$X = \{\text{red, blue}\}, \quad Y = \{\text{blue, green, orange}\}, \quad Z = \{\text{red, blue, white}\}$$
$$\mathbf{U} = \{\text{red, yellow, blue, green, orange, purple, black, white}\}$$

**1.95**   Describe in words the universal set $\mathbf{U}$.

**▮** $\mathbf{U}$ consists of the six colors of the rainbow together with black and white.

**1.96**   Find: **(a)** $X \cup Y$ and **(b)** $X \cup Z$.

**▮ (a)** $X \cup Y$ is obtained by listing the elements in both $X$ and $Y$; hence $X \cup Y = \{\text{red, blue, green, orange}\}$.
**(b)** Similarly, $X \cup Z = \{\text{red, blue, white}\}$. (Since $X \subseteq Z$, we have $X \cup Z = Z$ (Theorem 1.2).)

**1.97**   Find: **(a)** $X \cap Y$ and **(b)** $X \cap Z$.

**▮ (a)** $X \cap Y$ is obtained by listing the elements in both $X$ and $Y$; hence $X \cap Y = \{\text{blue}\}$.
**(b)** Similarly, $X \cap Z = \{\text{red, blue}\}$. (Since $X \subseteq Z$, we have $X \cap Z = X$ (Theorem 1.2).)

**1.98**   Find: **(a)** $X^c$, **(b)** $Y^c$, and **(c)** $Z^c$.

**▮ (a)** $X^c$ is obtained by listing the elements in $\mathbf{U}$ which do not belong to $X$. Hence

$$X^c = \{\text{yellow, green, orange, purple, black, white}\}$$

**(b)** Similarly, $Y^c = \{\text{red, yellow, purple, black, white}\}$,
**(c)** $Z^c = \{\text{yellow, green, orange, purple, black}\}$. (Since $X \subseteq Z$, we have $Z^c \subseteq X^c$.)

**1.99**   Find: **(a)** $X \backslash Y$ and **(b)** $X \backslash Z$.

**▮ (a)** $X \backslash Y$ is obtained by listing the elements in $X$ which do not belong to $Y$; hence $X \backslash Y = \{\text{red}\}$.
**(b)** Since $X \subseteq Z$, we have $X \backslash Z = \emptyset$.

**1.100**   Find: **(a)** $(X \cup Y)^c$ and **(b)** $Y^c \backslash Z$.

**▮ (a)** $X \cup Y = \{\text{red, blue, green, orange}\}$ and so $(X \cup Y)^c = \{\text{yellow, purple, black, white}\}$.
**(b)** List the elements in $Y^c$ (Problem 1.98) which do not belong to $Z$ to obtain $Y^c \backslash Z = \{\text{yellow, purple, black}\}$.

**1.101**   Find: **(a)** $X \cup Y \cup Z$ and **(b)** $X \cap Y \cap Z$.

**▮ (a)** List all elements appearing in any set to obtain $X \cup Y \cup Z = \{\text{red, blue, green, orange, white}\}$.

**(b)** List the elements belonging to all three sets to obtain

$$X \cap Y \cap Z = \{\text{blue}\}.$$

(Since $X \subseteq Z$, we have $X \cup Y \cup Z = Y \cup Z$ and $X \cap Y \cap Z = Y \cap Z$.)

**1.102** Find: **(a)** $Y \cap Z^c$ and **(b)** $X \cap Z^c$.

   ▌ **(a)** List the elements in both $Y$ and $Z^c$ (Problem 1.98) to obtain $Y \cap Z^c = \{\text{green, orange}\}$.
      **(b)** Since $X \subseteq Z$, we have $X \cap Z^c = \emptyset$.

**1.103** Determine whether or not each of the following is equal to $A$, the empty set $\emptyset$, or the universal set **U**:
    **(a)** $A \cup A$,     **(b)** $A \cup U$,     **(c)** $A \cup \emptyset$,     **(d)** $A \cup A^c$

   ▌ **(a)** $A \cup A = A$, **(b)** $A \cup U = U$, **(c)** $A \cup \emptyset = A$, and **(d)** $A \cup A^c = U$.

**1.104** Determine whether or not each of the following is equal to $A$, the empty set $\emptyset$, or the universal set **U**:
    **(a)** $A \cap A$,     **(b)** $A \cap U$,     **(c)** $A \cap \emptyset$,     **(d)** $A \cap A^c$

   ▌ **(a)** $A \cap A = A$, **(b)** $A \cap U = A$, **(c)** $A \cap \emptyset = \emptyset$, and **(d)** $A \cap A^c = \emptyset$.

**1.105** Determine whether or not each of the following is equal to $A$, the empty set $\emptyset$, or the universal set **U**:
    **(a)** $A \backslash A$,     **(b)** $A \backslash U$,     **(c)** $A \backslash \emptyset$,     **(d)** $A \backslash A^c$,     **(e)** $(A^c)^c$

   ▌ **(a)** $A \backslash A = \emptyset$, **(b)** $A \backslash U = \emptyset$, **(c)** $A \backslash \emptyset = A$, **(d)** $A \backslash A^c = A$, and **(e)** $(A^c)^c = A$.

**1.106** Prove $A \backslash B = A \cap B^c$, which defines the difference operation in terms of intersection and complement.

   ▌ $A \backslash B = \{x : x \in A, x \notin B\} = \{x : x \in A, x \in B^c\} = A \cap B^c$

**1.107** Prove: **(a)** $A \backslash B$ and $B$ are disjoint, and **(b)** $A \cup B = (A \backslash B) \cup B$.

   ▌ **(a)** Suppose $x \in A \backslash B$ and $x \in B$. The first condition implies $x \in A$ and $x \notin B$. However, $x \in B$ and $x \notin B$ is impossible. Therefore no such $x$ exists; that is, $(A \backslash B) \cap B = \emptyset$, as required.
      **(b)** Using properties in Table 1-1, page 19, we have

$$(A \backslash B) \cup B = (A \cap B^c) \cup B = (A \cup B) \cap (B^c \cup B) = (A \cup B) \cap U = A \cup B$$

**1.108** Determine which of the following is equivalent to $A \subseteq B$: **(a)** $A \cap B^c = \emptyset$, **(b)** $A^c \cup B = U$, **(c)** $B^c \subseteq A^c$, **(d)** $A \backslash B = \emptyset$. (Compare with Theorem 1.2.)

   ▌ They are all equivalent to $A \subseteq B$.

## 1.4 VENN DIAGRAMS AND SET OPERATIONS, FUNDAMENTAL PRODUCTS

This section refers to the Venn diagram of sets $A$ and $B$ and the Venn diagram of sets $A$, $B$ and $C$ as shown in Fig. 1-6(a) and (b) respectively.

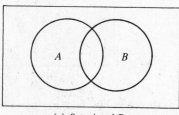

(a) Sets $A$ and $B$.

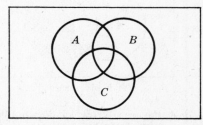

(b) Sets $A$, $B$, and C.     **Fig. 1-6**

**1.109** In the Venn diagram of Fig. 1-6(a), shade the area representing $(A \cup B)^c$.

   ▌ First shade $A \cup B$ with strokes in one direction as in Fig. 1-7(a). Then $(A \cup B)^c$ is the area outside of $A \cup B$ as shaded in Fig. 1-7(b).

**1.110** Shade the area representing $A^c \cap B^c$ in the Venn diagram of Fig. 1-6(a).

   ▌ First shade $A^c$, the area outside $A$, with strokes that slant upward to the right ($///$) and then shade $B^c$ with

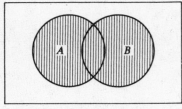

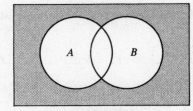

(a) $A \cup B$ is shaded.

(b) $(A \cup B)^c$ is shaded.

**Fig. 1-7**

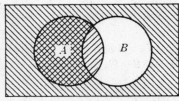

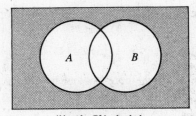

(a) $A^c$ is shaded with ////.
$B^c$ is shaded with \\\\.

(b) $A^c \cap B^c$ is shaded.

**Fig. 1-8**

strokes that slant downward to the right (\\\\) as in Fig. 1-8($a$). Then $A^c \cap B^c$ is the crosshatched area which is shaded in Fig. 1-8($b$). (By this and Problem 1.109, $(A \cup B)^c = A^c \cap B^c$ since they represent the same area. This property of sets is called DeMorgan's law.)

**1.111** Shade the set $A \cap B^c$ in the Venn diagram of Fig. 1-6($a$).

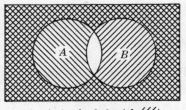

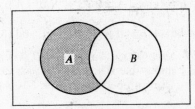

(a) $A$ and $B^c$ are shaded.

(b) $A \cap B^c$ is shaded.

**Fig. 1-9**

▌ First shade $A$ with strokes in one direction (////), and then shade $B^c$, the area outside of $B$, with strokes in another direction (\\\\) as shown in Fig. 1-9($a$); the crosshatched area is the intersection $A \cap B^c$ shown shaded in Fig. 1-9($b$). (Observe that $A \cap B^c = A \backslash B$. Compare with Problem 1.106.)

**1.112** Shade the set $(B \backslash A)^c$ in the Venn diagram of Fig. 1-6($a$).

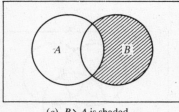

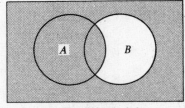

(a) $B \backslash A$ is shaded.

(b) $(B \backslash A)^c$ is shaded.

**Fig. 1-10**

▌ Shade $B \backslash A$, the area of $B$ which does not lie in $A$ as shown in Fig. 1-10($a$); then $(B \backslash A)^c$ is the area outside of $B \backslash A$, as shown in Fig. 1-10($b$).

**1.113** Shade the set $A \cap (B \cup C)$ in the Venn diagram of Fig. 1-6($b$).

▌ Shade $A$ with upward slanted strokes (///) and $B \cup C$ with downward slanted strokes (\\\) as shown in Fig. 1-11($a$). Then the crosshatched area is the intersection $A \cap (B \cup C)$, shown shaded in Fig. 1-11($b$).

**1.114** Shade the set $(A \cap B) \cup (A \cap C)$.

▌ Shade $A \cap B$ with upward slanted strokes (///) and $B \cap C$ with downward slanted strokes (\\\) as shown in

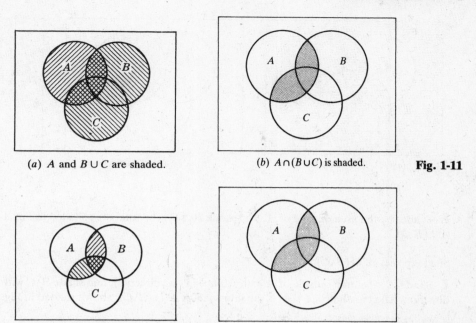

(a) A and B ∪ C are shaded.　　(b) A ∩ (B ∪ C) is shaded.　　**Fig. 1-11**

(a) A ∩ B and A ∩ C are shaded.　　(b) (A ∩ B) ∪ (A ∩ C) is shaded.　　**Fig. 1-12**

Fig. 1-12(a). Then the total area shaded is the union $(A \cap B) \cup (A \cap C)$ as shown in Fig. 1-12(b). [By Fig. 1-11(b) and 1-12(b), $A \cup (B \cap C) = (A \cap B) \cup (A \cap C)$. That is, the union operation distributes over the intersection operation for sets.]

**1.115**　Shade the set $A \cup (B \cap C)$.

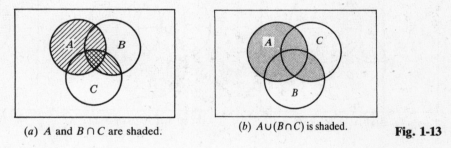

(a) A and B ∩ C are shaded.　　(b) A ∪ (B ∩ C) is shaded.　　**Fig. 1-13**

▌ Shade A with upward slanted strokes (///) and B ∩ C with downward slanted strokes (\\\) as shown in Fig. 1-13(a). Then the total area shaded is the union $A \cup (B \cup C)$ as shown in Fig. 1-13(b).

**1.116**　Shade the set $(A \cup B) \cap (A \cup C)$.

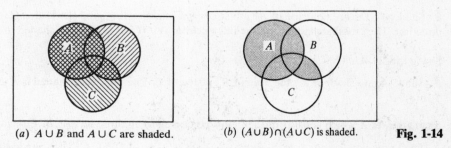

(a) A ∪ B and A ∪ C are shaded.　　(b) (A ∪ B) ∩ (A ∪ C) is shaded.　　**Fig. 1-14**

▌ Shade $A \cup B$ with upward slanted strokes (///) and $A \cup C$ with downward slanted strokes (\\\) as shown in Fig. 1-14(a). Then the crosshatched area is the intersection $(A \cup B) \cap (A \cup C)$ shown in Fig. 1-14(b). [By Fig. 1-13(b) and 1-14(b), $A \cup (B \cap C) = (A \cup B) \cap (A \cup C)$. That is, the intersection operation distributes over the union operation for sets.]

**1.117**　Shade the set $A^c \cup B \cup C$.

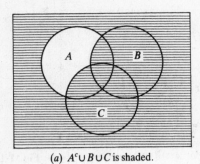
(a) $A^c \cup B \cup C$ is shaded.

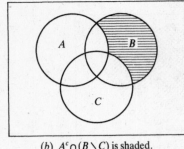
(b) $A^c \cap (B \setminus C)$ is shaded.

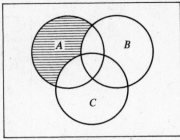
(c) $A \cap B^c \cap C^c$ is shaded.

**Fig. 1-15**

▌ Shade $A^c$, the area outside of $A$, and shade $B \cup C$. The total area shaded in Fig. 1-15(a) is the union $A^c \cup B \cup C$.

**1.118**   Shade the set $A^c \cap (B \setminus C)$.

▌ Shade $A^c$, the area outside of $A$ with strokes in one direction, and shade $B \setminus C$ with strokes in another direction. The crosshatched area is the intersection $A^c \cap (B \setminus C)$, shown shaded in Fig. 1-15(b).

**1.119**   Shade the set $A \cap B^c \cap C^c$.

▌ See Fig. 1-15(c). The shaded area which lies in $A$ but outside of $B$ and $C$ is the required result.

**1.120**   Shade the set $A \cap B \cap C^c$.

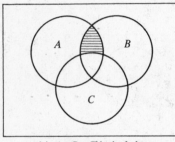
(a) $A \cap B \cap C^c$ is shaded.

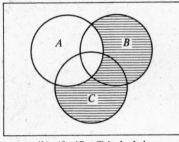
(b) $A^c \cap (B \cup C)$ is shaded.

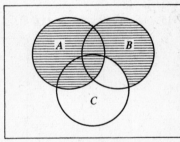
(c) $A \cup (B \setminus C)$ is shaded.

**Fig. 1-16**

▌ Shade the area in $A$ and in $B$ but outside of $C$ as shown in Fig. 1-16(a).

**1.121**   Shade the set $A^c \cap (B \cup C)$.

▌ Shade $A^c$, the area outside of $A$ with strokes in one direction, and shade $B \cup C$ with strokes in another direction. The crosshatched area is the intersection, $A^c \cap (B \cup C)$, shown shaded in Fig. 1-16(b).

**1.122**   Shade the set $A \cup (B \setminus C)$.

▌ Shade $A$ and shade $B \setminus C$, the area in $B$ outside of $C$. The total area shaded is $A \cup (B \setminus C)$ as shown in Fig. 1-16(c).

**1.123**   Shade the set $X$ which consists of the points belonging to all three sets $A$, $B$, $C$ or to none of the sets.

▌ Shade the area common to all three sets $A$, $B$, $C$, i.e., $A \cap B \cap C$. Then shade the area outside of all three sets, i.e., $A^c \cap B^c \cap C^c$. Then $X$ is the total area shaded as shown in Fig. 1-17(a).

**1.124**   Shade the set $Y$ which consists of those points belonging to exactly one of the three sets $A$, $B$, $C$.

▌ Shade the area of $A$ outside of $B$ and $C$, i.e., $A \cap B^c \cap C^c$. Then shade the area of $B$ outside of $A$ and $C$, i.e., $A^c \cap B \cap C^c$. Lastly, shade the area of $C$ outside of $A$ and $B$, i.e., $A^c \cap B^c \cap C$. The total area shaded is $Y$, shown in Fig. 1-17(b). [Note $Y = (A^c \cap B \cap C) \cup (A \cap B^c \cap C) \cup (A \cap B \cap C^c)$.]

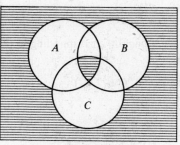
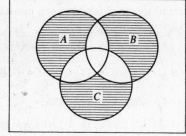
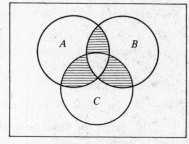

(a) $X$ is shaded.  (b) $Y$ is shaded.  (c) $Z$ is shaded.

**Fig. 1-17**

**1.125** Shade the set $Z$ which consists of those points belonging to exactly two of the three sets $A$, $B$, $C$.

▮ Shade the area common to $A$ and $B$ but outside of $C$, i.e., $A \cap B \cap C^c$. Then shade the area common to $A$ and $C$ but outside of $B$, i.e., $A \cap B^c \cap C$. Lastly, shade the area common to $B$ and $C$ but outside of $A$, i.e., $A^c \cap B \cap C$. The total area shaded is $Z$, shown in Fig. 1-17(c).

## Fundamental Products

**1.126** A *fundamental product* of sets $A_1$, $A_2$, . . . , $A_n$ is an expression of the form $A_1^{e_1} \cap A_2^{e_2} \cap \cdots \cap A_n^{e_n}$ where $A_i^{e_i}$ is either $A_i$ or $A_i^c$. Show that any two distinct fundamental products $P_1$ and $P_2$ are disjoint.

▮ Suppose $P_1$ and $P_2$ differ in the $i$th set, say $P_1$ contains $A_i$ and $P_2$ contains $A_i^c$. Then $P_1$ is a subset of $A_i$ and $P_2$ is a subset of $A_i^c$. Thus $P_1 \cap P_2 = \emptyset$, as claimed.

**1.127** Find the number of fundamental products of the $n$ sets $A_1$, $A_2$, . . . , $A_n$.

▮ The set $A_1^{e_1}$ can be chosen in two ways, $A_1$ or $A_1^c$. Similarly, the set $A_2^{e_2}$ can be chosen as $A_2$ or $A_2^c$. And so on. Thus there are $2 \times 2 \times \cdots \times 2 = 2^n$ such fundamental products.

**1.128** List all the fundamental products of the three sets $A$, $B$ and $C$.

▮ There are $2^3 = 8$ such products as follows:

$$P_1 = A \cap B \cap C \qquad P_3 = A \cap B^c \cap C \qquad P_5 = A^c \cap B \cap C \qquad P_7 = A^c \cap B^c \cap C$$
$$P_2 = A \cap B \cap C^c \qquad P_4 = A \cap B^c \cap C^c \qquad P_6 = A^c \cap B \cap C^c \qquad P_8 = A_c \cap B^c \cap C^c$$

**1.129** Each of the eight areas in the Venn diagram of sets $A$, $B$, $C$ in Fig. 1-6(b) represents a fundamental product. Label the areas by the fundamental products $P_1$ through $P_8$ appearing in Problem 1.128.

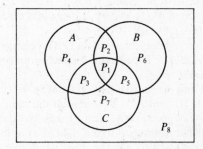

**Fig. 1-18**

▮ See Fig. 1-18. The area common to $A$, $B$, and $C$ is labeled $P_1 = A \cap B \cap C$; the area common to $A$ and $B$ but outside of $C$ is labeled $P_2 = A \cap B \cap C^c$; the area common to $A$ and $C$ but outside of $B$ is labeled $P_3 = A \cap B^c \cap C$; and so on.

**1.130** Write $A \cap (B \cup C)$ as the (disjoint) union of fundamental products.

▮ By Fig. 1-11(b), $A \cap (B \cup C)$ consists of three of the eight areas of the Venn diagram. The three areas correspond to the fundamental products $A \cap B \cap C$, $A \cap B \cap C^c$, and $A \cap B^c \cap C$. Thus

$$A \cap (B \cup C) = (A \cap B \cap C) \cup (A \cap B \cap C^c) \cup (A \cap B^c \cap C)$$

**1.131**    Write $A^c \cap (B \cup C)$ as the (disjoint) union of fundamental products.

$\blacksquare$    By Fig. 1-16(b), $A^c \cap (B \cup C)$ consists of the three areas of the Venn diagram corresponding to the fundamental products $A^c \cap B \cap C^c$, $A^c \cap B \cap C$, and $A^c \cap B^c \cap C$. Thus

$$A^c \cap (B \cup C) = (A^c \cap B \cap C^c) \cup (A^c \cap B \cap C) \cup (A^c \cap B^c \cap C)$$

**1.132**    Write $A \cup (B \cap C)$ as the union of fundamental products.

$\blacksquare$    Using the Venn diagram of $A \cup (B \cap C)$ in Fig. 1-13(b), we get

$$A \cup (B \cap C) = (A \cap B \cap C) \cup (A \cap B \cap C^c) \cup (A \cap B^c \cap C) \cup (A^c \cap B \cap C) \cup (A \cap B^c \cap C^c)$$

**1.133**    Write $A \cup (B \backslash C)$ as the union of fundamental products.

$\blacksquare$    Using the Venn diagram of $A \cup (B \backslash C)$ in Fig. 1-16(c) we get

$$A \cup (B \backslash C) = (A \cap B \cap C) \cup (A \cap B \cap C^c) \cup (A \cap B^c \cap C) \cup (A^c \cap B \cap C^c) \cup (A \cap B^c \cap C^c)$$

**1.134**    Find the number of fundamental products for the sets $A$, $B$, $C$, and $D$.

$\blacksquare$    Since there are four sets, there are $2^4 = 16$ such fundamental products.

**1.135**    Let $X = A \cap B \cap C$. Is $X$ a fundamental product?

$\blacksquare$    If $A$, $B$, and $C$ are the only sets involved, then $X$ is a fundamental product. However, if more sets are involved, say, $A$, $B$, $C$, and $D$, then $X$ is not a fundamental product. In particular,

$$X = (A \cap B \cap C \cap D) \cup (A \cap B \cap C \cap D^c)$$

expresses $X$ as the (disjoint) union of fundamental products (of $A$, $B$, $C$, and $D$).

## 1.5 ALGEBRA OF SETS, DUALITY

The following theorem is used throughout this section. (Although each part of the theorem follows from an analogous logical law discussed in Chapter 13, some parts of the theorem are proven below.)

**Theorem 1.3:**    Sets satisfy the laws in Table 1-1.

**1.136**    Prove DeMorgan's Laws: (**a**) $(A \cup B)^c = A^c \cap B^c$, and (**b**) $(A \cap B)^c = A^c \cup B^c$.

$\blacksquare$    (**a**)    Two methods are used to prove the set equation. The first method uses the fact that $X = Y$ is equivalent to $X \subseteq Y$ and $Y \subseteq X$. The second method uses Venn diagrams.
   *Method 1.*    We first show that $(A \cup B)^c \subseteq A^c \cap B^c$. If $x \in (A \cup B)^c$, then $x \notin A \cup B$. Thus $x \notin A$ and $x \notin B$, and so $x \in A^c$ and $x \in B^c$. Hence $x \in A^c \cap B^c$.
   Next we show that $A^c \cap B^c \subseteq (A \cup B)^c$. Let $x \in A^c \cap B^c$. Then $x \in A^c$ and $x \in B^c$, so $x \notin A$ and $x \notin B$. Hence $x \notin A \cup B$, so $x \in (A \cup B)^c$.
   We have proven that every element of $(A \cup B)^c$ belongs to $A^c \cap B^c$ and that every element of $A^c \cap B^c$ belongs to $(A \cup B)^c$. Together, these inclusions prove that the sets have the same elements, i.e., that $(A \cup B)^c = A^c \cap B^c$.
   *Method 2.*    The Venn diagram of $(A \cup B)^c$ in Fig. 1-7(b) and the Venn diagram of $A^c \cap B^c$ in Fig. 1-8(b) show that $(A \cup B)^c$ and $A^c \cap B^c$ represent the same area. Thus $(A \cup B)^c = A^c \cap B^c$.

(**b**)    First shade $A^c$, the area outside of $A$, with strokes that slant upward to the right (///) and then shade $B^c$ with strokes that slant downward to the right (\\\) as in Fig. 1-19(a). Then the total area shaded is $A^c \cup B^c$ as shown in Fig. 1-19(b). On the other hand, the area shaded in Fig. 1-19(b) is the area outside of $A \cap B$, i.e., $(A \cap B)^c$. Thus $(A \cap B)^c = A^c \cup B^c$.

**1.137**    Prove the Identity Laws: (**a**) $A \cup \varnothing = A$, and (**b**) $A \cap \mathbf{U} = A$.

$\blacksquare$    (**a**)    By Problem 1.79, $A \subseteq A \cup \varnothing$. Suppose $x \in A \cup \varnothing$. Then $x \in A$ or $x \in \varnothing$. Since $\varnothing$ is the empty set, $x \notin \varnothing$ and hence $x \in A$. Thus $A \cup \varnothing \subseteq A$. Both inclusions give $A \cup \varnothing = \varnothing$.

(**b**)    By Problem 1.79, $A \cap \mathbf{U} \subseteq A$. Suppose $x \in A$. Since $\mathbf{U}$ is the universal set, $x \in \mathbf{U}$; and hence $x \in A \cap \mathbf{U}$. Thus $A \subseteq A \cap \mathbf{U}$. Both inclusions give $A \cap \mathbf{U} = A$.

**1.138**    Prove the Identity Laws: (**a**) $A \cup \mathbf{U} = \mathbf{U}$, and (**b**) $A \cap \varnothing = \varnothing$.

**TABLE 1-1. Laws of the Algebra of Sets**

| Idempotent Laws | |
| --- | --- |
| 1a. $A \cup A = A$ | 1b. $A \cap A = A$ |

| Associative Laws | |
| --- | --- |
| 2a. $(A \cup B) \cup C = A \cup (B \cup C)$ | 2b. $(A \cap B) \cap C = A \cap (B \cap C)$ |

| Commutative Laws | |
| --- | --- |
| 3a. $A \cup B = B \cup A$ | 3b. $A \cap B = B \cap A$ |

| Distributive Laws | |
| --- | --- |
| 4a. $A \cup (B \cap C) = (A \cup B) \cap (A \cup C)$ | 4b. $A \cap (B \cup C) = (A \cap B) \cup (A \cap C)$ |

| Identity Laws | |
| --- | --- |
| 5a. $A \cup \emptyset = A$ | 5b. $A \cap \mathbf{U} = A$ |
| 6a. $A \cup \mathbf{U} = \mathbf{U}$ | 6b. $A \cap \emptyset = \emptyset$ |

| Involution Law | |
| --- | --- |
| 7. $(A^c)^c = A$ | |

| Complement Laws | |
| --- | --- |
| 8a. $A \cup A^c = \mathbf{U}$ | 8b. $A \cap A^c = \emptyset$ |
| 9a. $\mathbf{U}^c = \emptyset$ | 9b. $\emptyset^c = \mathbf{U}$ |

| DeMorgan's Laws | |
| --- | --- |
| 10a. $(A \cup B)^c = A^c \cap B^c$ | 10b. $(A \cap B)^c = A^c \cup B^c$ |

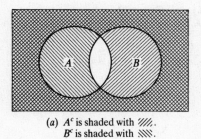

(a) $A^c$ is shaded with ▨. $B^c$ is shaded with ▨.

(b) $A^c \cup B^c$ is shaded.

**Fig. 1-19**

**(a)** By Problem 1.79, $\mathbf{U} \subseteq A \cup \mathbf{U}$. Since $\mathbf{U}$ is the universal set, $A \cup \mathbf{U} \subseteq \mathbf{U}$. Both inclusions imply $A \cup \mathbf{U} = \mathbf{U}$.

**(b)** By Problem 1.79, $A \cap \emptyset \subseteq \emptyset$. Since $\emptyset$ is the empty set, $\emptyset \subseteq A \cap \emptyset$. Both inclusions imply $A \cap \emptyset = \emptyset$.

**1.139** Prove the Distributive Laws: **(a)** $A \cup (B \cap C) = (A \cup B) \cap (A \cup C)$, and **(b)** $A \cap (B \cup C) = (A \cap B) \cup (A \cap C)$.

**(a)** By the Venn diagrams in Figs 1-13(b) and 1-14(b), $A \cup (B \cap C)$ and $(A \cup B) \cap (A \cup C)$ represent the same area. Thus $A \cup (B \cap C) = (A \cup B) \cap (A \cup C)$.

**(b)** By the Venn diagrams in Figs 1-11(b) and 1-12(b), $A \cap (B \cup C)$ and $(A \cap B) \cup (A \cap C)$ represent the same area. Thus $A \cap (B \cup C) = (A \cap B) \cup (A \cap C)$.

**1.140** Prove the Commutative Laws: **(a)** $A \cup B = B \cup A$, and **(b)** $A \cap B = B \cap A$.

**(a)** $A \cup B = \{x : x \in A \text{ or } x \in B\} = \{x : x \in B \text{ or } x \in A\} = B \cup A$.

**(b)** $A \cap B = \{x : x \in A \text{ and } x \in B\} = \{x : x \in B \text{ and } x \in A\} = B \cap A$.

**1.141** Prove the Idempotent Laws: **(a)** $A \cup A = A$, and **(b)** $A \cap A = A$.

**(a)** $A \cup A = \{x : x \in A \text{ or } x \in A\} = \{x : x \in A\} = A$.

**(b)** $A \cap A = \{x : x \in A \text{ and } x \in A\} = \{x : x \in A\} = A$.

**1.142**  Prove the Involution Law: $(A^c)^c = A$.

▮  $(A^c)^c = \{x : x \notin A^c\} = \{x : x \in A\} = A$

The following definition is used below.

**Definition:**  The dual $E^*$ of an equation $E$ involving sets is the equation obtained by interchanging $\cup$ and $\cap$ and also $\mathbf{U}$ and $\varnothing$ in $E$, i.e., by replacing each occurrence of $\cup$, $\cap$, $\mathbf{U}$, and $\varnothing$ in $E$ by $\cap$, $\cup$, $\varnothing$ and $\mathbf{U}$ respectively.

**1.143**  Write the dual of each set equation:
  (a)  $(\mathbf{U} \cap A) \cup (B \cap A) = A$,   (b)  $(A \cap \mathbf{U}) \cap (\varnothing \cup A^c) = \varnothing$

▮  Interchange $\cup$ and $\cap$ and also $\mathbf{U}$ and $\varnothing$ in each set equation:
  (a)  $(\varnothing \cup A) \cap (B \cup A) = A$,   (b)  $(A \cup \varnothing) \cup (\mathbf{U} \cap A^c) = \mathbf{U}$

**1.144**  Write the dual of each set equation:
  (a)  $(A \cup B) \cap (A \cup B^c) = A \cup \varnothing$,   (b)  $(A \cap \mathbf{U}) \cup (B \cap A) = A$

▮  Replace each occurrence of $\cup$, $\cap$, $\mathbf{U}$, and $\varnothing$ by $\cap$, $\cup$, $\varnothing$ and $\mathbf{U}$ respectively:
  (a)  $(A \cap B) \cup (A \cap B^c) = A \cap \mathbf{U}$,   (b)  $(A \cup \varnothing) \cap (B \cup A) = A$

**1.145**  Write the dual of each set equation:
  (a)  $A \cup (A \cap B) = A$   (c)  $(A \cup \mathbf{U}) \cap (A \cap \varnothing) = \varnothing$
  (b)  $(A \cap B) \cup (A^c \cap B) \cup (A \cap B^c) \cup (A^c \cap B^c) = \mathbf{U}$   (d)  $(A \cup B) \cap (B \cup C) = (A \cap C) \cup B$

▮  Replace each occurrence of $\cup$, $\cap$, $\mathbf{U}$ and $\varnothing$ by $\cap$, $\cup$, $\varnothing$ and $\mathbf{U}$ respectively:
  (a)  $A \cap (A \cup B) = A$   (c)  $(A \cap \varnothing) \cup (A \cup \mathbf{U}) = \mathbf{U}$
  (b)  $(A \cup B) \cap (A^c \cup B) \cap (A \cup B^c) \cap (A^c \cup B^c) = \varnothing$   (d)  $(A \cap B) \cup (B \cap C) = (A \cup C) \cap B$

**1.146**  Write the dual of each set equation:
  (a)  $(A \cup B \cup C)^c = (A \cup C)^c \cap (A \cup B)^c$   (c)  $(A \cap \mathbf{U})^c \cap A = \varnothing$
  (b)  $A \cup B = (B^c \cap A^c)^c$   (d)  $A = (B^c \cap A) \cup (A \cap B)$

▮  (a)  $(A \cap B \cap C)^c = (A \cap C)^c \cup (A \cap B)^c$   (c)  $(A \cup \varnothing)^c \cup A = \mathbf{U}$
  (b)  $A \cap B = (B^c \cup A^c)^c$   (d)  $A = (B^c \cup A) \cap (A \cup B)$

**1.147**  Write the dual of each set equation:
  (a)  $A^c \cup B^c \cup C^c = (A \cap B \cap C)^c$
  (b)  $(A \cap \mathbf{U}) \cap (B \cup C) = (A \cap B) \cup (A \cap C)$
  (c)  $A = (B^c \cap A) \cup (C^c \cap A) \cup (A \cap B \cap C)$

▮  (a)  $A^c \cap B^c \cap C^c = (A \cup B \cup C)^c$
  (b)  $(A \cup \varnothing) \cup (B \cap C) = (A \cup B) \cap (A \cup C)$
  (c)  $A = (B^c \cup A) \cap (C^c \cup A) \cap (A \cup B \cup C)$

**1.148**  Explain the *principle of duality*.

▮  The Principle of Duality states that if certain axioms imply their own duals, then the dual of any theorem that is a consequence of the axioms is also a consequence of the axioms. For, given any theorem and its proof, the dual of the theorem can be proven in the same way by using the dual of each step in the original proof.

## Algebra of Sets

**1.149**  Consider sets under the operations of union, intersection and complement. (a) Explain the meaning of the expression "algebra of sets". (b) Explain why the principle of duality applies to the algebra of sets.

▮  (a)  The algebra of sets refers to the laws in Table 1-1 and those theorems whose proofs require the use of those laws and no others, i.e., those theorems which are a consequence of those laws.
  (b)  The dual of every law in Table 1-1 is also a law in Table 1-1. Thus the principle of duality applies to the algebra of sets.

**1.150**  Use the laws in Table 1-1 to prove the identities: (a) $(\mathbf{U} \cap A) \cup (B \cap A) = A$, (b) $(\varnothing \cup A) \cap (B \cup A) = A$.

**(a)**

| Statement | Reason |
|---|---|
| $(\mathbf{U} \cap A) \cup (B \cap A) = (A \cap \mathbf{U}) \cup (A \cap B)$ | Commutative law 3*a* |
| $= A \cap (\mathbf{U} \cup B)$ | Distributive law 4*b* |
| $= A \cap (B \cup \mathbf{U})$ | Commutative law 3*a* |
| $= A \cap \mathbf{U}$ | Identity law 6*a* |
| $= A$ | Identity law 5*b* |

**(b)** This is the dual of the identity proved in **(a)** and hence is true by the principle of duality. In other words, replacing each step in the proof in **(a)** by dual statements gives a proof of this identity.

**1.151** Prove the Right Distributive Laws: **(a)** $(B \cup C) \cap A = (B \cap A) \cup (C \cap A)$, **(b)** $(B \cap C) \cup A = (B \cup A) \cap (C \cup A)$

**(a)**

| | Statement | | Reason |
|---|---|---|---|
| 1. | $(B \cup C) \cap A = A \cap (B \cup C)$ | 1. | Commutative law |
| 2. | $= (A \cap B) \cup (A \cap C)$ | 2. | Distributive law |
| 3. | $= (B \cap A) \cup (C \cap A)$ | 3. | Commutative law |

**(b)** Since this is the dual of the identity proven in **(a)**, simply replace each step in the above proof by its dual:

| | Statement | | Reason |
|---|---|---|---|
| 1. | $(B \cap C) \cup A = A \cup (B \cap C)$ | 1. | Commutative law |
| 2. | $= (A \cup B) \cap (A \cup C)$ | 2. | Distributive law |
| 3. | $= (B \cup A) \cap (C \cup A)$ | 3. | Commutative law |

**1.152** Prove the following set identities: **(a)** $(A \cup B) \cap (A \cup B^c) = A$, **(b)** $(A \cap B) \cup (A \cap B^c) = A$.

**(a)**

| | Statement | | Reason |
|---|---|---|---|
| 1. | $(A \cup B) \cap (A \cup B^c) = A \cup (B \cap B^c)$ | 1. | Distributive law |
| 2. | $B \cap B^c = \varnothing$ | 2. | Complement law |
| 3. | $\therefore (A \cup B) \cap (A \cup B^c) = A \cup \varnothing$ | 3. | Substitution |
| 4. | $A \cup \varnothing = A$ | 4. | Identity law |
| 5. | $\therefore (A \cup B) \cap (A \cup B^c) = A$ | 5. | Substitution |

**(b)** Follows from **(a)** and the principle of duality.

**1.153** Prove the Absorption Laws: **(a)** $A \cup (A \cap B) = A$, **(b)** $A \cap (A \cup B) = A$.

**(a)**

| | |
|---|---|
| $A \cup (A \cap B) = (A \cap \mathbf{U}) \cup (A \cap B)$ | Identity law |
| $= A \cap (\mathbf{U} \cup B)$ | Distributive law |
| $= A \cap (B \cup \mathbf{U})$ | Associative law |
| $= A \cap \mathbf{U}$ | Identity law |
| $= A$ | Identity law |

**(b)** Follows from **(a)** and the principle of duality.

**1.154** Prove: **(a)** $(B^c \cap \mathbf{U}) \cap (A^c \cup \varnothing) = (A \cup B)^c$, **(b)** $(B^c \cup \varnothing) \cup (A^c \cap \mathbf{U}) = (A \cap B)^c$.

**(a)**

| | |
|---|---|
| $(B^c \cap \mathbf{U}) \cap (A^c \cup \varnothing) = B^c \cap A^c$ | Identity law |
| $= A^c \cap B^c$ | Commutative law |
| $= (A \cup B)^c$ | DeMorgan's law |

**(b)** Follows from **(a)** and the principle of duality.

**1.155** The algebra of sets is defined in terms of the operations of union, intersection, and complement. Set inclusion is defined in the algebra of sets as follows:

$$A \subseteq B \quad \text{means} \quad A \cap B = A$$

Use this definition to prove that if $A \subseteq B$ and $B \subseteq C$, then $A \subseteq C$.

| Statement | Reason |
|-----------|--------|
| 1. $A = A \cap B$ and $B = B \cap C$ | 1. Definition of subset |
| 2. $\therefore A = A \cap (B \cap C)$ | 2. Substitution |
| 3. $A = (A \cap B) \cap C$ | 3. Associative law |
| 4. $\therefore A = A \cap C$ | 4. Substitution |
| 5. $\therefore A \subseteq C$ | 5. Definition of subset |

## 1.6 FINITE SETS, COUNTING PRINCIPLE

This section uses the following definition and notation.

**Definition:** A set is said to be *finite* if it contains exactly $m$ distinct elements where $m$ denotes some nonnegative integer. Otherwise, a set is said to be *infinite*.

**Notation:** If a set $A$ is finite, then $n(A)$ will denote the number of elements in $A$.

**1.156** Determine which of the following sets are finite.
- (a) $A = \{$seasons in the year$\}$
- (b) $B = \{$states in the Union$\}$
- (c) $C = \{$positive integers less than 1$\}$
- (d) $D = \{$odd integers$\}$
- (e) $E = \{$positive integral divisors of 12$\}$
- (f) $F = \{$cats living in the United States$\}$

- (a) $A$ is finite because there are four seasons in the year, i.e., $n(A) = 4$.
- (b) $B$ is finite because there are 50 states in the Union, i.e., $n(B) = 50$.
- (c) There are no positive integers less than 1; hence $C$ is empty. Thus $C$ is finite and $n(C) = 0$.
- (d) $D$ is infinite.
- (e) The positive integral divisors of 12 are 1, 2, 3, 4, 6 and 12. Hence $E$ is finite and $n(E) = 6$.
- (f) Although it may be difficult to count the number of cats living in the United States, there is still a finite number of them. Hence $F$ is finite.

**1.157** Identify whether each of the following sets is infinite or finite:
- (a) $\{$days in a week$\}$
- (b) $\{$different letters in the word "mathematics"$\}$
- (c) $\{$negative integers$\}$
- (d) $\{$ways to order the numbers 1 through 100$\}$

- (a) Finite. There are seven days in a week, hence the set is finite.
- (b) Finite. There are eight different letters in the word "mathematics", hence the set is finite.
- (c) Infinite. There are an infinite number of negative integers, hence the set is infinite.
- (d) Finite. Though the number of combinations is very large and listing them would be a lengthy task, there are a finite number of possibilities, hence the set is finite.

**1.158** Identify whether each of the following sets is infinite or finite:
- (a) $\{$lines through the origin$\}$
- (b) $\{$lines that satisfy the equation $3x = y\}$
- (c) $\{$sides of a cube$\}$
- (d) $\{$squares with the points $(0, 0)$, $(0, 1)$ and $(0, 4)$ as corners$\}$

- (a) Infinite. There are an infinite number of lines passing through any point, hence the set is infinite.
- (b) Finite. The equation specifies one single line passing through the origin, hence the set is finite.
- (c) Finite. There are six sides to a cube, hence the set is finite.
- (d) Finite. There are no squares that can satisfy the conditions, hence the set is empty and thus finite.

**1.159** Find the number of elements in each finite set:
- (a) $A = \{2, 4, 6, 8, 10\}$
- (b) $B = \{x: x^2 = 4\}$
- (c) $C = \{x: x > x + 2\}$
- (d) $D = \{x: x$ is a positive integer, $x$ is a divisor of 15$\}$
- (e) $E = \{$letters in the alphabet preceding the letter $m\}$
- (f) $F = \{x: x$ is a solution to $x^3 = 27\}$

- (a) There are five specified elements; hence $n(A) = 5$.
- (b) There are only two roots, $x = 2$ and $x = -2$. Thus $n(B) = 2$.
- (c) No $x$ satisfies the given condition. Thus $C = \emptyset$ and $n(C) = 0$.
- (d) The positive divisors of 15 are 1, 3, 5 and 15. Hence $n(D) = 4$.
- (e) There are 12 letters preceding $m$; hence $n(E) = 12$.
- (f) If $\mathbf{U}$ is the real field $\mathbf{R}$ then $x^3 = 27$ has only the solution $x = 3$; hence $n(F) = 1$. However, if $\mathbf{U}$ is the complex field $\mathbf{C}$ then $x^3 = 27$ has three distinct solutions; hence $n(F) = 3$.

## Counting (Inclusion-Exclusion) Principle

Problems 1.160–1.177 use the following theorems.

**Lemma 1.4:**   Suppose $A$ and $B$ are disjoint finite sets. Then $A \cup B$ is finite and

$$n(A \cup B) = n(A) + n(B)$$

**Theorem 1.5:**   Suppose $A$ and $B$ are finite sets. Then $A \cup B$ and $A \cap B$ are finite and

$$n(A \cup B) = n(A) + n(B) - n(A \cap B)$$

Thus $n(A \cap B) = n(A) + n(B) - n(A \cup B)$.

**Theorem 1.6:**   Suppose $A$, $B$, and $C$ are finite sets. Then $A \cup B \cup C$ is finite and

$$n(A \cup B \cup C) = n(A) + n(B) + n(C) - n(A \cap B) - n(A \cap C) - n(B \cap C) + n(A \cap B \cap C)$$

**Theorem 1.7   (Inclusion-Exclusion Principle):**   Suppose $A_1, A_2, \ldots, A_n$ are finite sets. Then $A_1 \cup A_2 \cup \cdots \cup A_n$ is finite and

$$n(A_1 \cup A_2 \cup \cdots \cup A_n) = \sum_{1 \le i \le n} n(A_i) - \sum_{1 \le i < j \le n} n(A_i \cap A_j) + \sum_{1 \le i < j < k \le n} n(A_i \cap A_j \cap A_k)$$
$$- \cdots + (-1)^{n-1} n(A_1 \cap A_2 \cap \cdots \cap A_n)$$

**Remark:**   Theorems 1.5 and 1.6 are special cases of Theorem 1.7.

**1.160**   Prove Lemma 1.4.

❚   In counting the elements of $A \cup B$, first count those that are in $A$. There are $n(A)$ of these. The only other elements of $A \cup B$ are those that are in $B$ but not in $A$. But since $A$ and $B$ are disjoint, no element of $B$ is in $A$, so there are $n(B)$ elements that are in $B$ but not in $A$. Therefore, $n(A \cup B) = n(A) + n(B)$.

**1.161**   Prove Theorem 1.5.

❚   In counting the elements of $A \cup B$, we count the elements in $A$ and count the elements in $B$. There are $n(A)$ in $A$ and $n(B)$ in $B$. However, the elements in $A \cap B$ were counted twice. Thus

$$n(A \cup B) = n(A) + n(B) - n(A \cap B)$$

as required. Alternately, we have the disjoint unions

$$A \cup B = A \cup (B \backslash A) \qquad \text{and} \qquad B = (A \cap B) \cup (B \backslash A)$$

Therefore, by Lemma 1.4,

$$n(A \cup B) = n(A) + n(B \backslash A) \qquad \text{and} \qquad n(B) = n(A \cap B) + n(B \backslash A)$$

Thus $n(B \backslash A) = n(B) - n(A \cap B)$ and hence

$$n(A \cup B) = n(A) + n(B) - n(A \cap B)$$

as required.

**1.162**   Prove Theorem 1.6.

❚   Using $(A \cup B) \cap C = (A \cap C) \cup (B \cap C)$ and $(A \cap C) \cap (B \cap C) = A \cap B \cap C$ and using Theorem 1.5 repeatedly, we have

$$n(A \cup B \cup C) = n(A \cup B) + n(C) - n[(A \cap C) \cup (B \cap C)]$$
$$= [n(A) + n(B) - n(A \cap B)] + n(C) - [n(A \cap C) + n(B \cap C) - n(A \cap B \cap C)]$$
$$= n(A) + n(B) + n(C) - n(A \cap B) - n(A \cap C) - n(B \cap C) + n(A \cap B \cap C)$$

as required.

**1.163**   Show that: (a) $A \backslash B$ and $A \cap B$ are disjoint and $A = (A \backslash B) \cup (A \cap B)$; (b) $n(A \backslash B) = n(A) - n(A \cap B)$.

❚   (a)   Suppose $x \in A \backslash B$ and $x \in A \cap B$. Then $x \notin B$ since $x \in A \backslash B$, and $x \in B$ since $x \in A \cap B$. This contradiction shows that no element $x$ can belong to both $A \backslash B$ and $A \cap B$; that is, $A \backslash B$ and $A \cap B$ are disjoint. Also,

$$(A \backslash B) \cup (A \cap B) = (A \cap B^c) \cup (A \cap B) = A \cap (B^c \cup B) = A \cap U = A$$

**(b)**  By **(a)** and Lemma 1.4, $n(A) = n(A \backslash B) + n(A \cap B)$ which gives us the result.

**1.164**  Suppose $A \subseteq B$. Show that $n(A \cup B) = n(B)$ and $n(A \cap B) = n(A)$.

❚  Since $A \subseteq B$, we have $A \cup B = B$ and $A \cap B = A$. Hence $n(A \cup B) = n(B)$ and $n(A \cap B) = n(A)$.

**1.165**  At dinner, five people order the special of the day, two people order from the list of entrees and one person orders only a salad. Find the number $m$ of people at dinner.

❚  Since the sets are disjoint (assuming no one orders more than one dinner), $m = 5 + 2 + 1 = 8$, the total number of dinners ordered.

**1.166**  There are 22 female students and 18 male students in a classroom. How many students are there in total?

❚  The sets of male and female students are disjoint; hence the total $t = 22 + 18 = 40$ students.

**1.167**  Twelve waiters with bachelor degrees and four waiters with masters degrees work at a restaurant. Find the number $d$ of waiters with degrees (assuming no waiter has a doctoral degree).

❚  The set $M$ of waiters with masters degrees is contained in the set $B$ of waiters with bachelor degrees. Hence $d = n(B \cup M) = n(B) = 12$.

**1.168**  Of 32 people who save paper or bottles (or both) for recycling, 30 save paper and 14 save bottles. Find the number $m$ of people who **(a)** save both, **(b)** save only paper, and **(c)** save only bottles.

❚  Let $P$ and $B$ denote the sets of people saving paper and bottles, respectively.
**(a)**  By Theorem 1.5,

$$m = n(P \cap B) = n(P) + n(B) - n(P \cup B) = 30 + 14 - 32 = 12$$

**(b)**  $m = n(P \backslash B) = n(P) - n(P \cap B) = 30 - 12 = 18$
**(c)**  $m = n(B \backslash P) = n(B) - n(P \cap B) = 14 - 12 = 2$

**1.169**  A sample of 80 car owners revealed that 24 owned station wagons and 62 owned cars which are not station wagons. Find the number $k$ of people who owned both a station wagon and some other car.

❚  By Theorem 1.5, $k = 62 + 24 - 80 = 6$.

**1.170**  You have interviewed a dozen people and found that all of them had been to Disney World or to Disneyland. If eight people had been to Disneyland, how many had been to Disney World?

❚  The answer is not four people unless we are told that no one went to both Disneyland and Disney World. That is, there is not enough information to determine the solution (unless, for example, we are told the number that have been to both).

**1.171**  Suppose 12 people read the *Wall Street Journal* ($W$) or *Business Week* ($B$) (or both). Given three people read only the *Journal* and six read both, find the number $k$ of people who read only *Business Week*.

❚  Note $W \cup B = (W \backslash B) \cup (W \cap B) \cup (B \backslash W)$ and the union is disjoint. Thus $12 = 3 + 6 + k$   or   $k = 3$.

**1.172**  Asked what pets they had, 10 families responded: (i) six had dogs, (ii) four had cats, and (iii) two had neither cats nor dogs. Find the number $k$ of families that had both cats and dogs.

❚  Here $10 - 2 = 8$ had either cats or dogs (or both). By Theorem 1.5, $k = 6 + 4 - 8 = 2$.

**1.173**  The students in a dormitory were asked whether they had a dictionary ($D$) or a thesaurus ($T$) in their rooms. The results showed that 650 students had a dictionary, 150 did not have a dictionary, 175 had a thesaurus, and 50 had neither a dictionary nor a thesaurus. Find the number $k$ of students who: **(a)** live in the dormitory, **(b)** have both a dictionary and a thesaurus, and **(c)** have only a thesaurus.

❚  Here $n(D) = 650$, $n(D^c) = 150$, $n(T) = 175$, and $n(D^c \cap T^c) = n((D \cup T)^c) = 50$.

**(a)**                                        $k = n(\mathbf{U}) = n(D) + n(D^c) = 650 + 150 = 800$

**(b)** First find $n(D \cup T) = n(\mathbf{U}) - n((D \cup T)^c) = 800 - 50 = 750$. Then, by Theorem 1.5,

$$k = n(D \cap T) = 650 + 175 - 750 = 75$$

**(c)**

$$k = n(T) - n(D \cap T) = 175 - 75 = 100$$

**1.174** In a survey of 60 people, it was found that 25 read *Newsweek* magazine, 26 read *Time*, and 26 read *Fortune*. Also 9 read both *Newsweek* and *Fortune*, 11 read both *Newsweek* and *Time*, 8 read both *Time* and *Fortune*, and 8 read no magazine at all.
   **(a)** Find the number of people who read all three magazines.
   **(b)** Fill in the correct number of people in each of the eight regions of the Venn diagram of Fig. 1-20(a). Here $N$, $T$, and $F$ denote the set of people who read *Newsweek*, *Time*, and *Fortune* respectively.
   **(c)** Determine the number of people who read exactly one magazine.

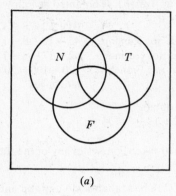   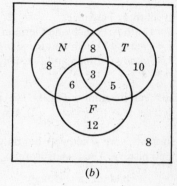

(a)                (b)                **Fig. 1-20**

▌ **(a)** Let $x = n(N \cap T \cap F)$, the number of people who read all three magazines. Note $n(N \cup T \cup F) = 52$ because 8 people read none of the magazines. We have

$$n(N \cup T \cup F) = n(N) + n(T) + n(F) - n(N \cap T) - n(N \cap F) - n(T \cap F) + n(N \cap T \cap F)$$

Hence, $52 = 25 + 26 + 26 - 11 - 9 - 8 + x$ or $x = 3$.
   **(b)** The required Venn diagram, Fig. 1-20(b), is obtained as follows:
       3 read all three magazines,
       $11 - 3 = 8$ read *Newsweek* and *Time* but not all three magazines,
       $9 - 3 = 6$ read *Newsweek* and Fortune but not all three magazines,
       $8 - 3 = 5$ read *Time* and *Fortune* but not all three magazines,
       $25 - 8 - 6 - 3 = 8$ read only *Newsweek*,
       $25 - 8 - 5 - 3 = 10$ read only *Time*,
       $26 - 6 - 5 - 3 = 12$ read only *Fortune*.
   **(c)** $8 + 10 + 12 = 30$ read only one magazine.

**1.175** Suppose that 100 of the 120 mathematics students at a college take at least one of the languages French, German, and Russian. Also suppose

| | |
|---|---|
| 65 study French | 20 study French and German |
| 45 study German | 25 study French and Russian |
| 42 study Russian | 15 study German and Russian |

**(a)** Find the number of students who study all three languages.
**(b)** Fill in the correct number of students in each of the eight regions of the Venn diagram of Fig. 1-21(a). Here $F$, $G$, and $R$ denote the sets of students studying French, German, and Russian, respectively.
**(c)** Determine the number $k$ of students who study (1) exactly one language, and (2) exactly two languages.

▌ **(a)** By Theorem 1.6,

$$n(F \cup G \cup R) = n(F) + n(G) + n(R) - n(F \cap G) - n(F \cap R) - n(G \cap R) + n(F \cap G \cap R)$$

Now, $n(F \cup G \cup R) = 100$ because 100 of the students study at least one of the languages. Substituting,

$$100 = 65 + 45 + 42 - 20 - 25 - 15 + n(F \cap G \cap R)$$

and so, $n(F \cap G \cap R) = 8$, i.e., eight students study all three languages.

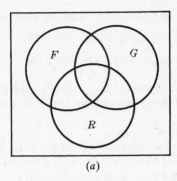 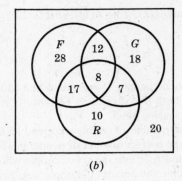

$(a)$           $(b)$      **Fig. 1-21**

**(b)** Using **(a)**, the required Venn diagram, Fig. 1-21(*b*), is obtained as follows:

8 study all three languages
$20 - 8 = 12$ study French and German but not Russian
$25 - 8 = 17$ study French and Russian but not German
$15 - 8 = 7$ study German and Russian but not French

$65 - 12 - 8 - 17 = 28$ study only French
$45 - 12 - 8 - 7 = 18$ study only German
$42 - 17 - 8 - 7 = 10$ study only Russian
$120 - 100 = 20$ do not study any of the languages

**(c)** Use the Venn diagram of Fig. 1-21(*b*) to obtain
(1) $k = 28 + 18 + 10 = 56$,    (2) $k = 12 + 17 + 7 = 36$

**1.176** One hundred students were asked whether they had taken courses in any of the three areas, sociology, anthropology, and history. The results were:

45 had taken sociology       18 had taken sociology and anthropology
38 had taken anthropology     9 had taken sociology and history
21 had taken history          4 had taken history and anthropology

and 23 had taken no courses in any of the areas.
**(a)** Draw a Venn diagram that will show the results of the survey.
**(b)** Determine the number $k$ of students who had taken classes in exactly (1) one of the areas, and (2) two of the areas.

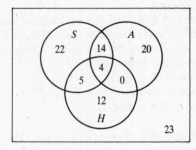

**Fig. 1-22**

❚ Let $S$, $A$ and, $H$ denote the sets of students who have taken courses in sociology, anthropology, and history, respectively.
**(a)** First find $n(S \cup A \cup H) = 100 - 23 = 77$. Next find $m = (S \cap A \cap H)$ using Theorem 1.6:

$$77 = 45 + 38 + 21 - 18 - 9 - 4 + m \quad \text{or} \quad m = 4$$

Now fill in the required Venn diagram of Fig. 1-22 as follows:
4 belong to all three sets,
$18 - 4 = 14$ belong to $S$ and $A$ but not $H$,
$9 - 4 = 5$ belong to $S$ and $H$ but not $A$,
$4 - 4 = 0$ belong to $A$ and $H$ but not $S$,
$45 - 14 - 4 - 5 = 22$ belong to only $S$,
$38 - 14 - 4 - 0 = 20$ belong to only $A$,
$21 - 5 - 4 - 0 = 12$ belong to only $H$,
23 belong to none of the three sets.
**(b)** Use the Venn diagram to obtain: (1) $k = 22 + 20 + 12 = 54$, and (2) $k = 14 + 5 + 0 = 19$.

**1.177** A survey on a sample of 25 new cars being sold at a local auto dealer was conducted to see which of three popular options, air-conditioning (A), radio (R), and power windows (W), were already installed. The survey found:

| | |
|---|---|
| 15 had air-conditioning | 4 had radio and power windows |
| 12 had radio | 3 had all three options |
| 5 had air-conditioning and power windows | 2 had no options |
| 9 had air-conditioning and radio | |

Find the number of cars that had: (**a**) only power windows, (**b**) only air-conditioning, (**c**) only radio, (**d**) radio and power windows but not air-conditioning, (**e**) air-conditioning and radio, but not power windows, (**f**) only one of the options.

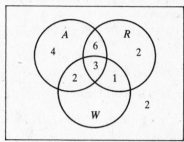

**Fig. 1-23**

    ▮ Use the data to first fill in the Venn diagram of A, R, and W in Fig. 1-23 as follows:

        3 had all three options,
        $9 - 3 = 6$ had A and R but not W,
        $5 - 3 = 2$ had A and W but not R,
        $4 - 3 = 1$ had R and W but not A,
        $15 - 6 - 3 - 2 = 4$ had only A,
        $12 - 6 - 3 - 1$ had only R,
        2 had none of the options.

Using the Venn diagram we obtain:

(**a**)  $25 - (6 + 4 + 2 + 3 + 2 + 1 + 2) = 5$ had only W,
(**b**)  4,    (**c**)  2,    (**d**)  $3 + 1 = 4$,    (**e**)  6,    (**f**)  $4 + 2 + 5 = 11$

## 1.7 CLASSES OF SETS, POWER SETS

**1.178** Explain the use of the term "class of sets" or "collection of sets" and the use of the term subclass or subcollection.

    ▮ Suppose X is a set whose elements are sets. To avoid confusion, we will refer to X as a *class* of sets or *collection* of sets rather than a set of sets. We will then refer to a subset of X as a *subclass* or *subcollection*.

**1.179** Let A be a given set. (**a**) Define the *power set* of A, denoted by $\mathscr{P}(A)$. (**b**) Find the number of elements in $\mathscr{P}(A)$ when A is finite.

    ▮ (**a**)  The power set $\mathscr{P}(A)$ of A is the collection of all subsets of A.
      (**b**)  The number of elements in $\mathscr{P}(A)$ is 2 raised to the power $n(A)$; that is, $n(\mathscr{P}(A)) = 2^{n(A)}$.

**1.180** Consider the set $A = [\{1, 2, 3\}, \{4, 5\}, \{6, 7, 8\}]$.
(**a**)  What are the elements of A?
(**b**)  Determine whether each of the following is true or false:

        (i)  $1 \in A$      (iii)  $\{6, 7, 8\} \in A$    (v)  $\emptyset \notin A$
        (ii)  $\{1, 2, 3\} \subseteq A$  (iv)  $\{\{4, 5\}\} \subseteq A$  (vi)  $\emptyset \subseteq A$

    ▮ (**a**)  A is a class of sets; its elements are the sets $\{1, 2, 3\}$, $\{4, 5\}$, and $\{6, 7, 8\}$.
      (**b**)  (i)  False. 1 is not one of the elements of A.
          (ii)  False. $\{1, 2, 3\}$ is not a subset of A; it is one of the elements of A.
          (iii)  True. $\{6, 7, 8\}$ is one of the elements of A.
          (iv)  True. $\{\{4, 5\}\}$, the set consisting of the element $\{4, 5\}$, is a subset of A.
          (v)  False. The empty set $\emptyset$ is not an element of A, i.e., it is not one of the three sets listed in the problem statement.
          (vi)  True. The empty set is a subset of every set; even a class of sets.

**1.181** Let $X = \{a, b, c\}$. Find the power set $\mathscr{P}(X)$ of $X$. List the elements (subsets of $X$) of each of the following subclasses of $\mathscr{P}(X)$.
(a) $Y_1$ = sets which contain two elements;
(b) $Y_2$ = sets which contain three elements;
(c) $Y_3$ = sets which contain the element "$a$";
(d) $Y_4$ = sets which contain the elements "$b$" and "$c$".

▌ $\mathscr{P}(X)$ consists of all the subsets of $X$:

$$\mathscr{P}(X) = [\emptyset, \{a\}, \{b\}, \{c\}, \{a, b\}, \{a, c\}, \{b, c\}, \{a, b, c\}]$$

Note the empty set $\emptyset$ belongs to $\mathscr{P}(X)$ since $\emptyset$ is a subset of $X$. Similarly, $X = \{a, b, c\}$ belongs to $\mathscr{P}(X)$. Note also that $\mathscr{P}(X)$ contains $2^3 = 8$ elements.
(a) $\{a, b\}, \{a, c\}, \{b, c\}$     (c) $\{a\}, \{a, b\}, \{a, c\}, \{a, b, c\}$
(b) $\{a, b, c\}$                 (d) $\{b, c\}, \{a, b, c\}$

**1.182** Determine the power set $\mathscr{P}(A)$ of $A = \{a, b, c, d\}$.

▌ The elements of $\mathscr{P}(A)$ are the subsets of $A$. Hence:

$$\mathscr{P}(A) = [A, \{a, b, c\}, \{a, b, d\}, \{a, c, d\}, \{b, c, d\}, \{a, b\}, \{a, c\}, \{a, d\},$$
$$\{b, c\}, \{b, d\}, \{c, d\}, \{a\}, \{b\}, \{c\}, \{d\}, \emptyset]$$

We note that $\mathscr{P}(A)$ has $2^4 = 16$ elements.

**1.183** Suppose $X = \{1, 2, 3, 4, 5\}$. List the elements of the following subclasses of $\mathscr{P}(X)$:
(a) $Y_1$ = sets which do not contain the elements 2 or 4;
(b) $Y_2$ = sets whose elements sum to 5;
(c) $Y_3$ = sets with 4 elements.

▌ List the subsets of $X$ with the given property:
(a) $\{1\}, \{3\}, \{5\}, \{1, 3\}, \{1, 5\}, \{3, 5\}, \{1, 3, 5\}$
(b) $\{2, 3\}, \{1, 4\}, \{5\}$
(c) $\{1, 2, 3, 4\}, \{1, 2, 3, 5\}, \{1, 2, 4, 5\}, \{1, 3, 4, 5\}, \{2, 3, 4, 5\}$

**1.184** Find the number of elements in the power set of each of the following sets:
(a) $\{$one, two$\}$        (c) $\{7\}$
(b) $\{$car, bus, train, plane$\}$       (d) $\{1, 2, 3, 4, 5\}$

▌ Recall $\mathscr{P}(A)$ contains $2^{n(A)}$ elements. Thus: (a) $2^2 = 4$, (b) $2^4 = 16$, (c) $2^1 = 2$, (d) $2^5 = 32$.

**1.185** Is the power set $\mathscr{P}(\emptyset)$ of the empty set $\emptyset$ empty?

▌ No. $\mathscr{P}(\emptyset) = \{\emptyset\}$, the class with one element, the empty set.

**1.186** Find the number of elements in the power set of each of the following sets:
(a) $\{x : x$ is a day of the week$\}$      (c) $\{x : x$ is a season of the year$\}$
(b) $\{x : x$ is a positive divisor of 6$\}$     (d) $\{x : x$ is a letter in the word "yes"$\}$

▌ (a) $2^7 = 128$; (b) $2^4 = 16$ since there are four divisors, 1, 2, 3, 6; (c) $2^4 = 16$; (d) $2^3 = 8$.

**1.187** Let $A = [\{a\}, \{b, c, d, e\}, \{c, d\}]$. List the elements of $A$ and determine whether each of the following statements is true or false:
(a) $a \in A$     (c) $\{\{a\}, \{c, d\}\} \subseteq A$     (e) $\emptyset \subseteq A$
(b) $\{a\} \in A$    (d) $\{b, c, d, e\} \subseteq A$      (f) $\emptyset \in A$

▌ The elements of $A$ are $\{a\}$, $\{b, c, d, e\}$ and $\{c, d\}$.
(a) False. The element $a$ is not one of the three elements of $A$.
(b) True. The set $\{a\}$ is one of the three elements of $A$.
(c) True. $\{\{a\}, \{c, d\}\}$ is a subset of $A$.
(d) False. $\{b, c, d, e\}$ is an element of $A$, not a subset.
(e) True. The empty set is a subset of every set, even a class of sets.
(f) False. The empty set is not specified as one of the elements of $A$.

**1.188**  Consider the class of sets $B = [\{1, 3, 5\}, \{2, 4, 6\}, \{0\}]$. List the elements of $B$ and determine whether each of the following statements is true or false:

(a) $\varnothing \subseteq B$   (c) $\{1, 3, 5\} \subseteq B$   (e) $\{\{2, 4, 6\}, \{0\}\} \subseteq B$
(b) $3 \in B$   (d) $\{1, 2, 3, 4, 5, 6\} \in B$   (f) $\{0\} \in B$

❙ The elements of $B$ are $\{1, 3, 5\}$, $\{2, 4, 6\}$, and $\{0\}$.

(a) True. The empty set is a subset of every set, even a class of sets.
(b) False. While 3 is an element of one of the sets which is an element of the class of sets $B$, it is not one of the elements of $B$.
(c) False. $\{1, 3, 5\}$ is an element of $B$ and is not a subset.
(d) False. $\{1, 2, 3, 4, 5, 6\}$ is not an element of $B$.
(e) True. $\{\{2, 4, 6\}, \{0\}\}$ is a set of elements from $B$ and is therefore a subset of $B$.
(f) True. $\{0\}$ is one of the elements of $B$.

Problems 1.189–1.191 refer to the following classes of sets:

$$E = [\{1, 2, 3\}, \{2, 3\}, \{a, b\}], \qquad F = [\{a, b\}, \{1, 2\}]$$

**1.189**  Find: (a) $E \cup F$, (b) $E \cap F$, (c) $E^c$, (d) $E \backslash F$.

❙ (a) $E \cup F = [\{1, 2, 3\}, \{2, 3\}, \{a, b\}, \{1, 2\}]$, the elements in $E$ or $F$.
(b) $E \cap F = [\{a, b\}]$ since $\{a, b\}$ is the only element in both sets.
(c) $E^c$ cannot be specified since the universal set $\mathbf{U}$ has not been given.
(d) $E \backslash F = [\{1, 2, 3\}, \{2, 3\}]$, the elements in $E$ which do not belong to $F$.

**1.190**  Find the power set $\mathscr{P}(E)$ of $E$.

❙ Here $\mathscr{P}(E)$ consists of the subsets of $E$ and there are $2^3 = 8$ of them:

$$\mathscr{P}(E) = \{\varnothing, [\{1, 2, 3\}], [\{2, 3\}], [\{a, b\}], [\{1, 2, 3\}, \{2, 3\}], [\{1, 2, 3\}, \{a, b\}], [\{2, 3\}, \{a, b\}], E\}$$

Note $\mathscr{P}(E)$ is a collection of classes of sets.

**1.191**  Determine whether the following statements are true or false:

(a) $\{a, b\} \subseteq F$   (c) $F \subseteq E$   (e) $1 \in E$
(b) $[\{1, 2, 3\}] \subseteq E$   (d) $\varnothing \subseteq F$   (f) $\{2, 3\} \in E$

❙ (a) False. $\{a, b\}$ is an element of $F$, not a subset.
(b) True.
(c) False. $\{1, 2\} \in F$ does not belong to $E$.
(d) True. The empty set $\varnothing$ is a subset of every set.
(e) False. The element 1 is not an element in $E$.
(f) True.

**1.192**  Find the power set $\mathscr{P}(A)$ of $A = \{1, 2, 3, 4, 5\}$.

❙ List all the subsets of $A$; there are $2^5 = 32$ of them:

$$\mathscr{P}(A) = [\varnothing, \{1\}, \{2\}, \{3\}, \{4\}, \{5\}, \{1, 2\}, \{1, 3\}, \{1, 4\}, \{1, 5\},$$
$$\{2, 3\}, \{2, 4\}, \{2, 5\}, \{3, 4\}, \{3, 5\}, \{4, 5\}, \{1, 2, 3\},$$
$$\{1, 2, 4\}, \{1, 2, 5\}, \{2, 3, 4\}, \{2, 3, 5\}, \{3, 4, 5\}, \{1, 3, 4\},$$
$$\{1, 3, 5\}, \{1, 4, 5\}, \{2, 4, 5\}, \{1, 2, 3, 4\}, \{1, 2, 3, 5\},$$
$$\{1, 2, 4, 5\}, \{1, 3, 4, 5\}, \{2, 3, 4, 5\}, A]$$

**1.193**  Find the power set $\mathscr{P}(A)$ of $A = [\{a, b\}, \{c\}, \{d, e, f\}]$.

❙ Since $A$ has 3 elements, $\mathscr{P}(A)$ has $2^3 = 8$ elements:

$$\mathscr{P}(A) = \{A, [\{a, b\}, \{c\}], [\{a, b\}, \{d, e, f\}], [\{c\}, \{d, e, f\}], [\{a, b\}], [\{c\}], [\{d, e, f\}], \varnothing\}$$

**1.194**  Suppose $A$ is a finite set with $m$ elements. Prove $\mathscr{P}(A)$ has $2^m$ elements.

▌ Let $X$ be an arbitrary member of $\mathscr{P}(A)$. For each $a \in A$, there are two possibilities: $a \in X$ or $a \notin X$. But there are $m$ elements in $A$; hence there are

$$\overbrace{2 \cdot 2 \cdot 2 \cdots \cdot 2}^{m \text{ times}} = 2^m$$

different sets $X$. That is, $\mathscr{P}(A)$ has $2^m$ members.

## 1.8 MATHEMATICAL INDUCTION

**1.195** State the *principle of mathematical induction* in two equivalent forms.

▌ *Form I*: Let $P$ be a proposition defined on the positive integers $\mathbf{N}$; i.e., $P(n)$ is either true or false for each $n$ in $\mathbf{N}$. Suppose $P$ has the following two properties:
(i) $P(1)$ is true.
(ii) $P(n + 1)$ is true whenever $P(n)$ is true.
Then $P$ is true for every positive integer.
*Form II* ("Complete Induction"): Let $P$ be a proposition defined on the positive integers $\mathbf{N}$, such that:
(i) $P(1)$ is true.
(ii) $P(n)$ is true whenever $P(k)$ is true for all $1 \le k < n$.
Then $P$ is true for every positive integer.

**Remark:** The above principle of mathematical induction begins at $n_0 = 1$ and proves that $P(n)$ is true for all $n \ge 1$. Alternately, one can begin at any integer $n_0 = m$ and prove that $P(n)$ is true for all $n \ge m$.

**1.196** Let $P$ be the proposition that the sum of the first $n$ odd numbers is $n^2$; that is,

$$P(n): \quad 1 + 3 + 5 + \cdots + (2n - 1) = n^2$$

(The $n$th odd number is $2n - 1$, and the next odd number is $2n + 1$.) Prove $P$ is true for every positive integer $n \in \mathbf{N}$.

▌ Since $1 = 1^2$, $P(1)$ is true. Assuming $P(n)$ is true, we add $2n + 1$ to both sides of $P(n)$, obtaining

$$1 + 3 + 5 + \cdots + (2n - 1) + (2n + 1) = n^2 + (2n + 1) = (n + 1)^2$$

which is $P(n + 1)$. That is, $P(n + 1)$ is true whenever $P(n)$ is true. By the principle of mathematical induction, $P$ is true of all $n$.

**1.197** Prove the proposition $P$ that the sum of the first $n$ positive integers is $\frac{1}{2}n(n + 1)$; that is,

$$P(n): \quad 1 + 2 + 3 + \cdots + n = \tfrac{1}{2}n(n + 1)$$

▌ The proposition holds for $n = 1$ since $1 = \frac{1}{2}(1)(1 + 1)$. That is, $P(1)$ is true. Assuming $P(n)$ is true, we add $n + 1$ to both sides of $P(n)$, obtaining

$$
\begin{aligned}
1 + 2 + 3 + \cdots + n + (n + 1) &= \tfrac{1}{2}n(n + 1) + (n + 1) \\
&= \tfrac{1}{2}[n(n + 1) + 2(n + 1)] \\
&= \tfrac{1}{2}[(n + 1)(n + 2)]
\end{aligned}
$$

which is $P(n + 1)$. That is, $P(n + 1)$ is true whenever $P(n)$ is true. By the principle of induction, $P$ is true for all $n$.

**1.198** Prove the following proposition:

$$P(n): \quad 1^2 + 2^2 + \cdots + n^2 = \frac{n(n + 1)(2n + 1)}{6}$$

▌ Since $1 = (1)(2)(3)/6$, we have $P(1)$ is true. Assuming $P(n)$ is true, we add $(n + 1)^2$ to both sides of $P(n)$, obtaining

$$1^2 + 2^2 + \cdots + n^2 + (n + 1)^2 = \frac{n(n + 1)(2n + 1)}{6} + (n + 1)^2$$

$$= \frac{n(n + 1)(2n + 1) + 6(n + 1)^2}{6} = \frac{(n + 1)[(2n^2 + n) + (6n + 6)]}{6}$$

$$= \frac{(n+1)(2n^2 + 7n + 6)}{6} = \frac{(n+1)(n+2)(2n+3)}{6}$$

$$= \frac{(n+1)(n+2)[2(n+1)+1]}{6}$$

which is $P(n+1)$. Thus $P(n+1)$ is true whenever $P(n)$ is true. By the principle of induction, $P$ is true for all $n$.

**1.199** Prove the following proposition:

$$P(n): \quad 1 + 4 + 7 + \cdots + (3n - 2) = \frac{n(3n-1)}{2}$$

▮ Since $1 = 1(3-1)/2$, we have $P(1)$ is true. Assuming $P(n)$ is true, we add $[3(n+1)-2] = (3n+1)$ to both sides of $P(n)$, obtaining

$$1 + 4 + 7 + \cdots + (3n-2) + (3n+1) = \frac{n(3n-1)}{2} + (3n+1)$$

$$= \frac{n(3n-1) + 2(3n+1)}{2} = \frac{3n^2 + 5n + 2}{2} = \frac{(n+1)(3m+2)}{2}$$

$$= \frac{(n+1)[3(n+1)-1]}{2}$$

which is $P(n+1)$. Thus $P(n+1)$ is true whenever $P(n)$ is true. By the principle of induction, $P$ is true for all $n$.

**1.200** Prove the following proposition:

$$P(n): \quad \frac{1}{1(3)} + \frac{1}{3(5)} + \frac{1}{5(7)} + \cdots + \frac{1}{(2n-1)(2n+1)} = \frac{n}{2n+1}$$

▮ Since $1/3 = 1/(2+1)$, we have $P(1)$ is true. Assuming $P(n)$ is true, we add $1/[(2n+1)(2n+3)]$ to both sides of $P(n)$, obtaining

$$\frac{1}{1(3)} + \frac{1}{3(5)} + \frac{1}{5(7)} + \cdots + \frac{1}{(2n-1)(2n+1)} + \frac{1}{(2n+1)(2n+3)}$$

$$= \frac{n}{2n+1} + \frac{1}{(2n+1)(2n+3)} = \frac{n(2n+3)+1}{(2n+1)(2n+3)} = \frac{2n^2 + 3n + 1}{(2n+1)(2n+3)}$$

$$= \frac{(n+1)(2n+1)}{(2n+1)(2n+3)} = \frac{n+1}{2n+3} = \frac{n+1}{2(n+1)+1}$$

which is $P(n+1)$. Thus $P(n+1)$ is true whenever $P(n)$ is true. By the principle of induction, $P$ is true for all $n$.

**1.201** Prove the following proposition (for $n \geq 0$):

$$P(n): \quad 1 + 2 + 2^2 + 2^3 + \cdots + 2^n = 2^{n+1} - 1$$

▮ Since $1 = 2^1 - 1$, we have $P(0)$ is true. Assuming $P(n)$ is true, we add $2^{n+1}$ to both sides of $P(n)$, obtaining

$$1 + 2 + 2^2 + \cdots + 2^n + 2^{n+1} = 2^{n+1} - 1 + 2^{n+1}$$

$$= 2(2^{n+1}) - 1 = 2^{n+2} - 1$$

which is $P(n+1)$. Thus $P(n+1)$ is true whenever $P(n)$ is true. By the principle of induction, $P$ is true for all $n \geq 0$.

**1.202** Prove $n! \geq 2^n$ for $n \geq 4$.

▮ Since $4! = 24 \geq 2^4 = 16$, the formula is true for $n = 4$. Assuming $n! \geq 2^n$, we have

$$(n+1)! = n!\,(n+1) \geq 2^n(n+1) \geq 2^n(2) = 2^{n+1}$$

Thus the formula is true for $n + 1$. By induction, the formula is true for all $n \geq 4$.

**1.203** Prove $n^2 \geq 2n + 1$ for $n \geq 3$.

▮ Since $3^2 = 9 \geq 2(3) + 1 = 7$, the formula is true for $n = 3$. Assuming $n^2 \geq 2n + 1$, we have

$$(n + 1)^2 = n^2 + 2n + 1 \geq 2n + 1 + 2n + 1 = 2n + 2 + 2n \geq 2n + 2 + 1 = 2(n + 1) + 1$$

Thus the formula is true for $n + 1$. By induction, the formula is true for all $n \geq 3$.

**1.204**   Prove $2^n \geq n^2$ for $n \geq 4$.

▮ Since $2^4 = 16 = 4^2$, the formula is true for $n = 4$. Assuming $2^n \geq n^2$ and also $n^2 \geq 2n + 1$ (Problem 1.203), we have

$$2^{n+1} = 2(2^n) \geq 2(n^2) = n^2 + n^2 \geq n^2 + 2n + 1 = (n + 1)^2$$

Thus the formula is true for $n + 1$. By induction, the formula is true for all $n \geq 4$.

**Theorem 1.8:**   Suppose $*$ is an associative operation on a set $S$, that is, $(a * b) * c = a(b * c)$ for any three elements $a, b, c \in S$. Prove that all possible "products" of $n$ ordered elements $a_1, a_2, \ldots, a_n$ are equal. (Thus, when dealing with an associative operation, we can dispense with parentheses and simply write $a_1 * a_2 * \cdots * a_m$.)

**1.205**   Prove Theorem 1.8.

▮ The proof is by induction on $n$. The cases $n = 1$ and $n = 2$ are trivially true, and the case $n = 3$ is true since $*$ is associative. Suppose $n > 3$ and use the notations (with $*$ replaced by juxtaposition)

$$(a_1 a_2 \cdots a_n) \equiv (\cdots ((a_1 a_2) a_3) \cdots) a_n \qquad \text{and} \qquad [a_1 a_2 \cdots a_n] \equiv \text{any product}$$

We shall show that $[a_1 a_2 \cdots a_n] = (a_1 a_2 \cdots a_n)$. In fact, since $[a_1 a_2 \cdots a_n]$ denotes some product, there exists an $r < n$ such that $[a_1 a_2 \cdots a_n] = [a_1 a_2 \cdots a_r][a_{r+1} \cdots a_n]$. Therefore, by induction,

$$\begin{aligned}
[a_1 a_2 \cdots a_n] &= [a_1 a_2 \cdots a_r][a_{r+1} \cdots a_n] = [a_1 a_2 \cdots a_r](a_{r+1} \cdots a_n) \\
&= [a_1 \cdots a_r]((a_{r+1} \cdots a_{n-1})a_n) = ([a_1 \cdots a_r](a_{r+1} \cdots a_{n-1}))a_n \\
&= [a_1 \cdots a_{n-1}]a_n = (a_1 \cdots a_{n-1})a_n = (a_1 a_2 \cdots a_n).
\end{aligned}$$

Thus the theorem is proved.

**1.206**   Show that the principle of mathematical induction (complete form) is equivalent to the assertion that every nonempty set of positive integers has a smallest member (the *well-ordering principle* for **N**).

▮ Suppose that **N** is well-ordered, and that we are given a proposition $P(n)$ satisfying the hypotheses (i) and (ii) of the induction principle. Let **F** denote the subset of **N** on which $P$ is false. If **F** is nonempty, it has a smallest member, $q$; by (i), $q \geq 2$. Then $P(1), \ldots, P(q - 1)$ are all true; hence, by (ii), $P(q)$ is true. This contradiction shows that **F** must be empty. Thus, $P$ is true for every positive integer, and the induction principle is valid.

Conversely, suppose that the induction principle holds and that there exists a subset, **S**, of **N** that has no smallest member. Let **S**\* be the complement of **S**, and define the proposition $P(n)$: $n$ belongs to **S**\*. $P(n)$ satisfies (i) and (ii) of complete induction (if it did not, **S** would have a smallest member); consequently, **S**\* = **N**, which means that **S** is empty. Thus, **N** is well-ordered.

## 1.9   ARGUMENTS AND VENN DIAGRAMS

This section uses Venn diagrams to determine the validity of an argument.

**1.207**   Translate each of the following statements into a Venn diagram.
(*a*)   All students are lazy.        (*c*)   No student is lazy.
(*b*)   Some students are lazy.       (*d*)   Not all students are lazy.

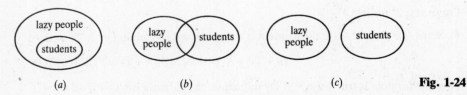

(*a*)                   (*b*)                   (*c*)                   **Fig. 1-24**

▮ (*a*)   The set of students are contained in the set of lazy people as shown in Fig. 1-24(*a*).

(**b**)   The set of students and set of lazy people have some elements in common as shown in Fig. 1-24(*b*).
(**c**)   The set of students and the set of lazy people are disjoint as pictured in Fig. 1-24(*c*).
(**d**)   Here the set of students is not contained in the set of lazy people. This leads to Fig. 1-24(*b*) (with the possibility that the intersection is empty).

**1.208**   Show that the following argument (adapted from a book on logic by Lewis Carroll, the author of *Alice in Wonderland*) is valid.

$S_1$:   My saucepans are the only things I have that are made of tin.
$S_2$:   I find all your presents very useful.
$S_3$:   None of my saucepans is of the slightest use.
_____

$S$:   Your presents to me are not made of tin.

(The statements $S_1$, $S_2$, and $S_3$ above the horizontal line denote the assumptions, and the statement $S$ below the line denotes the conclusion. The argument is valid if the conclusion $S$ follows logically from the assumptions $S_1$, $S_2$, and $S_3$.)

▮ By $S_1$ the tin objects are contained in the set of saucepans and by $S_3$ the set of saucepans and the set of useful things are disjoint: hence draw the Venn diagram of Fig. 1-25.

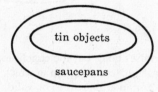 

Fig. 1-25

By $S_2$ the set of "your presents" is a subset of the set of useful things; hence draw Fig. 1-26.

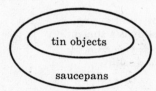 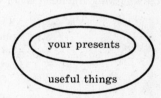

Fig. 1-26

The conclusion is clearly valid by the above Venn diagram because the set of "your presents" is disjoint from the set of tin objects.

**1.209**   Consider the following assumptions:

$S_1$:   Poets are happy people.
$S_2$:   Every doctor is wealthy.
$S_3$:   No one who is happy is also wealthy.

Determine the validity of each of the following conclusions: (**a**) No poet is wealthy. (**b**) Doctors are happy people. (**c**) No one can be both a poet and a doctor.

▮ By $S_1$ the set of poets is contained in the set of happy people, and by $S_3$ the set of happy people is disjoint from the set of wealthy people. Hence draw the Venn diagram of Fig. 1-27.

 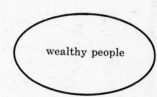

Fig. 1-27

By $S_2$ the set of doctors is contained in the set of wealthy people. So draw the Venn diagram of Fig. 1-28. From this diagram it is obvious that (*a*) and (*c*) are valid conclusions whereas (*b*) is not valid.

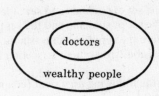

**Fig. 1-28**

**1.210** Show that the following argument is not valid by constructing a Venn diagram in which the premises hold but the conclusion does not hold:

$S_1$: Some students are lazy.
$S_2$: All males are lazy.

S: Some students are males.

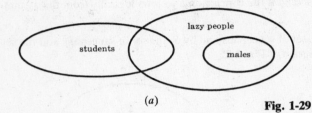

(a)     **Fig. 1-29**     (b)

▌ Consider the Venn diagram in Fig. 1-29(a). Both premises hold, but the conclusion does not hold. Thus the argument is not valid even though it is possible to construct a Venn diagram in which the premises and conclusion hold, such as in Fig. 1-29(b). In other words, for an argument to be valid, the conclusion must *always* be true when the premises are true.

**1.211** Show that the following argument is not valid:

$S_1$: All students are lazy.
$S_2$: Nobody who is wealthy is a student.

S: Lazy people are not wealthy.

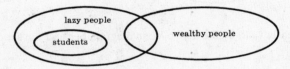

**Fig. 1-30**

▌ Figure 1-30 gives a Venn diagram where both premises hold, but the conclusion does not hold. Thus the argument is invalid.

**1.212** Show that the following argument is valid:

$S_1$: No student is lazy.
$S_2$: John is an artist.
$S_3$: All artists are lazy.

S: John is not a student.

**Fig. 1-31**

▌ By $S_3$ the set of artists is a subset of the set of lazy people, and by $S_1$ the set of lazy people and the set of students are disjoint. Thus draw the Venn diagram in Fig. 1-31. By $S_2$ John belongs to the set of artists; hence the conclusion "John is not a student" follows from the premises. In other words, the argument is valid.

**1.213**   Show that the following argument is valid:

$S_1$:   All lawyers are wealthy.
$S_2$:   Poets are temperamental.
$S_3$:   Audrey is a lawyer.
$S_4$:   No temperamental person is wealthy.

———————————————

$S$:   Audrey is not a poet.

**Fig. 1-32**

▌ The premises $S_1$, $S_4$, and then $S_2$ lead to the Venn diagram in Fig. 1-32. By $S_3$, Audrey belongs to the set of lawyers which is disjoint from the set of poets. Thus "Audrey is not a poet" is a valid conclusion.

**1.214**   Show that the following argument is not valid (even though each statement is true):

$S_1$;   Some animals can reason.
$S_2$:   Man is an animal.

———————————————

$S$:   Man can reason.

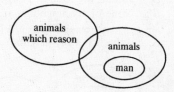

**Fig. 1-33**

▌ Figure 1-33 gives a Venn diagram in which both premises hold but the conclusion does not hold. Thus the argument is not valid.

**1.215**   Determine the validity of the argument:

$S_1$:   All red meat contains cholesterol.
$S_2$:   No expensive food contains cholesterol.

———————————————

$S$:   Read meat is not expensive.

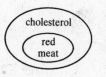 

**Fig. 1-34**

▌ The premises $S_1$ and $S_2$ lead to the Venn diagram in Fig. 1-34. Thus red meat is disjoint from food that is expensive. Accordingly, $S$ is a valid conclusion.

**1.216**   Determine the validity of the argument:

$S_1$:   New York is a big city.
$S_2$:   Erik lives in a city with trolley cars.
$S_3$:   No big city has trolley cars.

———————————————

$S$:   Erik does not live in New York.

▌ The premises $S_1$ and $S_3$ lead to the Venn diagram in Fig. 1-35. By $S_2$, Erik lives in a city with trolley cars. By the Venn diagram such cities do not include New York. Thus $S$ is a valid conclusion.

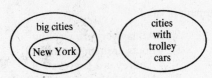

**Fig. 1-35**

**1.217**    Determine the validity of the following argument:

$S_1$:    All gold jewelry are expensive.
$S_2$;    No earrings are expensive.
_____

$S$:    Earrings are not made of gold.

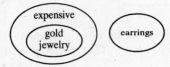

**Fig. 1-36**

▮ The premises $S_1$ and $S_2$ lead to the Venn diagram in Fig. 1-36. Thus the set of earrings is disjoint from the set of gold jewelry; that is, $S$ is a valid conclusion.

**1.218**    Determine the validity of the following argument:

$S_1$:    All my friends are musicians.
$S_2$;    John is my friend.
$S_3$;    None of my neighbors are musicians.
_____

$S$:    John is not my neighbor.

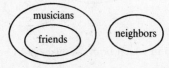

**Fig. 1-37**

▮ The premises $S_1$ and $S_3$ lead to the Venn diagram in Fig. 1-37. By $S_2$, John belongs to the set of friends which is disjoint from the set of neighbors. Thus $S$ is a valid conclusion and so the argument is valid.

**1.219**    Consider the following assumptions:

$S_1$:    All dictionaries are useful.
$S_2$:    Mary owns only romance novels.
$S_3$:    No romance novel is useful.

Determine the validity of each of the following conclusions:
**(a)**    Romance novels are not dictionaries.
**(b)**    Mary does not own a dictionary.
**(c)**    All useful books are dictionaries.

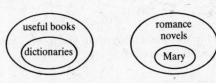

**Fig. 1-38**

▮ The three premises lead to the Venn diagram in Fig. 1-38. From this diagram it follows that **(a)** and **(b)** are valid conclusions. However, **(c)** is not a valid conclusion since there may be useful books which are not dictionaries.

**1.220**    Consider the following assumptions:

$S_1$:    All wool clothes are warm.
$S_2$;    None of my clothes is warm.
$S_3$:    Macy's only sells wool clothes.

Determine the validity of each of the following conclusions:
- (**a**) None of my clothes is made of wool.
- (**b**) All of Macy's clothes are warm.
- (**c**) None of my clothes comes from Macy's.

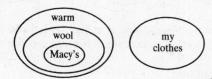

Fig. 1-39

▌ The three premises lead to the Venn diagram in Fig. 1-39 which shows that (**a**), (**b**), and (**c**) are valid conclusions.

**1.221** Consider the following assumptions:

$S_1$: I planted all my expensive trees last year.
$S_2$: All my fruit trees are in my orchard.
$S_3$: No tree in the orchard was planted last year.

Determine whether or not each of the following is a valid conclusion: (**a**) The fruit trees were planted last year. (**b**) No expensive tree is in the orchard. (**c**) No fruit tree is expensive.

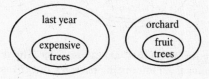

Fig. 1-40

▌ The three premises lead to the Venn diagram in Fig. 1-40. The diagram shows that (**b**) and (**c**) are valid conclusions, but (**a**) is not valid.

**1.222** Consider the following assumptions:

$S_1$: No practical car is expensive.
$S_2$: Cars with sunroofs are expensive.
$S_3$: All wagons are practical.

Determine the validity of each of the following conclusions:
- (**a**) No practical car has a sunroof.
- (**b**) Some wagons are expensive.
- (**c**) No wagon has a sunroof.
- (**d**) All practical cars are wagons.
- (**e**) Cars with sunroofs are not practical.

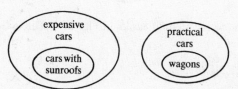

Fig. 1-41

▌ The three premises lead to the Venn diagram in Fig. 1-41. The diagram shows that (**a**), (**c**), and (**e**) are valid conclusions, but (**b**) and (**c**) are not valid.

**1.223** Determine the validity of the following argument:

$S_1$: Babies are illogical.
$S_2$: Nobody is despised who can manage a crocodile.
$S_3$: Illogical people are despised.

$S$: Babies cannot manage crocodiles.

(The above argument is adapted from Lewis Carrol, *Symbolic Logic*; he is also the author of *Alice in Wonderland*.)

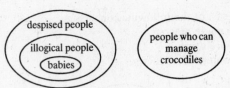

**Fig. 1-42**

▮ The three premises lead to the Venn diagram in Fig. 1-42. Since the set of babies and the set of people who can manage crocodiles are disjoint, "Babies cannot manage crocodiles" is a valid conclusion.

**1.224** Consider the following assumptions:

$S_1$: All mathematicians are interesting people.
$S_2$: Only uninteresting people become insurance sales persons.
$S_3$: Every genius is a mathematician.

Determine the validity of each of the following conclusions: (**a**) Insurance salespeople are not mathematicians. (**b**) Some geniuses are insurance salespersons. (**c**) Some geniuses are interesting people.

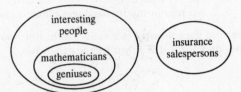

**Fig. 1-43**

▮ The three premises lead to the Venn diagram in Fig. 1-43. The diagram shows that (**a**) and (**c**) are valid conclusions (in fact, every genius is an interesting person), but (**b**) is not a valid conclusion.

**1.225** Consider the following assumptions:

$S_1$: All poets are poor.
$S_2$: In order to be a teacher, one must graduate from college.
$S_3$: No college graduate is poor.

Determine whether or not each of the following is a valid conclusion: (**a**) Teachers are not poor. (**b**) Poets are not teachers. (**c**) College graduates do not become poets.

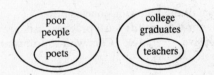

**Fig. 1-44**

▮ The three premises lead to the Venn diagram in Fig. 1-44. The diagram shows that (**a**), (**b**), and (**c**) are all valid conclusions.

## 1.10 SYMMETRIC DIFFERENCE

**1.226** The *symmetric difference* of sets $A$ and $B$ is denoted and defined by

$$A \oplus B = (A \cup B) \backslash (A \cap B)$$

That is, $A \oplus B$ consists of those elements which belong to either $A$ or $B$, but not both. (Figure 1-45 shows a Venn diagram of $A \oplus B$.) Prove

$$A \oplus B = (A \backslash B) \cup (B \backslash A)$$

▮ *Method 1.* Suppose $x \in A \oplus B$, that is, $x$ belongs to $A$ or $B$ but not both. If $x \in A$, then $x \notin B$ and so $x \in A \backslash B$. If $x \in B$, then $x \notin A$ and so $x \in B \backslash A$. Thus $x$ belongs to $A \backslash B$ or $B \backslash A$, i.e., $x \in (A \backslash B) \cup (B \backslash A)$. Accordingly $A \oplus B \subseteq (A \backslash B) \cup (B \backslash A)$.

Suppose $y \in (A \backslash B) \cup (B \backslash A)$. Then $y$ belongs to $A \backslash B$ or $B \backslash A$. If $y \in A \backslash B$, then $y$ belongs to $A$ but not both. If $y \in B \backslash A$, then $y$ belongs to $B$ but not both. Thus $y$ belongs to $A$ or $B$ but not both; that is, $y \in A \oplus B$. Accordingly, $(A \backslash B) \cup (B \backslash A) \subseteq A \oplus B$. Both inclusions imply $A \oplus B = (A \backslash B) \cup (B \backslash A)$.

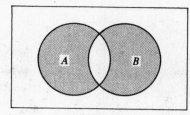

$A \oplus B$ is shaded.            **Fig. 1-45**

*Method 2.* The shaded area in the Venn diagram in Fig. 1-45 is also $(A\backslash B) \cup (B\backslash A)$. Thus $A \oplus B = (A\backslash B) \cup (B\backslash A)$.

Problems 1.227–1.230 refer to the sets:

$$A = \{1, 2, 3, 4, 5, 6\}, \quad B = \{4, 5, 6, 7, 8, 9\} \quad C = \{1, 3, 5, 7, 9\}, \quad D = \{2, 3, 5, 7, 8\}$$

**1.227** Find: **(a)** $A \oplus B$, and **(b)** $B \oplus C$.

   **(a)** First find $A\backslash B = \{1, 2, 3\}$ and $B\backslash A = \{7, 8, 9\}$. Then $A \oplus B$ is the union:

$$A \oplus B = (A\backslash B) \cup (B\backslash A) = \{1, 2, 3\} \cup \{7, 8, 9\} = \{1, 2, 3, 7, 8, 9\}$$

   **(b)** First find $B\backslash C = \{4, 6, 8\}$ and $C\backslash B = \{1, 3\}$. Then $B \oplus C = \{1, 3, 4, 6, 8\}$.

**1.228** Find: **(a)** $C \oplus D$, and **(b)** $A \oplus D$.

   **(a)** $C\backslash D = \{1, 9\}$ and $D\backslash C = \{2, 8\}$. Then $C \oplus D = \{1, 2, 8, 9\}$.
   **(b)** $A\backslash D = \{1, 4, 6\}$ and $D\backslash A = \{7, 8\}$. Then $A \oplus D = \{1, 4, 6, 7, 8\}$.

**1.229** Find: **(a)** $A \cap (B \oplus D)$, and **(b)** $(A \cap B) \oplus (A \cap D)$.

   **(a)** $B\backslash D = \{4, 6, 9\}$ and $D\backslash B = \{2, 3\}$. Then $B \oplus D = \{2, 3, 4, 6, 9\}$. Thus $A \cap (B \oplus D) = \{2, 3, 4, 6\}$.
   **(b)** First find $A \cap B = \{4, 5, 6\}$ and $A \cap D = \{2, 3, 5\}$. Next compute $(A \cap B)\backslash(A \cap D) = \{4, 6\}$ and $(A \cap D)\backslash(A \cap B) = \{2, 3\}$. Thus $(A \cap B) \oplus (A \cap D) = \{2, 3, 4, 6\}$.
[Note $A \cap (B \oplus D) = (A \cap B) \oplus (A \cap D)$.]

**1.230** Find: **(a)** $A \cup (B \oplus D)$, and **(b)** $(A \cup B) \oplus (A \cup D)$.

   **(a)** By Problem 1.229(a), $B \oplus D = \{2, 3, 4, 6, 9\}$; hence $A \cup (B \oplus D) = \{1, 2, 3, 4, 5, 6, 9\}$.
   **(b)** $A \cup B = \{1, 2, 3, 4, 5, 6, 7, 8, 9\}$ and $A \cup D = \{1, 2, 3, 4, 5, 6, 7, 8\}$. Hence $(A \cup B)\backslash(A \cup D) = \{9\}$ and $(A \cup D)\backslash(A \cup B) = \varnothing$. Thus $(A \cup B) \oplus (A \cup D) = \{9\}$.
[Note that $A \cup (B \oplus D) \neq (A \cup B) \oplus (A \cup D)$. Compare with Problem 1.229.]

**Theorem 1.9:** Symmetric difference satisfies the following properties:
   (i)   $(A \oplus B) \oplus C = A \oplus (B \oplus C)$ (associative law)
   (ii)   $A \oplus B = B \oplus A$ (commutative law)
   (iii)  If $A \oplus B = A \oplus C$, then $B = C$ (cancellation law)
   (iv)  $A \cap (B \oplus C) = (A \cap B) \oplus (A \cap C)$ (distributive law)

**1.231** Prove Theorem 1.9(i).

   Consider a Venn diagram of sets $A$, $B$, $C$. Shade $A \oplus B$ with strokes in one direction (///) and shade $C$ with strokes in another direction (\\\\\\) as shown in Fig. 1-46(a). Then $(A \oplus B) \oplus C$ consists of the areas in Fig. 1-46(a) with strokes in one direction or another but not both, as shown in Fig. 1-46(b).

   Now shade $A$ with strokes in one direction (///) and shade $B \oplus C$ with strokes in another direction (\\\\\\) as shown in Fig. 1-46(c). Then $A \oplus (B \oplus C)$ consists of the areas in Fig. 1-46(c) with strokes in one direction or the other but not both, as shown in Fig. 1-46(d).

   Figures 1-46(b) and 1-46(d) show the same areas shaded. Thus $(A \oplus B) \oplus C = A \oplus (B \oplus C)$ as required.

**1.232** Prove Theorem 1.9(ii).

   $A \oplus B = (A\backslash B) \cup (B\backslash A) = (B\backslash A) \cup (A\backslash B) = B \oplus A$

**1.233** Prove Theorem 1.9(iii).

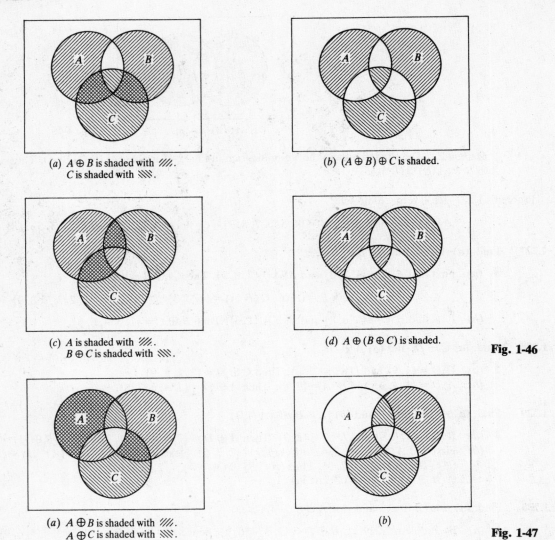

(a)  $A \oplus B$ is shaded with ///.
  $C$ is shaded with \\\\.

(b)  $(A \oplus B) \oplus C$ is shaded.

(c)  $A$ is shaded with ///.
  $B \oplus C$ is shaded with \\\\.

(d)  $A \oplus (B \oplus C)$ is shaded.

**Fig. 1-46**

(a)  $A \oplus B$ is shaded with ///.
  $A \oplus C$ is shaded with \\\\.

(b)

**Fig. 1-47**

▌ Consider a Venn diagram of sets $A$, $B$, $C$. Shade $A \oplus B$ with strokes in one direction ($///$) and shade $A \oplus C$ with strokes in another direction ($\backslash\backslash\backslash$) as in Fig. 1-47(a). Now Fig. 1-47(b) shows those areas in Fig. 1-47(a) which have strokes in one direction or the other, but not both. If $A \oplus B = A \oplus C$, then the areas shaded in Fig. 1-47(b) must be empty. Thus $B = B \cap C = C$, as claimed.

**1.234** Prove Theorem 1.9(iv).

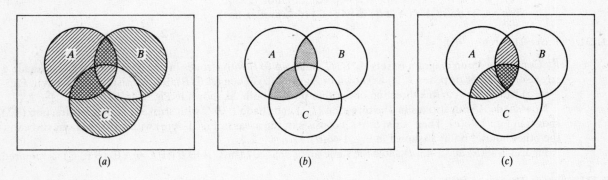

(a)

(b)

(c)

**Fig. 1-48**

▌ Consider a Venn diagram of sets $A$, $B$, $C$. Shade $A$ with strokes in one direction ($///$) and shade $B \oplus C$ with strokes in another direction ($\backslash\backslash\backslash$), as in Fig. 1-48(a). Then the crosshatched area is $A \cap (B \oplus C)$ which is shaded in Fig. 1-48($b$). Now shade $A \cap B$ with strokes in one direction ($///$) and shade $A \cap C$ with strokes in another direction ($\backslash\backslash\backslash$), as in Fig. 1-48($c$). Then $(A \cap B) \oplus (A \cap C)$ consists of the areas in Fig. 1-48($c$) with strokes in one direction or another, but not both. These areas are the same as those shaded in Fig. 1-48($b$). Thus $A \cap (B \oplus C) = (A \cap B) \oplus (A \cap C)$.

**1.235** Describe the set $A \oplus B \oplus C$ [shown in Fig. 1-46($b$)]. Are parentheses needed for the symmetric difference of four $(A \oplus B \oplus C \oplus D)$ or more sets?

▮ $A \oplus B \oplus C$ consists of those elements in exactly one of the three sets or in all of the three sets. Theorem 1.9(i) states that the symmetric difference satisfies the associative law and hence, by Theorem 1.8, no parentheses are needed for the symmetric difference of any number of sets [which consists of those elements in an odd number of the given sets].

## 1.11 REAL NUMBER SYSTEM R, SETS OF NUMBERS

This section deals with subsets of the real number system $\mathbf{R}$, including the rational numbers $\mathbf{Q}$, the integers $\mathbf{Z}$, and the natural numbers (positive integers) $\mathbf{N}$.

**1.236** Let $A$ and $B$ be sets of numbers and let $k$ be a number. Define: (*a*) $A + B$, (*b*) $AB$, (*c*) $k + A$, (*d*) $kA$.

▮ (*a*) $A + B$ is the set obtained by adding each number of $A$ to each number of $B$ (omitting repetitions); that is,

$$A + B = \{x : x = a + b,\, a \in A,\, b \in B\}$$

(*b*) $AB$ is the set obtained by multiplying each number of $A$ with each number of $B$; that is,

$$AB = \{x : x = ab,\, a \in A,\, b \in B\}$$

(*c*) The set $k + A$ is obtained by adding $k$ to each element of $A$.
(*d*) The set $kA$ is obtained by multiplying $k$ with each element of $A$.

Problems 1.237–1.240 concern sets $A = \{3, 4, 5, 6\}$, $B = \{2, 3, 5\}$, and $C = \{1, 4\}$.

**1.237** Find: (*a*) $2 + A$, (*b*) $3B$.

▮ (*a*) Add 2 to each element of $A$ to obtain $2 + A = \{5, 6, 7, 8\}$.
(*b*) Multiply each element of $B$ by 3 to obtain $3B = \{6, 9, 15\}$.

**1.238** Find: $A + C$.

▮ Add each element of $A$ to each element of $C$ to obtain

$$A + C = \{3 + 1, 3 + 4, 4 + 1, 4 + 4, 5 + 1, 5 + 4, 6 + 1, 6 + 4\}$$
$$= \{4, 7, 5, 8, 6, 9, 7, 10\} = \{4, 5, 6, 7, 8, 9, 10\}$$

**1.239** Find $B + B$.

▮ Add each element of $B$ to each element of $B$ to obtain

$$B + B = \{2 + 2, 2 + 3, 2 + 5, 3 + 2, 3 + 3, 3 + 5, 5 + 2, 5 + 3, 5 + 5\}$$
$$= \{4, 5, 7, 5, 6, 8, 7, 8, 10\} = \{4, 5, 6, 7, 8, 10\}$$

**1.240** Find $BB$.

▮ Multiply each element of $B$ by each element of $B$ to obtain

$$BB = \{4, 6, 10, 6, 9, 15, 10, 15, 25\} = \{4, 6, 9, 10, 15, 25\}$$

**1.241** Find an infinite set $A$ such that $A + A$ and $A$ are disjoint.

▮ Let $A = \{1, 3, 5, \ldots\} = \{\text{positive odd integers}\}$. Then $A + A$ consists only of even integers.

**1.242** Find an infinite set $B$ such that $B + B = B$.

▮ Let $B = \{0, 1, 2, \ldots\} = \{\text{nonnegative integers}\}$. Then $B + B = B$.

**1.243** Find a finite set $C$ such that: (a) $C + C = C$, (b) $CC = C$.

▮ (a) Let $C = \{0\}$. Then $C + C = C$.
(b) Let $C = \{0, 1\}$. Then $CC = C$.

**1.244** What are the inclusion relations between the sets $\mathbf{Q}$, $\mathbf{Z}$, $\mathbf{N}$, and $\mathbf{R}$? What is $\mathbf{Q}^c$ called?

▮ The set of positive integers $\mathbf{N}$ is contained in the set of integers $\mathbf{Z}$ which, in turn, is contained in the set of rational numbers $\mathbf{Q}$, and all are subsets of the set of real numbers $\mathbf{R}$. That is, $\mathbf{N} \subseteq \mathbf{Z} \subseteq \mathbf{Q} \subseteq \mathbf{R}$. The elements of $\mathbf{Q}^c$ are called *irrational numbers*.

**1.245** Discuss the meaning of the expression "real line $\mathbf{R}$".

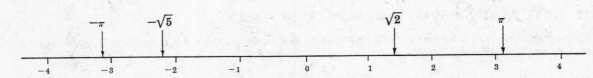

**Fig. 1-49** The real line $\mathbf{R}$.

▮ One of the most important properties of the real number system $\mathbf{R}$ is that $\mathbf{R}$ can be represented by points on a straight line. Specifically, as in Fig. 1-49, a point, called the *origin,* is chosen to represent 0 and another point, usually to the right of 0, to represent 1. Then there is a natural way to pair off the points on the line and the real numbers, i.e., each point will represent a unique real number and each real number will be represented by a unique point. For this reason we refer to $\mathbf{R}$ as the *real line* and use the words point and number interchangeably.

## Positive Numbers

**1.246** Describe geometrically the positive and negative (real) numbers and explain how the positive real numbers are defined axiomatically.

▮ Those numbers to the right of 0 on the real line $\mathbf{R}$, i.e., on the same side as 1, are the *positive numbers*; those numbers to the left of 0 are the *negative numbers*. The set of positive numbers can be completely described by the following axioms:
[$\mathbf{P}_1$] If $a \in \mathbf{R}$, then exactly one of the following is true: $a$ is positive; $a = 0$; $-a$ is positive.
[$\mathbf{P}_2$] If $a, b \in \mathbf{R}$ are positive, then their sum $a + b$ and their product $a \cdot b$ are also positive.
We then say $a$ is *negative* if $-a$ is positive. Thus, by [$\mathbf{P}_1$], any nonzero $a$ is positive or negative, but not both.

**1.247** Prove, using only axioms [$\mathbf{P}_1$] and [$\mathbf{P}_2$], that the real number 1 is positive.

▮ By [$\mathbf{P}_1$], either 1 or $-1$ is positive. If $-1$ is positive then, by [$\mathbf{P}_2$], the product $(-1)(-1) = 1$ is positive. But this contradicts [$\mathbf{P}_1$] which states that 1 and $-1$ cannot both be positive. Hence the assumption that $-1$ is positive is false and so 1 is positive.

**1.248** Prove that the real number $-2$ is negative.

▮ By Problem 1.247, 1 is positive and so, by [$\mathbf{P}_2$], the sum $1 + 1 = 2$ is positive; hence $-2$ is not positive, i.e., $-2$ is negative.

**1.249** Prove that $1/2$ is a positive number.

▮ By [$\mathbf{P}_1$], either $-1/2$ or $1/2$ is positive. Suppose $-1/2$ is positive and so, by [$\mathbf{P}_2$], the sum $(-1/2) + (-1/2) = -1$ is also positive. But by Problem 1.247, the number 1, and not $-1$, is positive. Thus we have a contradiction, and so $1/2$ is positive.

**1.250** Prove that the product $a \cdot b$ of a positive number $a$ and a negative number $b$ is negative.

▮ If $b$ is negative then $-b$ is positive; hence by [$\mathbf{P}_2$] the product $a \cdot (-b)$ is also positive. But $a \cdot (-b) = -(a \cdot b)$. Thus $-(a \cdot b)$ is positive and so $a \cdot b$ is negative.

**1.251** Prove that the product $a \cdot b$ of negative numbers $a$ and $b$ is positive.

▮ If $a$ and $b$ are negative then, $-a$ and $-b$ are positive. Hence by [$P_2$], the product $(-a) \cdot (-b)$ is positive. But $a \cdot b = (-a) \cdot (-b)$, and so $a \cdot b$ is positive.

## Order Inequalities

**1.252**   Explain how the concept of "order" is introduced in the real number system **R**.

▮ An order relation is defined in **R** using the concept of positiveness as follows. The real number $a$ is less than the real number $b$, written $a < b$, if $b - a$ is a positive number. The following notation is also used:

$$a > b, \text{ read } a \text{ is greater than } b, \qquad\qquad \text{means } b < a$$
$$a \leq b, \text{ read } a \text{ is less than or equal to } b, \qquad \text{means } a < b \text{ or } a = b$$
$$a \geq b, \text{ read } a \text{ is greater than or equal to } b, \qquad \text{means } b \leq a$$

Geometrically speaking,

$$a < b \text{ means } a \text{ is to the left of } b \text{ on the real line } \mathbf{R};$$
$$a > b \text{ means } a \text{ is to the right of } b \text{ on the real line } \mathbf{R}.$$

Note also that $a$ is positive or negative according as $a > 0$ or $a < 0$. We refer to the relations $<, >, \leq$, and $\geq$ as inequalities in order to distinguish them from the equality relation $=$. We also shall refer to $<$ and $>$ as strict inequalities.

**1.253**   Write each statement in notational form:
(**a**)   $a$ is less than $b$.       (**d**)   $a$ is greater than $b$.
(**b**)   $a$ is not greater than $b$.       (**e**)   $a$ is not less than $b$.
(**c**)   $a$ is less than or equal to $b$.       (**f**)   $a$ is not greater than or equal to $b$.

▮ A vertical or slant line through a symbol denotes the negation of that symbol. (**a**) $a < b$, (**b**) $a \not> b$, (**c**) $a \leq b$, (**d**) $a > b$, (**e**) $a \not< b$, (**f**) $a \not\geq b$

**1.254**   Explain the meaning and geometrical significance of $a < x < b$.

▮ Here $a < x < b$ means $a < x$ and also $x < b$. Thus $x$ will lie between $a$ and $b$ on the real line.

**1.255**   Rewrite the following geometric relationships between the given real numbers using the inequality notation:
(**a**)   $y$ lies to the right of 8.       (**c**)   $x$ lies between $-3$ and 7.
(**b**)   $z$ lies to the left of $-3$.       (**d**)   $w$ lies between 5 and 1.

▮ Recall that $a < b$ means $a$ lies to the left of $b$ on the real line:
(**a**)   $y > 8$ or $8 < y$.       (**c**)   $-3 < x$ and $x < 7$ or, more concisely, $-3 < x < 7$.
(**b**)   $z < -3$.       (**d**)   $1 < w < 5$.

**Theorem 1.10:**   (i)   If $a < b$, then $b \not< a$.
(ii)   If $a < b$ and $b < c$, then $a < c$.

**1.256**   Prove Theorem 1.10(i).

▮ By definition, $a < b$ means $b - a$ is positive. Then, by [$P_1$], $-(b - a) = a - b$ is not positive. Hence $b \not< a$, as claimed.

**1.257**   Prove Theorem 1.10(ii).

▮ By definition, $a < b$ and $b < c$ means $b - a$ and $c - b$ are positive. By [$P_2$], the sum of two positive numbers $(b - a) + (c - b) = c - a$ is positive. Thus, by definition, $a < c$.

**Theorem 1.11:**   Let $a$, $b$, and $c$ be real numbers.
(i)   If $a < b$, then $a + c < b + c$.
(ii)   If $a < b$ and $c$ is positive, then $ac < bc$.
(iii)   If $a < b$ and $c$ is negative, then $ac > bc$.

**1.258**   Prove Theorem 1.11(i).

▌ By definition, $a < b$ means $b - a$ is positive. But

$$(b + c) - (a + c) = b - a$$

Hence $(b + c) - (a + c)$ is positive and so $a + c < b + c$.

**1.259** Prove Theorem 1.11(ii).

▌ By definition, $a < b$ means $b - a$ is positive. But $c$ is also positive; hence by $[\mathbf{P}_2]$ the product $c(b - a) = bc - ac$ is positive. Accordingly, $ac < bc$.

**1.260** Prove Theorem 1.11(iii).

▌ By definition, $a < b$ means $b - a$ is positive. By $[\mathbf{P}_1]$, if $c$ is negative then $-c$ is positive; hence by $[\mathbf{P}_2]$ the product $(b - a)(-c) = ac - bc$ is also positive. Thus, by definition, $bc < ac$ or, equivalently, $ac > bc$.

**1.261** Prove: Suppose $a$ and $b$ are positive. Then $a < b$ if and only if $a^2 < b^2$.

▌ Suppose $a < b$. Since $a$ and $b$ are positive, $a^2 < ab$ and $ab < b^2$; hence $a^2 < b^2$.
  On the other hand, suppose $a^2 < b^2$. Then $b^2 - a^2 = (b + a)(b - a)$ is positive. Since $a$ and $b$ are positive, the sum $b + a$ is positive; hence $b - a$ is positive or else the product $(b + a)(b - a)$ would be negative. Thus, by definition, $a < b$.

**1.262** Prove that the sum of a positive number $a$ and its reciprocal $1/a$ is greater than or equal to 2; that is, if $a > 0$, then $a + 1/a \geq 2$.

▌ If $a = 1$, then $1/a = 1$ and so $a + 1/a = 1 + 1 = 2$. On the other hand, if $a \neq 1$, then $a - 1 \neq 0$ and so

$$(a - 1)^2 > 0 \quad \text{or} \quad a^2 - 2a + 1 > 0 \quad \text{or} \quad a^2 + 1 > 2a$$

Since $a$ is positive, we can divide both sides of the inequality by $a$ to obtain $a + 1/a > 2$.

## Intervals

**1.263** Let $a$ and $b$ be the real numbers such that $a < b$. Define the (finite) intervals from $a$ to $b$. Show the intervals on the real line.

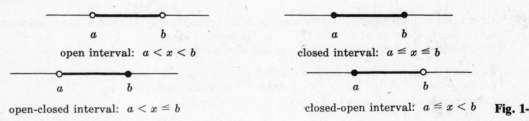

open interval: $a < x < b$     closed interval: $a \leq x \leq b$

open-closed interval: $a < x \leq b$     closed-open interval: $a \leq x < b$     **Fig. 1-50**

▌ The set of all real numbers $x$ satisfying:

$a < x < b$   is called the open interval from $a$ to $b$,
$a \leq x \leq b$   is called the closed interval from $a$ to $b$,
$a < x \leq b$   is called the open-closed interval from $a$ to $b$,
$a \leq x < b$   is called the closed-open interval from $a$ to $b$.

The points $a$ and $b$ are called the endpoints of the interval. Observe that a closed interval contains both its endpoints, an open interval contains neither endpoint, and an open-closed and a closed-open interval contains exactly one of its endpoints.
  Figure 1-50 shows these four intervals. Note that in each diagram the endpoints $a$ and $b$ are circled, the line between $a$ and $b$ is thickened, and the circle about the endpoint is shaded if the endpoint belongs to the interval.

**1.264** Define and show the infinite intervals.

$x < a$          $x \leq a$          $x > a$          $x \geq a$

**Fig. 1-51**

▌ Let $a$ be any real number. Then the set of all real numbers $x$ satisfying $x < a$, $x \le a$, $x > a$ or $x \ge a$ is called an *infinite interval*. These intervals are shown in Fig. 1-51.

**1.265** Describe and plot each of the following intervals: (a) $2 < x < 4$, (b) $-1 \le x \le 2$, and (c) $-3 < x \le 1$.

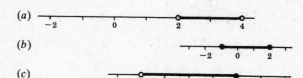

Fig. 1-52

▌ (a) All numbers greater than 2 and less than 4, i.e., all points between 2 and 4; see Fig. 1-52(a).
(b) All numbers between $-1$ and 2, including $-1$ and 2; see Fig. 1-52(b).
(c) All numbers greater than $-3$ and less than or equal to 1; see Fig. 1-52(c).

**1.266** Describe and plot each interval: (a) $x > -1$, and (b) $x \le 2$.

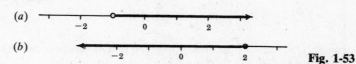

Fig. 1-53

▌ (a) All numbers greater than $-1$, i.e., all points to the right of $-1$; see Fig. 1-53(a).
(b) All numbers less than or equal to 2, i.e., all points to the left of 2, including 2; see Fig. 1-53(b).

**1.267** Find the interval satisfying each inequality, i.e., rewrite the inequality in terms of $x$ alone.
(a) $3 \le x - 4 \le 8$, (b) $-1 \le x + 3 \le 2$, (c) $-9 \le 3x \le 12$, (d) $-6 \le -2x \le 4$.

▌ (a) Add 4 to each side to obtain $7 \le x \le 12$.
(b) Add $-3$ to each side to obtain $-4 \le x \le -1$.
(c) Divide each side by 3 (or: multiply by $\frac{1}{3}$) to obtain $-3 \le x \le 4$.
(d) Divide each side by $-2$ (or: multiply by $-\frac{1}{2}$) and reverse the inequalities to obtain $-2 \le x \le 3$.

**1.268** Find the interval satisfying each inequality, i.e., solve each inequality: (a) $3 < 2x - 5 < 7$, and (b) $-7 \le -2x + 3 \le 5$.

▌ (a) Add 5 to each side to obtain: $8 < 2x < 12$
Divide each side by 2: $4 < x < 6$
(b) Add $-3$ to each side to obtain: $-10 \le -2x \le 2$.
Divide each side by $-2$ and reverse the inequalities: $-1 \le x \le 5$.

## Absolute Values

**1.269** Define and describe geometrically the absolute value of a real number.

▌ The absolute value of a real number $x$, written $|x|$, is defined by

$$|x| = \begin{cases} x & \text{if } x \ge 0 \\ -x & \text{if } x < 0 \end{cases}$$

that is, if $x$ is nonnegative then $|x| = x$, and if $x$ is negative then $|x| = -x$. Thus $|x| \ge 0$ for every $x \in \mathbf{R}$.

Geometrically speaking, the absolute value of $x$ is the distance between the point $x$ on the real line and the origin, i.e., the point 0. Furthermore, the distance between any two points $a$, $b \in \mathbf{R}$ is $|a - b| = |b - a|$.

**1.270** Find (a) $|-7|$, (b) $|4|$, (c) $|-\pi|$, (d) $|\sqrt{5}|$.

▌ The absolute value of a number gives the magnitude of that number. Thus
(a) $|-7| = 7$, (b) $|4| = 4$, (c) $|-\pi| = \pi$, (d) $|\sqrt{5}| = \sqrt{5}$.

**1.271** Evaluate: (a) $|3 - 5|$, (b) $|-3 + 5|$, and (c) $|-3 - 5|$,

▌ (a) $|3 - 5| = |-2| = 2$, (b) $|-3 + 5| = |2| = 2$, (c) $|-3 - 5| = |-8| = 8$.

**1.272** Evaluate: **(a)** $|-4| + |2 - 5|$, and **(b)** $|3 - 7| - |-5|$.

▌ **(a)** $|-4| + |2 - 5| = 4 + |-3| = 4 + 3 = 7$,     **(b)** $|3 - 7| - |-5| = |-4| - |-5| = 4 - 5 = -1$

**1.273** Evaluate: **(a)** $|2 - 8| + |3 - 1|$, and **(b)** $|2 - 5| - |4 - 7|$.

▌ **(a)** $|2 - 8| + |3 - 1| = |-6| + |2| = 6 + 2 = 8$,     **(b)** $|2 - 5| - |4 - 7| = |-3| - |-3| = 3 - 3 = 0$.

**1.274** Evaluate: **(a)** $4 + |-1 - 5| - |-8|$, and **(b)** $|3 - 6| - |-2 + 4| - |-2 - 3|$.

▌ **(a)** $4 + |-1 - 5| - |-8| = 4 + |-6| - |-8| = 4 + 6 - 8 = 2$
  **(b)** $|3 - 6| - |-2 + 4| - |-2 - 3| = 3 - 2 - 5 = -4$

**1.275** Give a geometrical interpretation of the inequality $|x| < 5$, and rewrite the inequality without the absolute value sign.

**Fig. 1-54**

▌ The statement $|x| < 5$ can be interpreted to mean that the distance between $x$ and the origin is less than 5; hence $x$ must lie between $-5$ and 5 on the real line. In other words,

$$|x| < 5 \quad \text{and} \quad -5 < x < 5 \quad \text{and, similarly,} \quad |x| \le 5 \quad \text{and} \quad -5 \le x \le 5$$

have identical meaning. [See Fig. 1-54.]

**1.276** Rewrite without the absolute value sign: **(a)** $|x| \le 3$, **(b)** $|x - 2| < 5$, **(c)** $|2x - 3| \le 7$.

▌ **(a)** $-3 \le x \le 3$
  **(b)** $-5 < x - 2 < 5$   or   $-3 < x < 7$
  **(c)** $-7 \le 2x - 3 \le 7$   or   $-4 \le 2x \le 10$   or   $-2 \le x \le 5$

**Theorem 1.12:** Let $a$ and $b$ be any real numbers. Then
   (i)   $|a| \ge 0$, and $|a| = 0$ iff $a = 0$      (iv)   $|a + b| \le |a| + |b|$
   (ii)   $-|a| \le a \le |a|$                  (v)   $|a + b| \ge |a| - |b|$
   (iii)   $|ab| = |a| \cdot |b|$

**1.277** Prove Theorem 1.12(iii).

▌ The theorem holds if $a = 0$ or $b = 0$. Hence we can assume $a \ne 0$ and $b \ne 0$. There are four cases:
*Case (a).* Both $a$ and $b$ are positive. Then $ab$ is positive, and $|a| = a$, $|b| = b$, and $|ab| = ab$. Then $|ab| = ab = |a| \cdot |b|$.
*Case (b).* Here $a$ is positive and $b$ is negative. Then $ab$ is negative, and $|a| = a$, $|b| = -b$, and $|ab| = -ab$. Then $|ab| = -ab = a(-b) = |a| \cdot |b|$.
*Case (c).* Here $a$ is negative and $b$ is positive. The proof is similar to case (b).
*Case (d).* Both $a$ and $b$ are negative. Then $ab$ is positive, and $|a| = -a$, $|b| = -b$, and $|ab| = ab$. Then $|ab| = ab = (-a)(-b) = |a| \cdot |b|$.

**1.278** Prove Theorem 1.12(iv).

▌ Since $|a| = \pm a$, $-|a| \le a \le |a|$; also, $-|b| \le b \le |b|$. Then, adding,

$$-(|a| + |b|) \le a + b \le |a| + |b|$$

Therefore $|a + b| \le ||a| + |b|| = |a| + |b|$.

**1.279** Prove: $|a - b| \le |a| + |b|$.

▌ Using the result of Problem 1.278, we have $|a - b| = |a + (-b)| \le |a| + |-b| = |a| + |b|$.

**1.280** Prove: $|a - c| \le |a - b| + |b - c|$.

▌ $$|a - c| = |(a - b) + (b - c)| \le |a - b| + |b - c|$$

**1.281**   Plot and describe the graph of the absolute value function $f(x) = |x|$.

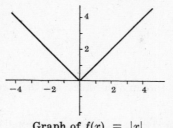

Graph of $f(x) = |x|$       **Fig. 1-55**

▌ For nonnegative values of $x$ we have $f(x) = x$ and hence we obtain the points of the form $(a, a)$, e.g.,

$$(0, 0), (1, 1), (2, 2), \ldots$$

For negative values of $x$ we have $f(x) = -x$ and hence we obtain the points of the form $(-a, a)$, e.g.,

$$(-1, 1), (-2, 2), (-3, 3), \ldots$$

This yields the graph in Fig. 1-55. Observe that the graph of $f(x) = |x|$ lies entirely in the upper half plane since $f(x) \geq 0$ for every $x \in \mathbf{R}$. Also, the graph consists of the line $y = x$ in the right half plane and of the line $y = -x$ in the left half plane.

## Bounded Sets

**1.282**   Define a bounded set $A$.

▌ A set $A$ of real numbers is said to be:

(i)   bounded,      (ii)   bounded from above,      (iii)   bounded from below

according as there exists a real number $M$ such that:

(i)   $|x| \leq M$,      (ii)   $x \leq M$,      (iii)   $M \leq x$

for every $x \in A$. The number $M$ is called a *bound* in (i), an *upper bound* in (ii), and a *lower bound* in (iii). Note that $A$ is bounded if and only if $A$ is a subset of some finite interval.

**Remark:**   If a set $A$ is finite, then $A$ is necessarily bounded. If $A$ is infinite, then $A$ may be bounded, only bounded from above (below), or not bounded at all.

**1.283**   State whether each of the following sets is bounded, bounded from below, or bounded from above:
**(a)** $A = \{1, 1/2, 1/3, \ldots, 1/n, \ldots\}$, **(b)** $B = \{2, 4, 6, \ldots\}$, **(c)** $C = \{4, 780, -3355, 22, 5678, -99\}$,

▌ **(a)**   $A$ is bounded since $A$ is certainly a subset of the interval $[0, 1]$. Alternatively, $M = 1$ is a bound for $A$.
    **(b)**   $B$ is bounded from below, e.g., 0 is a lower bound, but not bounded from above. Thus $B$ is unbounded.
    **(c)**   $C$ is finite and hence bounded. In particular, 5678 is an upper bound and $-3355$ is a lower bound.

**1.284**   State whether each of the following sets is bounded, bounded from below, or bounded from above:
**(a)** $A = \{x : x < 4\}$, **(b)** $B = \{1, -1, 3, -3, 5, -5, 7, -7, \ldots\}$, **(c)** $C = \{1, -1, 1/2, -1/2, 1/3, -1/3, \ldots\}$.

▌ **(a)**   $A$ is bounded from above, e.g., 4 is an upper bound, but not bounded from below since there are negative numbers whose absolute values are arbitrarily large. Thus, in particular, $A$ is not bounded.
    **(b)**   $B$ has neither an upper bound nor a lower bound. Thus $B$ is not bounded.
    **(c)**   Although there are an infinite number of numbers in $C$, the set $C$ is still bounded. It certainly is contained in the interval $[-1, 1]$.

**1.285**   Suppose sets $A$ and $B$ are bounded. What can be said about the intersection and union of $A$ and $B$?

▌ Both the union and intersection of bounded sets are bounded.

**1.286**   Suppose sets $C$ and $D$ are unbounded. What can be said about the union and intersection of $C$ and $D$?

▌ The union of $C$ and $D$ must be unbounded, but the intersection could be either bounded or unbounded.

# CHAPTER 2
# Relations

## 2.1 PRODUCT SETS

This section covers ordered pairs and (ordered) $n$-tuples, and the (cartesian) product of sets, using the following notation:

$$(a, b) \qquad \text{ordered pair of elements } a \text{ and } b;$$

$$(a_1, a_2, \ldots, a_n) \qquad n\text{-tuple of elements } a_1, \ldots, a_n;$$

$$A \times B = \{(a, b): a \in A, b \in B\} \qquad \text{product of sets } A \text{ and } B;$$

$$A_1 \times A_2 \times \cdots \times A_n \text{ or } \prod_{i=1}^{n} A_i \qquad \text{product of sets } A_1, A_2, \ldots, A_n.$$

We also use $A^2 = A \times A$ and $A^n = A \times A \times \cdots \times A$ ($n$ factors).

**2.1** Explain the main difference between an ordered pair $(a, b)$ and the set $\{a, b\}$ with two elements.

▌ The order of the elements in $(a, b)$ does make a difference; here $a$ is designated as the first element and $b$ as the second element. Thus $(a, b) \neq (b, a)$ unless $a = b$. On the other hand, $\{a, b\}$ and $\{b, a\}$ represent the same set.

**2.2** Explain when: (*a*) ordered pairs $(a, b)$ and $(c, d)$ are equal; (*b*) $n$-tuples $(a_1, a_2, \ldots, a_n)$ and $(b_1, b_2, \ldots, b_n)$ are equal.

▌ (*a*) These two ordered pairs are equal if and only if $a = c$ and $b = d$.
    (*b*) Similarly, $(a_1, a_2, \ldots, a_n) = (b_1, b_2, \ldots, b_n)$ if and only if the corresponding elements (components) are equal, i.e., $a_1 = b_1, a_2 = b_2, \ldots, a_n = b_n$.

**2.3** Find $x$ and $y$ given $(3x, x - 2y) = (6, -8)$.

▌ Two ordered pairs are equal if and only if the corresponding components are equal. Hence we obtain the equations $3x = 6$ and $x - 2y = -8$ from which $x = 2$, $y = 5$.

**2.4** Find $x$ and $y$ if $(x - 3y, 5) = (7, x - y)$.

▌ Set corresponding components equal to each other to obtain

$$x - 3y = 7 \qquad \text{and} \qquad x - y = 5$$

This yields $x = 4$, $y = -1$.

**2.5** Find $x$, $y$, and $z$ if $(2x, x + y, x - y - 2z) = (4, -1, 3)$.

▌ Since the two ordered triples are equal, set the three corresponding components equal to each other to obtain

$$2x = 4, \qquad x + y = -1, \qquad x - y - 2z = 3$$

Solving the system yields $x = 2$, $y = -3$, $z = 1$.

**2.6** Let $A = \{1, 2, 3\}$ and $B = \{a, b\}$. Find (*a*) $A \times B$, (*b*) $B \times A$.

▌ (*a*) $A \times B$ consists of all ordered pairs with the first component from $A$ and the second component from $B$. Thus

$$A \times B = \{(1, a), (1, b), (2, a), (2, b), (3, a), (3, b)\}$$

    (*b*) Here the first component is from $B$ and the second component is from $A$:

$$B \times A = \{(a, 1), (a, 2), (a, 3), (b, 1), (b, 2), (b, 3)\}$$

**2.7** Suppose $A = \{1, 2\}$. Find (*a*) $A^2$, (*b*) $A^3$.

▮ **(a)** Here $A^2 = A \times A$. Hence $A^2 = \{(1, 1), (1, 2), (2, 1), (2, 2)\}$.

**(b)** $A^3 = A \times A \times A$. Thus form all ordered triples with the elements in $A$:

$$A^3 = \{(1, 1, 1), (1, 1, 2), (1, 2, 1), (1, 2, 2), (2, 1, 1), (2, 1, 2), (2, 2, 1), (2, 2, 2)\}$$

(We may view $A^3$ as $A \times A^2$.)

**2.8**   Let $A = \{1, 2\}$ and $B = \{a, b\}$. Determine whether or not each of the following is equal to $A \times B$.

**(a)** $E = [\{1, a\}, \{1, b\}, \{2, a\}, \{2, b\}]$   **(c)** $G = [(1, a), (1, b), (2, a), (b, 2)]$

**(b)** $F = [(a, 1), (a, 2), (b, 1), (b, 2)]$   **(d)** $H = [(1, b), (2, a), (1, a), (2, b)]$

▮ **(a)** No. $E$ is a set of sets, not a set of ordered pairs.

**(b)** No. $F = B \times A$, not $A \times B$.

**(c)** No. $G$ would be equal to $A \times B$ if the last pair were $(2, b)$, not $(b, 2)$.

**(d)** Yes, even though its elements are not listed in a systematic way.

**2.9**   Let $A = \{\text{male, female}\}$ and $B = \{\text{cat, dog, fish}\}$. Find: **(a)** $A \times B$, **(b)** $B \times A$.

▮ **(a)** Form all ordered pairs where the first element is from $A$ and the second element is from $B$:

$$A \times B = \{(\text{male, cat}), (\text{male, dog}), (\text{male, fish}), (\text{female, cat}),$$
$$(\text{female, dog}), (\text{female, fish})\}$$

**(b)** Form all ordered pairs where the first element is from $B$ and the second element is from $A$, or simply reverse the pairs in $A \times B$:

$$B \times A = \{(\text{cat, male}), (\text{dog, male}), (\text{fish, male}), (\text{cat, female}),$$
$$(\text{dog, female}), (\text{fish, female})\}$$

**2.10**   Let $Y = \{0, 1\}$ and $Z = \{1, 0\}$. Find: **(a)** $Y \times Z$ and **(b)** $Z \times Y$. **(c)** What do you notice about $Y \times Z$ and $Z \times Y$?

▮ **(a)** $\{(0, 1), (0, 0), (1, 1), (1, 0)\}$

**(b)** $\{(1, 0), (1, 1), (0, 0), (0, 1)\}$

**(c)** $Y \times Z$ and $Z \times Y$ are equal since $Y$ and $Z$ are equal.

**2.11**   Discuss the geometrical representation of $\mathbf{R}^2 = \mathbf{R} \times \mathbf{R}$ as points in the plane.

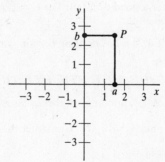

**Fig. 2-1**

▮ Here each point $P$ in the plane represents an ordered pair $(a, b)$ of real numbers and vice versa as shown in Fig. 2-1. That is, the vertical line through $P$ meets the $x$ axis at $a$, and the horizontal line through $P$ meets the $y$ axis at $b$. $\mathbf{R}^2$ is frequently called the *cartesian plane*.

**2.12**   Show that $n(A \times B) = n(A) \cdot n(B)$ where $A$ and $B$ are finite sets and $n(A)$ denotes the number of elements in $A$. State the general result.

▮ For each ordered pair $(a, b)$ in $A \times B$ there are $n(A)$ choices for $a$ and there are $n(B)$ choices for $b$. Thus there are $n(A) \cdot n(B)$ such ordered pairs. That is, $n(A \times B) = n(A) \cdot n(B)$. Similarly, one can show that if $A_1, A_2, \ldots, A_m$ are finite sets, then

$$n(A_1 \times A_2 \times \cdots \times A_m) = n(A_1)n(A_2) \cdots n(A_m)$$

**2.13**   Let $A = \{1, 2, 3, \ldots, 8, 9, 10\}$ and $B = \{a, b, c, \ldots, x, y, z\}$. How many elements are in $A \times B$?

▌ Here $n(A) = 10$ and $n(B) = 26$. Thus $A \times B$ contain $(10)(26) = 260$ elements.

**2.14** Let $A = \{1, 2, 3, 6\}$ and $B = \{8, 9, 10\}$. Determine the number of elements in: **(a)** $A \times B$, **(b)** $B \times A$, **(c)** $A^2$, **(d)** $B^4$, **(e)** $A \times A \times B$, **(f)** $B \times A \times B$.

▌ Here $n(A) = 4$ and $n(B) = 3$. To obtain the number of elements in each product set, multiply the numbers of elements in each set:

**(a)** $n(A \times B) = 4 \cdot 3 = 12$      **(d)** $n(B^4) = 3^4 = 81$
**(b)** $n(B \times A) = 3 \cdot 4 = 12$      **(e)** $n(A \times A \times B) = 4 \cdot 4 \cdot 3 = 48$
**(c)** $n(A^2) = 4 \cdot 4 = 16$      **(f)** $n(B \times A \times B) = 3 \cdot 4 \cdot 3 = 36$

**2.15** Given $A = \{1, 2\}$, $B = \{x, y, z\}$, and $C = \{3, 4\}$. Find $A \times B \times C$ and $n(A \times B \times C)$.

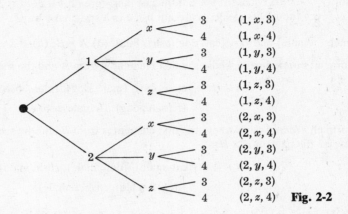

**Fig. 2-2**

▌ $A \times B \times C$ consists of all ordered triplets $(a, b, c)$ where $a \in A$, $b \in B$, $c \in C$. These elements of $A \times B \times C$ can be systematically obtained by a so-called tree diagram shown in Fig. 2-2. The elements of $A \times B \times C$ are precisely the 12 ordered triplets to the right of the tree diagram.

Observe that $n(A) = 2$, $n(B) = 3$, and $n(C) = 2$; hence

$$n(A \times B \times C) = 12 = n(A) \cdot n(B) \cdot n(C)$$

**2.16** Each toss of a coin will yield either a head or a tail. Let $C = \{H, T\}$ denote the set of outcomes. Find $C^3$, $n(C^3)$, and explain what $C^3$ represents.

▌ Since $n(C) = 2$, we have $n(C^3) = 2^3 = 8$. Omitting certain commas and parentheses for notational convenience,

$$C^3 = \{HHH, HHT, HTH, HTT, THH, THT, TTH, TTT\}$$

$C^3$ represents all possible sequences of outcomes of three tosses of the coin.

**2.17** Let $S = \{a, b, c\}$, $T = \{b, c, d\}$, and $W = \{a, d\}$. Construct the tree diagram of $S \times T \times W$ and then find $S \times T \times W$.

▌ Choose a point $P$ on the left as a "root" and draw three lines to the right representing the elements of the first set $S$ as shown in Fig. 2-3. At each endpoint draw three lines representing the elements of the second set $T$, and then at each new endpoint draw two lines representing the elements of the third set $W$. Each element of $S \times T \times W$ corresponds to a path from $P$ to an endpoint. Thus

$$S \times T \times W = \{(a, b, a), (a, b, d), (a, c, a), (a, c, d), (a, d, a), (a, d, d), (b, b, a), (b, b, d), (b, c, a),$$
$$(b, c, d), (b, d, a), (b, d, d), (c, b, a), (c, b, d), (c, c, a), (c, c, d), (c, d, a), (c, d, d)\}$$

**2.18** Let $W = \{\text{Mark, Eric, Paul}\}$ and let $V = \{\text{Eric, David}\}$. Find: **(a)** $W \times V$, **(b)** $V \times W$, **(c)** $V \times V$.

▌ Write all the ordered pairs for each product set:

**(a)** $W \times V = \{(\text{Mark, Eric}), (\text{Mark, David}), (\text{Eric, Eric}), (\text{Eric, David}), (\text{Paul, Eric}), (\text{Paul, David})\}$.
**(b)** $V \times W = \{(\text{Eric, Mark}), (\text{David, Mark}), (\text{Eric, Eric}), (\text{David, Eric}), (\text{Eric, Paul}), (\text{David, Paul})\}$.
**(c)** $V \times V = \{(\text{Eric, Eric}), (\text{Eric, David}), (\text{David, Eric}), (\text{David, David})\}$.

**2.19** Given $A = \{1, 2\}$, $B = \{a, b, c\}$, and $C = \{c, d\}$. Find: **(a)** $(A \times B) \cap (A \times C)$ and **(b)** $A \times (B \cap C)$.

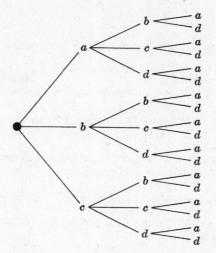

**Fig. 2-3**

**(a)** First find

$$A \times B = \{(1, a), (1, b), (1, c), (2, a), (2, b), (2, c)\}, \qquad A \times C = \{(1, c), (1, d), (2, c), (2, d)\}$$

Then $(A \times B) \cap (A \times C) = \{(1, c), (2, c)\}$.

**(b)** Here $B \cap C = \{c\}$. Thus $A \times (B \cap C) = \{(1, c), (2, c)\}$.

Note that $(A \times B) \cap (A \times C) = A \times (B \cap C)$. This is true for any sets $A$, $B$, and $C$.

**2.20** Let $A = \{a, b\}$, $B = \{1, 2\}$, and $C = \{2, 3\}$. Find: **(a)** $(A \times B) \cup (A \times C)$, **(b)** $A \times (B \cup C)$.

**(a)** First find $A \times B = \{(a, 1), (a, 2), (b, 1), (b, 2)\}$, and $A \times C = \{(a, 2), (a, 3), (b, 2), (b, 3)\}$. Then

$$(A \times B) \cup (A \times C) = \{(a, 1), (a, 2), (a, 3), (b, 1), (b, 2), (b, 3)\}$$

**(b)** First find $B \cup C = \{1, 2, 3\}$. Then $A \times (B \cup C) = \{(a, 1), (a, 2), (a, 3), (b, 1), (b, 2), (b, 3)\}$.

Note that $(A \times B) \cup (A \times C) = A \times (B \cup C)$. This is true for any sets $A$, $B$ and $C$.

**2.21** Prove $(A \times B) \cap (A \times C) = A \times (B \cap C)$.

$$(A \times B) \cap (A \times C) = \{(x, y): (x, y) \in A \times B \text{ and } (x, y) \in A \times C\}$$
$$= \{(x, y): x \in A, y \in B \text{ and } x \in A, y \in C\}$$
$$= \{(x, y): x \in A, y \in B \cap C\} = A \times (B \cap C)$$

**2.22** Prove $(A \times B) \cup (A \times C) = A \times (B \cup C)$.

$$(A \times B) \cup (A \times C) = \{(x, y): (x, y) \in A \times B \text{ or } (x, y) \in A \times C\}$$
$$= \{(x, y): x \in A, y \in B \text{ or } x \in A, y \in C\}$$
$$= \{(x, y): x \in A, \text{ and } y \in B \text{ or } y \in C\}$$
$$= \{(x, y): x \in A, y \in B \cup C\} = A \times (B \cup C)$$

**2.23** Let $A_1 = \{b, c, f\}$, $A_2 = \{a\}$, and $A_3 = \{r, t\}$. Find $\prod A_i$.

Here $\prod A_i = A_1 \times A_2 \times A_3$. Hence

$$\prod A_i = \{(b, a, r), (b, a, t), (c, a, r), (c, a, t), (f, a, r), (f, a, t)\}$$

**2.24** Let $B_1 = \{1, 2\}$, $B_2 = \{3, 4\}$, $B_3 = \{5, 6\}$. Find $\prod B_i$.

Here $\prod B_i = B_1 \times B_2 \times B_3$. Thus

$$\prod B_i = \{(1, 3, 5), (1, 3, 6), (1, 4, 5), (1, 4, 6), (2, 3, 5), (2, 3, 6), (2, 4, 5), (2, 4, 6)\}$$

## 2.2 RELATIONS

A *binary relation*, or simply *relation*, from a set $A$ to a set $B$ is a subset $R$ of $A \times B$. Given $a \in A$ and $b \in B$, we write

$$a \, R \, b \quad \text{or} \quad a \, \not{R} \, b \qquad \text{according as} \qquad (a, b) \in R \text{ or } (a, b) \notin R$$

If $R$ is a relation from $A$ to $A$, i.e., if $R \subseteq A \times A$, then we say $R$ is a relation *on* $A$.

**2.25** Let $R$ be a relation from $A$ to $B$. Define the domain of $R$, written dom $(R)$, and the range of $R$, written range $(R)$.

▮ The domain of $R$ is the subset of $A$ consisting of the first elements of the ordered pairs of $R$, and the range of $R$ is the subset of $B$ consisting of the second elements.

**2.26** Define the inverse of a relation $R$ from $A$ to $B$.

▮ The inverse of $R$, denoted $R^{-1}$, is the relation from $B$ to $A$ which consists of those ordered pairs which when reversed belong to $R$; that is,

$$R^{-1} = \{(b, a): (a, b) \in R\}$$

In other words, $b R^{-1} a$ if and only if $a R b$.

**2.27** Determine which of the following are relations from $A = \{a, b, c\}$ to $B = \{1, 2\}$:
   (a)   $R_1 = \{(a, 1), (a, 2), (c, 2)\}$     (d)   $R_4 = \{(b, 2)\}$
   (b)   $R_2 = \{(a, 2), (b, 1)\}$     (e)   $R_5 = \emptyset$, the empty set
   (c)   $R_3 = \{(c, 1), (c, 2), (c, 3)\}$     (f)   $R_6 = A \times B$

▮ They are all relations from $A$ to $B$ since they are all subsets of $A \times B$. $R_5 = \emptyset$, the empty set, is called the *empty relation* from $A$ to $B$, and $R_6 = A \times B$ is called the *universal relation* from $A$ to $B$.

**2.28** Find the inverse of each relation in Problem 2.27.

▮ Reverse the ordered pairs of each relation $R_k$ to obtain $R_k^{-1}$:
   (a)   $R_1^{-1} = \{(1, a), (2, a), (2, c)\}$     (d)   $R_4^{-1} = \{(2, b)\}$
   (b)   $R_2^{-1} = \{(2, a), (1, b)\}$     (e)   $R_5^{-1} = \emptyset$
   (c)   $R_3^{-1} = \{(1, c), (2, c), (3, c)\}$     (f)   $R_6^{-1} = B \times A$

**2.29** Find the number of relations from $A = \{a, b, c\}$ to $B = \{1, 2\}$.

▮ There are $3 \cdot 2 = 6$ elements in $A \times B$ and hence there are $m = 2^6 = 64$ subsets of $A \times B$. Thus there are $m = 64$ relations from $A$ to $B$.

**2.30** Let $R$ be the relation on $A = \{1, 2, 3, 4\}$ defined by "$x$ is less than $y$", that is, $R$ is the relation $<$. Write $R$ as a set of ordered pairs.

▮ $R$ consists of the ordered pairs $(a, b)$ where $a < b$. Thus

$$R = \{(1, 2), (1, 3), (1, 4), (2, 3), (2, 4), (3, 4)\}$$

**2.31** Find the inverse $R^{-1}$ of the relation $R$ in Problem 2.30. Can $R^{-1}$ be described in words?

▮ Reverse the ordered pairs of $R$ to obtain $R^{-1}$:

$$R^{-1} = \{(2, 1), (3, 1), (4, 1), (3, 2), (4, 2), (4, 3)\}$$

$R^{-1}$ is the relation $>$, that is, $R^{-1}$ can be described by the statement "$x$ is greater than $y$".

**2.32** Let $R$ be the relation from $A = \{1, 2, 3, 4\}$ to $B = \{x, y, z\}$ defined by

$$R = \{(1, y), (1, z), (3, y), (4, x), (4, z)\}$$

   (a)   Determine the domain and range of $R$.
   (b)   Find the inverse relation $R^{-1}$ of $R$.

▮ (a)   The domain of $R$ consists of the first elements of the ordered pairs of $R$, and the range consists of the second elements. Thus dom $(R) = \{1, 3, 4\}$ and range $(R) = \{x, y, z\}$.
   (b)   $R^{-1}$ is obtained by reversing the ordered pairs in $R$. Thus

$$R^{-1} = \{(y, 1), (z, 1), (y, 3), (x, 4), (z, 4)\}$$

**2.33**   Let $R$ be the relation "is located in" from the set $X$ of cities to the set $Y$ of countries. State each of the following in words and indicate whether the statement is true or false:

(**a**)  (Paris, France) $\in R$,        (**c**)  (Washington, Canada) $\in R$,

(**b**)  (Moscow, Italy) $\in R$,        (**d**)  (London, England) $\in R$.

▌ (**a**)  Paris is located in France. True.
   (**b**)  Moscow is located in Italy. False.
   (**c**)  Washington is located in Canada. False.
   (**d**)  London is located in England. True.

**2.34**   Let $A = \{1, 2, 3\}$ and let $R = \{(1, 1), (2, 1), (3, 2), (1, 3)\}$ be a relation on $A$ (i.e., a relation from $A$ to $A$). Determine whether each of the following is true or false:

(**a**)  $1\,R\,1$,   (**b**)  $1\,\not R\,2$,   (**c**)  $2\,R\,3$,   (**d**)  $2\,\not R\,1$,   (**e**)  $3\,R\,2$,   (**f**)  $3\,\not R\,1$

▌ The statement $a\,R\,b$ is true if and only if $(a, b) \in R$. Accordingly

(**a**)  True, since $(1, 1) \in R$       (**d**)  False, since $(2, 1) \in R$
(**b**)  True since $(1, 2) \notin R$       (**e**)  True, since $(3, 2) \in R$
(**c**)  False, since $(2, 3) \notin R$       (**f**)  True, since $(3, 1) \notin R$

**2.35**   Consider the relation $=$ (equality) on $A = \{1, 2, 3, 4\}$. Write $=$ as a set of ordered pairs.

▌ Here $(a, b) \in \,=\,$ means $a = b$. Thus $=$ is the following set of ordered pairs, $\{(1, 1), (2, 2), (3, 3), (4, 4)\}$.

**2.36**   Let $A = \{1, 2, 3, 4, 6\}$, and let $R$ be the relation on $A$ defined by "$x$ divides $y$", written $x \mid y$. (Note $x \mid y$ if there exists an integer $z$ such that $xz = y$, e.g., $2 \mid 6$ since $2 \cdot 3 = 6$.) Write $R$ as a set of ordered pairs.

▌ Find those numbers in $A$ divisible by 1, 2, 3, 4 and then 6. These are:

$$1 \mid 1,\ 1 \mid 2,\ 1 \mid 3,\ 1 \mid 4,\ 1 \mid 6,\ 2 \mid 2,\ 2 \mid 4,\ 2 \mid 6,\ 3 \mid 3,\ 3 \mid 6,\ 4 \mid 4,\ 6 \mid 6$$

Thus   $R = \{(1, 1), (1, 2), (1, 3), (1, 4), (1, 6), (2, 2), (2, 4), (2, 6), (3, 3), (3, 6), (4, 4), (6, 6)\}$.

**2.37**   Find the inverse $R^{-1}$ of the relation $R$ in Problem 2.36. Can $R^{-1}$ be described in words?

▌ Reverse the ordered pairs of $R$ to obtain $R^{-1}$:

$$R^{-1} = \{(1, 1), (2, 1), (3, 1), (4, 1), (6, 1), (2, 2), (4, 2), (6, 2), (3, 3), (6, 3), (4, 4), (6, 6)\}$$

$R^{-1}$ can be described by the statement "$x$ is a multiple of $y$".

**2.38**   Let $S$ be the relation on the set $\mathbf{N}$ of positive integers defined by the equation $x + 3y = 13$, that is,

$$S = \{(x, y): x + 3y = 13\}$$

(Unless otherwise stated or implied, $x$ denotes the first coordinate and $y$ the second coordinate in an ordered pair.) Write $S$ as a set of ordered pairs.

▌ Assign values to one of the variables, say $y$, and solve for the other variable $x$ in the equation. Thus
(i)   $y = 1$ yields $x = 10$.        (iii)   $y = 3$ yields $x = 4$.
(ii)  $y = 2$ yields $x = 7$.        (iv)   $y = 4$ yields $x = 1$.
Any other value of $y$ does not yield a positive integer for $x$. Accordingly,

$$S = \{(10, 7), (7, 2), (4, 3), (1, 4)\}$$

**2.39**   Let $S$ be the relation in Problem 2.38. Find the domain and range of $S$.

▌ The domain consists of the first elements in the ordered pairs and the range the second elements; hence dom $(S) = \{10, 7, 4, 1\}$ and range $(S) = \{1, 2, 3, 4\}$.

**2.40**   Let $S$ be the relation in Problem 2.38. Find the inverse relation $S^{-1}$ and describe $S^{-1}$ by an equation.

▌ Reverse the ordered pairs in $S$ to obtain

$$S^{-1} = \{(1, 10), (2, 7), (3, 4), (4, 1)\}$$

Interchange $x$ and $y$ in the equation defining $S$ to obtain an equation defining $S^{-1}$; hence $3x + y = 13$ defines $S^{-1}$.

**2.41**   Let $R$ be the relation on the set $X = \{0, 1, 2, 3, \ldots\}$ of nonnegative integers defined by the equation $x^2 + y^2 = 25$. Write $R$ as a set of ordered pairs.

▌ The only nonnegative integer solutions of the given equation are when $x = 0, 3, 4, 5$ and when, respectively, $y = 5, 4, 3, 0$. Thus $R = \{(0, 5), (3, 4), (4, 3), (5, 0)\}$.

**2.42** Let $S$ be the relation on the set **N** of positive integers defined by the equation $3x + 4y = 17$. Write $S$ as a set of ordered pairs.

▌ Here $3x = 17 - 4y$. Thus no value of $y$ can exceed 4, since $x$ must be positive. Testing $y = 1, 2, 3, 4$, only $y = 2$ yields an integer value for $x$, i.e., $x = 3$. Thus $S = \{(3, 2)\}$.

**2.43** Let $R$ be the relation on the set **N** of positive integers defined by the equation $2x + 4y = 17$. Write $R$ as a set of ordered pairs.

▌ No value of $y$ can exceed 4 (as in Problem 2.42). Testing $y = 1, 2, 3, 4$, we see that no value of $x$ yields an integer value for $x$. Thus $R = \emptyset$, the empty relation on **N**. (Alternately, any integer values for $x$ and $y$ must yield an even number for $2x + 4y$ which can never equal the odd number 17.)

**2.44** Describe the inverse of the following relations on the set $A$ of people: **(a)** "is taller than", **(b)** "is older than", **(c)** "is a parent of", **(d)** "is a sibling of".

▌ **(a)** "is shorter than",    **(c)** "is a child of"
　**(b)** "is younger than",    **(d)** "is a sibling of" (This relation is symmetric.)

**2.45** Describe the inverse of the following relations on the set $X$ of lines in a plane: **(a)** "is parallel to", **(b)** "lies above", **(c)** "is perpendicular to".

▌ **(a)** "is parallel to",    **(b)** "lies below",    **(c)** "is perpendicular to"
(Here both **(a)** and **(c)** are symmetric relations.)

**2.46** Let $R$ be the relation from $X = \{1, 2, 3, 4\}$ to $Y = \{a, b, c, d\}$ defined by
$$R = \{(1, a), (1, b), (3, b), (3, d), (4, b)\}$$
Find each of the following subsets of $X$: **(a)** $E = \{x : x R b\}$, **(b)** $F = \{x : x R d\}$.

▌ **(a)** $E$ consists of the elements related to $b$. There are three ordered pairs, $(1, b)$, $(3, b)$, and $(4, b)$, with $b$ as the second element. Thus 1, 3, and 4 are related to $b$ and so $E = \{1, 3, 4\}$.
　**(b)** $F = \{3\}$ since there is only one ordered pair $(3, d)$ with the second element $d$.

**2.47** Let $R$ be the relation from $X$ to $Y$ in Problem 2.46. Find each of the following subsets of $Y$: **(a)** $G = \{y : 1 R y\}$, **(b)** $H = \{y : 2 R y\}$.

▌ **(a)** $G$ consists of the elements of $Y$ to which 1 is related. There are two ordered pairs, $(1, a)$ and $(1, b)$, with 1 as the first element. Thus 1 is related to $a$ and $b$ and hence $G = \{a, b\}$.
　**(b)** $H = \emptyset$, the empty subset of $Y$, since there is no ordered pair with 2 as the first element.

**2.48** Let $A$ be any set. Define the *diagonal relation* on $A$, frequently denoted by $\Delta_A$ or simply $\Delta$. Can you give another name of this relation?

▌ The diagonal relation consists of all ordered pairs $(a, b)$ such that $a = b$; that is, $\Delta = \{(a, a) : a \in A\}$. This is the same as the relation = of equality.

**2.49** Suppose $A$ is a finite set. Find the number $m$ of relations on $A$ where: **(a)** $A$ has 3 elements, **(b)** $A$ has $n$ elements.

▌ **(a)** $A \times A$ has $3^2 = 9$ elements. Therefore, there are $2^9 = 512$ subsets of $A \times A$ and hence $m = 512$ relations on $A$.
　**(b)** $A \times A$ has $n^2$ elements and so $m = 2^{n^2}$.

**2.50** Let $R$ and $S$ be the relations on $A = \{1, 2, 3\}$ defined by
$$R = \{(1, 1), (1, 2), (2, 3), (3, 1), (3, 3)\}, \qquad S = \{(1, 2), (1, 3), (2, 1), (3, 3)\}$$
Find $R \cap S$ and $R \cup S$.

▌ Treat $R$ and $S$ simply as sets, and take the usual intersection and union.
$$R \cap S = \{(1, 2), (3, 3)\} \quad \text{and} \quad R \cup S = \{(1, 1), (1, 2), (1, 3), (2, 1), (2, 3), (3, 1), (3, 3)\}$$

**2.51** Let $R$ be the relation on $A = \{1, 2, 3\}$ in Problem 2.50. Find $R^c$.

▋ Use the fact that $A \times A$ is the universal relation on $A$ to obtain

$$R^c = (A \times A)\backslash R = \{(1, 3), (2, 1), (2, 2), (3, 2)\}$$

(Note $A \times A$ has $3 \cdot 3 = 9$ elements and $R$ has 5 elements; hence $R^c$ has 4 elements.)

**2.52** Let $R$ and $S$ be the relations from $A = \{1, 2, 3\}$ to $B = \{a, b\}$ defined by

$$R = \{(1, a), (3, a), (2, b), (3, b)\}, \qquad S = \{(1, b), (2, b)\}$$

Find $R \cap S$ and $R \cup S$.

▋ Treat $R$ and $S$ simply as sets: $R \cap S = \{(2, b)\}$ and $R \cup S = \{(1, a), (3, a), (2, b), (3, b), (1, b)\}$.

**2.53** Let $R$ be the relation from $A$ to $B$ in Problem 2.52. Find $R^c$.

▋ Use the fact that $A \times B$ is the universal relation from $A$ to $B$ to obtain

$$R^c = (A \times B)\backslash R = \{(1, b), (2, a)\}$$

(Note $A \times B$ has $3 \cdot 2 = 6$ elements and $R$ has 4 elements; hence $R^c$ will have 2 elements.)

**2.54** Describe the inverse of the following relations on a collection $X$ of sets: (a) $\subseteq$ (subset), (b) $x$ is disjoint from $y$.

▋ (a) $\supseteq$ (contains or superset).
(b) $y$ is disjoint from $x$. (Relation is symmetric.)

**2.55** Let $R$ be the relation on the set $\mathbf{N}$ of positive integers defined by the equation $x^2 + 2y = 100$. Find the domain of $R$.

▋ Here $2y = 100 - x^2$. Thus $x$ cannot exceed 9 since $y$ is positive. Also, $x$ cannot be odd since $100 - x^2$ must be even. Accordingly, dom $(R) = \{2, 4, 6, 8\}$.

**2.56** Let $R$ be the relation on $\mathbf{N}$ in Problem 2.55. Write $R$ as a set of ordered pairs and find the range of $R$.

▋ Substitute $x = 2, 4, 6, 8$ in the equation $2y = 100 - x^2$ to obtain, respectively, $y = 48, 42, 32, 18$. Thus

$$R = \{(2, 48), (4, 42), (6, 32), (8, 18)\} \qquad \text{and} \qquad \text{range } (R) = \{48, 42, 32, 18\}$$

**2.57** Let $R$ be the relation on $\mathbf{N}$ in Problem 2.55. Find $R^{-1}$ and describe $R^{-1}$ by an equation.

▋ Reverse the ordered pairs in $R$ to obtain

$$R^{-1} = \{(48, 2), (42, 4), (32, 6), (18, 8)\}$$

Interchange $x$ and $y$ in the equation defining $R$ to obtain an equation defining $R^{-1}$; hence $y^2 + 2x = 100$ defines $R^{-1}$.

**2.58** Consider the relations $<$ (less than), $\Delta$ (diagonal or equality) and $|$ (divides) on $A = \{1, 2, 3\}$. (Recall $x \mid y$ if $xz = y$ for some integer $z$.) Find: (a) $< \cup \Delta$, (b) $< \cap |$.

▋ First write $<$, $\Delta$, and $|$ as sets of ordered pairs:

$$< = \{(1, 2), (1, 3), (2, 3\ \ )\}, \qquad \Delta = \{(1, 1), (2, 2), (3, 3)\}$$
$$| = \{(1, 1), (1, 2), (1, 3), (2, 2), (3, 3)\}$$

Then treat $<$, $\Delta$, and $|$ simply as sets.
(a) $< \cup \Delta = \{(1, 2), (1, 3), (2, 3), (1, 1), (2, 2), (3, 3)\}$. (Note that $< \cup \Delta$ is identical with $\leq$.)
(b) $< \cap | = \{(1, 2), (1, 3)\}$.

**2.59** Let $X = \{a, b, c, d, e, f\}$ and $Y = \{\text{bed, dead, bad, feed, face}\}$, and let $R$ be the relation from $X$ to $Y$ defined by "$x$ is a letter in $y$". Describe in words and find the sets: (a) $E = \{x : (x, \text{dead}) \in R\}$, (b) $F = \{y : b\,R\,y\}$

▋ (a) $E$ consists of the letters in dead; hence $E = \{d, e, a\}$.
(b) $f$ consists of the words containing the letter $b$; hence $F = \{\text{bed, bad}\}$.

**2.60** Let $R$ be the relation "is adjacent to" on the set of countries in the world. (Country $x$ is adjacent to country $y$ if they have a common border.) State each of the following in words and indicate whether the statement is true or false:

(**a**)   (France, Spain) $\in R$    (**c**)   (China, Japan) $\notin R$

(**b**)   (Canada, Mexico) $\in R$    (**d**)   (Germany, Poland) $\notin R$

▮ (**a**)   France is adjacent to Spain. True.

(**b**)   Canada is adjacent to Mexico. False.

(**c**)   China is not adjacent to Japan. True.

(**d**)   Germany is not adjacent to Poland. False.

## 2.3   REPRESENTATION OF RELATIONS

This section investigates a number of ways of representing and picturing relations.

**2.61**   Describe the "arrow diagram" of a relation $R$ from a finite set $A$ to a finite set $B$. Illustrate using the relation $R$ from set $A = \{1, 2, 3, 4\}$ to set $B = \{x, y, z\}$ defined by

$$R = \{(1, y), (1, z), (3, y), (4, x), (4, z)\}$$

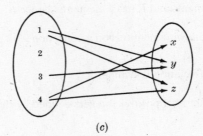

(*c*)                          **Fig. 2-4**

▮ Write down the elements of $A$ and the elements of $B$ in two columns within two disjoint disks, and then draw an arrow from $a \in A$ to $b \in B$ whenever $a$ is related to $b$, i.e., whenever $(a, b) \in R$, as shown in Fig. 2-4. This figure is called the arrow diagram of $R$.

**2.62**   Define the matrix representation $M_R$ of a relation $R$ from a finite set $A$ to a finite set $B$. Illustrate with the relation $R$ of Problem 2.61.

▮ Form a rectangular array whose rows are labeled by the elements of $A$ and whose columns are labeled by the elements of $B$ as in Fig. 2-5(*a*). Then put the integer 1 in each position of the array where $a \in A$ is related to $b \in B$, i.e., where $(a, b) \in R$, and put 0 in the remaining positions, i.e., where $(a, b) \notin R$. This final array, in Fig. 2-5(*b*), is the the matrix $M_R$ of the relation $R$.

$$
\begin{array}{c}
\begin{array}{ccc} x & y & x \end{array} \\
\begin{array}{c} 1 \\ 2 \\ 3 \\ 4 \end{array}
\left(\begin{array}{ccc} & & \\ & \cdot & \\ & & \\ & & \end{array}\right)
\end{array}
\qquad
\begin{array}{c}
\begin{array}{ccc} x & y & x \end{array} \\
\begin{array}{c} 1 \\ 2 \\ 3 \\ 4 \end{array}
\left(\begin{array}{ccc} 0 & 1 & 1 \\ 0 & 0 & 0 \\ 0 & 1 & 0 \\ 1 & 0 & 1 \end{array}\right)
\end{array}
$$

(*a*)                     (*b*)        **Fig. 2-5**

**2.63**   Let $R$ be a relation from a finite set $A$ to a finite set $B$. Explain how we may obtain: (**a**) the arrow diagram of $R^{-1}$ from the arrow diagram of $R$; (**b**) the matrix $N$ representing $R^{-1}$ from the matrix $M_R$ representing $R$.

▮ (**a**)   Simply reverse the arrows in the arrow diagram of $R$ to obtain the arrow diagram of $R^{-1}$.

(**b**)   Take the transpose, i.e., write the rows as columns, of the matrix $M_R$ representing $R$ to obtain the matrix $N$ representing $R^{-1}$.

**2.64**   Consider the relation $R$ in Problem 2.61. (**a**) Draw the arrow diagram of the inverse relation $R^{-1}$. (**b**) Find the matrix $N$ representing $R^{-1}$.

▮ (**a**)   Reverse the arrows in Fig. 2-4, the arrow diagram of $R$, to obtain Fig. 2-6, which is the arrow diagram of $R^{-1}$.

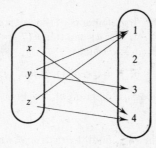

**Fig. 2-6**

(b)  Simply take the transpose, i.e., write the rows as columns, of the matrix $M_R$ in Fig. 2-5 to obtain

$$N = \begin{pmatrix} 0 & 0 & 0 & 1 \\ 1 & 0 & 1 & 0 \\ 1 & 0 & 0 & 1 \end{pmatrix}$$

**2.65**  Let $S$ be the relation from $A = \{$Ellen, Stephanie, Audrey, Jane$\}$ to $B = \{$yes, no$\}$ defined by

$$S = \{(\text{Ellen, no}), (\text{Stephanie, yes}), (\text{Audrey, yes}), (\text{Jane, no})\}$$

Find the matrix $M$ representing the relation $S$.

❙  Order the elements of $A$ and $B$, say, as given. Then

$$M = \begin{pmatrix} 0 & 1 \\ 1 & 0 \\ 1 & 0 \\ 0 & 1 \end{pmatrix}$$

(A different ordering of the elements may give a different matrix.)

**2.66**  Find the inverse $S^{-1}$ of the relation $S$ in Problem 2.65 and find the matrix $N$ which represents $S^{-1}$.

❙  Simply reverse the ordered pairs in $S$ to obtain

$$S^{-1} = \{(\text{no, Ellen}), (\text{yes, Stephanie}), (\text{yes, Audrey}), (\text{no, Jane})\}$$

The matrix $N$ representing $S^{-1}$ can be obtained by taking the transpose of the matrix $M$ representing $S$. Thus

$$N = M^T = \begin{pmatrix} 0 & 1 & 1 & 0 \\ 1 & 0 & 0 & 1 \end{pmatrix}$$

(Here we assume the same ordering of $A$ and $B$ which determined $M$.)

**2.67**  Let $T$ be the relation from $A = \{1, 2, 3, 4, 5\}$ to $B = \{$red, white, blue, green$\}$ defined by

$$T = \{(1, \text{red}), (1, \text{blue}), (3, \text{blue}), (4, \text{green})\}$$

(a)  Draw an arrow diagram of the relation $T$. (b) Find the domain and range of $T$. (c) Find the inverse $T^{-1}$ and its arrow diagram.

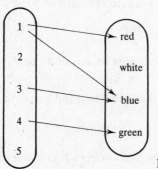

**Fig. 2-7**

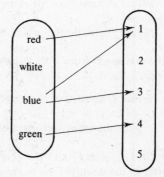

**Fig. 2-8**

❙  (a)  Draw an arrow from $x \in A$ to $y \in B$ for each $(x, y) \in T$. The required arrow diagram is shown in Fig. 2-7.

**(b)** The domain consists of the first elements of the ordered pairs of $T$ and the range consists of the second elements. Hence dom $(T) = \{1, 3, 4\}$ and range $(T) = \{\text{red, blue, green}\}$.

**(c)** Reverse the ordered pairs in $T$ to obtain

$$T^{-1} = \{(\text{red}, 1), (\text{blue}, 1), (\text{blue}, 3), (\text{green}, 4)\}$$

Reverse the arrows in the arrow diagram of $T$ in Fig. 2-7 to obtain the arrow diagram of $T^{-1}$ as shown in Fig. 2-8.

**2.68** Consider the relation $T$ in Problem 2.67. Find the matrix $M$ which represents $T$ and the matrix $N$ which represents $T^{-1}$.

▌ Order the elements of $A$ and $B$, say, as given. Then

$$M = \begin{pmatrix} 1 & 0 & 1 & 0 \\ 0 & 0 & 0 & 0 \\ 0 & 0 & 1 & 0 \\ 0 & 0 & 0 & 1 \\ 0 & 0 & 0 & 0 \end{pmatrix} \quad \text{and} \quad N = M^T = \begin{pmatrix} 1 & 0 & 0 & 0 & 0 \\ 0 & 0 & 0 & 0 & 0 \\ 1 & 0 & 1 & 0 & 0 \\ 0 & 0 & 0 & 1 & 0 \end{pmatrix}$$

Note that the number of 1s in each matrix is equal to the number of ordered pairs in $T$.

**2.69** Let $R$ be the relation from $X = \{1, 2, 3, 4\}$ to $Y = \{a, b, c, d\}$ shown in Fig. 2-9. State whether or not each of the following is true: **(a)** $1Rb$, **(b)** $2Rc$, **(c)** $3Rs$, **(d)** $4Rc$. Also, **(e)** write $R$ as a set of ordered pairs.

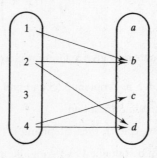

**Fig. 2-9**

▌ **(a)** Yes, there is an arrow from 1 to $b$.
  **(b)** No, there is no arrow from 2 to $c$.
  **(c)** No, there is no arrow from 3 to $a$.
  **(d)** Yes, there is an arrow from 4 to $c$.
  **(e)** Each arrow in the diagram, say from $x$ to $y$, determines an ordered pair $(x, y)$ in $R$. Thus

$$R = \{(1, b), (2, b), (2, d), (4, c), (4, d)\}$$

**2.70** Given the relation $R$ from $X$ to $Y$ shown in Fig. 2-9, find each of the following subsets of $Y$: **(a)** $E = \{y: 2Ry\}$, **(b)** $F = \{y: 1Ry\}$.

▌ **(a)** Subset $E$ consists of the elements to which 2 is related. There are arrows from 2 to $b$ and 2 to $d$; hence $E = \{b, d\}$.
  **(b)** $F = \{b\}$ since there is only one arrow which goes from 1 to $b$.

**2.71** Given the relation $R$ from $X$ to $Y$ shown in Fig. 2-9, find each of the following subsets of $X$: **(a)** $G = \{x: xRd\}$, **(b)** $H = \{x: xRa\}$.

▌ **(a)** Subset $G$ consists of the elements related to $d$. There are arrows from 2 to $d$ and 4 to $d$; hence $G = \{2, 4\}$.
  **(b)** $H = \varnothing$, the empty set, since there is no arrow to $a$.

**2.72** Let $X = \{a, b, c, d, e, f\}$ and $Y = \{\text{beef, dad, ace, cab}\}$ and let $R$ be the relation from $X$ to $Y$ where $(x, y) \in R$ if $x$ is a letter in the word $y$. Find the matrix $M$ which represents $R$.

▌ Order the elements of $X$ and $Y$, say, as given. Notice $M$ will have six rows, labeled by the elements of $X$, and four columns, labeled by the elements of $Y$. Then put 1 in the row $x$ and column $y$ if $x$ is a letter in $y$ and 0 otherwise. Thus

$$M = \begin{array}{c} \\ a \\ b \\ c \\ d \\ e \\ f \end{array} \begin{array}{c} \text{beef} \quad \text{dad} \quad \text{ace} \quad \text{cab} \end{array} \\ \begin{pmatrix} 0 & 1 & 1 & 1 \\ 1 & 0 & 0 & 1 \\ 0 & 0 & 1 & 1 \\ 0 & 1 & 0 & 0 \\ 1 & 0 & 1 & 0 \\ 1 & 0 & 0 & 0 \end{pmatrix}$$

**2.73**   Consider a relation $S$ from $X = \{1, 2, 3\}$ to $Y = \{a, b, c, d\}$ whose matrix representation is

$$M = \begin{array}{c} \\ 1 \\ 2 \\ 3 \end{array} \begin{array}{c} a \quad b \quad c \quad d \end{array} \\ \begin{pmatrix} 0 & 1 & 0 & 1 \\ 0 & 0 & 1 & 1 \\ 1 & 1 & 0 & 1 \end{pmatrix}$$

State whether each of the following is true: **(a)** $1\,S\,b$, **(b)** $2\,S\,a$, **(c)** $3\,S\,d$.

▌ **(a)**   Yes, there is a 1 in row 1, column $b$.
   **(b)**   No, there is a 0 in row 2, column $a$.
   **(c)**   Yes, there is a 1 in row 3, column $d$.

**2.74**   Write the relation $S$ in Problem 2.73 as a set of ordered pairs.

▌ Each 1 in the matrix, say, in row $x$ and column $y$, determines an ordered pair $(x, y) \in S$. Thus

$$S = \{(1, b), (1, d), (2, c), (2, d), (3, a), (3, b), (3, d)\}$$

**2.75**   Let $S$ be the relation in Problem 2.73. Find the following subsets of $X$ and $Y$:
**(a)**   $E = \{x : x\,S\,b\}$,   **(b)**   $F = \{y : 3\,R\,y\}$.

▌ **(a)**   Subset $E$ consists of the elements related to $b$. In column $b$ of the matrix $M$, there is a 1 in rows 1 and 3. Hence $E = \{1, 3\}$.
   **(b)**   Subset $F$ consists of the elements to which 3 is related. In row 3 of the matrix $M$, there is a 1 in columns $a$, $b$, and $d$. Hence $F = \{a, b, d\}$.

### Directed Graph of a Relation on a Set

**2.76**   Describe the "directed graph" of a relation $R$ on a set $A$. Illustrate using the relation $R$ on $A = \{1, 2, 3, 4\}$ defined by

$$R = \{(1, 2), (2, 2), (2, 4), (3, 2), (3, 4), (4, 1), (4, 3)\}$$

(We emphasize that a directed graph is not defined for a relation from one set to another set.)

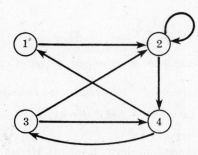

$$R = \{(1, 2), (2, 2), (2, 4), (3, 2), (3, 4), (4, 1), (4, 3)\} \quad \textbf{Fig. 2-10}$$

▌ Write down the elements of $A$, and then draw an arrow from an element $x$ to an element $y$ whenever $(x, y) \in R$. The directed graph for the given relation is shown in Fig. 2-10.

**2.77**  Let $A = \{1, 2, 3, 4, 6\}$ and let $R$ be the relation on $A$ defined by "$x$ divides $y$", written $x \mid y$. Recall (Problem 2.36) that

$$R = \{(1, 1), (1, 2), (1, 3), (1, 4), (1, 6), (2, 2), (2, 4), (2, 6), (3, 3), (3, 6), (6, 6)\}$$

Draw the directed graph of $R$.

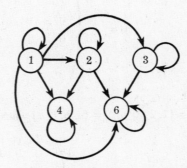

**Fig. 2-11**

▌ Write down the integers 1, 2, 3, 4, 6 and draw an arrow from the integer $x$ to the integer $y$ if $x$ divides $y$ as in Fig. 2-11.

**2.78**  Find the matrix $M$ of the relation $R$ in Problem 2.77.

▌ Assume the rows and columns of $M$ are each labeled 1, 2, 3, 4, 6. Then put 1 in row $x$ and column $y$ if $x$ divides $y$ and 0 otherwise. Thus

$$M = \begin{array}{c} \\ 1 \\ 2 \\ 3 \\ 4 \\ 6 \end{array} \begin{array}{c} \begin{array}{ccccc} 1 & 2 & 3 & 4 & 6 \end{array} \\ \left(\begin{array}{ccccc} 1 & 1 & 1 & 1 & 1 \\ 0 & 1 & 0 & 1 & 1 \\ 0 & 0 & 1 & 0 & 1 \\ 0 & 0 & 0 & 1 & 0 \\ 0 & 0 & 0 & 0 & 1 \end{array}\right) \end{array}$$

(Note that since $R$ is a relation on the set $A$ the matrix $M$ is square, i.e., $M$ has the same number of rows as columns.)

**2.79**  Let $S$ be the relation on $X = \{a, b, c, d, e, f\}$ defined by

$$S = \{(a, b), (b, b), (b, c), (c, f), (d, b), (e, a), (e, b), (e, f)\}$$

Draw the directed graph of $S$.

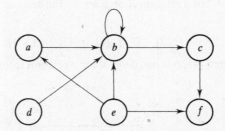

**Fig. 2-12**

▌ Write down the letters in $X$ and draw an arrow from the letter $x$ to the letter $y$ if $(x, y) \in S$ as in Fig. 2-12.

**2.80**  Let $S$ be the relation on $X$ in Problem 2.79. Find each of the following subsets of $X$:

     **(a)** $E = \{x : e\,S\,x\}$,    **(b)** $F = \{x : x\,S\,b\}$,    **(c)** $G = \{x : x\,S\,e\}$.

▌ Use the directed graph of $S$ in Fig. 2-12.
**(a)** Subset $E$ consists of the elements to which $e$ is related. Hence $E = \{a, b, f\}$ since there are arrows from $e$ to $a$, $b$, and $f$.
**(b)** Subset $F$ consists of the elements related to $b$. Thus $F = \{a, b, d, e\}$ since there are arrows from $a$, $b$, $d$, and $e$ to $b$.
**(c)** Subset $G$ consists of the elements related to $e$. Hence $G = \varnothing$, the empty set, since there is no arrow to $e$.

**2.81** Draw the directed graph of the relation $T$ on $X = \{1, 2, 3, 4\}$ defined by

$$T = \{(1, 1), (2, 2), (2, 3), (3, 2), (4, 2), (4, 4)\}$$

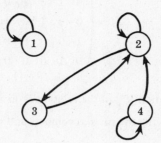

**Fig. 2-13**

▮ Draw an arrow from $x$ to $y$ when $(x, y) \in T$ as in Fig. 2-13. Note that there is an arrow for each ordered pair in $T$.

**2.82** Find the matrix $M$ which represents the relation $T$ in Problem 2.81.

▮ Each $(x, y) \in T$ determines a 1 in $M$ as follows:

$$M = \begin{pmatrix} 1 & 0 & 0 & 0 \\ 0 & 1 & 1 & 0 \\ 0 & 1 & 0 & 0 \\ 0 & 1 & 0 & 1 \end{pmatrix}$$

**2.83** Let $R$ be the relation on $A = \{1, 2, 3, 4, 5\}$ described by the directed graph in Fig. 2-14. Write $R$ as a set of ordered pairs.

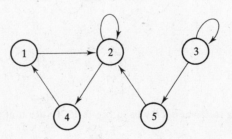

**Fig. 2-14**

▮ Each arrow in the diagram, say from $x$ to $y$, determines an ordered pair $(x, y)$ in $R$. Thus

$$R = \{(1, 2), (2, 2), (2, 4), (3, 3), (3, 5), (4, 1), (5, 2)\}$$

**2.84** Let $R$ be the relation on $A$ shown in Fig. 2-14. Find each of the following subsets of $A$: **(a)** $E = \{a : a\,R\,2\}$, **(b)** $F = \{a : a\,R\,3\}$.

▮ **(a)** Subset $E$ consists of the elements related to 2; hence $E = \{1, 2, 5\}$ since there are arrows from 1, 2, and 5 to 2.

**(b)** $F = \{3\}$ since there is only one arrow to 3, namely from 3 to itself.

**2.85** Let $R$ be the relation on $A$ shown in Fig. 2-14. Find each of the following subsets of $A$: **(a)** $G = \{a : 2\,R\,a\}$, **(b)** $H = \{a : 3\,R\,a\}$.

▮ **(a)** Subset $G$ consists of the elements to which 2 is related; hence $G = \{2, 4\}$ since there are arrows from 2 to 2 and 4.

**(b)** $H = \{3, 5\}$ since there are arrows from 3 to 3 and 5.

**2.86** Find the matrix $M$ of the relation $R$ on $A$ shown in Fig. 2-14.

▮ The matrix $M$ will have 5 rows and 5 columns (labeled by the elements 1, 2, 3, 4, 5 of $A$, respectively). Put the integer 1 in row $x$ and column $y$ whenever $x \, R \, y$, and put 0 in the remaining positions to obtain the matrix

$$M = \begin{pmatrix} 0 & 1 & 0 & 0 & 0 \\ 0 & 1 & 0 & 1 & 0 \\ 0 & 0 & 1 & 0 & 1 \\ 1 & 0 & 0 & 0 & 0 \\ 0 & 1 & 0 & 0 & 0 \end{pmatrix}$$

**2.87**  Find the matrix $N$ of the inverse relation $R^{-1}$ of the relation $R$ on $A$ in Fig. 2-14.

    ❚  Simply take the transpose (i.e., write the rows as columns and vice versa) of the matrix $M$ of $R$ in Problem 2.86 to obtain

$$N = M^{T} = \begin{pmatrix} 0 & 0 & 0 & 1 & 0 \\ 1 & 1 & 0 & 0 & 1 \\ 0 & 0 & 1 & 0 & 0 \\ 0 & 1 & 0 & 0 & 0 \\ 0 & 0 & 1 & 0 & 0 \end{pmatrix}$$

**2.88**  Let $R$ be the relation on $A = \{2, 3, 4, 6, 9\}$ defined by "$x$ is relatively prime to $y$", i.e., the only positive divisor of $x$ and $y$ is 1. Write $R$ as a set of ordered pairs.

    ❚  $R = \{(2, 3), (2, 9), (3, 2), (3, 4), (4, 3), (4, 9), (9, 2), (9, 4)\}$.

**2.89**  Draw the directed graph of the relation $R$ in Problem 2.88.

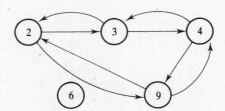

**Fig. 2-15**

    ❚  Draw an arrow from $x$ to $y$ when $x \, R \, y$ as in Fig. 2-15. (Note that 6 is not related to any of the elements.)

**2.90**  Find the matrix $M$ representing the relation $R$ in Problem 2.88.

    ❚  Here $M$ has five rows and five columns labeled, say, by 2, 3, 4, 6, 9, respectively. Then

$$M = \begin{array}{c} \\ 2 \\ 3 \\ 4 \\ 6 \\ 9 \end{array} \begin{array}{c} \begin{array}{ccccc} 2 & 3 & 4 & 6 & 9 \end{array} \\ \begin{pmatrix} 0 & 1 & 0 & 0 & 1 \\ 1 & 0 & 1 & 0 & 0 \\ 0 & 1 & 0 & 0 & 1 \\ 0 & 0 & 0 & 0 & 0 \\ 1 & 0 & 1 & 0 & 0 \end{pmatrix} \end{array}$$

## Graphs of Relations on R

This subsection considers relations on the set **R** of real numbers. Such a relation $S$ frequently consists of all ordered pairs of real numbers satisfying some given equation

$$E(x, y) = 0$$

The relation $S$ is identified with this equation, i.e., we speak of the relation $E(x, y) = 0$. Furthermore, since $\mathbf{R}^2$ can be represented by points in the plane, we can picture $S$ by emphasizing those points in the plane which belong to $S$. This pictorial representation of the relation is sometimes called the *graph* of the relation.

**2.91** Find the inverse of each of the following relations on **R**:

    (**a**) $x^2 + xy = 100$,    (**b**) $5x^2 - 3y^2 = 15$,    (**c**) $y = \sin x$

▌ Since $(a, b)$ belongs to a relation if and only if $(b, a)$ belongs to the inverse relation, the inverse is obtained by interchanging $x$ and $y$ in the given equations. Thus

    (**a**) $y^2 + xy = 100$,    (**b**) $5y^2 - 3x^2 = 15$,    (**c**) $x = \sin y$

**2.92** Figure 2-16 shows the graph of the relation $S$ defined by the equation $4x^2 + 9y^2 = 36$. Find: (**a**) the domain of $S$, and (**b**) the range of $S$.

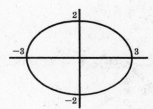

**Fig. 2-16**

▌ (**a**) The domain of $S$ is the interval $[-3, 3]$ since the vertical line through each of these points on the $x$ axis, and only these points, contains at least one point of $S$.

    (**b**) The range of $S$ is the interval $[-2, 2]$, since the horizontal line through each of these points on the $y$ axis, and only these points, contains at least one point of $S$.

**2.93** Describe the relationship between the graph of a relation $S$ on **R** and the graph of the inverse relation $S^{-1}$.

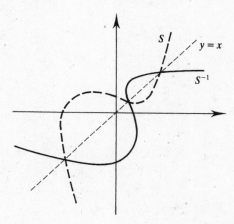

**Fig. 2-17**

▌ The ordered pair $(a, b)$ belongs to $S$ if and only if the reverse pair $(b, a)$ belongs to $S^{-1}$. Thus the graph of $S^{-1}$ may be obtained from the graph of $S$ by reflecting $S$ in the line $y = x$ as shown in Fig. 2-17.

**2.94** Figure 2-18 shows the graph of the relation $S$ defined by the equation $y = x^2$. Find the domain and range of $S$.

▌ Here dom $(S) = \mathbf{R}$ since every vertical line contains a point of $S$; but range $(S) = [0, \infty) = \{x: x \geq 0\}$ since only the horizontal lines on and above the $x$ axis intersect the graph of $S$.

**2.95** Let $S$ be the relation in Problem 2.94. (**a**) Find the equation which determines the inverse relation $S^{-1}$. (**b**) Draw the graph of $S^{-1}$.

▌ (**a**) Interchange $x$ and $y$ in the given equation to obtain $x = y^2$.

    (**b**) Reflect the graph of $S$ in the line $y = x$ as in Fig. 2-19.

**2.96** Explain how to plot a relation $S$ on **R** of the form:

        (**a**) $y > f(x)$,    (**b**) $y \geq f(x)$,    (**c**) $y < f(x)$,    (**d**) $y \leq f(x)$

▌ First plot $y = f(x)$. Then the relation $S$ will consist of all the points: (**a**) above $y = f(x)$, (**b**) above and on $y = f(x)$, (**c**) below $y = f(x)$, (**d**) below and on $y = f(x)$.

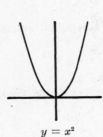

$y = x^2$    **Fig. 2-18**

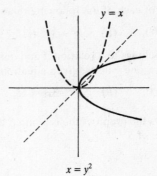

$x = y^2$    **Fig. 2-19**

**2.97**    Sketch each of the following relations on **R**: *(a)* $y \leq x^2$, *(b)* $y < 3 - x$, *(c)* $y > x^3$.

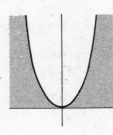

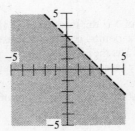

*(a)* $y \leq x^2$            *(b)* $y < 3 - x$

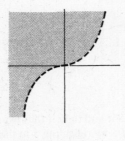

*(c)* $y > x^3$            **Fig. 2-20**

**❙**    Use the procedure in Problem 2.96 to obtain Fig. 2-20. Note that the curves $y = f(x)$ in Figs 2-20(*b*) and (*c*) are drawn with dashes since the points on each $y = f(x)$ do not belong to the corresponding relation.

**2.98**    Explain how to plot a relation $S$ on **R** of the form $E(x, y) < 0$ (or $\leq$, $>$, $\geq$).

**❙**    First plot $E(x, y) = 0$. The curve $E(x, y) = 0$ will, in simple situations, partition the plane into two or more regions. The relation will consist of all the points in possibly one or more of the regions. Then test one or more points in each region to determine whether or not all the points in that region belong to the relation.

**2.99**    Sketch each of the following relations on **R**: *(a)* $x^2 + y^2 < 16$, *(b)* $x^2 - 4y^2 \geq 9$.

**❙**    Use the procedure in Problem 2.98 to obtain Fig. 2-21.

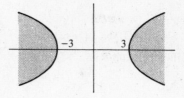

(a) $x^2 + y^2 < 16$   (b) $x^2 - 4y^2 \geq 9$   **Fig. 2-21**

**2.100** Consider the following relations on **R**:

(**a**)  $y = \sin \pi x$,   (**b**)  $x^2 + 4y^2 = 4$,   (**c**)  $x^2 - y^2 = 1$

and the corresponding graphs shown in Fig. 2-22. Draw the graph of each of the inverse functions.

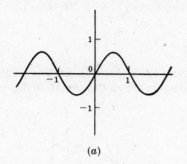 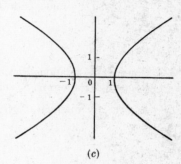

(a)    (b)    (c)

**Fig. 2-22**

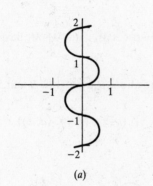 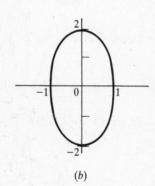 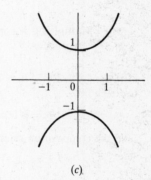

(a)    (b)    (c)

**Fig. 2-23**

▌ Reflect each graph in the line $y = x$ to obtain the corresponding graph of the inverse function (see Fig. 2-23).

## 2.4 COMPOSITION OF RELATIONS

**2.101** Define the composition of relations.

▌ Let $A$, $B$, and $C$ be sets, and let $R$ be a relation from $A$ to $B$ and let $S$ be a relation from $B$ to $C$. That is, $R$ is a subset of $A \times B$ and $S$ is a subset of $B \times C$. Then $R$ and $S$ give rise to a relation from $A$ to $C$ denoted by $R \circ S$ and defined by

$$a(R \circ S)c \text{ if for some } b \in B \text{ we have } a\,R\,b \text{ and } b\,S\,c$$

That is,

$$R \circ S = \{(a, c): \text{there exists } b \in B \text{ for which } (a, b) \in R \text{ and } (b, c) \in S\}$$

The relation $R \circ S$ is called the *composition* of $R$ and $S$; it is sometimes denoted simply by $RS$.

**2.102** Let $A = \{1, 2, 3\}$, $B = \{a, b, c\}$, and $C = \{x, y, z\}$. Consider the following relations $R$ from $A$ to $B$ and $S$ from

$B$ to $C$:

$$R = \{(1, b), (2, a), (2, c)\} \quad \text{and} \quad S = \{(a, y), (b, x), (c, y), (c, z)\}$$

Find the composition relation $R \circ S$.

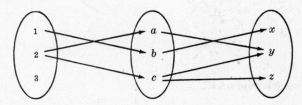

**Fig. 2-24**

▌ Draw the arrow diagrams of $R$ and $S$ as in Fig. 2-24. There is an arrow from 1 to $b$ which is followed by an arrow from $b$ to $x$. Thus $1(R \circ S)x$ since $1 R b$ and $b S x$; that is, $(1, x)$ belongs to $R \circ S$. Similarly there is a path from 2 to $a$ to $y$ and a path from 2 to $c$ to $z$. Thus $(2, y)$ and $(2, z)$ also belong to $R \circ S$. No other pairs belong to $R \circ S$. Thus

$$R \circ S = \{(1, x), (2, y), (2, z)\}$$

**2.103** Consider the relations $R$, $S$, and $R \circ S$ in Problem 2.102. **(a)** Find the matrices $M_R$, $M_S$, and $M_{R \circ S}$ of the respective relations $R$, $S$, and $R \circ S$. **(b)** Multiply $M_R$ and $M_S$ and compare the product $M_R M_S$ to the matrix $M_{R \circ S}$.

▌ **(a)** The matrices of $M_R$, $M_S$, and $M_{R \circ S}$ follow:

$$M_R = \begin{array}{c} 1 \\ 2 \\ 3 \end{array}\begin{pmatrix} 0 & 1 & 0 \\ 1 & 0 & 1 \\ 0 & 0 & 0 \end{pmatrix}, \quad M_S = \begin{array}{c} a \\ b \\ c \end{array}\begin{pmatrix} 0 & 1 & 0 \\ 1 & 0 & 0 \\ 0 & 1 & 1 \end{pmatrix}, \quad M_{R \circ S} = \begin{array}{c} 1 \\ 2 \\ 3 \end{array}\begin{pmatrix} 1 & 0 & 0 \\ 0 & 1 & 1 \\ 0 & 0 & 0 \end{pmatrix}$$

**(b)** Multiplying $M_R$ and $M_S$ we obtain $M_R M_S = \begin{pmatrix} 1 & 0 & 0 \\ 0 & 2 & 1 \\ 0 & 0 & 0 \end{pmatrix}$. The matrices $M_{R \circ S}$ and $M_R M_S$ have the same zero entries.

**2.104** Let $A = \{1, 2, 3, 4\}$, $B = \{a, b, c, d\}$, and $C = \{x, y, z\}$. Consider the relations $R$ from $A$ to $B$ and $S$ from $B$ to $C$ defined by

$$R = \{(1, a), (2, d), (3, a), (3, b), (3, d)\}, \quad S = \{(b, x), (b, z), (c, y), (d, z)\}$$

Find the composition relation $R \circ S$.

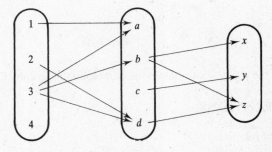

**Fig. 2-25**

▌ Draw the arrow diagrams of $R$ and $S$ as in Fig. 2-25. There is an arrow from 2 to $d$ which is followed by an arrow from $d$ to $z$. Thus

$$2(R \circ S)z \quad \text{since} \quad 2 R d \text{ and } d S z$$

Similarly there is a path from 3 to $b$ to $x$ and a path from 3 to $b$ to $z$. Thus

$$3(R \circ S)x \quad \text{and} \quad 3(R \circ S)z$$

No other element of $A$ is connected to an element of $C$. Accordingly,

$$R \circ S = \{(2, z), (3, x), (3, z)\}$$

**2.105** Use matrices to find the composition $R \circ S$ of the relations $R$ and $S$ in Problem 2.104.

❙ First find the matrices $M_R$ and $M_S$ representing $R$ and $S$, respectively, as follows:

$$M_R = \begin{array}{c} 1 \\ 2 \\ 3 \\ 4 \end{array} \begin{pmatrix} a & b & c & d \\ 1 & 0 & 0 & 0 \\ 0 & 0 & 0 & 1 \\ 1 & 1 & 0 & 1 \\ 0 & 0 & 0 & 0 \end{pmatrix} \quad \text{and} \quad M_S = \begin{array}{c} a \\ b \\ c \\ d \end{array} \begin{pmatrix} x & y & z \\ 0 & 0 & 0 \\ 1 & 0 & 1 \\ 0 & 1 & 0 \\ 0 & 0 & 1 \end{pmatrix}$$

Multiply $M_R$ and $M_S$ to obtain the matrix

$$M = M_R M_S = \begin{array}{c} 1 \\ 2 \\ 3 \\ 4 \end{array} \begin{pmatrix} x & y & z \\ 0 & 0 & 0 \\ 0 & 0 & 1 \\ 1 & 0 & 2 \\ 0 & 0 & 0 \end{pmatrix}$$

The nonzero entries in this matrix tell us which elements are related by $R \circ S$; that is, $M_{R \circ S}$ and $M$ have the same nonzero entries. Thus

$$R \circ S = \{(2, z), (3, x), (3, z)\}$$

which agrees with the result in Problem 2.104.

**Theorem 2.1:** Let $A$, $B$, $C$ and $D$ be sets. Suppose $R$ is a relation from $A$ to $B$, $S$ is a relation from $B$ to $C$, and $T$ is a relation from $C$ to $D$. Then

$$(R \circ S) \circ T = R \circ (S \circ T)$$

(That is, the composition of relations satisfies the associative law.)

**2.106** Prove Theorem 2.1.

❙ We need to show that each ordered pair in $(R \circ S) \circ T$ belongs to $R \circ (S \circ T)$, and vice versa.

Suppose $(a, d)$ belongs to $(R \circ S) \circ T$. Then there exists a $c$ in $C$ such that $(a, c) \in R \circ S$ and $(c, d) \in T$. Since $(a, c) \in R \circ S$, there exists a $b$ in $B$ such that $(a, b) \in R$ and $(b, c) \in S$. Since $(b, c) \in S$ and $(c, d) \in T$, we have $(b, c) \in S \circ T$; and since $(a, b) \in R$ and $(b, d) \in S \circ T$, we have $(a, d) \in R \circ (S \circ T)$. Thus $(R \circ S) \circ T \subseteq R \circ (S \circ T)$. Similarly, $R \circ (S \circ T) \subseteq (R \circ S) \circ T$. Both inclusion relations prove $(R \circ S) \circ T = R \circ (S \circ T)$.

**2.107** Let $A = \{a, b, c, d\}$, $B = \{1, 2, 3\}$, and $C = \{w, x, y, z\}$. Consider the relations $R$ from $A$ to $B$ and $S$ from $B$ to $C$ defined by

$$R = \{(a, 3), (b, 3), (c, 1), (c, 3), (d, 2)\}, \qquad S = \{(1, x), (2, y), (2, z)\}$$

**(a)** Draw an arrow diagram for both $R$ and $S$. **(b)** Find the composition relation $R \circ S$.

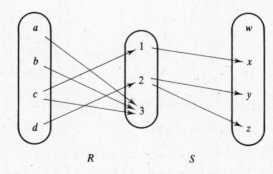

$$R \qquad\qquad S \qquad\qquad \textbf{Fig. 2-26}$$

❙ **(a)** Draw the sets $A$, $B$, and $C$ and then draw the arrows corresponding to the pairs in $R$ and $S$ as in Fig. 2-26.

**(b)** There is a path from $c$ to 1 to $x$, $d$ to 2 to $y$, and $d$ to 2 to $z$. No other paths connect elements of $A$ to $C$. Thus $R \circ S = \{(c, x), (d, y), (d, z)\}$.

**2.108** Let $R$ and $S$ be the relations on $A = \{1, 2, 3, 4\}$ defined by:

$$R = \{(1, 1), (3, 1), (3, 4), (4, 2), (4, 3)\}, \qquad S = \{(1, 3), (2, 1), (3, 1), (3, 2), (4, 4)\}$$

Find the composition relation $R \circ S$.

▌ First find those elements to which 1 is related by $R \circ S$. Note $1\,R\,1$ and $1\,S\,3$; hence $(1, 3)$ belongs to $R \circ S$.
Next find those elements to which 2 is related by $R \circ S$. No such elements exist since no pair in $R$ begins with 2.
Next find those elements to which 3 is related by $R \circ S$. Note $3\,R\,1$ and $3\,R\,4$, and $1\,S\,3$ and $4\,S\,4$. Thus $(3, 3)$ and $(3, 4)$ belong to $R \circ S$.
Lastly, find those elements to which 4 is related by $R \circ S$. Note $4\,R\,2$ and $4\,R\,3$, and $2\,S\,1$, $3\,S\,1$, and $3\,S\,2$. Thus $(4, 1)$ and $(4, 2)$ belong to $R \circ S$.
Accordingly, $R \circ S = \{(1, 3), (3, 3), (3, 4), (4, 1), (4, 2)\}$.

**2.109** Find the composition $S \circ R$ for the relations in Problem 2.108.

▌ First use $S$ and then $R$ to obtain the following paths:
(i)   $1 \to 3 \to 1$ and $1 \to 3 \to 4$;   (iii)   $3 \to 1 \to 1$;
(ii)   $2 \to 1 \to 1$;   (iv)   $4 \to 4 \to 2$ and $4 \to 4 \to 3$
Thus $S \circ R = \{(1, 1), (1, 4), (2, 1), (3, 1), (4, 2), (4, 3)\}$.

**2.110** Find the composition $R^2 = R \circ R$ for the relation $R$ in Problem 2.108.

▌ Use $R$ twice to obtain the following paths:

$$1 \to 1 \to 1, \quad 3 \to 1 \to 1, \quad 3 \to 4 \to 2, \quad 3 \to 4 \to 3, \quad 4 \to 3 \to 1, \quad 4 \to 3 \to 4$$

Thus $R^2 = \{(1, 1), (3, 1), (3, 2), (3, 3), (4, 1), (4, 4)\}$.

**2.111** Find the composition $R^3 = R \circ R \circ R$ for the relation $R$ in Problem 2.108.

▌ Use $R$ three times or find the composition of $R^2$ with $R$ to obtain the paths

$$1 \to 1 \to 1, \quad 3 \to 1 \to 1, \quad 3 \to 3 \to 1, \quad 3 \to 3 \to 4, \quad 4 \to 1 \to 1, \quad 4 \to 4 \to 2, \quad 4 \to 4 \to 3$$

Thus $R^3 = \{(1, 1), (3, 1), (3, 4), (4, 1), (4, 2)\}$.

**2.112** Let $R$ and $S$ be the relations on $X = \{a, b, c\}$ defined by

$$R = \{(a, b), (a, c), (b, a)\} \qquad \text{and} \qquad S = \{(a, c), (b, a), (b, b), (c, a)\}$$

Find the matrices $M_R$ and $M_S$ representing $R$ and $S$ respectively.

▌ Order the elements of $X$, say, $a, b, c$. Then

$$M_R = \begin{matrix} & \begin{matrix} a & b & c \end{matrix} \\ \begin{matrix} a \\ b \\ c \end{matrix} & \begin{pmatrix} 0 & 1 & 1 \\ 1 & 0 & 0 \\ 0 & 0 & 0 \end{pmatrix} \end{matrix}, \qquad \text{and} \qquad M_S = \begin{matrix} & \begin{matrix} a & b & c \end{matrix} \\ \begin{matrix} a \\ b \\ c \end{matrix} & \begin{pmatrix} 0 & 0 & 1 \\ 1 & 1 & 0 \\ 1 & 0 & 0 \end{pmatrix} \end{matrix}$$

**2.113** Find the composition $R \circ S$ for the relations $R$ and $S$ in Problem 2.112.

▌ Multiply the matrices $M_R$ and $M_S$ to obtain

$$M_R M_S = \begin{pmatrix} 0+1+1 & 0+1+0 & 0+0+0 \\ 0+0+0 & 0+0+0 & 1+0+0 \\ 0+0+0 & 0+0+0 & 0+0+0 \end{pmatrix} = \begin{pmatrix} 2 & 1 & 0 \\ 0 & 0 & 1 \\ 0 & 0 & 0 \end{pmatrix}$$

The nonzero entries of $M_R M_S$ indicate that $R \circ S = \{(a, a), (a, b), (b, c)\}$.

**2.114** Find the composition $S \circ R$ for the relations $S$ and $R$ in Problem 2.112.

▌ Multiply the matrices $M_S$ and $M_R$ to obtain

$$M_S M_R = \begin{pmatrix} 0+0+0 & 0+0+0 & 0+0+0 \\ 0+1+0 & 1+0+0 & 1+0+0 \\ 0+0+0 & 1+0+0 & 1+0+0 \end{pmatrix} = \begin{pmatrix} 0 & 0 & 0 \\ 1 & 1 & 1 \\ 0 & 1 & 1 \end{pmatrix}$$

The nonzero entries of $M_S M_R$ indicate that $S \circ R = \{(b, a), (b, b), (b, c), (c, b), (c, c)\}$.

**2.115** Find the composition $R^2 = R \circ R$ for the relation $R$ in Problem 2.112.

▌ Multiply the matrix $M_R$ by itself to obtain

$$M_R^2 = \begin{pmatrix} 0+1+0 & 0+0+0 & 0+0+0 \\ 0+0+0 & 1+0+0 & 1+0+0 \\ 0+0+0 & 0+0+0 & 0+0+0 \end{pmatrix} = \begin{pmatrix} 1 & 0 & 0 \\ 0 & 1 & 1 \\ 0 & 0 & 0 \end{pmatrix}$$

Thus $R^2 = \{(a, a), (b, b), (b, c)\}$.

**2.116** Find the composition $S^2 = S \circ S$ for the relation $S$ in Problem 2.112.

▌ Multiply the matrix $M_S$ by itself to obtain

$$M_S^2 = \begin{pmatrix} 0+0+1 & 0+0+0 & 0+0+0 \\ 0+1+0 & 0+1+0 & 1+0+0 \\ 0+0+0 & 0+0+0 & 1+0+0 \end{pmatrix} = \begin{pmatrix} 1 & 0 & 0 \\ 1 & 1 & 1 \\ 0 & 0 & 1 \end{pmatrix}$$

Thus $S^2 = \{(a, a), (b, a), (b, b), (b, c), (c, c)\}$.

**2.117** Find $R^{-1}$ and the matrix $N_R$ representing $R^{-1}$ for the relation $R$ in Problem 2.112.

▌ Reverse the elements of $R$ to get $R^{-1} = \{(b, a), (c, a), (a, b)\}$. Use $R^{-1}$ or take the transpose of $M_R$ to obtain $N_R = \begin{pmatrix} 0 & 1 & 0 \\ 1 & 0 & 0 \\ 1 & 0 & 0 \end{pmatrix}$.

**2.118** Find the composition $R \circ R^{-1}$ for the relation $R$ in Problem 2.112.

▌ Multiply the corresponding matrices $M_R$ and $N_R$ to obtain

$$M_R N_R = \begin{pmatrix} 0+1+1 & 0+0+0 & 0+0+0 \\ 0+0+0 & 1+0+0 & 0+0+0 \\ 0+0+0 & 0+0+0 & 0+0+0 \end{pmatrix} = \begin{pmatrix} 2 & 0 & 0 \\ 0 & 1 & 0 \\ 0 & 0 & 0 \end{pmatrix}$$

Thus $R \circ R^{-1} = \{(a, a), (b, b)\}$.

**2.119** Find the composition $R^{-1} \circ R$ for the relation $R$ in Problem 2.112.

▌ Multiply the corresponding matrices $N_R$ and $M_R$ to obtain

$$N_R M_R = \begin{pmatrix} 0+1+0 & 0+0+0 & 0+0+0 \\ 0+0+0 & 1+0+0 & 1+0+0 \\ 0+0+0 & 1+0+0 & 1+0+0 \end{pmatrix} = \begin{pmatrix} 1 & 0 & 0 \\ 0 & 1 & 1 \\ 0 & 1 & 1 \end{pmatrix}$$

Thus $R^{-1} \circ R = \{(a, a), (b, b), (b, c), (c, b), (c, c)\}$.

**2.120** Give advantages and disadvantages of representing a relation $R$ by a matrix $M_R$.

▌ One main advantage is that, using matrices, compositions and inverses are readily obtained. The main disadvantage is that the memory space required is of order $n^2$ whereas the relation may be of order $n$. For example, $A$ may be a set with 100 elements and $R$ may be a relation with 200 elements; hence approximately 300 memory locations would be required to store $A$ and $R$. However, $M_R$ would require $(100)^2 = 10\,000$ memory locations.

## 2.5 TYPES OF RELATIONS

**2.121** Let $R$ be a relation on a set $A$. Define the following four types of relations: **(a)** reflexive, **(b)** symmetric, **(c)** antisymmetric, **(d)** transitive. (Note that these properties are only defined for a relation on a set, i.e., they are not defined for a relation from one set to another set.)

▌ **(a)** $R$ is *reflexive* if $a\,R\,a$ for every $a$ in $A$.
 **(b)** $R$ is *symmetric* if $a\,R\,b$ implies $b\,R\,a$.
 **(c)** $R$ is *antisymmetric* if $a\,R\,b$ and $b\,R\,a$ implies $a = b$.
 **(d)** $R$ is *transitive* if $a\,R\,b$ and $b\,R\,c$ implies $a\,R\,c$.

**2.122** Determine when a relation $R$ on a set $A$ is **(a)** not reflexive, **(b)** not symmetric, **(c)** not transitive, **(d)** not antisymmetric.

▌ **(a)** There exists $a \in A$ such that $(a, a)$ does not belong to $R$.
 **(b)** There exists $(a, b)$ in $R$ such that $(b, a)$ does not belong to $R$.
 **(c)** There exist $(a, b)$ and $(b, c)$ in $R$ such that $(a, c)$ does not belong to $R$.
 **(d)** There exist distinct elements $a$ and $b$ such that $(a, b)$ and $(b, a)$ belong to $R$.

**2.123** Consider the following five relations on the set $A = \{1, 2, 3\}$:

$$R = \{(1, 1), (1, 2), (1, 3), (3, 3)\} \qquad \varnothing = \text{empty relation}$$
$$S = \{(1, 1), (1, 2), (2, 1), (2, 2), (3, 3)\} \qquad A \times A = \text{universal relation}$$
$$T = \{(1, 1), (1, 2), (2, 2), (2, 3)\}$$

Determine which of the relations are reflexive.

▌ $R$ is not reflexive since $2 \in A$ but $(2, 2) \notin R$. $T$ is not reflexive since $(3, 3) \notin T$ and, similarly, $\varnothing$ is not reflexive. $S$ and $A \times A$ are reflexive.

**2.124** Determine which of the five relations in Problem 2.123 are symmetric.

▌ $R$ is not symmetric since $(1, 2) \in R$ but $(2, 1) \notin R$, and similarly $T$ is not symmetric. $S$, $\varnothing$, and $A \times A$ are symmetric.

**2.125** Determine which of the five relations in Problem 2.123 are transitive.

▌ $T$ is not transitive since $(1, 2)$ and $(2, 3)$ belong to $T$, but $(1, 3)$ does not belong to $T$. The other four relations are transitive.

**2.126** Determine which of the five relations in Problem 2.123 are antisymmetric.

▌ $S$ is not antisymmetric since $1 \neq 2$, and $(1, 2)$ and $(2, 1)$ both belong to $S$. Similarly, $A \times A$ is not antisymmetric. The other three relations are antisymmetric.

**2.127** Let $R$ be the relation on $A = \{1, 2, 3, 4\}$ defined by

$$R = \{(1, 1), (2, 2), (2, 3), (3, 2), (4, 2), (4, 4)\}$$

Show that $R$ is neither **(a)** reflexive, nor **(b)** transitive.

▌ **(a)** $R$ is not reflexive because $3 \in A$ but $3\,\not\!R\,3$, i.e., $(3, 3) \notin R$.
 **(b)** $R$ is not transitive because $4\,R\,2$ and $2\,R\,3$ but $4\,\not\!R\,3$, i.e., $(4, 2) \in R$ and $(2, 3) \in R$ but $(4, 3) \notin R$.

**2.128** Show that the relation $R$ in Problem 2.127 is neither **(a)** symmetric, nor **(b)** antisymmetric.

▌ **(a)** $R$ is not symmetric because $4\,R\,2$ but $2\,\not\!R\,4$, i.e., $(4, 2) \in R$ but $(2, 4) \notin R$.
 **(b)** $R$ is not antisymmetric becaue $2\,R\,3$ and $3\,R\,2$ but $2 \neq 3$.

**2.129** Give examples of relations $R$ on $A = \{1, 2, 3\}$ having the stated property:
 **(a)** $R$ is both symmetric and antisymmetric.
 **(b)** $R$ is neither symmetric nor antisymmetric.
 **(c)** $R$ is transitive but $R \cup R^{-1}$ is not transitive.

▌ There are several possible examples for each answer. One possible set of examples follows:
(a)  $R = \{(1, 1), (2, 2)\}$
(b)  $R = \{(1, 2), (2, 1), (2, 3)\}$
(c)  $R = \{1, 2\}$

**2.130**  Let $R$, $S$, and $T$ be the relations on $A = \{1, 2, 3\}$ defined by

$$R = \{(1, 1), (2, 2), (3, 3)\} = \Delta_A, \quad S = \{(1, 2), (2, 1), (3, 3)\}, \quad T = \{(1, 2), (2, 3), (1, 3)\}$$

Determine which of the relations are reflexive.

▌ $S$ and $T$ are not reflexive since $1 \not{S} 1$ and $1 \not{T} 1$. The diagonal relation $R$ is reflexive.

**2.131**  Determine which of the relations in Problem 2.130 are symmetric.

▌ $T$ is not symmetric since $1 \, T \, 2$ but $2 \not{T} 1$. The relations $R$ and $S$ are symmetric.

**2.132**  Determine which of the relations in Problem 2.130 are antisymmetric.

▌ $S$ is not antisymmetric since $1 \, S \, 2$ and $2 \, S \, 1$ but $1 \neq 2$. The relations $R$ and $T$ are antisymmetric.

**2.133**  Determine which of the relations in Problem 2.130 are transitive.

▌ $S$ is not transitive since $1 \, S \, 2$ and $2 \, S \, 1$, but $1 \not{S} 1$. The relations $R$ and $T$ are transitive.

**2.134**  Consider the relation $\perp$ of perpendicularity on the set $L$ of lines in the Euclidean plane. Determine whether or not $\perp$ is reflexive, symmetric, antisymmetric, or transitive.

▌ Clearly, if line $a$ is perpendicular to line $b$, then $b$ is perpendicular to $a$, that is, if $a \perp b$, then $b \perp a$. Thus $\perp$ is symmetric. However, $\perp$ is neither reflexive, antisymmetric, nor transitive.

**2.135**  Consider the relation $|$ of division on the set $\mathbf{N}$ of positive integers. (Recall $x \mid y$ if there exists a $z$ such that $xz = y$, i.e., $2 \mid 6$, $5 \mid 15$ and $7 \mid 21$.) Determine whether or not $|$ is reflexive, symmetric, antisymmetric, or transitive.

▌ Clearly, $|$ is not symmetric since, e.g., $2 \mid 6$ but $6 \nmid 2$. However, $|$ is reflexive since $n \mid n$ for every $n \in \mathbf{N}$, $|$ is antisymmetric since if $n \mid m$ and $m \mid n$ then $n = m$, and $|$ is transitive since if $r \mid s$ and $s \mid t$ then $r \mid t$. (Note that $|$ is not antisymmetric on the set $\mathbf{Z}$ of integers since, e.g., $2 \mid -2$ and $-2 \mid 2$ but $2 \neq -2$.)

**2.136**  Each of the following defines a relation on the set $\mathbf{N}$ of positive integers:

$$R: \quad x \text{ is greater than } y, \qquad S: \quad x + y = 10, \qquad T: \quad x + 4y = 10$$

Determine which of the relations are reflexive.

▌ None are reflexive, e.g., $(1, 1)$ belongs to neither $R$, $S$, nor $T$.

**2.137**  Determine which of the relations in Problem 2.136 are symmetric.

▌ $R$ is not symmetric since, e.g., $6 > 3$ but $3 \not> 6$. Also, $T$ is not symmetric since $6 \, T \, 1$ but $1 \not{T} 6$. However, $S$ is symmetric.

**2.138**  Determine which of the relations in Problem 2.136 are transitive.

▌ $R$ is transitive since, if $x > y$ and $y > z$, then $x > z$. However, $S$ is not transitive since, e.g., $3 \, S \, 7$ and $7 \, S \, 3$ but $3 \not{S} 3$. On the other hand, $T = \{(6, 1), (2, 2)\}$ is transitive.

**2.139**  Determine which of the relations in Problem 2.136 are antisymmetric.

▌ $S$ is not antisymmetric since, e.g., $2 \, S \, 8$ and $8 \, S \, 2$ but $2 \neq 8$. However, $R$ and $T$ are antisymmetric.

**2.140**  Let $P(X)$ be the collection of all subsets of a set $X$ with at least three elements. Each of the following defines a relation on $P(X)$:

$$R: \quad A \subseteq B, \qquad S: \quad A \text{ is disjoint from } B, \qquad T: \quad A \cup B = X$$

Determine which of the above relations are reflexive.

**▮** $R$ is reflexive since $A \subseteq A$ for any set $A$. However, $S$ and $T$ are not reflexive.

**2.141** Determine which of the relations in Problem 2.140 are symmetric.

**▮** $R$ is not symmetric since $A \subseteq B$ does not imply $B \subseteq A$. On the other hand, $S$ and $T$ are symmetric.

**2.142** Determine which of the relations in Problem 2.140 are antisymmetric.

**▮** If $A \subseteq B$ and $B \subseteq A$, then $A = B$; hence $R$ is antisymmetric. Clearly, $S$ and $T$ are not antisymmetric.

**2.143** Determine which of the relations in Problem 2.140 are transitive.

**▮** If $A \subseteq B$ and $B \subseteq C$, then $A \subseteq C$; hence $R$ is transitive. However, $S$ and $T$ are not transitive.

**2.144** Let $R$ be a relation on a set $A$. Redefine the following properties using the diagonal $\Delta_A$, $R^{-1}$, and composition of relations: **(a)** reflexive, **(b)** symmetric, **(c)** antisymmetric, **(d)** transitive.

**▮** **(a)** $R$ is reflexive if $\Delta_A \subseteq R$.    **(c)** $R$ is antisymmetric if $R \cap R^{-1} \subseteq \Delta_A$.
    **(b)** $R$ is symmetric if $R = R^{-1}$.    **(d)** $R$ is transitive if $R \circ R \subseteq R$.

**2.145** Suppose $R$ and $S$ are reflexive relations on a set $A$. Show that $R \cap S$ is reflexive.

**▮** Let $a \in A$. Then $(a, a) \in R$ and $(a, a) \in S$ since $R$ and $S$ are reflexive. Hence $(a, a) \in R \cap S$. Thus $R \cap S$ is reflexive.

**2.146** Suppose $R$ and $S$ are symmetric operations on a set $A$. Show that $R \cap S$ is also symmetric.

**▮** Suppose $(a, b) \in R \cap S$. Then $(a, b)$ belongs to both $R$ and $S$. Since $R$ and $S$ are symmetric, $(b, a)$ belongs to both $R$ and $S$. Hence $(b, a) \in R \cap S$, and so $R \cap S$ is symmetric.

**2.147** Suppose $R$ and $S$ are transitive relations on a set $A$. Show that $R \cap S$ is transitive.

**▮** Suppose $(a, b)$ and $(b, c)$ are in $R \cap S$. Then $(a, b)$ and $(b, c)$ are in both $R$ and $S$. Since both relations are transitive, $(a, c) \in R$ and $(a, c) \in S$. Thus $(a, c) \in R \cap S$, and so $R \cap S$ is transitive.

**2.148** Suppose $R$ is a reflexive relation on a set $A$. Show that $R^{-1}$ and $R \cup S$ are reflexive for any relation $S$ on $A$.

**▮** Let $a \in A$. Then $(a, a) \in R$ since $R$ is reflexive. Thus $(a, a) \in R^{-1}$ and $(a, a) \in R \cup S$; hence $R^{-1}$ and $R \cup S$ are reflexive.

**2.149** Suppose $R$ is an antisymmetric relation on a set $A$. Show that: **(a)** $R^{-1}$ is antisymmetric, and **(b)** $R \cap S$ is antisymmetric for any relation $S$ on $A$.

**▮** **(a)** Suppose $(a, b)$ and $(b, a)$ belong to $R^{-1}$. Then $(b, a)$ and $(a, b)$ belong to $R$. Since $R$ is antisymmetric, $a = b$. Thus $R^{-1}$ is antisymmetric.
    **(b)** Suppose $(a, b)$ and $(b, a)$ are both in $R \cap S$. Then, in particular, $(a, b)$ and $(b, a)$ are both in $R$. Since $R$ is antisymmetric, $a = b$. Hence $R \cap S$ is antisymmetric.

**2.150** Show, by a counterexample, that $R$ and $S$ may be transitive relations on $A$, but $R \cup S$ need not be transitive.

**▮** Let $R = \{(1, 2)\}$ and $S = \{(2, 3)\}$. Then $R$ and $S$ are transitive, but $R \cup S = \{(1, 2), (2, 3)\}$ is not transitive.

**2.151** Suppose $R$ is any relation on $A$. Show that $R \cup R^{-1}$ is symmetric.

**▮** Suppose $(a, b) \in R \cup R^{-1}$. If $(a, b) \in R$, then $(b, a) \in R^{-1}$ and hence $(b, a) \in R \cup R^{-1}$. Similarly, if $(a, b) \in R^{-1}$, then $(b, a) \in R$ and hence $(b, a) \in R \cup R^{-1}$. Thus $R \cup R^{-1}$ is symmetric.

## Closure Properties

**2.152** Let $R$ be a relation on a set $A$. Define the transitive (symmetric, reflexive) closure of $R$.

**▮** A relation $R^*$ is the transitive (symmetric, reflexive) closure of $R$ if $R^*$ is the smallest relation containing $R$ which is transitive (symmetric, reflexive).

**2.153** Let $R$ be a relation on a set $A$. Give a procedure to find the symmetric and reflexive closures of $R$.

▐ $R \cup R^{-1}$ is the symmetric closure of $R$, and $R \cup \Delta_A$ is the reflexive closure of $R$.

**2.154** Let $R$ be the relation on $A = \{1, 2, 3\}$ defined by $R = \{(1, 1), (1, 2), (2, 3)\}$ Find: (a) the reflexive closure of $R$, and (b) the symmetric closure of $R$.

▐ (a) $R \cup \Delta_A = \{(1, 1), (1, 2), (2, 3), (2, 2), (3, 3)\}$ is the reflexive closure of $R$.
(b) $R \cup R^{-1} = \{(1, 1), (1, 2), (2, 3), (2, 1), (3, 2)\}$ is the symmetric closure of $R$.

**2.155** Let $R$ be a relation on a finite set $A$, and let $D$ be the directed graph of $R$. Suppose there is a path, say,

$$a \rightarrow b_1 \rightarrow b_2 \rightarrow \cdots \rightarrow b_m \rightarrow c$$

from $a$ to $c$ in the directed graph $D$. Show that $(a, c)$ belongs to the transitive closure $R^*$ of $R$. [In fact, $R^*$ consists of all pairs $(x, y)$ such that there is a path from $x$ to $y$ in $D$.]

▐ We have $(a, b_1)$ and $(b_1, b_2)$ belong to $R$ and hence to $R^*$. Thus $(a, b_2)$ belongs to $R^*$ since $R^*$ is transitive. Since $(a, b_2)$ belongs to $R^*$ and we have that $(b_2, b_3)$ belongs to $R$ and hence $R^*$ then $(a, b_3)$ belongs to $R^*$. Continuing, we finally obtain that $(a, c)$ belongs to $R^*$.

**2.156** Find the transitive closure $R^*$ of the relation $R$ on $A = \{1, 2, 3, 4\}$ defined by the directed graph in Fig. 2-27.

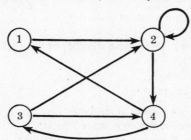

$$R = \{(1, 2), (2, 2), (2, 4), (3, 2), (3, 4), (4, 1), (4, 3)\} \quad \textbf{Fig. 2-27}$$

▐ There is a path from every point in $A$ to every other point in $A$ and also a path from each point to itself. Thus $R^* = A \times A$, the universal relation.

**2.157** Find the transitive closure $R^*$ of the relation $R$ on $A = \{1, 2, 3, 4\}$ defined by the directed graph in Fig. 2-28.

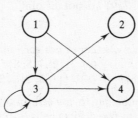

**Fig. 2-28**

▐ There is a path from 1 to points 2, 3, and 4. There is no path from 2 to any point. There is a path from 3 to the points 2, 3, and 4. There is no path from 4 to any point. Thus

$$R^* = \{(1, 2), (1, 3), (1, 4), (3, 2), (3, 3), (3, 4)\}$$

**2.158** Suppose $A$ has $n$ elements, say $A = \{1, 2, \ldots, n\}$. Find a relation $R$ on $A$ with $n$ pairs whose transitive closure $R^*$ is the universal relation $A \times A$ (containing $n^2$ pairs).

▐ Let $R = \{(1, 2), (2, 3), (3, 4), \ldots, (n-1, n), (n, 1)\}$. Then $R$ has $n$ elements and there is a path from each element of $A$ to any other element and itself. Thus $R^* = A \times A$.

## 2.6 PARTITIONS

**2.159** Define a partition of a nonempty set $S$.

▐ A *partition* of $S$ is a collection $P = \{A_i\}$ of nonempty subsets of $S$ such that:
(i) Each $a$ in $S$ belongs to one of the $A_i$.

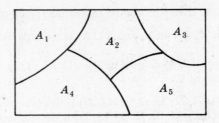

**Fig. 2-29**

(ii)   The sets of $P$ are mutually disjoint; that is, if $A_i \neq A_j$ then $A_i \cap A_j = \varnothing$.

The subsets in a partition are called *cells*. Figure 2-29 is a Venn diagram of a partition of the rectangular set of points into five cells.

**2.160**   Let $S = \{1, 2, 3, 4, 5, 6\}$. Determine whether or not each of the following is a partition of $S$:
   (a)   $P_1 = [\{1, 2, 3\}, \{1, 4, 5, 6\}]$       (c)   $P_3 = [\{1, 3, 5\}, \{2, 4\}, \{6\}]$
   (b)   $P_2 = [\{1, 2\}, \{3, 5, 6\}]$       (d)   $P_4 = [\{1, 3, 5\}, \{2, 4, 6, 7\}]$

   ▐   (a)   No, since $1 \in S$ belongs to two cells.
       (b)   No, since $4 \in S$ does not belong to any cell.
       (c)   $P_3$ is a partition of $S$.
       (d)   No, since $\{2, 4, 6, 7\}$ is not a subset of $S$.

**2.161**   Let $S = \{$red, blue, green, yellow$\}$. Determine whether or not each of the following is a partition of $S$:
   (a)   $P_1 = [\{$red$\}, \{$blue, green$\}]$.
   (b)   $P_2 = [\{$red, blue, green, yellow$\}]$.
   (c)   $P_3 = [\varnothing, \{$red, blue$\}, \{$green, yellow$\}]$.

   ▐   (a)   No, since yellow does not belong to any cell.
       (b)   $P_2$ is a partition of $S$ whose only element is $S$ itself.
       (c)   No, since the empty set $\varnothing$ cannot belong to a partition.

**2.162**   Let $S = \{1, 2, \ldots, 8, 9\}$. Determine whether or not each of the following is a partition of $S$:
   (a)   $[\{1, 3, 5\}, \{2, 6\}, \{4, 8, 9\}]$       (c)   $[\{1, 3, 5\}, \{2, 4, 6, 8\}, \{7, 9\}]$
   (b)   $[\{1, 3, 5\}, \{2, 4, 6, 8\}, \{5, 7, 9\}]$       (d)   $[\{S\}]$

   ▐   (a)   No, since $7 \in S$ does not belong to any cell.
       (b)   No, since $\{1, 3, 5\}$ and $\{5, 7, 9\}$ are not disjoint.
       (c)   and (d) are partitions of $S$.

**2.163**   Let $X = \{1, 2, \ldots, 8, 9\}$. Determine whether or not each of the following is a partition of $X$:
   (a)   $[\{1, 3, 6\}, \{2, 8\}, \{5, 7, 9\}]$       (c)   $[\{2, 4, 5, 8\}, \{1, 9\}, \{3, 6, 7\}]$
   (b)   $[\{1, 5, 7\}, \{2, 4, 8, 9\}, \{3, 5, 6\}]$       (d)   $[\{1, 2, 7\}, \{3, 5\}, \{4, 6, 8, 9\}, \{3, 5\}]$

   ▐   (a)   No; because $4 \in X$ does not belong to any cell. In other words, $X$ is not the union of the cells.
       (b)   No; because $5 \in X$ belongs to two distinct cells, $\{1, 5, 7\}$ and $\{3, 5, 6\}$. In other words, the two distinct cells are not disjoint.
       (c)   Yes; because each element of $X$ belongs to exactly one cell. In other words, the cells are disjoint and their union is $X$.
       (d)   Yes. Although 3 and 5 appear in two places, the cells are not distinct.

**2.164**   Find all the partitions of $S = \{1, 2, 3\}$.

   ▐   Note that each partition of $S$ contains either 1, 2, or 3 distinct cells. The partitions are as follows:
   (1)   $[S]$.
   (2)   $[\{1\}, \{2, 3\}], [\{2\}, \{1, 3\}], [\{3\}, \{1, 2\}]$.
   (3)   $[\{1\}, \{2\}, \{3\}]$.
   There are five different partitions of $S$.

**2.165**   Find all the partitions of $X = \{a, b, c, d\}$.

   ▐   Note first that each partition of $X$ contains either 1, 2, 3, or 4 distinct sets. The partitions are as follows:
   (1)   $[\{a, b, c, d\}]$.

(2)  [{a}, {b, c, d}], [{b}, {a, c, d}], [{c}, {a, b, d}], [{d}, {a, b, c}],
    [{a, b}, {c, d}], [{a, c}, {b, d}], [{a, d}, {b, c}].
(3)  [{a}, {b}, {c, d}], [{a}, {c}, {b, d}], [{a}, {d}, {b, c}],
    [{b}, {c}, {a, d}], [{b}, {d}, {a, c}], [{c}, {d}, {a, b}].
(4)  [{a}, {b}, {c}, {d}].
There are fifteen different partitions of $X$.

**2.166**  Determine whether or not each of the following is a partition of the set $\mathbf{N}$ of positive integers:
(a)  $[\{n: b > 5\}, \{n: n < 5\}]$,  (b)  $[\{n: n > 5\}, \{0\}, \{1, 2, 3, 4, 5\}]$,  (c)  $[\{n: n^2 > 11\}, \{n: n^2 < 11\}$

■ (a)  No, since $5 \in \mathbf{N}$ does not belong to any cell.
(b)  No, since $\{0\}$ is not a subset of $\mathbf{N}$.
(c)  Yes, the two cells are disjoint and their union is $\mathbf{N}$.

**2.167**  Determine whether or not each of the following is a partition of the set $\mathbf{R}$ of real numbers:
(a)  $[\{x: x > 4\}, \{x: x < 5\}]$,  (b)  $[\{x: x > 0\}, \{0\}, \{x: x < 0\}]$,  (c)  $[\{x: x^2 > 11\}, \{x: x^2 < 11\}]$

■ (a)  No, since the two cells are not disjoint, e.g., 4.5 belongs to both cells.
(b)  Yes, since the three cells are mutually disjoint and their union is $\mathbf{R}$.
(c)  No, since $\sqrt{11}$ in $\mathbf{R}$ does not belong to either cell.

**2.168**  Let $[A_1, A_2, \ldots, A_m]$ and $[B_1, B_2, \ldots, B_n]$ be partitions of a set $X$. Show that the collection of sets

$$P = [A_i \cap B_j: i = 1, \ldots, m, j = 1, \ldots, n]\setminus\emptyset$$

is also a partition (called the *cross partition*) of $X$. (Observe that we have deleted the empty set $\emptyset$.)

■ Let $x \in X$. Then $x$ belongs to $A_r$ for some $r$, and to $B_s$ for some $s$; hence $x$ belongs to $A_r \cap B_s$. Thus the union of the $A_i \cap B_j$ is equal to $X$. Now suppose $A_r \cap B_s$ and $A_{r'} \cap B_{s'}$ are not disjoint, say $y$ belongs to both sets. Then $y$ belongs to $A_r$ and $A_{r'}$; hence $A_r = A_{r'}$. Similarly $y$ belongs to $B_s$ and $B_{s'}$; hence $B_s = B_{s'}$. Accordingly, $A_r \cap B_s = A_{r'} \cap B_{s'}$. Thus the cells are mutually disjoint or equal. Accordingly, $P$ is a partition of $X$.

**2.169**  Let $S = \{1, 2, 3, 4, 5, 6\}$. Find the cross partition $P$ of the following partitions of $S$:

$$P_1 = [\{1, 2, 3\}, \{4, 5, 6\}] \quad \text{and} \quad P_2 = [\{1, 3, 4, 6\}, \{2, 5\}]$$

■ The intersection of each cell in $P_1$ with each cell in $P_2$ yields

$$P = [\{1, 3\}, \{2\}, \{4, 6\}, \{5\}]$$

**2.170**  Let $X = \{1, 2, 3, \ldots, 8, 9\}$. Find the cross partition $P$ of the following partitions of $X$:

$$P_1 = [\{1, 3, 5, 7, 9\}, \{2, 4, 6, 8\}] \quad \text{and} \quad P_2 = [\{1, 2, 3, 4\}, \{5, 7\}, \{6, 8, 9\}]$$

■ Intersect each cell in $P_1$ with each cell in $P_2$ (omitting empty intersections) to obtain

$$P = [\{1, 3\}, \{5, 7\}, \{9\}, \{2, 4\}, \{8\}]$$

**2.171**  Let $P$ be the cross partition of partitions $P_1$ and $P_2$ of a set $X$. Under what condition will $P = P_1$?

■ If each cell in $P_1$ is a subset of a cell in $P_2$, then $P = P_1$.

**2.172**  Let $P$ be the cross partition of partitions $P_1$ and $P_2$ of a set $X$. Suppose $P_1$ has $r$ cells and $P_2$ has $s$ cells. Find bounds on the number $n$ of cells in $P$.

■ $P$ cannot have more than $rs$ cells, and cannot have less cells than in $P_1$ or $P_2$. In other words, $\max(r, s) \le n \le rs$.

**2.173**  Let $f(n, k)$ represent the number of partitions of a set $S$ of $n$ elements into $k$ cells ($k = 1, 2, \ldots, n$). Find a recursion formula for $f(n, k)$.

■ Note first that $f(n, 1) = 1$ and $f(n, n) = 1$ since there is only one way to partition $S$ with $n$ elements into either one cell or $n$ cells. Now suppose $n > 1$ and $1 < k < n$. Let $b$ be some distinguished element of $S$. If $\{b\}$ constitutes a cell, then $S\setminus\{b\}$ can be partitioned into $k - 1$ cells in $f(n - 1, k - 1)$ ways. On the other hand, each partition of $S\backslash\{b\}$ into $k$ cells allows $b$ to be admitted into a cell in $k$ ways. We have thus shown that

$$f(n, k) = f(n-1, k-1) + kf(n-1, k)$$

which is the desired recursion formula.

**2.174**  Consider the recursion formula in Problem 2.173. (*a*) Find the solution for $n = 1, 2, 3, 4, 5, 6$ in a form similar to Pascal's triangle. (*b*) Find the number $m$ of partitions of a set with $n = 6$ elements.

▮ (*a*)  Use the recursion formula (e.g. $f(6, 4) = f(5, 3) + 4f(5, 4) = 25 + (4)(10) = 65$) to obtain the triangle

```
1
1    1
1    3    1
1    7    6    1
1    15   25   10   1
1    31   90   65   15   1
```

(*b*)  $m = 1 + 31 + 90 + 65 + 15 + 1 = 203$.

## 2.7  EQUIVALENCE RELATIONS

**2.175**  What is an *equivalence relation*?

▮ A relation $R$ on a set $A$ is called an equivalence relation if it is reflexive, symmetric, and transitive. (Ordinary equality is obviously the model for equivalence relations.)

**2.176**  Let $L$ be the set of lines in the Euclidean plane. Let $R$ be the relation on $L$ defined by "is parallel to (‖) or coincident with (≡)". Show that $R$ is an equivalence relation.

▮ Since $a = a$, for any line $a$ in $L$, $R$ is reflexive. If $a \parallel b$, then $b \parallel a$; so $R$ is symmetric. If $a \parallel b$ and $b \parallel c$, then $a \parallel c$ or $a = c$; hence $R$ is transitive. Thus $R$ is an equivalence relation.

**2.177**  On the set $L$ of lines in the Euclidean plane, let $S$ be the relation "has a point in common with". Is $S$ an equivalence relation?

▮ No. For example, if $a$ and $c$ are distinct horizontal lines and $b$ is a vertical line, then $a \, S \, b$ and $b \, S \, c$, but $a \, \cancel{S} \, c$.

**2.178**  Consider the relation $\perp$ of perpendicularity on the set $L$ of lines in the Euclidean plane. Is $\perp$ an equivalence relation?

▮ No. Although $\perp$ is symmetric, it is neither reflexive nor transitive.

**2.179**  Let $T$ be the set of triangles in the Euclidean plane. Show that the relation $R$ of similarity is an equivalence relation on $T$.

▮ Every triangle is similar to itself, so $R$ is reflexive. If triangle $a$ is similar to triangle $b$, then $b$ is similar to $a$: hence $R$ is symmetric. If $a$ is similar to $b$, and $b$ is similar to $c$, then $a$ is similar to $c$. Hence $R$ is an equivalence relation.

**2.180**  Let $R$ be the relation on the set $\mathbf{N}$ of positive integers defined by $R = \{(a, b): a + b \text{ is even}\}$. Is $R$ an equivalence relation?

▮ Yes. Clearly, for any $a \in \mathbf{N}$, $a + a$ is even; and if $a + b$ is even, then $b + a$ is even. Thus $R$ is reflexive and symmetric. To show that $R$ is transitive, we note that $aRb$ if and only if both $a$ and $b$ have the same "parity", i.e., $a$ and $b$ are both even or both odd. Accordingly, if $aRb$ and $bRc$, then $a$ and $b$ have the same parity and $b$ and $c$ have the same parity; and hence $a$ and $c$ have the same parity, that is, $aRc$. Thus $R$ is also transitive. Hence $R$ is an equivalence relation.

**2.181**  Let $S$ be the relation "is a blood relative of" on the set $X$ of people. Is $S$ an equivalence relation?

▮ No. Although $S$ is clearly, reflexive, and symmetric, it is not transitive. For example, $b$ may have a cousin $a$ through his mother's family and have a cousin $c$ through his father's family; hence $a \, R \, b$ and $b \, R \, c$. However, $a$ and $c$ need not be blood relatives.

**2.182** Let $R = \{(1, 1), (1, 3), (3, 1), (3, 3)\}$. Is $R$ an equivalence relation on $A = \{1, 2, 3\}$? on $B = \{1, 3\}$?

▮ Clearly $R$ is symmetric and transitive. However, $R$ is not an equivalence relation on $A$ since $2 \not\!R 2$ and so $R$ is not reflexive on $A$. On the other hand, $R$ is reflexive on $B$ and hence $R$ is an equivalence relation on $B$.

**2.183** Show that the relation $\subseteq$ of set inclusion is not an equivalence relation on, say, the subsets of **N**.

▮ The relation $\subseteq$ is reflexive and transitive, but $\subseteq$ is not symmetric, that is, $A \subseteq B$ does not imply that $B \subseteq A$.

**2.184** Consider the set **Z** of integers and an integer $m > 1$. We say that $x$ is congruent to $y$ modulo $m$, written

$$x \equiv y \pmod{m}$$

if $x - y$ is divisible by $m$ or, equivalently, if $x = y + km$ for some integer $k$. Show that this defines an equivalence relation on **Z**.

▮ For any $x$ in **Z**, we have $x \equiv x \pmod{m}$ because $x - x = 0$ is divisible by $m$. Hence the relation is reflexive.
   Suppose $x \equiv y \pmod{m}$, so $x - y$ is divisible by $m$. Then $-(x - y) = y - x$ is also divisible by $m$, so $y \equiv x \pmod{m}$. Thus the relation is symmetric.
   Now suppose $x \equiv y \pmod{m}$ and $y \equiv z \pmod{m}$, so $x - y$ and $y - z$ are each divisible by $m$. Then the sum

$$(x - y) + (y - z) = x - z$$

is also divisible by $m$; hence $x \equiv z \pmod{m}$. Thus the relation is transitive.
   We have shown that the relation of congruence modulo $m$ on **Z** is reflexive, symmetric, and transitive; hence it is an equivalence relation.

**2.185** Let $A$ be a set of nonzero integers and let $\simeq$ be the relation on $A \times A$ defined by

$$(a, b) \simeq (c, d) \qquad \text{whenever} \qquad ad = bc$$

Prove that $\simeq$ is an equivalence relation.

▮ We must show that $\simeq$ is reflexive, symmetric, and transitive.
   (i) Reflexivity. We have $(a, b) \simeq (a, b)$ since $ab = ba$. Hence $\simeq$ is reflexive.
   (ii) Symmetry. Suppose $(a, b) \simeq (c, d)$. Then $ad = bc$. Accordingly, $cb = da$ and hence $(c, d) \simeq (a, b)$. Thus $\simeq$ is symmetric.
   (iii) Transitivity. Suppose $(a, b) \simeq (c, d)$ and $(c, d) \simeq (e, f)$. Then $ad = bc$ and $cf = de$. Multiplying corresponding terms of the equations gives $(ad)(cf) = (bc)(de)$. Canceling $c \neq 0$ and $d \neq 0$ from both sides of the equation yields $af = be$, and hence $(a, b) \simeq (e, f)$. Thus $\simeq$ is transitive.
   Accordingly, $\simeq$ is an equivalence relation.

**2.186** Let $A$ be a set of integers and let $\sim$ be the relation on $A \times A$ defined by

$$(a, b) \sim (c, d) \qquad \text{if} \qquad a + d = b + c$$

Prove that $\sim$ is an equivalence relation.

▮ We must show that $\sim$ is reflexive, symmetric, and transitive.
   (i) Reflexivity. We have $(a, b) \sim (a, b)$ since $a + b = b + a$. Hence $\sim$ is reflexive.
   (ii) Symmetry. Suppose $(a, b) \sim (c, d)$. Then $a + d = b + c$. Accordingly, $c + b = d + a$ and hence $(c, d) \sim (a, b)$. Thus $\sim$ is symmetric.
   (iii) Transitivity. Suppose $(a, b) \sim (c, d)$ and $(c, d) \sim (e, f)$. Then $a + d = b + c$ and $c + f = d + e$. Adding the equations gives

$$(a + d) + (c + f) = (b + c) + (d + e)$$

Subtracting $c$ and $d$ from both sides of the equation yields $a + f = b + e$, and hence $(a, b) \sim (e, f)$. Thus $\sim$ is transitive.
   Accordingly, $\sim$ is an equivalence relation.

## Equivalence Relations and Partitions

This subsection examines the fundamental relationship between equivalence relations and partitions.

**2.187** Let $R$ be an equivalence relation on a nonempty set $A$. **(a)** Define the *equivalence class* of an element $a \in A$, denoted by $[a]$. **(b)** Define the *quotient of A by R*, denoted by $A/R$.

▎**(a)** The equivalence class $[a]$ is the set of elements of $A$ to which $a$ is related; that is, $[a] = \{x: (a, x) \in R\}$.
    **(b)** $A/R$ is the collection of equivalence classes; that is, $A/R = \{[a]: a \in A\}$.

**Theorem 2.2:** Let $R$ be an equivalence relation on a nonempty set $A$. Then the quotient set $A/R$ is a partition of $A$.
    Specifically,
      (i)   $a \in [a]$, for every $a \in A$;
      (ii)  $[a] = [b]$ if and only if $(a, b) \in R$;
      (iii) if $[a] \neq [b]$, then $[a]$ and $[b]$ are disjoint.

**2.188** Prove Theorem 2.2.

▎  *Proof of* (i).  Since $R$ is reflexive, $(a, a) \in R$ for every $a \in A$ and therefore $a \in [a]$.
    *Proof of* (ii).  Suppose $(a, b) \in R$. We want to show that $[a] = [b]$. Let $x \in [b]$; then $(b, x) \in R$. But, by hypothesis, $(a, b) \in R$ and so, by transitivity, $(a, x) \in R$. Accordingly, $x \in [a]$. Thus $[b] \subseteq [a]$. To prove that $[a] \subseteq [b]$, we observe that $(a, b) \in R$ implies, by symmetry, that $(b, a) \in R$. Then, by a similar argument, we obtain $[a] \subseteq [b]$. Consequently, $[a] = [b]$. On the other hand, if $[a] = [b]$, then, by (i), $b \in [b] = [a]$; hence $(a, b) \in R$.
    *Proof of* (iii).  We prove the equivalent contrapositive statement:

$$\text{if} \quad [a] \cap [b] \neq \emptyset \quad \text{then} \quad [a] = [b]$$

If $[a] \cap [b] \neq \emptyset$, then there exists an element $x \in A$ with $x \in [a] \cap [b]$. Hence $(a, x) \in R$ and $(b, x) \in R$. By symmetry, $(x, b) \in R$ and, by transitivity, $(a, b) \in R$. Consequently, by (ii), $[a] = [b]$.

**2.189** Let $A = \{1, 2, 3, 4, 5, 6\}$ and let $R$ be the equivalence relation on $A$ defined by

$$R = \{(1, 1), (1, 5), (2, 2), (2, 3), (2, 6), (3, 2), (3, 3), (3, 6), (4, 4), (5, 1), (5, 5), (6, 2), (6, 3), (6, 6)\}$$

Find the partition of $A$ induced by $R$, i.e., find the equivalence classes of $R$.

▎Those elements related to 1 are 1 and 5 hence

$$[1] = \{1, 5\}$$

We pick an element which does not belong to $[1]$, say 2. Those elements related to 2 are 2, 3, and 6; hence

$$[2] = \{2, 3, 6\}$$

The only element which does not belong to $[1]$ or $[2]$ is 4. The only element related to 4 is 4. Thus

$$[4] = \{4\}$$

Accordingly, $[\{1, 5\}, \{2, 3, 6\}, \{4\}]$ is the partition of $A$ induced by $R$.

**2.190** The relation $R = \{(1, 1), (1, 2), (2, 1), (3, 3)\}$ is an equivalence relation of the set $S = \{1, 2, 3\}$. Find the quotient set $S/R$.

▎Under the relation $R$, $[1] = \{1, 2\}$, $[2] = \{1, 2\}$, and $[3] = \{3\}$. Noting that $[1] = [2]$, we have $S/R = \{[1], [3]\}$.

**2.191** Let $A = \{1, 2, 3, \ldots, 13, 14, 15\}$. Let $R$ be the relation on $A$ defined by congruence modulo 4. Find the equivalence classes determined by $R$.

▎Recall (Problem 2.184) that $a \equiv b$ (mod 4) if 4 divides $a - b$ or, equivalently, if $a = b + 4k$ for some integer $k$. Thus:
(1)  Add multiples of 4 to 1 to obtain the equivalence class $[1] = \{1, 5, 9, 13\}$.
(2)  Add multiples of 4 to 2 to obtain $[2] = \{2, 6, 10, 14\}$.
(3)  Add multiples of 4 to 3 to obtain $[3] = \{3, 7, 11, 14\}$.
(4)  Add multiples of 4 to 4 to obtain $[4] = \{4, 8, 12\}$.
Then $[1], [2], [3], [4]$ are all the equivalence classes since they include all the elements of $A$.

**2.192** Consider the set of words $W = \{\text{sheet, last, sky, wash, wind, sit}\}$. Find $W/R$ where $R$ is the equivalence relation on $W$ defined by **(a)** "has the same number of letters as", and **(b)** "begins with the same letter as".

▎**(a)**  Those words with the same number of letters belong to the same cell; hence
      $W/R = [\{\text{sheet}\}, \{\text{last, wash, wind}\}, \{\text{sky, sit}\}]$.
  **(b)**  Those words beginning with the same letter belong to the same cell; hence
      $W/R = [\{\text{sheet, sky, sit}\}, \{\text{last}\}, \{\text{wash, wind}\}]$.

**2.193**  Let $A = \{1, 2, 3, \ldots, 14, 15\}$. Consider the equivalence relation $\simeq$ on $A \times A$ defined by $(a, b) \simeq (c, d)$ if $ad = bc$. (See Problem 2.185.) Find the equivalence class of $(3, 2)$.

*❚* We seek all $(m, n)$ such that $(3, 2) \simeq (m, n)$, that is, such that $3n = 2m$ or $3/2 = m/n$. (In other words, if $(3, 2)$ is written as a fraction $3/2$, then we seek all fractions $m/n$ which are equal to $3/2$.) Thus

$$[(3, 2)] = \{(3, 2), (6, 4), (9, 6), (12, 8), (15, 10)\}$$

**2.194**  Let $A = \{1, 2, 3, \ldots, 14, 15\}$. Consider the equivalence relation $\sim$ on $A \times A$ defined by $(a, b) \sim (c, d)$ if $a + d = b + c$. (See Problem 2.186.) Find the equivalence class of $(2, 7)$.

*❚* We seek all $(m, n)$ such that $(2, 11) \sim (m, n)$, that is, such that $2 + n = 11 + m$ or $n = 9 + m$. Set $m = 1, 2, \ldots$ to obtain

$$[(2, 11)] = \{(1, 10), (2, 11), (3, 12), (4, 13), (5, 14), (6, 15)\}$$

**2.195**  Let $R_5$ be the equivalence relation on the set $\mathbf{Z}$ of integers defined by $x \equiv y \pmod 5$. (See Problem 2.184.) Find $\mathbf{Z}/R_5$, the induced equivalence classes.

*❚* There are exactly five distinct equivalence classes in $\mathbf{Z}/R_5$:

$$A_0 = \{\ldots, -10, -5, 0, 5, 10, \ldots\} \qquad A_3 = \{\ldots, -7, -2, 3, 8, 13, \ldots\}$$
$$A_1 = \{\ldots, -9, -4, 1, 6, 11, \ldots\} \qquad A_4 = \{\ldots, -6, -1, 4, 9, 14, \ldots\}$$
$$A_2 = \{\ldots, -8, -3, 2, 7, 12, \ldots\}$$

Specifically, $A_r = [r]$ is obtained by adding multiples of 5 to $r$. Note that any integer $x$ is uniquely expressible in the form $x = 5q + r$, where $0 \le r \le 4$, so that $x \in A_r$.

**Theorem 2.3:**  Let $P = \{A_k\}$ be a partition of a set $S$. Then there is an equivalence relation $\sim$ on $S$ such that $S/\sim$ is the same as the partition $P = \{A_k\}$.

**2.196**  Prove Theorem 2.3.

*❚* Define $a \sim b$ if $a$ and $b$ belong to the same cell $A_k$. Clearly, $\sim$ is reflexive and symmetric. The fact that the $A_k$ are mutually exclusive guarantees that $\sim$ is also transitive. Thus $\sim$ is an equivalence relation. Also,

$$[a] = \{x : a \sim x\} = \{x : x \text{ is in the same cell } A_k \text{ as } a\}$$

Thus the equivalence classes under $\sim$ are the same as the cells in the partition $P$.

## 2.8  TERNARY AND $n$-ARY RELATIONS

**2.197**  Define a ternary relation and give an example.

*❚* A *ternary* relation is a set of ordered triples. In particular, if $S$ is a set, then a subset of $S^3$ is called a ternary relation on $S$. For example, if $L$ is a line, then "betweenness" is a ternary relation among points of $L$.

**2.198**  Let $A = \{1, 2, 3, \ldots, 14, 15\}$. Let $R$ be the ternary relation on $A$ defined by the equation $x^2 + 5y = z$. Write $R$ as a set of ordered triples.

*❚* Since $x^2 > 15$ for $x > 3$, we need only find solutions for $y$ and $z$ when $x = 1, 2, 3$. Thus

$$R = \{(1, 1, 6), (1, 2, 11), (2, 1, 9), (2, 2, 14), (3, 1, 14)\}$$

**2.199**  Show how a binary operation, say addition $(+)$, may be viewed as a ternary relation.

*❚* The operation $+$ may be defined as a set of ordered triples as follows:

$$+ = \{(x, y, z) : x + y = z\}$$

Thus, for example, $(2, 5, 7)$ belongs to $+$ but $(3, 4, 5)$ does not belong to $+$.

**2.200**  Define an $n$-ary relation with an example.

*❚* An $n$-ary relation is a set of $n$-tuples. In particular, if $S$ is a set, then a subset of $S^n$ is called an $n$-ary relation

on $S$. For example, the set $W$ of solutions of an equation, say,

$$x_1 + 2x_2 + 3x_3 + \cdots + nx_n = 0$$

may be viewed as an $n$-ary relation on $R$.

**2.201**  Let $A = \{1, 2, 3, \ldots, 14, 15\}$. Let $R$ be the 4-ary relation on $A$ defined by $R = \{(x, y, z, t): 4x + 3y + z^2 = t\}$. Write $R$ as a set of 4-tuples.

❚  Note we can only have $x = 1, 2, 3$. Thus

$R = \{(1, 1, 1, 8), (1, 1, 2, 11), (1, 2, 1, 11), (1, 2, 2, 14), (1, 3, 1, 14), (2, 1, 1, 12), (2, 1, 2, 15), (2, 2, 1, 15)\}$

# CHAPTER 3
# Functions

## 3.1 FUNCTIONS, MAPPINGS

**3.1** Define a function from a set $A$ into a set $B$.

▐ Suppose that to each element of $A$ there is assigned a unique element of $B$; the collection of such assignments is called a *function* (or *mapping* or *map*) from $A$ into $B$. We denote a function $f$ from $A$ into $B$ by

$$f: A \to B$$

We write $f(a)$, read "$f$ of $a$", for the element of $B$ that $f$ assigns to $a \in A$; it is called the *value* of $f$ at $a$ or the *image* of $a$ under $f$.

**Remark:** The terms function and mapping are frequently used synonymously, although some texts reserve the word function for a real-valued or complex-valued mapping, that is, which maps a set into **R** or **C**.

**3.2** What is the **(a)** domain, **(b)** codomain, **(c)** image of a function $f: A \to B$?
**(a)** The set $A$ is the *domain* of $f$.
**(b)** The set $B$ is the *codomain* of $f$.
**(c)** The set of all image values of $f$ is called the *image* (or *range*) of $f$ and is denoted by $\operatorname{Im} f$ or $f(A)$. That is,

$$\operatorname{Im} f = \{b \in B: \text{there exists } a \in A \text{ such that } f(a) = b\}$$

[Observe that $\operatorname{Im} f$ is a subset (perhaps a proper subset) of $B$.]

**3.3** Consider a function $f: A \to B$. **(a)** Let $S$ be a subset of $A$. Define the image of $S$ under $f$, denoted by $f(S)$. **(b)** Let $T$ be a subset of $B$. Define the inverse image or *preimage* of $T$ under $f$, denoted by $f^{-1}(T)$.

▐ **(a)** Here $f(S) = \{f(a): a \in S\} = \{b \in B: \exists a \in S \text{ such that } f(a) = b\}$. In other words, $f(S)$ consists of all images of the elements in $S$. (Here $\exists$ is short for "there exists".)
**(b)** Here $f^{-1}(T) = \{a \in A: f(a) \in T\}$. In other words, $f^{-1}(T)$ consists of the elements of $A$ whose images belong to $T$.

**3.4** Define the equality of functions.

▐ Two functions $f: A \to B$ and $g: A \to B$ are defined to be equal, written $f = g$, if $f(a) = g(a)$ for every $a \in A$. The negation of $f = g$ is written $f \neq g$ and is the statement: There exists an $a \in A$ for which $f(a) \neq g(a)$.

**3.5** Define the graph of a function $f: A \to B$.

▐ To each function $f: A \to B$ there corresponds the subset of $A \times B$ given by $\{(a, f(a)): a \in A\}$. We call this set the *graph* of $f$. We note that two functions $f: A \to B$ and $g: A \to B$ are equal if and only if they have the same graph. Thus we do not distinguish between a function and its graph.

**3.6** Consider the function $f$ from $A = \{a, b, c, d\}$ into $B = \{x, y, z, w\}$ defined by Fig. 3-1. Find: **(a)** the image of each element of $A$; **(b)** the image of $f$; and **(c)** the graph of $f$, i.e., write $f$ as a set of ordered pairs.

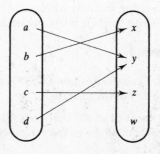

**Fig. 3-1**

▌ **(a)** The arrow indicates the image of an element. Thus

$$f(a) = y, \qquad f(b) = x, \qquad f(c) = z, \qquad f(d) = y$$

**(b)** The image $f(A)$ of $f$ consists of all image values. Only $x$, $y$, $z$ appear as image values; hence $f(A) = \{x, y, z\}$.

**(c)** The ordered pairs $(a, f(a))$, where $a \in A$ form the graph of $f$. Thus $f = \{(a, y), (b, x), (c, z), (d, y)\}$.

**3.7** Consider the function $f$ defined by Fig. 3-1. Find: **(a)** $f(S)$ where $S = \{a, b, d\}$; **(b)** $f^{-1}(T)$ where $T = \{y, z\}$; and **(c)** $f^{-1}(w)$.

▌ **(a)** $f(S) = f(\{a, b, d\}) = \{f(a), f(b), f(d)\} = \{y, x, y\} = \{x, y\}$.

**(b)** The elements $a$, $c$, and $d$ have images in $T$, hence $f^{-1}(T) = \{a, c, d\}$.

**(c)** No element has the image $w$ under $f$; hence $f^{-1}(w) = \varnothing$, the empty set.

**3.8** State whether or not each diagram in Fig. 3-2 defines a function from $A = \{a, b, c\}$ into $B = \{x, y, z\}$

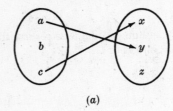  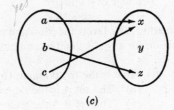

(a)  (b)  (c)

**Fig. 3-2**

▌ **(a)** No. There is no element of $B$ assigned to the element $b \in A$.

**(b)** No. Two elements, $x$ and $z$, are assigned to $c \in A$.

**(c)** Yes, since each element of $A$ is assigned a unique element of $B$.

**3.9** State whether or not each diagram of Fig. 3-3 defines a function from $C = \{1, 2, 3\}$ into $D = \{4, 5, 6\}$.

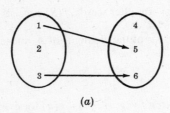  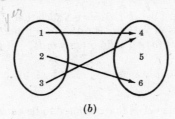  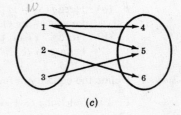

(a)  (b)  (c)

**Fig. 3-3**

▌ **(a)** No. There is no element of $D$ assigned to the element $2 \in C$.

**(b)** Yes, since each element of $C$ is assigned a unique element of $D$.

**(c)** No. Two elements, 4 and 5, are assigned to $1 \in C$.

**3.10** Let $A$ be the set of students in a school. Determine which of the following assignments defines a function on $A$. **(a)** To each student assign his or her age. **(b)** To each student assign his or her teacher. **(c)** To each student assign his or her sex. **(d)** To each student assign his or her spouse.

▌ A collection of assignments is a function on $A$ providing each element $a \in A$ is assigned exactly one element. Thus:

**(a)** Yes, because each student has one and only one age.

**(b)** Yes, if each student has only one teacher; no, if any student has more than one teacher.

**(c)** Yes.

**(d)** No, if any student is not married.

**3.11** Consider the set $A = \{1, 2, 3, 4, 5\}$ and the function $f: A \rightarrow A$ defined by Fig. 3-4. Find: **(a)** the image of each element of $A$, and **(b)** the image $f(A)$ of the function $f$.

▌ **(a)** The arrow indicates the image of an element; thus $f(1) = 3$, $f(2) = 5$, $f(3) = 5$, $f(4) = 2$, $f(5) = 3$.

**(b)** The image $f(A)$ of $f$ consists of all the image values. Now only 2, 3, and 5 appear as the image of any elements of $A$; hence $f(A) = \{2, 3, 5\}$.

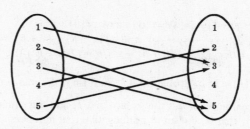

**Fig. 3-4**

**3.12**   Find the graph of the function $f$ defined by Fig. 3-4, i.e., write $f$ as a set of ordered pairs.

▮   The ordered pairs $(a, f(a))$, where $a \in A$ form the graph of $f$. Thus

$$f = \{(1, 3), (2, 5), (3, 5), (4, 2), (5, 3)\}$$

**3.13**   Consider the function $f$ defined by Fig. 3-4. Find: (a) $f(S)$ where $S = \{1, 3, 5\}$; (b) $f^{-1}(T)$ where $T = \{1, 2\}$; and (c) $f^{-1}(3)$.

▮   (a)   $f(S) = f(\{1, 3, 5\}) = \{f(1), f(3), f(5)\} = \{3, 5, 3\} = \{3, 5\}$.
(b)   Only 4 has its image in $T = \{1, 2\}$. Thus $f^{-1}(T) = \{4\}$.
(c)   The elements 1 and 5 have image 3; hence $f^{-1}(3) = \{1, 5\}$.

**3.14**   Let $f$ be a subset of $A \times B$. When does $f$ define a function from $A$ into $B$?

▮   A subset $f$ of $A \times B$ is a function $f: A \to B$ if and only if each $a \in A$ appears as the first coordinate in exactly one ordered pair in $f$.

**3.15**   Let $X = \{1, 2, 3, 4\}$. Determine whether each of the following relations on $X$ (set of ordered pairs) is a function from $X$ into $X$.
(a)   $f = \{(2, 3), (1, 4), (2, 1), (3, 2), (4, 4)\}$    (c)   $h = \{(2, 1), (3, 4), (1, 4), (2, 1), (4, 4)\}$
(b)   $g = \{(3, 1), (4, 2), (1, 1)\}$

▮   Recall that a subset $f$ of $X \times X$ is a function $f: X \to X$ if and only if each $a \in X$ appears as the first coordinate in exactly one ordered pair in $f$.
(a)   No. Two different ordered pairs (2, 3) and (2, 1) in $f$ have the same number 2 as their first coordinate.
(b)   No. The element $2 \in X$ does not appear as the first coordinate in any ordered pair in $g$.
(c)   Yes. Although $2 \in X$ appears as the first coordinte in two ordered pairs in $h$, these two ordered pairs are equal.

**3.16**   Let $W = \{a, b, c, d\}$. Determine whether each of the following sets of ordered pairs is a function from $W$ into $W$.
(a)   $\{(b, a), (c, d), (d, a), (c, d), (a, d)\}$    (c)   $\{(a, b), (b, b), (c, b), (d, b)\}$
(b)   $\{(d, d), (c, a), (a, b), (d, b)\}$    (d)   $\{(a, a), (b, a), (a, b), (c, d), (d, a)\}$

▮   (a)   Yes. Although $c$ appears as the first coordinate in two ordered pairs, these two ordered pairs are equal.
(b)   No. The element $b$ does not appear as the first coordinate in any ordered pair.
(c)   Yes, since each element of $W$ appears as the first coordinate in exactly one ordered pair.
(d)   No. The element $a$ appears as the first coordinate in two different ordered pairs.

**3.17**   Let $f: \mathbf{R} \to \mathbf{R}$ be the function which assigns to each real number $x$ its square $x^2$. Describe different ways of defining $f$.

▮   The function $f$ may be described by any of the following:

$$f(x) = x^2 \quad \text{or} \quad x \mapsto x^2 \quad \text{or} \quad y = x^2$$

Here the barred arrow $\mapsto$ is read "goes into". In the last notation, $x$ is called the *independent variable* and $y$ is called the *dependent variable* since the value of $y$ will depend on the value that $x$ takes.

**Remark:**   Whenever a function $f$ is given by a formula using the independent variable $x$, as in Problem 3.17, we assume unless otherwise stated or implied, that $f$ is a function from $\mathbf{R}$ (or the largest subset of $\mathbf{R}$ for which $f$ has meaning) into $\mathbf{R}$. (See Section 3.2.)

**3.18**   Consider the above function $f(x) = x^2$ in Problem 3.17. Find: (a) the value of $f$ at 5, $-4$, and 0; (b) $f(y + 2)$ and $f(x + h)$; and (c) $[f(x + h) - f(x)]/h$.

▌ (a) $f(5) = 5^2 = 25$, $f(-4) = (-4)^2 = 16$, and $f(0) = 0^2 = 0$.
  (b) $f(y + 2) = (y + 2)^2 = y^2 + 4y + 4$, and $f(x + h) = (x + h)^2 = x^2 + 2xh + h^2$.
  (c) $[f(x + h) - f(x)]/h = (x^2 + 2xh + h^2 - x^2)/h = (2xh + h^2)/h = 2x + h$.

**3.19** Consider the function $f(x) = x^2$ in Problem 3.17. Find $\operatorname{Im} f$, the image of $f$.

▌ Every nonnegative real number $a$ is the square of $\sqrt{a}$, and the square of any number cannot be negative. Hence $\operatorname{Im} f = \{x : x \geq 0\}$, that is, the set of nonnegative real numbers.

**3.20** Let $f$ assign to each country in the world its capital city. Find: (a) the domain of $f$, and (b) $f(\text{France})$, $f(\text{Canada})$, $f(\text{Japan})$.

▌ (a) The domain of $f$ is the set of countries of the world.
  (b) Here $f(\text{France}) = \text{Paris}$ since Paris is the capital of France. Similarly, $f(\text{Canada}) = \text{Ottawa}$, and $f(\text{Japan}) = \text{Tokyo}$.

**3.21** Let $g$ assign to each word in the English language the number of distinct letters needed to spell the word. Find $g(\text{letter})$, $g(\text{mathematics})$, and $g(\text{amour})$.

▌ Here $g(\text{letter}) = 4$ since there are four letters, $l$, $e$, $t$, and $r$, required to spell "letter". Similarly, $g(\text{mathematics}) = 8$. However, $g(\text{amour})$ is not defined since the domain of $g$ is the set of English words and "amour" is a French word.

**3.22** Let $A$ be the set of polygons in the plane. Let $h: A \to \mathbf{N}$ assign to each polygon $P$ its number of sides. Find $h(\text{triangle})$, $h(\text{square})$, $h(\text{hexagon})$, and $h(\text{trapezoid})$.

▌ Here $h(\text{triangle}) = 3$ since a triangle has three sides. Also, $h(\text{square}) = 4$, $h(\text{hexagon}) = 6$, and $h(\text{trapezoid}) = 4$.

**3.23** Let $X = \{a, b\}$ and $Y = \{1, 2, 3\}$. Find the number $n$ of functions: (a) from $X$ into $Y$, and (b) from $Y$ into $X$.

▌ (a) There are three choices, 1, 2, or 3, for the image of $a$ and there are the same three choices for the image of $b$. Thus there are $n = 3 \cdot 3 = 3^2 = 9$ possible functions from $X$ into $Y$.
  (b) There are two choices, $a$ or $b$, for each of the three elements of $Y$. Thus there are $n = 2 \cdot 2 \cdot 2 = 2^3 = 8$ possible functions from $Y$ into $X$.

**3.24** Suppose $X$ has $|X|$ elements and $Y$ has $|Y|$ elements. Show that there are $|Y|^{|X|}$ functions from $X$ into $Y$. (For this reason, one frequently writes $Y^X$ for the collection of all functions from $X$ into $Y$.)

▌ There are $|Y|$ choices for the image of each of the $|X|$ elements of $X$; hence there are $|Y|^{|X|}$ possible functions from $X$ into $Y$.

**3.25** Let $A$ be any nonempty set. (a) Define the identity mapping on $A$, denoted by $1_A$ or 1. (b) Find $1_A(3)$, $1_A(6)$, $1_A(8)$ where $A = \{1, 2, 3, \ldots, 9\}$.

▌ (a) The identity map on $A$ is the function $1_A: A \to A$ defined by $1_A(x) = x$ for every $x \in A$.
  (b) Under the identity map, the image of an element is the element itself; so $1_A(3) = 3$, $1_A(6) = 6$, $1_A(8) = 8$.

**3.26** Define a constant map.

▌ Let $f$ be a function with domain $A$. Then $f$ is a constant map if every $a \in A$ is assigned the same element.

**3.27** Given sets $A$ and $B$, how many constant maps are there from $A$ into $B$?

▌ Each $b \in B$ defines the constant map $f(x) = b$ for every $x \in A$. Hence there are $|B|$ constant maps where $|B|$ denotes the number of elements in $B$.

**3.28** Let $S$ be a subset of $A$ and let $f: A \to B$. Define the restriction of $f$ to $S$.

▌ The *restriction* of $f$ to $S$ is the mapping $\hat{f}: S \to B$ defined by $\hat{f}(s) = f(s)$ for every $s \in S$. One usually writes $f|_S$ to denote the restriction of $f$ to $S$.

**3.29** Let $f: \mathbf{R} \to \mathbf{R}$ be defined by $f(x) = x^2$. Let $\hat{f}: \mathbf{Z} \to \mathbf{R}$ be the restriction of $f$ to $\mathbf{Z}$, that is, let $\hat{f} = f|_Z$. Find $f(4)$, $f(-3)$, and $f(1/2)$.

▮ By definition, $\hat{f}(n) = f(n)$ for every $n \in \mathbf{Z}$. Thus $\hat{f}(4) = f(4) = 4^2 = 16$ and $\hat{f}(-3) = f(-3) = (-3)^2 = 9$. However, $\hat{f}(1/2)$ is not defined since $1/2$ is not in the domain of $\hat{f}$.

**3.30** Let $S$ be a subset of $A$. Define the inclusion map from $S$ into $A$.

▮ The *inclusion* map from $S$ into $A$, denoted by $i: S \hookrightarrow A$, is defined by $i(x) = x$ for every $x \in S$. In other words, the inclusion map of $S$ into $A$ is the restriction of the identity map on $A$ to $S$.

**3.31** Consider the inclusion map $i: \mathbf{N} \hookrightarrow \mathbf{R}$. Find $i(4)$, $i(8)$, $i(23)$, $i(-6)$.

▮ The inclusion map sends each element into itself. Thus $i(4) = 4$, $i(8) = 8$ and $i(23) = 23$. However, $i(-6)$ is not defined since $-6$ does not belong to $\mathbf{N}$ and hence $-6$ is not in the domain of $i: \mathbf{N} \hookrightarrow \mathbf{R}$.

## 3.2 REAL-VALUED FUNCTIONS

This section covers real-valued functions, that is, functions $f$ which map sets into $\mathbf{R}$. Frequently, the domain of $f$ is $\mathbf{R}$ or an interval subset of $\mathbf{R}$ and hence the function $f$ can be plotted in the coordinate plane $\mathbf{R} \times \mathbf{R} = \mathbf{R}^2$. In particular, when the functions are piecewise continuous and differentiable, such as polynomial, rational, trigonometric, exponential, and logarithmic functions, the graph of such a function $f$ can be approximated by first plotting some of its points and then drawing a smooth curve through these points. The points are usually obtained from a table where various values are assigned to $x$ and the corresponding values $f(x)$ computed.

The following notation is also used for intervals from $a$ to $b$ where $a$ and $b$ are real numbers such that $a < b$:

$$[a, b] = \{x: a \le x \le b\}, \text{ called the closed interval from } a \text{ to } b,$$
$$[a, b) = \{x: a \le x < b\}, \text{ called a half-open interval from } a \text{ to } b,$$
$$(a, b] = \{x: a < x \le b\}, \text{ called a half-open interval from } a \text{ to } b,$$
$$(a, b) = \{x: a < x < b\}, \text{ called the open interval from } a \text{ to } b.$$

**3.32** What is the domain $D$ of a real-valued function $f(x)$ (where $x$ is a real variable) when $f(x)$ is given by a formula?

▮ The domain $D$ consists of the largest subset of $\mathbf{R}$ for which $f(x)$ has meaning and is real, unless otherwise specified.

**3.33** Find the domain $D$ of each of the following functions:
   (a) $f(x) = 1/(x - 2)$,   (b) $g(x) = x^2 - 3x - 4$,   (c) $h(x) = \sqrt{25 - x^2}$

▮ (a) $f$ is not defined for $x - 2 = 0$, i.e., for $x = 2$; hence $D = \mathbf{R} \backslash \{2\}$.
   (b) $g$ is defined for every real number; hence $D = \mathbf{R}$.
   (c) $h$ is not defined when $25 - x^2$ is negative; hence $D = [-5, 5] = \{x: -5 \le x \le 5\}$.

**3.34** Find the domain $D$ of the function $f(x) = x^2$ where $0 \le x \le 2$.

▮ Although the formula for $f$ is meaningful for every real number, the domain of $f$ is explicitly given as $D = \{x: 0 \le x \le 2\}$.

**3.35** Use a formula to define each of the following functions from $\mathbf{R}$ into $\mathbf{R}$:
   (a) To each number let $f$ assign its cube.
   (b) To each number let $g$ assign the number 5.
   (c) To each positive number let $h$ assign its square, and to each nonpositive number let $h$ assign the number 6.

▮ (a) Since $f$ assigns to any number $x$ its cube $x^3$, we can define $f$ by $f(x) = x^3$.
   (b) Since $g$ assigns 5 to any number $x$, we can define $g$ by $g(x) = 5$.
   (c) Two different rules are used to define $h$ as follows: $h(x) = \begin{cases} x^2 & \text{if } x > 0 \\ 6 & \text{if } x \le 0 \end{cases}$.

**3.36** Consider the functions $f$, $g$, and $h$ of Problem 3.35. Find: (a) $f(4)$, $f(-2)$, $f(0)$; (b) $g(4)$, $g(-2)$, $g(0)$; (c) $h(4)$, $h(-2)$, $h(0)$.

▮ (a) Now $f(x) = x^3$ for every number $x$; hence $f(4) = 4^3 = 64$, $f(-2) = (-2)^3 = -8$, and $f(0) = 0^3 = 0$.
   (b) The image of every number is 5, so $g(4) = 5$, $g(-2) = 5$, and $g(0) = 5$.
   (c) Since $4 > 0$, $h(4) = 4^2 = 16$. On the other hand, $-2, 0 \le 0$, and so $h(-2) = 6$, $h(0) = 6$.

**3.37** Use a formula to define each of the following functions from **R** into **R**:
  **(a)** To each number let $f$ assign its square plus 3.
  **(b)** To each number let $g$ assign its cube plus twice the number.
  **(c)** To each number greater than or equal to 3 let $h$ assign the number squared, and to each number less than 3 let $h$ assign the number $-2$.

▮ **(a)** $f(x) = x^3 + 3$. **(b)** $g(x) = x^3 + 2x$. **(c)** Two different rules are used to define $h$; $h(x) = \begin{cases} x^2 & \text{if } x \geq 3 \\ -2 & \text{if } x < 3 \end{cases}$.

**3.38** Let $g: \mathbf{R} \rightarrow \mathbf{R}$ be defined by $g(x) = \begin{cases} x^2 - 3x & \text{if } x \geq 2 \\ x + 2 & \text{if } x < 2 \end{cases}$. Find: **(a)** $g(5)$, **(b)** $g(0)$, and **(c)** $g(-2)$.

▮ **(a)** Since $5 \geq 2$, $g(5) = 5^2 - 3(5) = 25 - 15 = 10$.
  **(b)** Since $0 < 2$, $g(0) = 0 + 2 = 2$.
  **(c)** Since $-2 < 2$, $g(-2) = -2 + 2 = 0$.

**3.39** Consider the function $f(x) = x^2 - 3x + 2$. Find: **(a)** $f(-3)$, **(b)** $f(2) - f(-4)$, **(c)** $f(y)$, and **(d)** $f(a^2)$.

▮ The function assigns to any element the square of the element minus 3 times the element plus 2.
  **(a)** $f(-3) = (-3)^2 - 3(-3) + 2 = 9 + 9 + 2 = 20$
  **(b)** $f(2) = (2)^2 - 3(2) + 2 = 0$, $f(-4) = (-4)^2 - 3(-4) + 2 = 30$. Then

$$f(2) - f(-4) = 0 - 30 = -30$$

  **(c)** $f(y) = (y)^2 - 3(y) + 2 = y^2 - 3y + 2$
  **(d)** $f(a^2) = (a^2)^2 - 3(a^2) + 2 = a^4 - 3a^2 + 2$

**3.40** Given the function $f(x)$ of Problem 3.39, find: **(a)** $f(x^2)$, **(b)** $f(y - z)$, **(c)** $f(x + 3)$, and **(d)** $f(2x - 3)$.

▮ **(a)** $f(x^2) = (x^2)^2 - 3(x^2) + 2 = x^4 - 3x^2 + 2$
  **(b)** $f(y - z) = (y - z)^2 - 3(y - z) + 2 = y^2 - 2yz + z^2 - 3y + 3z + 2$
  **(c)** $f(x + 3) = (x + 3)^2 - 3(x + 3) + 2 = (x^2 + 6x + 9) - 3x - 9 + 2 = x^2 + 3x + 2$
  **(d)** $f(2x - 3) = (2x - 3)^2 - 3(2x - 3) + 2 = 4x^2 - 12x + 9 - 6x + 9 + 2 = 4x^2 - 18x + 20$

**3.41** Given the function $f(x)$, of Problem 3.39, find: **(a)** $f(x + h)$, **(b)** $f(x + h) - f(x)$, **(c)** $[f(x + h) - f(x)]/h$.

▮ **(a)** $f(x + h) = (x + h)^2 - 3(x + h) + 2 = x^2 + 2xh + h^2 - 3x - 3h + 2$
  **(b)** Using **(a)**, we obtain

$$f(x + h) - f(x) = (x^2 + 2xh + h^2 - 3x - 3h + 2) - (x^2 - 3x + 2) = 2xh + h^2 - 3h$$

  **(c)** Using **(b)**, we have

$$[f(x + h) - f(x)]/h = (2xh + h^2 - 3h)/h = 2x + h - 3$$

**3.42** Determine which of the graphs in Fig. 3-5 are functions from **R** into **R**.

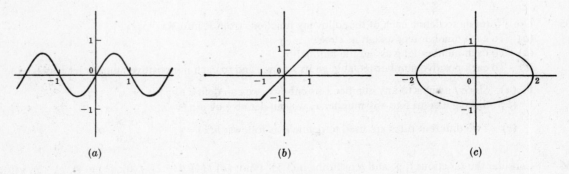

(a)                    (b)                    (c)

**Fig. 3-5**

▮ Geometrically speaking, a set of points on a coordinate diagram is a function if and only if every vertical line contains exactly one point of the set. **(a)** Yes. **(b)** Yes. **(c)** No.

**3.43**    Determine which of the graphs in Fig. 3-6 are functions from **R** into **R**.

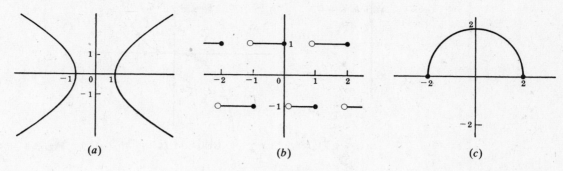

(a)                                    (b)                                    (c)

**Fig. 3-6**

▌ (**a**)  No. (**b**) Yes. (**c**) No; however the graph does define a function from $D$ into **R** where $D = \{x: -2 \le x \le 2\}$.

**3.44**    Sketch the graph of $f(x) = 3x - 2$.

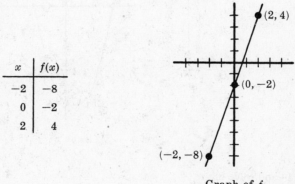

| $x$ | $f(x)$ |
|-----|--------|
| $-2$ | $-8$ |
| $0$ | $-2$ |
| $2$ | $4$ |

Graph of $f$        **Fig. 3-7**

▌ Since $f$ is linear, only two points (three as a check) are needed to sketch its graph. Set up a table with three values of $x$, say, $x = -2, 0, 2$ and find the corresponding values of $f(x)$:

$$f(-2) = 3(-2) - 2 = -8, \qquad f(0) = 3(0) - 2 = -2, \qquad f(2) = 3(2) - 2 = 4$$

Draw the line through these points as in Fig. 3-7.

**3.45**    Consider the function $f: \mathbf{R} \to \mathbf{R}$ defined by $f(x) = x^3$. Find: (**a**) $f(3)$ and $f(-5)$, (**b**) $f(y)$ and $f(y + 1)$, (**c**) $f(x + h)$, (**d**) $[f(x + h) - f(x)]/h$.

▌ (**a**)  $f(3) = 3^3 = 27$,     $f(-5) = (-5)^3 = -125$
(**b**)  $f(y) = (y)^3 = y^3$,     $f(y + 1) = (y + 1)^3 = y^3 + 3y^2 + 3y + 1$
(**c**)  $f(x + h) = (x + h)^3 = x^3 + 3x^2h + 3xh^2 + h^3$
(**d**)  $[f(x + h) - f(x)]/h = (x^3 + 3x^2h + 3xh^2 + h^3 - x^3)/h = (3x^2h + 3xh^2 + h^3)/h = 3x^2 + 3xh + h^2$

**3.46**    Sketch the graph of the function in Problem 3.45.

▌ Since $f$ is a polynomial function, it can be sketched by first plotting some points of its graph and then drawing a smooth curve through these points as in Fig. 3-8.

**3.47**    Sketch the graph of the function $g(x) = x^2 + x - 6$.

▌ Set up a table of values for $x$ and then find the corresponding values of the function. Plot the points in a coordinate diagram, and then draw a smooth continuous curve through these points as in Fig. 3-9.

**3.48**    Given the function of Problem 3.47, find (**a**) $g^{-1}(14)$, (**b**) $g^{-1}(-8)$.

| $x$ | $f(x)$ |
|---|---|
| $-3$ | $-27$ |
| $-2$ | $-8$ |
| $-1$ | $-1$ |
| $0$ | $0$ |
| $1$ | $1$ |
| $2$ | $8$ |
| $3$ | $27$ |

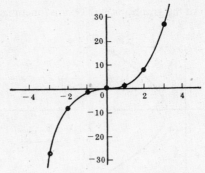

Graph of $f(x) = x^3$ **Fig. 3-8**

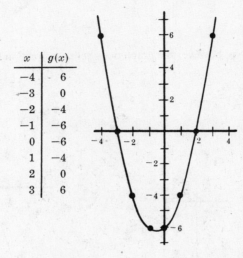

| $x$ | $g(x)$ |
|---|---|
| $-4$ | $6$ |
| $-3$ | $0$ |
| $-2$ | $-4$ |
| $-1$ | $-6$ |
| $0$ | $-6$ |
| $1$ | $-4$ |
| $2$ | $0$ |
| $3$ | $6$ |

Graph of $g$ **Fig. 3-9**

**(a)** Set $g(x) = 14$ and solve for $x$:

$$x^2 + x - 6 = 14 \quad \text{or} \quad x^2 + x - 20 = 0 \quad \text{or} \quad (x + 5)(x - 4) = 0$$

Thus $x = -5$ and $x = 4$. In other words, $g^{-1}(-4) = \{-5, 4\}$.

**(b)** Set $g(x) = -8$ and solve for $x$: $x^2 + x - 6 = -8$ or $x^2 + x + 2 = 0$. Using the quadratic formula, the discriminant $D = b^2 - 4ac = 1^2 - 4(1 \cdot 2) = -7$ is negative and hence there are no real solutions. Thus $g^{-1}(-8) = \emptyset$, the empty set.

**3.49** Sketch the graph of $h(x) = x^3 - 3x^2 - x + 3$.

❚ Draw a smooth curve through some of the points of the graph of $h$ as in Fig. 3-10.

**3.50** Consider the function $h(x) = x^3 - 3x^2 - x + 3$ (Problem 3.49). **(a)** Find $h(\mathbf{R})$, the image of $h$. **(b)** How many real roots does $h$ have? **(c)** Find $h^{-1}(A)$ where $A = [-15, 15]$.

❚ Use the graph of $h$ in Fig. 3-10.
**(a)** Since every horizontal line intersects the graph of $h$, every real number is an image value. Thus $f(\mathbf{R}) = \mathbf{R}$.
**(b)** Since the graph crosses the $x$ axis in three points, $h$ has three real roots. That is, $x^3 - 3x^2 - x + 3 = 0$ has three real roots.
**(c)** The graph indicates that the image of every $x$-value between $-2$ and $4$, and only these $x$-values, lies between $-15$ and $15$. Thus $f^{-1}(A) = [-2, 4]$.

**3.51** Sketch the graph of $f(x) = 2$.

❚ For any value of $x$, we have $f(x) = 2$. Thus, for example, $(-3, 2)$, $(0, 2)$, $(1, 2)$, $(3, 2)$ lie on the graph of $f$ given by the horizontal line through $y = 2$ as shown in Fig. 3-11.

**3.52** Sketch the graph of $g(x) = (1/2)x - 1$.

| $x$ | $h(x)$ |
|-----|--------|
| $-2$ | $-15$ |
| $-1$ | $0$ |
| $0$ | $3$ |
| $1$ | $0$ |
| $2$ | $-3$ |
| $3$ | $0$ |
| $4$ | $15$ |

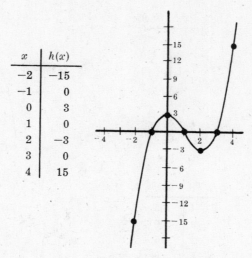

Graph of $h$      **Fig. 3-10**

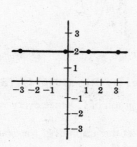

Graph of $f$      **Fig. 3-11**

| $x$ | $g(x)$ |
|-----|--------|
| $-2$ | $-2$ |
| $0$ | $-1$ |
| $2$ | $0$ |

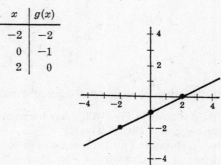

Graph of $g$      **Fig. 3-12**

▌ Since $g$ is linear, only two points (three as a check) are needed to sketch its graph. Set up a table with three values of $x$, say, $x = -2, 0, 2$ and find the corresponding values of $g(x)$:

$$g(-2) = -1 - 1 = -2, \qquad g(0) = 0 - 1 = -1, \qquad g(2) = 1 - 1 = 0.$$

Draw the line through these points as in Fig. 3-12.

**3.53** Sketch the graph of the function $h(x) = 2x^2 - 4x - 3$.

| $x$ | $h(x)$ |
|-----|--------|
| $-2$ | $13$ |
| $-1$ | $3$ |
| $0$ | $-3$ |
| $1$ | $-5$ |
| $2$ | $-3$ |
| $3$ | $3$ |

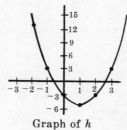

Graph of $h$      **Fig. 3-13**

▌ Draw a smooth continuous curve through some of the points of the graph of $h$ as in Fig. 3-13.

**3.54** Sketch the graph of the function $f(x) = x^3 - 3x + 2$.

▌ Draw a smooth continuous curve through some of the points of the graph of $f$ as in Fig. 3-14.

**3.55** Sketch the graph of the function $g(x) = x^4 - 10x^2 + 9$.

▌ Draw a smooth continuous curve through some of the points of the graph of $g$ as in Fig. 3-15.

| $x$ | $f(x)$ |
|---|---|
| -3 | -16 |
| -2 | 0 |
| -1 | 4 |
| 0 | 2 |
| 1 | 0 |
| 2 | 4 |
| 3 | 20 |

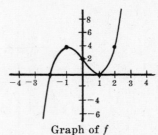

Graph of $f$     **Fig. 3-14**

| $x$ | $g(x)$ |
|---|---|
| -4 | 105 |
| -3 | 0 |
| -2 | -15 |
| -1 | 0 |
| 0 | 9 |
| 1 | 0 |
| 2 | -15 |
| 3 | 0 |
| 4 | 105 |

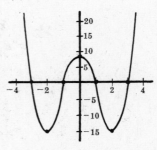

Graph of $g$     **Fig. 3-15**

**3.56**   Consider the functions $f$ and $g$ in Problems 3.54 and 3.55 respectively. **(a)** Is $f(\mathbf{R}) = \mathbf{R}$? **(b)** Is $g(\mathbf{R}) = \mathbf{R}$?

   **▌**   **(a)**   Yes. As shown in Fig. 3-14, every horizontal line intersects the graph of $f$; hence every value of $y$ is in the image of $f$. Thus $f(\mathbf{R}) = \mathbf{R}$.

       **(b)**   No. As shown in Fig. 3–15, some horizontal lines do not intersect the graph of $g$, for example, the horizontal line through $y = -20$. Thus $-20 \notin g(\mathbf{R})$, and so $g(\mathbf{R}) \neq \mathbf{R}$.

**3.57**   Sketch the graph of $h(x) = \begin{cases} 0 & \text{if } x = 0 \\ 1/x & \text{if } x \neq 0 \end{cases}$.

| $x$ | $h(x)$ |
|---|---|
| 4 | $\frac{1}{4}$ |
| 2 | $\frac{1}{2}$ |
| 1 | 1 |
| $\frac{1}{2}$ | 2 |
| $\frac{1}{4}$ | 4 |
| 0 | 0 |
| $-\frac{1}{4}$ | $-4$ |
| $-\frac{1}{2}$ | $-2$ |
| $-1$ | $-1$ |
| $-2$ | $-\frac{1}{2}$ |
| $-4$ | $-\frac{1}{4}$ |

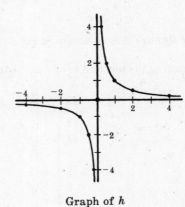

Graph of $h$     **Fig. 3-16**

   **▌**   See Fig. 3-16. (Note that this graph is only piecewise continuous. Specifically, $h$ is continuous for $x < 0$ and for $x > 0$.)

**3.58**   A function $f: \mathbf{R} \to \mathbf{R}$ is a *polynomial function* if $f(x) \equiv 0$, the zero function, or $f$ can be expressed in the form

$$f(x) = a_n x^n + a_{n-1} x^{n-1} + \cdots + a_1 x + a_0$$

where the $a_i$ are real numbers and $a_n \neq 0$. Define: **(a)** the leading coefficient of $f$; **(b)** monic polynomial; **(c)** the degree of $f$, written deg $f$.

   **▌**   **(a)**   The leading coefficient of $f$ is the nonzero coefficient of the highest power of $x$ or, in other words, $a_n$.

**(b)** A polynomial $f$ is monic if its leading coefficient is 1, i.e., if $a_n = 1$.

**(c)** The degree of the zero function $f(x) \equiv 0$ is not defined; otherwise, $\deg f = n$, the highest power of $x$ with a nonzero coefficient.

**3.59** Suppose $f(x)$ and $g(x)$ are polynomial functions such that $\deg f = m$ and $\deg g = n$. Find the degree of the product $h(x) = f(x)g(x)$.

▮ The degree of the product $h$ is the sum of the degrees of its factors $f$ and $g$; that is; $\deg h = \deg f + \deg g = m + n$.

**3.60** Let $f(x) = a_n x^n + \cdots + a_1 x + a_0$ be a polynomial function of odd degree. Argue that $f(\mathbf{R}) = \mathbf{R}$.

▮ We want to show that for every $k \in \mathbf{R}$, the equation $f(x) = k$ has a solution $x \in \mathbf{R}$. We may always suppose $a_n = +1$, so that $f(x) \approx x^n$ when $|x|$ is very large. Then there must exist a (large) positive real number $a$ such that both $f(a) > |k|$ and $f(-a) < -|k|$, which imply

$$f(-a) < k < f(a) \qquad (*)$$

Now, the graph of $f$ is an unbroken curve connecting the points $P_1 = (-a, f(-a))$ and $P_2 = (a, f(a))$; it must therefore intersect any horizontal line included between the horizontals through $P_1$ and $P_2$. By $(*)$, $y = k$ is just such a horizontal line; in other words, $f(x) = k$ for some $-a < x < a$.

## 3.3 COMPOSITION OF FUNCTIONS

**3.61** Consider functions $f: A \to B$ and $g: B \to C$; that is, where the codomain of $f$ is the domain of $g$. Define the composition function of $f$ and $g$.

▮ The *composition* of $f$ and $g$, written $g \circ f$, is the function from $A$ into $C$ defined by

$$(g \circ f)(a) \equiv g(f(a))$$

That is, to find the image of $a$ under $g \circ f$, we first find the image of $a$ under $f$ and then we find the image of $f(a)$ under $g$.

**Remark:** If we view $f$ and $g$ as relations, then the function in Problem 3.61 is the same as the composition of $f$ and $g$ as relations (see Section 2.4) except that here we use the functional notation $g \circ f$ for the composition of $f$ and $g$ instead of the notation $f \circ g$ which was used for the composition of relations.

**3.62** Let the functions $f: A \to B$ and $g: B \to C$ be defined by Fig. 3-17. Find the composition function $g \circ f: A \to C$.

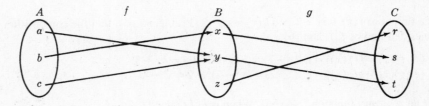

Fig. 3-17

▮ We use the definition of the composition function to compute:

$$(g \circ f)(a) = g(f(a)) = g(y) = t$$
$$(g \circ f)(b) = g(f(b)) = g(x) = s$$
$$(g \circ f)(c) = g(f(c)) = g(y) = t$$

Note that we arrive at the same answer if we "follow the arrows" in the diagram:

$$a \to y \to t, \qquad b \to x \to s, \qquad c \to y \to t$$

**3.63** Give the images of the functions $f$ and $g$ in Fig. 3-17.

▮ The image values under the mapping $f$ are $x$ and $y$, and the image values under $g$ are $r$, $s$ and $t$; hence $\operatorname{Im} f = \{x, y\}$ and $\operatorname{Im} g = \{r, s, t\}$.

**3.64** Figure 3-18 defines functions $f: A \to B$, $g: B \to C$, and $h: C \to D$. Find the composition function $h \circ g \circ f$.

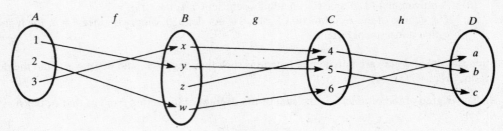

**Fig. 3-18**

▌ Follow the arrows from $A$ to $B$ to $C$ to $D$ as follows:

$$1 \rightarrow y \rightarrow 5 \rightarrow c \qquad \text{hence} \qquad (h \circ g \circ f)(1) = c$$
$$2 \rightarrow w \rightarrow 6 \rightarrow a \qquad \text{hence} \qquad (h \circ g \circ f)(2) = a$$
$$3 \rightarrow x \rightarrow 4 \rightarrow b \qquad \text{hence} \qquad (h \circ g \circ f)(3) = b$$

**3.65**  Let functions $f$ and $g$ be defined by $f(x) = 2x + 1$ and $g(x) = x^2 - 2$ respectively. Find: **(a)** $(g \circ f)(4)$ and $(f \circ g)(4)$; **(b)** $(g \circ f)(a + 2)$; and **(c)** $(f \circ g)(a + 2)$.

▌ **(a)** $f(4) = 2 \cdot 4 + 1 = 9$. Hence $(g \circ f)(4) = g(f(4)) = g(9) = 9^2 - 2 = 79$. $g(4) = 4^2 - 2 = 14$. Hence $(f \circ g)(4) = f(g(4)) = f(14) = 2 \cdot 14 + 1 = 29$. (Note that $f \circ g \neq g \circ f$ since they differ on $x = 4$.)

**(b)** $f(a + 2) = 2(a + 2) + 1 = 2a + 5$. Hence

$$(g \circ f)(a + 2) = g(f(a + 2)) = g(2a + 5) = (2a + 5)^2 - 2 = 4a^2 + 20a + 23$$

**(c)** $g(a + 2) = (a + 2)^2 - 2 = a^2 + 4a + 2$. Hence

$$(f \circ g)(a + 2) = f(g(a + 2)) = f(a^2 + 4a + 2) = 2(a^2 + 4a + 2) + 1 = 2a^2 + 8a + 5$$

**3.66**  Given the functions $f(x) = 2x + 1$ and $g(x) = x^2 - 2$ (Problem 3.65), find the composition functions **(a)** $g \circ f$, and **(b)** $f \circ g$.

▌ **(a)** Compute the formula for $g \circ f$ as follows:

$$(g \circ f)(x) = g(f(x)) = g(2x + 1) = (2x + 1)^2 - 2 = 4x^2 + 4x - 1$$

Observe that the same answer can be found by writing $y = f(x) = 2x + 1$ and $z = g(y) = y^2 - 2$, and then eliminating $y$: $z = y^2 - 2 = (2x + 1)^2 - 2 = 4x^2 + 4x - 1$.

**(b)** $(f \circ g)(x) = f(g(x)) = f(x^2 - 2) = 2(x^2 - 2) + 1 = 2x^2 - 3$.

**3.67**  Given the functions $f(x) = 2x + 1$ and $g(x) = x^2 - 2$ (Problem 3.65), find the composition functions: **(a)** $f \circ f$ (sometimes denoted by $f^2$), and **(b)** $g \circ g$.

▌ **(a)** $(f \circ f)(x) = f(f(x)) = f(2x + 1) = 2(2x + 1) + 1 = 4x + 3$.

**(b)** $(g \circ g)(x) = g(g(x)) = g(x^2 - 2) = (x^2 - 2)^2 - 2 = x^4 - 4x^2$.

**3.68**  Consider an arbitrary function $f: A \rightarrow B$. When is $f \circ f$ defined?

▌ The composition $f \circ f$ is defined when the domain of $f$ is equal to the codomain of $f$, that is, when $A = B$.

**3.69**  Consider any function $f: A \rightarrow B$. Show that: **(a)** $1_B \circ f = f$, **(b)** $f \circ 1_A = f$. (Here $1_B: B \rightarrow B$ and $1_A: A \rightarrow A$ are the identity functions on $B$ and $A$ respectively.) (See Problem 3.25.)

▌ **(a)** $(1_B \circ f)(a) = 1_B(f(a)) = f(a)$, for every $a \in A$. Thus $1_B \circ f = f$.

**(b)** $(f \circ 1_A)(a) = f(1_A(a)) = f(a)$, for every $a \in A$. Thus $f \circ 1_B = f$.

**Theorem 3.1:**  Consider functions $f: A \rightarrow B$, $g: B \rightarrow C$, and $h: C \rightarrow D$. Then $h \circ (g \circ f) = (h \circ g) \circ f$.

**3.70**  Prove Theorem 3.1 which states that composition of functions satisfies the associative law.

▌ Consider any element $a \in A$. Then

$$(h \circ (g \circ f))(a) = h((g \circ f)(a)) = h(g(f(a))) \quad \text{and} \quad ((h \circ g) \circ f)(a) = (h \circ g)(f(a)) = h(g(f(a)))$$

Thus $(h \circ (g \circ f))(a) = ((h \circ g) \circ f)(a)$ for every $a \in A$, and so $h \circ (g \circ f) = (h \circ g) \circ f$.

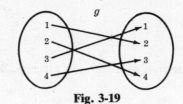
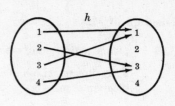

**Fig. 3-19**

Problems 3.71–3.76 refer to the functions $f$, $g$, and $h$ in Fig. 3-19 where each function maps the set $A = \{1, 2, 3, 4\}$ into itself.

**3.71**   Find the composition function $f \circ g$.

▌ First apply $g$ and then $f$ as follows:

$$(f \circ g)(1) = f(g(1)) = f(2) = 1 \qquad (f \circ g)(3) = f(g(3)) = f(1) = 2$$
$$(f \circ g)(2) = f(g(2)) = f(4) = 4 \qquad (f \circ g)(4) = f(g(4)) = f(3) = 1$$

**3.72**   Find the composition function $g \circ h$.

▌ Follow the arrows using $h$ first and then $g$ as follows:

$$1 \to 1 \to 2, \qquad 2 \to 3 \to 1, \qquad 3 \to 1 \to 2, \qquad 4 \to 3 \to 1$$

Thus $(g \circ h)(1) = 2$, $(g \circ h)(2) = 1$, $(g \circ h)(3) = 2$, $(g \circ h)(3) = 1$.

**3.73**   Find the composition function $g^2 = g \circ g$.

▌ Follow the arrows using $g$ twice:

$$1 \to 2 \to 4, \qquad 2 \to 4 \to 3, \qquad 3 \to 1 \to 2, \qquad 4 \to 3 \to 1$$

Thus $g^2(1) = 4$, $g^2(2) = 3$, $g^2(3) = 2$, $g^2(4) = 1$.

**3.74**   Find the composition function $h^2 = h \circ h$.

▌ Follow the arrows using $h$ twice:

$$1 \to 1 \to 1, \qquad 2 \to 3 \to 1, \qquad 3 \to 1 \to 1, \qquad 4 \to 3 \to 1$$

Here $h^2$ is the constant function $h^2(x) = 1$.

**3.75**   Find the composition function $f \circ h \circ g$.

▌ Follow the arrows using $g$ first, then $h$ and finally $f$, that is, in reverse order:

$$1 \to 2 \to 3 \to 1, \qquad 2 \to 4 \to 3 \to 1, \qquad 3 \to 1 \to 1 \to 2, \qquad 4 \to 3 \to 1 \to 2$$

Thus $f \circ h \circ g = \{(1, 1), (2, 1), (3, 2), (4, 2)\}$.

**3.76**   Find the composition function $f^3 = f \circ f \circ f$.

▌ Follow the arrows using $f$ three times as follows:

$$1 \to 2 \to 1 \to 2, \qquad 2 \to 1 \to 2 \to 1, \qquad 3 \to 1 \to 2 \to 1, \qquad 4 \to 4 \to 4 \to 4$$

Thus $f \circ f \circ f = \{(1, 2), (2, 1), (3, 1), (4, 4)\}$.

**3.77**   Consider the functions $f(x) = 2x - 3$ and $g(x) = x^2 + 3x + 5$. Find a formula for the composition functions (**a**) $g \circ f$ and (**b**) $f \circ g$.

▌ (**a**)   $(g \circ f)(x) = g(f(x)) = g(2x - 3) = (2x - 3)^2 + 3(2x - 3) + 5 = 4x^2 - 6x + 9 + 6x - 9 + 5 = 4x^2 + 5$.
(**b**)   $(f \circ g)(x) = f(g(x)) = f(x^2 + 3x + 5) = 2(x^2 + 3x + 5) - 3 = 2x^2 + 6x + 7$.

**3.78**   Consider the above function $f(x) = 2x - 3$. Find a formula for the composition functions (**a**) $f^2 = f \circ f$ and (**b**) $f^3 = f \circ f \circ f$.

▌ (**a**)   $f^2(x) = f(f(x)) = f(2x - 3) = 2(2x - 3) - 3 = 4x - 9$.
(**b**)   $f^3(x) = f(f^2(x)) = f(4x - 9) = 2(4x - 9) - 3 = 8x - 21$.

## Diagram of Maps

**3.79**    Define a *diagram of maps*.

▌ A directed graph in which the vertices are sets and the edges denote maps between the sets is called a diagram of maps.

Problems 3.80–3.83 refer to maps $f: A \rightarrow B$, $g: B \rightarrow A$, $h: C \rightarrow B$, $F: B \rightarrow C$, and $G: A \rightarrow C$ which are pictured in the diagram of maps in Fig. 3-20.

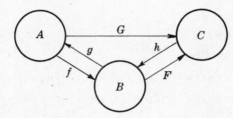

**Fig. 3-20**

**3.80**    Is $g \circ f$ defined? If so, what is its domain and codomain?

▌ Since $f$ goes from $A$ to $B$ and $g$ goes from $B$ to $A$, $g \circ f$ is defined and $A$ is its domain and codomain.

**3.81**    Is $h \circ f$ defined? If so, what is its domain and codomain?

▌ Note that $h$ does not "follow" $f$ in the diagram, i.e., the codomain $B$ of $f$ is not the domain of $h$. Hence $h \circ f$ is not defined.

**3.82**    Is $F \circ h \circ G$ defined? If so, what is its domain and codomain?

▌ The arrows representing $G$, $h$, and $F$ do follow each other in the diagram and go from $A$ to $C$ to $B$ to $C$. Thus $F \circ h \circ G$ is defined with domain $A$ and codomain $C$. (We emphasize that compositions are "read" from right to left.)

**3.83**    Is $G \circ F \circ h$ defined? If so, what is its domain and codomain?

▌ $F$ follows $h$ in the diagram, but $G$ does not follow $F$, i.e., the codomain $C$ of $F$ is not the domain of $G$. Hence $G \circ F \circ h$ is not defined.

**3.84**    Define a commutative diagram of maps.

▌ A diagram of maps is commutative if any two paths with the same initial and terminal vertices are equal.

Problems 3.85–3.90 refer to the commutative diagram of maps in Fig. 3-21.

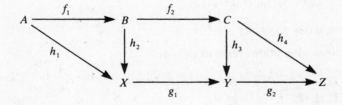

**Fig. 3-21**

**3.85**    Represent $h_2 \circ f_1$ by a single map.

▌ The composition map $h_2 \circ f_1$ goes from $A$ to $B$ to $X$. Since the diagram is commutative, $h_2 \circ f_1 = h_1$.

**3.86**    Represent $h_3 \circ f_2$ in as many ways as possible.

▌ The map $h_3 \circ f_2$ goes from $B$ to $C$ to $Y$. The only other path from $B$ to $Y$ is the map $g_1 \circ h_2$.

**3.87**    Represent the map $g_2 \circ h_3$ by a single map.

▌ The map $g_2 \circ h_3$ goes from $C$ to $Y$ to $Z$. The map $h_4$ goes from $C$ to $Z$. Since the diagram is commutative, $g_2 \circ h_3 = h_4$.

**3.88**    Represent the map $g_1 \circ h_3$ by a single map.

▮ The map $g_1 \circ h_3$ is not defined since the codomain $Y$ of $h_3$ is not the domain of $g_1$.

**3.89**    Represent the map $g_2 \circ h_3 \circ f_2 \circ f_1$ in as many ways as possible.

▮ The map $g_2 \circ h_3 \circ f_2 \circ f_1$ goes from $A$ to $B$ to $C$ to $Y$ to $Z$. There are three other paths from $A$ to $Z$:
(i) $g_2 \circ g_1 \circ h_1$, (ii) $g_2 \circ g_1 \circ h_2 \circ f_1$, and (iii) $h_4 \circ f_2 \circ f_1$.

**3.90**    Find all maps: **(a)** from $A$ to $Y$, **(b)** from $X$ to $Z$, **(c)** from $C$ to $X$.

▮ **(a)**    There are three paths from $A$ to $Y$ which are $A$ to $B$ to $C$ to $Y$, $A$ to $B$ to $X$ to $Y$, and $A$ to $X$ to $Y$. Thus there are three maps from $A$ to $Y$ which are $h_3 \circ f_2 \circ f_1$, $g_1 \circ h_2 \circ f_1$ and $g_1 \circ h_1$.
   **(b)**    There is only one path from $X$ to $Z$ which is $X$ to $Y$ to $Z$. This corresponds to the map $g_2 \circ g_1$.
   **(c)**    There is no path and hence no map from $C$ to $X$.

## 3.4  ONE-TO-ONE, ONTO, AND INVERTIBLE FUNCTIONS

**3.91**    Define a one-to-one (or injective) function.

▮ A function $f: A \rightarrow B$ is said to be *one-to-one* (written 1-1) if different elements in the domain $A$ have distinct images. Another way of saying the same thing is that $f$ is *one-to-one* if $f(a) = f(a')$ implies $a = a'$.

**3.92**    Define an onto (or surjective) function.

▮ A function $f: A \rightarrow B$ is said to be an *onto* function if each element of $B$ is the image of some element of $A$. In other words, $f: A \rightarrow B$ is onto if the image of $f$ is the entire codomain, i.e., if $f(A) = B$. In such a case we say that $f$ is a function from $A$ *onto* $B$ or that $f$ maps $A$ *onto* $B$.

**3.93**    Define a one-to-one correspondence (or bijective function).

▮ A function $f: A \rightarrow B$ is called a *one-to-one correspondence* or a *bijective* function between $A$ and $B$ if $f$ is both one-to-one and onto. This terminology comes from the fact that each element of $A$ will then correspond to a unique element of $B$ and vice versa.

**3.94**    Define an invertible function.

▮ A function $f: A \rightarrow B$ is said to be *invertible* if there exists a function $g: B \rightarrow A$ such that $f \circ g = 1_B$ and $g \circ f = 1_A$ (where $1_A$ and $1_B$ are the identity maps). In such a case, the function $g$ is called the inverse of $f$ and is denoted by $f^{-1}$. Alternatively, $f$ is invertible if the inverse relation $f^{-1}$ is a function from $B$ to $A$. Also, if $b \in B$ then $f^{-1}(b) = a$ where $a$ is the unique element of $A$ for which $f(a) = b$. The following theorem gives a simple criterion.

**Theorem 3.2:**    A function $f: A \rightarrow B$ is invertible if and only if $f$ is bijective.

Problems 3.95–3.97 refer to the functions $f_1: A \rightarrow B$, $f_2: B \rightarrow C$, $f_3: C \rightarrow D$ and $f_4: D \rightarrow E$ defined in Fig. 3-22.

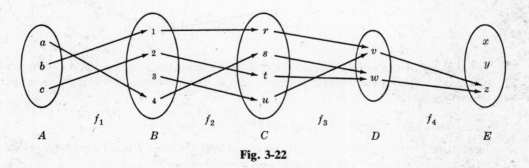

**Fig. 3-22**

**3.95**    Which of the functions in Fig. 3-22 are one-to-one?    $A \; ; \; B$

▮ The function $f_1$ is one-to-one since no element of $B$ is the image of more than one element of $A$. Similarly, $f_2$ is one-to-one. However, neither $f_3$ nor $f_4$ is one-to-one since $f_3(r) = f_3(u)$ and $f_4(v) = f_4(w)$.

**3.96** Which of the functions in Fig. 3-22 are onto functions?

▌ The functions $f_2$ and $f_3$ are both onto functions since every element of $C$ is the image under $f_2$ of some element of $B$ and every element of $D$ is the image under $f_3$ of some element of $C$, i.e., $f_2(B) = C$ and $f_3(C) = D$. On the other hand, $f_1$ is not onto since $3 \in B$ is not the image under $f_1$ of any element of $A$, and $f_4$ is not onto since $x \in E$ is not the image under $f_4$ of any element of $D$.

**3.97** Which of the functions in Fig. 3-22 are invertible.

▌ The function $f_1$ is one-to-one but not onto, $f_3$ is onto but not one-to-one and $f_4$ is neither one-to-one nor onto. However, $f_2$ is both one-to-one and onto, i.e., $f_2$ is a bijective function between $A$ and $B$. Hence $f_2$ is invertible and $f_2^{-1}$ is a function from $C$ to $B$.

**3.98** Let $A = \{a, b, c, d, e\}$, and let $B$ be the set of letters in the alphabet. Let the functions $f$, $g$ and $h$ from $A$ into $B$ be defined as follows:

(a) $a \xrightarrow{f} r$    (b) $a \xrightarrow{g} z$    (c) $a \xrightarrow{h} a$
    $b \rightarrow a$        $b \rightarrow y$        $b \rightarrow c$
    $c \rightarrow s$        $c \rightarrow x$        $c \rightarrow e$
    $d \rightarrow r$        $d \rightarrow y$        $d \rightarrow r$
    $e \rightarrow e$        $e \rightarrow z$        $e \rightarrow s$

Are any of these functions one-to-one?

▌ Recall that a function is one-to-one if it assigns distinct image values to distinct elements in the domain.
(a) No. For $f$ assigns $r$ to both $a$ and $d$.
(b) No. For $g$ assigns $z$ to both $a$ and $e$.
(c) Yes. For $h$ assigns distinct images to different elements in the domain.

**3.99** Determine if each function is one-to-one.
(a) To each person on the earth assign the number which corresponds to his age.
(b) To each country in the world assign the latitude and longitude of its capital.
(c) To each book written by only one author assign the author.
(d) To each country in the world which has a prime minister assign its prime minister.

▌ (a) No. Many people in the world have the same age.
(b) Yes.
(c) No. There are different books with the same author.
(d) Yes. Different countries in the world have different prime ministers.

**3.100** Let the functions $f: A \rightarrow B$, $g: B \rightarrow C$, and $h: C \rightarrow D$ be defined by Fig. 3-23. Determine which of the functions are onto.

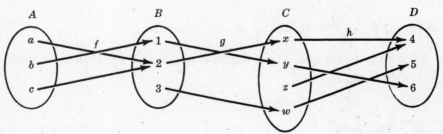

**Fig. 3-23**

▌ The function $f: A \rightarrow B$ is not onto since $3 \in B$ is not the image of any element in $A$. The function $g: B \rightarrow C$ is not onto since $z \in C$ is not the image of any element in $B$. The function $h: C \rightarrow D$ is onto since each element in $D$ is the image of some element of $C$.

**3.101** Determine which of the functions $f$, $g$, and $h$ in Fig. 3-23 are one-to-one.

▌ The function $f$ is not one-to-one since $f(a) = f(c) = 2$. The function $h$ is not one-to-one since $h(x) = h(z) = 4$. The function $g$ is one-to-one since the images of 1, 2, and 3 are distinct.

**3.102** Which of the functions $f$, $g$, and $h$ in Fig. 3-23 are invertible?

▌ The function $f$ is neither one-to-one nor onto, $g$ is one-to-one but not onto, and $h$ is onto but not one-to-one. Thus none of the functions is bijective, and thus none is invertible.

**3.103** Find the composition $h \circ g \circ f$ of the functions in Fig. 3-23.

▮ Now $a \to 2 \to x \to 4$, $b \to 1 \to y \to 6$, $c \to 2 \to x \to 4$. Hence $h \circ g \circ f = \{(a, 4), (b, 6), (c, 4)\}$.

**3.104** Recall that a function $f: \mathbf{R} \to \mathbf{R}$ may be identified with its graph. Give a geometrical condition which is equivalent to the property that (a) $f$ is one-to-one, (b) $f$ is onto, and (c) $f$ is invertible.

▮ (a) To say that $f$ is one-to-one means that there are no two distinct pairs $(a_1, b)$ and $(a_2, b)$ in the graph of $f$; hence each horizontal line can intersect the graph of $f$ in at most one point.

(b) To say that $f$ is an onto function means that for every $b \in \mathbf{R}$ there must be at least one $a \in \mathbf{R}$ such that $(a, b)$ belongs to the graph of $f$; hence each horizontal line must intersect the graph of $f$ at least once.

(c) If $f$ is invertible, i.e., both one-to-one and onto, then each horizontal line will intersect the graph of $f$ in exactly one point.

**3.105** Consider the functions $f(x) = 2^x$, $g(x) = x^3 - x$, and $h(x) = x^2$ whose graphs appear in Fig. 3-24. Determine which of the functions are one-to-one.

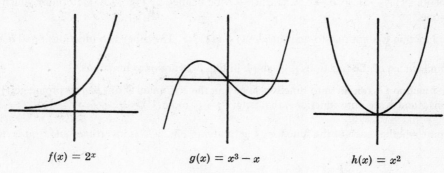

$f(x) = 2^x$      $g(x) = x^3 - x$      $h(x) = x^2$

**Fig. 3-24**

▮ The function $g$ is not one-to-one since there are horizontal lines which contain more than one point of the graph of $g$, e.g., $y = 0$ contains three points of $g$. The function $h$ is not one-to-one since $h(2) = h(-2) = 4$, i.e., the horizontal line $y = 4$ contains two points of $h$. However, $f$ is one-to-one since no horizontal line contains more than one point of $f$.

**3.106** Determine which of the functions $f$, $g$, and $h$ in Fig. 3-24 are onto functions.

▮ The function $f$ is not an onto function since some horizontal lines (those below the $x$ axis) contain no point of $f$. Similarly, $h$ is not an onto function since $k = -16$ (and any other negative number) has no preimage, i.e., the horizontal line $y = -16$ contains no point of $h$. However, $g$ is an onto function since every horizontal line contains at least one point of $g$.

**3.107** Which of the functions $f$, $g$, and $h$ in Fig. 3-24 are invertible?

▮ None of the functions $f$, $g$, and $h$ are invertible since no function is both one-to-one and onto.

**3.108** Some texts say that $f(x) = 2^x$ in Fig. 3-24 has an inverse. Why?

▮ The function $f(x) = 2^x$ is one-to-one with image $D = \{x: x > 0\}$, the positive real numbers. Suppose we redefine $f$ to be the function $f: \mathbf{R} \to D$, that is, with $D$ as the codomain. Then $f$ is bijective (one-to-one and onto) and hence has an inverse function $f^{-1}: D \to \mathbf{R}$ (see Theorem 3.2).

**3.109** Let $W = \{1, 2, 3, 4, 5\}$ and let $f: W \to W$, $g: W \to W$, and $h: W \to W$ be defined by the diagrams in Fig. 3-25. Determine whether each function is invertible, and, if it is, find its inverse function.

▮ In order for a function to be invertible, the function must be both one-to-one and onto. Only $h$ is one-to-one and onto, so only $h$ is invertible. To find $h^{-1}$, the inverse of $h$, reverse the ordered pairs which belong to $h$.

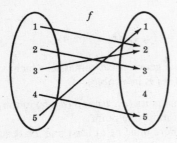 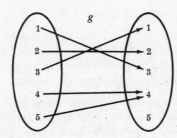 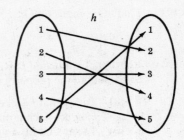

**Fig. 3-25**

Note

$$h = \{(1, 2), (2, 4), (3, 3), (4, 5), (5, 1)\}$$

hence

$$h^{-1} = \{(2, 1), (4, 2), (3, 3), (5, 4), (1, 5)\}$$

Observe that $h^{-1}$ can be obtained by reversing the arrows in the diagram for $h$.

**3.110** Let functions $f: A \to B$, $g: B \to C$, and $h: C \to D$ be defined by Fig. 3-26. Determine which of the functions are one-to-one.

▮ The function $g$ is not one-to-one since $g(1) = g(3) = r$. The other two functions $f$ and $h$ are one-to-one.

**3.111** Determine which of the functions $f$, $g$, and $h$ in Fig. 3-26 are onto functions.

▮ The function $f$ is not an onto function since 3 in the codomain $B$ of $f$ has no preimage. The other two functions $g$ and $h$ are onto functions, that is, $g(B) = C$ and $h(C) = D$.

**3.112** Determine whether each of the functions $f$, $g$, and $h$ in Fig. 3-26 is invertible, and, if it is, find its inverse.

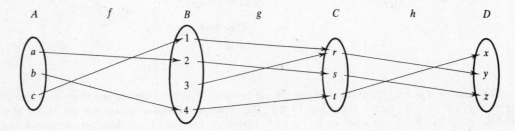

**Fig. 3-26**

▮ Only $h$ is both one-to-one and onto; hence only $h$ is invertible. The inverse $h^{-1}$ of $h$ is obtained by reversing the ordered pairs in $h$. Thus

$$h = \{(r, y), (s, z), (t, x)\} \quad \text{and so} \quad h^{-1} = \{(y, r), (z, s), (x, t)\}$$

**3.113** Find the composition function $h \circ g \circ f$ for the functions $f$, $g$, and $h$ in Fig. 3-26.

▮ Follow the arrows from $A$ to $B$ to $C$ to $D$ as follows:

$$a \to 2 \to s \to z, \qquad b \to 4 \to t \to x, \qquad c \to 1 \to r \to y$$

Thus $h \circ g \circ f = \{(a, z), (b, x), (c, y)\}$.

**3.114** Let $f: \mathbf{R} \to \mathbf{R}$ be defined by $f(x) = 2x - 3$. Now $f$ is one-to-one and onto; hence $f$ has an inverse mapping $f^{-1}$. Find a formula for $f^{-1}$.

▮ Let $y$ be the image of $x$ under the mapping $f$, that is, set $y = 2x - 3$. Interchange $x$ and $y$ to obtain $x = 2y - 3$. Solve for $y$ in terms of $x$ to get $y = (x + 3)/2$. Thus the formula defining the inverse mapping is $f^{-1}(x) = (x + 3)/2$.

**3.115** Find a formula for the inverse of $g(x) = x^2 - 1$.

▮ Set $y = x^2 - 1$. Interchange $x$ and $y$ to get $x = y^2 - 1$. Solve for $y$ to get $y = \pm\sqrt{x + 1}$. The inverse of $g$ does not exist unless the domain of $g^{-1}$ is restricted to $x \geq -1$. In this case assume only the positive value of $\sqrt{x + 1}$

and so $g^{-1}(x) = \sqrt{x+1}$.

**3.116**   Find a formula for the inverse of $h(x) = \dfrac{2x-3}{5x-7}$.

▐   Set $y = h(x)$ and then interchange $x$ and $y$ as follows:

$$y = \frac{2x-3}{5x-7} \quad \text{and then} \quad x = \frac{2y-3}{5y-7}$$

Now solve for $y$ in terms of $x$:

$$5xy - 7x = 2y - 3 \quad \text{or} \quad 5xy - 2y = 7x - 3 \quad \text{or} \quad (5x-2)y = 7x - 3$$

Thus   $\qquad\qquad\qquad y = \dfrac{7x-3}{5x-2} \quad \text{and so} \quad h^{-1}(x) = \dfrac{7x-3}{5x-2}$

(Here the domain of $h^{-1}$ excludes $x = 2/5$.)

**3.117**   Suppose $f: A \to B$ and $g: B \to C$ are one-to-one functions. Show that $g \circ f: A \to C$ is one-to-one.

▐   Suppose $(g \circ f)(x) = (g \circ f)(y)$. Then $g(f(x)) = g(f(y))$. Since $g$ is one-to-one, $f(x) = f(y)$. Since $f$ is one-to-one, $x = y$. We have proven that $(g \circ f)(x) = (g \circ f)(y)$ implies $x = y$; hence $g \circ f$ is one-to-one.

**3.118**   Suppose $f: A \to B$ and $g: B \to C$ are onto functions. Show that $g \circ f: A \to C$ is an onto function.

▐   Suppose $c \in C$. Since $g$ is onto, there exists $b \in B$ for which $g(b) = c$. Since $f$ is onto, there exists $a \in A$ for which $f(a) = b$. Thus $(g \circ f)(a) = g(f(a)) = g(b) = c$; hence $g \circ f$ is onto.

**3.119**   Given $f: A \to B$ and $g: B \to C$. Show that if $g \circ f$ is one-to-one, then $f$ is one-to-one.

▐   Suppose $f$ is not one-to-one. Then there exists distinct elements $x, y \in A$ for which $f(x) = f(y)$. Thus $(g \circ f)(x) = g(f(x)) = g(f(y)) = (g \circ f)(y)$; hence $g \circ f$ is not one-to-one. Therefore, if $g \circ f$ is one-to-one, then $f$ must be one-to-one.

**3.120**   Given $f: A \to B$ and $g: B \to C$. Show that if $g \circ f$ is onto, then $g$ is onto.

▐   If $a \in A$, then $(g \circ f)(a) = g(f(a)) \in g(B)$; hence $(g \circ f)(A) \subseteq g(B)$. Suppose $g$ is not onto. Then $g(B)$ is properly contained in $C$ and so $(g \circ f)(A)$ is properly contained in $C$; thus $g \circ f$ is not onto. Accordingly, if $g \circ f$ is onto, then $g$ must be onto.

**3.121**   Prove Theorem 3.2. A function $f: A \to B$ has an inverse if and only if $f$ is bijective (one-to-one and onto).

▐   Suppose $f$ has an inverse, i.e., there exists a function $f^{-1}: B \to A$ for which $f^{-1} \circ f = 1_A$ and $f \circ f^{-1} = 1_B$. Since $1_A$ is one-to-one, $f$ is one-to-one by Problem 3.119; and since $1_B$ is onto, $f$ is onto by Problem 3.120. That is, $f$ is both one-to-one and onto.

Now suppose $f$ is both one-to-one and onto. Then each $b \in B$ is the image of a unique element in $A$, say $\hat{b}$. Thus if $f(a) = b$, then $a = \hat{b}$; hence $f(\hat{b}) = b$. Now let $g$ denote the mapping from $B$ to $A$ defined by $g(b) = \hat{b}$. We have:
  (i)   $(g \circ f)(a) = g(f(a)) = g(b) = \hat{b} = a$, for every $a \in A$; hence $g \circ f = 1_A$.
  (ii)   $(f \circ g)(b) = f(g(b)) = f(\hat{b}) = b$, for every $b \in B$; hence $f \circ g = 1_B$.
Accordingly, $f$ has an inverse. Its inverse is the mapping $g$.

**3.122**   Let $P = \{A_i\}$ be a partition of a set $S$. **(a)** Define the natural (or canonical) map $f$ from $S$ to $P$. **(b)** Prove that the natural map $f: S \to P$ is an onto function.

▐   **(a)**   Let $s \in S$. Since $P$ is a partition of $S$, there is a unique index $i_0$ such that $s \in A_{i_0}$. Define $f: S \to P$ by $f(s) = A_{i_0}$. This is the natural map.
    **(b)**   Let $A_i \in P$. Then $A_i \neq \emptyset$. Thus there exists $s \in S$ such that $s \in A_i$ and so $f(s) = A_i$. Thus $f$ is an onto mapping.

**3.123**   Let $S$ be a subset of $A$ and let $i: S \hookrightarrow A$ be the inclusion map (Problem 3.30). Show that the inclusion map $i$ is one-to-one.

▐   Suppose $i(x) = i(y)$. Note $i(x) = x$ and $i(y) = y$. Hence $x = y$ and $i$ is one-to-one.

**3.124** Determine whether or not a constant function can be *(a)* one-to-one, *(b)* an onto function.

 ▎ *(a)* A constant function is one-to-one if and only if the domain consists of exactly one element.
   *(b)* A constant function is an onto function if and only if the codomain consists of exactly one element.

**3.125** On which sets $A$ will the identity function $1_A: A \rightarrow A$ be *(a)* one-to-one? *(b)* an onto function?

 ▎ For any set $A$, the identity function $1_A$ is both one-to-one and onto (and hence invertible).

**3.126** Find the "largest" interval $D$ on which the formula $f(x) = x^2$ defines a one-to-one function.

 ▎ As long as the interval $D$ contains either positive or negative numbers, but not both, the function will be one-to-one. Thus $D$ can be the infinite interval

$$[0, \infty) = \{x : x \geq 0\} \qquad \text{or} \qquad (-\infty, 0] = \{x : x \leq 0\}$$

There can be other intervals on which $f$ will be one-to-one, but they will be subsets of one of these two intervals.

**3.127** Describe the relationship between the graph of a function $y = f(x)$ and the graph of the inverse function $y = f^{-1}(x)$.

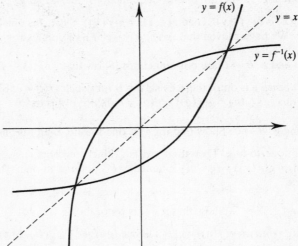

**Fig. 3-27**

 ▎ The ordered pair $(a, b)$ belongs to the graph of $f$ if and only if the reversed pair $(b, a)$ belongs to $f^{-1}$. Thus the graph of $f^{-1}$ may be obtained from the graph of $f$ by reflecting $f$ in the line $y = x$ as shown in Fig. 3-27.

**3.128** Find the graphs of the inverses of the functions $f(x) = 2^x$, $g(x) = x^3 - x$, and $h(x) = x^2$ sketched in Fig. 3-24. Which of these graphs define a function?

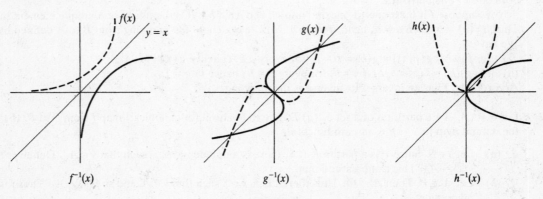

**Fig. 3-28**

 ▎ Reflect each graph in the line $y = x$ as in Fig. 3-28. The graphs $g^{-1}$ and $h^{-1}$ are not functions since there are vertical lines which intersect the graph in more than one point. However, as noted in Problem 3.108, $f^{-1}$ does define a function with domain $D = \{x : x > 0\}$.

## 3.5 MATHEMATICAL FUNCTIONS AND COMPUTER SCIENCE

This section gives various mathematical functions which also appear in computer science, together with their notation.

### Floor and Ceiling Functions

**3.129** Define the floor and ceiling functions.

▎ Let $x$ be any real number. Then $x$ lies between two integers called the floor and the ceiling of $x$. Specifically;
$\lfloor x \rfloor$, called the *floor* of $x$, denotes the greatest integer that does not exceed $x$.
$\lceil x \rceil$, called the *ceiling* of $x$, denotes the least integer that is not less than $x$.
If $x$ is itself an integer, then $\lfloor x \rfloor = \lceil x \rceil$; otherwise $\lfloor x \rfloor + 1 = \lceil x \rceil$.

**3.130** Find: **(a)** $\lfloor 7.5 \rfloor$, $\lfloor -7.5 \rfloor$, $\lfloor -18 \rfloor$; and **(b)** $\lceil 7.5 \rceil$, $\lceil -7.5 \rceil$, $\lceil -18 \rceil$,

▎ **(a)** By definition, $\lfloor x \rfloor$ denotes the greatest integer that does not exceed $x$, hence $\lfloor 7.5 \rfloor = 7$, $\lfloor -7.5 \rfloor = -8$, $\lfloor -18 \rfloor = -18$.

**(b)** By definition, $\lceil x \rceil$ denotes the least integer that is not less than $x$, hence $\lceil 7.5 \rceil = 8$, $\lceil -7.5 \rceil = -7$, $\lceil -18 \rceil = -18$.

**3.131** Find: **(a)** $\lfloor 3.14 \rfloor$, $\lfloor \sqrt{5} \rfloor$, $\lfloor -8.5 \rfloor$, $\lfloor 7 \rfloor$; and **(b)** $\lceil 3.14 \rceil$, $\lceil \sqrt{5} \rceil$, $\lceil -8.5 \rceil$, $\lceil 7 \rceil$.

▎ **(a)** $\lfloor 3.14 \rfloor = 3$, $\lfloor \sqrt{5} \rfloor = 2$, $\lfloor -8.5 \rfloor = -9$, $\lfloor 7 \rfloor = 7$;　　**(b)** $\lceil 3.14 \rceil = 4$, $\lceil \sqrt{5} \rceil = 3$, $\lceil -8.5 \rceil = -8$, $\lceil 7 \rceil = 7$.

**3.132** Find: **(a)** $\lfloor \sqrt{30} \rfloor$, $\lfloor \sqrt[3]{30} \rfloor$, $\lfloor \pi \rfloor$; and **(b)** $\lceil \sqrt{30} \rceil$, $\lceil \sqrt[3]{30} \rceil$, $\lceil \pi \rceil$.

▎ **(a)** $\lfloor \sqrt{30} \rfloor = 5$, $\lfloor \sqrt[3]{30} \rfloor = 3$, $\lfloor \pi \rfloor = 3$;　　**(b)** $\lceil \sqrt{30} \rceil = 6$, $\lceil \sqrt[3]{30} \rceil = 4$, $\lceil \pi \rceil = 4$.

**3.133** Plot the graph of $f(x) = \lceil x \rceil - \lfloor x \rfloor$.

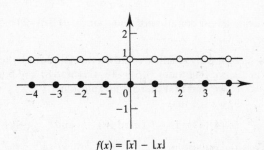

$$f(x) = \lceil x \rceil - \lfloor x \rfloor$$　　　　**Fig. 3-29**

▎ Here $f(x) = 0$ if $x$ is an integer and $f(x) = 1$ otherwise, as shown in Fig. 3-29.

### Remainder Function; Modular Arithmetic

**3.134** Let $k$ be any integer and let $M$ be a positive integer. Define $k \pmod M$ which is read "$k$ modulo $M$".

▎ Now $k \pmod M$ denotes the integer remainder when $k$ is divided by $M$. More exactly, $k \pmod M$ is the unique integer $r$ such that $k = Mq + r$ where $0 \le r < M$ and $q$ is the quotient.

**3.135** Find $25 \pmod 7$, $25 \pmod 5$, $35 \pmod{11}$, $3 \pmod 8$.

▎ When $k$ is positive, simply divide $k$ by $M$ to obtain the remainder $r$. Then $r = k \pmod M$. Thus

$$25 \pmod 7 = 4, \qquad 25 \pmod 5 = 0, \qquad 35 \pmod{11} = 2, \qquad 3 \pmod 8 = 3$$

**3.136** Find $26 \pmod 7$, $34 \pmod 8$, $2345 \pmod 6$, $495 \pmod{11}$.

▎ Since $k$ is positive, simply divide $k$ by $M$ to obtain the remainder $r$. Then $r = k \pmod M$ and so

$$26 \pmod 7 = 5, \qquad 34 \pmod 8 = 2, \qquad 2345 \pmod 6 = 5, \qquad 495 \pmod{11} = 0$$

**3.137** Find $-26 \pmod 7$, $-2345 \pmod 6$, $-371 \pmod 6$, $-39 \pmod 3$.

▎ Since $k$ is negative, divide $|k|$ by the modulus to obtain the remainder $r'$. Then $k \pmod M = M - r'$ when

$r' \neq 0$. Thus

$$-26 \,(\text{mod } 7) = 7 - 5 = 2, \qquad -2345 \,(\text{mod } 6) = 6 - 5 = 1, \qquad -371 \,(\text{mod } 8) = 8 - 3 = 5, \qquad -39 \,(\text{mod } 3) = 0$$

**Remark:** The term "mod" is also used for the mathematical congruence relation, which is denoted and defined as follows:

$$a \equiv b \,(\text{mod } M) \qquad \text{if and only if} \qquad M \text{ divides } b - a$$

$M$ is called the *modulus*, and $a \equiv b \,(\text{mod } M)$ is read "$a$ is congruent to $b$ modulo $M$". The following aspects of the congruence relation are frequently useful:

$$0 \equiv M \,(\text{mod } M) \qquad \text{and} \qquad a \pm M \equiv a \,(\text{mod } M)$$

**3.138** Explain the meaning of the expression "arithmetic modulo $M$".

▮ *Arithmetic modulo $M$* refers to the arithmetic operations of addition, multiplication, and subtraction where the arithmetic value is replaced by its equivalent value in the set

$$\{0, 1, 2, \ldots, M-1\} \quad \text{or in the set} \quad \{1, 2, 3, \ldots, M\}$$

For example, in arithmetic modulo 12, sometimes called "clock" arithmetic,

$$6 + 9 \equiv 3, \quad 7 \times 5 \equiv 11, \quad 1 - 5 \equiv 8, \quad 2 + 10 \equiv 0 \equiv 12$$

(The use of 0 or $M$ depends on the application.)

**3.139** Using arithmetic modulo 15, evaluate $9 + 13$, $7 + 11$, $4 - 9$, $2 - 10$.

▮ Use $a \pm M \equiv a \,(\text{mod } M)$:

$$9 + 13 = 22 \equiv 22 - 15 = 7, \quad 7 + 11 = 18 \equiv 18 - 15 = 3, \quad 4 - 9 = -5 \equiv -5 + 15 = 10, \quad 2 - 10 = -8 \equiv -8 + 15 = 7$$

**3.140** Solve each of the following linear congruence equations: (**a**) $3x \equiv 2 \,(\text{mod } 8)$, (**b**) $6x \equiv 5 \,(\text{mod } 9)$, (**c**) $4x \equiv 6 \,(\text{mod } 10)$.

▮ Since each modulus is relatively small, we find all the solutions by testing:
(**a**) Testing $0, 1, 2, \ldots, 7$, we find that $(3)(6) = 18 \equiv 2 \,(\text{mod } 8)$ and 6 is the only solution.
(**b**) Testing $0, 1, 2, \ldots, 8$, we find that there is no solution.
(**c**) Testing $0, 1, 2, \ldots, 9$, we see that

$$(4)(4) = 16 \equiv 6 \,(\text{mod } 10) \qquad \text{and} \qquad (4)(9) = 36 \equiv 6 \,(\text{mod } 10)$$

and that 4 and 9 are the only solutions.

## Factorial Function

**3.141** Define the factorial function.

▮ The product of the positive integers from 1 to $n$, inclusive, is denoted by $n!$ (read "$n$ factorial"). That is,

$$n! = 1 \cdot 2 \cdot 3 \cdots (n-2)(n-1)n$$

It is also convenient to define $0! = 1$.

**3.142** Find $2!$, $3!$, and $4!$

▮ Multiply the integers from 1 to $n$:

$$2! = 1 \cdot 2 = 2, \qquad 3! = 1 \cdot 2 \cdot 3 = 6, \qquad 4! = 1 \cdot 2 \cdot 3 \cdot 4 = 24$$

**3.143** Find $5!$, $6!$, $7!$, and $8!$.

▮ For $n > 1$, we have $n! = n \cdot (n-1)!$ Hence

$$5! = 5 \cdot 4! = 5 \cdot 24 = 120, \quad 6! = 6 \cdot 5! = 6 \cdot 120 = 720, \quad 7! = 7 \cdot 6! = 7 \cdot 720 = 5040, \quad 8! = 8 \cdot 7! = 8 \cdot 5040 = 40\,320$$

**3.144** Compute: (**a**) $\dfrac{13!}{11!}$, and (**b**) $\dfrac{7!}{10!}$.

**(a)** $\dfrac{13!}{11!} = \dfrac{13 \cdot 12 \cdot 11 \cdot 10 \cdot 9 \cdot 8 \cdot 7 \cdot 6 \cdot 5 \cdot 4 \cdot 3 \cdot 2 \cdot 1}{11 \cdot 10 \cdot 9 \cdot 8 \cdot 7 \cdot 6 \cdot 5 \cdot 4 \cdot 3 \cdot 2 \cdot 1} = 13 \cdot 12 = 156$ or $\dfrac{13!}{11!} = \dfrac{13 \cdot 12 \cdot 11!}{11!} = 13 \cdot 12 = 156$

**(b)** $\dfrac{7!}{10!} = \dfrac{7!}{10 \cdot 9 \cdot 8 \cdot 7!} = \dfrac{1}{10 \cdot 9 \cdot 8} = \dfrac{1}{720}$

**3.145** Find all solutions of $(n!)! = (2n)!$.

By trial: $n = 0$ (*yes*); $n = 1$ (*no*); $n = 2$ (*no*); $n = 3$ (*yes*). For $n \geq 4$,

$$n! = n[(n-1)\cdots 3]2 \geq n[3]2 > 2n$$

so that $(n!)! > (2n)!$; thus no further solutions exist.

**3.146** Simplify: **(a)** $\dfrac{n!}{(n-1)!}$, and **(b)** $\dfrac{(n+2)!}{n!}$.

**(a)** $\dfrac{n!}{(n-1)!} = \dfrac{n(n-1)(n-2)\cdots 3 \cdot 2 \cdot 1}{(n-1)(n-2)\cdots 3 \cdot 2 \cdot 1} = n$ or, simply, $\dfrac{n!}{(n-1)!} = \dfrac{n(n-1)!}{(n-1)!} = n$

**(b)** $\dfrac{(n+2)!}{n!} = \dfrac{(n+2)(n+1)n(n-1)(n-2)\cdots 3 \cdot 2 \cdot 1}{n(n-1)(n-2)\cdots 3 \cdot 2 \cdot 1} = (n+2)(n+1) = n^2 + 3n + 2$

or, simply, $\dfrac{(n+2)!}{n!} = \dfrac{(n+2)(n+1) \cdot n!}{n!} = (n+2)(n+1) = n^2 + 3n + 2$

**3.147** Simplify: **(a)** $\dfrac{(n+1)!}{(n-1)!}$, and **(b)** $\dfrac{(n-1)!}{(n+2)!}$.

**(a)** $\dfrac{(n+1)!}{(n-1)!} = \dfrac{(n+1)n(n-1)(n-2)\cdots 3 \cdot 2 \cdot 1}{(n-1)(n-2)\cdots 3 \cdot 2 \cdot 1} = (n+1) \cdot n = n^2 + n$

or, simply, $\dfrac{(n+1)!}{(n-1)!} = \dfrac{(n+1) \cdot n \cdot (n-1)!}{(n-1)!} = (n+1) \cdot n = n^2 + n$

**(b)** $\dfrac{(n-1)!}{(n+2)!} = \dfrac{(n-1)!}{(n+2)(n+1) \cdot n \cdot (n-1)!} = \dfrac{1}{(n+2)(n+1) \cdot n} = \dfrac{1}{n^3 + 3n^2 + 2n}$

## Exponential and Logarithmic Functions

**3.148** Explain how the exponential function $f(x) = a^x$ is defined.

The function $f(x) = a^x$ is defined for integer exponents (where $m$ is a positive integer) by

$$a^m = a \cdot a \cdots a \ (m \text{ times}), \qquad a^0 = 1, \qquad a^{-m} = \frac{1}{a^m}$$

Exponents are extended to include all rational numbers by defining, for any rational number $m/n$,

$$a^{m/n} = \sqrt[n]{a^m} = (\sqrt[n]{a})^m$$

Exponents are extended to include all real numbers by defining, for any real number $x$,

$$a^x = \lim_{r \to x} a^r$$

where $r$ approaches $x$ through rational values.

**3.149** Evaluate $2^4$, $2^{-4}$, and $125^{2/3}$.

By definition,

$$2^4 = 2 \cdot 2 \cdot 2 \cdot 2 = 16, \qquad 2^{-4} = \frac{1}{2^4} = \frac{1}{16}, \qquad 125^{2/3} = (\sqrt[3]{125})^2 = 5^2 = 25$$

**3.150** Evaluate $2^{-5}$, $8^{2/3}$, and $25^{-3/2}$.

By definition,

$$2^{-5} = 1/2^5 = 1/32, \quad 8^{2/3} = (\sqrt[3]{8})^2 = 2^2 = 4, \qquad 25^{-3/2} = 1/25^{3/2} = 1/5^3 = 1/125$$

**3.151** Explain how the logarithmic function $g(x) = \log_b (x)$ is defined.

**❙** Logarithms are related to exponents as follows. Let $b$ be a positive number. The logarithm of any positive number $x$ to the base $b$, written

$$\log_b x$$

represents the exponent to which $b$ must be raised to obtain $x$. That is,

$$y = \log_b x \quad \text{and} \quad b^y = x$$

are equivalent statements. Accordingly, for any base $b$, $\log_b 1 = 0$ since $b^0 = 1$, and $\log_b b = 1$ since $b^1 = b$.
The logarithm of a negative number and the logarithm of 0 are not defined.

**3.152** Evaluate: **(a)** $\log_2 8$, **(b)** $\log_2 64$, **(c)** $\log_{10} 100$, and **(d)** $\log_{10} 0.001$.

**❙** **(a)** $\log_2 8 = 3$ since $2^3 = 8$      **(c)** $\log_{10} 100 = 2$ since $10^2 = 100$
    **(b)** $\log_2 64 = 6$ since $2^6 = 64$    **(d)** $\log_{10} 0.001 = -3$ since $10^{-3} = 0.001$

**Remark:** Frequently, logarithms are expressed using approximate values. For example, using tables or calculators, we obtain

$$\log_{10} 300 = 2.4771 \quad \text{and} \quad \log_e 40 = 3.6889$$

as approximate answers. (Here $e = 2.718281 \cdots$.)

**3.153** Evaluate: **(a)** $\log_2 32$, **(b)** $\log_{10} 1000$, and **(c)** $\log_2 (1/16)$.

**❙** **(a)** $\log_2 32 = 5$ since $2^5 = 32$,     **(b)** $\log_{10} 1000 = 3$ since $10^3 = 1000$,     **(c)** $\log_2 (1/16) = -4$ since $2^{-4} = 1/2^4 = 1/16$.

**3.154** Find: **(a)** $\lfloor \log_2 1000 \rfloor$, **(b)** $\lfloor \log_2 0.01 \rfloor$.

**❙** **(a)** $\lfloor \log_2 1000 \rfloor = 9$ since $2^9 = 512$ but $2^{10} = 1024$.
    **(b)** $\lfloor \log_2 0.01 \rfloor = -7$ since $2^{-7} = 1/128 < 0.01 < 2^{-6} = 1/64$.

**Remark:** The exponential and logarithmic functions $f(x) = b^x$ and $g(x) = \log_b x$ may also be viewed as inverse functions of each other. Accordingly, the graphs of these two functions are related as illustrated in Problem 3.155.

**3.155** Plot the graphs of the exponential function $f(x) = 2^x$, the logarithmic function $g(x) = \log_2 x$, and the linear function $h(x) = x$ on the same coordinate axes. **(a)** Describe a geometric property of the graphs $f(x)$ and $g(x)$. **(b)** For any positive number $c$, how are $f(c)$, $g(c)$, and $h(c)$ related?

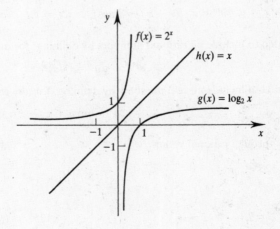

**Fig. 3-30**

**❙** The graphs of the three functions are shown in Fig. 3-30.
**(a)** Since $f(x) = 2^x$ and $g(x) = \log_2 x$ are inverse functions, they are symmetric with respect to the line $y = x$.
**(b)** For any positive number $c$, we have

$$g(c) < h(c) < f(c)$$

In fact, as $c$ increases in value, the vertical distances $h(c) - g(c)$ and $f(c) - h(c)$ increase in value. Moreover, the logarithmic function $g(x)$ grows very slowly compared with the linear function $h(x)$, and the exponential function $f(x)$ grows very quickly compared with $h(x)$.

## Rate of Growth; Big $O$ Notation

**3.156** Discuss the rate of growth of the following standard functions:

$$\log_2 n, \quad n, \quad n \log_2 n, \quad n^2, \quad n^3, \quad 2^n$$

▌ The rates of growth for these standard functions are indicated in Fig. 3-31, which gives their approximate values for certain values of $n$. Observe that the functions are listed in the order of their rates of growth: the logarithmic function $\log_2 n$ grows most slowly, the exponential function $2^n$ grows most rapidly, and the polynomial functions $n^c$ grow according to the exponent $c$.

| $n$ ＼ $g(n)$ | $\log_2 n$ | $n$ | $n \log_2 n$ | $n^2$ | $n^3$ | $2^n$ |
|---|---|---|---|---|---|---|
| 5 | 3 | 5 | 15 | 25 | 125 | 32 |
| 10 | 4 | 10 | 40 | 100 | $10^3$ | $10^3$ |
| 100 | 7 | 100 | 700 | $10^4$ | $10^6$ | $10^{30}$ |
| 1000 | 10 | $10^3$ | $10^4$ | $10^6$ | $10^9$ | $10^{300}$ |

**Fig. 3-31** Rate of growth of standard functions.

**3.157** Interpret the rate of increase of an arbitrary function $f(n)$.

▌ This is usually accomplished comparing $f(n)$ with some standard function, such as one of the functions in Problem 3.156. One way to do this is to use the functional "Big $O$" notation defined in Problem 3.158.

**3.158** Explain the meaning of the "Big $O$" notation.

▌ Suppose $f(n)$ and $g(n)$ are functions defined on the positive integers with the property that $f(n)$ is bounded by some multiple of $g(n)$ for almost all $n$. That is, suppose there exist a positive integer $n_0$ and a positive number $M$ such that, for all $n > n_0$, we have

$$|f(n)| \leq M \, |g(n)|$$

In this event we write $\qquad f(n) = O(g(n))$

which is read "$f(n)$ is of order $g(n)$". We also write

$$f(n) = h(n) + O(g(n)) \qquad \text{when} \qquad f(n) - h(n) = O(g(n))$$

(This is called the "big $O$" notation since $f(n) = o(g(n))$ has an entirely different meaning.)

**3.159** Suppose $P(n) = a_0 + a_1 n + a_2 n^2 + \cdots + a_m n^m$; that is, suppose degree $P(n) = m$. Prove that $P(n) = O(n^m)$.

▌ Let $b_0 = |a_0|$, $b_1 = |a_1|$, ..., $b_m = |a_m|$. Then, for $n \geq 1$,

$$P(n) \leq b_0 + b_1 n + b_2 n^2 + \cdots + b_m n^m = \left( \frac{b_0}{n^m} + \frac{b_1}{n^{m-1}} + \cdots + b_m \right) n^m$$

$$\leq (b_0 + b_1 + \cdots + b_m) n^m = M n^m$$

where $M = |a_0| + |a_1| + \cdots + |a_m|$. Hence $P(n) = O(n^m)$. [Also recall Problem 3.60.]
  For example, $5x^3 + 3x = O(x^3)$ and $x^5 - 4\,000\,000 x^2 = O(x^5)$.

**3.160** Compare the rate of growth of the factorial function $f(n) = n!$ to the functions in Fig. 3-31.

▌ The factorial function $f(n) = n!$ grows faster than the exponential function $2^n$. Clearly, for $n \geq 4$,

$$2^n = 2 \cdot 2 \cdot \cdots \cdot 2 \leq 1 \cdot 2 \cdot 3 \cdot \cdots \cdot (n-1) n$$

In fact, $f(n) = n!$ grows faster than the exponential function $c^n$ for any constant $c$.

## 3.6 RECURSIVELY DEFINED FUNCTIONS

**3.161** What is meant by a *recursively defined* function?

❚ A function is said to be recursively defined if the function definition refers to itself. In order for the definition not to be circular, it must have the following two properties:
(1) There must be certain arguments, called *base values,* for which the function does not refer to itself.
(2) Each time the function does refer to itself, the argument of the function must be closer to a base value.
A recursive function with these two properties is also said to be well-defined.

**3.162** Consider the following definition of *n* factorial:
*Definition* (Factorial Function):
      **(a)** If $n = 0$, then $n! = 1$.
      **(b)** If $n > 0$, then $n! = n \cdot (n - 1)!$
Show that this definition is recursive and that the function is well-defined.

❚ This definition of $n!$ is recursive, since it refers to itself when it uses $(n - 1)!$ However, **(a)** the value of $n!$ is explicitly given when $n = 0$ (thus 0 is the base value); and **(b)** the value of $n!$ for arbitrary $n$ is defined in terms of a smaller value of $n$ which is closer to the base value 0. Accordingly, the definition is not circular, or in other words, the factorial function is well-defined.

**3.163** Calculate 4! using the recursive definition in Problem 3.162.

❚ This calculation requires the following nine steps:
(1)   $4! = 4 \cdot 3!$
(2)       $3! = 3 \cdot 2!$
(3)           $2! = 2 \cdot 1!$
(4)              $1! = 1 \cdot 0!$
(5)                 $0! = 1$
(6)              $1! = 1 \cdot 1 \ = 1$
(7)           $2! = 2 \cdot 1 \ = 2$
(8)       $3! = 3 \cdot 2 = 6$
(9)   $4! = 4 \cdot 6 \ = 24$
That is:
*Step 1:* This defines 4! in terms of 3!, so we must postpone evaluating 4! until we evaluate 3! This postponement is indicated by indenting the next step.
*Step 2:* Here 3! is defined in terms of 2! so we must postpone evaluating 3! until we evaluate 2!.
*Step 3:* This defines 2! in term of 1!.
*Step 4:* This defines 1! in terms of 0!.
*Step 5:* This step can explicitly evaluate 0!, since 0 is the base value of the recursive definition.
*Steps 6 to 9:* We backtrack, using 0! to find 1!, using 1! to find 2!, using 2! to find 3!, and finally using 3! to find 4!. This backtracking is indicated by the "reverse" indention.

**3.164** Let $a$ and $b$ denote positive integers. Suppose a function $Q$ is defined recursively as follows:

$$Q(a, b) = \begin{cases} 0 & \text{if} \quad a < b \\ Q(a - b, b) + 1 & \text{if} \quad b \le a \end{cases}$$

**(a)** Find the value of $Q(2, 3)$ and $Q(14, 3)$.
**(b)** What does this function do? Find $Q(5861, 7)$.

❚ **(a)**                         $Q(2, 3) = 0$     since     $2 < 3$
$$Q(14, 3) = Q(11, 3) + 1$$
$$= [Q(8, 3) + 1] + 1 = Q(8, 3) + 2$$
$$= [Q(5, 3) + 1] + 2 = Q(5, 3) + 3$$
$$= [Q(2, 3) + 1] + 3 = Q(2, 3) + 4$$
$$= 0 + 4 = 4$$

**(b)** Each time $b$ is subtracted from $a$, the value of $Q$ is increased by 1. Hence $Q(a, b)$ finds the quotient when $a$ is divided by $b$. Thus $Q(5861, 7) = 837$.

**3.165** Let $n$ denote a positive integer. Suppose a function $L$ is defined recursively as follows:

$$L(n) = \begin{cases} 0 & \text{if } n = 1 \\ L(\lfloor n/2 \rfloor) + 1 & \text{if } n > 1 \end{cases}$$

(Here $\lfloor k \rfloor$ denotes the "floor" of $k$, that is, the greatest integer which does not exceed $k$.)
**(a)** Find $L(25)$. **(b)** What does this function do?

**█ (a)**
$$L(25) = L(12) + 1$$
$$= [L(6) + 1] + 1 = L(6) + 2$$
$$= [L(3) + 1] + 2 = L(3) + 3$$
$$= [L(1) + 1] + 3 = L(1) + 4$$
$$= 0 + 4 = 4$$

**(b)** Each time $n$ is divided by 2, the value of $L$ is increased by 1. Hence $L$ is the greatest integer such that

$$2^L \le n$$

Accordingly, $L(n) = \lfloor \log_2 n \rfloor$.

## Fibonacci Sequence

**3.166** The celebrated Fibonacci sequence (usually denoted by $F_0, F_1, F_2, \ldots$) is as follows:

$$0, 1, 1, 2, 3, 5, 8, 13, 21, 34, 55, \ldots$$

That is, $F_0 = 0$ and $F_1 = 1$ and each succeeding term is the sum of the two preceding terms. A formal definition of this function follows:
*Definition* (Fibonacci Sequence):
    **(a)** If $n = 0$ or $n = 1$, then $F_n = n$.
    **(b)** If $n > 1$, then $F_n = F_{n-2} + F_{n-1}$.
Show that this definition is recursive and that the function is well-defined.

**█** The above is a recursive definition, since the definition refers to itself when it uses $F_{n-2}$ and $F_{n-1}$. Here **(a)** the base values are 0 and 1, and **(b)** the value of $F_n$ is defined in terms of smaller values of $n$ which are closer to the base values. Accordingly, this function is well-defined.

**3.167** Find the next two terms of the Fibonacci sequence in Problem 3.166, i.e., find the next two terms after 55.

**█** We have $F_{11} = 34 + 55 = 89$ and $F_{12} = 55 + 89 = 144$.

**3.168** Find $F_{16}$ in the Fibonacci sequence.

**█** Although $F_n$ is defined recursively, it is easier to evaluate $F_{16}$ by using iteration (that is, by evaluating from the bottom up), rather than by using recursion (that is, evaluating from the top down). In particular, each Fibonacci number is the sum of the two preceding Fibonacci numbers. Beginning with $F_{11} = 89$ and $F_{12} = 144$ (see Problem 3.167), we have

$$F_{13} = 89 + 144 = 233, \qquad F_{14} = 144 + 233 = 377, \qquad F_{15} = 233 + 377 = 610$$

and hence $F_{16} = 377 + 610 = 987$.

## Ackermann Function

**3.169** The Ackermann function is a function with two arguments each of which can be assigned any nonnegative integer: $0, 1, 2, \ldots$. This function is defined as follows:
*Definition* (Ackermann Function):
    **(a)** If $m = 0$, then $A(m, n) = n + 1$.
    **(b)** If $m \ne 0$ but $n = 0$, then $A(m, n) = A(m - 1, 1)$.
    **(c)** If $m \ne 0$ and $n \ne 0$, then $A(m, n) = A(m - 1, A(m, n - 1))$
Show that this function is recursively defined. What are the base values?

**█** The above is a recursive definition, since the definition refers to itself in parts **(b)** and **(c)**. Observe that $A(m, n)$ is explicitly given only when $m = 0$. Thus the base values are the pairs

$$(0, 0), (0, 1), (0, 2), (0, 3), \ldots, (0, n), \ldots$$

Although it is not obvious from the definition, the value of any $A(m, n)$ may eventually be expressed in terms of the value of the function on one or more of the base pairs.

**Remark:** The value of $A(1, 3)$ is calculated in Problem 3.170. Even this simple case requires 15 steps. Generally speaking, the Ackermann function is too complex to evaluate except in trivial cases. Its importance comes from its use in mathematical logic.

**3.170** Use the definition of the Ackermann function to find $A(1, 3)$.

▮ We have the following 15 steps:
(1)  $A(1, 3) = A(0, A(1, 2))$
(2)   $A(1, 2) = A(0, A(1, 1))$
(3)    $A(1, 1) = A(0, A(1, 0))$
(4)     $A(1, 0) = A(0, 1)$
(5)      $A(0, 1) = 1 + 1 = 2$
(6)     $A(1, 0) = 2$
(7)    $A(1, 1) = A(0, 2)$
(8)     $A(0, 2) = 2 + 1 = 3$
(9)    $A(1, 1) = 3$
(10)   $A(1, 2) = A(0, 3)$
(11)    $A(0, 3) = 3 + 1 = 4$
(12)   $A(1, 2) = 4$
(13)  $A(1, 3) = A(0, 4)$
(14)   $A(0, 4) = 4 + 1 = 5$
(15)  $A(1, 3) = 5$

The forward indention indicates that we are postponing an evaluation and are recalling the definition, and the backward indention indicates that we are backtracking.

Observe that (**a**) of the definition is used in Steps 5, 8, 11 and 14; (**b**) in Step 4; and (**c**) in Steps 1, 2 and 3. In the other Steps we are backtracking with substitutions.

## 3.7 INDEXED CLASSES OF SETS

**3.171** Explain the meaning of an indexing function.

▮ Let $I$ be a nonempty set, and let $S$ be a collection of sets. An indexing function from $I$ to $S$ is a function $f: I \rightarrow S$. For any $i \in I$, we denote the image $f(i)$ by $A_i$. Thus the indexing function $f$ is usually denoted by

$$\{A_i: i \in I\} \quad \text{or} \quad \{A_i\}_{i \in I} \quad \text{or simply} \quad \{A_i\}$$

The set $I$ is called the *indexing set*, and the elements of $I$ are called *indices*. If $f$ is one-to-one and onto, we say that $S$ is indexed by $I$.

**3.172** Show how the set operations of union and intersection may be defined for classes of sets.

▮ The union and intersection of an indexed class of sets, say $\{A_i: i \in I\}$, are defined, respectively, as follows:

$$\bigcup_{i \in I} A_i = \{x: x \in A_i \text{ for some } i \in I\}$$

and

$$\bigcap_{i \in I} A_i = \{x: x \in A_i \text{ for all } i \in I\}$$

In the case that $I$ is a finite set, these are just the same as our previous definitions of union and intersection. If $I$ is **N**, we may denote the union and intersection by

$$A_1 \cup A_2 \cup \cdots \quad \text{and} \quad A_1 \cap A_2 \cap \cdots$$

respectively.

**3.173** For each positive integer $n$ in **N**, let $D_n$ be the following subset of **N**:

$$D_n = \{n, 2n, 3n, 4n, \ldots\} = \{\text{multiples of } n\}$$

Find: (**a**) $D_3 \cap D_5$, (**b**) $D_4 \cup D_8$, and (**c**) $D_3 \cap D_6$.

▮ (**a**) $D_3 \cap D_5$ consists of multiples of 3 and also multiples of 5, and so consists of multiples of 15. Thus $D_3 \cap D_5 = D_{15}$.

(b)   $D_8 \subseteq D_4$ because every multiple of 8 is also a multiple of 4; hence $D_4 \cup D_8 = D_4$.

(c)   $D_6 \subseteq D_3$ because every multiple of 6 is also a multiple of 3; hence $D_3 \cap D_6 = D_6$.

**3.174**   For the sets $D_n = \{n, 2n, 3n, \ldots\}$ in Problem 3.173, find: (a) $\bigcup \{D_n: n \in \mathbf{N}\}$, (b) $\bigcap \{D_n: n \in \mathbf{N}\}$, and (c) $\bigcup \{D_p: p$ is a prime number$\}$.

   (a)   Each $m \in \mathbf{N}$ belongs to $D_m$; hence $\bigcup \{D_n: n \in \mathbf{N}\} = \mathbf{N}$.

   (b)   For any $m \in \mathbf{N}$, we have $m \notin D_{m+1}$. Thus $\bigcap \{D_n: n \in \mathbf{N}\} = \varnothing$.

   (c)   $\bigcup_p D_p = \{2, 3, \ldots\} = \mathbf{N} \backslash \{1\}$ because every positive integer except 1 is a multiple of a prime number.

**3.175**   Let $I$ be the set $\mathbf{Z}$ of integers. To each integer $n$ we assign the following subset of $\mathbf{R}$:

$$A_n = \{x: x \le n\}$$

(In other words, $A_n$ is the infinite interval $(-\infty, n]$.) Find $\bigcup_n A_n$ and $\bigcap_n A_n$.

   For any real number $a$, there exist integers $n_1$ and $n_2$ such that $n_1 < a < n_2$; so $a \in A_{n_2}$ but $a \notin A_{n_1}$. Hence

$$a \in \bigcup_n A_n \qquad \text{but} \qquad a \notin \bigcap_n A_n$$

Accordingly

$$\bigcup_n A_n = \mathbf{R} \qquad \text{but} \qquad \bigcap_n A_n = \varnothing$$

**3.176**   For any $i \in \mathbf{Z}$, let $B_i = [i, i + 1]$, the closed interval from $i$ to $i + 1$. Find (a) $B_1 \cup B_2$, (b) $B_3 \cap B_4$, (c) $\bigcup_{i=7}^{18} B_i$, and (d) $\bigcup_{i \in \mathbf{Z}} B_i$.

   (a)   $B_1 \cup B_2$ consists of all points in the intervals $[1, 2]$ and $[2, 3]$; hence

$$B_1 \cup B_2 = [1, 3]$$

   (b)   $B_3 \cap B_4$ consists of the points which lie in both $[3, 4]$ and $[4, 5]$; thus

$$B_3 \cap B_4 = \{4\}$$

   (c)   $\bigcup_{i=7}^{18} B_i$ means the union of the sets $[7, 8], [8, 9], \ldots, [18, 19]$; thus

$$\bigcup_{i=7}^{18} B_i = [7, 19]$$

   (d)   Since every real number belongs to at least one interval $[i, i + 1]$, then $\bigcup_{i \in \mathbf{Z}} B_i = \mathbf{R}$.

**3.177**   For any $n \in \mathbf{N}$, let $D_n = (0, 1/n)$, the open interval from 0 to $1/n$. Find: (a) $D_3 \cup D_7$, (b) $D_3 \cap D_{20}$, (c) $D_s \cup D_t$, and (d) $D_s \cap D_t$.

   (a)   Since $(0, 1/3)$ is a superset of $(0, 1/7)$, $D_3 \cup D_7 = D_3$.

   (b)   Since $(0, 1/20)$ is a subset of $(0, 1/3)$, $D_3 \cap D_{20} = D_{20}$.

   (c)   Let $m = \min(s, t)$, that is, the smaller of the two numbers $s$ and $t$; then $D_m$ is equal to $D_s$ or $D_t$ and contains the other as a subset. Hence $D_s \cup D_t = D_m$.

   (d)   Let $M = \max(s, t)$, that is, the larger of the two numbers $s$ and $t$; then $D_s \cap D_t = D_M$.

**3.178**   For the open intervals $D_n = (0, 1/n)$ in Problem 3.177 find: (a) $\bigcup_{n \in A} D_n$, where $A$ is a subset of $\mathbf{N}$, and (b) $\bigcap_{n \in \mathbf{N}} D_n$.

   (a)   Let $a$ be the smallest member of $A$. Then $\bigcup_{n \in A} D_n = D_a$.

   (b)   If $x$ is a real number, then there is at least one natural number $n$ such that $x \notin (0, 1/n)$. Hence $\bigcap_{n \in \mathbf{N}} D_n = \varnothing$.

**3.179**   Show how any collection $\mathscr{B}$ of sets may be viewed as an indexed class of sets.

   The collection $\mathscr{B}$ of sets may be indexed by itself. Specifically, the identity function $i: \mathscr{B} \to \mathscr{B}$ is an indexed class of sets $\{A_i\}_{i \in \mathscr{B}}$ where $A_i \in \mathscr{B}$ and where $i = A_i$. In other words, the index of any set in $\mathscr{B}$ is the set itself.

**3.180**   Prove $B \cap (\bigcup_{i \in I} A_i) = \bigcup_{i \in I} (B \cap A_i)$.

   Let $x$ belong to $B \cap (\bigcup_{i \in I} A_i)$. Then $x \in B$ and $x \in (\bigcup_{i \in I} A_i)$; thus there exists an $i_0$ such that $x \in A_{i_0}$. Hence $x$ belongs to $B \cap A_{i_0}$, which implies $x$ belongs to $\bigcup_{i \in I} (B \cap A_i)$. Therefore,

$$B \cap \left(\bigcup_{i \in I} A_i\right) \subseteq \bigcup_{i \in I} (B \cap A_i)$$

Let $y$ belong to $\bigcup_{i \in I}(B \cap A_i)$. Then there exists an $i_0$ such that $y \in B \cap A_{i_0}$; thus $y \in B$ and $y \in A_{i_0}$. Hence $y$ is a member of $\bigcup_{i \in I} A_i$. Since $y \in B$ and $y \in \bigcup_{i \in I} A_i$, $y$ belongs to $B \cap (\bigcup_{i \in I} A_i)$. Consequently,

$$\bigcup_{i \in I}(B \cap A_i) \subseteq B \cap \left(\bigcup_{i \in I} A_i\right)$$

Both inclusions imply

$$B \cap \left(\bigcup_{i \in I} A_i\right) = \bigcup_{i \in I}(B \cap A_i)$$

**3.181** Let $\{A_i\}_{i \in I}$ be any indexed class of sets and let $i_0 \in I$. Prove:

$$\bigcap_{i \in I} A_i \subseteq A_{i_0} \subseteq \bigcup_{i \in I} A_i$$

▮ Let $x \in \bigcap_{i \in I} A_i$; then $x \in A_i$ for every $i \in I$. In particular, $x \in A_{i_0}$. Hence

$$\bigcap_{i \in I} A_i \subseteq A_{i_0}$$

Let $y \in A_{i_0}$. Since $i_0 \in I$, $y \in \bigcup_{i \in I} A_i$. Consequently, $A_{i_0} \subseteq \bigcup_{i \in I} A_i$.

**3.182** Prove the following generalization of DeMorgan's law: For any class of sets $\{A_i\}$, we have $(\bigcup_i A_i)^c = \bigcap_i A_i^c$.

▮ We have:

$$x \in \left(\bigcup_i A_i\right)^c \quad \text{iff} \quad x \notin \bigcup_i A_i$$
$$\text{iff} \quad \forall i \in I, x \notin A_i$$
$$\text{iff} \quad \forall i \in I, x \in A_i^c$$
$$\text{iff} \quad x \in \bigcap_i A_i^c$$

Therefore, $(\bigcup_i A_i)^c = \bigcap_i A_i^c$. (Here we have used the logical notations iff for "if and only if" and $\forall$ for "for all".)

## 3.8 CARDINALITY, CARDINAL NUMBERS

**3.183** Explain what it means for two sets to have the "same number of elements". How is this related to the notion of a cardinal number?

▮ Two sets $A$ and $B$ are said to have the same number of elements or the same cardinality, or are said to be equipotent, written

$$|A| = |B| \quad \text{or} \quad \text{card}(A) = \text{card}(B)$$

if there exists a one-to-one correspondence $f : A \to B$. This is an equivalence relation on any collection of sets and a cardinal number may be viewed as an equivalence class determined by this relation or simply as a symbol attached to the equivalence class.

**3.184** Define the finite and infinite sets. Give examples of infinite sets.

▮ A set $A$ is finite if $A$ is empty or if $A$ has the same cardinality as the set $\{1, 2, \ldots, n\}$ for some positive integer $n$. A set is infinite if it is not finite. (Alternatively, a set is infinite if it is equipotent to a proper subset of itself.) Familiar examples of infinite sets are the natural numbers $\mathbf{N}$, the integers $\mathbf{Z}$, the rational numbers $\mathbf{Q}$, and the real numbers $\mathbf{R}$.

**Remarks:** (*a*) We use the obvious symbols for the cardinal numbers of finite sets. That is, 0 is assigned to the empty set $\emptyset$, and $n$ is assigned to the set $\{1, 2, \ldots, n\}$. Thus $|A| = n$ if and only if $A$ has the same cardinality as $\{1, 2, \ldots, n\}$ which implies that $A$ has $n$ elements.

(*b*) The cardinal number of the infinite set $\mathbf{N}$ of positive integers is $\aleph_0$ ("aleph-naught"). This symbol was introduced by Cantor. Thus $|A| = \aleph_0$ if and only if $A$ has the same cardinality as $\mathbf{N}$. A set with cardinality $\aleph_0$ is said to be *denumerable* or *countably infinite*. A set which is finite or denumerable is said to be *countable*.

**(c)** The cardinal number of the set $\mathbf{R}$ of real numbers is denoted by $c$. We will show (Problem 3.196) that $|I| = |\mathbf{R}| = c$, where $I = [0, 1]$ is the closed unit interval, and that $\aleph_0 \neq c$. A set $A$ with cardinality $c$ is said to have the power of the continuum.

**3.185** Let $E = \{2, 4, 6, \ldots\}$, the set of even positive integers. Show that $|E| = \aleph_0$.

    ▌ The function $f: \mathbf{N} \to E$, defined by $f(n) = 2n$, is a one-to-one correspondence between the positive integers $\mathbf{N}$ and $E$. Thus $E$ has the same cardinality as $\mathbf{N}$ and so we may write $|E| = \aleph_0$.

**3.186** Find the cardinal number of each set: **(a)** $A = \{a, b, c, \ldots, y, z\}$, **(b)** $B = \{1, -3, 5, 11, -28\}$, and **(c)** $C = \{x : x \in \mathbf{N}, x^2 = 5\}$.

    ▌ **(a)** $|A| = 26$ since there are 26 letters in the English alphabet.
    **(b)** $|B| = 5$.
    **(c)** $|C| = 0$ since there is no positive integer whose square is 5, i.e., since $C$ is empty.

**3.187** Find the cardinal number of each set: **(a)** $A = \{10, 20, 30, 40, \ldots\}$ and **(b)** $B = \{6, 7, 8, 9, \ldots\}$.

    ▌ **(a)** $|A| = \aleph_0$ because $f: \mathbf{N} \to A$, defined by $f(n) = 10n$, is a one-to-one correspondence between $\mathbf{N}$ and $A$.
    **(b)** $|B| = \aleph_0$ because $g: \mathbf{N} \to B$, defined by $g(n) = n + 5$, is a one-to-one correspondence between $\mathbf{N}$ and $B$.

**3.188** Find the cardinal number of each set:
**(a)** $A = \{\text{Monday, Tuesday}, \ldots, \text{Sunday}\}$,
**(b)** $B = \{x : x^2 = 25, 3x = 6\}$,
**(c)** The power set $P(A)$ of $A = \{1, 4, 5, 9\}$.

    ▌ **(a)** $|A| = 7$, since there are seven days in a week.
    **(b)** Here $B$ is empty since no number satisfies both $x^2 = 25$ and $3x = 6$. Thus $|B| = 0$.
    **(c)** Here $A$ has 4 elements, so $P(A)$ has $2^4 = 16$ elements, or $|P(A)| = 16$.

**3.189** Find the cardinal number of each set: **(a)** The collection $X$ of functions from $A = \{a, b, c\}$ into $B = \{1, 2, 3, 4\}$, and **(b)** The set $Y$ of all relations on $A = \{a, b, c\}$.

    ▌ **(a)** Since $A$ has 3 elements and $B$ has 4 elements, $X$ has $4^3 = 64$ elements. Thus $|X| = 64$.
    **(b)** Since $A$ has 3 elements, $A \times A$ has 9 elements. Thus there are $2^9 = 512$ subsets of $A \times A$, i.e., there are 512 relations on $A$. Hence $|Y| = 512$.

**3.190** Show that the set $\mathbf{Z}$ of integers has cardinality $\aleph_0$.

    ▌ The following diagram shows a one-to-one correspondence between $\mathbf{N}$ and $\mathbf{Z}$:

$$\begin{array}{ccccccccc} \mathbf{N} = 1 & 2 & 3 & 4 & 5 & 6 & 7 & 8 & \cdots \\ \downarrow & \downarrow & \downarrow & \downarrow & \downarrow & \downarrow & \downarrow & \downarrow & \\ \mathbf{Z} = 0 & 1 & -1 & 2 & -2 & 3 & -3 & 4 & \cdots \end{array}$$

That is, the following function $f: \mathbf{N} \to \mathbf{Z}$ is one-to-one and onto:

$$f(n) = \begin{cases} n/2 & \text{if } n \text{ is even} \\ (1-n)/2 & \text{if } n \text{ is odd} \end{cases}$$

Accordingly, $|\mathbf{Z}| = |\mathbf{N}| = \aleph_0$.

**3.191** Let $A_1, A_2, \ldots$ be a countable number of finite sets. Prove that the union $S = \bigcup_i A_i$ is countable.

    ▌ Essentially, we list the elements of $A_1$, then we list the elements of $A_2$ which do not belong to $A_1$, then we list the elements of $A_3$ which do not belong to $A_1$ or $A_2$, i.e., which have not already been listed, and so on. Since the $A_i$ are finite, we can always list the elements of each set. This process is done formally as follows.

First we define sets $B_1, B_2, \ldots$ where $B_i$ contains the elements of $A_i$ which do not belong to preceding sets, i.e., we define

$$B_1 = A_1 \quad \text{and} \quad B_k = A_k \backslash (A_1 \cup A_2 \cup \cdots \cup A_{k-1})$$

Then the $B_i$ are disjoint and $S = \bigcup_i B_i$. Let $b_{i1}, b_{i2}, \ldots, b_{im_i}$ be the elements of $B_i$. Then $S = \{b_{ij}\}$. Let $f: S \to \mathbf{N}$ be defined as follows:

$$f(b_{ij}) = m_1 + m_2 + \cdots + m_{i-1} + j$$

If $S$ is finite, then $S$ is countable. If $S$ is infinite, then $f$ is a one-to-one correspondence between $S$ and $\mathbf{N}$. Thus $S$ is countable.

**Theorem 3.3:** A countable union of countable sets is countable.

**3.192** Prove Theorem 3.3.

▌ Suppose $A_1, A_2, A_3, \ldots$ are a countable number of countable sets. In particular, suppose $a_{i1}, a_{i2}, a_{i3}, \ldots$ are elements of $A_i$. Define sets $B_2, B_3, B_4, \ldots$ as follows:

$$B_k = \{a_{ij} : i + j = k\}$$

Observe that each $B_k$ is finite and

$$S = \bigcup_i A_i = \bigcup_k B_k$$

By Problem 3.191, $\bigcup_k B_k$ is countable. Hence $S = \bigcup_i A_i$ is countable and the theorem is proved.

**3.193** Let $A = \{a_1, a_2, a_3, \ldots\}$ be an infinite sequence of distinct elements. Show that $|A| = \aleph_0$.

▌ The function $f : \mathbf{N} \to A$, defined by $f(n) = a_n$, is one-to-one and onto; hence $|A| = |\mathbf{N}| = \aleph_0$.

**3.194** Show that the product set $\mathbf{N} \times \mathbf{N}$ has cardinality $\aleph_0$.

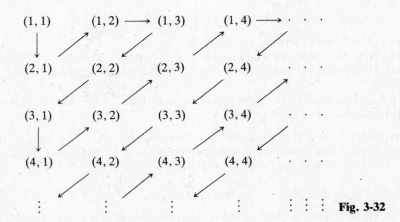

**Fig. 3-32**

▌ Figure 3-32 shows that the set $\mathbf{N} \times \mathbf{N}$ can be written as an infinite sequence of distinct elements as follows:

$$\{(1, 1), \quad (2, 1), \quad (1, 2), \quad (1, 3), \quad (2, 2), \quad \ldots\}$$

(Specifically, the sequence is determined by "following the arrows" in Fig. 3-32.) Then, by Problem 3.193, $|\mathbf{N} \times \mathbf{N}| = \aleph_0$.

**Theorem 3.4:** The set $I = [0, 1]$ of all real numbers between 0 and 1 inclusive is uncountable.

**3.195** Prove Theorem 3.4.

▌ The set $I$ is clearly infinite, since it contains $1, 1/2, 1/3, \ldots$. Suppose $I$ is denumerable. Then there exists a one-to-one correspondence $f : \mathbf{N} \to I$. Let $f(1) = a_1, f(2) = a_2, \ldots$; that is, $I = \{a_1, a_2, a_3, \ldots\}$. We list the elements $a_1, a_2, \ldots$ in a column and express each in its decimal expansion:

$$a_1 = 0.x_{11}x_{12}x_{13}x_{14} \cdots$$
$$a_2 = 0.x_{21}x_{22}x_{23}x_{24} \cdots$$
$$a_3 = 0.x_{31}x_{32}x_{33}x_{34} \cdots$$
$$a_4 = 0.x_{41}x_{42}x_{43}x_{44} \cdots$$
$$\cdots\cdots\cdots\cdots\cdots\cdots\cdots\cdots$$

where $x_{ij} \in \{0, 1, 2, \ldots, 9\}$. (For those numbers which can be expressed in two different decimal expansions, e.g., $0.2000000 \cdots = 0.1999999 \cdots$, we choose the expansion which ends with nines.)

Let $b = 0.y_1 y_2 y_3 y_4 \cdots$ be the real number obtained as follows:

$$y_i = \begin{cases} 1 & \text{if} \quad x_{ii} \neq 1 \\ 2 & \text{if} \quad x_{ii} = 1 \end{cases}$$

Now $b \in I$. But

$$b \neq a_1 \text{ because } y_1 \neq x_{11}$$
$$b \neq a_2 \text{ because } y_2 \neq x_{22}$$
$$b \neq a_3 \text{ because } y_3 \neq x_{33}$$
$$\dots\dots\dots\dots\dots\dots\dots\dots\dots$$

Therefore $b$ does not belong to $I = \{a_1, a_2, \ldots\}$. This contradicts the fact that $b \in I$. Hence the assumption that $I$ is denumerable must be false, so $I$ is uncountable.

**3.196**    Consider the closed unit interval $I = [0, 1]$ and the open unit interval $I' = (0, 1)$. Prove: **(a)** $|I| = |I'|$, and **(b)** $|\mathbf{R}| = |I'| = |I|$. (Thus by Theorem 3.4, we have $\mathfrak{c} \neq \aleph_0$.)

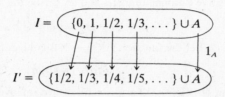

**Fig. 3-33**

**▌** **(a)** Note that

$$I = [0, 1] = \{0, 1, 1/2, 1/3, \ldots\} \cup A \qquad \text{and} \qquad I' = (0, 1) = \{1/2, 1/3, 1/4, \ldots\} \cup A$$

where $A = [0, 1] - \{0, 1, 1/2, 1/3, \ldots\} = (0, 1) - \{1/2, 1/3, \ldots\}$. Consider the function $f: I \to I'$ defined by Fig. 3-33, that is,

$$f(x) = \begin{cases} 1/2 & \text{if} \quad x = 0 \\ 1/(n + 2) & \text{if} \quad x = 1/n \quad (n \in \mathbf{N}) \\ x & \text{if} \quad x \neq 0, 1/n \quad (n \in \mathbf{N}) \end{cases}$$

Then $f$ is one-to-one and onto. Consequently, $|I| = |I'|$.

**(b)** The trigonometric function $f: I' \to \mathbf{R}$ defined by $f(x) = \tan(\pi x - \pi/2)$ is one-to-one and onto. Thus $|\mathbf{R}| = |I'| = |I|$.

**3.197**    Prove: The set $P$ of all polynomials

$$p(x) = a_0 + a_1 x + \cdots + a_m x^m$$

with integral coefficients, that is, where $a_0, a_1, \ldots, a_m$ are integers, is denumerable.

**▌** For each pair of natural numbers $(n, m)$, let $P_{(n,m)}$ be the set of polynomials of degree $m$ in which

$$|a_0| + |a_1| + \cdots + |a_m| = n$$

Note that $P_{(n,m)}$ is finite. Therefore $P = \bigcup_{i \in \mathbf{N} \times \mathbf{N}} P_i$ is countable since it is a countable family of countable sets. But $P$ is not finite; hence $P$ is denumerable.

**3.198**    A real number $r$ is called an *algebraic number* if $r$ is a solution to a polynomial equation

$$p(x) = a_0 + a_1 x + \cdots + a_n x^n = 0$$

with integral coefficients. Prove that the set $A$ of algebraic numbers is denumerable.

**▌** Note, by Problem 3.197, that the set $E$ of polynomial equations is denumerable:

$$E = \{p_1(x) = 0, p_2(x) = 0, p_3(x) = 0, \ldots\}$$

Define

$$A_i = \{x \mid x \text{ is a solution of } p_i(x) = 0\}$$

Since a polynomial of degree $n$ can have at most $n$ roots, each $A_i$ is finite. Therefore $A = \bigcup_{i \in \mathbf{N}} A_i$ is a countable family of countable sets. Accordingly, $A$ is countable and, since $A$ is not finite, therefore denumerable.

**3.199**   Prove: A subset of a denumerable set is either finite or denumerable. (Thus a subset of a countable set is countable.)

▮   Let

$$A = \{a_1, a_2, \ldots\} \tag{1}$$

be any denumerable set and let $B$ be a subset of $A$. If $B = \emptyset$, then $B$ is finite. If $B \neq \emptyset$, then let $a_{n_1}$ be the first element in the sequence in (1) such that $a_{n_1} \in B$; let $a_{n_2}$ be the first element which follows $a_{n_1}$ in the sequence in (1) such that $a_{n_2} \in B$; etc. Then

$$B = \{a_{n_1}, a_{n_2}, \ldots\}$$

If the set of integers $\{n_1, n_2, \ldots\}$ is bounded, then $B$ is finite. Otherwise $B$ is denumerable.

**3.200**   Prove that the set $\mathbf{Q}$ of rational numbers is denumerable, i.e., that $|\mathbf{Q}| = \aleph_0$.

▮   Let $Q^+$ be the set of positive rational numbers and let $Q^-$ be the set of negative rational numbers. Then

$$\mathbf{Q} = Q^- \cup \{0\} \cup Q^+$$

is the set of rational numbers. Let the function $f: Q^+ \to \mathbf{N} \times \mathbf{N}$ be defined by

$$f(p/q) = (p, q)$$

where $p/q$ is any member of $Q^+$ expressed as the ratio of two relatively prime positive integers. Then $f$ is one-to-one and hence $Q^+$ has the same cardinality as a subset of $\mathbf{N} \times \mathbf{N}$. By Problem 3.199, $Q^+$ is denumerable. Similarly, $Q^-$ is denumerable. Hence the set $\mathbf{Q}$ of rational numbers, which is the union of $Q^+$, $\{0\}$, and $Q^-$, is also denumerable.

**3.201**   Let $A$ and $B$ be any two sets. Problem 3.183 defined the relation card $(A) = |A| = |B|$ in terms of a bijective function.
**(a)**   How do we define the relation $|A| \leq |B|$ and the relation $|A| < |B|$?
**(b)**   State the classical Schroeder–Bernstein Theorem and the Law of Trichotomy for cardinal numbers.

▮   **(a)**   Suppose there exists an injective function $f: A \to B$. Then we write $|A| \leq |B|$. Also, if $|A| \leq |B|$ but $|A| \neq |B|$, then we write $|A| < |B|$.

**(b)**   The Schroeder–Bernstein Theorem states that if $|A| \leq |B|$ and $|B| \leq |A|$, then $|A| = |B|$. The Law of Trichotomy states that, for any two sets $A$ and $B$, we have $|A| < |B|$, $|B| < |A|$ or $|A| = |B|$.

**Theorem 3.5 (Cantor):**   For any set $A$, we have $|A| < |P(A)|$ where $P(A)$ is the power set of $A$.

**3.202**   Prove Theorem 3.5.

▮   The function $g: A \to P(A)$, defined by $g(a) = \{a\}$, is injective. Hence $|A| \leq |P(A)|$. We need only show that $|A| \neq |P(A)|$, and then the theorem will follow.

Suppose the contrary, that is, that $|A| = |P(A)|$. Then there exists a function $f: A \to P(A)$ which is one-to-one and onto. Let $a \in A$ be called a "bad" element if $a$ does not belong to the set which is its image, i.e., if $a \notin f(a)$. Let $B$ be the set of "bad" elements. Specifically,

$$B = \{x : x \in A, x \notin f(x)\}$$

Now $B$ is a subset of $A$. Since $f: A \to P(A)$ is onto, there exists an element $b \in A$ such that $f(b) = B$. Is $b$ "bad" or "good"? If $b \notin B$, then $b \notin f(b) = B$, which is a contradiction. If $b \notin B$, then $b \in f(b) = B$, which is also a contradiction. Thus the original assumption that $|A| = |P(A)|$ has led to a contradiction. Thus $|A| \neq |P(A)|$ and the theorem has been proved.

# CHAPTER 4
# Vectors and Matrices

## 4.1 VECTORS IN $\mathbf{R}^n$

This section considers the following vector operations:

$$\text{Vector Addition: } u + v = (a_1 + b_1, a_2 + b_2, \ldots, a_n + b_n)$$
$$\text{Scalar Multiplication: } ku = (ka_1, ka_2, \ldots, ka_n)$$
$$\text{Negation: } -u = (-1)u = (-a_1, -a_2, \ldots, -a_n)$$

where $u = (a_1, a_2, \ldots, a_n)$ and $v = (b_1, b_2, \ldots, b_n)$ are vectors in $\mathbf{R}^n$ and $k$ is a real number (scalar).

**4.1** Let $u_1 = (1, 3, 5)$, $u_2 = (3, 5, 1)$, $u_3 = (1, 5, 3)$, $u_4 = (3, 5, 1)$ be vectors in $\mathbf{R}^3$. Which of the vectors, if any, are equal?

▮ Only $u_2$ and $u_4$ are componentwise equal; hence only $u_2 = u_4$.

**4.2** Let $u = (2, -7, 1)$, $v = (-3, 0, 4)$, $w = (0, 5, -8)$. Find: **(a)** $u + v$, **(b)** $v + w$, **(c)** $-3u$, **(d)** $-w$.

▮ **(a)** Add corresponding components:

$$u + v = (2, -7, 1) + (-3, 0, 4) = (2 - 3, -7 + 0, 1 + 4) = (-1, -7, 5)$$

**(b)** Add corresponding components:

$$v + w = (-3, 0, 4) + (0, 5, -8) = (-3 + 0, 0 + 5, 4 - 8) = (-3, 5, -4)$$

**(c)** Multiply each component of $u$ by the scalar $-3$:

$$-3u = -3(2, -7, 1) = (-6, 21, -3)$$

**(d)** Multiply each component of $w$ by $-1$, i.e., change the sign of each component:

$$-w = -(0, 5, -8) = (0, -5, 8)$$

**4.3** Let $u$, $v$, and $w$ be the vectors of Problem 4.2. Find: **(a)** $3u - 4v$ and **(b)** $2u + 3v - 5w$.

▮ First perform the scalar multiplication and then the vector addition.
**(a)** $3u - 4v = 3(2, -7, 1) - 4(-3, 0, 4) = (6, -21, 3) + (12, 0, -16) = (18, -21, -13)$
**(b)** $2u + 3v - 5w = 2(2, -7, 1) + 3(-3, 0, 4) - 5(0, 5, -8)$

$$= (4, -14, 2) + (-9, 0, 12) + (0, -25, 40)$$
$$= (4 - 9 + 0, -14 + 0 - 25, 2 + 12 + 40) = (-5, -39, 54)$$

**4.4** Let $u = (2, 3, -4)$ and $v = (1, -5, 8)$. Find: **(a)** $u + v$, **(b)** $5u$, and **(c)** $-v$.

▮ **(a)** $u + v = (2 + 1, 3 - 5, -4 + 8) = (3, -2, 4)$
**(b)** $5u = (5 \cdot 2, 5 \cdot 3, 5 \cdot (-4)) = (10, 15, -20)$
**(c)** $-v = -1 \cdot (1, -5, 8) = (-1, 5, -8)$

**4.5** Let $u$ and $v$ be the vectors in Problem 4.4. Find: **(a)** $2u - 3v$ and **(b)** $3u + 5v$.

▮ **(a)** $2u - 3v = (4, 6, -8) + (-3, 15, -24) = (1, 21, -32)$
**(b)** $3u + 5v = (6, 9, -12) + (5, -25, 40) = (11, -16, 28)$

**4.6** Let $u = (3, -2, 1, 4)$ and $v = (7, 1, -3, 6)$. Find: **(a)** $u + v$, **(b)** $4u$, and **(c)** $2u - 3v$.

▮ **(a)** $u + v = (3 + 7, -2 + 1, 1 - 3, 4 + 6) = (10, -1, -2, 10)$
**(b)** $4u = (4 \cdot 3, 4 \cdot (-2), 4 \cdot 1, 4 \cdot 4) = (12, -8, 4, 16)$
**(c)** $2u - 3v = (6, -4, 2, 8) + (-21, -3, 9, -18) = (-15, -7, 11, -10)$

**4.7** Define the zero vector 0 in $\mathbf{R}^n$.

▮ The *zero vector* is the vector whose components are all zero, i.e., $0 = (0, 0, \ldots, 0)$.

**4.8**   Explain the difference between column vectors and row vectors, with examples.

▌ A *column vector u* is a vector whose components are written vertically, e.g.,

$$\begin{pmatrix} 7 \\ -4 \\ 5 \end{pmatrix}, \quad \begin{pmatrix} 3 \\ -7 \end{pmatrix}, \quad \text{and} \quad \begin{pmatrix} 2 \\ -3 \\ 0 \\ 6 \end{pmatrix}$$

are column vectors with three, two, and four components, respectively. A *row vector* is a vector whose components are written horizontally, as given in the previous problems. (Vectors will normally be written as row vectors.)

**4.9**   Compute: (*a*) $\begin{pmatrix} 3 \\ -4 \\ 5 \end{pmatrix} + \begin{pmatrix} 1 \\ 1 \\ -2 \end{pmatrix}$, (*b*) $\begin{pmatrix} 1 \\ 2 \\ -3 \end{pmatrix} + \begin{pmatrix} 4 \\ -5 \end{pmatrix}$, (*c*) $-3\begin{pmatrix} 4 \\ -5 \\ -6 \end{pmatrix}$, (*d*) $-\begin{pmatrix} -6 \\ 7 \\ -8 \end{pmatrix}$.

▌ (*a*)   Add corresponding components:

$$\begin{pmatrix} 3 \\ -4 \\ 5 \end{pmatrix} + \begin{pmatrix} 1 \\ 1 \\ -2 \end{pmatrix} = \begin{pmatrix} 3+1 \\ -4+1 \\ 5-2 \end{pmatrix} = \begin{pmatrix} 4 \\ -3 \\ 3 \end{pmatrix}$$

   (*b*)   The sum is not defined since the column vectors have different numbers of components.
   (*c*)   Multiply each component by the scalar:

$$-3\begin{pmatrix} 4 \\ -5 \\ -6 \end{pmatrix} = \begin{pmatrix} -3 \cdot 4 \\ -3 \cdot -5 \\ -3 \cdot -6 \end{pmatrix} = \begin{pmatrix} -12 \\ 15 \\ 18 \end{pmatrix}$$

   (*d*)   Multiply each component by $-1$; i.e., change the sign of each component:

$$-\begin{pmatrix} -6 \\ 7 \\ -8 \end{pmatrix} = \begin{pmatrix} 6 \\ -7 \\ 8 \end{pmatrix}$$

**4.10**   Compute: (*a*) $2\begin{pmatrix} 1 \\ -1 \\ 3 \end{pmatrix} - 3\begin{pmatrix} 2 \\ 3 \\ -4 \end{pmatrix}$, (*b*) $-2\begin{pmatrix} 5 \\ 3 \\ -4 \end{pmatrix} + 4\begin{pmatrix} -1 \\ 5 \\ 2 \end{pmatrix} - 3\begin{pmatrix} 3 \\ -1 \\ -1 \end{pmatrix}$.

▌ First perform the scalar multiplication and then the vector addition:

(*a*) $2\begin{pmatrix} 1 \\ -1 \\ 3 \end{pmatrix} - 3\begin{pmatrix} 2 \\ 3 \\ -4 \end{pmatrix} = \begin{pmatrix} 2 \\ -2 \\ 6 \end{pmatrix} + \begin{pmatrix} -6 \\ -9 \\ 12 \end{pmatrix} = \begin{pmatrix} -4 \\ -11 \\ 18 \end{pmatrix}$

(*b*) $-2\begin{pmatrix} 5 \\ 3 \\ -4 \end{pmatrix} + 4\begin{pmatrix} -1 \\ 5 \\ 2 \end{pmatrix} - 3\begin{pmatrix} 3 \\ -1 \\ -1 \end{pmatrix} = \begin{pmatrix} -10 \\ -6 \\ 8 \end{pmatrix} + \begin{pmatrix} -4 \\ 20 \\ 8 \end{pmatrix} + \begin{pmatrix} -9 \\ 3 \\ 2 \end{pmatrix} = \begin{pmatrix} -23 \\ 17 \\ 19 \end{pmatrix}$

**4.11**   Find $x$ and $y$ if $(x, 3) = (2, x + y)$.

▌ Since the two vectors are equal, the corresponding components are equal to each other:

$$x = 2, \qquad 3 = x + y$$

Substitute $x = 2$ into the second equation to obtain $y = 1$. Thus $x = 2$ and $y = 1$.

**4.12**   Find $x$ and $y$ if $(4, y) = x(2, 3)$.

▌ Multiply by the scalar $x$ to obtain $(4, y) = x(2, 3) = (2x, 3x)$. Set the corresponding components equal to each other: $4 = 2x$, $y = 3x$. Solve the linear equations for $x$ and $y$: $x = 2$ and $y = 6$.

**4.13**   Find $x$, $y$, and $z$ if $(2x, 3, y) = (4, x + z, 2z)$.

❙ Set corresponding components equal to each other to obtain the system of equations

$$2x = 4, \qquad 3 = x + z, \qquad y = 2z$$

Then $x = 2$, $z = 1$, and $y = 2$.

**4.14** Find $x$ and $y$ if $x(1, 1) + y(2, -1) = (1, 4)$.

❙ First multiply by the scalars $x$ and $y$ and then add:

$$x(1, 1) + y(2, -1) = (x, x) + (2y, -y) = (x + 2y, x - y) = (1, 4)$$

Now set corresponding components equal to each other to obtain

$$x + 2y = 1, \qquad x - y = 4$$

Solve the system of equations to find $x = 3$ and $y = -1$.

**4.15** Explain what it means for one vector to be a linear combination of other vectors.

❙ A vector $v$ is a linear combination of vectors $u_1, u_2, \ldots, u_m$ if there exist scalars $a_1, a_2, \ldots, a_m$ such that $v = a_1 u_1 + a_2 u_2 + \cdots + a_m u_m$.

**4.16** Write $v = (1, 4)$ as a linear combination of $u_1 = (1, 1)$ and $u_2 = (2, -1)$.

❙ We want to express $v$ in the form

$$v = x u_1 + y u_2 \qquad\qquad (1)$$

with $x$ and $y$ as yet unknown. Thus we require

$$(1, 4) = x(1, 1) + y(2, -1)$$

From Problem 4.14, $x = 3$ and $y = -1$. Thus, substituting into $(1)$, we have $v = 3u_1 - u_2$.

**4.17** Write the vector $v = (1, -2, 5)$ as a linear combination of the vectors $u_1 = (1, 1, 1)$, $u_2 = (1, 2, 3)$, and $u_3 = (2, -1, 1)$.

❙ We want to express $v$ in the form $v = x u_1 + y u_2 + z u_3$ with $x$, $y$, and $z$ as yet unknown. Thus we have

$$\begin{pmatrix} 1 \\ -2 \\ 5 \end{pmatrix} = x \begin{pmatrix} 1 \\ 1 \\ 1 \end{pmatrix} + y \begin{pmatrix} 1 \\ 2 \\ 3 \end{pmatrix} + z \begin{pmatrix} 2 \\ -1 \\ 1 \end{pmatrix} = \begin{pmatrix} x + y + 2z \\ x + 2y - z \\ x + 3y + z \end{pmatrix}$$

(It is more convenient to write the vectors as columns when forming linear combinations.) Setting corresponding components equal to each other we obtain

$$\begin{array}{lll} x + y + 2z = 1 & \qquad x + y + 2z = 1 & \qquad x + y + 2z = 1 \\ x + 2y - z = -2 \quad \text{or} & \qquad y - 3z = -3 \quad \text{or} & \qquad y - 3z = -3 \\ x + 3y + z = 5 & \qquad 2y - z = 4 & \qquad 5z = 10 \end{array}$$

The unique solution of the triangular system is $x = -6$, $y = 3$, $z = 2$; thus $v = -6u_1 + 3u_2 + 2u_3$.

**4.18** Write $v = (2, 3, -5)$ as a linear combination of $u_1 = (1, 2, -3)$, $u_2 = (2, -1, -4)$, and $u_3 = (1, 7, -5)$.

❙ Find the equivalent system of equations and then solve. Thus

$$\begin{pmatrix} 2 \\ 3 \\ -5 \end{pmatrix} = x \begin{pmatrix} 1 \\ 2 \\ -3 \end{pmatrix} + y \begin{pmatrix} 2 \\ -1 \\ -4 \end{pmatrix} + z \begin{pmatrix} 1 \\ 7 \\ -5 \end{pmatrix} = \begin{pmatrix} x + 2y + z \\ 2x - y + 7z \\ -3x - 4y - 5z \end{pmatrix}$$

Set corresponding components equal to each other to obtain

$$\begin{array}{lll} x + 2y + z = 2 & \qquad x + 2y + z = 2 & \qquad x + 2y + z = 2 \\ 2x - y + 7z = 3 \quad \text{or} & \qquad -5y + 5z = -1 \quad \text{or} & \qquad -5y + 5z = -1 \\ -3x - 4y - 5z = -5 & \qquad 2y - 2z = 1 & \qquad 0 = 3 \end{array}$$

The third equation $0 = 3$ indicates that the system has no solution. Thus $v$ cannot be written as a linear combination of the vectors $u_1$, $u_2$, and $u_3$.

**Theorem 4.1:**  For any vectors $u = (u_i)$, $v = (v_i)$, and $w = (w_i)$ in $\mathbf{R}^n$, and any scalars $k$, $k'$; in $\mathbf{R}$:

    (i)   $(u + v) + w = u + (v + w)$       (v)   $k(u + v) = ku + kv$

    (ii)  $u + 0 = u$                       (vi)  $(k + k')u = ku + k'u$

    (iii) $u + (-u) = 0$               (vii) $(kk')u = k(k'u)$

    (iv) $u + v = v + u$              (viii) $1u = u$

**4.19**    Prove Theorem 4.1(i): $(u + v) + w = u + (v + w)$.

    ▌ By definition, $u_i + v_i$ is the $i$th component of $u + v$ and so $(u_i + v_i) + w_i$ is the $i$th component of $(u + v) + w$. On the other hand, $v_i + w_i$ is the $i$th component of $v + w$ and so $u_i + (v_i + w_i)$ is the $i$th component of $u + (v + w)$. But $u_i$, $v_i$, and $w_i$ are real numbers for which the associative law holds; that is,

$$(u_i + v_i) + w_i = u_i + (v_i + w_i) \qquad (i = 1, \ldots, n)$$

Accordingly, $(u + v) + w = u + (v + w)$, since their corresponding components are equal.

**4.20**    Prove Theorem 4.1(ii): $u + 0 = u$.

    ▌ $u + 0 = (u_1, u_2, \ldots, u_n) + (0, 0, \ldots, 0) = (u_1 + 0, u_2 + 0, \ldots, u_n) = (u_1, u_2, \ldots, u_n) = u$

**4.21**    Prove Theorem 4.1(iii): $u + (-u) = 0$.

    ▌ $u + (-u) = (u_1, u_2, \ldots,) + (-u_1, -u_2, \ldots, -u_n)$

                $= (u_1 - u_1, u_2 - u_2, \ldots, u_n - u_n) = (0, 0, \ldots, 0) = 0$

**4.22**    Prove Theorem 4.1(iv): $u + v = v + u$.

    ▌ By definition, $u_i + v_i$ is the $i$th component of $u + v$, and $v_i + u_i$ is the $i$th component of $v + u$. But $u_i$ and $v_i$ are real numbers for which the commutative law holds, that is,

$$u_i + v_i = v_i + u_i \qquad (i = 1, \ldots, n)$$

Hence $u + v = v + u$, since their corresponding components are equal.

**4.23**    Prove Theorem 4.1(v): $k(u + v) = ku + kv$.

    ▌ Since $u_i + v_i$ is the $i$th component of $u + v$, $k(u_i + v_i)$ is the $i$th component of $k(u + v)$. Since $ku_i$ and $kv_i$ are the $i$th components of $ku$ and $kv$ respectively, $ku_i + kv_i$ is the $i$th component of $ku + kv$. But $k$, $u_i$, and $v_i$ are real numbers; hence

$$k(u_i + v_i) = ku_i + kv_i \qquad (i = 1, \ldots, n)$$

Thus $k(u + v) = ku + kv$, as corresponding components are equal.

**4.24**    Prove Theorem 4.1(vi): $(k + k')u = ku + k'u$.

    ▌ By definition, $(k + k')u_i$ is the $i$th component of the vector $(k + k')u$. Since $ku_i$ and $k'u_i$ are the $i$th components of $ku$ and $k'u$, respectively, $ku_i + k'u_i$ is the $i$th component of $ku + k'u$. But $k$, $k'$, and $u_i$ are real numbers; hence

$$(k + k')u_i = ku_i + k'u_i \qquad (i = 1, \ldots, n)$$

Thus $(k + k')u = ku + k'u$, as corresponding components are equal.

**4.25**    Prove Theorem 4.1(vii): $(kk')u = k(k'u)$.

    ▌ Since $k'u_i$ is the $i$th component of $k'u$, $k(k'u_i)$ is the $i$th component of $k(k'u)$. But $(kk')u_i$ is the $i$th component of $(kk')u$ and, since $k$, $k'$, and $u_i$ are real numbers,

$$(kk')u_i = k(k'u_i) \qquad (i = 1, \ldots, n)$$

Hence $(kk')u = k(k'u)$, as corresponding components are equal.

**4.26**    Prove Theorem 4.1(viii): $1u = u$.

    ▌ $1 \cdot u = 1(u_1, u_2, \ldots, u_n) = (1u_1, 1u_2, \ldots, 1u_n) = (u_i, u_2, \ldots, u_n) = u$

**4.27**    Show that (*a*) $0u = \mathbf{0}$ for any vector $u$; and (*b*) $k\mathbf{0} = \mathbf{0}$ for any scalar $k$. Here $\mathbf{0} = $ zero vector.

**(a)** $0u = 0(u_1, u_2, \ldots, u_n) = (0u_1, 0u_2, \ldots, 0u_n) = (0, 0, \ldots, 0) = \mathbf{0}$.
**(b)** $k0 = k(0, 0, \ldots, 0) = (k \cdot 0, k \cdot 0, \ldots, k \cdot 0) = (0, 0, \ldots, 0) = \mathbf{0}$.

**4.28**  Show that $(-1)u = -u$.

From the previously proved properties,

$$u + (-u) = 0 = 0u = (1 + (-1))u = 1u + (-1)u = u + (-1)u$$

and the result follows upon adding $-u$ to both sides.

## Dot (Inner) Products, Norms

This subsection considers the following vector operations:

$$\text{Dot (Inner) Product: } u \cdot v = a_1b_1 + a_2b_2 + \cdots + a_nb_n = \sum_{i=1}^{n} a_ib_i$$

$$\text{Norm (Length): } \|u\| = \sqrt{u \cdot u} = \sqrt{a_1^2 + a_2^2 + \cdots + a_n^2}$$

where $u = (a_1, a_2, \ldots, a_n)$ and $v = (b_1, b_2, \ldots, b_n)$ are vectors in $\mathbf{R}^n$.

**4.29**  Compute $u \cdot v$ where **(a)** $u = (2, -3, 6)$, $v = (8, 2, -3)$; **(b)** $u = (1, -8, 0, 5)$, $v = (3, 6, 4)$.

**(a)**  Multiply corresponding components and add:

$$u \cdot v = (2)(8) + (-3)(2) + (6)(-3) = 16 - 6 - 18 = -8$$

**(b)**  The dot product is not defined between vectors with different numbers of components.

**4.30**  Compute $u \cdot v$ where: **(a)** $u = (3, -5, 2, 1)$, $v = (4, 1, -2, 5)$; **(b)** $u = (1, -2, 3, -4)$, $v = (6, 7, 1, -2)$.

Multiply corresponding components and add:
**(a)**  $u \cdot v = (3)(4) + (-5)(1) + (2)(-2) + (1)(5) = 12 - 5 - 4 + 5 = 8$
**(b)**  $u \cdot v = 6 - 14 + 3 + 8 = 3$

**4.31**  Let $u = (2, -7, 1)$, $v = (-3, 0, 4)$, and $w = (0, 5, -8)$. Find: **(a)** $u \cdot v$, **(b)** $u \cdot w$, and **(c)** $v \cdot w$.

Multiply corresponding components and then add:
**(a)**  $u \cdot v = 2 \cdot (-3) + (-7) \cdot 0 + 1 \cdot 4 = -6 + 0 + 4 = -2$
**(b)**  $u \cdot w = 0 - 35 - 8 = -43$
**(c)**  $v \cdot w = 0 + 0 - 32 = -32$

**4.32**  Suppose $u = (3, 2, 1)$, $v = (5, -3, 4)$, $w = (1, 6, -7)$. Find: **(a)** $(u + v) \cdot w$, **(b)** $u \cdot w + v \cdot w$.

**(a)**  First calculate $u + v$ by adding corresponding components;

$$u + v = (3 + 5, 2 - 3, 1 + 4) = (8, -1, 5)$$

Then compute $(u + v) \cdot w = (8)(1) + (-1)(6) + (5)(-7) = 8 - 6 - 35 = -33$.
**(b)**  First find $u \cdot w = 3 + 12 - 7 = 8$ and $v \cdot w = 5 - 18 - 28 = -41$. Then

$$u \cdot w + v \cdot w = 8 - 41 = -33$$

Note: As expected from Theorem 4.2(i) both values are equal.

**4.33**  Let $u = (1, 2, 3, -4)$, $v = (5, -6, 7, 8)$; and $k = 3$. Find: **(a)** $k(u \cdot v)$, **(b)** $(ku) \cdot v$, **(c)** $u \cdot (kv)$.

**(a)**  First find $u \cdot v = 5 - 12 + 21 - 32 = -18$. Then $k(u \cdot v) = 3(-18) = -54$.
**(b)**  First find $ku = (3(1), 3(2), 3(3), 3(-4)) = (3, 6, 9, -12)$. Then

$$(ku) \cdot v = (3)(5) + (6)(-6) + (9)(7) + (-12)(8) = 15 - 36 + 63 - 96 = -54$$

**(c)**  First find $kv = (15, -18, 21, 24)$. Then

$$u \cdot (kv) = (1)(15) + (2)(-18) + (3)(21) + (-4)(24) = 15 - 36 + 63 - 96 = -54$$

Note: As expected from Theorem 4.2(ii) and (iii), all three values are equal.

**4.34**  Find: **(a)** $\|u\|$ if $u = (3, -12, -4)$, and **(b)** $\|v\|$ if $v = (2, -3, 8, -5)$.

■ **(a)** First find $\|u\|^2 = u \cdot u$ by squaring the components of $u$ and adding:

$$\|u\|^2 = 3^2 + (-12)^2 + (-4)^2 = 9 + 144 + 16 = 169$$

Then $\|u\| = \sqrt{169} = 13$.

**(b)** Square each component of $v$ and then add to obtain $\|v\|^2 = v \cdot v$:

$$\|v\|^2 = 2^2 + (-3)^2 + 8^2 + (-5)^2 = 4 + 9 + 64 + 25 = 102.$$

Then $\|v\| = \sqrt{102}$.

**4.35**    Find $\|w\|$ if $w = (-3, 1, -2, 4, -5)$.

■ We have $\|w\|^2 = 9 + 1 + 4 + 16 + 25 = 55$; hence $\|w\| = \sqrt{55}$.

**4.36**    Determine $k$ such that $\|u\| = \sqrt{39}$ where $u = (1, k, -2, 5)$.

■ $\|u\|^2 = 1^2 + k^2 + (-2)^2 + 5^2 = k^2 + 30$. Now solve $k^2 + 30 = 39$ to obtain $k = 3, -3$.

**4.37**    Let $v$ be an nonzero vector. Show that $\hat{v} \equiv \dfrac{1}{\|v\|} v = \dfrac{v}{\|v\|}$ is a unit vector in the same direction as $v$. (The process of finding $\hat{v}$ is called *normalizing v*.)

■ The vector $\hat{v}$ is a unit vector since

$$\hat{v} \cdot \hat{v} = \left(\frac{v}{\|v\|}\right) \cdot \left(\frac{v}{\|v\|}\right) = \frac{1}{\|v\|^2} (v \cdot v) = \frac{1}{\|v\|^2} \|v\|^2 = 1$$

Moreover, $\hat{v}$ is in the same direction as $v$, since $\hat{v}$ is a positive scalar multiple of $v$.

**4.38**    Normalize: **(a)** $v = (12, -3, -4)$; **(b)** $w = (4, -2, -3, 8)$.

■ **(a)** First find $\|v\|^2 = v \cdot v = 12^2 + (-3)^2 + (-4)^2 = 144 + 9 + 16 = 169$. Then divide each component of $v$ by $\|v\| = \sqrt{169} = 13$ to obtain

$$\hat{v} = \frac{v}{\|v\|} = \left(\frac{12}{13}, \frac{-3}{13}, \frac{-4}{13}\right)$$

**(b)** First find $\|w\|^2 = w \cdot w = 42 + (-2)^2 + (-3)^2 + 8^2 = 16 + 4 + 9 + 64 = 93$. Divide each component of $w$ by $\|w\| = \sqrt{93}$ to obtain

$$\hat{w} = \frac{w}{\|w\|} = \left(\frac{4}{\sqrt{93}}, \frac{-2}{\sqrt{93}}, \frac{-3}{\sqrt{93}}, \frac{8}{\sqrt{93}}\right)$$

**4.39**    Normalize $v = (1/2, 2/3, -1/4)$.

■ Note that $v$ and any positive multiple of $v$ will have the same normalized form. Hence, first multiply $v$ by 12 to "clear" fractions: $12v = (6, 8, -3)$. Then

$$\|12v\|2 = 36 + 64 + 9 = 109 \qquad \text{and} \qquad \hat{v} = \widehat{12v} = \frac{12v}{\|12v\|} = \left(\frac{6}{\sqrt{109}}, \frac{8}{\sqrt{109}}, \frac{-3}{\sqrt{109}}\right)$$

**4.40**    Let $u = (2, -7, 1)$, $v = (-3, 0, 4)$, and $w = (0, 5, -8)$. Find: **(a)** $\|u\|$, **(b)** $\|v\|$, and **(c)** $\|w\|$.

■ Take the square root of the sum of the squares of the components:
**(a)**    $\|u\| = \sqrt{2^2 + (-7)^2 + 1^2} = \sqrt{4 + 49 + 1} = \sqrt{54} = 3\sqrt{6}$
**(b)**    $\|v\| = \sqrt{9 + 0 + 16} = \sqrt{25} = 5$
**(c)**    $\|w\| = \sqrt{0 + 25 + 64} = \sqrt{89}$

**4.41**    Define orthogonal vectors in $\mathbf{R}^n$.

■ Vectors $u$ and $v$ in $\mathbf{R}^n$ are said to be *orthogonal* (or *perpendicular*) if their dot product is zero, that is, if $u \cdot v = 0$. (Note that in physics the dot product of two nonzero vectors $u$ and $v$ in $\mathbf{R}^3$ is defined as $u \cdot v = |u| \, |v| \cos \theta$ where $\theta$ is the angle between $u$ and $v$. When the two vectors are perpendicular to each other, $\theta = 90°$, and so $u \cdot v = 0$. This agrees with the statement above.)

**4.42**    Let $u = (5, 4, 1)$, $v = (3, -4, 1)$, and $w = (1, -2, 3)$. Which of the vectors, if any, are orthogonal?

▮ Find the dot product of each pair of vectors:

$$u \cdot v = 15 - 16 + 1 = 0, \qquad v \cdot w = 3 + 8 + 3 = 14, \qquad u \cdot w = 5 - 8 + 3 = 0$$

Hence $u$ and $v$ are orthogonal, $u$ and $w$ are orthogonal, but $v$ and $w$ are not.

**4.43** Determine $k$ so that the vectors $u$ and $v$ are orthogonal where
(a) $u = (1, k, -3)$ and $v = (2, -5, 4)$
(b) $u = (2, 3k, -4, 1, 5)$ and $v = (6, -1, 3, 7, 2k)$

▮ In each case, compute $u \cdot v$, set it equal to 0, and solve for $k$.
(a) $u \cdot v = (1)(2) + (k)(-5) + (-3)(4) = 2 - 5k - 12 = 0$ or $-5k - 10 = 0$. Solving, $k = -2$.
(b) $u \cdot v = 12 - 3k - 12 + 7 + 10k = 7k + 7 = 0$. Solving, $k = -1$.

## Summation Symbol, Theorems and Proofs

**4.44** Let $f(k)$ be an algebraic expresion involving an integer variable $k$.

(a) Define the expression $S_n = \sum_{k=1}^{n} f(k)$ where $n \geq 1$. (Here 1 is called the *lower limit*, $n$ is called the *upper limit*, and the Greek letter sigma functions as the *summation symbol*.)

(b) Suppose $n_1$ and $n_2$ are any integers such that $n_1 \leq n_2$. Define $\sum_{k=n_1}^{n_2} f(k)$.

▮ (a) $S_n = f(1) + f(2) + \cdots + f(n-1) + f(n)$. From this definition, it is obvious that, for $n \geq 2$, $S_n = S_{n-1} + f(n)$.

(b) $\sum_{k=n_1}^{n_2} f(k) = f(n_1) + f(n_1 + 1) + f(n_1 + 2) + \cdots + f(n_2)$. For $n_2 \leq n_1$, the summation is usually defined to be zero.

**4.45** Find: (a) $\sum_{k=1}^{4} k^3$, (b) $\sum_{j=2}^{5} j^2$, and (c) $\sum_{k=1}^{5} x_k$.

▮ (a) $\sum_{k=1}^{4} k^3 = 1^3 + 2^3 + 3^3 + 4^3 = 1 + 8 + 27 + 64 = 100$
(c) $\sum_{k=1}^{5} x_k = x_1 + x_2 + x_3 + x_4 + x_5$

(b) $\sum_{j=2}^{5} j^2 = 2^2 + 3^2 + 4^2 + 5^2 = 4 + 9 + 16 + 25 = 54$

**4.46** Rewrite using the summation symbol:
(a) $a_1 b_1 + a_2 b_2 + \cdots + a_n b_n$
(c) $a_{i1} b_{1j} + a_{i2} b_{2j} + a_{i3} b_{3j} + \cdots + a_{ip} b_{pj}$
(b) $a_0 + a_1 x + a_2 x^2 + \cdots + a_n x^n$

▮ (a) $\sum_{i=1}^{n} a_i b_i$,
(b) $\sum_{i=0}^{n} a_i x^i$,
(c) $\sum_{k=1}^{p} a_{ik} b_{kj}$.

**4.47** Prove: $\sum_{k=1}^{n} [f(k) + g(k)] = \sum_{k=1}^{n} f(k) + \sum_{k=1}^{n} g(k)$.

▮ The proof is by induction on $n$. For $n = 1$,

$$\sum_{k=1}^{1} [f(k) + g(k)] = f(1) + g(1) = \sum_{k=1}^{1} f(k) + \sum_{k=1}^{1} g(k)$$

Suppose $n > 1$, and that the theorem holds for $n - 1$; i.e.,

$$\sum_{k=1}^{n-1} [f(k) + g(k)] = \sum_{k=1}^{n-1} f(k) + \sum_{k=1}^{n-1} g(k)$$

Then [see Problem 4.44(a)],

$$\sum_{k=1}^{n} [f(k) + g(k)] = \sum_{k=1}^{n-1} [f(k) + g(k)] + [f(n) + g(n)] = \sum_{k=1}^{n-1} f(k) + \sum_{k=1}^{n-1} g(k) + f(n) + g(n)$$

$$= \left[ \sum_{k=1}^{n-1} f(k) + f(n) \right] + \left[ \sum_{k=1}^{n-1} g(k) + g(n) \right] = \sum_{k=1}^{n} f(k) + \sum_{k=1}^{n} g(k)$$

Thus the theorem is proved.

**4.48** Prove: $\sum\limits_{k=1}^{n} cf(k) = c \sum\limits_{k=1}^{n} f(k)$.

▌ The proof is immediate from the distributive law, $a(b + c + \cdots) = ab + ac + \cdots$, for real numbers.

**Theorem 4.2:** For any vectors $u = (u_i)$, $v = (v_i)$, and $w = (w_i)$ in $\mathbf{R}^n$, and any scalar $k$ in $\mathbf{R}$:
   (i)   $(u + v) \cdot w = u \cdot w + v \cdot w$      (iii)  $u \cdot v = v \cdot u$
   (ii)  $(ku) \cdot v = k(u \cdot v)$      (iv)  $u \cdot u \geq 0$, and $u \cdot u = 0$ iff $u = 0$

**4.49** Prove Theorem 4.2(i): $(u + v) \cdot w = u \cdot w + v \cdot w$.

▌ Using Problem 4.47,

$$(u + v) \cdot w = \sum_{i=1}^{n} (u_i + v_i)w_i = \sum_{i=1}^{n} (u_i w_i + v_i w_i) = \sum_{i=1}^{n} u_i w_i + \sum_{i=1}^{n} v_i w_i = u \cdot w + v \cdot w$$

**4.50** Prove Theorem 4.2(ii): $(ku) \cdot v = k(u \cdot v)$.

▌ Using Problem 4.48,

$$(ku) \cdot v = \sum_{i=1}^{n} (ku_i)v_i = \sum_{i=1}^{n} k(u_i v_i) = k \sum_{i=1}^{n} u_i v_i = k(u \cdot v).$$

**4.51** Prove Theorem 4.2(iii): $u \cdot v = v \cdot u$.

▌ $u \cdot v = \sum\limits_{i=1}^{n} u_i v_i = \sum\limits_{i=1}^{n} v_i u_i = v \cdot u.$

**4.52** Prove Theorem 4.2(iv): $u \cdot u \geq 0$, and $u \cdot u = 0$ iff $u = 0$.

▌ Since $u_i^2$ is nonnegative for each $i$, $u \cdot u = u_1^2 + u_2^2 + \cdots + u_n^2 \geq 0$. Furthermore, $u \cdot u = 0$ iff $u_i = 0$ for each $i$; that is, iff $u = 0$. (Here, iff is short for "if and only if.")

**Theorem 4.3 (Cauchy–Schwarz inequality):**   $|u \cdot v| \leq \|u\| \, \|v\|$, for arbitrary $u$ and $v$ in $\mathbf{R}^n$.

**4.53** Prove Theorem 4.3.

▌ We shall prove the following stronger statement:

$$|u \cdot v| \leq \sum_{i=1}^{n} |u_i v_i| \leq \|u\| \, \|v\|.$$

First, if $u = 0$ or $v = 0$, then the inequality reduces to $0 \leq 0 \leq 0$ and is therefore true. Hence we need only consider the case in which $u \neq 0$ and $v \neq 0$, i.e., where $\|u\| \neq 0$ and $\|v\| \neq 0$. Furthermore, because

$$|u \cdot v| = \left| \sum u_i v_i \right| \leq \sum |u_i v_i|$$

we need only prove the second inequality.
   Now, for any real numbers $x, y \in \mathbf{R}$, $0 \leq (x - y)^2 = x^2 - 2xy + y^2$ or, equivalently,

$$2xy \leq x^2 + y^2 \tag{1}$$

Set $x = |u_i|/\|u\|$ and $y = |v_i|/\|v\|$ in (1) to obtain, for any $i$,

$$2 \frac{|u_i|}{\|u\|} \frac{|v_i|}{\|v\|} \leq \frac{|u_i|^2}{\|u\|^2} + \frac{|v_i|^2}{\|v\|^2} \tag{2}$$

But, by definition of the norm of a vector, $\|u\| = \sum u_i^2 = \sum |u_i|^2$ and $\|v\| = \sum v_i^2 = \sum |v_i|^2$. Thus summing (2) with respect to $i$ and using $|u_i v_i| = |u_i| \, |v_i|$, we have

$$2 \frac{\sum |u_i v_i|}{\|u\| \, \|v\|} \leq \frac{\sum |u_i|^2}{\|u\|^2} + \frac{\sum |v_i|^2}{\|v\|^2} = \frac{\|u\|^2}{\|u\|^2} + \frac{\|v\|^2}{\|v\|^2} = 2 \quad \text{and hence} \quad \frac{\sum |u_i v_i|}{\|u\| \, \|v\|} \leq 1$$

Multiplying both sides by $\|u\| \, \|v\|$, we obtain the required inequality.

**Theorem 4.4 (Minkowski's inequality):**   $\|u + v\| \leq \|u\| + \|v\|$, for arbitrary $u$ and $v$ in $\mathbf{R}^n$.

**4.54** Prove Theorem 4.4.

▮ By the Cauchy–Schwarz inequality and the other properties of the inner product,

$$\|u+v\|^2 = (u+v)\cdot(u+v) = u\cdot u + 2(u\cdot v) + v\cdot v$$
$$\leq \|u\|^2 + 2\|u\|\,\|v\| + \|v\|^2 = (\|u\| + \|v\|)^2$$

Taking the square roots of both sides yields the desired inequality.

**4.55** Prove that the norm in $\mathbf{R}^n$ satisfies the following laws:
[$N_1$]: For any vector $u$, $\|u\| \geq 0$; and $\|u\| = 0$ iff $u = 0$.
[$N_2$]: For any vector $u$ and any scalar $k$, $\|ku\| = |k|\,\|u\|$.
[$N_3$]: For any vectors $u$ and $v$, $\|u+v\| \leq \|u\| + \|v\|$.

▮ [$N_1$] follows from Theorem 4.2(iv) and the fact that $\|u\| = \sqrt{u\cdot u}$; [$N_3$] is Minkowski's inequality. Hence we need only prove that [$N_2$] holds. Suppose $u = (u_1, u_2, \ldots, u_n)$ and so $ku = (ku_1, ku_2, \ldots, ku_n)$. Then

$$\|ku\|^2 = (ku_1)^2 + (ku_2)^2 + \cdots + (ku_n)^2 = k^2(u_1^2 + u_2^2 + \cdots + u_n^2) = k^2\|u\|^2$$

Taking square roots gives [$N_2$].

## 4.2 MATRICES, MATRIX ADDITION, AND SCALAR MULTIPLICATION

This chapter uses capital letters $A, B, C, \ldots$ to denote matrices and lowercase letters $a, b, c, x, y, \ldots$ to denote scalars. Unless otherwise stated or implied, scalars will be real numbers; in other words, the matrices will be over $\mathbf{R}$.

**4.56** Let $A$ be an arbitrary matrix (rectangular array of scalars), say

$$A = \begin{pmatrix} a_{11} & a_{12} & \cdots & a_{1n} \\ a_{21} & a_{22} & \cdots & a_{2n} \\ \cdots & \cdots & \cdots & \cdots \\ a_{m1} & a_{m2} & \cdots & a_{mn} \end{pmatrix}$$

**(a)** What are the rows and columns of $A$? **(b)** What is the size of $A$? **(c)** When are two such matrices equal?

▮ **(a)** The $m$ horizontal $n$-tuples

$$(a_{11}, a_{12}, \ldots, a_{1n}), (a_{21}, a_{22}, \ldots, a_{2n}), \ldots, (a_{m1}, a_{m2}, \ldots, a_{mn})$$

are called the *rows* of $A$ and the $n$ vertical $m$-tuples

$$\begin{pmatrix} a_{11} \\ a_{21} \\ \cdots \\ a_{m1} \end{pmatrix}, \begin{pmatrix} a_{12} \\ a_{22} \\ \cdots \\ a_{m2} \end{pmatrix}, \ldots, \begin{pmatrix} a_{1n} \\ a_{21} \\ \cdots \\ a_{mn} \end{pmatrix}$$

its *columns*.
**(b)** Since $A$ has $m$ rows and $n$ columns, it is said to be an $m$ by $n$ matrix, written $m \times n$. The pair of numbers $m$ and $n$ is called the *size* of the matrix.
**(c)** Two matrices $A$ and $B$ are *equal*, written $A = B$, if they have the same size and if their corresponding elements are equal.

**4.57** The notation $A = (a_{ij})$ is used to denote the matrix in Problem 4.56 (or $A = (a_{ij})_{m \times n}$ if the size is not understood). What is the significance of the first subscript, $i$, and the second subscript, $j$?

▮ The scalar $a_{ij}$ is the element of $A$ in row $i$ and column $j$. Thus, the first subscript tells the row of the element and the second subscript tells the column.

**4.58** Find the rows, columns, and size of the matrix $A = \begin{pmatrix} 1 & 2 & 3 \\ 4 & 5 & 6 \end{pmatrix}$.

▮ The *rows* of $A$ are the horizontal lines of numbers; there are two of them: $(1, 2, 3)$ and $(4, 5, 6)$. The *columns* of $A$ are the vertical lines of numbers; there are three of them:

$$\begin{pmatrix} 1 \\ 4 \end{pmatrix}, \qquad \begin{pmatrix} 2 \\ 5 \end{pmatrix}, \qquad \begin{pmatrix} 3 \\ 6 \end{pmatrix}$$

The *size* of $A$ is $2 \times 3$ (read: 2 by 3), the number of rows by the number of columns.

**4.59**   Which of the following matrices, if any, are equal?

$$A = \begin{pmatrix} 4 & 1 \\ 2 & 3 \end{pmatrix}, \qquad B = \begin{pmatrix} 2 & 3 \\ 4 & 1 \end{pmatrix}, \qquad C = \begin{pmatrix} 4 & 2 \\ 1 & 3 \end{pmatrix}, \qquad D = \begin{pmatrix} 4 & 1 \\ 3 & 2 \end{pmatrix}, \qquad E = \begin{pmatrix} 2 & 3 \\ 4 & 1 \end{pmatrix}$$

▐   Although all five matrices have the same size and contain the scalars 1, 2, 3, 4, only $B$ and $E$ contain equal corresponding entries. Thus only $B = E$.

**4.60**   Find $x, y, z, w$ if $\begin{pmatrix} x+y & 2z+w \\ x-y & z-w \end{pmatrix} = \begin{pmatrix} 3 & 5 \\ 1 & 4 \end{pmatrix}$.

▐   Equate corresponding entries to obtain the system of equations

$$x + y = 3, \qquad x - y = 1, \qquad 2z + w = 5, \qquad z - w = 4$$

The solution of the system of equations is $x = 2$, $y = 1$, $z = 3$, $w = -1$.

**4.61**   The $m \times n$ zero matrix, denoted by $0_{m \times n}$ or simply 0, is the matrix whose elements are all zero. Display the $2 \times 2$, $2 \times 3$, and $1 \times 4$ zero matrices.

▐   Simply let each entry be the scalar 0:

$$\begin{pmatrix} 0 & 0 \\ 0 & 0 \end{pmatrix}, \qquad \begin{pmatrix} 0 & 0 & 0 \\ 0 & 0 & 0 \end{pmatrix}, \qquad (0, 0, 0, 0)$$

**4.62**   The *negative* of an $m \times n$ matrix $A = (a_{ij})$ is the $m \times n$ matrix $-A \equiv (-a_{ij})$. Find the negatives of

$$A = \begin{pmatrix} 1 & -3 & 4 & 7 \\ 2 & -5 & 0 & -8 \end{pmatrix}, \qquad B = \begin{pmatrix} 2 & -3 \\ -6 & 1 \end{pmatrix}$$

▐   Take the negative of each element:

$$-A = \begin{pmatrix} -1 & -(-3) & -4 & -7 \\ -2 & -(-5) & -0 & -(-8) \end{pmatrix} = \begin{pmatrix} -1 & 3 & -4 & -7 \\ -2 & 5 & 0 & 8 \end{pmatrix}, \qquad -B = \begin{pmatrix} -2 & 3 \\ 6 & -1 \end{pmatrix}$$

**4.63**   A matrix $A$ with only one row is called a *row matrix* or a *row vector* and is frequently denoted by $A = (a_1, a_2, \ldots, a_n)$; we omit its first subscript since it must be one. Analogously, a matrix $B$ with only one column is called a *column matrix* or a *column vector* and is frequently denoted by

$$B = \begin{pmatrix} b_1 \\ b_2 \\ \cdots \\ b_m \end{pmatrix}$$

(here we omit the second subscript since, again, it must be one). Discuss the difference, if any between the following

$$u = (1, 2, 3) \qquad \text{and} \qquad v = \begin{pmatrix} 1 \\ 2 \\ 3 \end{pmatrix}$$

▐   Viewed as vectors in $\mathbf{R}^3$, $u$ and $v$ may be considered equal. However, as matrices, they cannot be equal, for they have different sizes.

## Matrix Addition and Scalar Multiplication

This subsection considers the following operations of matrix addition and scalar multiplication where $A = (a_{ij})$ and $B = (b_{ij})$ are matrices with the same size and $k$ is a scalar:

$$A + B = \begin{pmatrix} a_{11}+b_{11} & a_{12}+b_{12} & \cdots & a_{1n}+b_{1n} \\ a_{21}+b_{21} & a_{22}+b_{22} & \cdots & a_{2n}+b_{2n} \\ \cdots\cdots\cdots\cdots\cdots\cdots\cdots\cdots\cdots\cdots \\ a_{m1}+b_{m1} & a_{m2}+b_{m2} & \cdots & a_{mn}+b_{mn} \end{pmatrix} \quad \text{and} \quad kA = \begin{pmatrix} ka_{11} & ka_{12} & \cdots & ka_{1n} \\ ka_{21} & ka_{22} & \cdots & ka_{2n} \\ \cdots\cdots\cdots\cdots\cdots\cdots\cdots \\ ka_{m1} & ka_{m2} & \cdots & ka_{mn} \end{pmatrix}$$

That is, $A + B$ is the matrix obtained by adding corresponding entries from $A$ and $B$ and $kA$ is the matrix obtained by multiplying each entry of $A$ by $k$.

**4.64** Find $A + B$ where: **(a)** $A = \begin{pmatrix} 1 & -2 & 3 \\ 4 & 5 & -6 \end{pmatrix}$ and $B = \begin{pmatrix} 3 & 0 & 2 \\ -7 & 1 & 8 \end{pmatrix}$, **(b)** $A = \begin{pmatrix} 1 & 2 & -3 \\ 0 & -4 & 1 \end{pmatrix}$ and $B = \begin{pmatrix} 3 & 5 \\ 1 & -2 \end{pmatrix}$.

▌ **(a)** Add corresponding entries: $A + B = \begin{pmatrix} 1+3 & -2+0 & 3+2 \\ 4-7 & 5+1 & -6+8 \end{pmatrix} = \begin{pmatrix} 4 & -2 & 5 \\ -3 & 6 & 2 \end{pmatrix}$.

**(b)** The sum is not defined, since the matrices have different sizes.

**4.65** Find $C + D$ where:

**(a)** $C = \begin{pmatrix} 1 & 2 & 3 \\ 4 & 5 & 6 \end{pmatrix}$ and $D = \begin{pmatrix} 1 & -1 & 2 \\ 0 & 3 & -5 \end{pmatrix}$, **(b)** $C = \begin{pmatrix} 1 & 2 & -3 & 4 \\ 0 & -5 & 1 & -1 \end{pmatrix}$ and $D = \begin{pmatrix} 3 & -5 & 6 & -1 \\ 2 & 0 & -2 & -3 \end{pmatrix}$

▌ Add corresponding elements:

**(a)** $C + D = \begin{pmatrix} 1+1 & 2+(-1) & 3+2 \\ 4+0 & 5+3 & 6+(-5) \end{pmatrix} = \begin{pmatrix} 2 & 1 & 5 \\ 4 & 8 & 1 \end{pmatrix}$

**(b)** $C + D = \begin{pmatrix} 1+3 & 2+(-5) & (-3)+6 & 4+(-1) \\ 0+2 & (-5)+0 & 1+(-2) & (-1)+(-3) \end{pmatrix} = \begin{pmatrix} 4 & -3 & 3 & 3 \\ 2 & -5 & -1 & -4 \end{pmatrix}$

**4.66** Find $3A$ and $-5A$, where $A = \begin{pmatrix} 1 & -2 & 3 \\ 4 & 5 & -6 \end{pmatrix}$.

▌ Multiply each entry by the given scalar:

$$3A = \begin{pmatrix} 3\cdot 1 & 3\cdot(-2) & 3\cdot 3 \\ 3\cdot 4 & 3\cdot 5 & 3\cdot(-6) \end{pmatrix} = \begin{pmatrix} 3 & -6 & 9 \\ 12 & 15 & -18 \end{pmatrix}$$

$$-5A = \begin{pmatrix} -5\cdot 1 & -5\cdot(-2) & -5\cdot 3 \\ -5\cdot 4 & -5\cdot 5 & -5\cdot(-6) \end{pmatrix} = \begin{pmatrix} -5 & 10 & -15 \\ -20 & -25 & 30 \end{pmatrix}$$

**4.67** Compute: **(a)** $3\begin{pmatrix} 2 & 4 \\ -3 & 1 \end{pmatrix}$, **(b)** $-2\begin{pmatrix} 1 & 7 \\ 2 & -3 \\ 0 & -1 \end{pmatrix}$.

▌ **(a)** 
$$3\begin{pmatrix} 2 & 4 \\ -3 & 1 \end{pmatrix} = \begin{pmatrix} 3\cdot 2 & 3\cdot 4 \\ 3\cdot(-3) & 3\cdot 1 \end{pmatrix} = \begin{pmatrix} 6 & 12 \\ -9 & 3 \end{pmatrix}$$

▌ **(b)**
$$-2\begin{pmatrix} 1 & 7 \\ 2 & -3 \\ 0 & -1 \end{pmatrix} = \begin{pmatrix} (-2)\cdot 1 & (-2)\cdot 7 \\ (-2)\cdot 2 & (-2)\cdot(-3) \\ (-2)\cdot 0 & (-2)\cdot(-1) \end{pmatrix} = \begin{pmatrix} -2 & -14 \\ -4 & 6 \\ 0 & 2 \end{pmatrix}$$

**4.68** The *difference*, $A - B$, of two matrices $A$ and $B$ of the same size is defined by $A - B = A + (-B)$. Find $A - B$ if

$$A = \begin{pmatrix} 4 & -5 & 6 \\ 2 & 3 & -1 \end{pmatrix} \quad \text{and} \quad B = \begin{pmatrix} 2 & -3 & 8 \\ 1 & -2 & -6 \end{pmatrix}$$

▌
$$A - B = A + (-B) = \begin{pmatrix} 4 & -5 & 6 \\ 2 & 3 & -1 \end{pmatrix} + \begin{pmatrix} -2 & 3 & -8 \\ -1 & 2 & 6 \end{pmatrix} = \begin{pmatrix} 2 & -2 & -2 \\ 1 & 5 & 5 \end{pmatrix}$$

**4.69** Find $2A - 3B$, where $A = \begin{pmatrix} 1 & -2 & 3 \\ 4 & 5 & -6 \end{pmatrix}$ and $B = \begin{pmatrix} 3 & 0 & 2 \\ -7 & 1 & 8 \end{pmatrix}$.

▌ First perform the scalar multiplications, and then a matrix addition:

$$2A - 3B = \begin{pmatrix} 2 & -4 & 6 \\ 8 & 10 & -12 \end{pmatrix} + \begin{pmatrix} -9 & 0 & -6 \\ 21 & -3 & -24 \end{pmatrix} = \begin{pmatrix} -7 & -4 & 0 \\ 29 & 7 & -36 \end{pmatrix}$$

(Note that we multiply $B$ by $-3$ and then add, rather than multiplying $B$ by 3 and subtracting. This usually avoids errors.)

**4.70** If $A = \begin{pmatrix} 2 & -5 & 1 \\ 3 & 0 & -4 \end{pmatrix}$, $B = \begin{pmatrix} 1 & -2 & -3 \\ 0 & -1 & 5 \end{pmatrix}$, and $C = \begin{pmatrix} 0 & 1 & -2 \\ 1 & -1 & -1 \end{pmatrix}$, find $3A + 4B - 2C$.

▎ First perform the scalar multiplications, and then the matrix additions:

$$3A + 4B - 2C = \begin{pmatrix} 6 & -15 & 3 \\ 9 & 0 & -12 \end{pmatrix} + \begin{pmatrix} 4 & -8 & -12 \\ 0 & -4 & 20 \end{pmatrix} + \begin{pmatrix} 0 & -2 & 4 \\ -2 & 2 & 2 \end{pmatrix} = \begin{pmatrix} 10 & -25 & -5 \\ 7 & -2 & 10 \end{pmatrix}$$

**4.71**  Find $2A + 5B$, where $A = \begin{pmatrix} 1 & 3 \\ 2 & -5 \end{pmatrix}$ and $B = \begin{pmatrix} 4 & -3 & -6 \\ 3 & 7 & -8 \end{pmatrix}$,

▎ Although $2A$ and $5B$ are defined, the sum $2A + 5B$ is not defined since $2A$ and $5B$ have different sizes.

**4.72**  Find $x, y, z$, and $t$, if $3\begin{pmatrix} x & y \\ z & t \end{pmatrix} = \begin{pmatrix} x & 6 \\ -1 & 2t \end{pmatrix} + \begin{pmatrix} 4 & x+y \\ z+t & 3 \end{pmatrix}$.

▎ First write each side as a single matrix:

$$\begin{pmatrix} 3x & 3y \\ 3z & 3t \end{pmatrix} = \begin{pmatrix} x+4 & x+y+6 \\ z+t-1 & 2t+3 \end{pmatrix}$$

Set corresponding entries equal to each other to obtain the system of four equations,

$$3x = x + 4 \qquad\qquad 2x = 4$$
$$3y = x + y + 6 \qquad\qquad 2y = 6 + x$$
$$\qquad\qquad\qquad \text{or}$$
$$3z = z + t - 1 \qquad\qquad 2z = t - 1$$
$$3t = 2t + 3 \qquad\qquad t = 3$$

The solution is: $x = 2$, $y = 4$, $z = 1$, $t = 3$.

**Theorem 4.5:**  Let **M** be the collection of all $m \times n$ matrices over **R**. Then, for any matrices $A = (a_{ij})$, $B = (b_{ij})$, and $C = (c_{ij})$ in **M**, and any scalars $k_1, k_2$ in **R**,

   (i)   $(A + B) + C = A + (B + C)$      (v)   $k_1(A + B) = k_1 A + k_1 B$

  (ii)   $A + 0 = A$                    (vi)   $(k_1 + k_2)A = k_1 A + k_2 A$

 (iii)   $A + (-A) = 0$           (vii)   $(k_1 k_2)A = k_1(k_2 A)$

 (iv)   $A + B = B + A$        (viii)   $1A = A$

**4.73**  Prove Theorem 4.5.

▎ The proof may be obtained directly from the proof of Theorem 4.1 in Problems 4.19–4.26 by replacing the $u_i$, $v_i$, $w_i$ in the proof of Theorem 4.1 by the entries $a_{ij}$, $b_{ij}$, $c_{ij}$, respectively. (In fact, Theorem 4.1 may be viewed as a special case of Theorem 4.5 by viewing the vectors $u$, $v$, and $w$ as row matrices.)

**4.74**  Comment on the difference, if any, between the $+$ signs in (vi) of Theorem 4.5.

▎ On the left, the $+$ sign refers to addition of scalars in **R**; on the right, to addition of matrices in **M**.

## 4.3  MATRIX MULTIPLICATION

    This section considers the following operation of matrix multiplication. Suppose $A$ and $B$ are two matrices such that the number of columns of $A$ is equal to the number of rows of $B$, say $A$ is an $m \times p$ matrix and $B$ is a $p \times n$ matrix. Then the product of $A$ and $B$, written $AB$, is the $m \times n$ matrix whose $ij$-entry is obtained by multiplying the elements of the $i$th row of $A$ by the corresponding elements of the $j$th column of $B$ and then adding;

$$\begin{pmatrix} a_{11} & \cdots & a_{1p} \\ \cdot & \cdots & \cdot \\ \boxed{a_{i1} & \cdots & a_{ip}} \\ \cdot & \cdots & \cdot \\ a_{m1} & \cdots & a_{mp} \end{pmatrix} \begin{pmatrix} b_{11} & \cdots & \boxed{b_{1j}} & \cdots & b_{1n} \\ \cdot & \cdots & \cdot & \cdots & \cdot \\ \cdot & \cdots & \cdot & \cdots & \cdot \\ \cdot & \cdots & \cdot & \cdots & \cdot \\ b_{p1} & \cdots & \boxed{b_{pj}} & \cdots & b_{pn} \end{pmatrix} = \begin{pmatrix} c_{11} & \cdots & c_{1n} \\ \cdot & \cdots & \cdot \\ \cdot & \boxed{c_{ij}} & \cdot \\ \cdot & \cdots & \cdot \\ c_{m1} & \cdots & c_{mn} \end{pmatrix}$$

where $$c_{ij} = a_{i1}b_{1j} + a_{i2}b_{2j} + \cdots + a_{ip}b_{pj} = \sum_{k=1}^{p} a_{ik}b_{kj}$$

In particular, the product of a row matrix and a column matrix with the same number of elements is their dot product as defined in Section 4.1:

$$(a_1, a_2, \ldots, a_n)\begin{pmatrix} b_1 \\ b_2 \\ \cdots \\ b_n \end{pmatrix} = a_1 b_2 + a_2 b_2 + \cdots + a_n b_n \equiv \sum_{k=1}^{n} a_k b_k$$

If the number of columns of $A$ is not equal to the number of rows of $B$, say $A$ is $m \times p$ and $B$ is $q \times n$ where $p \neq q$, then the product $AB$ is not defined.

**4.75** Calculate: **(a)** $(8, -4, 5)\begin{pmatrix} 3 \\ 2 \\ -1 \end{pmatrix}$, **(b)** $(6, -1, 7, 5)\begin{pmatrix} 4 \\ -9 \\ -3 \\ 2 \end{pmatrix}$, and **(c)** $(3, 8, -2, 4)\begin{pmatrix} 5 \\ -1 \\ 6 \end{pmatrix}$.

**▌ (a)** Multiply corresponding entries and add:

$$(8, -4, 5)\begin{pmatrix} 3 \\ 2 \\ -1 \end{pmatrix} = (8)(3) + (-4)(2) + (5)(-1) = 24 - 8 - 5 = 11$$

**(b)** Multiply corresponding entries and add:

$$(6, -1, 7, 5)\begin{pmatrix} 4 \\ -9 \\ -3 \\ 2 \end{pmatrix} = 24 + 9 - 21 + 10 = 22$$

**(c)** This product is not defined since the row matrix and column matrix have different numbers of elements.

**4.76** Let $(r \times s)$ denote a matrix with size $r \times s$. Find the size of each product that is defined:

**(a)** $(2 \times 3)(3 \times 4)$    **(c)** $(1 \times 2)(3 \times 1)$    **(e)** $(3 \times 4)(3 \times 4)$

**(b)** $(4 \times 1)(1 \times 2)$    **(d)** $(5 \times 2)(2 \times 3)$    **(f)** $(2 \times 2)(2 \times 4)$

**▌** An $m \times p$ matrix is multipliable on the right by a $q \times n$ matrix only when $p = q$, that is, only when the "inner" numbers are equal. In such a case, the product in an $m \times n$ matrix, that is, the size is the "outer" numbers in the given order. Thus **(a)** $2 \times 4$, **(b)** $4 \times 2$, **(c)** not defined since the inner numbers 2 and 3 are not equal, **(d)** $5 \times 3$, **(e)** not defined since the inner numbers 4 and 3 are distinct, and **(f)** $2 \times 4$.

**4.77** Find the product $AB$ of the matrices $A = \begin{pmatrix} 1 & 3 \\ 2 & -1 \end{pmatrix}$ and $B = \begin{pmatrix} 2 & 0 & -4 \\ 3 & -2 & 6 \end{pmatrix}$.

**▌** Since $A$ is $2 \times 2$ and $B$ is $2 \times 3$, the product $AB$ is defined as a $2 \times 3$ matrix. To obtain the entries in the first row of $AB$, multiply the first row $(1, 3)$ of $A$ by the columns $\begin{pmatrix} 2 \\ 3 \end{pmatrix}$, $\begin{pmatrix} 0 \\ -2 \end{pmatrix}$, and $\begin{pmatrix} -4 \\ 6 \end{pmatrix}$ of $B$, respectively:

$$\begin{pmatrix} \boxed{1 \quad 3} \\ 2 \quad -1 \end{pmatrix}\left(\boxed{\begin{matrix}2\\3\end{matrix}} \quad \boxed{\begin{matrix}0\\-2\end{matrix}} \quad \boxed{\begin{matrix}-4\\6\end{matrix}}\right) = \begin{pmatrix} (1)(2) + (3)(3) & (1)(0) + (3)(-2) & (1)(-4) + (3)(6) \end{pmatrix}$$

$$= \begin{pmatrix} 2+9 & 0-6 & -4+18 \end{pmatrix} = \begin{pmatrix} 11 & -6 & 14 \end{pmatrix}$$

To obtain the entries in the second row of $AB$, multiply the second row $(2, -1)$ of $A$ by the columns of $B$, respectively:

$$\begin{pmatrix} 1 \quad 3 \\ \boxed{2 \quad -1} \end{pmatrix}\left(\boxed{\begin{matrix}2\\3\end{matrix}} \quad \boxed{\begin{matrix}0\\-2\end{matrix}} \quad \boxed{\begin{matrix}-4\\6\end{matrix}}\right) = \begin{pmatrix} 11 & -6 & 14 \\ (2)(2) + (-1)(3) & (2)(0) + (-1)(-2) & (2)(-4) + (-1)(6) \end{pmatrix}$$

Thus 
$$AB = \begin{pmatrix} 11 & -6 & 14 \\ 1 & 2 & -14 \end{pmatrix}$$

**4.78** Find the product $BA$ of the matrices $A$ and $B$ in Problem 4.77.

▌ Note that $B$ is $2 \times 3$ and $A$ is $2 \times 2$. Since the inner numbers 3 and 2 are not equal, the product $BA$ is not defined.

**4.79** Find the product $AB$ where $A = (2 \quad 1)$ and $B = \begin{pmatrix} 1 & -2 & 0 \\ 4 & 5 & -3 \end{pmatrix}$.

▌ Since $A$ is $1 \times 2$ and $B$ is $2 \times 3$, the product $AB$ is defined as a $1 \times 3$ matrix, or row vector with 3 components. To obtain the components of $AB$, multiply the row of $A$ by each column of $B$:

$$AB = (\boxed{2, 1})\begin{pmatrix} \boxed{1} & \boxed{-2} & \boxed{0} \\ 4 & 5 & -3 \end{pmatrix} = (2+4, \, -4+5, \, 0-3) = (6, \, 1, \, -3)$$

**4.80** Find the product $AB$ where $A = \begin{pmatrix} 2 & -1 \\ 1 & 0 \\ -3 & 4 \end{pmatrix}$ and $B = \begin{pmatrix} 1 & -2 & -5 \\ 3 & 4 & 0 \end{pmatrix}$.

▌ Now $A$ is $3 \times 2$ and $B$ is $2 \times 3$, so the product $AB$ is defined and is a $3 \times 3$ matrix. To obtain the first row of the product matrix $AB$, multiply the first row of $A$ by each column of $B$, respectively:

$$\begin{pmatrix} \boxed{2 \;\; -1} \\ 1 \quad 0 \\ -3 \quad 4 \end{pmatrix}\begin{pmatrix} \boxed{1} & \boxed{-2} & \boxed{-5} \\ 3 & 4 & 0 \end{pmatrix} = \begin{pmatrix} 2-3 & -4-4 & -10+0 \end{pmatrix} = \begin{pmatrix} -1 & -8 & -10 \end{pmatrix}$$

To obtain the second row of the product matrix $AB$, multiply the second row of $A$ by each column of $B$, respectively:

$$\begin{pmatrix} 2 \quad -1 \\ \boxed{1 \quad 0} \\ -3 \quad 4 \end{pmatrix}\begin{pmatrix} \boxed{1} & \boxed{-2} & \boxed{-5} \\ 3 & 4 & 0 \end{pmatrix} = \begin{pmatrix} -1 & -8 & -10 \\ 1+0 & -2+0 & -5+0 \end{pmatrix} = \begin{pmatrix} -1 & -8 & -10 \\ 1 & -2 & -5 \end{pmatrix}$$

To obtain the third row of the product matrix $AB$, multiply the third row of $A$ by each column of $B$, respectively:

$$\begin{pmatrix} 2 \quad -1 \\ 1 \quad 0 \\ \boxed{-3 \quad 4} \end{pmatrix}\begin{pmatrix} \boxed{1} & \boxed{-2} & \boxed{-5} \\ 3 & 4 & 0 \end{pmatrix} = \begin{pmatrix} -1 & -8 & -10 \\ 1 & -2 & -5 \\ -3+12 & 6+16 & 15+0 \end{pmatrix} = \begin{pmatrix} -1 & -8 & -10 \\ 1 & -2 & -5 \\ 9 & 22 & 15 \end{pmatrix}$$

Thus

$$AB = \begin{pmatrix} -1 & -8 & -10 \\ 1 & -2 & -5 \\ 9 & 22 & 15 \end{pmatrix}$$

**4.81** Find the product $BA$ where $A$ and $B$ are the matrices of Problem 4.80.

▌ Since $B$ is $2 \times 3$ and $A$ is $3 \times 2$, the product $BA$ is defined as a $2 \times 2$ matrix. To obtain the first row of $BA$, multiply the first row of $B$ by each column of $A$, respectively:

$$\begin{pmatrix} \boxed{1 \;\; -2 \;\; -5} \\ 3 \quad 4 \quad 0 \end{pmatrix}\begin{pmatrix} \boxed{2} & \boxed{-1} \\ 1 & 0 \\ -3 & 4 \end{pmatrix} = \begin{pmatrix} 2-2+15 & -1+0-20 \end{pmatrix} = \begin{pmatrix} 15 & -21 \end{pmatrix}$$

To obtain the second row of $BA$, multiply the second row of $B$ by each column of $A$, respectively:

$$\begin{pmatrix} 1 \quad -2 \quad -5 \\ \boxed{3 \;\; 4 \;\; 0} \end{pmatrix}\begin{pmatrix} \boxed{2} & \boxed{-1} \\ 1 & 0 \\ -3 & 4 \end{pmatrix} = \begin{pmatrix} 15 & -21 \\ 6+4+0 & -3+0+0 \end{pmatrix} = \begin{pmatrix} 15 & -21 \\ 10 & -3 \end{pmatrix}$$

Thus

$$BA = \begin{pmatrix} 15 & -21 \\ 10 & -3 \end{pmatrix}$$

**4.82** Find $AB$ where $A = \begin{pmatrix} 2 & 3 & -1 \\ 4 & -2 & 5 \end{pmatrix}$ and $B = \begin{pmatrix} 2 & -1 & 0 & 6 \\ 1 & 3 & -5 & 1 \\ 4 & 1 & -2 & 2 \end{pmatrix}$.

▮ Since $A$ is $2 \times 3$ and $B$ is $3 \times 4$, the product is defined as a $2 \times 4$ matrix. Multiply the rows of $A$ by the columns of $B$ to obtain:

$$AB = \begin{pmatrix} 4+3-4 & -2+9-1 & 0-15+2 & 12+3-2 \\ 8-2+20 & -4-6+5 & 0+10-10 & 24-2+10 \end{pmatrix} = \begin{pmatrix} 3 & 6 & -13 & 13 \\ 26 & -5 & 0 & 32 \end{pmatrix}$$

**4.83**   Find the size of the product $AB$, where $A = \begin{pmatrix} 2 & -1 & 0 \\ 1 & 0 & -3 \end{pmatrix}$ and $B = \begin{pmatrix} 1 & -4 & 0 & 1 \\ 2 & -1 & 3 & -1 \\ 4 & 0 & -2 & 0 \end{pmatrix}$. Furthermore,

suppose $AB = (c_{ij})$. Find: **(a)**: $c_{23}$, **(b)** $c_{14}$, **(c)** $c_{21}$, **(d)** $c_{32}$.

▮ Since $A$ is $2 \times 3$ and $B$ is $3 \times 4$, the product $AB$ is a $2 \times 4$ matrix. Also, the element $c_{ij}$, the $ij$-entry of $AB$, is the product of row $i$ of $A$ by column $j$ of $B$. Therefore:

**(a)**   $c_{23} = (1, 0, -3)\begin{pmatrix} 0 \\ 3 \\ -2 \end{pmatrix} = (1)(0) + (0)(3) + (-3)(-2) = 0 + 0 + 6 = 6$

**(b)**   $c_{14} = (2, -1, 0)\begin{pmatrix} 1 \\ -1 \\ 0 \end{pmatrix} = (2)(1) + (-1)(-1) + (0)(0) = 2 + 1 + 0 = 3$

**(b)**   $c_{21} = (1, 0, -3)\begin{pmatrix} 1 \\ 2 \\ 4 \end{pmatrix} = (1)(1) + (0)(2) + (-3)(4) = 1 + 0 - 12 = -11$

**(d)**   The element $c_{32}$ does not exist, since $A$, and with it $AB$, has only two rows.

**4.84**   Find: **(a)** $\begin{pmatrix} 1 & 6 \\ -3 & 5 \end{pmatrix}\begin{pmatrix} 2 \\ -7 \end{pmatrix}$, **(b)** $\begin{pmatrix} 2 \\ -7 \end{pmatrix}\begin{pmatrix} 1 & 6 \\ -3 & 5 \end{pmatrix}$, **(c)** $(2, -7)\begin{pmatrix} 1 & 6 \\ -3 & 5 \end{pmatrix}$, **(d)** $\begin{pmatrix} 1 & 6 \\ -3 & 5 \end{pmatrix}(2, -7)$.

▮ **(a)**   The first factor is $2 \times 2$ and the second is $2 \times 1$, so the product is defined as a $2 \times 1$ matrix.

$$\begin{pmatrix} 1 & 6 \\ -3 & 5 \end{pmatrix}\begin{pmatrix} 2 \\ -7 \end{pmatrix} = \begin{pmatrix} 2 - 42 \\ -6 - 35 \end{pmatrix} = \begin{pmatrix} -40 \\ -41 \end{pmatrix}$$

**(b)**   The product is not defined since the first factor is $2 \times 1$ and the second factor is $2 \times 2$.

**(c)**   The first factor is $1 \times 2$ and the second factor is $2 \times 2$, so the product is defined as a $1 \times 2$ (row) matrix.

$$(2, -7)\begin{pmatrix} 1 & 6 \\ -3 & 5 \end{pmatrix} = (2 + 21, 12 - 35) = (23, -23)$$

**(d)**   The product is not defined, since the first factor is $2 \times 2$ and the second factor is $1 \times 2$.

**4.85**   Let $A$ be an $m \times n$ matrix, with $m > 1$ and $n > 1$. Assuming $u$ and $v$ are vectors, discuss the conditions under which **(a)** $Au$ and **(b)** $vA$ are defined.

▮ **(a)** The product $Au$ is defined only when $u$ is a column vector with $n$ components; i.e., an $n \times 1$ matrix. In such case, $Au$ is a column vector with $m$ components. **(b)** The product $vA$ is defined only when $v$ is a row vector with $m$ components; i.e., a $1 \times m$ matrix. In such case, $vA$ is a row vector with $n$ components.

**4.86**   Compute: **(a)** $\begin{pmatrix} 2 \\ 3 \\ -1 \end{pmatrix}(6, -4, 5)$ and **(b)** $(6, -4, 5)\begin{pmatrix} 2 \\ 3 \\ -1 \end{pmatrix}$.

▮ **(a)**   The first factor is $3 \times 1$ and the second factor is $1 \times 3$, so the product is defined as a $3 \times 3$ matrix.

$$\begin{pmatrix} 2 \\ 3 \\ -1 \end{pmatrix}(6, -4, 5) = \begin{pmatrix} (2)(6) & (2)(-4) & (2)(5) \\ (3)(6) & (3)(-4) & (3)(5) \\ (-1)(6) & (-1)(-4) & (-1)(5) \end{pmatrix} = \begin{pmatrix} 12 & -8 & 10 \\ 18 & -12 & 15 \\ -6 & 4 & -5 \end{pmatrix}$$

**(b)**   The first factor is $1 \times 3$ and the second factor is $3 \times 1$, so the product is defined as a $1 \times 1$ matrix, which we frequently write as a scalar.

$$(6, -4, 5)\begin{pmatrix} 2 \\ 3 \\ -1 \end{pmatrix} = (12 - 12 - 5) = (-5) = -5$$

**4.87** Display two matrices $A$ and $B$ such that $AB$ and $BA$ are defined and have the same size, but $AB \neq BA$.

▮ Let $A = \begin{pmatrix} 1 & 6 \\ -3 & 5 \end{pmatrix}$ and $B = \begin{pmatrix} 4 & 0 \\ 2 & -1 \end{pmatrix}$. Then

$$AB = \begin{pmatrix} 1 & 6 \\ -3 & 5 \end{pmatrix}\begin{pmatrix} 4 & 0 \\ 2 & -1 \end{pmatrix} = \begin{pmatrix} 4+12 & 0-6 \\ -12+10 & 0-5 \end{pmatrix} = \begin{pmatrix} 16 & -6 \\ -2 & -5 \end{pmatrix}$$

$$BA = \begin{pmatrix} 4 & 0 \\ 2 & -1 \end{pmatrix}\begin{pmatrix} 1 & 6 \\ -3 & 5 \end{pmatrix} = \begin{pmatrix} 4+0 & 24+0 \\ 2+3 & 12-5 \end{pmatrix} = \begin{pmatrix} 4 & 24 \\ 5 & 7 \end{pmatrix}$$

*Matrix multiplication does not obey the commutative law.*

**4.88** Clearly $0A = 0$ (where the two zero matrices may be of different sizes) and $A0 = 0$. Show that we can have $AB = 0$, with $A \neq 0$ and $B \neq 0$.

▮ Let $A = \begin{pmatrix} 1 & 2 \\ 2 & 4 \end{pmatrix}$ and $B = \begin{pmatrix} 6 & 2 \\ -3 & -1 \end{pmatrix}$. Then

$$AB = \begin{pmatrix} 1 & 2 \\ 2 & 4 \end{pmatrix}\begin{pmatrix} 6 & 2 \\ -3 & -1 \end{pmatrix} = \begin{pmatrix} 6-6 & 2-2 \\ 12-12 & 4-4 \end{pmatrix} = \begin{pmatrix} 0 & 0 \\ 0 & 0 \end{pmatrix}$$

(In other words, matrix multiplication has zero divisors.)

Problems 4.89–4.92 establish the following theorem, where we assume that all products are defined.

**Theorem 4.6:**  Suppose that $A$, $B$, $C$ are matrices and $k$ is a scalar. Then:

   (i)   $(AB)C = A(BC)$  associative law
   (ii)  $A(B + C) = AB + AC$  left distributive law
   (iii) $(B + C)A = BA + CA$  right distributive law
   (iv)  $k(AB) = (kA)B = A(kB)$

**4.89** Prove Theorem 4.6(i): $(AB)C = A(BC)$.

▮ Let $A = (a_{ij})$, $B = (b_{jk})$, and $C = (c_{kl})$. Furthermore, let $AB = S = (s_{ik})$ and $BC = T = (t_{jl})$. Then

$$s_{ik} = \sum_{j=1}^{m} a_{ij}b_{jk} \qquad t_{jl} = \sum_{k=1}^{n} b_{jk}c_{kl}$$

Now multiplying $S$ by $C$, i.e., $(AB)$ by $C$, the element in the $i$th row and $l$th column of the matrix $(AB)C$ is

$$\sum_{k=1}^{n} s_{ik}c_{kl} = \sum_{k=1}^{n}\sum_{j=1}^{m} (a_{ij}b_{jk})c_{kl}$$

On the other hand, multiplying $A$ by $T$, i.e., $A$ by $BC$, the element in the $i$th row and $l$th column of the matrix $A(BC)$ is

$$\sum_{j=1}^{m} a_{ij}t_{jl} = \sum_{j=1}^{m}\sum_{k=1}^{n} a_{ij}(b_{jk}c_{kl})$$

The associative law in the field of scalars implies that the two double sums are equal, proving (i).

**4.90** Prove Theorem 4.6(ii): $A(B + C) = AB + AC$.

▮ Let $A = (a_{ik})$, $B = (b_{kj})$, and $C = (c_{kj})$. (Since $AB$ and $AC$ are defined, we can use the same index $k$ for the columns of $A$ and the rows of $B$ and $C$.) Let $D = B + C = (d_{kj})$, $E = AB = (e_{ij})$, and $F = AC = (f_{ij})$. Then

$$d_{kj} = b_{kj} + c_{kj}, \qquad e_{ij} = \sum_{k=1}^{p} a_{ik}b_{kj}, \qquad f_{ij} = \sum_{k=1}^{p} a_{ik}c_{kj}$$

Hence the $ij$-entry of the matrix $AB + AC$ is

$$e_{ij} + f_{ij} = \sum_{k=1}^{p} a_{ik}b_{kj} + \sum_{k=1}^{p} a_{ik}c_{kj} = \sum_{k=1}^{p} (a_{ik}b_{kj} + a_{ik}c_{kj}) \tag{1}$$

On the other hand, the $ij$-entry of the matrix $AD = A(B + C)$ is

$$\sum_{k=1}^{p} a_{ik}d_{kj} = \sum_{k=1}^{p} a_{ik}(b_{kk} + c_{kj}) \tag{2}$$

The right sides of (1) and (2) are equal by virtue of the distributive law in the scalar field; this proves (ii).

**4.91**   Prove Theorem 4.6(iii): $(B + C)A = BA + CA$.

▮ The proof is as in Problem 4.90. (There is no distinction between left and right multiplication in the field of scalars.)

**4.92**   Prove Theorem 4.6(iv): $k(AB) = (kA)B = A(kB)$.

▮
$$k\left(\sum_{r} a_{ir}b_{rj}\right) = \sum_{r}(ka_{ir})b_{rj} = \sum_{r} a_{ir}(kb_{rj})$$

## 4.4   TRANSPOSE OF A MATRIX

This section considers the transpose operation on matrices where the *transpose* of a matrix $A$, written $A^T$, is the matrix obtained by writing the rows of $A$, in order, as columns:

$$\begin{pmatrix} a_1 & a_2 & \cdots & a_n \\ b_1 & b_2 & \cdots & b_n \\ \cdots\cdots\cdots\cdots\cdots \\ c_1 & c_2 & \cdots & c_n \end{pmatrix}^T = \begin{pmatrix} a_1 & b_1 & \cdots & c_1 \\ a_2 & b_2 & \cdots & c_2 \\ \cdots\cdots\cdots\cdots\cdots \\ a_n & b_n & \cdots & c_n \end{pmatrix}$$

In other words, if $A = (a_{ij})$ is an $m \times n$ matrix, then $A^T = (a_{ij}^T)$ is the $n \times m$ matrix where $a_{ij}^T = a_{ji}$, for all $i$ and $j$.

**4.93**   Given $A = \begin{pmatrix} 1 & 3 & 5 \\ 6 & -7 & -8 \end{pmatrix}$, find $A^T$ and $(A^T)^T$.

▮ Rewrite the rows of $A$ as columns to obtain $A^T$, and then rewrite the rows of $A^T$ as columns to obtain $(A^T)^T$:

$$A^T = \begin{pmatrix} 1 & 6 \\ 3 & -7 \\ 5 & -8 \end{pmatrix}, \qquad (A^T)^T = \begin{pmatrix} 1 & 3 & 5 \\ 6 & -7 & -8 \end{pmatrix}$$

(As expected [see Theorem 4.7(ii)], $(A^T)^T = A$.)

**4.94**   Transpose: (a) $\begin{pmatrix} a_1 & a_2 & a_3 & a_4 \\ a_4 & a_3 & a_2 & a_1 \end{pmatrix}$, and (b) $\begin{pmatrix} 1 & 2 & 3 \\ -4 & -4 & -4 \\ 5 & 6 & 7 \end{pmatrix}$.

▮ Rewrite the rows as columns in (a) and the columns as rows in (b):

$$(a)\ \begin{pmatrix} a_1 & a_4 \\ a_2 & a_3 \\ a_3 & a_2 \\ a_4 & a_1 \end{pmatrix}, \qquad (b)\ \begin{pmatrix} 1 & -4 & 5 \\ 2 & -4 & 6 \\ 3 & -4 & 7 \end{pmatrix}$$

**4.95**   Find $u^T$, $v^T$, $w^T$ for the row vectors $u = (2, 4)$, $v = (1, 3, 5)$, and $w = (6, 6, 6)$.

▮ The transpose of a row vector will be a column vector:

$$u^T = \begin{pmatrix} 2 \\ 4 \end{pmatrix}, \qquad v^T = \begin{pmatrix} 1 \\ 3 \\ 5 \end{pmatrix} \qquad w^T = \begin{pmatrix} 6 \\ 6 \\ 6 \end{pmatrix}$$

**4.96** Find the transposes of the column vectors $u = \begin{pmatrix} 1 \\ 1 \end{pmatrix}$, $v = \begin{pmatrix} 2 \\ 4 \\ 6 \end{pmatrix}$, $w = \begin{pmatrix} -5 \\ -6 \\ 7 \end{pmatrix}$.

▌ The transpose of a column vector will be a row vector: $u^T = (1, 1)$, $v^T = (2, 4, 6)$, $w^T = (-5, -6, 7)$.

**4.97** Show that the matrices $AA^T$ and $A^TA$ are defined for any matrix $A$.

▌ If $A$ is an $m \times n$ matrix, then $A^T$ is an $n \times m$ matrix. Hence $AA^T$ is defined as an $m \times m$ matrix, and $A^TA$ is defined as an $n \times n$ matrix.

**4.98** Find $AA^T$ and $A^TA$, where $A = \begin{pmatrix} 1 & 2 & 0 \\ 3 & -1 & 4 \end{pmatrix}$.

▌ Obtain $A^T$ by rewriting the rows of $A$ as columns:

$$A^T = \begin{pmatrix} 1 & 3 \\ 2 & -1 \\ 0 & 4 \end{pmatrix} \quad \text{whence} \quad AA^T = \begin{pmatrix} 1 & 2 & 0 \\ 3 & -1 & 4 \end{pmatrix} \begin{pmatrix} 1 & 3 \\ 2 & -1 \\ 0 & 4 \end{pmatrix} = \begin{pmatrix} 5 & 1 \\ 1 & 26 \end{pmatrix}$$

$$A^TA = \begin{pmatrix} 1 & 3 \\ 2 & -1 \\ 0 & 4 \end{pmatrix} \begin{pmatrix} 1 & 2 & 0 \\ 3 & -1 & 4 \end{pmatrix} = \begin{pmatrix} 1+9 & 2-3 & 0+12 \\ 2-3 & 4+1 & 0-4 \\ 0+12 & 0-4 & 0+16 \end{pmatrix} = \begin{pmatrix} 10 & -1 & 12 \\ -1 & 5 & -4 \\ 12 & -4 & 16 \end{pmatrix}$$

**4.99** Given $A = \begin{pmatrix} 1 & 2 \\ 3 & -4 \end{pmatrix}$ and $B = \begin{pmatrix} 5 & 0 \\ -6 & 7 \end{pmatrix}$. Find $(AB)^T$.

▌ $$AB = \begin{pmatrix} 5-12 & 0+14 \\ 15+24 & 0-28 \end{pmatrix} = \begin{pmatrix} -7 & 14 \\ 39 & -28 \end{pmatrix} \quad \text{and so} \quad (AB)^T = \begin{pmatrix} -7 & 39 \\ 14 & -28 \end{pmatrix}$$

**4.100** Find $A^TB^T$ for the matrices in Problem 4.99.

▌ We have

$$A^T = \begin{pmatrix} 1 & 3 \\ 2 & -4 \end{pmatrix} \quad \text{and} \quad B^T = \begin{pmatrix} 5 & -6 \\ 0 & 7 \end{pmatrix} \quad \text{and so} \quad A^TB^T = \begin{pmatrix} 5+0 & -6+21 \\ 10+0 & -12-28 \end{pmatrix} = \begin{pmatrix} 5 & 15 \\ 10 & -40 \end{pmatrix}$$

Note that $(AB)^T \neq A^TB^T$.

**4.101** Find $B^TA^T$ for the matrices in Problem 4.99.

▌ $$B^TA^T = \begin{pmatrix} 5 & -6 \\ 0 & 7 \end{pmatrix} \begin{pmatrix} 1 & 3 \\ 2 & -4 \end{pmatrix} = \begin{pmatrix} 5-12 & 15+24 \\ 0+14 & 0-28 \end{pmatrix} = \begin{pmatrix} -7 & 39 \\ 14 & -28 \end{pmatrix}$$

(As expected [see Theorem 4.7(iv)], $(AB)^T = B^TA^T$.)

**Theorem 4.7:** The transpose operation on matrices satisfies
- (i)  $(A + B)^T = A^T + B^T$
- (ii)  $(A^T)^T = A$
- (iii)  $(kA)^T = kA^T$ ($k$ a scalar)
- (iv)  $(AB)^T = B^TA^T$

**4.102** Prove Theorem 4.7(i): $(A + B)^T = A^T + B^T$.

▌ If $A = (a_{ij})$ and $B = (b_{ij})$, then $a_{ij} + b_{ij}$ is the $ij$-entry of $A + B$; hence $a_{ij} + b_{ij}$ is the $ji$-entry (reverse order) of $(A + B)^T$. On the other hand, $a_{ij}$ is the $ji$-entry of $A^T$ and $b_{ij}$ is the $ji$-entry of $B^T$; so $a_{ij} + b_{ij}$ is the $ji$-entry of $A^T + B^T$. Thus $(A + B)^T = A^T + B^T$, since corresponding entries are equal.

**4.103** Prove Theorem 4.7(ii): $(A^T)^T = A$.

▌ Suppose $A = (a_{ij})$, $A^T = (b_{ij})$, and $(A^T)^T = (c_{ij})$. Then, for every $i$ and $j$, we have $b_{ij} = a_{ji}$ and hence $c_{ij} = b_{ji} = a_{ij}$. Thus $(A^T)^T = A$, since corresponding elements are equal. (In other words, a double interchange of rows and columns is equivalent to no interchange.)

**4.104** Prove Theorem 4.7(iii): $(kA)^T = kA^T$ where $k$ is a scalar.

▌ If $A = (a_{ij})$, then $ka_{ij}$ is the $ij$-entry of $kA$, and so $ka_{ij}$ is the $ji$-entry (reverse order) of $(kA)^T$. On the other hand, $a_{ij}$ is the $ji$-entry of $A^T$, and hence $ka_{ij}$ is the $ji$-entry of $kA^T$. Thus $(kA)^T = kA^T$, since corresponding entries are equal.

**4.105** Prove Theorem 4.7(iv): $(AB)^T = B^T A^T$.

❙ If $A = (a_{ij})$ and $B = (b_{kj})$, the $ij$-entry of $AB$ is

$$a_{i1}b_{1j} + a_{i2}b_{2j} + \cdots + a_{im}b_{mj} \tag{1}$$

Thus (1) is the $ji$-entry [reverse order] of $(AB)^T$.

On the other hand, column $j$ of $B$ becomes row $j$ of $B^T$, and row $i$ of $A$ becomes column $i$ of $A^T$. Consequently, the $ji$-entry of $B^T A^T$ is

$$(b_{1j} \quad b_{2j}, \cdots, b_{mj})\begin{pmatrix} a_{i1} \\ a_{i2} \\ \cdots \\ a_{im} \end{pmatrix} = b_{ij}a_{i1} + b_{2j}a_{i2} + \cdots + b_{mj}a_{im}$$

Thus, $(AB)^T = B^T A^T$, since corresponding entries are equal.

## 4.5 SQUARE MATRICES

This section investigates *square matrices*, that is, those matrices with the same number $n$ of rows as columns; such matrices are said to be of *order n* and are called *n-square matrices*. The (*main*) *diagonal* of a square matrix $A = (a_{ij})$ consists of the scalars $a_{11}, a_{22}, \ldots, a_{nn}$, and the *trace* of $A$, written tr $(A)$, is the sum of its diagonal elements.

**Remark 1:** The collection $M_n$ of all $n$-square matrices is closed under the operations of matrix addition, scalar product, matrix multiplication, and transpose, that is, the sum, scalar multiple, product, and transpose of $n$-square matrices are again $n$-square matrices.

**Remark 2:** The $n$-square matrix with 1s along the main diagonal and 0s elsewhere is called the *unit* or *identity matrix* and will be denoted by $I$. The unit matrix $I$ plays the same role in matrix multiplication as the number 1 does in the usual multiplication of numbers. Specifically,

$$AI = IA = A$$

for any square matrix $A$.

**Remark 3:** We form powers of a square matrix $A$ by defining

$$A^2 = AA, \quad A^3 = A^2 A, \quad \ldots, \quad \text{and } A^0 = I$$

We also form polynomials in $A$. That is, for any polynomial

$$f(x) = a_0 + a_1 x + a_2 x^2 + \cdots + a_n x^n$$

we define $f(A)$ to be the matrix

$$f(A) = a_0 I + a_1 A + a_2 A^2 + \cdots + a_n A^n$$

In the case that $f(A)$ is the zero matrix, then $A$ is said to be a *zero* or *root* of the polynomial $f(x)$.

**4.106** Find the diagonal of each of the following matrices:

(a) $A = \begin{pmatrix} 1 & 3 & 6 \\ 2 & -5 & 8 \\ 4 & -2 & 7 \end{pmatrix}$, (b) $B = \begin{pmatrix} t-2 & 3 \\ -4 & t+5 \end{pmatrix}$, (c) $C = \begin{pmatrix} 1 & 2 & -3 \\ 4 & -5 & 6 \end{pmatrix}$.

❙ (a) The diagonal consists of the elements from the upper left corner to the lower right corner of the matrix, that is, the elements $a_{11}, a_{22}, a_{33}$. Thus the diagonal of $A$ consists of the scalars 1, $-5$, and 7.
(b) The diagonal consists of the pair $[t-2, t+5]$.
(c) The diagonal is defined only for square matrices.

**4.107** Find the trace of each matrix in Problem 4.106.

❙ (a) The trace of $A$ is the sum of its diagonal elements: tr $(A) = 1 - 5 + 7 = 3$.
(b) Add the diagonal elements: tr $(B) = (t-2) + (t+5) = 2t + 3$.
(c) The trace, like the diagonal, is not defined for nonsquare matrices.

**4.108** Find the identity matrix $I_n$ of order $n$ for $n = 2, 3$, and 4. Display using *Kronecker delta notation*.

▮ Write 1s on the diagonal and 0s elsewhere:

$$I_2 = \begin{pmatrix} 1 & 0 \\ 0 & 1 \end{pmatrix}, \qquad I_3 = \begin{pmatrix} 1 & 0 & 0 \\ 0 & 1 & 0 \\ 1 & 0 & 1 \end{pmatrix}, \qquad I_4 = \begin{pmatrix} 1 & 0 & 0 & 0 \\ 0 & 1 & 0 & 0 \\ 0 & 0 & 1 & 0 \\ 0 & 0 & 0 & 1 \end{pmatrix}$$

The Kronecker delta is defined as $\delta_{ij} = \begin{cases} 0 & \text{if } i \neq j \\ 0 & \text{if } i = j \end{cases}$. Accordingly, $I = (\delta_{ij})$.

**4.109** Let $A = \begin{pmatrix} 1 & 2 \\ 4 & -3 \end{pmatrix}$. Find: (**a**) $A^2$, (**b**) $A^3$.

▮ (**a**) $A^2 = AA = \begin{pmatrix} 1 & 2 \\ 4 & -3 \end{pmatrix}\begin{pmatrix} 1 & 2 \\ 4 & -3 \end{pmatrix} = \begin{pmatrix} 1+8 & 2-6 \\ 4-12 & 8+9 \end{pmatrix} = \begin{pmatrix} 9 & -4 \\ -8 & 17 \end{pmatrix}$

▮ (**b**) $A^3 = AA^2 = \begin{pmatrix} 1 & 2 \\ 4 & -3 \end{pmatrix}\begin{pmatrix} 9 & -4 \\ -8 & 17 \end{pmatrix} = \begin{pmatrix} 9-16 & -4+34 \\ 36+24 & -16-51 \end{pmatrix} = \begin{pmatrix} -7 & 30 \\ 60 & -67 \end{pmatrix}$

**4.110** Referring to Problem 4.109, evaluate $f(A)$ for the polynomial $f(x) = 2x^3 - 4x + 5$.

▮ First substitute $A$ for $x$ and $5I$ for the constant 5 in the given polynomial $f(x) = 2x^3 - 4x + 5$:

$$f(A) = 2A^3 - 4A + 5I = 2\begin{pmatrix} -7 & 30 \\ 60 & -67 \end{pmatrix} - 4\begin{pmatrix} 1 & 2 \\ 4 & -3 \end{pmatrix} + 5\begin{pmatrix} 1 & 0 \\ 0 & 1 \end{pmatrix}$$

Then multiply each matrix by its respective scalar:

$$f(A) = \begin{pmatrix} -14 & 60 \\ 120 & -134 \end{pmatrix} + \begin{pmatrix} -4 & -8 \\ -16 & 12 \end{pmatrix} + \begin{pmatrix} 5 & 0 \\ 0 & 5 \end{pmatrix}$$

Lastly, add the corresponding elements in the matrices:

$$f(A) = \begin{pmatrix} -14-4+5 & 60-8+0 \\ 120-16+0 & -134+12+5 \end{pmatrix} = \begin{pmatrix} -13 & 52 \\ 104 & -117 \end{pmatrix}$$

**4.111** Show that the matrix $A$ of Problem 4.109 is a root of the polynomial $g(x) = x^2 + 2x - 11$.

▮ Now $A$ is a zero of $g(x)$ if the matrix $g(A)$ is the zero matrix. Thus compute $g(A)$ by first substituting $A$ for $x$ and $11I$ for the constant 11 in $g(x) = x^2 + 2x - 11$:

$$g(A) = A^2 + 2A - 11I = \begin{pmatrix} 9 & -4 \\ -8 & 17 \end{pmatrix} + 2\begin{pmatrix} 1 & 2 \\ 4 & -3 \end{pmatrix} - 11\begin{pmatrix} 1 & 0 \\ 0 & 1 \end{pmatrix}$$

Then multiply each matrix by the scalar preceding it:

$$g(A) = \begin{pmatrix} 9 & -4 \\ -8 & 17 \end{pmatrix} + \begin{pmatrix} 2 & 4 \\ 8 & -6 \end{pmatrix} + \begin{pmatrix} -11 & 0 \\ 0 & -11 \end{pmatrix}$$

Lastly, add the corresponding elements in the matrices:

$$g(A) = \begin{pmatrix} 9+2-11 & -4+4+0 \\ -8+8+0 & 17-6-11 \end{pmatrix} = \begin{pmatrix} 0 & 0 \\ 0 & 0 \end{pmatrix}$$

Since $g(A) = 0$, $A$ is a zero of the polynomial $g(x)$.

**4.112** Let $B = \begin{pmatrix} 1 & 3 \\ 5 & 3 \end{pmatrix}$. Find $f(B)$, where $f(x) = 2x^2 - 4x + 3$.

▮ First find

$$B^2 = BB = \begin{pmatrix} 1 & 3 \\ 5 & 3 \end{pmatrix}\begin{pmatrix} 1 & 3 \\ 5 & 3 \end{pmatrix} = \begin{pmatrix} 1+15 & 3+9 \\ 5+15 & 15+9 \end{pmatrix} = \begin{pmatrix} 16 & 12 \\ 20 & 24 \end{pmatrix}$$

Then

$$f(B) = 2B^2 - 4B + 3I = 2\begin{pmatrix} 16 & 12 \\ 20 & 24 \end{pmatrix} - 4\begin{pmatrix} 1 & 3 \\ 5 & 3 \end{pmatrix} + 3\begin{pmatrix} 1 & 0 \\ 0 & 1 \end{pmatrix}$$

$$= \begin{pmatrix} 32 & 24 \\ 40 & 48 \end{pmatrix} + \begin{pmatrix} -4 & -12 \\ -20 & -12 \end{pmatrix} + \begin{pmatrix} 3 & 0 \\ 0 & 3 \end{pmatrix} = \begin{pmatrix} 31 & 12 \\ 20 & 39 \end{pmatrix}$$

**4.113** Referring to Problem 4.112, find $g(B)$ for the polynomial $g(x) = x^2 - 4x - 12$.

$$g(B) = B^2 - 4B - 12I = \begin{pmatrix} 16 & 12 \\ 20 & 24 \end{pmatrix} - 4\begin{pmatrix} 1 & 3 \\ 5 & 3 \end{pmatrix} - 12\begin{pmatrix} 1 & 0 \\ 0 & 1 \end{pmatrix}$$

$$= \begin{pmatrix} 16 & 12 \\ 20 & 24 \end{pmatrix} + \begin{pmatrix} -4 & -12 \\ -20 & -12 \end{pmatrix} + \begin{pmatrix} -12 & 0 \\ 0 & -12 \end{pmatrix}$$

$$= \begin{pmatrix} 0 & 0 \\ 0 & 0 \end{pmatrix}$$

[Thus $B$ is a root of the polynomial $g(x)$.]

**4.114** Let $A = \begin{pmatrix} 1 & 2 \\ 0 & 1 \end{pmatrix}$. Find: **(a)** $A^2$, **(b)** $A^3$, and **(c)** $AS_k$ for $S_k = \begin{pmatrix} 1 & k \\ 0 & 1 \end{pmatrix}$.

**(a)** $A^2 = AA = \begin{pmatrix} 1 & 2 \\ 0 & 1 \end{pmatrix}\begin{pmatrix} 1 & 2 \\ 0 & 1 \end{pmatrix} = \begin{pmatrix} 1+0 & 2+2 \\ 0+0 & 0+1 \end{pmatrix} = \begin{pmatrix} 1 & 4 \\ 0 & 1 \end{pmatrix}$

**(b)** $A^3 = AA^2 = \begin{pmatrix} 1 & 2 \\ 0 & 1 \end{pmatrix}\begin{pmatrix} 1 & 4 \\ 0 & 1 \end{pmatrix} = \begin{pmatrix} 1+0 & 4+2 \\ 0+0 & 0+1 \end{pmatrix} = \begin{pmatrix} 1 & 6 \\ 0 & 1 \end{pmatrix}$

**(c)** $AS_k = \begin{pmatrix} 1 & 2 \\ 0 & 1 \end{pmatrix}\begin{pmatrix} 1 & k \\ 0 & 1 \end{pmatrix} = \begin{pmatrix} 1+0 & k+2 \\ 0+0 & 0+1 \end{pmatrix} = \begin{pmatrix} 1 & k+2 \\ 0 & 1 \end{pmatrix}$

**4.115** Find $A^n$ for the matrix $A$ of Problem 4.114.

Referring to Problem 4.114, multiplying $A^m$ by $A$ adds 2 to the upper right entry; hence $A^n = \begin{pmatrix} 1 & 2n \\ 0 & 1 \end{pmatrix}$

**4.116** Matrices $A$ and $B$ commute if $AB = BA$. Show that $A = \begin{pmatrix} 1 & 2 \\ 3 & 4 \end{pmatrix}$ and $B = \begin{pmatrix} 5 & 4 \\ 6 & 11 \end{pmatrix}$ commute.

$$AB = \begin{pmatrix} 5+12 & 4+22 \\ 15+24 & 12+44 \end{pmatrix} = \begin{pmatrix} 17 & 26 \\ 39 & 56 \end{pmatrix} \quad \text{and} \quad BA = \begin{pmatrix} 5+12 & 10+16 \\ 6+33 & 12+44 \end{pmatrix} = \begin{pmatrix} 17 & 26 \\ 39 & 56 \end{pmatrix}$$

Since $AB = BA$, the matrices commute.

**4.117** Find all matrices $M = \begin{pmatrix} x & y \\ z & t \end{pmatrix}$ that commute with $A = \begin{pmatrix} 1 & 1 \\ 0 & 1 \end{pmatrix}$.

$$AM = \begin{pmatrix} x+z & y+t \\ z & t \end{pmatrix} \quad \text{and} \quad MA = \begin{pmatrix} x & x+y \\ z & z+t \end{pmatrix}$$

Set $AM = MA$, to obtain the four equations

$$x+z = x, \quad y+t = x+y, \quad z = z, \quad t = z+t$$

From the first or last equation, $z = 0$; from the second equation, $x = t$. Thus $M$ is any matrix of the form $\begin{pmatrix} x & y \\ 0 & x \end{pmatrix}$.

## Square Matrices as Functions

**4.118** Show that an $n$-square matrix $A$ defines a function from $\mathbf{R}^n$ into $\mathbf{R}^n$ in two different ways.

Let $u$ be a vector in $\mathbf{R}^n$. Then $A$ defines a function $A: \mathbf{R}^n \to \mathbf{R}^n$ by either $A(u) = Au$ or $A(u) = uA$ according as $u$ is a column vector or a row vector.

**Remark:** Unless otherwise stated or implied, in subsequent problems vectors in $\mathbf{R}^n$ will be defined as column vectors, and the function defined by the matrix $A$ will be $A(u) = Au$. For typographical reasons, column vectors will often be indicated as transposed row vectors.

**4.119** Let $A = \begin{pmatrix} 1 & -2 & 3 \\ 4 & 5 & -6 \\ 2 & 0 & -1 \end{pmatrix}$. Find $A(u)$ where $u = (1, -3, 7)^T$. (Note $u$ is a column vector.)

∎ $$A(u) = Au = \begin{pmatrix} 1 & -2 & 3 \\ 4 & 5 & -6 \\ 2 & 0 & -1 \end{pmatrix} \begin{pmatrix} 1 \\ -3 \\ 7 \end{pmatrix} = \begin{pmatrix} 1+6+21 \\ 4-15-42 \\ 2+0-7 \end{pmatrix} = \begin{pmatrix} 28 \\ -53 \\ -5 \end{pmatrix}$$

**4.120** For the matrix $A$ in Problem 4.119, find $A(v)$ where:
(a) $v = (2, -1, 4)^T$,     (b) $v = (1, -7, 6, -4)^T$,     (c) $v = (3, -2, 6)$

∎ (a) $A(v) = Av = \begin{pmatrix} 1 & -2 & 3 \\ 4 & 5 & -6 \\ 2 & 0 & -1 \end{pmatrix} \begin{pmatrix} 2 \\ -1 \\ 4 \end{pmatrix} = \begin{pmatrix} 2+2+12 \\ 8-5-24 \\ 4+0-4 \end{pmatrix} = \begin{pmatrix} 16 \\ -21 \\ 0 \end{pmatrix}$

(b) Since $A$ is a 3-square matrix, $A(v)$ is not defined because $v$ belongs to $\mathbf{R}^4$ and not to $\mathbf{R}^3$ as required.

(c) By our convention, $A(v)$ is not defined since the given $v$ is a row vector.

**4.121** Given $A = \begin{pmatrix} 1 & 3 \\ 4 & -3 \end{pmatrix}$. Find a *nonzero* column vector $u = \begin{pmatrix} x \\ y \end{pmatrix}$ such that $A(u) = 3u$.

∎ First set up the matrix equation $Au = 3u$:

$$\begin{pmatrix} 1 & 3 \\ 4 & -3 \end{pmatrix} \begin{pmatrix} x \\ y \end{pmatrix} = 3 \begin{pmatrix} x \\ y \end{pmatrix}$$

Write each side as a single matrix (column vector):

$$\begin{pmatrix} x + 3y \\ 4x - 3y \end{pmatrix} = \begin{pmatrix} 3x \\ 3y \end{pmatrix}$$

Set corresponding elements equal to each other to obtain the system of equations, and reduce it to echelon form:

$$\begin{matrix} x + 3y = 3x \\ 4x - 3y = 3y \end{matrix} \Big\} \to \begin{cases} 2x - 3y = 0 \\ 4x - 6y = 0 \end{cases} \to \begin{cases} 2x - 3y = 0 \\ \phantom{2x - 3y} 0 = 0 \end{cases} \to 2x - 3y = 0$$

The system reduces to one homogeneous equation in two unknowns, and so has an infinite number of solutions. To obtain a nonzero solution let, say, $y = 2$; then $x = 3$. That is, $u = (3, 2)^T$ is a desired vector.

**4.122** Given $B = \begin{pmatrix} 1 & 3 \\ 5 & 3 \end{pmatrix}$. Find a *nonzero* vector $u = \begin{pmatrix} x \\ y \end{pmatrix}$ such that $B(u) = 6u$.

∎ Proceed as in Problem 4.121:

$$\begin{pmatrix} 1 & 3 \\ 5 & 3 \end{pmatrix} \begin{pmatrix} x \\ y \end{pmatrix} = 6 \begin{pmatrix} x \\ y \end{pmatrix} \qquad \text{or} \qquad \begin{pmatrix} x + 3y \\ 5x + 3y \end{pmatrix} = \begin{pmatrix} 6x \\ 6y \end{pmatrix}$$

Then $\qquad \begin{matrix} x + 3y = 6x \\ 5x + 3y = 6y \end{matrix} \Big\} \to \begin{cases} -5x + 3y = 0 \\ 5x - 3y = 0 \end{cases} \to 5x - 3y = 0$

There are an infinite number of solutions. To obtain a nonzero solution, set $y = 5$; hence $x = 3$. Thus, $u = (3, 5)^T$.

**4.123** Given $A = \begin{pmatrix} 1 & 2 & -3 \\ 2 & 5 & -1 \\ 5 & 12 & -5 \end{pmatrix}$. Find all vectors $u = (x, y, z)^T$ such that $A(u) = 0$.

▌ Set up the equation $Au = 0$ and then write each side as a single matrix:

$$\begin{pmatrix} 1 & 2 & -3 \\ 2 & 5 & -1 \\ 5 & 12 & -5 \end{pmatrix}\begin{pmatrix} x \\ y \\ z \end{pmatrix} = \begin{pmatrix} 0 \\ 0 \\ 0 \end{pmatrix} \quad \text{or} \quad \begin{pmatrix} x + 2y - 3z \\ 2x + 5y - z \\ 5x + 12y - 5z \end{pmatrix} = \begin{pmatrix} 0 \\ 0 \\ 0 \end{pmatrix}$$

Set corresponding elements equal to each other to obtain a homogeneous system, and reduce the system to echelon form:

$$\left.\begin{matrix} x + 2y - 3z = 0 \\ 2x + 5y - z = 0 \\ 5x + 12y - 5z = 0 \end{matrix}\right\} \rightarrow \left\{\begin{matrix} x + 2y - 3z = 0 \\ y + 5z = 0 \\ 2y + 10z = 0 \end{matrix}\right\} \rightarrow \left\{\begin{matrix} x + 2y - 3z = 0 \\ y + 5z = 0 \end{matrix}\right.$$

In the echelon form, $z$ is the free variable. To obtain the general solution, set $z = a$ where $a$ is a parameter. Back substitution yields $y = -5a$, and then $x = 13a$. Thus, $u = (13a, -5a, a)^T$ represents all vectors such that $Au = 0$.

## Invertible Matrices

This subsection considers invertible matrices. A square matrix $A$ is said to be *invertible* or *nonsingular* if there exists a matrix $B$ with the property that

$$AB = BA = I, \text{ the identity matrix}$$

Such a matrix $B$ is unique; it is called the *inverse* of $A$ and is denoted by $A^{-1}$.

**Remark:** It is known that $AB = I$ if and only if $BA = I$; hence it is necessary to test only one product to determine whether two given matrices are inverses.

**4.124** Show that the above inverse matrix $B$ is unique.

▌ If $AB_1 = B_1A = I$ and $AB_2 = B_2A = 1$, then $B_1 = B_1I = B_1(AB_2) = (B_1A)B_2 = IB_2 = B_2$.

**4.125** Show that the inverse relation is symmetric; i.e., $(A^{-1})^{-1} = A$.

▌ If $AB = BA = I$, then $BA = AB = I$; so, if $B$ is the inverse of $A$, then $B$ is invertible and $A$ is the inverse of $B$. In other words, $(A^{-1})^{-1} = A$.

**4.126** Show that $A = \begin{pmatrix} 2 & 5 \\ 1 & 3 \end{pmatrix}$ and $B = \begin{pmatrix} 3 & -5 \\ -1 & 2 \end{pmatrix}$ are inverses.

▌ Compute $AB$ and $BA$:

$$AB = \begin{pmatrix} 2 & 5 \\ 1 & 3 \end{pmatrix}\begin{pmatrix} 3 & -5 \\ -1 & 2 \end{pmatrix} = \begin{pmatrix} 6-5 & -10+10 \\ 3-3 & -5+6 \end{pmatrix} = \begin{pmatrix} 1 & 0 \\ 0 & 1 \end{pmatrix} = I$$

$$BA = \begin{pmatrix} 3 & -5 \\ -1 & 2 \end{pmatrix}\begin{pmatrix} 2 & 5 \\ 1 & 3 \end{pmatrix} = \begin{pmatrix} 6-5 & 15-15 \\ -2+2 & -5+6 \end{pmatrix} = \begin{pmatrix} 1 & 0 \\ 0 & 1 \end{pmatrix} = I$$

Thus $A$ and $B$ are inverses since $AB = BA = I$.

**4.127** Show that $A = \begin{pmatrix} 1 & 0 & 2 \\ 2 & -1 & 3 \\ 4 & 1 & 8 \end{pmatrix}$ and $B = \begin{pmatrix} -11 & 2 & 2 \\ -4 & 0 & 1 \\ 6 & -1 & -1 \end{pmatrix}$ are inverses.

▌

$$AB = \begin{pmatrix} -11+0+12 & 2+0-2 & 2+0-2 \\ -22+4+18 & 4+0-3 & 4-1-3 \\ -44-4+48 & 8+0-8 & 8+1-8 \end{pmatrix} = \begin{pmatrix} 1 & 0 & 0 \\ 0 & 1 & 0 \\ 0 & 0 & 1 \end{pmatrix} = I$$

By the above remark, $AB = I$ if and only if $BA = I$; hence we do not need to test if $BA = I$. Thus $A$ and $B$ are inverses of each other.

**4.128** Find the inverse of $\begin{pmatrix} 3 & 5 \\ 2 & 3 \end{pmatrix}$.

▮ We seek scalars $x$, $y$, $z$, and $t$ for which

$$\begin{pmatrix} 3 & 5 \\ 2 & 3 \end{pmatrix}\begin{pmatrix} x & y \\ z & t \end{pmatrix} = \begin{pmatrix} 1 & 0 \\ 0 & 1 \end{pmatrix} \quad \text{or} \quad \begin{pmatrix} 3x + 5z & 3y + 5t \\ 2x + 3z & 2y + 3t \end{pmatrix} = \begin{pmatrix} 1 & 0 \\ 0 & 1 \end{pmatrix}$$

or which satisfy

$$\begin{cases} 3x + 5z = 1 \\ 2x + 3z = 0 \end{cases} (1), \qquad \begin{cases} 3y + 5t = 0 \\ 2y + 3t = 1 \end{cases} (2)$$

To solve (1), multiply the first equation by 2 and the second equation by $-3$ and then add:

$$\begin{array}{ll} 2 \times \text{first:} & 6x + 10z = 2 \\ -3 \times \text{second:} & -6x - 9z = 0 \\ \hline \text{Addition:} & z = 2 \end{array}$$

Substitute $z = 2$ into the first equation to obtain

$$3x + 5 \cdot 2 = 1 \quad \text{or} \quad 3x + 10 = 1 \quad \text{or} \quad 3x = -9 \quad \text{or} \quad x = -3$$

To solve (2), multiply the first equation by 2 and the second equation by $-3$ and then add:

$$\begin{array}{ll} 2 \times \text{first:} & 6y + 10t = 0 \\ -3 \times \text{second:} & -6y - 9t = -3 \\ \hline \text{Addition:} & t = -3 \end{array}$$

Substitute $t = -3$ in the first equation to obtain

$$3y + 5 \cdot (-3) = 0 \quad \text{or} \quad 3y - 15 = 0 \quad \text{or} \quad 3y = 15 \quad \text{or} \quad y = 5$$

Thus the inverse of the given matrix is $\begin{pmatrix} -3 & 5 \\ 2 & -3 \end{pmatrix}$.

**4.129** When is the general $2 \times 2$ matrix $A = \begin{pmatrix} a & b \\ c & d \end{pmatrix}$ invertible? What then is its inverse?

▮ We seek scalars $x$, $y$, $z$, $t$ such that

$$\begin{pmatrix} a & b \\ c & d \end{pmatrix}\begin{pmatrix} x & y \\ z & t \end{pmatrix} = \begin{pmatrix} 1 & 0 \\ 0 & 1 \end{pmatrix} \quad \text{or} \quad \begin{pmatrix} ax + bz & ay + bt \\ cx + dz & cy + dt \end{pmatrix} = \begin{pmatrix} 1 & 0 \\ 0 & 1 \end{pmatrix}$$

which reduces to solving the following two systems

$$\begin{cases} ax + bz = 1 \\ cx + dz = 0 \end{cases} \quad \text{and} \quad \begin{cases} ay + bt = 0 \\ cy + dt = 1 \end{cases}$$

Set $|A| = ad - bc$ [the *determinant* of $A$]. The two systems have a solution if and only if $|A| \neq 0$. In this case the first system has the unique solution $x = d/|A|$, $z = -c/|A|$, and the second system has the unique solution $y = -b/|A|$, $t = a/|A|$. Accordingly,

$$A^{-1} = \begin{pmatrix} d/|A| & -b/|A| \\ -c/|A| & a/|A| \end{pmatrix} = \frac{1}{|A|}\begin{pmatrix} d & -b \\ -c & a \end{pmatrix}$$

In words: When $|A| \neq 0$, the inverse of a $2 \times 2$ matrix $A$ is obtained by (i) interchanging the elements on the main diagonal, (ii) taking the negatives of the other elements, and (iii) multiplying the matrix by $1/|A|$.

**4.130** Find the inverse of $A = \begin{pmatrix} 5 & 3 \\ 4 & 2 \end{pmatrix}$.

▮ Use the explicit formula in Problem 4.129. First find $|A| = (5)(2) - (3)(4) = -2$. Next interchange the diagonal elements, take the negatives of the nondiagonal elements and multiply by $1/|A|$:

$$A^{-1} = -\frac{1}{2}\begin{pmatrix} 2 & -3 \\ -4 & 5 \end{pmatrix} = \begin{pmatrix} -1 & 3/2 \\ 2 & -5/2 \end{pmatrix}$$

**4.131** Find the inverse of $B = \begin{pmatrix} 2 & -3 \\ 1 & 3 \end{pmatrix}$.

❚ First find $|B| = (2)(3) - (-3)(1) = 9$. Next interchange the diagonal elements, take the negatives of the nondiagonal elements, and multiply by $1/|B|$:

$$B^{-1} = \frac{1}{9}\begin{pmatrix} 3 & 3 \\ -1 & 2 \end{pmatrix} = \begin{pmatrix} 1/3 & 1/3 \\ -1/9 & 2/9 \end{pmatrix}$$

**4.132** Try to find the inverse of $C = \begin{pmatrix} -2 & 6 \\ 3 & -9 \end{pmatrix}$.

❚ First find $|C| = (-2)(-9) - (6)(3) = 0$. Since $|C| = 0$, $C$ has no inverse.

Problems 4.133–4.136 assume that the reader is familiar with the elementary row operations and the Gaussian algorithm which row reduces a matrix to an echelon form and to its row canonical form.

**4.133** Give the Gaussian elimination algorithm which either finds the inverse of an $n$-square matrix $A$ or determines that $A$ is not invertible.

❚ *Step 1:* Form the $n \times 2n$ (block) matrix $M = (A \,\vdots\, I)$; that is, $A$ is in the left half of $M$ and $I$ is in the right half of $M$.

*Step 2:* Row reduce $M$ to echelon form. If the process generates a zero now in the $A$-half of $M$, STOP ($A$ is not invertible). Otherwise, the $A$-half will assume triangular form.

*Step 3:* Further row reduce $M$ to the row canonical form $(I \,\vdots\, B)$, where $I$ has replaced $A$ in the left half of the matrix.

*Step 4:* Set $A^{-1} = B$.

**4.134** Find the inverse of $A = \begin{pmatrix} 1 & 0 & 2 \\ 2 & -1 & 3 \\ 4 & 1 & 8 \end{pmatrix}$.

❚ Form the block matrix $M = (A \,\vdots\, I)$ and reduce $M$ to echelon form:

$$M = \begin{pmatrix} 1 & 0 & 2 & \vdots & 1 & 0 & 0 \\ 2 & -1 & 3 & \vdots & 0 & 1 & 0 \\ 4 & 1 & 8 & \vdots & 0 & 0 & 1 \end{pmatrix} \sim \begin{pmatrix} 1 & 0 & 2 & \vdots & 1 & 0 & 0 \\ 0 & -1 & -1 & \vdots & -2 & 1 & 0 \\ 0 & 1 & 0 & \vdots & -4 & 0 & 1 \end{pmatrix} \sim \begin{pmatrix} 1 & 0 & 2 & \vdots & 1 & 0 & 0 \\ 0 & -1 & -1 & \vdots & -2 & 1 & 0 \\ 0 & 0 & -1 & \vdots & -6 & 1 & 1 \end{pmatrix}$$

In echelon form, the left half of $M$ is in triangular form; hence $A$ is invertible. Further row reduce $M$ to row canonical form:

$$M \sim \begin{pmatrix} 1 & 0 & 0 & \vdots & -11 & 2 & 2 \\ 0 & -1 & 0 & \vdots & 4 & 0 & -1 \\ 0 & 0 & 1 & \vdots & 6 & -1 & -1 \end{pmatrix} \sim \begin{pmatrix} 1 & 0 & 0 & \vdots & -11 & 2 & 2 \\ 0 & 1 & 0 & \vdots & -4 & 0 & 1 \\ 0 & 0 & 1 & \vdots & 6 & -1 & -1 \end{pmatrix}$$

The final block matrix is in the form $(I \,\vdots\, A^{-1})$; hence $A^{-1} = \begin{pmatrix} -11 & 2 & 2 \\ -4 & 0 & 1 \\ 6 & -1 & -1 \end{pmatrix}$.

**4.135** Find the inverse of $B = \begin{pmatrix} 1 & -2 & 2 \\ 2 & -3 & 6 \\ 1 & 1 & 7 \end{pmatrix}$.

❚ Form the block matrix $M = (B \,\vdots\, I)$ and reduce $M$ to echelon form:

$$M = \begin{pmatrix} 1 & -2 & 2 & \vdots & 1 & 0 & 0 \\ 2 & -3 & 6 & \vdots & 0 & 1 & 0 \\ 1 & 1 & 7 & \vdots & 0 & 0 & 1 \end{pmatrix} \sim \begin{pmatrix} 1 & -2 & 2 & \vdots & 1 & 0 & 0 \\ 0 & 1 & 2 & \vdots & -2 & 1 & 0 \\ 0 & 3 & 5 & \vdots & -1 & 0 & 1 \end{pmatrix} \sim \begin{pmatrix} 1 & -2 & 2 & \vdots & 1 & 0 & 0 \\ 0 & 1 & 2 & \vdots & -2 & 1 & 0 \\ 0 & 0 & -1 & \vdots & 5 & -3 & 1 \end{pmatrix}$$

In echelon form, the left half of $M$ is in triangular form; hence $B$ has an inverse. Further row reduce $M$ to row canonical form:

$$M \sim \begin{pmatrix} 1 & -2 & 0 & \vdots & 11 & -6 & 2 \\ 0 & 1 & 0 & \vdots & 8 & -5 & 2 \\ 0 & 0 & 1 & \vdots & -5 & 3 & -1 \end{pmatrix} \sim \begin{pmatrix} 1 & 0 & 0 & \vdots & 27 & -16 & 6 \\ 0 & 1 & 0 & \vdots & 8 & -5 & 2 \\ 0 & 0 & 1 & \vdots & -5 & 3 & -1 \end{pmatrix}$$

The final matrix has the form $(I \mid B^{-1})$; hence $B^{-1}$ is the right half of the last matrix.

**4.136** Apply the Gaussian algorithm to $C = \begin{pmatrix} 1 & 3 & -4 \\ 1 & 5 & -1 \\ 3 & 13 & -6 \end{pmatrix}$.

▌ Form the block matrix $M = (C \mid I)$ and row reduce to echelon form:

$$\begin{pmatrix} 1 & 3 & -4 & \vdots & 1 & 0 & 0 \\ 1 & 5 & -1 & \vdots & 0 & 1 & 0 \\ 3 & 13 & -6 & \vdots & 0 & 0 & 1 \end{pmatrix} \sim \begin{pmatrix} 1 & 3 & -4 & \vdots & 1 & 0 & 0 \\ 0 & 2 & 3 & \vdots & -1 & 1 & 0 \\ 0 & 4 & 6 & \vdots & -3 & 0 & 1 \end{pmatrix} \sim \begin{pmatrix} 1 & 3 & -4 & \vdots & 1 & 0 & 0 \\ 0 & 2 & 3 & \vdots & -1 & 1 & 0 \\ 0 & 0 & 0 & \vdots & -1 & -2 & 1 \end{pmatrix}$$

In echelon form, $M$ has a zero row in its left half; that is, $C$ is not row reducible to triangular form. Accordingly, $C$ is not invertible.

**4.137** Suppose $A$, $B$ and $A_1, A_2, \ldots, A_n$ are invertible matrices of the same order. Show that: **(a)** $AB$ is invertible and $(AB)^{-1} = B^{-1}A^{-1}$; **(b)** $A_1 A_2 \cdots A_n$ is invertible and $(A_1 A_2 \cdots A_n)^{-1} = A_n^{-1} \cdots A_2^{-1} A_1^{-1}$.

▌ **(a)** We have

$$(AB)(B^{-1}A^{-1}) = A(BB^{-1})A^{-1} = AIA^{-1} = AA^{-1} = I$$
$$(B^{-1}A^{-1})(AB) = B^{-1}(A^{-1}A)B = B^{-1}IB = B^{-1}B = I$$

Thus $B^{-1}A^{-1}$ is the inverse of $AB$, that is, $(AB)^{-1} = B^{-1}A^{-1}$.

**(b)** The proof is by induction on $n$. For $n = 1$, we have $A_1^{-1} = A_1^{-1}$. Suppose $n > 1$ and the theorem holds for $n$. We prove it is true for $n + 1$. Using part **(a)**, we have

$$(A_1 A_2 \cdots A_n A_{n+1})^{-1} = [(A_1 A_2 \cdots A_n)A_{n+1}]^{-1} = A_{n+1}^{-1}(A_1 A_2 \cdots A_n)^{-1} = A_{n+1}^{-1} A_n^{-1} \cdots A_2^{-1} A_1^{-1}$$

Thus the theorem holds for $n + 1$. Accordingly, the theorem holds for every positive $n$.

**4.138** If $A$ is invertible, show that $kA$ is invertible when $k \neq 0$, with inverse $k^{-1}A^{-1}$.

▌ Since $k \neq 0$, $k^{-1} = 1/k$ exists. Then $(kA)(k^{-1}A^{-1}) = (kk^{-1})(AA^{-1}) = 1 \cdot I = I$. Hence $k^{-1}A^{-1}$ is the inverse of $kA$.

**4.139** Show that $A$ is invertible if and only if $A^T$ is invertible.

▌ If $A$ is invertible, then there exists a matrix $B$ such that $AB = BA = I$. Then $(AB)^T = (BA)^T = I^T$ and so $B^T A^T = A^T B^T = I$. Hence $A^T$ is invertible, with inverse $B^T$. The converse follows from the fact that $(A^T)^T = A$.

**4.140** Show that the operations of inversion and transposition commute; that is, $(A^T)^{-1} = (A^{-1})^T$.

▌ By Problem 4.139, $B^T$ is the inverse of $A^T$; that is $B^T = (A^T)^{-1}$. But $B = A^{-1}$; hence $(A^{-1})^T = (A^T)^{-1}$.

## 4.6 SPECIAL TYPES OF SQUARE MATRICES

This section considers the following square matrices:
**(a)** $D = (d_{ij})$ is *diagonal*, denoted by $D = \text{diag}(d_{11}, d_{22}, \ldots, d_{nn})$, if its nondiagonal elements are all zero.
**(b)** $A = (a_{ij})$ is *upper (lower) triangular* if its elements below (above) the diagonal are all zero, i.e., if $a_{ij} = 0$ when $i < j$ $(i > j)$.
**(c)** $A$ is *symmetric* if $A^T = A$, i.e., if $a_{ij} = a_{ji}$ for all $i$ and $j$. ($A$ is *skew-symmetric* or *antisymmetric* if $A^T = -A$.)
**(d)** $A$ is *orthogonal* if $A^T = A^{-1}$, i.e., if $AA^T = A^T A = I$.

**4.141** Write out diag $(3, -7, 2)$, diag $(4, -5)$, and diag $(6, -3, 0, 1)$.

▌ Put the given scalars on the diagonal, with 0s elsewhere:

$$\begin{pmatrix} 3 & 0 & 0 \\ 0 & -7 & 0 \\ 0 & 0 & 2 \end{pmatrix}, \qquad \begin{pmatrix} 4 & 0 \\ 0 & -5 \end{pmatrix}, \qquad \begin{pmatrix} 6 & & & \\ & -3 & & \\ & & 0 & \\ & & & 1 \end{pmatrix}$$

(It is common practice to omit blocks or patterns of 0s as in the third matrix.)

**4.142** Find $AB$ where $A = \text{diag}(2, -3, 5)$ and $B = \text{diag}(7, 4, 6)$.

▮ The product is a diagonal matrix obtained by multiplying corresponding diagonal entries:

$$AB = \text{diag}\,(2 \cdot 7, -3 \cdot 4, 5 \cdot 6) = \text{diag}\,(14, -12, 30)$$

**4.143** Find the inverse of each of the following matrices; (*a*) $A = \text{diag}\,(2, -3, 4)$, (*b*) $B = \text{diag}\,(1, 3, -1, 5)$, (*c*) $C = \text{diag}\,(4, 1, 0, -3)$.

▮ The inverse of $D = \text{diag}\,(a_1, a_2, \ldots, a_n)$ is the diagonal matrix $D^{-1} = \text{diag}\,(a_1^{-1}, a_2^{-1}, \ldots, a_n^{-1})$ providing no $a_i = 0$.

(*a*) $A^{-1} = (1/2, -1/3, 1/4)$
(*b*) $B^{-1} = (1, 1/3, -1, 1/5)$
(*c*) $C$ has no inverse since the third diagonal entry, is 0.

**4.144** Display the generic upper triangular matrices of orders 2, 3, and 4.

▮
$$\begin{pmatrix} a_{11} & a_{12} \\ 0 & a_{22} \end{pmatrix}, \qquad \begin{pmatrix} b_{11} & b_{12} & b_{13} \\ & b_{22} & b_{23} \\ & & b_{33} \end{pmatrix}, \qquad \begin{pmatrix} c_{11} & c_{12} & c_{13} & c_{14} \\ & c_{22} & c_{23} & c_{24} \\ & & c_{33} & c_{34} \\ & & & c_{44} \end{pmatrix}$$

(As in diagonal matrices, it is common practice to omit patterns of 0s.)

**4.145** Using only the elements 0 and 1, find: (*a*) all $2 \times 2$ diagonal matrices, (*b*) all $2 \times 2$ upper triangular matrices.

▮ (*a*) Diagonal matrices must have 0s off the diagonal:

$$\begin{pmatrix} 1 & 0 \\ 0 & 1 \end{pmatrix}, \qquad \begin{pmatrix} 1 & 0 \\ 0 & 0 \end{pmatrix}, \qquad \begin{pmatrix} 0 & 0 \\ 0 & 1 \end{pmatrix}, \qquad \begin{pmatrix} 0 & 0 \\ 0 & 0 \end{pmatrix}$$

(*b*) Upper triangular matrices must have 0s below the diagonal. This gives the four matrices of (*a*), plus the following four matrices:

$$\begin{pmatrix} 1 & 1 \\ 0 & 1 \end{pmatrix}, \qquad \begin{pmatrix} 1 & 1 \\ 0 & 0 \end{pmatrix}, \qquad \begin{pmatrix} 0 & 1 \\ 0 & 1 \end{pmatrix}, \qquad \begin{pmatrix} 0 & 1 \\ 0 & 0 \end{pmatrix}$$

**4.146** Suppose $A = (a_{ij})$ and $B = (b_{ij})$ are upper triangular matrices. Clearly the sum $A + B$ and any scalar multiple $kA$ are again upper triangular. Show that:
(*a*) The product $AB$ is upper triangular.
(*b*) The diagonal entries of $AB$ are $a_1 b_1, a_2 b_2, \ldots, a_n b_n$.

▮ (*a*) Let $AB = (c_{ij})$; then

$$c_{ij} = \sum_{k=1}^{n} a_{jk} b_{kj}$$

If $i > j$, then, for any $k$, either $i > k$ or $k > j$, so that either $a_{ik} = 0$ or $b_{kj} = 0$. Thus, $c_{ik} = 0$, and $AB$ is upper triangular.
(*b*) If $AB = (c_{ij})$, then

$$c_{ii} = \sum_{k=1}^{n} a_{ik} b_{ki}$$

But, for $k < i$, $a_{ik} = 0$; and, for $k > i$, $b_{ki} = 0$. Hence $c_{ii} = a_{ii} b_{ii}$, as claimed.

**4.147** Find an upper triangular matrix $A$ such that $A^3 = \begin{pmatrix} 8 & -57 \\ 0 & 27 \end{pmatrix}$.

▮ Set $A = \begin{pmatrix} x & y \\ 0 & z \end{pmatrix}$. Then $x^3 = 8$, so $x = 2$; $z^3 = 27$, so $z = 3$. Next calculate $A^3$ using $x = 2$ and $z = 3$:

$$A^2 = \begin{pmatrix} 2 & y \\ 0 & 3 \end{pmatrix}\begin{pmatrix} 2 & y \\ 0 & 3 \end{pmatrix} = \begin{pmatrix} 4 & 5y \\ 0 & 9 \end{pmatrix} \quad \text{and} \quad A^3 = \begin{pmatrix} 2 & y \\ 0 & 3 \end{pmatrix}\begin{pmatrix} 4 & 5y \\ 0 & 9 \end{pmatrix} = \begin{pmatrix} 8 & 19y \\ 0 & 27 \end{pmatrix}$$

Thus $19y = -57$, or $y = -3$. Accordingly, $A = \begin{pmatrix} 2 & -3 \\ 0 & 3 \end{pmatrix}$.

**4.148** Exhibit the generic lower triangular matrices of orders 2, 3, and 4.

▮ In each case put 0s above the diagonal:

$$\begin{pmatrix} a_{11} & 0 \\ a_{21} & a_{22} \end{pmatrix}, \qquad \begin{pmatrix} b_{11} & & \\ b_{21} & b_{22} & \\ b_{31} & b_{32} & b_{33} \end{pmatrix}, \qquad \begin{pmatrix} c_{11} & & & \\ c_{21} & c_{22} & & \\ c_{31} & c_{32} & c_{33} & \\ c_{41} & c_{42} & c_{43} & c_{44} \end{pmatrix}$$

## Symmetric and Skew-Symmetric Matrices

**4.149** Determine if each of the following matrices is symmetric or skew-symmetric:

$$\textbf{(a)} \quad A = \begin{pmatrix} 0 & 5 & -2 \\ -5 & 0 & 3 \\ 2 & -3 & 0 \end{pmatrix}, \qquad \textbf{(b)} \quad B = \begin{pmatrix} 4 & -7 & 1 \\ -7 & 3 & 2 \\ 1 & 2 & -5 \end{pmatrix}, \qquad \textbf{(c)} \quad C = \begin{pmatrix} 1 & 1 & 1 \\ 1 & 1 & 1 \end{pmatrix}$$

▮ **(a)** By inspection, the diagonal elements are all 0 and symmetric elements (mirror images in the diagonal), 5 and −5, −2 and 2, and 3 and −3, are negatives of each other; hence $A$ is skew-symmetric.

**(b)** By inspection, the symmetric elements, −7 and −7, 1 and 1, and 2 and 2, are equal; hence $B$ is symmetric.

**(c)** Since $C$ is not square, $C$ is neither symmetric nor skew-symmetric.

**4.150** Determine if each of the following matrices is symmetric or skew-symmetric:

$$\textbf{(a)} \quad D = \begin{pmatrix} 1 & 1 \\ 1 & 0 \end{pmatrix}, \qquad \textbf{(b)} \quad E = \begin{pmatrix} 1 & 1 \\ -1 & 0 \end{pmatrix}, \qquad \textbf{(c)} \quad F = \begin{pmatrix} 0 & 1 \\ -1 & 0 \end{pmatrix}, \qquad \textbf{(d)} \quad G = \begin{pmatrix} 0 & 0 \\ 0 & 0 \end{pmatrix}$$

▮ **(a)** By inspection $D^T = D$; hence $D$ is symmetric.

**(b)** We see that $E^T \neq \pm E$. Accordingly, $E$ is neither symmetric nor skew-symmetric.

**(c)** By inspection, $F^T = -F$; hence $F$ is skew-symmetric.

**(d)** Both, since $0^T = 0 = -0$ when 0 is square.

**4.151** Find $x, y, z, t$ if $A = \begin{pmatrix} 5 & 2 & x \\ y & z & -3 \\ 4 & t & -7 \end{pmatrix}$ is symmetric.

▮ Equate symmetric elements (mirror images in the diagonal) to obtain $x = 4$, $y = 2$, $t = -3$. The unknown $z$, on the diagonal, is indeterminate.

**4.152** Find $x$ and $B$ if $B = \begin{pmatrix} 4 & x+2 \\ 2x-3 & x+1 \end{pmatrix}$ is symmetric.

▮ Set the symmetric elements $x+2$ and $2x+3$ equal to each other to obtain $x = 5$; hence $B = \begin{pmatrix} 4 & 7 \\ 7 & 6 \end{pmatrix}$.

**4.153** Suppose $A = (a_{ij})$ and $B = (b_{ij})$ are symmetric. Show that **(a)** $A + B$ is symmetric, and **(b)** $kA$ is symmetric.

▮ **(a)** If $A + B = (c_{ij})$, then $c_{ij} = a_{ij} + b_{ij} = a_{ji} + b_{ji} = c_{ji}$.

**(b)** If $kA = (c_{ij})$, then $c_{ij} = ka_{ij} = ka_{ji} = c_{ji}$.

**4.154** Show that $AB$ need not be symmetric, even though $A$ and $B$ are symmetric.

▮ Let $A = \begin{pmatrix} 1 & 2 \\ 2 & 3 \end{pmatrix}$ and $B = \begin{pmatrix} 4 & 5 \\ 5 & 6 \end{pmatrix}$. Then $AB = \begin{pmatrix} 14 & 17 \\ 23 & 28 \end{pmatrix}$ is not symmetric.

**Theorem 4.8:** Let $A$ be a square matrix. Then: (i) $A + A^T$ is symmetric; (ii) $A - A^T$ is skew-symmetric; (iii) $A = B + C$ where $B = \frac{1}{2}(A + A^T)$ is symmetric and $C = \frac{1}{2}(A - A^T)$ is skew-symmetric.

**4.155** Prove Theorem 4.8(i).

▮ $(A + A^T)^T = A^T + (A^T)^T = A^T + A = A + A^T$.

**4.156** Prove Theorem 4.8(ii).

∎ $(A - A^T)^T = A^T - (A^T)^T = A^T - A = -(A - A^T)$.

**4.157** Prove Theorem 4.8(iii).

∎ The proof follows from the fact that $A = B + C$ and that any multiple of a symmetric (skew-symmetric) matrix is symmetric (skew-symmetric).

**4.158** Write $A = \begin{pmatrix} 2 & 3 \\ 7 & 8 \end{pmatrix}$ as the sum of a symmetric matrix $B$ and a skew-symmetric matrix $C$.

∎ Calculate

$$A^T = \begin{pmatrix} 2 & 7 \\ 3 & 8 \end{pmatrix}, \qquad A + A^T = \begin{pmatrix} 4 & 10 \\ 10 & 16 \end{pmatrix}, \qquad A - A^T = \begin{pmatrix} 0 & -4 \\ 4 & 0 \end{pmatrix}$$

Then $B = \frac{1}{2}(A + A^T) = \begin{pmatrix} 2 & 5 \\ 5 & 8 \end{pmatrix}$ and $C = \frac{1}{2}(A - A^T) = \begin{pmatrix} 0 & -2 \\ 2 & 0 \end{pmatrix}$.

**4.159** Suppose $A$ is symmetric. Show that $A^2$ and, in general, $A^n$ is symmetric.

∎ $(A^2)^T = (AA)^T = A^T A^T = AA = A^2$. Also, by induction, $(A^n)^T = (AA^{n-1})^T = (A^{n-1})^T A^T = A^{n-1}A = A_n$.

**4.160** Let $A$ be an $n$-square symmetric matrix and $P$ any $n \times m$ matrix. Show that $P^T A P$ is also symmetric.

∎ $(P^T A P)^T = P^T A^T (P^T)^T = P^T A P$.

## Orthogonal Matrices

**4.161** Show that $A = \begin{pmatrix} 1/9 & 8/9 & -4/9 \\ 4/9 & -4/9 & -7/9 \\ 8/9 & 1/9 & 4/9 \end{pmatrix}$ is orthogonal.

∎ We need only show $AA^T = I$:

$$AA^T = \begin{pmatrix} 1/9 & 8/9 & -4/9 \\ 4/9 & -4/9 & -7/9 \\ 8/9 & 1/9 & 4/9 \end{pmatrix} \begin{pmatrix} 1/9 & 4/9 & 8/9 \\ 8/9 & -4/9 & 1/9 \\ -4/9 & -7/9 & 4/9 \end{pmatrix} = \frac{1}{81} \begin{pmatrix} 1+64+16 & 4-32+28 & 8+8-16 \\ 4-32+28 & 16+16+49 & 32-4-28 \\ 8+8-16 & 32-4-28 & 64+1+16 \end{pmatrix}$$

$$= \frac{1}{81} \begin{pmatrix} 81 & 0 & 0 \\ 0 & 81 & 0 \\ 0 & 0 & 81 \end{pmatrix} = \begin{pmatrix} 1 & 0 & 0 \\ 0 & 1 & 0 \\ 0 & 0 & 1 \end{pmatrix} = I$$

**4.162** Define an orthogonal set and an orthonormal set of vectors in $\mathbf{R}^n$.

∎ The vectors $u_1, u_2, \ldots, u_r$ form an orthogonal set of vectors if the vectors are pairwise orthogonal, that is, if $u_i \cdot u_j = 0$ for $i \neq j$. They form an orthonormal set if they are orthogonal and if they are also unit vectors, that is, if $u_i \cdot u_i = 1$ for each $i$. In terms of the Kronecker delta, the condition for orthonormality is $u_i \cdot u_j = \delta_{ij}$.

**4.163** Show that

$$A = \begin{pmatrix} a_1 & a_2 & a_3 \\ b_1 & b_2 & b_3 \\ c_1 & c_2 & c_3 \end{pmatrix}$$

is orthogonal if and only if its rows $u_1 = (a_1, a_2, a_3)$, $u_2 = (b_1, b_2, b_3)$, and $u_3 = (c_1, c_2, c_3)$ form an orthonormal set.

∎ If $A$ is orthogonal, then

$$AA^T = \begin{pmatrix} a_1 & a_2 & a_3 \\ b_1 & b_2 & b_3 \\ c_1 & c_2 & c_3 \end{pmatrix} \begin{pmatrix} a_1 & b_1 & c_1 \\ a_2 & b_2 & c_2 \\ a_3 & b_3 & c_3 \end{pmatrix} = \begin{pmatrix} 1 & 0 & 0 \\ 0 & 1 & 0 \\ 0 & 0 & 1 \end{pmatrix} = I$$

This yields

$$a_1^2 + a_2^2 + a_3^2 = u_1 \cdot u_1 = 1 \quad a_1b_1 + a_2b_2 + a_3b_3 = u_1 \cdot u_2 = 0 \quad a_1c_1 + a_2c_2 + a_3c_3 = u_1 \cdot u_3 = 0$$
$$b_1a_1 + b_2a_2 + b_3a_3 = u_2 \cdot u_1 = 0 \quad b_1^2 + b_2^2 + b_3^2 = u_2 \cdot u_2 = 1 \quad b_1c_1 + b_2c_2 + b_3c_3 = u_2 \cdot u_3 = 0$$
$$c_1a_1 + c_2a_2 + c_3a_3 = u_3 \cdot u_1 = 0 \quad c_1b_1 + c_2b_2 + c_3b_3 = u_3 \cdot u_2 = 0 \quad c_1^2 + c_2^2 + c_3^2 = u_3 \cdot u_3 = 1$$

that is, $u_i \cdot u_j = \delta_{ij}$. Accordingly, $u_1$, $u_2$, $u_3$ form an orthonormal set. The converse follows from the fact that each step is reversible.

**Theorem 4.9:** Let $A$ be a real matrix. Then the following are equivalent: **(a)** $A$ is orthogonal; **(b)** the rows of $A$ form an orthonormal set; **(c)** the columns of $A$ form an orthonormal set.

**4.164** Prove Theorem 4.9.

▌ First we prove that **(a)** and **(b)** are equivalent. Let $R_1, R_2, \ldots, R_n$ denote the rows of $A$; then $R_1^T, R_2^T, \ldots, R_n^T$ are the columns of $A^T$. Now let $AA^T = (c_{ij})$. By matrix multiplication, $c_{ij} = R_iR_j^T = R_i \cdot R_j$. Thus $AA^T = I$ iff $R_i \cdot R_j = \delta_{ij}$ iff the rows $R_1, R_2, \ldots, R_n$ form an orthonormal set. Thus **(a)** and **(b)** are equivalent. The proof that **(a)** and **(c)** are equivalent is similar except we use $A^TA = I$ instead of $AA^T = I$. Thus the theorem is proved. (Problem 4.163 is essentially the proof for the case when $A$ has order 3.)

**4.165** Find $x, y, z, s, t$ if $A = \begin{pmatrix} x & 2/3 & 2/3 \\ 2/3 & 1/3 & y \\ z & s & t \end{pmatrix}$ is orthogonal.

▌ Let $R_1, R_2, R_3$ denote the rows of $A$, and let $C_1, C_2, C_3$ denote the columns of $A$. Since $R_1$ is a unit vector, $x^2 + 4/9 + 4/9 = 1$, or $x = \pm 1/3$. Since $R_2$ is a unit vector, $4/9 + 1/9 + y^2 = 1$, or $y = \pm 2/3$. Since $R_1 \cdot R_2 = 0$, we get $2x/3 + 2/9 + 2y/3 = 0$, or $3x + 3y = -1$. The only possibility is that $x = 1/3$ and $y = -2/3$. Thus

$$A = \begin{pmatrix} 1/3 & 2/3 & 2/3 \\ 2/3 & 1/3 & -2/3 \\ x & s & t \end{pmatrix}$$

Since the columns are unit vectors,

$$1/9 + 4/9 + z^2 = 1, \qquad 4/9 + 1/9 + s^2 = 1, \qquad 4/9 + 4/9 + t^2 = 1$$

Thus $z = \pm 2/3$, $s = \pm 2/3$, and $t = \pm 1/3$.
Case (i): $z = 2/3$. Since $C_1$ and $C_2$ are orthogonal, $s = -2/3$; since $C_1$ and $C_3$ are orthogonal, $t = 1/3$.
Case (ii): $z = -2/3$. Since $C_1$ and $C_2$ are orthogonal, $s = 2/3$; since $C_1$ and $C_3$ are orthogonal, $t = -1/3$.
Hence there are exactly two possible solutions:

$$A = \begin{pmatrix} 1/3 & 2/3 & 2/3 \\ 2/3 & 1/3 & -2/3 \\ 2/3 & -2/3 & 1/3 \end{pmatrix} \qquad \text{and} \qquad A = \begin{pmatrix} 1/3 & 2/3 & 2/3 \\ 2/3 & 1/3 & -2/3 \\ -2/3 & 2/3 & -1/3 \end{pmatrix}$$

**4.166** Suppose $A = \begin{pmatrix} a & b \\ c & d \end{pmatrix}$ is orthogonal. Show that $a^2 + b^2 = 1$ and

$$A = \begin{pmatrix} a & b \\ b & -a \end{pmatrix} \qquad \text{or} \qquad A = \begin{pmatrix} a & b \\ -b & a \end{pmatrix}$$

▌ Since $A$ is orthogonal, the rows of $A$ form an orthonormal set. Hence

$$a^2 + b^2 = 1, \qquad c^2 + d^2 = 1, \qquad ac + bd = 0$$

Similarly, the columns form an orthonormal set, so

$$a^2 + c^2 = 1, \qquad b^2 + d^2 = 1, \qquad ab + cd = 0$$

Therefore, $c^2 = 1 - a^2 = b^2$, whence $c = \pm b$.

Case (i): $c = +b$. Then $b(a + d) = 0$ or $d = -a$; the corresponding matrix is $\begin{pmatrix} a & b \\ b & -a \end{pmatrix}$.

Case (ii): $c = -b$. Then $b(d - a) = 0$ or $d = a$; the corresponding matrix is $\begin{pmatrix} a & b \\ -b & a \end{pmatrix}$.

**4.167** Find a $2 \times 2$ orthogonal matrix $P$ whose first row is **(a)** $(1/\sqrt{5}, 2/\sqrt{5})$ **(b)** a multiple of $u = (2, 3)$.

▌ **(a)** By Problem 4.166, $P = \begin{pmatrix} 1/\sqrt{5} & 2/\sqrt{5} \\ 2/\sqrt{5} & -1/\sqrt{5} \end{pmatrix}$ or $P = \begin{pmatrix} 1/\sqrt{5} & 2/\sqrt{5} \\ -2/\sqrt{5} & 1/\sqrt{5} \end{pmatrix}$.

**(b)** First normalize $u$ to obtain the first row of $P$. We have $\|u\| = \sqrt{4 + 9} = \sqrt{13}$. Hence

$$P = \begin{pmatrix} 2/\sqrt{13} & 3/\sqrt{13} \\ 3/\sqrt{13} & -2/\sqrt{13} \end{pmatrix} \quad \text{or} \quad P = \begin{pmatrix} 2/\sqrt{13} & 3/\sqrt{13} \\ -3/\sqrt{13} & 2/\sqrt{13} \end{pmatrix}$$

**4.168** Show that every $2 \times 2$ orthogonal matrix has the form

$$\begin{pmatrix} \cos \theta & \sin \theta \\ -\sin \theta & \cos \theta \end{pmatrix} \quad \text{or} \quad \begin{pmatrix} \cos \theta & \sin \theta \\ \sin \theta & -\cos \theta \end{pmatrix}$$

for some real number $\theta$.

▌ Let $a$ and $b$ be any real numbers such that $a^2 + b^2 = 1$. Then there exists a real number $\theta$ such that $a = \cos \theta$ and $b = \sin \theta$. The result now follows from Problem 4.166.

**4.169** Suppose $A$ and $B$ are $n$-square orthogonal matrices. Show that $AB$ is an ($n$-square) orthogonal matrix.

▌ It suffices to show that $(AB)(AB)^T = I$:

$$(AB)(AB)^T = (AB)(B^T A^T) = A(BB^T)A^T = AIA^T = AA^T = I$$

**4.170** Suppose $A$ is orthogonal. Show that $A^{-1}$ is orthogonal.

▌ We need to show that $(A^{-1})^T = (A^{-1})^{-1}$. Since $A$ is orthogonal, $A^T = A^{-1}$. Since transposition commutes with inverse (Problem 4.140), $(A^{-1})^T = (A^T)^{-1} = (A^{-1})^{-1}$. Thus $A^{-1}$ is orthogonal.

**4.171** Find a $3 \times 3$ orthogonal matrix $P$ whose first two rows are multiples of $u_1 = (1, 1, 1)$ and $u_2 = (0, -1, 1)$ respectively.

▌ Let $u_3 = (x, y, z)$ be a nonzero vector orthogonal to $u_1$ and $u_2$. Then

$$x + y + z = 0 \quad \text{and} \quad -y + z = 0$$

Here $z$ is a free variable. Set $z = -1$ to obtain $y = -1$ and $x = 2$. So $u_3 = (2, -1, -1)$. Let $A$ be the matrix whose rows are $u_1$, $u_2$, $u_3$; and let $P$ be the matrix obtained from $A$ by normalizing the rows of $A$. Thus

$$A = \begin{pmatrix} 1 & 1 & 1 \\ 0 & -1 & 1 \\ 2 & -1 & -1 \end{pmatrix} \quad \text{and} \quad P = \begin{pmatrix} 1/\sqrt{3} & 1/\sqrt{3} & 1/\sqrt{3} \\ 0 & -1/\sqrt{2} & 1/\sqrt{2} \\ 2/\sqrt{6} & -1/\sqrt{6} & -1/\sqrt{6} \end{pmatrix}$$

## 4.7 DETERMINANTS

The *determinant* of an $n$-square matrix $A = (a_{ij})$ is a certain scalar assigned to the matrix $A$. The determinant is denoted by det $(A)$ or $|A|$ or

$$\begin{vmatrix} a_{11} & a_{12} & \cdots & a_{1n} \\ a_{21} & a_{22} & \cdots & a_{2n} \\ \cdots\cdots\cdots\cdots\cdots\cdots \\ a_{n1} & a_{n2} & \cdots & a_{nn} \end{vmatrix}$$

The number $n$ is called the *order* of the determinant.

**Remark 1:** The determinants of orders one, two, and three are defined as follows:

$$|a_{11}| = a_{11}$$

$$\begin{vmatrix} a_{11} & a_{12} \\ a_{21} & a_{22} \end{vmatrix} = a_{11}a_{22} - a_{12}a_{21}$$

$$\begin{vmatrix} a_{11} & a_{12} & a_{13} \\ a_{21} & a_{22} & a_{23} \\ a_{31} & a_{32} & a_{33} \end{vmatrix} = a_{11}a_{22}a_{33} + a_{12}a_{23}a_{31} + a_{13}a_{21}a_{32} - a_{13}a_{22}a_{31} - a_{12}a_{21}a_{33} - a_{11}a_{23}a_{32}$$

**Remark 2:**   The general definition of a determinant of order $n$ is as follows:

$$\det (A) = \sum \text{sgn} (\sigma) a_{1j_1} a_{2j_2} \cdots a_{nj_n}$$

where the sum is taken over all permutations $\sigma = \{j_1, j_2, \ldots, j_n\}$ of $\{1, 2, \ldots, n\}$. Here $\text{sgn} (\sigma)$ equals plus or minus one according as an even or an odd number of interchanges are required to change $\sigma$ so that its numbers are in the usual order. We have included the general definition of the determinant function for completeness. The reader is referred to texts in matrix theory or linear algebra for techniques for computing determinants of order greater than three. (We do briefly treat such determinants later in the section.) Permutations are introduced in Chapter 8.

**Remark 3:**   The following two theorems, whose proofs lie beyond the scope of this text, play an important role in matrix theory.

**Theorem 4.10:**   For any two $n$-square matrices $A$ and $B$, we have

$$\det (AB) = \det (A) \cdot \det (B)$$

(That is, the determinant function is multiplicative.)

**Theorem 4.11:**   A matrix is invertible if and only if it has a nonzero determinant.

## Determinants of Orders One and Two

**4.172**   Find det (24), det $(-6)$, and det $(t + 2)$.

▮   The determinant is the scalar itself; hence, det $(24) = 24$, det $(-6) = -6$, and det $(t + 2) = t + 2$.

**4.173**   Show that the equation $ax = b$ has a unique solution if and only if det $(a) \neq 0$.

▮   The equation $ax = b$ has a unique solution if and only if $a \neq 0$. However, det $(a) = a$. Thus $ax = b$ has a unique solution if and only if det $(a) \neq 0$. [Analogously, the matrix equation $AX = B$ has a unique solution if and only if det $(A) \neq 0$.]

**4.174**   Give a mnemonic for the evaluation of the determinant of order two.

▮
$$
\begin{array}{c}
{}^{+}\left[\begin{array}{cc} a_{11} & a_{22} \\ a_{21} & a_{22} \end{array}\right]{}^{-}
\end{array}
$$

The determinant is equal to the product of the elements along the plus-labeled arrow minus the product of the elements along the minus-labeled arrow. [There is an analogous scheme (Problem 4.185) for determinants of order three, but not for higher-order determinants.]

**4.175**   Compute the determinant of each matrix: **(a)** $\begin{pmatrix} 5 & 4 \\ 2 & 3 \end{pmatrix}$, **(b)** $\begin{pmatrix} 2 & 1 \\ -4 & 6 \end{pmatrix}$, **(c)** $\begin{pmatrix} 3 & -2 \\ 4 & 5 \end{pmatrix}$.

▮   **(a)**  $\begin{vmatrix} 5 & 4 \\ 2 & 3 \end{vmatrix} = (5)(3) - (4)(2) = 15 - 8 = 7$     **(b)**  $\begin{vmatrix} 2 & 1 \\ -4 & 6 \end{vmatrix} = (2)(6) - (1)(-4) = 12 + 4 = 16$

**(c)**  $\begin{vmatrix} 3 & -2 \\ 4 & 5 \end{vmatrix} = 15 + 8 = 23$

**4.176**   Compute the determinant of each matrix: **(a)** $\begin{pmatrix} 4 & -5 \\ -1 & -2 \end{pmatrix}$, **(b)** $\begin{pmatrix} 3 & -8 \\ 0 & 5 \end{pmatrix}$, **(c)** $\begin{pmatrix} a & b \\ c & d \end{pmatrix}$.

▮   **(a)**  $\begin{vmatrix} 4 & -5 \\ -1 & -2 \end{vmatrix} = -8 - 5 = -13$,     **(b)**  $\begin{vmatrix} 3 & -8 \\ 0 & 5 \end{vmatrix} = 15 - 0 = 15$,     **(c)**  $\begin{vmatrix} a & b \\ c & d \end{vmatrix} = ad - bc$

**4.177**   Find the determinant of: **(a)** $A = \begin{pmatrix} a - b & a \\ a & a + b \end{pmatrix}$, **(b)** $B = \begin{pmatrix} t - 5 & 7 \\ -1 & t + 3 \end{pmatrix}$.

▮   **(a)**   det $(A) = \begin{vmatrix} a - b & a \\ a & a + b \end{vmatrix} = (a - b)(a + b) - (a)(a) = -b^2$

**(b)**   det $(B) = \begin{vmatrix} t - 5 & 7 \\ -1 & t + 3 \end{vmatrix} = (t - 5)(t + 3) + 7 = t^2 - 2t - 15 + 7 = t^2 - 2t - 8$

**4.178** Determine those values of $k$ for which $\begin{vmatrix} k & k \\ 4 & 2k \end{vmatrix} = 0$.

▮ $\begin{vmatrix} k & k \\ 4 & 2k \end{vmatrix} = 2k^2 - 4k = 0$, or $2k(k-2) = 0$. Hence $k = 0$ or $k = 2$.

**4.179** Determine those values of $t$ for which $\begin{vmatrix} t-2 & 3 \\ 4 & t-1 \end{vmatrix} = 0$.

▮ $\qquad \begin{vmatrix} t-2 & 3 \\ 4 & t-1 \end{vmatrix} = t^2 - 3t + 2 - 12 = t^2 - 3t - 10 = 0 \qquad$ or $\qquad (t-5)(t+2) = 0$

Here $t = 5$ or $t = -2$.

**4.180** Consider the following two equations in the two unknowns $x$ and $y$:

$$a_1 x + b_1 y = c_1$$
$$a_2 x + a_2 y = c_2$$

The system has a unique solution if and only if $D \equiv a_1 b_2 - a_2 b_1 \neq 0$; that solution is

$$x = \frac{b_2 c_1 - b_1 c_2}{a_1 b_2 - a_2 b_1}, \qquad y = \frac{a_1 c_1 - a_2 c_1}{a_1 b_2 - a_2 b_1}$$

Express the solution completely in terms of determinants.

▮ $\qquad x = \dfrac{N_x}{D} = \dfrac{b_2 c_1 - b_1 c_2}{a_1 b_2 - a_2 b_1} = \dfrac{\begin{vmatrix} c_1 & b_1 \\ c_2 & b_2 \end{vmatrix}}{\begin{vmatrix} a_1 & b_1 \\ a_2 & b_2 \end{vmatrix}}, \qquad y = \dfrac{N_y}{D} = \dfrac{a_1 c_2 - a_2 c_1}{a_1 b_2 - a_2 b_1} = \dfrac{\begin{vmatrix} a_1 & c_1 \\ a_2 & c_2 \end{vmatrix}}{\begin{vmatrix} a_1 & b_1 \\ a_2 & b_2 \end{vmatrix}}$

Here $D$, the determinant of the matrix of coefficients, appears in the denominator of both quotients. The numerators $N_x$ and $N_y$ of the quotients for $x$ and $y$, respectively, can be obtained by substituting the column of constant terms in place of the column of coefficients of the given unknown in the matrix of coefficients.

**4.181** Solve by determinants: $\begin{cases} 2x - 3y = 7 \\ 3x + 5y = 1 \end{cases}$.

▮ The determinant $D$ of the matrix of coefficients is

$$D = \begin{vmatrix} 2 & -3 \\ 3 & 5 \end{vmatrix} = (2)(5) - (3)(-3) = 10 + 9 = 19$$

Since $D \neq 0$, the system has a unique solution. To obtain the numerator $N_x$ replace, in the matrix of coefficients, the coefficients of $x$ by the constant terms:

$$N_x = \begin{vmatrix} 7 & -3 \\ 1 & 5 \end{vmatrix} = (7)(5) - (1)(-3) = 35 + 3 = 38$$

To obtain the numerator $N_y$ replace, in the matrix of coefficients, the coefficients of $y$ by the constant terms:

$$N_y = \begin{vmatrix} 2 & 7 \\ 3 & 1 \end{vmatrix} = (2)(1) - (3)(7) = 2 - 21 = -19$$

Thus the unique solution of the system is

$$x = \frac{N_x}{D} = \frac{38}{19} = 2 \qquad \text{and} \qquad y = \frac{N_y}{D} = \frac{-19}{19} = -1$$

**4.182** Solve by determinants: $\begin{cases} 2x - 4y = 7 \\ 3x - 6y = 5 \end{cases}$.

▮ The determinant $D$ of the matrix of coefficients is

$$D = \begin{vmatrix} 2 & -4 \\ 3 & -6 \end{vmatrix} = (2)(6) - (3)(-4) = -12 + 12 = 0$$

Since $D = 0$, the system does not have a unique solution, and we cannot solve the system by determinants.

**4.183** If $ab \neq 0$, solve using determinants: $\begin{cases} ax - 2by = c \\ 3ax - 5by = 2c \end{cases}$.

▮ First find $D = \begin{vmatrix} a & -2b \\ 3a & -5b \end{vmatrix} = -5ab + 6ab = ab$. Since $D = ab \neq 0$, the system has a unique solution. Next find

$$N_x = \begin{vmatrix} c & -2b \\ 2c & -5b \end{vmatrix} = -5bc + 4bc = -bc \quad \text{and} \quad N_y = \begin{vmatrix} a & c \\ 3a & 2c \end{vmatrix} = 2ac - 3ac = -ac$$

Then $x = N_x/D = -bc/ab = -c/a$ and $y = N_y/D = -ac/ab = -c/b$.

**4.184** Verify the multiplicative property (Theorem 4.10) for determinants of order two.

▮
$$AB = \begin{pmatrix} a_{11} & a_{12} \\ a_{21} & a_{22} \end{pmatrix} \begin{pmatrix} b_{11} & b_{12} \\ b_{21} & b_{22} \end{pmatrix} = \begin{pmatrix} a_{11}b_{11} + a_{12}b_{21} & a_{11}b_{12} + a_{12}b_{22} \\ a_{21}b_{11} + a_{22}b_{21} & a_{21}b_{12} + a_{22}b_{22} \end{pmatrix}$$

$$\det(AB) = (a_{11}b_{11} + a_{12}b_{21})(a_{21}b_{12} + a_{22}b_{22}) - (a_{11}b_{12} + a_{12}b_{22})(a_{21}b_{11} + a_{22}b_{21})$$

$$= a_{11}b_{11}a_{21}b_{12}^{(1)} + a_{11}b_{11}a_{22}b_{22} + a_{12}b_{21}a_{21}b_{12} + a_{12}b_{21}a_{22}b_{22}^{(4)}$$

$$- a_{11}b_{12}a_{21}b_{11} - a_{11}b_{12}a_{22}b_{21}^{(2)} - a_{12}b_{22}a_{21}b_{11}^{(3)} - a_{12}b_{22}a_{22}b_{21}$$

On the other hand,

$$\det(A) \cdot \det(B) = (a_{11}a_{22} - a_{12}a_{21})(b_{11}b_{22} - b_{12}b_{21})$$

$$= a_{11}a_{22}b_{11}b_{22}^{(1)} - a_{11}a_{22}b_{12}b_{21}^{(2)} - a_{12}a_{21}b_{11}b_{22}^{(3)} + a_{12}a_{21}b_{12}b_{21}^{(4)}$$

The four nonlabeled terms in $\det(AB)$ cancel each other; hence $\det(AB) = \det(A) \cdot \det(B)$.

## Determinants of Order Three

**4.185** Use Fig. 4-1 to obtain the determinant of $A = \begin{pmatrix} a_1 & b_1 & c_1 \\ a_2 & b_2 & c_2 \\ a_3 & b_3 & c_3 \end{pmatrix}$.

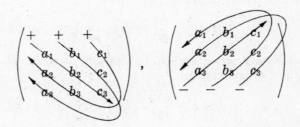

**Fig. 4-1**

▮ Form the product of each of the three numbers joined by an arrow in the diagram on the left, and precede each product by a plus sign as follows:

$$+ a_1b_2c_3 + b_1c_2a_3 + c_1a_2b_2$$

Now form the product of each of the three numbers joined by an arrow in the diagram on the right, and precede each product by a minus sign as follows:

$$- a_3b_2c_1 - b_3c_2a_1 - c_3a_2b_3$$

Then the determinant of $A$ is precisely the sums of the above two expressions:

$$|A| = \begin{vmatrix} a_1 & b_1 & c_1 \\ a_2 & b_2 & c_2 \\ a_3 & b_3 & c_3 \end{vmatrix} = a_1b_2c_3 + b_1c_2a_3 + c_1a_2b_3 - a_3b_2c_1 - b_3c_2a_1 - c_3a_2b_1$$

(The above method of computing $|A|$ does not hold for determinants of order greater than 3.)

**4.186** Find the determinant of: **(a)** $A = \begin{pmatrix} 2 & 1 & 1 \\ 0 & 5 & -2 \\ 1 & -3 & 4 \end{pmatrix}$ and **(b)** $B = \begin{pmatrix} 3 & -2 & -4 \\ 2 & 5 & -1 \\ 0 & 6 & 1 \end{pmatrix}$.

▮ Use Fig. 4-1 to obtain

**(a)** $\det(A) = \begin{vmatrix} 2 & 1 & 1 \\ 0 & 5 & -2 \\ 1 & -3 & 4 \end{vmatrix} = (2)(5)(4) + (1)(-2)(1) + (1)(-3)(0) - (1)(5)(1) - (-3)(-2)(2) - (4)(1)(0)$

$$= 40 - 2 + 0 - 5 - 12 - 0 = 21$$

**(b)** $\det(B) = \begin{vmatrix} 3 & -2 & -4 \\ 2 & 5 & -1 \\ 0 & 6 & 1 \end{vmatrix} = (3)(5)(1) + (-2)(-1)(0) + (-4)(6)(2) - (0)(5)(-4) - (6)(-1)(3) - (1)(-2)(2)$

$$= 15 + 0 - 48 - 0 + 18 + 4 = -11$$

**4.187** Find the determinant of: **(a)** $C = \begin{pmatrix} -2 & -1 & 4 \\ 6 & -3 & -2 \\ 4 & 1 & 2 \end{pmatrix}$ and **(b)** $D = \begin{pmatrix} 7 & 6 & 5 \\ 1 & 2 & 1 \\ 3 & -2 & 1 \end{pmatrix}$.

**(a)** $\det(C) = \begin{vmatrix} -2 & -1 & 4 \\ 6 & -3 & -2 \\ 4 & 1 & 2 \end{vmatrix} = 12 + 8 + 24 + 48 - 4 + 12 = 100$

**(b)** $\det(D) = \begin{vmatrix} 7 & 6 & 5 \\ 1 & 2 & 1 \\ 3 & -2 & 1 \end{vmatrix} = 14 + 18 - 10 - 30 + 14 - 6 = 0$

**4.188** Show that

$$\begin{vmatrix} a_{11} & a_{12} & a_{13} \\ a_{21} & a_{22} & a_{23} \\ a_{31} & a_{32} & a_{33} \end{vmatrix} = a_{11} \begin{vmatrix} a_{22} & a_{23} \\ a_{32} & a_{33} \end{vmatrix} - a_{12} \begin{vmatrix} a_{21} & a_{23} \\ a_{31} & a_{33} \end{vmatrix} + a_{13} \begin{vmatrix} a_{21} & a_{22} \\ a_{31} & a_{32} \end{vmatrix}$$

▮ Expand the determinants of order two to obtain

$$a_{11}(a_{22}a_{33} - a_{23}a_{32}) - a_{12}(a_{21}a_{33} - a_{23}a_{31}) + a_{13}(a_{21}a_{32} - a_{22}a_{31})$$
$$= a_{11}a_{22}a_{33} - a_{12}a_{23}a_{32} - a_{12}a_{21}a_{33} + a_{12}a_{23}a_{31} + a_{13}a_{21}a_{32} - a_{13}a_{22}a_{31}$$

Except for order, this is the expansion originally given for a determinant of order three.

Note that each $2 \times 2$ matrix can be obtained by deleting, in the original matrix, the row and column containing its coefficient (an element of the first row). Note that the coefficients are taken with alternating signs.

$$= a_{11} \begin{vmatrix} a_{11} & a_{12} & a_{13} \\ a_{21} & a_{22} & a_{23} \\ a_{31} & a_{32} & a_{33} \end{vmatrix} - a_{12} \begin{vmatrix} a_{11} & a_{12} & a_{13} \\ a_{21} & a_{22} & a_{23} \\ a_{31} & a_{32} & a_{33} \end{vmatrix} + a_{13} \begin{vmatrix} a_{11} & a_{12} & a_{13} \\ a_{21} & a_{22} & a_{23} \\ a_{31} & a_{32} & a_{33} \end{vmatrix}$$

**4.189** Find the determinant of: **(a)** $A = \begin{pmatrix} 1 & 2 & 3 \\ 4 & -2 & 3 \\ 0 & 5 & -1 \end{pmatrix}$, **(b)** $B = \begin{pmatrix} 2 & 3 & 4 \\ 5 & 6 & 7 \\ 8 & 9 & 1 \end{pmatrix}$.

▮ Expand by the first row as in Problem 4.188:

**(a)** $\det(A) = \begin{vmatrix} 1 & 2 & 3 \\ 4 & -2 & 3 \\ 0 & 5 & -1 \end{vmatrix} = \begin{vmatrix} 1 & 2 & 3 \\ 4 & -2 & 3 \\ 0 & 5 & -1 \end{vmatrix} - 2 \begin{vmatrix} 1 & 2 & 3 \\ 4 & -2 & 3 \\ 0 & 5 & -1 \end{vmatrix} + 3 \begin{vmatrix} 1 & 2 & 3 \\ 4 & -2 & 3 \\ 0 & 5 & -1 \end{vmatrix}$

$$= 1 \begin{vmatrix} -2 & 3 \\ 5 & -1 \end{vmatrix} - 2 \begin{vmatrix} 4 & 3 \\ 0 & -1 \end{vmatrix} + 3 \begin{vmatrix} 4 & -2 \\ 0 & 5 \end{vmatrix}$$

$$= 1(2 - 15) - 2(-4 + 0) + 3(20 + 0) = -13 + 8 + 60 = 55$$

**(b)** $\det(B) = \begin{vmatrix} 2 & 3 & 4 \\ 5 & 6 & 7 \\ 8 & 9 & 1 \end{vmatrix} = 2\begin{vmatrix} 6 & 7 \\ 9 & 1 \end{vmatrix} - 3\begin{vmatrix} 5 & 7 \\ 8 & 1 \end{vmatrix} + 4\begin{vmatrix} 5 & 6 \\ 8 & 9 \end{vmatrix}$

$$= 2(6-63) - 3(5-56) + 4(45-48) = 27$$

**4.190** Find the determinant of: **(a)** $C = \begin{pmatrix} 2 & 3 & -4 \\ 0 & -4 & 2 \\ 1 & -1 & 5 \end{pmatrix}$ and **(b)** $D = \begin{pmatrix} 2 & 0 & 1 \\ 4 & 2 & -3 \\ 5 & 3 & 1 \end{pmatrix}$.

**(a)** $\det(C) = \begin{vmatrix} 2 & 3 & -4 \\ 0 & -4 & 2 \\ 1 & -1 & 5 \end{vmatrix} = 2\begin{vmatrix} -4 & 2 \\ -1 & 5 \end{vmatrix} - 3\begin{vmatrix} 0 & 2 \\ 1 & 5 \end{vmatrix} + (-4)\begin{vmatrix} 0 & -4 \\ 1 & -1 \end{vmatrix}$

$$= 2(-20+2) - 3(0-2) - 4(0+4) = -46$$

**(b)** $\det(D) = \begin{vmatrix} 2 & 0 & 1 \\ 4 & 2 & -3 \\ 5 & 3 & 1 \end{vmatrix} = 2\begin{vmatrix} 2 & -3 \\ 3 & 1 \end{vmatrix} - 0\begin{vmatrix} 4 & -3 \\ 5 & 1 \end{vmatrix} + 1\begin{vmatrix} 4 & 2 \\ 5 & 3 \end{vmatrix} = 2(2+9) + (12-10) = 24$

**4.191** Let $A = \begin{pmatrix} a_1 & b_1 & c_1 \\ a_2 & b_2 & c_2 \\ a_3 & b_3 & c_3 \end{pmatrix}$. Express $\det(A)$ as a linear combination of determinants of order two with coefficients from: **(a)** the second row, and **(b)** the third row.

**(a)** $\det(A) = a_1b_2c_3 + a_2b_3c_1 + a_3b_1c_2 - a_1b_3c_2 - a_2b_1c_3 - a_3b_2c_1$

$$= -a_2(b_1c_3 - b_3c_1) + b_2(a_1c_3 - a_3c_1) - c_2(a_1b_3 - a_3b_1)$$

$$= -a_2\begin{vmatrix} a_1 & b_1 & c_1 \\ a_2 & b_2 & c_2 \\ a_3 & b_3 & c_3 \end{vmatrix} + b_2\begin{vmatrix} a_1 & b_1 & c_1 \\ a_2 & b_2 & c_2 \\ a_3 & b_3 & c_3 \end{vmatrix} - c_2\begin{vmatrix} a_1 & b_1 & c_1 \\ a_2 & b_2 & c_2 \\ a_3 & b_3 & c_3 \end{vmatrix}$$

$$= -a_2\begin{vmatrix} b_1 & c_1 \\ b_3 & c_3 \end{vmatrix} + b_2\begin{vmatrix} a_1 & c_1 \\ a_3 & c_3 \end{vmatrix} - c_2\begin{vmatrix} a_1 & b_1 \\ a_3 & b_3 \end{vmatrix}$$

**(b)** $\det(A) = a_1b_2c_3 + b_1c_2a_3 + c_1a_2b_3 - a_3b_2c_1 - b_3c_2a_1 - c_3a_2b_1$

$$= a_3(b_1c_2 - b_2c_1) - b_3(a_1c_2 - a_2c_1) + c_3(a_1b_2 - a_2b_1)$$

$$= a_3\begin{vmatrix} a_1 & b_1 & c_1 \\ a_2 & b_2 & c_2 \\ a_3 & b_3 & c_3 \end{vmatrix} - b_3\begin{vmatrix} a_1 & b_1 & c_1 \\ a_2 & b_2 & c_2 \\ a_3 & b_3 & c_3 \end{vmatrix} + c_3\begin{vmatrix} a_1 & b_1 & c_1 \\ a_2 & b_2 & c_2 \\ a_3 & b_3 & c_3 \end{vmatrix}$$

$$= a_3\begin{vmatrix} b_1 & c_1 \\ b_2 & c_2 \end{vmatrix} - b_3\begin{vmatrix} a_1 & c_1 \\ a_2 & c_2 \end{vmatrix} + c_3\begin{vmatrix} a_1 & b_1 \\ a_2 & b_2 \end{vmatrix}$$

**4.192** The signs of the coefficients in the row-expansions of the third-order determinant of Problem 4.191 form a checkerboard pattern in the original matrix as follows:

$$\begin{pmatrix} + & - & + \\ - & + & - \\ + & - & + \end{pmatrix}$$

We can also expand the determinant so that the coefficients come from a column rather than from a row. The same checkerboard pattern works for the columns. Exhibit the three column-expansions of $\det(A)$.

$$\det(A) = a_1\begin{vmatrix} b_2 & c_2 \\ b_3 & c_3 \end{vmatrix} - a_2\begin{vmatrix} b_1 & c_1 \\ b_3 & c_3 \end{vmatrix} + a_3\begin{vmatrix} b_1 & c_1 \\ b_2 & c_2 \end{vmatrix} \quad \text{first column}$$

$$= -b_1\begin{vmatrix} a_2 & c_2 \\ a_3 & c_3 \end{vmatrix} + b_2\begin{vmatrix} a_1 & c_1 \\ a_3 & c_3 \end{vmatrix} - b_3\begin{vmatrix} a_1 & c_1 \\ a_2 & c_2 \end{vmatrix} \quad \text{second column}$$

$$= c_1\begin{vmatrix} a_2 & b_2 \\ a_3 & b_3 \end{vmatrix} - c_2\begin{vmatrix} a_1 & b_1 \\ a_3 & b_3 \end{vmatrix} + c_3\begin{vmatrix} a_1 & b_1 \\ a_2 & b_2 \end{vmatrix} \quad \text{third column}$$

**4.193** Consider three linear equations in the three unknowns $x$, $y$, and $z$:

$$a_1 x + b_1 y + c_1 z = d_1$$
$$a_2 x + b_2 y + c_2 z = d_2$$
$$a_3 x + b_3 y + c_3 z = d_3$$

Give a condition (in terms of determinants) which determines when the system has a unique solution, and express such a unique solution in terms of determinants.

❚ The above system has a unique solution if and only if the determinant of the matrix of coefficients is not zero:

$$D = \begin{vmatrix} a_1 & b_1 & c_1 \\ a_2 & b_2 & c_2 \\ a_3 & b_3 & c_3 \end{vmatrix} \neq 0 \qquad (1)$$

In this case, the unique solution of the system can be expressed as quotients of determinants,

$$x = \frac{N_x}{D}, \qquad y = \frac{N_y}{D}, \qquad z = \frac{N_z}{D}$$

where the denominator $D$ in each quotient is the determinant $(1)$ and the numerators $N_x$, $N_y$, and $N_z$ are obtained by replacing the column of coefficients of the unknown in the matrix of coefficients by the column of constant terms:

$$N_x = \begin{vmatrix} d_1 & b_1 & c_1 \\ d_2 & b_2 & c_2 \\ d_3 & b_3 & c_3 \end{vmatrix}, \qquad N_y = \begin{vmatrix} a_1 & d_1 & c_1 \\ a_2 & d_2 & c_2 \\ a_3 & d_3 & c_3 \end{vmatrix}, \qquad N_z = \begin{vmatrix} a_1 & b_1 & d_1 \\ a_2 & b_2 & d_2 \\ a_3 & b_3 & d_3 \end{vmatrix}$$

(We emphasize that if the determinant $D$ of the matrix of coefficients is zero then the system has either no solution or an infinite number of solutions.)

**4.194** Solve using determinants: $\begin{cases} 2x + y + z = 3 \\ x + y + z = 1 \\ x - 2y - 3z = 4 \end{cases}$.

❚ First compute the determinant $D$ of the matrix of coefficients:

$$D = \begin{vmatrix} 2 & 1 & -1 \\ 1 & 1 & 1 \\ 1 & -2 & -3 \end{vmatrix} = -6 + 1 + 2 + 1 + 4 + 3 = 5$$

Since $D \neq 0$, the system has a unique solution. Next evaluate $N_x$, $N_y$, and $N_z$, the numerators for $x$, $y$, and $z$ respectively:

$$N_x = \begin{vmatrix} 3 & 1 & -1 \\ 1 & 1 & 1 \\ 4 & -2 & -3 \end{vmatrix} = -9 + 4 + 2 + 4 + 6 + 3 = 10$$

$$N_y = \begin{vmatrix} 2 & 3 & -1 \\ 1 & 1 & 1 \\ 1 & 4 & -3 \end{vmatrix} = -6 + 3 - 4 + 1 - 8 + 9 = -5$$

$$N_x = \begin{vmatrix} 2 & 1 & 3 \\ 1 & 1 & 1 \\ 1 & -2 & 4 \end{vmatrix} = 8 + 1 - 6 - 3 + 4 - 4 = 0$$

Thus the unique solution is

$$x = \frac{N_x}{D} = \frac{10}{5} = 2, \qquad y = \frac{N_y}{D} = \frac{-5}{5} = -1, \qquad z = \frac{N_z}{D} = \frac{0}{5} = 0$$

## General Order Determinants

This subsection considers general order determinants. The following remarks are in order.

**Remark 1:** The expansion of a third order determinant in terms of second order determinants (Problem 4.191), credited to Laplace, is true in general. That is, any determinant can be similarly expressed as a linear combination of determinants of lower order using any row or any column as coefficients, with the coefficient $a_{ij}$ multiplied by $(-1)^{i+j}$ (i.e., the signs follow a checkerboard pattern).

**Remark 2:** The elementary row operation $(kR_i + R_j) \to (R_j)$, which adds $k$ times row $i$ to row $j$, does not change the value of the determinant. [A similar result is true for the elementary column operation $(kC_i + C_j) \to (C_j)$.]

**Remark 3:** The determinant of a triangular matrix is equal to the product of its diagonal elements. In particular, $\det(I) = 1$ and $\det(0) = 0$.

**4.195** Let $A = (a_{ij})$ be a nonzero $n$-square matrix with $n > 1$. Give an algorithm which reduces the determinant of $A$ to a determinant of order $n - 1$.

▮ *Step 1:* Choose an element $a_{ij} = 1$ or, if lacking, $a_{ij} \neq 0$.
    *Step 2:* Using $a_{ij}$ as a pivot, apply elementary row (column) operations to put 0s in all the other positions in column $j$ (row $i$).
    *Step 3:* Expand the determinant using the column (row) containing $a_{ij}$.
(The validity of the above algorithm follows from the above remarks.)

**4.196** Compute the determinant of $A = \begin{pmatrix} 5 & 4 & 2 & 1 \\ 2 & 3 & 1 & -2 \\ -5 & -7 & -3 & 9 \\ 1 & -2 & -1 & 4 \end{pmatrix}$.

▮ Use $a_{23} = 1$ as a pivot to put 0s in the other entries in the third column, that is, apply the row operations

$$(-2R_2 + R_1) \to (R_1), \qquad (3R_2 + R_3) \to (R_3), \qquad (R_2 + R_4) \to (R_4)$$

The value of the determinant does not change by these operations; that is,

$$|A| = \begin{vmatrix} 5 & 4 & 2 & 1 \\ 2 & 3 & 1 & -2 \\ -5 & -7 & -3 & 9 \\ 1 & -2 & -1 & 4 \end{vmatrix} = \begin{vmatrix} 1 & -2 & 0 & 5 \\ 2 & 3 & 1 & -2 \\ 1 & 2 & 0 & 3 \\ 3 & 1 & 0 & 2 \end{vmatrix}$$

Now if we expand by the third column, we may neglect all terms which contain 0. Thus

$$|A| = (-1)^{2+3} \begin{vmatrix} 1 & -2 & \boxed{0} & 5 \\ \boxed{2} & \boxed{3} & \boxed{1} & \boxed{-2} \\ 1 & 2 & \boxed{0} & 3 \\ 3 & 1 & \boxed{0} & 2 \end{vmatrix} = - \begin{vmatrix} 1 & -2 & 5 \\ 1 & 2 & 3 \\ 3 & 1 & 2 \end{vmatrix}$$

$$= -(4 - 18 + 5 - 30 - 3 + 4) = -(-38) = 38$$

**4.197** Evaluate the determinant of $B = \begin{pmatrix} 3 & -2 & -5 & 4 \\ 1 & -2 & -2 & 3 \\ -2 & 4 & 7 & -3 \\ 2 & -3 & -5 & 8 \end{pmatrix}$.

▮ Use $b_{21} = 1$ as a pivot and put 0s in the other entries in the second row by the column operations

$$(2C_1 + C_2) \to (C_2), \qquad (2C_1 + C_3) \to (C_3), \qquad \text{and} \qquad (-3C_1 + C_4) \to (C_4)$$

Then

$$|B| = \begin{vmatrix} 3 & -2 & -5 & 4 \\ 1 & -2 & -2 & 3 \\ -2 & 4 & 7 & -3 \\ 2 & -3 & -5 & 8 \end{vmatrix} = \begin{vmatrix} 3 & -2+2(3) & -5+2(3) & 4-3(3) \\ 1 & -2+2(1) & -2+2(1) & 3-3(1) \\ -2 & 4+2(-2) & 7+2(-2) & -3-3(-2) \\ 2 & -3+2(2) & -5+2(2) & 8-3(2) \end{vmatrix}$$

$$= \begin{vmatrix} 3 & 4 & 1 & -5 \\ 1 & 0 & 0 & 0 \\ -2 & 0 & 3 & 3 \\ 2 & 1 & -1 & 2 \end{vmatrix} = - \begin{vmatrix} 4 & 1 & -5 \\ 0 & 3 & 3 \\ 1 & -1 & 2 \end{vmatrix} = -(24 + 3 + 0 + 15 + 12 - 0) = -54$$

**4.198** Evaluate the determinant of $C = \begin{pmatrix} 2 & 5 & -3 & -2 \\ -2 & -3 & 2 & -5 \\ 1 & 3 & -2 & 2 \\ -1 & -6 & 4 & 3 \end{pmatrix}$.

▮ Use $c_{31} = 1$ as a pivot and apply the row operations

$$(-2R_3 + R_1) \rightarrow (R_1), \qquad (2R_3 + R_2) \rightarrow (R_2), \qquad \text{and} \qquad (R_3 + R_4) \rightarrow (R_4)$$

Then

$$|C| = \begin{vmatrix} 2 & 5 & -3 & -2 \\ -2 & -3 & 2 & -5 \\ 1 & 3 & -2 & 2 \\ -1 & -6 & 4 & 3 \end{vmatrix} = \begin{vmatrix} 0 & -1 & 1 & -6 \\ 0 & 3 & -2 & -1 \\ 1 & 3 & -2 & 2 \\ 0 & -3 & 2 & 5 \end{vmatrix} = + \begin{vmatrix} -1 & 1 & -6 \\ 3 & -2 & -1 \\ -3 & 2 & 5 \end{vmatrix} = 10 + 3 - 36 + 36 - 2 - 15 = -4$$

**4.199** Evaluate the determinant of each matrix:

$$(a) \; A = \begin{pmatrix} 3 & -2 & 5 & -8 \\ 0 & 7 & -4 & 9 \\ 0 & 0 & -6 & 4 \\ 0 & 0 & 0 & 2 \end{pmatrix}, \quad (b) \; B = \begin{pmatrix} 1 & 2 & 2 & 3 \\ 1 & 0 & -2 & 0 \\ 3 & -1 & 1 & -2 \\ 4 & -3 & 0 & 2 \end{pmatrix}, \quad (c) \; C = \begin{pmatrix} 0 & 0 & 0 & 0 \\ 0 & 0 & 0 & 0 \\ 0 & 0 & 0 & 0 \end{pmatrix}$$

▮ (a) Since $A$ is triangular, simply find the product of the diagonal elements: $|A| = (3)(7)(-6)(2) = -252$
(b) Use $b_{21} = 1$ as a pivot and apply the column operation $(2C_1 + C_3) \rightarrow (C_3)$:

$$|B| = \begin{vmatrix} 1 & 2 & 4 & 3 \\ 1 & 0 & 0 & 0 \\ 3 & -1 & 7 & -2 \\ 4 & -3 & 6 & 2 \end{vmatrix} = - \begin{vmatrix} 2 & 4 & 3 \\ -1 & 7 & -2 \\ -3 & 8 & 2 \end{vmatrix} = -(28 + 24 - 24 + 63 + 32 + 8) = -131$$

(c) Although $C$ is a zero matrix, it is not a square matrix; hence its determinant is not defined.

**4.200** Evaluate the determinant of $A = \begin{pmatrix} 6 & 2 & 1 & 0 & 5 \\ 2 & 1 & 1 & -2 & 1 \\ 1 & 1 & 2 & -2 & 3 \\ 3 & 0 & 2 & 3 & -1 \\ -1 & -1 & -3 & 4 & 2 \end{pmatrix}$.

▮ First reduce $|A|$ to a determinant of order four, and then to a determinant of order three. First use $a_{22} = 1$ as a pivot and apply $(-2R_2 + R_1) \rightarrow (R_1)$, $(-R_2 + R_3) \rightarrow (R_3)$, and $(R_2 + R_5) \rightarrow (R_5)$. Then

$$|A| = \begin{vmatrix} 2 & 0 & -1 & 4 & 3 \\ 2 & 1 & 1 & -2 & 1 \\ -1 & 0 & 1 & 0 & 2 \\ 3 & 0 & 2 & 3 & -1 \\ 1 & 0 & -2 & 2 & 3 \end{vmatrix} = \begin{vmatrix} 2 & -1 & 4 & 3 \\ -1 & 1 & 0 & 2 \\ 3 & 2 & 3 & -1 \\ 1 & -2 & 2 & 3 \end{vmatrix}$$

Use again $a_{22} = 1$ as a pivot and apply $(C_1 + C_2) \rightarrow (C_1)$ and $(-C_2 + C_4) \rightarrow (C_4)$:

$$|A| = \begin{vmatrix} 1 & -1 & 4 & 5 \\ 0 & 1 & 0 & 0 \\ 5 & 2 & 3 & -5 \\ -1 & -2 & 2 & 7 \end{vmatrix} = \begin{vmatrix} 1 & 4 & 5 \\ 5 & 3 & -5 \\ -1 & 2 & 7 \end{vmatrix} = 21 + 20 + 50 + 15 + 10 - 140 = -24$$

**4.201** If $P$ is nonsingular, show that $|P^{-1}| = |P|^{-1}$.

▮ $P^{-1}P = I$. Hence $1 = |I| = |P^{-1}P| = |P^{-1}| \, |P|$, and so $|P^{-1}| = |P|^{-1}$.

**4.202** Suppose that $B$ is *similar* to $A$; that is, suppose that there is a nonsingular matrix $P$ such that $B = P^{-1}AP$. Show that $|B| = |A|$.

▮ We have $|B| = |P^{-1}AP| = |P^{-1}| \, |A| \, |P| = |A| \, |P^{-1}| \, |P| = |A|$. (Although the matrices $P^{-1}$ and $A$ need not commute, their determinants, as scalars, do commute.)

**4.203** Suppose $A$ is orthogonal. Using the fact that $|A| = |A^T|$, show that $|A| = \pm 1$.

▮ Since $A$ is orthogonal, $AA^T = I$. Thus $1 = |I| = |AA^T| = |A| \, |A^T| = |A|^2$. Accordingly, $|A| = \pm 1$.

### Volume As a Determinant

Determinants are related to area and volume as follows: Let $u_1, u_2, \ldots, u_n$ be vectors (arrows) in $\mathbf{R}^n$. Let $S$ be the parallelepiped formed by the vectors. Let $A$ be the matrix with rows $u_1, u_2, \ldots, u_n$. Then the volume of $S$ (or area of $S$ when $n = 2$), denoted by $V(S)$, is equal to the absolute value of det $(A)$.

**4.204** Let $u_1 = (2, 3)$ and $u_2 = (5, 1)$ be vectors in $\mathbf{R}^2$. (*a*) Draw the parallelogram $S$ determined by the vectors (arrows). (*b*) Find the area of $S$.

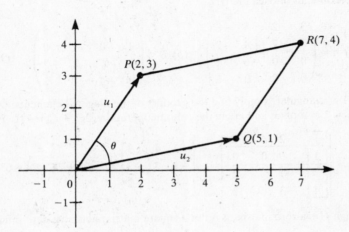

**Fig. 4-2**

▮ (*a*)  Draw the arrows from the origin $O$ to the points $P(2, 3)$ and $Q(5, 1)$ in the plane $\mathbf{R}^2$ as in Fig. 4-2. Then complete $S$ by drawing parallels to $u_1$ and $u_2$ as shown in Fig. 4-2.

(*b*)  Find the determinant of the matrix $A = \begin{pmatrix} 2 & 3 \\ 5 & 1 \end{pmatrix}$ whose rows are $u_1$ and $u_2$. Here $|A| = 2 - 15 = -13$. Hence area of $S = |-13| = 13$.

**4.205** Find the volume $V(S)$ of the parallelepiped $S$ in $\mathbf{R}^3$ determined by the vectors $u_1 = (2, 5, 2)$, $u_2 = (4, 2, 3)$, and $u_3 = (1, 1, 4)$ in $\mathbf{R}^3$.

▮ Evaluate the determinant of the matrix $A = \begin{pmatrix} 2 & 5 & 2 \\ 4 & 2 & 3 \\ 1 & 1 & 4 \end{pmatrix}$ (whose rows are the vectors $u_1, u_2, u_3$):

$|A| = 16 + 15 + 8 - 4 - 6 - 80 = -51$. Then $V(S) = 51$.

**4.206** Let $u_1$ and $u_2$ be vectors (arrows) in $\mathbf{R}^2$ and let $A$ be the matrix with rows $u_1$ and $u_2$. Give a geometric condition that determines whether det $(A)$ is positive, zero, or negative.

▮ If the smallest rotation that brings $u_1$ into $u_2$ is counterclockwise (clockwise), det $(A)$ is positive (negative). If $u_1$ is in the same or opposite direction as $u_2$, then det $(A)$ is zero.

**4.207** Let $u_1, u_2$, and $u_3$ be vectors (arrows) in $\mathbf{R}^3$. Let $A$ be the matrix with rows $u_1, u_2, u_3$. Give a geometric condition that determines whether det $(A)$ is positive, zero, or negative.

▮ det $(A)$ is positive or negative according as $u_1, u_2, u_3$ form a right- or left-handed coordinate system. If the three vectors lie in a plane, then det $(A)$ is zero.

**4.208** Show that the vectors $u_1 = (1, 2, 4)$, $u_2 = (2, 1, -3)$, and $u_3 = (5, 7, 9)$ lie in a plane.

$$\begin{vmatrix} 1 & 2 & 4 \\ 2 & 1 & -3 \\ 5 & 7 & 9 \end{vmatrix} = 9 - 30 + 56 - 20 + 21 - 36 = 0$$

(or else note that $u_3 = 3u_1 + u_2$).

**4.209** Find the volume $V(S)$ of the parallelepiped $S$ in $\mathbf{R}^4$ determined by the vectors $u_1 = (2, -1, 4, -3)$, $u_2 = (-1, 1, 0, 2)$, $u_3 = (3, 2, 3, -1)$, and $u_4 = (1, -2, 2, 3)$.

Evaluate the following determinant:

$$\begin{vmatrix} 2 & -1 & 4 & -3 \\ -1 & 1 & 0 & 2 \\ 3 & 2 & 3 & -1 \\ 1 & -2 & 2 & 3 \end{vmatrix} = \begin{vmatrix} 1 & -1 & 4 & -1 \\ 0 & 1 & 0 & 0 \\ 5 & 2 & 3 & -5 \\ -1 & -2 & 2 & 7 \end{vmatrix} = \begin{vmatrix} 1 & 4 & -1 \\ 5 & 3 & -5 \\ -1 & 2 & 7 \end{vmatrix}$$

$$= 21 + 20 - 10 - 3 + 10 - 140 = -102$$

Hence $V(S) = 102$.

# CHAPTER 5
# Graph Theory

## 5.1 GRAPHS AND MULTIGRAPHS

The study of graph theory is introduced in this chapter and it will be continued in the next two chapters.

**5.1**   Define a graph.

▮   A *graph* $G$ consists of two parts:
(i)   A set $V = V(G)$ whose elements are called *vertices, points,* or *nodes*.
(ii)   A collection $E = E(G)$ of unordered pairs of distinct vertices called *edges*.
We write $G(V, E)$ when we want to emphasize the two parts of $G$.

**5.2**   Define a multigraph.

▮   A *multigraph* $G = G(V, E)$ also consists of a set $V$ of vertices and a set $E$ of edges except that $E$ may contain *multiple* edges, i.e., edges connecting the same endpoints, and $E$ may contain one or more *loops*, i.e., an edge whose endpoints are the same vertex.

**5.3**   Describe a diagram of a graph (multigraph).

▮   Graphs (multigraphs) $G = G(V, E)$ are pictured by diagrams in the plane as follows. Each vertex $v$ in $V$ is represented by a dot (or small circle) and each edge $e = \{u, v\}$ is represented by a curve which connects its *endpoints u* and *v*. (In fact, we usually denote a graph, when possible, by drawing its diagram rather than explicitly listing its vertices and edges.)

**5.4**   Describe formally the graph shown in Fig. 5-1.

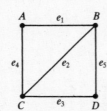

**Fig. 5-1**

▮   Figure 5-1 shows the graph $G = G(V, E)$ where: (i) $V$ consists of the vertices $A, B, C, D$; and (ii) $E$ consists of the five edges $e_1 = \{A, B\}$, $e_2 = \{B, C\}$, $e_3 = \{C, D\}$, $e_4 = \{A, C\}$, $e_5 = \{B, D\}$.

**5.5**   The diagram in Fig. 5-2 shows a multigraph $G$. Why is $G$ not a graph?

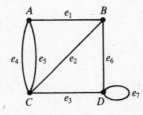

**Fig. 5-2**

▮   $G$ contains multiple edges, $e_4$ and $e_5$, which connect the same two vertices $A$ and $C$. Also, $G$ contains a loop $e_7$ whose endpoints are the same vertex $D$. A graph does not have multiple edges or loops.

**5.6**   Describe formally the graph shown in Fig. 5-3.

▮   Figure 5-3 shows a graph $G = G(V, E)$ where (i) $V$ consists of four vertices $A, B, C, D$; and (ii) $E$ consists of five edges $e_1 = \{A, B\}$, $e_2 = \{B, C\}$, $e_3 = \{C, D\}$, $e_4 = \{A, C\}$, $e_5 = \{B, D\}$.

**5.7**   Consider the multigraph $G = G(V, E)$ shown in Fig. 5-4.
**(a)**   Find the number of vertices and edges. **(b)** Are there any multiple edges or loops? If so, what are they?

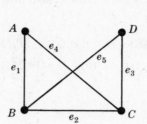

Fig. 5-3

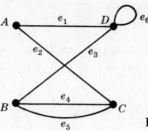

Fig. 5-4

■ **(a)** $G$ contains four vertices $A$, $B$, $C$, $D$; and six edges, $e_1$, $e_2$, ..., $e_6$. (Although the edges $e_2$ and $e_3$ cross at a point, the diagram does not indicate that the intersection point is a vertex of $G$.)

**(b)** The edges $e_4$ and $e_5$ are multiple edges since they both have the same endpoints $B$ and $C$. The edge $e_6$ is a loop.

**5.8** Draw a diagram for each of the following graphs $G = G(V, E)$:
**(a)** $V = \{A, B, C, D\}$, $E = [\{A, B\}, \{D, A\}, \{C, A\}, \{C, D\}]$
**(b)** $V = \{a, b, c, d, e, f\}$, $E = [\{a, d\}, \{a, f\}, \{b, c\}, \{b, f\}, \{c, e\}]$

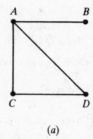

(a)

(b)

Fig. 5-5

■ First draw vertices of the graph, and then connect the appropriate vertices to indicate the edges of the graph, as shown in Fig. 5-5.

**5.9** Draw a diagram of each of the following multigraphs $G(V, E)$ where $V = \{P_1, P_2, P_3, P_4, P_5\}$ and
**(a)** $E = [\{P_2, P_4\}, \{P_2, P_3\}, \{P_3, P_5\}, \{P_5, P_4\}]$
**(b)** $E = [\{P_1, P_1\}, \{P_2, P_3\}, \{P_2, P_4\}, \{P_3, P_2\}, \{P_4, P_1\}, \{P_5, P_4\}]$

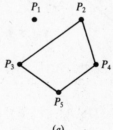

(a)

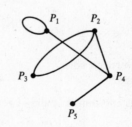

(b)

Fig. 5-6

■ As with graphs, draw the vertices and then indicate the edges by connecting the appropriate vertices, as in Fig. 5-6. [Note that **(a)** is a graph, besides being a multigraph.]

**5.10** Draw the diagram of each of the following graphs $G(V, E)$:
**(a)** $V = \{A, B, C, D\}$, $E = [\{A, B\}, \{A, D\}, \{B, C\}, \{B, D\}, \{C, D\}]$
**(b)** $V = \{a, b, c, d, e\}$, $E = [\{a, b\}, \{a, c\}, \{b, c\}, \{d, e\}]$

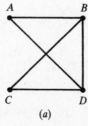

(a)

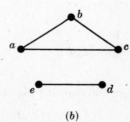

(b)

Fig. 5-7

❚ Draw a dot for each vertex $v$ in $V$, and for each edge $\{x, y\}$ in $E$ draw a curve from the vertex $x$ to the vertex $y$, as shown in Fig. 5-7.

**5.11**    Draw a diagram of each of the following multigraphs $G(V, E)$ where $V = \{P_1, P_2, P_3, P_4, P_5\}$ and

(a)  $E = [\{P_1, P_5\}, \{P_3, P_4\}, \{P_2, P_3\}, \{P_2, P_5\}, \{P_1, P_5\}]$,    (b)  $E = [\{P_2, P_4\}, \{P_2, P_3\}, \{P_5, P_1\}]$

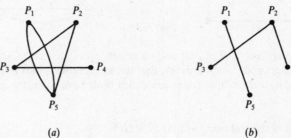

(a)                                              (b)            **Fig. 5-8**

❚ Draw diagrams as in Fig. 5-8.

**5.12**    Determine whether or not each of the following multigraphs $G(V, E)$ is a graph where $V = \{A, B, C, D\}$ and
(a)  $E = [\{A, B\}, \{A, C\}, \{A, D\}, \{B, C\}, \{C, D\}]$    (c)  $E = [\{A, B\}, \{C, D\}, \{A, B\}, \{B, D\}]$
(b)  $E = [\{A, B\}, \{B, B\}, \{A, D\}]$    (d)  $E = [\{A, B\}, \{B, C\}, \{C, B\}, \{B, B\}]$

❚ Recall a multigraph $G(V, E)$ is a graph if it has neither multiple edges nor loops. Thus
(a)  Yes.
(b)  No, since $\{B, B\}$ is a loop.
(c)  No, since $\{A, B\}$ and $\{A, B\}$ are multiple edges.
(d)  No, since $\{B, C\}$ and $\{C, B\}$ are multiple edges, and, moreover, $\{B, B\}$ is a loop.

**5.13**    Describe formally the graph shown in Fig. 5-9.

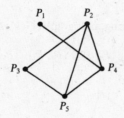

**Fig. 5-9**

❚ There are five vertices, so
$$V = \{P_1, P_2, P_3, P_4, P_5\}$$

There are six edges and thus six pairs of vertices; hence
$$E = [\{P_1, P_4\}, \{P_2, P_3\}, \{P_2, P_4\}, \{P_2, P_5\}, \{P_4, P_5\}, \{P_3, P_5\}]$$

**5.14**    Describe formally the graph shown in Fig. 5-10.

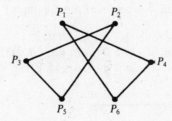

**Fig. 5-10**

❚ There are six vertices, so
$$V = \{P_1, P_2, P_3, P_4, P_5, P_6\}$$

There are six edges and thus six pairs of vertices; hence
$$E = [\{P_1, P_4\}, \{P_1, P_6\}, \{P_4, P_6\}, \{P_3, P_2\}, \{P_3, P_5\}, \{P_2, P_5\}]$$

**5.15**    Describe formally the multigraph shown in Fig. 5-11.

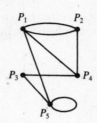

**Fig. 5-11**

   ❚   There are five vertices, so

$$V = \{P_1, P_2, P_3, P_4, P_5\}$$

There are eight edges (of which two are multiple edges and one is a loop) and thus eight pairs of vertices; hence

$$E = [\{P_1, P_2\}, \{P_1, P_2\}, \{P_1, P_4\}, \{P_1, P_5\}, \{P_2, P_4\}, \{P_3, P_4\}, \{P_3, P_5\}, \{P_5, P_5\}]$$

**5.16**    Describe formally the multigraph shown in Fig. 5-12.

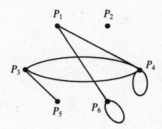

**Fig. 5-12**

   ❚   There are six vertices, so

$$V = \{P_1, P_2, P_3, P_4, P_5, P_6\}$$

There are seven edges (of which two are multiple edges and two are loops) and thus seven pairs of vertices; hence

$$E = [\{P_1, P_4\}, \{P_1, P_6\}, \{P_3, P_4\}, \{P_3, P_4\}, \{P_4, P_4\}, \{P_3, P_5\}, \{P_6, P_6\}]$$

**5.17**    Define a finite multigraph.

   ❚   A multigraph $G = G(V, E)$ is *finite* if both $V$ is finite and $E$ is finite. Note that a graph $G$ with a finite number of vertices $V$ must automatically have a finite number of edges and so must be finite.

**5.18**    What is the trivial graph?   empty or null graph?

   ❚   The *trivial* graph is the graph with one vertex and no edges. The empty graph is the graph with no vertices and no edges.

**5.19**    What is an isolated vertex? Which vertex in Fig. 5-6 is isolated?

   ❚   A vertex $V$ is *isolated* if it does not belong to any edge. The vertex $P_1$ in Fig. 5-6($a$) is isolated.

**5.20**    Suppose $G = G(V, E)$ has five vertices. Find the maximum number $m$ of edges in $E$ if: (**a**) $G$ is a graph, and (**b**) $G$ is a multigraph.

   ❚   (**a**)    There are $C(5, 2) = 10$ ways of choosing two vertices from $V$; hence $m = 10$.
       (**b**)    Since multiple edges are permitted, $G$ can have any number of edges (and loops), finite or infinite; hence no such maximum number $m$ exists.

## 5.2   DEGREE OF A VERTEX

**5.21**    Define the relation of adjacency and incidence in a graph $G$.

   ❚   Suppose $e = \{u, v\}$ is an edge in $G$, i.e., $u$ and $v$ are *endpoints* of $e$. Then the vertex $u$ is said to be *adjacent* to the vertex $v$, and the edge $e$ is said to be *incident* on $u$ and on $v$.

**5.22**  Define the degree and parity (even or odd) of a vertex.

▎ The *degree* of a vertex $v$ in a graph $G$, written deg $(v)$, is equal to the number of edges which are incident on $v$ or, in other words, the number of edges which contain $v$ as an endpoint. The vertex $v$ is said to be *even* or *odd* according as deg $(v)$ is even or odd.

**Theorem 5.1:**  The sum of the degrees of the vertices of a graph is equal to twice the number of edges.

**5.23**  Prove Theorem 5.1.

▎ Follows directly from the fact that each edge is counted twice in counting the degrees of the vertices of a graph $G$.

**5.24**  Does Theorem 5.1 hold for a multigraph?

▎ Yes. Note that a loop must be counted twice towards the degree of its endpoint.

**5.25**  Consider the graph $G = G(V, E)$ in Fig. 5-13. (*a*) Describe $G$ formally. (*b*) Find the degree and parity of each vertex of $G$. (*c*) Verify Theorem 5.1 for $G$.

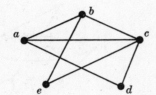

**Fig. 5-13**

▎ (*a*)  There are five vertices, so $V = \{a, b, c, d, e\}$. There are seven pairs $\{x, y\}$ of vertices where the vertex $x$ is connected with the vertex $y$: hence

$$E = [\{a, b\}, \{a, c\}, \{a, d\}, \{b, c\}, \{b, e\}, \{c, d\}, \{c, e\}]$$

  (*b*)  The degree of a vertex is equal to the number of edges to which it belongs; e.g., deg $(a) = 3$ since $a$ belongs to $\{a, b\}$, $\{a, c\}$, $\{a, d\}$ or, equivalently, there are three edges leaving $a$ in the diagram of $G$ in Fig. 5-13. Similarly, deg $(b) = 3$, deg $(c) = 4$, deg $(d) = 2$, deg $(e) = 2$. Thus $c$, $d$, and $e$ are even vertices and $a$ and $b$ are odd.

  (*c*)  The sum of the degrees of the vertices is $m = 3 + 3 + 4 + 2 + 2 = 14$ which does equal twice the number of edges.

**5.26**  Consider the graph $G$ where

$$V(G) = \{A, B, C, D\} \quad \text{and} \quad E(G) = [\{A, B\}, \{B, C\}, \{B, D\}, \{C, D\}]$$

Find the degree and parity of each vertex in $G$.

▎ Count the number of edges to which each vertex belongs to obtain

$$\deg(A) = 1, \quad \deg(B) = 3, \quad \deg(C) = 2, \quad \deg(D) = 2$$

Thus $C$ and $D$ are even and $A$ and $B$ are odd.

**5.27**  Find the degree of each vertex in the multigraph in Fig. 5-11.

▎ Count the number of edges leaving each vertex to obtain

$$\deg(P_1) = 4, \quad \deg(P_2) = 3, \quad \deg(P_3) = 2, \quad \deg(P_4) = 3, \quad \deg(P_5) = 4$$

(Here the loop at $P_5$ is counted twice toward the degree of $P_5$.)

**5.28**  Find the degree of each vertex in the multigraph in Fig. 5-12.

▎ Count the number of edges leaving each vertex to obtain:

$$\deg(P_1) = 2, \quad \deg(P_2) = 0, \quad \deg(P_3) = 3, \quad \deg(P_4) = 5, \quad \deg(P_5) = 1, \quad \deg(P_6) = 3$$

(Here the loops at $P_4$ and $P_6$ are counted twice toward the degree of their corresponding vertices.)

**5.29**   Find the degree and parity of each vertex in the graph in Fig. 5-9.

▌  Count the number of edges leaving each vertex to obtain

$$\deg(P_1) = 1, \quad \deg(P_2) = 3, \quad \deg(P_3) = 2, \quad \deg(P_4) = 3, \quad \deg(P_5) = 3$$

Thus $P_1$, $P_2$, $P_4$, and $P_5$ are odd and $P_3$ is even.

**5.30**   Find the degree and parity of each vertex in the graph in Fig. 5-10.

▌  Count the number of edges leaving each vertex to see that each vertex has degree 2 and hence each vertex is even.

**5.31**   Consider the multigraph $G$ where $V(G) = \{A, B, C, D\}$ and

$$E(G) = [\{A, C\}, \{A, D\}, \{B, B\}, \{B, C\}, \{C, A\}, \{C, B\}, \{D, B\}, \{D, D\}]$$

(a)   Find the degree and parity of each vertex in $G$.
(b)   Verify Theorem 5.1 for the multigraph $G$.

▌  (a)   Count the number of edges to which each vertex belongs or, equivalently, count the number of times each vertex appears in $E(G)$ to obtain

$$\deg(A) = 3, \quad \deg(B) = 5, \quad \deg(C) = 4, \quad \deg(D) = 4$$

Thus $A$ and $B$ are odd, and $C$ and $D$ are even.

(b)   The sum of the degrees of the vertices is $m = 3 + 5 + 4 + 4 = 16$ which does equal twice the number (eight) of edges.

**5.32**   Find the sum $m$ of the degrees of the vertices of $G$ where $V(G) = \{A, B, C, D\}$ and
(a)   $E(G) = [\{A, B\}, \{A, C\}, \{B, D\}, \{C, D\}]$
(b)   $E(G) = [\{A, B\}, \{A, C\}, \{A, D\}, \{B, A\}, \{B, B\}, \{C, B\}, \{C, D\}]$

▌  One way to determine $m$ is to find the degree of each vertex, and sum the degrees over all vertices. However, a faster approach would be to apply Theorem 5.1, i.e., the required result is to double the number of edges. Hence
(a)   There are 4 edges, so $m = 2(4) = 8$.
(b)   There are 7 edges, so $m = 2(7) = 14$.

**5.33**   Suppose $v$ is an isolated vertex in a graph (multigraph) $G$. What is its degree?

▌  The vertex $v$ is isolated if it does not belong to any edge. Thus $v$ is isolated if and only if $\deg(v) = 0$.

**5.34**   Consider $G = G(V, E)$ where $V = \{u, v, w\}$ and $\deg(v) = 4$. (a) Does such a graph $G$ exist? If not, why not? (b) Does such a multigraph $G$ exist? If yes, give an example.

▌  (a)   No. Since multiple edges and loops are not permitted, there can only be one edge from $v$ to each of the other two edges; hence $\deg(v) \leq 2$.
(b)   Yes. For example, $E = [\{u, v\}, \{u, v\}, \{v, w\}, \{v, w\}]$.

**5.35**   Consider $G = G(V, E)$ where $V = \{A, B, C, D\}$ and

$$\deg(A) = 2, \quad \deg(B) = 3, \quad \deg(C) = 2, \quad \deg(D) = 2$$

(a)   Does such a graph $G$ exist; If not, why not? (b) Does such a multigraph $G$ exist?

▌  (a)   No. The sum $m$ of the degrees of the vertices must be even, since $m$ is twice the number of edges (Theorem 5.1). Here $m = 7$, an odd number. Thus no such graph $G$ exists.
(b)   No, since Theorem 5.1 also holds for multigraphs.

## 5.3   PATHS, CONNECTIVITY

**5.36**   Define a path and its length in a graph (multigraph) $G$.

▌  A *path* $\alpha$ in $G$ with *origin* $v_0$ and *end* $v_n$ is an alternating sequence of vertices and edges of the form

$$v_0, e_1, v_1, e_2, v_2, \ldots, e_{n-1}, v_{n-1}, e_n, v_n$$

where each edge $e_i$ is incident on vertices $v_{i-1}$ and $v_i$. The number $n$ of edges is called the *length* of $\alpha$. When there is no ambiguity, we denote $\alpha$ by its sequence of edges, $\alpha = (e_1, e_2, \ldots, e_n)$, or by its sequence of vertices, $\alpha = (v_0, v_1, \ldots, v_n)$.

**5.37**   Define a simple path and a trail in a graph (multigraph) $G$.

▌ A path $\alpha = (v_0, v_1, \ldots, v_n)$ is *simple* if all the vertices are distinct. The path is a *trail* if all the edges are distinct.

**5.38**   Consider a graph (multigraph) $G$. Define a closed path and a cycle in $G$.

▌ A path $\alpha = (v_0, v_1, \ldots, v_n)$ is *closed* if $v_0 = v_n$, that is, if origin $(\alpha) =$ end $(\alpha)$. The path $\alpha$ is a *cycle* if it is closed and if all vertices are distinct except $v_0 = v_n$. A cycle of length $k$ is called a $k$-cycle. A cycle in a graph must therefore have length three or more.

**5.39**   Let $u$ and $v$ be vertices in a graph $G$. Define the distance between $u$ and $v$, written $d(u, v)$.

▌ If $u = v$, then $d(u, u) = 0$. Otherwise, $d(u, v)$ is equal to the length of a shortest path between $u$ and $v$. If no path between $u$ and $v$ exists, then $d(u, v)$ is not defined.

**5.40**   Let $G$ be the graph shown in Fig. 5-14. Consider the following paths in $G$:

(*a*)   $\alpha = (e_1, e_4, e_6, e_5)$,      (*b*)   $\beta = (e_2, e_5, e_3, e_4, e_6, e_3, e_1)$

Convert each sequence of edges into the corresponding sequence of vertices.

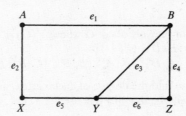

**Fig. 5-14**

▌ List the initial vertex of the first edge followed by the terminal (end) vertex of each edge in the sequence to obtain

(*a*)   $\alpha = (A, B, Z, Y, X)$,      and      (*b*)   $\beta = (A, X, Y, B, Z, Y, B, A)$.

**5.41**   Let $G$ be the graph in Fig. 5-14. Find: (*a*) all simple paths from vertex $A$ to vertex $Z$, and (*b*) $d(A, Z)$.

▌ (*a*)   A path from $A$ to $Z$ is simple if no vertex is repeated. There are four such simple paths as follows:

$$(A, B, Z), \quad (A, B, Y, Z), \quad (A, X, Y, Z), \quad (A, X, Y, B, Z)$$

(*b*)   $d(A, Z) = 2$ since the path $\alpha = (A, B, Z)$, of length 2, is the shortest path from $A$ to $Z$.

**5.42**   Let $G$ be the graph in Fig. 5-14. Find a $k$-cycle for: (*a*) $k = 3$, (*b*) $k = 4$, (*c*) $k = 5$, and (*d*) $k = 6$.

▌ A $k$-cycle is a closed path of length $k$ where all vertices are distinct (except $v_0 = v_n$). Thus (*a*) $(B, Y, Z, B)$, (*b*) $(A, B, Y, X, A)$, (*c*) $(A, B, Z, Y, X, A)$, and (*d*) No 6-cycle exists.

**5.43**   Let $G$ be the graph in Fig. 5-15. Determine whether or not each of the following sequences of edges forms a path:

(*a*)   $(\{A, X\}, \{X, B\}, \{C, Y\}, \{Y, X\})$      (*c*)   $(\{X, B\}, \{B, Y\}, \{Y, C\})$

(*b*)   $(\{A, X\}, \{X, Y\}, \{Y, Z\}, \{Z, A\})$      (*d*)   $(\{B, Y\}, \{X, Y\}, \{A, X\})$

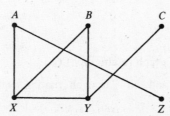

**Fig. 5-15**

❚ A sequence of edges is a path if the edges can be directed so that the end vertex of one edge is the initial vertex of the next edge.

(a) No. The edge $\{X, B\}$ is not followed by the edge $\{C, Y\}$.

(b) No. The pair $\{Y, Z\}$ is not an edge.

(c) Yes.

(d) Yes, since the sequence can be rewritten as $(\{B, Y\}, \{Y, X\}, \{X, A\})$.

**5.44** Let $G$ be the graph in Fig. 5-15. Find: (a) all simple paths from $A$ to $C$, and (b) $d(A, C)$.

❚ (a) There are only two simple paths from $A$ to $C$: $(A, X, Y, C)$ and $(A, X, B, Y, C)$.

(b) $d(A, C) = 3$ since 3 is the length of the shortest path from $A$ to $C$.

**5.45** Find all cycles in the graph $G$ in Fig. 5-15.

❚ There is only one cycle in $G$, the 3-cycle $\alpha = (B, X, Y, B)$. [Here we identify $\alpha$ with the other cycles that have the same vertices as $\alpha$, e.g., $(X, Y, B, X)$, and those cycles obtained by reversing the order of the vertices, e.g., $(B, Y, X, B]$.

**Theorem 5.2:** There is a path from a vertex $u$ to a vertex $v$ if and only if there is a simple path from $u$ to $v$.

**5.46** Prove Theorem 5.2.

❚ Since every simple path is a path, we need only prove that if there is a path $\alpha$ from $u$ to $v$, then there is a simple path from $u$ to $v$. The proof is by induction on the length $n$ of $\alpha$. Suppose $n = 1$, i.e., $\alpha = (u, v)$. Then $\alpha$ is a simple path from $u$ to $v$. Suppose $n > 1$, say

$$\alpha = (u = v_0, v_1, v_2, \ldots, v_{n-1}, v = v_n)$$

If no vertex is repeated, then $\alpha$ is a simple path from $u$ to $v$. Suppose a vertex is repeated, say $v_i = v_j$ where $i < j$. Then

$$\beta = (v_0, v_1, \ldots, v_i, v_{j+1}, \ldots, v_n)$$

is a path from $u = v_0$ to $v = v_n$ of length less than $n$. By induction, there is a simple path from $u$ to $v$.

**5.47** Is there any inclusion relation between closed paths, trails, simple paths, and cycles?

❚ Yes. Every cycle is a closed path since, by definition, a cycle is a closed path with distinct vertices. Also, every simple path is a trail since a path with distinct vertices must have distinct edges. (A cycle is a trail, but not a simple path.)

**5.48** Let $G$ be the graph in Fig. 5-16. Determine whether each of the following is a closed path, trail, simple path, or cycle: (a) $(B, A, X, C, B)$, (b) $(X, A, B, Y)$, (c) $(B, X, Y, B)$.

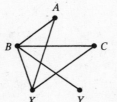

**Fig. 5-16**

❚ (a) This path is a cycle since it is closed and has distinct vertices.

(b) This path is simple since its vertices are distinct. It is not a cycle since it is not closed.

(c) This is not even a path since $\{X, Y\}$ is not an edge.

**5.49** Repeat Problem 5.48 for each of the following: (a) $(B, A, X, C, B, Y)$, (b) $(X, C, A, B, Y)$, and (c) $(X, B, A, X, C)$.

❚ (a) This path is a trail since its edges are distinct. It is not a simple path since the vertex $B$ is repeated.

(b) This is not even a path since $\{C, A\}$ is not an edge.

(c) This path is a trail since the edges are distinct. It is not a simple path since the vertex $X$ is repeated.

**5.50** Repeat Problem 5.48 for each of the following: (a) $(X, B, A, X, B)$, (b) $(A, B, C, X, B, A)$, (c) $(X, C, B, A)$.

▐ **(a)** This path is neither closed nor a trail. [The edge $\{X, B\}$ is repeated.] Thus it is neither a cycle nor a simple path.

**(b)** This is a closed path. It is not a cycle since the vertex $B$ is repeated.

**(c)** This is a simple path since the vertices are distinct.

**5.51** Let $G$ be the graph in Fig. 5-17. Find: **(a)** all simple paths from $A$ to $Z$, **(b)** all trails from $A$ to $Z$.

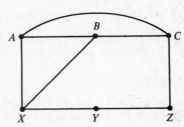

**Fig. 5-17**

▐ **(a)** A path from $A$ to $Z$ is simple if no vertex (and hence no edge) is repeated. There are five such simple paths:

$$(A, C, Z), \quad (A, B, C, Z), \quad (A, X, Y, Z), \quad (A, B, X, Y, Z), \quad (A, X, B, C, Z)$$

**(b)** A path from $A$ to $Z$ is a trail if no edge is repeated. There are eight such trails, the five simple paths from **(a)** together with

$$(A, X, B, A, C, Z), \quad (A, C, B, A, X, Y, Z), \quad (A, B, C, A, X, Y, Z)$$

**5.52** Find $d(A, Z)$ for the graph $G$ in Fig. 5-17.

▐ Here $d(A, Z) = 2$ since there is a path $\alpha = (A, C, Z)$ of length two from $A$ to $Z$ and none shorter. (Remember, length is the number of edges, not vertices, in a path.)

## Connected Graphs

**5.53** Define a connected graph (multigraph).

▐ A graph (multigraph) $G$ is *connected* if there is a path between any two of its vertices.

**5.54** Determine whether or not each of the graphs in Fig. 5-18 is connected.

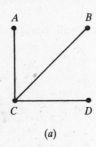 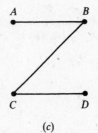 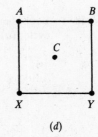

       (a)                  (b)                  (c)                  (d)

**Fig. 5-18**

▐ **(a)** Yes. There is a path between any two vertices of the graph.

**(b)** No. Here $A$, $B$, and $Y$ are connected, and $C$ and $X$ are connected, but there is no path from $A$, $B$, or $Y$ to either $C$ or $X$.

**(c)** Yes. There is a path between any two vertices of the graph.

**(d)** No. There is no path from $C$ to any other vertex of the graph.

**5.55** Consider the multigraphs in Fig. 5-19. Which of them are **(a)** connected, **(b)** loop-free (i.e., have no loops), **(c)** graphs?

▐ **(a)** Only (i) and (iii) are connected.

**(b)** Only (iv) has a loop, i.e., an edge with the same endpoints.

**(c)** Only (i) and (ii) are graphs. The multigraph (iii) has multiple edges and (iv) has multiple edges and a loop.

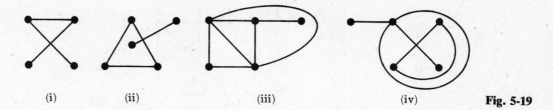

(i)        (ii)          (iii)              (iv)          **Fig. 5-19**

**5.56**    Consider the multigraphs in Fig. 5-20. Which of them are **(a)** connected, **(b)** graphs?

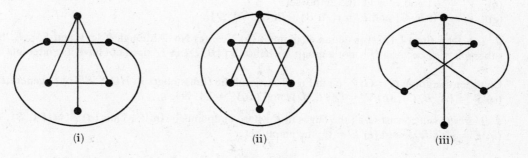

(i)                    (ii)                    (iii)

**Fig. 5-20**

▌ **(a)**    Only (iii) is connected. **(b)** They are all graphs.

**5.57**    Define the diameter of a connected graph $G$.

▌ The *diameter* of $G$, written diam $(G)$, is the maximum distance between any two of its vertices.

**5.58**    Find the diameter of the connected graph in Fig. 5-17.

▌ Here diam $(G) = 2$ since it is the maximum distance between any two vertices.

**5.59**    Find the diameter of the connected graph $G$ in Fig. 5-15.

▌ Note $d(C, Z) = 4$ and this is the maximum distance between any two vertices in $G$. Thus diam $(G) = 4$.

**5.60**    Find the diameter of the connected graph in Fig. 5-14.

▌ Here $d(A, Z) = 2$ and this is the maximum distance between any two vertices in $G$. Thus diam $(G) = 2$.

## 5.4  SUBGRAPHS, CONNECTED COMPONENTS, CUT POINTS, BRIDGES

**5.61**    Define the terms **(a)** subgraph and **(b)** full subgraph.

▌ **(a)**    Let $G$ be a graph. Then $H$ is a *subgraph* of $G$ if $V(H) \subseteq V(G)$, i.e., the vertices of $H$ are also vertices of $G$, and $E(H) \subseteq E(G)$, i.e., the edges of $H$ are also edges of $G$. In other words, $H(V', E')$ is a subgraph of $G(V, E)$ if $V' \subseteq V$ and $E' \subseteq E$.

**(b)**    Suppose $H = H(V', E')$ is a subgraph of $G = G(V, E)$. Then $H$ is called a *full subgraph* of $G$ if $E'$ contains all the edges of $E$ whose endpoints lie in $V'$. In this case $H$ is called the subgraph of $G$ *generated* by $V'$.

**5.62**    Consider the graph $G = G(V, E)$ in Fig. 5-21. Determine whether or not $H = H(V', E')$ is a subgraph of $G$ where
**(a)**    $V' = \{A, B, F\}$ and $E' = [\{A, B\}, \{A, F\}]$,
**(b)**    $V' = \{B, C, D\}$ and $E' = [\{B, C\}, \{B, D\}]$,
**(c)**    $V' = \{A, B, C\}$ and $E' = [\{A, B\}, \{A, C\}]$.

▌ $H$ is a subgraph of $G$ if $H$ is a graph and its vertices are contained in $V$ and its edges are contained in $E$.
**(a)**    No, the vertex $F$ is not a vertex in $G$. **(b)** Yes. **(c)** No, since $\{A, C\}$ is not an edge in $G$.

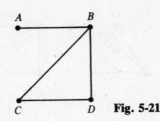

Fig. 5-21

**5.63** Consider the graph $G = G(V, E)$ in Fig. 5-21. Determine whether or not $H = H(V', E')$ is a subgraph of $G$ where
(**a**) $V' = \{A, B, D\}$ and $E' = [\{A, B\}, \{A, D\}]$,
(**b**) $V' = \{B\}$ and $E' = \emptyset$, the empty set,
(**c**) $V' = \{A, B, C\}$ and $E' = [\{A, B\}, \{B, C\}, \{B, D\}]$.

❙ (**a**) No, since $\{A, D\}$ is not an edge in $G$. (**b**) Yes. (**c**) No. Although $V' \subseteq V$ and $E' \subseteq E$, $H$ is not a subgraph of $G$ because $H$ is not a graph. Specifically, $\{B, D\}$ in $E'$ does not have its endpoints in $V'$.

**5.64** Consider the graph $G = G(V, E)$ in Fig. 5-21. Find the (full) subgraph $H(V', E')$ of $G$ generated by
(**a**) $V' = \{A, B, C\}$, (**b**) $V' = \{A, C, D\}$, and (**c**) $V' = \{A, D\}$.

❙ Here $E'$ will consist of all the edges in $E$ whose endpoints lie in $V'$. Thus (**a**) $E' = [\{A, B\}, \{B, C\}]$, (**b**) $E' = [\{C, D\}]$, and (**c**) $E' = \emptyset$, the empty set.

**5.65** Consider the graph $G = G(V, E)$ in Fig. 5-21. Find the number of full subgraphs of $G$.

❙ Each subset of $V = \{A, B, C, D\}$ determines a full subgraph of $G$. There are $m = 2^4 = 16$ subsets of $V$ and hence there are $m = 16$ full subgraphs of $G$. (We are including the empty graph, the graph with no vertices and no edges.)

## Connected Components

**5.66** Let $G$ be a graph (multigraph). Define a connected component of $G$. Illustrate with an example.

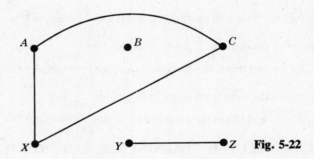

Fig. 5-22

❙ A *connected component* of $G$ is a subgraph of $G$ which is not contained in any larger connected subgraph of $G$. It is clear that a connected component is the full subgraph spanned by its vertices; hence we can designate a connected component by listing its vertices. It is also clear that $G$ can be partitioned into its connected components. Figure 5-22 shows a graph with three connected components, $\{A, C, X\}$, $\{B\}$, and $\{Y, Z\}$.

**5.67** Find the connected components of the graph $G$ in Fig. 5-23.

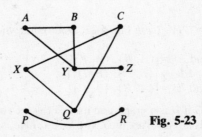

Fig. 5-23

❙ Start with any vertex, say $A$, and find all vertices connected to $A$; this gives the component $\{A, B, Y, Z\}$. Next select a vertex not included in this component and repeat the process to obtain another component. Continue in this way until all the components have been identified. For this graph, we obtain two additional components, $\{C, X, Q\}$ and $\{P, R\}$. Thus the components of $G$ are $\{A, B, Y, Z\}$, $\{C, X, Q\}$, $\{P, R\}$.

**5.68** Find the connected components of the graph $G$ in Fig. 5-24.

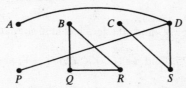

**Fig. 5-24**

❙ Proceed as in Problem 5.67 to obtain the connected components $\{A, D, P, S, C\}$ and $\{B, Q, R\}$.

**5.69** Find the connected components of $G$ where $V(G) = \{A, B, C, X, Y, Z\}$ and **(a)** $E(G) = [\{A, X\}, \{C, X\}]$, **(b)** $E(G) = [\{A, Y\}, \{B, C\}, \{Z, Y\}, \{X, Z\}]$.

❙ **(a)** Here $A$ is connected to $C$ and $X$; and $B$, $Y$, and $Z$ are isolated vertices; hence $\{A, C, X\}$, $\{B\}$, $\{Y\}$, and $\{Z\}$ are the connected components of $G$.

**(b)** Here $A$, $Y$, $Z$, and $X$ are connected; and $B$ and $C$ are connected. Thus $\{A, X, Y, Z\}$ and $\{B, C\}$ are the connected components of $G$.

**5.70** Find the connected components of $G$ where $V(G) = \{A, B, C, P, Q\}$ and **(a)** $E(G) = [\{A, C\}, \{B, Q\}, \{P, C\}, \{Q, A\}]$, **(b)** $E(G) = \emptyset$, the empty set.

❙ **(a)** Here $G$ is connected, i.e., each vertex is connected to the other vertices. Thus $G$ has one component $V(G) = \{A, B, C, P, Q\}$.

**(b)** Since $E(G)$ is empty, all the vertices are isolated; hence $\{A\}$, $\{B\}$, $\{C\}$, $\{P\}$, and $\{Q\}$ are the connected components of $G$.

**5.71** Let $G$ be a graph. For vertices $u$ and $v$, define $u \sim v$ if $u = v$ or if there is a path from $u$ to $v$. Show that $\sim$ is an equivalence relation on $V(G)$. How can one describe the equivalence classes induced by $\sim$?

❙ By definition, $u \sim u$ for every $u \in V(G)$, hence $\sim$ is reflexive. Suppose $u \sim v$. Then there is a path $\alpha$ from $u$ to $v$. Reversing $\alpha$ gives a path from $v$ back to $u$. Thus $v \sim u$ and therefore $\sim$ is symmetric. Lastly, suppose $u \sim v$ and $v \sim w$. Then there is a path $\alpha$ from $u$ to $v$ and a path $\beta$ from $v$ to $w$. However, end $(\alpha) = v = $ initial $(\beta)$. Thus $\alpha$ may be continued by $\beta$ to give a path $\alpha\beta$ from $u$ to $w$. Thus $u \sim w$ and therefore $\sim$ is transitive. Accordingly, $\sim$ is an equivalence relation.

The equivalence classes determined by $\sim$ are the connected components of $G$.

## Subgraph $G - v$, Cut Points

**5.72** Define the subgraph $G - v$ where $v$ is a vertex in $G$.

❙ $G - v$ is the subgraph of $G$ obtained by deleting the vertex $v$ from the vertex set $V(G)$ and deleting all edges in $E(G)$ which are incident on $v$. Alternately, $G - v$ is the full subgraph of $G$ generated by the remaining vertices.

**5.73** Define a cut point for a connected graph $G$.

❙ A vertex $v$ is called a *cut point* for $G$ if $G - v$ is disconnected. (More generally, $v$ is a cut point for any graph $G$ if $G - v$ has more connected components than $G$.)

**5.74** Let $G$ be the graph in Fig. 5-25. Find: **(a)** $G - A$, **(b)** $G - B$, and **(c)** $G - C$.

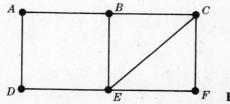

**Fig. 5-25**

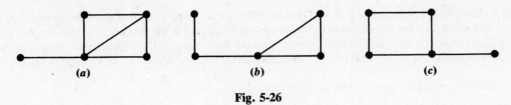

**Fig. 5-26**

▌ Delete the given vertex from $G$ and all edges incident on that vertex to obtain the graphs in Fig. 5-26.

**5.75**   Let $G$ be the graph in Fig. 5-25. Find: (**a**) $G - X$, (**b**) $G - Y$, and (**c**) $G - Z$.

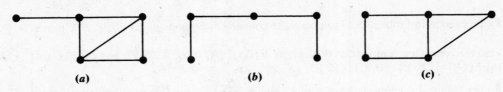

**Fig. 5-27**

▌ See Fig. 5-27.

**5.76**   Let $G$ be the graph in Fig. 5-25. Does $G$ have any cut points?

▌ Figures 5-26 and 5-27 show that $G - v$ is connected for any vertex $v$ of $G$. Thus $G$ has no cut points.

**5.77**   Let $G$ be the graph in Fig. 5-28. Find: (**a**) $G - A$, (**b**) $G - B$, and (**c**) $G - C$.

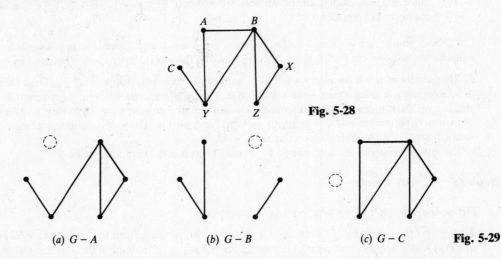

Fig. 5-28

(a) $G - A$          (b) $G - B$          (c) $G - C$          **Fig. 5-29**

▌ Delete the given vertex from the diagram and all edges incident on that vertex to obtain the graphs in Fig. 5-29.

**5.78**   Let $G$ be the graph in Fig. 5-28. Find: (**a**) $G - X$, (**b**) $G - Y$, and (**c**) $G - Z$.

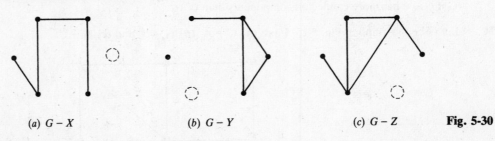

(a) $G - X$          (b) $G - Y$          (c) $G - Z$          **Fig. 5-30**

▌ See Fig. 5-30.

**5.79**  Let $G$ be the graph in Fig. 5-28. Does $G$ have any cut points?

▌ Figures 5-29($b$) and 5-30($b$) show that only $G - B$ and $G - Y$ are disconnected. Thus $B$ and $Y$ are cut points of $G$.

**5.80**  Let $G$ be the graph where $V(G) = \{A, B, C, X, Y, Z\}$ and $E(G) = [\{A, C\}, \{A, X\}, \{A, Y\}, \{B, Y\}, \{B, Z\}]$. (*a*) Find $G - A$. (*b*) Determine the number of connected components of $G - A$.

▌ (*a*)  Delete $A$ from $V(G)$ and delete all edges incident on $A$ from $E(G)$ to obtain

$$V(G - A) = \{B, C, X, Y, Z\} \qquad \text{and} \qquad E(G - A) = [\{B, Y\}, \{B, Z\}]$$

(*b*)  Here $B$, $Y$, and $Z$ are connected and $C$ and $X$ are isolated vertices (in $G - A$). Thus $\{B, Y, Z\}$, $\{C\}$, and $\{X\}$ are the connected components of $G - A$.

**5.81**  Let $G$ be the graph in Fig. 5-15. Does $G$ have any cut points?

▌ Deleting $A$, $X$, or $Y$ (and the edges incident on these vertices) disconnects $G$; hence $A$, $X$, and $Y$ are cut points.

**5.82**  Let $G$ be the graph in Fig. 5-16. Does $G$ have any cut points?

▌ Only removal of $B$ (and the edges incident on $B$) disconnects $G$; hence only $B$ is a cut point.

## Subgraph $G - e$, Bridges

**5.83**  Define the subgraph $G - e$ where $e$ is an edge in $G$.

▌ $G - e$ is the graph obtained by simply deleting $e$ from the edge set of $G$. Thus $V(G - e) = V(G)$ and $E(G - e) = E(G) \backslash \{e\}$.

**5.84**  Define a bridge for a connected graph $G$.

▌ An edge $e$ is a bridge for $G$ if $G - e$ is disconnected. (In general, $e$ is a bridge for any graph $G$ if $G - e$ has more connected components than $G$ has.)

**5.85**  Let $G$ be the graph in Fig. 5-21. Find (*a*) $G - \{A, B\}$, (*b*) $G - \{B, C\}$, (*c*) $G - \{B, D\}$, (*d*) $G - \{C, D\}$.

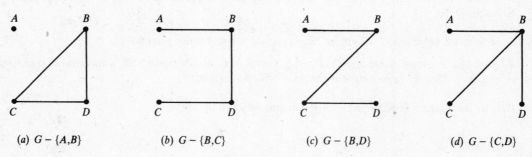

(*a*) $G - \{A,B\}$      (*b*) $G - \{B,C\}$      (*c*) $G - \{B,D\}$      (*d*) $G - \{C,D\}$

**Fig. 5-31**

▌ Simply delete the given edge from the graph to obtain the corresponding graphs in Fig. 5-31.

**5.86**  Let $G$ be the graph in Fig. 5-21. Does $G$ have any bridges?

▌ Figure 5-31 shows that only $G - \{A, B\}$ is disconnected; hence $\{A, B\}$ is a bridge and the only bridge for $G$.

**5.87**  Let $G$ be the graph in Fig. 5-15. Does $G$ have any bridges?

▌ $G$ has three bridges $\{A, X\}$, $\{A, Z\}$, and $\{Y, C\}$. Deleting any other edge of $G$ does not disconnect $G$.

**5.88**  Let $G$ be the graph in Fig. 5-16. Does $G$ have any bridges?

▌ Only $\{B, Y\}$ disconnects $G$ and hence $\{B, Y\}$ is the only bridge for $G$.

**5.89**    Let $G$ be the graph in Fig. 5-24. Does $G$ have any bridges?

❚ Here $G$ has two connected components. Deleting $\{C, S\}$ or $\{D, S\}$ partitions $V(G)$ into three (more than two) connected components; hence $\{C, S\}$ and $\{D, S\}$ are bridges.

**5.90**    Let $G$ be the connected graph in Problem 5.80. Does $G$ have any bridges?

❚ Each one of the edges disconnects $G$. Thus $G$ has five bridges.

## 5.5  TRAVERSABLE MULTIGRAPHS

This section discusses traversable multigraphs. Unless the distinction is vital and implied by the discussion, the term graph may be used when referring to both graphs and multigraphs.

**5.91**    Define a traversable multigraph with an example.

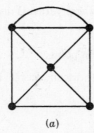  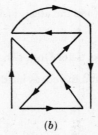

(a)                        (b)                    **Fig. 5-32**

❚ A multigraph $G$ is said to be *traversable* if it "can be drawn without any breaks in the curve and without repeating any edge", that is, if there is a path which includes all vertices and uses each edge exactly once. Such a path must be a trail (since no edge is used twice) and it will be called a traversable trail. Clearly a traversable multigraph must be connected. Figure 5-32(b) shows a traversable trail of the multigraph in Fig. 5-32(a). (To indicate the direction of the trail, the diagram misses touching vertices which are actually traversed.)

**5.92**    Suppose a multigraph $G$ is traversable and that a traversable trail does not begin or end at a vertex $P$. Show that $P$ is an even vertex.

❚ Whenever the traversable trail enters $P$ by an edge, there must always be an edge not previously used by which the trail can leave $P$. Thus the trail exhausts the edges incident on $P$ in pairs, and so $P$ has even degree, as claimed.

**5.93**    Show that a multigraph $G$ with more than two odd vertices is not traversable.

❚ Suppose $G$ is traversable and $Q$ is an odd vertex of $G$. By Problem 5.92, a traversable trail must either begin or end at $Q$. Thus $G$ cannot have more than two odd vertices.

**5.94**    Discuss the Bridges of Königsberg problem and its solution.

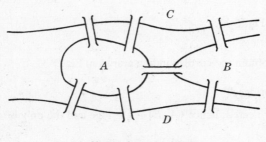  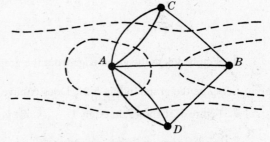

(a) Königsberg in 1736                    (b) Euler's graphical representation

**Fig. 5-33**

❚ The eighteenth-century East Prussian town of Königsberg included two islands and seven bridges as shown in Fig. 5-33(a). Question: Beginning anywhere and ending anywhere, can a person walk through town crossing all seven bridges but not crossing any bridge twice? The people of Königsberg wrote to the celebrated Swiss mathematician L. Euler about this question. Euler proved in 1736 that such a walk is impossible. He replaced the islands and the two sides of the river by points and the bridges by curves, thus obtaining Fig. 5-33(b). It is not difficult to see that the walk in Königsberg is possible if and only if the multigraph in Fig. 5-33(b) is traversable. But this multigraph has four odd vertices, and hence it is not traversable. Thus one cannot walk through Königsberg so that each bridge is crossed exactly once.

**5.95**   Define an eulerian graph and an eulerian trail.

▌ A graph (multigraph) $G$ is an *eulerian* graph if there exists a closed traversable trail, called an *eulerian* trail.

**Theorem 5.3 (Euler):**   A finite connected graph $G$ is eulerian if and only if each vertex has even degree.

**Corollary 5.4:**   Any finite connected graph with two odd vertices is traversable. A traversable trail may begin at either odd vertex and will end at the other odd vertex.

**5.96**   Prove Theorem 5.3.

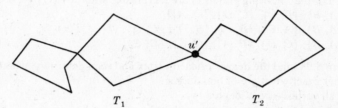

Fig. 5-34

▌ Suppose $G$ is eulerian and $T$ is a closed eulerian trail. For any vertex $v$ of $G$, the trail $T$ enters and leaves $v$ the same number of times without repeating any edge. Hence $v$ has even degree.

Suppose conversely that each vertex of $G$ has even degree. We construct an eulerian trail. We begin a trail $T_1$ at any edge $e$. We extend $T_1$ by adding one edge after the other. If $T_1$ is not closed at any step, say $T_1$ begins at $u$ but ends at $v \neq u$, then only an odd number of the edges incident on $v$ appear in $T_1$; hence we can extend $T_1$ by another edge incident on $v$. Thus we can continue to extend $T_1$ until $T_1$ returns to its initial vertex $u$, i.e., until $T_1$ is closed. If $T_1$ includes all the edges of $G$, then $T_1$ is our eulerian trail.

Suppose $T_1$ does not include all edges of $G$. Consider the graph $H$ obtained by deleting all edges of $T_1$ from $G$. $H$ may not be connected, but each vertex of $H$ has even degree since $T_1$ contains an even number of the edges incident on any vertex. Since $G$ is connected, there is an edge $e'$ of $H$ which has an endpoint $u'$ in $T_1$. We construct a trail $T_2$ in $H$ beginning at $u'$ and using $e'$. Since all vertices in $H$ have even degree, we can continue to extend $T_2$ in $H$ until $T_2$ returns to $u'$ as pictured in Fig. 5-34. We can clearly put $T_1$ and $T_2$ together to form a larger closed trail in $G$. We continue this process until all the edges of $G$ are used. We finally obtain an eulerian trail, and so $G$ is eulerian.

**5.97**   Prove Corollary 5.4.

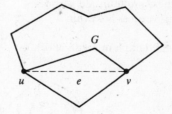

Fig. 5-35

▌ Suppose $G$ is the finite connected graph with exactly two odd vertices, say $u$ and $v$. Add another edge $e$ from $u$ to $v$ to the graph $G$ to form the new graph $G' = G \cup \{e\}$, as shown in Fig. 5-35. Then all the vertices of the graph $G'$ are even. By Theorem 5.3, there is a closed traversable trail $\alpha$ of $G'$. Since $\alpha$ is closed, we can assume, without loss of generality, that $\alpha$ begins with $e$. Let $\beta$ be the path $\alpha$ without its first edge $e$. Then $\beta$ is a traversable trail of $G$ beginning at $v$ and ending at $u$, as required.

**5.98**   Determine whether or not each of the graphs in Fig. 5-36 is traversable.

▌ Find the degree of each vertex and then determine whether all the vertices are of even degree or exactly two are of odd degree. If either condition is met, the graph is traversable.

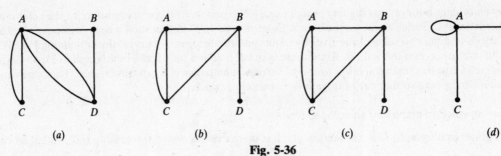

Fig. 5-36

(a)  Yes, since exactly two of its vertices, A and D, are of odd degree.
(b)  Yes, since all vertices are of even degree.
(c)  No, since all four vertices are of odd degree.
(d)  Yes, since exactly two of its vertices, B and C, are of odd degree.

**5.99**  Determine which of the following graphs $G$ are traversable where: $V(G) = \{A, B, C, D\}$ and
(a)  $E(G) = [\{A, B\}, \{B, C\}, \{C, D\}, \{D, A\}]$
(b)  $E(G) = [\{A, B\}, \{A, C\}, \{B, C\}, \{B, D\}, \{C, D\}, \{D, A\}]$
(c)  $E(G) = [\{A, B\}, \{C, D\}, \{B, A\}, \{C, C\}, \{D, C\}]$

▌ As in Problem 5.98, find the degree of each vertex and then determine whether all vertices are of even degree or whether exactly two are of odd degree.
(a)  Yes, since all vertices are of degree two.
(b)  No, since all four vertices are of degree three.
(c)  No. Although all vertices are of even degree, the graph is not connected.

**5.100**  Determine which of the graphs in Fig. 5-37 are traversable.

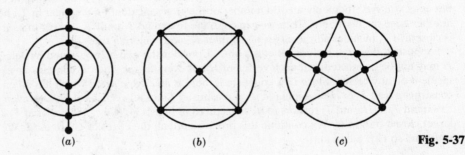

(a)                (b)                (c)                Fig. 5-37

▌ (a)  Traversable since six vertices are even and two are odd.
    (b)  Not traversable since there are four odd vertices.
    (c)  Traversable since all ten vertices are even.

**5.101**  Find a traversable trail for the multigraph in Fig. 5-38(a).

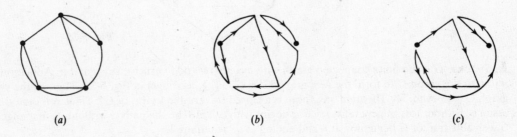

(a)                (b)                (c)

Fig. 5-38

▌ There are many possible solutions, but all of them will start at one of the odd vertices and end at the other. Figures 5-38(b) and 5-38(c) give two possible solutions.

**5.102** Determine which of the graphs in Fig. 5-39 are traversable.

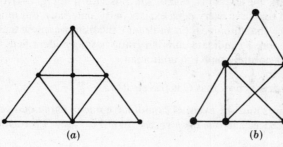

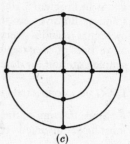

(a)  (b)  (c)

**Fig. 5-39**

▌ **(a)** Traversable since five vertices are even and two are odd.
**(b)** Traversable since five vertices are even and two are odd.
**(c)** Not traversable since the four outer vertices are odd.

**5.103** Find a traversable trail for the multigraph in Fig. 5-40(a).

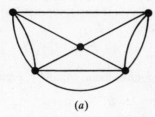   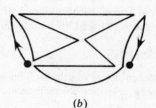

(a)  (b)

**Fig. 5-40**

▌ There are many possible solutions, but all of them must begin at one of the odd vertices and end at the other odd vertex. Figure 5-40(b) gives one such solution.

**5.104** Define a hamiltonian graph.

▌ A *hamiltonian graph* is a graph with a closed path that includes every vertex exactly once. Such a path is a cycle and is called a *hamiltonian cycle*. Note that an eulerian cycle uses every edge exactly once but may repeat vertices, while a hamiltonian cycle uses each vertex exactly once (except for the first and last) but may skip edges.

**5.105** Draw a graph with six vertices which is hamiltonian but not eulerian.

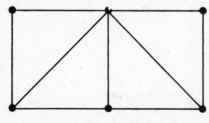   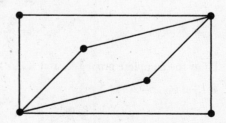

(a) Hamiltonian and noneulerian   (b) Eulerian and nonhamiltonian

**Fig. 5-41**

▌ There are many possible solutions to this problem and one of these is shown in Fig. 5-41(a). Every solution, however, must have a cycle that includes every vertex exactly once (hamiltonian), but must not have a closed trail that uses every edge exactly once. (eulerian). Note that when a candidate hamiltonian graph has been identified, one can easily determine if it is eulerian by looking for vertices of odd degree. Should at least one such vertex exist, the graph is not eulerian.

**5.106** Draw a graph with six vertices which is eulerian but not hamiltonian.

❚ As in Problem 5.105, there are many possible solutions, one of which is shown in Fig. 5-41(*b*). Every solution, however, must have a closed trail that uses every edge exactly once (eulerian), but must not have a cycle that includes every vertex exactly once (hamiltonian). From Euler's theorem we know that any graph with all vertices of even degree is eulerian. But once a candidate eulerian graph has been identified, there is no simple criterion for determining whether or not the graph is hamiltonian.

**5.107** Let $G$ be a connected graph with three vertices. Show that $G$ is traversable.

❚ Since the sum of the degree of the vertices must be even, $G$ cannot have one or three odd vertices. Thus $G$ must have only even vertices or two odd vertices and one even vertex. In either case, $G$ is traversable.

**5.108** Find a traversable trail $\alpha$ for the graph $G$ where

$$V(G) = \{A, B, C, D\} \qquad \text{and} \qquad E(G) = [\{A, C\}, \{A, D\}, \{B, C\}, \{B, D\}, \{C, D\}]$$

❚ Here $C$ and $D$ are odd vertices; hence one must begin at $C$ and end at $D$ or vice versa. One such trail is $\alpha = (C, A, D, B, C, D)$.

**5.109** Show that one can add or delete loops from a multigraph $G$ and the graph $G$ remains traversable or nontraversable.

❚ The degree of a vertex $v$ in $G$ is increased or decreased by two according as one adds or deletes a loop at $v$. Thus the parity (evenness or oddness) of $v$ is not changed. Accordingly, the condition that $G$ has zero or two odd vertices is not changed by adding or deleting loops.

## 5.6 SPECIAL GRAPHS

There are many different types of graphs. This section defines four of them: complete, regular, bipartite, and tree graphs. (Here the term graph does not include multigraphs.)

**5.110** Define a complete graph.

❚ A graph $G$ is *complete* if each vertex is connected to every other vertex. The complete graph with $n$ vertices is denoted by $K_n$.

**5.111** Draw a diagram of the complete graphs $K_1$, $K_2$, $K_3$, and $K_4$.

❚ First draw the appropriate number $n$ of vertices. Then draw an edge from each vertex to every other vertex. The required diagrams appear in Fig. 5-42(*a*).

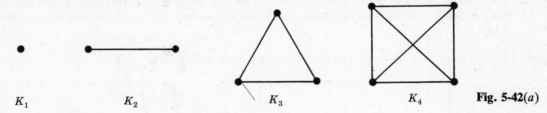

$K_1 \qquad\qquad K_2 \qquad\qquad K_3 \qquad\qquad K_4 \qquad$ **Fig. 5-42(*a*)**

**5.112** Draw the complete graphs $K_5$ and $K_6$.

❚ See Fig. 5-42(*b*).

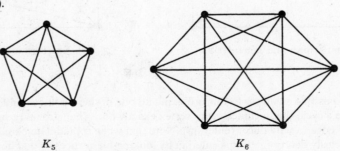

$K_5 \qquad\qquad\qquad K_6$

**Fig. 5-42(*b*)**

**5.113**    Find the number $m$ of edges in the complete graph $K_n$.

▌ Each pair of vertices determines an edge. Thus $m = C(n, 2) = n(n - 1)/2$ since there are $C(n, 2)$ ways of selecting two vertices out of $n$ vertices.

**5.114**    Find the number $m$ of edges in the graphs **(a)** $K_8$, **(b)** $K_{12}$, and **(c)** $K_{15}$.

▌ **(a)**  $m = \dfrac{8 \cdot 7}{2} = 28,$  **(b)**  $m = \dfrac{12 \cdot 11}{2} = 66,$  **(c)**  $m = \dfrac{15 \cdot 14}{2} = 105.$

**5.115**    The complete graph $K_n$ is connected since each vertex is connected to every other vertex. Find diam $(K_n)$.

▌ Here $d(u, v) = 1$ for any two distinct vertices $u$ and $v$ in $K_n$; hence diam $(K_n) = 1$.

**5.116**    Find the degree of each vertex in $K_n$.

▌ Each vertex $v$ is connected to the other $n - 1$ vertices; hence deg $(v) = n - 1$ for every $v$ in $K_n$.

**5.117**    Find those values of $n$ for which $K_n$ is traversable.

▌ If $n$ is odd, then every vertex $v$ is even since deg $(v) = n - 1$. Thus $K_n$ is traversable for $n$ odd. Also, $K_2$ is traversable since it has only one edge connecting the two vertices. However, for $n > 2$ and $n$ even, the complete graph will have $n$ (more than two) odd vertices and hence will not be traversable.

**5.118**    Define a regular graph.

▌ A graph $G$ is *regular of degree k* or *k-regular* if every vertex has degree $k$. In other words, a graph is regular if every vertex has the same degree.

**5.119**    Describe and draw the connected regular graphs of degrees 0, 1, and 2.

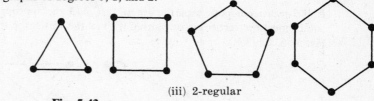

(i) 0-regular        (ii) 1-regular                    (iii) 2-regular

**Fig. 5-43**

▌ The connected 0-regular graph is the trivial graph with one vertex and no edges. The connected 1-regular graph is the graph with two vertices and one edge connecting them. The connected 2-regular graph with $n$ vertices is the graph which consists of a single $n$-cycle. Figure 5-43 shows the connected 0-regular and 1-regular graphs and some of the connected 2-regular graphs.

**5.120**    Suppose $r$ is an odd integer. Show that an $r$-regular graph must have an even number $n$ of vertices.

▌ Let $S$ be the sum of the degrees of an $r$-regular graph with $n$ vertices. Then $S = rn$. By Theorem 5.1, the sum $S$ must be even. If $r$ is odd, then $n$ must be even.

**5.121**    Find those values of $n$ for which the complete graph $K_n$ is regular.

▌ Every vertex in $K_n$ has degree $n - 1$. Thus, for every $n$, the graph $K_n$ is regular of degree $n - 1$.

**5.122**    Draw two 3-regular graphs with six vertices.

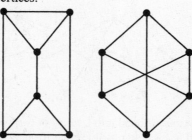

**Fig. 5-44**

▌ See Fig. 5-44.

**5.123**  Draw two 3-regular graphs with seven vertices.

❚ No such graphs exist since a 3-regular graph must have an even number of vertices. (See Problem 5.120.)

**5.124**  Draw two 3-regular graphs with eight vertices.

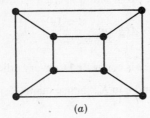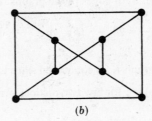

(a)  (b)  **Fig. 5-45**

❚ See Fig. 5.45. The two graphs are distinct since only graph (b) has a 5-cycle.

**5.125**  Define a bipartite graph and a complete bipartite graph.

❚ A graph $G$ is said to be *bipartite* if its vertices $V$ can be partitioned into two subsets $M$ and $N$ such that each edge of $G$ connects a vertex of $M$ to a vertex of $N$. By a complete bipartite graph, we mean that each vertex of $M$ is connected to each vertex of $N$; this graph is denoted by $K_{m,n}$ where $m$ is the number of vertices in $M$ and $n$ is the number of vertices in $N$, and for standardization, we assume $m \leq n$.

**5.126**  Find the number of edges in the complete bipartite graph $K_{m,n}$.

❚ Each of $m$ vertices is connected to each of $n$ vertices; hence $K_{m,n}$ has $mn$ edges.

**5.127**  Draw the complete bipartite graphs $K_{2,3}$, $K_{3,3}$, and $K_{2,4}$.

❚ To draw a complete bipartite graph, just place the appropriate number of vertices in two parallel columns and connect the vertices in one group with all the vertices in the other. The resulting graphs are shown in Fig. 5-46.

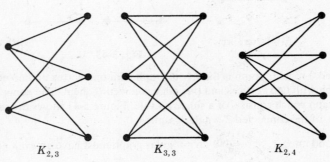

$K_{2,3}$  $K_{3,3}$  $K_{2,4}$  **Fig. 5-46**

**5.128**  Determine the diameter of any complete bipartite graph.

❚ The diameter of $K_{1,1}$ will be one since there are only two vertices and the shortest path between them is length one. All other bipartite graphs will have diameter two since any two points in either $M$ or $N$ will be exactly distance 2 apart. (One edge to reach the other subgroup of vertices and one to return.)

**5.129**  Draw the graph $K_{2,5}$.

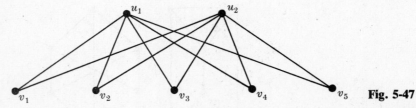

**Fig. 5-47**

❚ $K_{2,5}$ consists of seven vertices partitioned into a set $M$ of two vertices, say $u_1$ and $u_2$, and a set $N$ of five vertices, say $v_1$, $v_2$, $v_3$, $v_4$, and $v_5$, and all possible edges from a vertex $u_i$ to a vertex $v_j$. The required graph is shown in Fig. 5-47.

**5.130** Which connected graphs can be both regular and bipartite?

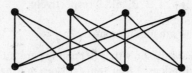

Fig. 5-48

▌ The bipartite graph $K_{m,m}$ is regular of degree $m$ since each vertex is connected to $m$ other vertices and hence its degree is $m$. Subgraphs of $K_{m,m}$ can also be regular if $m$ disjoint edges are deleted. For example, the subgraph of $K_{4,4}$ shown in Fig. 5-48 is 3-regular. We can continue to delete $m$ disjoint edges and each time obtain a regular graph of one less degree. These graphs may be disconnected, but in any case their connected components have the desired properties.

## Trees

This subsection introduces the notion of a tree graph. Such tree graphs will be covered more thoroughly in the next two chapters. Here we simply give its definition and some examples.

**5.131** Define a cycle-free graph and a tree graph.

▌ A graph $G$ is said to be *cycle-free* or *acyclic* if it has no cycles. If $G$ has no cycles and is connected, then $G$ is called a *tree*.

**5.132** Draw all trees with four or fewer vertices.

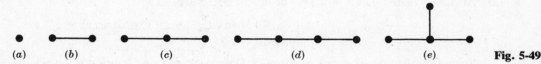

Fig. 5-49

▌ See Fig. 5-49. Note there are two trees with four vertices. The graph with one vertex and no edge is called the trivial tree [Fig. 5-49(a)].

**5.133** Draw all trees with five vertices.

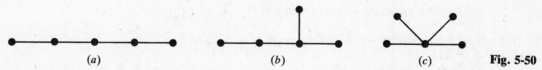

Fig. 5-50

▌ First draw five vertices. Then connect them so that no cycles are created. In this exercise, we must be careful not to repeat trees since two trees which appear different may just be drawn differently. There are three trees with five vertices as shown in Fig. 5-50.

**5.134** Draw all trees with six vertices.

▌ As in Problem 5.133, we must be careful not to repeat any trees. There are six trees with six vertices as shown in Fig. 5-51.

**5.135** Find the diameters of the trees in Fig. 5-51.

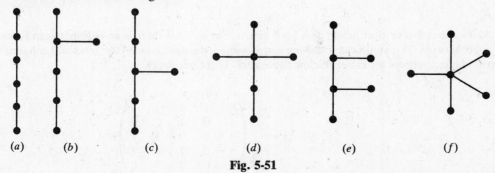

Fig. 5-51

▌ Recall that diam $(G)$ is the maximum distance between any two points in $G$. Thus the diameters of the graphs $(a)$, $(b)$, . . . , $(f)$ are 5, 4, 4, 3, 3, and 2 respectively.

**5.136**    Show that the trees in Fig. 5-51 are all different.

▌ By Problem 5.135, we need only show that $(b)$ and $(c)$ are different and that $(d)$ and $(e)$ are different. The tree $(d)$ has a vertex with degree four, but $(e)$ does not; hence $(d)$ and $(e)$ are different trees.

Deleting the vertex of degree three in either $(b)$ or $(c)$ results in three connected components. However, the connected components have different numbers of vertices, that is, 1, 1, and 3 in $(b)$ but 1, 2, and 2 in $(c)$. Thus the trees $(b)$ and $(c)$ are also different.

**5.137**    Prove that a finite tree $G$ (with at least one edge) has at least two vertices of degree 1.

▌ Let $\alpha = (u = v_0, v_1, \ldots, v_n = v)$ be a simple path of maximum length in $G$. If deg $(u) > 1$, then there is an edge $e = \{u, w\}$. If $w$ is not one of the vertices in $\alpha$, then $\alpha$ does not have maximum length. If $w$ is one of the vertices in $\alpha$, say $w = v_k$, then $(w, v_0, \ldots, v_k)$ is a cycle which cannot exist in a tree. Thus deg $(u) = 1$. Similarly, deg $(v) = 1$.

## 5.7  MATRICES AND GRAPHS, LINKED REPRESENTATION

This section considers two important matrices associated with a graph $G$.

**5.138**    Let $G$ be a graph with vertices $v_1, v_2, \ldots, v_m$ and edges $e_1, e_2, \ldots, e_n$. Define: $(a)$ the adjacency matrix of $G$; $(b)$ the incidence matrix of $G$.

▌ $(a)$    Adjacency matrix. Let $A = (a_{ij})$ be the $m \times m$ matrix defined by

$$a_{ij} = \begin{cases} 1 & \text{if } \{v_i, v_j\} \text{ is an edge, i.e., if } v_i \text{ is adjacent to } v_j \\ 0 & \text{otherwise} \end{cases}$$

Then $A$ is called the *adjacency matrix* of $G$. Observe that $a_{ij} = a_{ji}$; hence $A$ is a symmetric matrix. (We define an adjacency matrix for a multigraph by letting $a_{ij}$ denote the number of edges $\{v_i, v_j\}$.)

$(b)$    Incidence matrix. Let $M = (m_{ij})$ be the $m \times n$ matrix defined by

$$m = \begin{cases} 1 & \text{if the vertex } v_i \text{ is incident on the edge } e_j \\ 0 & \text{otherwise} \end{cases}$$

Then $M$ is called the *incidence matrix* of $G$.

**5.139**    Find the adjacency matrix $A = (a_{ij})$ of the graph $G$ in Fig. 5-52.

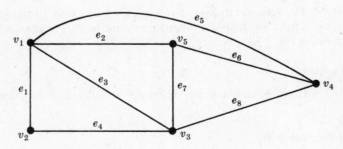

**Fig. 5-52**

▌ Since $G$ has five vertices, $a$ will be a $5 \times 5$ matrix. Set $a_{ij} = 1$ if there is an edge between $v_i$ and $v_j$, and set $a_{ij} = 0$ otherwise. This yields the following matrix (where we have labeled the rows and columns by the corresponding vertices for easier reading though this is not necessary):

$$A = \begin{array}{c} \\ v_1 \\ v_2 \\ v_3 \\ v_4 \\ v_5 \end{array} \begin{pmatrix} \begin{array}{ccccc} v_1 & v_2 & v_3 & v_4 & v_5 \end{array} \\ 0 & 1 & 1 & 1 & 1 \\ 1 & 0 & 1 & 0 & 0 \\ 1 & 1 & 0 & 1 & 1 \\ 1 & 0 & 1 & 0 & 1 \\ 1 & 0 & 1 & 1 & 0 \end{pmatrix}$$

**5.140** Find the incidence matrix $M = (m_{ij})$ of the graph $G$ in Fig. 5-52.

▌ Since $G$ has five vertices and eight edges, $M$ will be a $5 \times 8$ matrix. Set $m_{ij} = 1$ if vertex $v_i$ belongs to the edge $e_j$, and set $m_{ij} = 0$ otherwise. This yields the following matrix (where we have labeled the rows and columns by the corresponding vertices and edges for easier reading though this is not necessary):

$$
M = \begin{array}{c} \\ v_1 \\ v_2 \\ v_3 \\ v_4 \\ v_5 \end{array}
\begin{array}{c} \begin{array}{cccccccc} e_1 & e_2 & e_3 & e_4 & e_5 & e_6 & e_7 & e_8 \end{array} \\
\left( \begin{array}{cccccccc}
1 & 1 & 1 & 0 & 1 & 0 & 0 & 0 \\
1 & 0 & 0 & 1 & 0 & 0 & 0 & 0 \\
0 & 0 & 1 & 1 & 0 & 0 & 1 & 1 \\
0 & 0 & 0 & 0 & 1 & 1 & 0 & 1 \\
0 & 1 & 0 & 0 & 0 & 1 & 1 & 0
\end{array} \right) \end{array}
$$

**5.141** Find the adjacency matrix $A = (a_{ij})$ of the multigraph $G$ in Fig. 5-53.

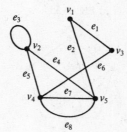

**Fig. 5-53**

▌ Since $G$ has five vertices, $A$ will be a $5 \times 5$ matrix. Set $a_{ij} = n$ where $n$ is the number of edges between $v_i$ and $v_j$, and set $a_{ij} = 0$ otherwise. This yields the following matrix:

$$
A = \begin{array}{c} \\ v_1 \\ v_2 \\ v_3 \\ v_4 \\ v_5 \end{array}
\begin{array}{c} \begin{array}{ccccc} v_1 & v_2 & v_3 & v_4 & v_5 \end{array} \\
\left( \begin{array}{ccccc}
0 & 0 & 1 & 0 & 1 \\
0 & 1 & 0 & 1 & 1 \\
1 & 0 & 0 & 1 & 0 \\
0 & 1 & 1 & 0 & 2 \\
1 & 1 & 0 & 2 & 0
\end{array} \right) \end{array}
$$

**5.142** Find the incidence matrix $M = (m_{ij})$ of the multigraph $G$ in Fig. 5-53.

▌ Since $G$ has five vertices and eight edges, $m$ will be a $5 \times 8$ matrix. Set $m_{ij} = 1$ if vertex $v_i$ belongs to the edge $e_j$, and set $m_{ij} = 0$ otherwise. This yields

$$
M = \begin{array}{c} \\ v_1 \\ v_2 \\ v_3 \\ v_4 \\ v_5 \end{array}
\begin{array}{c} \begin{array}{cccccccc} e_1 & e_2 & e_3 & e_4 & e_5 & e_6 & e_7 & e_8 \end{array} \\
\left( \begin{array}{cccccccc}
1 & 1 & 0 & 0 & 0 & 0 & 0 & 0 \\
0 & 0 & 1 & 1 & 1 & 0 & 0 & 0 \\
1 & 0 & 0 & 0 & 0 & 1 & 0 & 0 \\
0 & 0 & 0 & 0 & 1 & 1 & 1 & 1 \\
0 & 1 & 0 & 1 & 0 & 0 & 1 & 1
\end{array} \right) \end{array}
$$

**5.143** Find the adjacency matrix $A$ of the graph $G$ in Fig. 5-54.

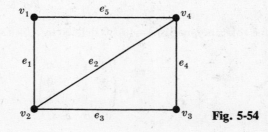

**Fig. 5-54**

▮ The adjacency matrix $A = (a_{ij})$ is defined by $a_{ij} = 1$ if there is an edge $\{v_i, v_j\}$ and $a_{ij} = 0$ otherwise. Hence

$$A = \begin{pmatrix} 0 & 1 & 0 & 1 \\ 1 & 0 & 1 & 1 \\ 0 & 1 & 0 & 1 \\ 1 & 1 & 1 & 0 \end{pmatrix}$$

**5.144** Find the incidence matrix $M$ of the graph $G$ in Fig. 5-54.

▮ The incidence matrix $M = (m_{ij})$ is defined by $m_{ij} = 1$ if edge $e_j$ is incident on vertex $v_i$ and $m_{ij} = 0$ otherwise. Hence

$$M = \begin{pmatrix} 1 & 0 & 0 & 0 & 1 \\ 1 & 1 & 1 & 0 & 0 \\ 0 & 0 & 1 & 1 & 0 \\ 0 & 1 & 0 & 1 & 1 \end{pmatrix}$$

**5.145** Find the adjacency matrix $A$ of the graph $G$ in Fig. 5-55.

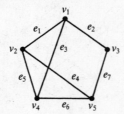

**Fig. 5-55**

▮ The adjacency matrix $A = (a_{ij})$ is defined by $a_{ij} = 1$ if there is an edge $\{v_i, v_j\}$ and $a_{ij} = 0$ otherwise. Hence

$$A = \begin{pmatrix} 0 & 1 & 1 & 1 & 0 \\ 1 & 0 & 0 & 1 & 1 \\ 1 & 0 & 0 & 0 & 1 \\ 1 & 1 & 0 & 0 & 1 \\ 0 & 1 & 1 & 1 & 0 \end{pmatrix}$$

**5.146** Find the incidence matrix $M$ of the graph $G$ in Fig. 5-55.

▮ The incidence matrix $M = (m_{ij})$ is defined by $m_{ij} = 1$ if edge $e_j$ is incident on vertex $v_i$ and $m_{ii} = 0$ otherwise. Hence

$$M = \begin{pmatrix} 1 & 1 & 1 & 0 & 0 & 0 & 0 \\ 1 & 0 & 0 & 1 & 1 & 0 & 0 \\ 0 & 1 & 0 & 0 & 0 & 0 & 1 \\ 0 & 0 & 1 & 0 & 1 & 1 & 0 \\ 0 & 0 & 0 & 1 & 0 & 1 & 1 \end{pmatrix}$$

**5.147** Find the adjacency matrix $A$ for the multigraph in Fig. 5-56.

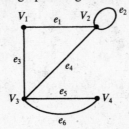

**Fig. 5-56**

▮ For a multigraph, the adjacency matrix $A = (a_{ij})$ is defined by $a_{ij} = n$ where $n \geq 0$ is the number of edges $\{v_i, v_j\}$

$$A = \begin{pmatrix} 0 & 1 & 1 & 0 \\ 1 & 1 & 1 & 0 \\ 1 & 1 & 0 & 2 \\ 0 & 0 & 2 & 0 \end{pmatrix}$$

**5.148**    Find the incidence matrix $M$ of the multigraph $G$ in Fig. 5-56.

❚ The incidence matrix $M = (m_{ij})$ is defined by $m_{ij} = 1$ if vertex $v_i$ is incident on edge $e_j$ and $m_{ij} = 0$ otherwise. Hence

$$M = \begin{pmatrix} 1 & 0 & 1 & 0 & 0 & 0 \\ 1 & 1 & 0 & 1 & 0 & 0 \\ 0 & 0 & 1 & 1 & 1 & 1 \\ 0 & 0 & 0 & 0 & 1 & 1 \end{pmatrix}$$

**5.149**    Draw the graph $G$ whose adjacency matrix $A = (a_{ij})$ follows:

$$A = \begin{pmatrix} 0 & 1 & 0 & 1 & 0 \\ 1 & 0 & 0 & 1 & 1 \\ 0 & 0 & 0 & 1 & 1 \\ 1 & 1 & 1 & 0 & 1 \\ 0 & 1 & 1 & 1 & 0 \end{pmatrix}$$

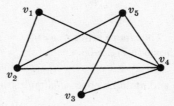

Fig. 5-57

❚ Since $A$ is a 5-square matrix, $G$ has five vertices, say $v_1, \ldots, v_5$. Draw an edge from $v_i$ to $v_j$ if $a_{ij} = 1$. The graph is shown in Fig. 5-57.

**5.150**    Draw the multigraph $G$ whose adjacency matrix $A = (a_{ij})$ follows:

$$A = \begin{pmatrix} 1 & 3 & 0 & 0 \\ 3 & 0 & 1 & 1 \\ 0 & 1 & 2 & 2 \\ 0 & 1 & 2 & 0 \end{pmatrix}$$

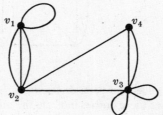

Fig. 5-58

❚ Since $A$ is a 4-square matrix, $G$ has four vertices, say $v_1, \ldots, v_4$. Draw $n$ edges from $v_i$ to $v_j$ if $a_{ij} = n$. Note that $v_i$ has $n$ loops if $a_{ii} = n$. The multigraph is shown in Fig. 5-58.

**5.151**    Draw the graph $G$ whose adjacency matrix $A$ is

$$A = \begin{pmatrix} 0 & 1 & 1 & 1 & 0 \\ 1 & 0 & 0 & 1 & 0 \\ 1 & 0 & 0 & 1 & 1 \\ 1 & 1 & 1 & 0 & 1 \\ 0 & 0 & 1 & 1 & 0 \end{pmatrix}$$

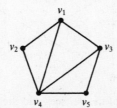

Fig. 5-59

❚ Since $A$ is a 5-square matrix, $G$ has five vertices, say $v_1, \dots, v_5$. We draw an edge from $v_i$ to $v_j$ if $a_{ij} = 1$. The resulting graph is shown in Fig. 5-59.

**5.152**    Draw the multigraph $G$ whose adjacency matrix $A$ is

$$A = \begin{pmatrix} 0 & 1 & 2 & 0 \\ 1 & 1 & 1 & 1 \\ 2 & 1 & 0 & 0 \\ 0 & 1 & 0 & 1 \end{pmatrix}$$

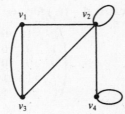

**Fig. 5-60**

❚ Since $A$ is a 4-square matrix, $G$ has four vertices, say $v_1, \dots, v_4$. For each $a_{ij} = n$ we draw $n$ edges from $v_i$ to $v_j$. The resulting multigraph is shown in Fig. 5-60.

**5.153**    Determine the number of loops and multiple edges in a multigraph $G$ from its adjacency matrix

$$A = \begin{pmatrix} 1 & 1 & 2 & 0 \\ 1 & 2 & 1 & 3 \\ 2 & 1 & 0 & 1 \\ 0 & 3 & 1 & 0 \end{pmatrix}$$

Draw the graph $G$ and check your answer.

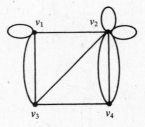

**Fig. 5-61**

❚ Since $A$ is a 4-square matrix, $g$ has four vertices, say $v_1, \dots, v_4$. We can find the number of loops by looking along the main diagonal of $A$ since these entries indicate the number of edges originating and terminating at the same vertex. Thus there are three loops: one at vertex $v_1$ and two at vertex $v_2$.

To find the number of multiple edges, we simply sum the number of entries greater than one below the main diagonal and add the number of entries greater than one along the main diagonal. We include the main diagonal since multiple loops are also multiple edges. We exclude the entries above the main diagonal since the matrix is symmetric and thus all the off diagonal entries are repeated. Thus there are seven multiple edges: two edges from $v_3$ to $v_1$, three edges from $v_4$ to $v_2$, and two loops at $v_2$.

The diagram of $G$ is shown in Fig. 5-61. The number of multiple edges and loops are as predicted.

**5.154**    Find the adjacency matrix $A$ and the incidence matrix $M$ for the graph $G$ in Fig. 5-62.

**Fig. 5-62**

❚ The matrices depend on the ordering of the vertices and the edges. One such ordering yields the following matrices:

$$A = \begin{pmatrix} 0 & 1 & 1 & 1 \\ 1 & 0 & 0 & 1 \\ 1 & 0 & 0 & 0 \\ 1 & 1 & 0 & 0 \end{pmatrix}, \qquad M = \begin{pmatrix} 1 & 1 & 1 & 0 \\ 1 & 0 & 0 & 1 \\ 0 & 1 & 0 & 0 \\ 0 & 0 & 1 & 1 \end{pmatrix}$$

**5.155** Draw the multigraph corresponding to each of the following adjacency matrices:

$$(\textit{a}) \quad A = \begin{pmatrix} 0 & 2 & 0 & 1 \\ 2 & 1 & 1 & 1 \\ 0 & 1 & 0 & 1 \\ 1 & 1 & 1 & 0 \end{pmatrix}, \qquad (\textit{b}) \quad A = \begin{pmatrix} 1 & 1 & 1 & 2 \\ 1 & 0 & 0 & 0 \\ 1 & 0 & 0 & 2 \\ 2 & 0 & 2 & 2 \end{pmatrix}$$

▐ See Fig. 5-63.

**5.156** Suppose a graph $G$ has $m$ vertices. Define the connection matrix $C$ of $G$. Characterize $C$ when $G$ is a connected graph.

▐ The connection matrix of $G$ is the $m \times m$ matrix $C = (c_{ij})$ where

$$c_{ij} = \begin{cases} 1 & \text{if } i = j \text{ or there is a path from } v_i \text{ to } v_j \\ 0 & \text{otherwise} \end{cases}$$

Thus $G$ is connected if and only if $C$ has no zero entry.

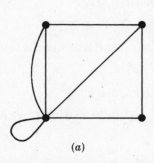
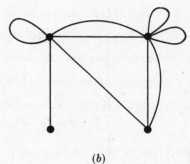

(a)  (b)  **Fig. 5-63**

**Theorem 5.5:** Let $A$ be the adjacency matrix of a graph $G$ with $m$ vertices where $m > 1$. Then the $ij$ entry of the matrix $A^n$ gives the number of paths of length $n$ from the vertex $v_i$ to the vertex $v_j$.

**5.157** Show the relationship between the adjacency matrix $A$ and the connection matrix $C$ of a graph $G$ with $m$ vertices.

▐ Since $G$ has $m$ vertices, any simple path from $v_i$ to $v_j$ must have length $m - 1$ or less. Thus the matrix

$$A + A^2 + \cdots + A^{m-1}$$

can have a zero $ij$ entry only if there is no path from $v_i$ to $v_j$. [By Theorem 5.2, no simple path means no path.] Hence the matrix $C$ and the matrix $A + A^2 + \cdots + A^{m-1}$ have the same zero entries off the main diagonal.

**5.158** Let $G$ be a graph with $m$ vertices. Describe two major drawbacks in the computer storage of $G$ as its adjacency matrix $A$.

▐ First of all, if the vertex and/or edge set of $G$ is subject to change, it may be difficult to effect the required alterations of $A$. Secondly, the number of edges in $G$ may be of order $m$ or of order $m \log m$, so the adjacency matrix $A$ will be sparse (will contain many zeros). Accordingly, a great deal of space will be wasted when $A$ is stored in memory. (Therefore, $G$ will usually be represented in memory by an AS representation discussed in Problem 5.159.)

## Adjacency-Structure (Linked) Representation of a Graph

**5.159** Define the adjacency-structure (AS) or linked representation of a graph using, as an example, the graph $G$ in Fig. 5-64($a$).

▐ The *adjacency-structure* (AS) *representation* of $G$ shows each vertex $u$ of $G$ followed by its set of adjacent

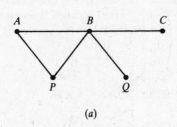

Adjacency Lists

$A: B, P$
$B: A, C, P, Q$
$C: B$
$P: A, B$
$Q: B$

(a)          (b)          **Fig. 5-64**

vertices. Such a representation may be presented as in Fig. 5-64(b) or in the compact form:

$$G = [A: B, P; B: A, C, P, Q; C: B; P: A, B; Q: B]$$

Notice that a colon ":" separates a vertex from its list of adjacent vertices, and that a semicolon ";" separates the different lists. This representation is sometimes called the *linked* representation of $G$ since the lists of adjacency vertices are frequently represented in memory by means of linked lists.

**5.160** Find the AS representation of the graph $G$ in Fig. 5-21.

▮ List each vertex of $G$ followed by its list of adjacent nodes, that is,

$$G = [A: B; B: A, C, D; C: B, D; D: B, C]$$

**5.161** Find the AS representation of the graph $G$ in Fig. 5-22.

▮ List each vertex of $G$ followed by its list of adjacent nodes, that is,

$$G = [A: C, X; B; C: A, X; Y: Z; Z: Y]$$

Note that the list following $B$ is empty which reflects the fact that $B$ is an isolated vertex.

**5.162** Find the AS representation of the graph $G$ in Fig. 5-28.

▮ List each vertex of $G$ followed by its list of adjacent nodes, that is,

$$G = [A: B, Y; B: A, X, Y, Z; C: Y; X: B, Z; Y: A, B, C; Z: B, X]$$

**5.163** Find the AS representation of the graph $G$ in Fig. 5-1.

▮ List each vertex of $G$ followed by its list of adjacent nodes, that is,

$$G = [A: B, C; B: A, C, D; C: A, B, D; D: C, B]$$

**5.164** Find the AS representation of the multigraph $G$ in Fig. 5-2.

▮ List each vertex of $G$ followed by its list of adjacent nodes, including multiplicity. Thus

$$G = [A: B, C, C; B: A, C, D; C: A, A, B, D; D: B, C, D]$$

**5.165** Find the AS representation of the graph $G$ in Fig. 5-15.

▮ List each vertex of $G$ followed by its list of adjacent nodes, that is,

$$G = [A: X, Z; B: X, Y; C: Y; X: A, B, Y; Y: B, C, X; Z: A]$$

## 5.8 LABELED GRAPHS

**5.166** Explain the meaning of a labeled graph with an example.

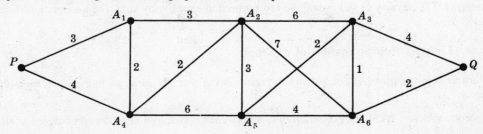

**Fig. 5-65**

▮ A graph $G$ is called a *labeled graph* if its edges and/or vertices are assigned data of one kind or another. In particular, if each edge $e$ of $G$ is assigned a nonnegative number $\ell(e)$ then $\ell(e)$ is called the *weight* or *length* of $e$. Figure 5-65 shows a labeled graph where the length of each edge is given in the obvious way.

**5.167**   Let $G$ be a labeled graph with lengths (weights) assigned to its edges. Explain the minimum path problem using Fig. 5-65 as an example.

▮ Let $P$ and $Q$ be vertices in $G$. The minimum path problem refers to finding a path of minimum length between $P$ and $Q$ where the length of the path is the sum of the lengths of its edges. Clearly, such a minimum path must be a simple path. A minimum path between $P$ and $Q$ in Fig. 5-65 is

$$(P, A_1, A_2, A_5, A_3, A_6, Q)$$

which has length 15. (The reader can try to find another minimum path.)

**5.168**   Let $G$ be the labeled graph in Fig. 5-66. Find a minimum path $\alpha$ between $A$ and $D$.

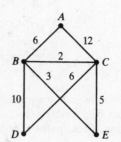

**Fig. 5-66**

▮ There are six sample paths between $A$ and $D$. These paths and their corresponding lengths follow:

| | | | |
|---|---|---|---|
| $(A, B, D)$: | 16 | $(A, C, D)$: | 18 |
| $(A, B, C, D)$: | 14 | $(A, C, B, D)$: | 24 |
| $(A, B, E, C, D)$: | 20 | $(A, C, E, B, D)$: | 30 |

Thus $\alpha = (A, B, C, D)$ and its length is 14.

**5.169**   Let $G$ be the labeled graph in Fig. 5-67. Find: (*a*) all simple paths between $A$ and $F$, and (*b*) a minimum path $\alpha$ between $A$ and $F$.

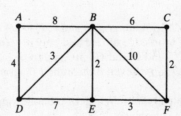

**Fig. 5-67**

▮ (*a*)   There are ten such paths:

| | | |
|---|---|---|
| $(A, B, F)$ | $(A, D, B, F)$ | $(A, D, E, F)$ |
| $(A, B, C, F)$ | $(A, D, B, C, F)$ | $(A, D, E, B, F)$ |
| $(A, B, E, F)$ | $(A, D, B, E, F)$ | $(A, D, E, B, C, F)$ |
| $(A, B, D, E, F)$ | | |

(*b*)   Find the length of each of the simple paths in (*a*) to obtain $\alpha = (A, D, B, E, F)$ which has length 12.

**5.170**   Give a "real life" example of a graph $G$ where both the vertices and edges are assigned data.

▮ Let the vertices of $G$ denote cities with their population, and let the edges of $G$ denote the distances between the cities.

**5.171**   Show how every connected graph $G$ may be viewed as a (weighted) labeled graph. What is a minimum path in such a graph?

▌ Here we can assume that every edge in $G$ has length 1. Then a minimum path $\alpha$ between vertices $P$ and $Q$ is a path of minimum length in the original sense, i.e., a path with a minimum number of edges.

5.172 Consider the following shopping problem: You are refurnishing your house and have decided to purchase the following items, each from a different store: ($A$) matching sofa and chair, ($B$) coffee table, ($C$) rug, ($D$) T.V., and ($E$) floor lamp. There are a few restrictions on the order in which these items can be purchased. First, the rug must be purchased before the sofa and chair set and coffee table (because this furniture must match the rug). Second, the lamp must be purchased last because, if there is no money left, it is the most expendable item.

You have determined the traveling time (in minutes) between stores and have organized this information into the graph $G$ in Fig. 5-68. Find the most efficient sequence $\alpha$ of purchases, that is, find the shopping order that will minimize the traveling time.

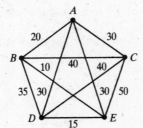

**Fig. 5-68**

▌ Here the required path $\alpha$ must include all five vertices. It must begin at $C$ or begin at $D$ followed by $C$. In all cases it must end at $E$. Assuming that back-tracking will not decrease the time, there are eight possible simple paths which meet the given conditions. These paths and their corresponding traveling times follow:

$CABDE$: 100    $CBADE$: 110    $CDABE$: 100    $DCABE$: 100
$CADBE$: 105    $CBDAE$: 135    $CDBAE$: 125    $DCBAE$: 130

Thus $\alpha = (D, C, A, B, E)$ or $\alpha = (C, A, B, D, E)$ or $\alpha = \{C, D, A, B, E\}$ and the minimum traveling time is 100 minutes.

## 5.9 ISOMORPHIC AND HOMEOMORPHIC GRAPHS

5.173 Define isomorphism of graphs.

▌ Suppose $G(V, E)$ and $G^*(V^*, E^*)$ are graphs and $f: V \to V^*$ is a one-to-one correspondence between the sets of vertices such that $\{u, v\}$ is an edge of $G$ if and only if $\{f(u), f(v)\}$ is an edge of $G^*$. Then $f$ is called an *isomorphism* between $G$ and $G^*$, and $G$ and $G^*$ are said to be *isomorphic* graphs. Normally, we do not distinguish between isomorphic graphs (even though their diagrams may "look different").

5.174 Suppose $G$ and $G^*$ are isomorphic graphs. Which of the following two conditions must hold for corresponding vertices: **(a)** degree, **(b)** being a cut point?

▌ Both must hold for corresponding vertices.

5.175 Suppose $G$ and $G^*$ are isomorphic graphs. Find the number of connected components of $G^*$ if $G$ has eight connected components.

▌ The graph $G^*$ must also have eight connected components.

7.176 Suppose $G$ and $G^*$ are isomorphic graphs and $G$ is traversable. Is $G^*$ traversable? If yes, what would be a traversable path for $G^*$?

▌ Yes, $G^*$ is traversable. Also, if $\alpha$ is a traversable path for $G$, then the corresponding path, say $\alpha'$, would be a traversable path for $G^*$.

5.177 Figure 5-69 shows ten graphs pictured as letters. Which of the ten graphs are isomorphic to M?

▌ M consists of five vertices in a single line. Thus S, V, and Z (and M itself) are isomorphic to M.

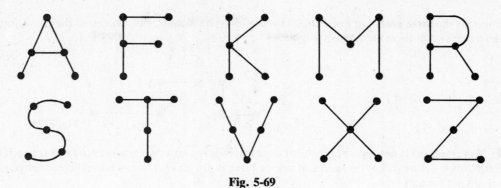

**Fig. 5-69**

**5.178**    Consider the "letters" A, F, K, R, T, and X in Fig. 5-69. Which of them are isomorphic?

▮ The letters A and R, F and T, and K and X are isomorphic.

**5.179**    Define homeomorphic graphs.

▮ Given any graph $G$, we can obtain a new graph by dividing an edge of $G$ with additional vertices. Two graphs $G$ and $G^*$ are said to be *homeomorphic* if they can be obtained from isomorphic graphs by this method.

**5.180**    Give an example of graphs which are homeomorphic, but not isomorphic.

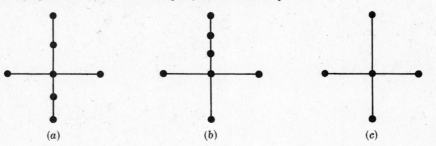

(a)                    (b)                    (c)                    **Fig. 5-70**

▮ The graphs (a) and (b) in Fig. 5-70 are not isomorphic; but they are homeomorphic since each can be obtained from (c) by adding appropriate vertices.

**5.181**    Find all (nonisomorphic) connected graphs with four vertices.

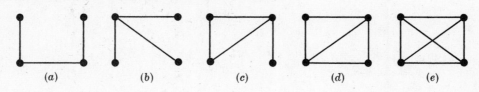

(a)            (b)            (c)            (d)            (e)            **Fig. 5-71**

▮ There are five of them, as shown in Fig. 5-71.

**5.182**    Can a finite graph $G$ be isomorphic to one of its subgraphs (other than itself)?

▮ No since isomorphic graphs must have the same number of elements.

**5.183**    Can a finite graph $G$ be homeomorphic to one of its subgraphs (other than itself)?

▮ Yes. For example, let $G$ be the graph in Fig. 5-71(a). Deleting one or both of the vertices of degree 1 from $G$ yields a subgraph which is homeomorphic to $G$ itself.

**5.184**    Give an example of an infinite graph $G$ which is isomorphic to one of its subgraphs (other than itself).

▮ Let $V(G) = \{1, 2, 3, \ldots\}$ and let $E(G) = [\{1, 2\}, \{2, 3\}, \ldots, \{n, n+1\}, \ldots]$. Consider the subgraph $G'$ where $V(G') = \{2, 3, 4, \ldots\}$ and $E(G') = [\{2, 3\}, \{3, 4\}, \ldots]$. Then $G$ is isomorphic to $G'$ under the isomorphism $f(n) = n + 1$.

**5.185**    Consider the three graphs in Fig. 5-26. Show that they are distinct, i.e., no two of them are isomorphic. Also show that two of them are homeomorphic.

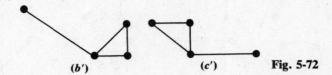

(b′)                    (c′)                    **Fig. 5-72**

▌ The graph **(a)** is not isomorphic to **(b)** or **(c)** since it has six edges whereas **(b)** and **(c)** each have five edges. Furthermore, if we delete the vertex of degree three in **(b)** and **(c)**, we obtain different subgraphs. Thus **(b)** and **(c)** are not isomorphic.

On the other hand, (b) and (c) are homeomorphic since they can be obtained, respectively, from the isomorphic graphs in Fig. 5-72 by adding an appropriate "internal" vertex.

# CHAPTER 6

# Planar Graphs and Trees

## 6.1 PLANAR GRAPHS

A graph or multigraph that can be drawn in a plane or on a sphere so that its edges do not cross is said to be *planar*.

**6.1** The graph $K_4$, which is a planar graph, is usually drawn with crossing edges as shown in Fig. 6-1(a). Draw this graph so that none of its edges cross.

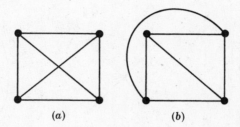

(a)          (b)          **Fig. 6-1**

▌ A drawing of $K_4$ without crossing edges is shown in Fig. 6-1(b).

**6.2** Draw the planar graph shown in Fig. 6-2(a) so that none of its edges cross.

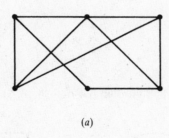          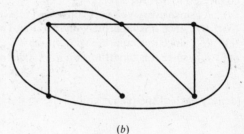

(a)                                    (b)          **Fig. 6-2**

▌ A solution is shown in Fig. 6-2(b).

**6.3** Draw the planar graph shown in Fig. 6.3(a) so that none of its edges cross.

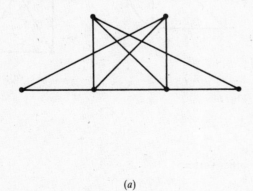          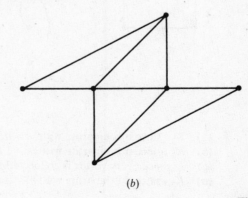

(a)                                    (b)

**Fig. 6-3**

▌ Rearrange the position of one of the vertices to obtain a solution as shown in Fig. 6-3(b).

**6.4** Draw the planar graph shown in Fig. 6-4(a) so that none of its edges cross.

▌ A solution is shown in Fig. 6-4(b).

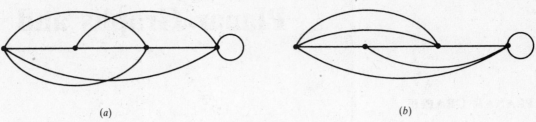

(a)                                    (b)

**Fig. 6-4**

**6.5**    Identify each of the planar graphs shown in Fig. 6-5 as one of the following: $K_4$, $K_{2,2}$, $K_{1,4}$, $K_{2,3}$.

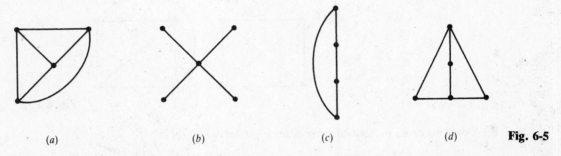

(a)                    (b)                    (c)                    (d)          **Fig. 6-5**

&#9612;    Recall $K_n$ is the complete graph with $n$ vertices and $K_{m,n}$ is the complete bipartite graph with $m$ vertices connected to $n$ vertices.

(a)    $K_4$ since every vertex is connected to every other vertex.
(b)    $K_{1,4}$ since it is bipartite with $m = 1$ and $n = 4$.
(c)    $K_{2,2}$ since it is bipartite with $m = n = 2$.
(d)    $K_{2,3}$ since it is bipartite with $m = 2$ and $n = 3$.

**6.6**    Identify each of the planar graphs shown in Fig. 6-6 as one of the following: $K_4$, $K_{2,2}$, $K_{1,4}$, $K_{2,3}$.

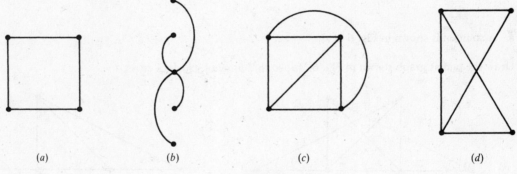

(a)                    (b)                    (c)                    (d)

**Fig. 6-6**

&#9612;    (a)    $K_{2,2}$ since it is bipartite with $m = n = 2$.
(b)    $K_{1,4}$ since it is bipartite with $m = 1$ and $n = 4$.
(c)    $K_4$ since every vertex is connected to every other vertex.
(d)    $K_{2,3}$ since it is bipartite with $m = 2$ and $n = 3$.

**6.7**    Identify which of the graphs in Fig. 6-7 are planar.

&#9612;    Only graphs (a) and (b) are planar, i.e., they can be drawn so that no edges cross. [The fact that (c) and (d) are not planar is not easily determined without the simple criterion that will be developed in Section 6.4.]

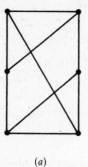 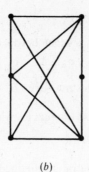 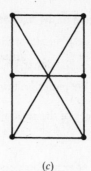 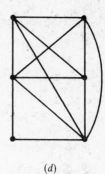

$(a)$          $(b)$          $(c)$          $(d)$

**Fig. 6-7**

**6.8**    Prove that a tree (Problem 5.131) is a special planar graph.

▌ Make an induction on the number $n$ of vertices of $T_n$. Clearly, the unique tree $T_2$ can be realized in the plane [Fig. 6-8($a$)]. For any $T_n$ ($n > 2$) choose a first-degree vertex (Problem 5.137) as $v_1$. Then the graph $T_n - v_1$, being connected and acyclic, is a $T_{n-1}$ which, by hypothesis, can be realized in the plane [Fig. 6-8($b$)]. One can obviously find a point $v_1$ of the plane such that the straight-line segment $v_1 v_2$ does not cut $T_{n-1}$. Thus $T_n$ can also be realized in the plane, and the induction is complete.

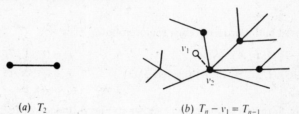

$(a)$  $T_2$          $(b)$  $T_n - v_1 = T_{n-1}$          **Fig. 6-8**

## 6.2  MAPS AND REGIONS

**6.9**    Explain the term map. What is a connected map?

▌ A particular planar representation of a finite planar multigraph is called a *map*. We say the map is *connected* if the underlying multigraph is connected.

**6.10**    Explain what is meant by a region of a map and give an example.

▌ A given map will divide the plane or sphere into connected areas called *regions*. For example, the connected map $M$ in Fig. 6-9 with six vertices and nine edges divides the plane into five regions as indicated.

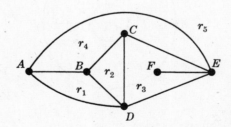

**Fig. 6-9**

**6.11**    Define the degree of a region.

▌ The border of each region $r$ of a map $M$ consists of a sequence of edges forming a closed path. The *degree* of the region $r$, denoted by deg $(r)$, is the length of the closed path bordering $r$. Sometimes the closed path is a cycle. If not, then some edge occurs twice in the path. For example, in Fig. 6-9, the borders of all the regions are cycles except for $r_3$. However, if we do move counterclockwise around $r_3$ starting, say, at the vertex $C$, then we obtain the closed path $(C, D, E, F, E, C)$, where the edge $\{E, F\}$ occurs twice.

**6.12**    Find the degree of each region of the map $M$ in Fig. 6-9.

    **❚**    The degree of a region is the length of the closed path which borders the region. Thus

$$\deg(r_1) = 3, \qquad \deg(r_2) = 3, \qquad \deg(r_3) = 5, \qquad \deg(r_4) = 4, \qquad \deg(r_5) = 3$$

Note that $\deg(r_3) = 5$ since the path bordering $r_3$ includes the edge $\{E, F\}$ twice.

**Theorem 6.1:**    The sum of the degrees of the regions of a map $M$ is equal to twice the number of edges in $M$.

**6.13**    Prove Theorem 6.1.

    **❚**    Each edge $e$ of the map $M$ either borders two regions or is contained in a region and will therefore occur twice in any path along the border of that region. Thus every edge contained in a region will be counted twice in determining the degrees of the regions of $M$.

**6.14**    Identify the cycle or closed path that borders each region of the map $Q$ shown in Fig. 6-10.

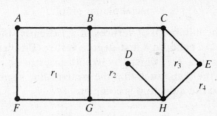

                                                 **Fig. 6-10**

    **❚**    The cycle or closed path bordering each region follows.

        $r_1 = (A, B, G, F, A)$ (cycle)                    $r_3 = (C, E, H, C)$ (cycle)

        $r_2 = (B, C, H, D, H, G, B)$ (closed path)       $r_4 = (A, B, C, E, H, G, F, A)$ (cycle)

**6.15**    Find the degree of each region of the map $Q$ shown in Fig. 6-10 and verify Theorem 6.1.

    **❚**    Counting the number of edges included in each cycle or closed path identified in Problem 6.14, the degree of each region is

$$\deg(r_1) = 4, \qquad \deg(r_2) = 6, \qquad \deg(r_3) = 3, \qquad \deg(r_4) = 7$$

The sum of the degrees is $4 + 6 + 3 + 7 = 20$. Since $Q$ has ten edges and $2 \cdot 10 = 20$, Theorem 6.1 is verified.

**6.16**    Identify the cycle or closed path that borders each region of the map $R$ shown in Fig. 6-11.

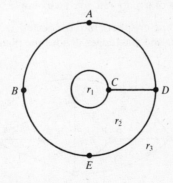

                                               **Fig. 6-11**

    **❚**    The cycle or closed path bordering each region follows.

        $r_1 = (C, C)$ (closed path),    $r_2 = (A, D, C, C, D, E, B, A)$ (closed path),    $r_3 = (A, D, E, B, A)$ (cycle)

**6.17**    Find the degree of each region of the map $R$ shown in Fig. 6-11 and verify Theorem 6.1.

    **❚**    Counting the number of edges included in each cycle or closed path identified in Problem 6.16, the degree of each region is

$$\deg(r_1) = 1, \qquad \deg(r_2) = 7, \qquad \deg(r_3) = 4$$

The sum of the degrees is $1 + 7 + 4 = 12$. Since there are six edges in the map $R$ and $2 \cdot 6 = 12$, Theorem 6.1 is verified.

**6.18** Identify the cycle or closed path that borders each region of the map $S$ shown in Fig. 6-12.

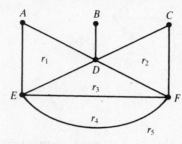

Fig. 6-12

▍ The cycle or closed path bordering each region follows.

$$r_1 = (A, D, E, A) \qquad r_3 = (D, F, E, D) \qquad r_5 = (A, D, B, D, C, F, E, A)$$
$$r_2 = (C, F, D, C) \qquad r_4 = (E, F, E)$$

**6.19** Find the degree of each region of the map $S$ of Problem 6.18 and verify Theorem 6.1.

▍ Counting the number of edges of each of the closed paths identified in Problem 6.18, the degree of each region is

$$\deg(r_1) = 3, \qquad \deg(r_2) = 3, \qquad \deg(r_3) = 3, \qquad \deg(r_4) = 2, \qquad \deg(r_5) = 7$$

The sum of the degrees is $3 + 3 + 3 + 2 + 7 = 18$ and, since $S$ has nine edges and thus $2 \cdot 9 = 18$, Theorem 6.1 is verified.

**6.20** The two multigraphs shown in Fig. 6-13 are the same (isomorphic). However, their maps are different. For each map, identify the border and the degree of each region, and verify Theorem 6.1.

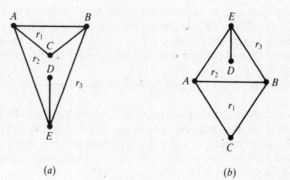

$(a)$ $(b)$ Fig. 6-13

▍ The border for each region in Fig. 6-13$(a)$ is

$$r_1 = (A, B, C, A), \qquad r_2 = (A, C, B, E, D, E, A), \qquad r_3 = (A, B, E, A)$$

Thus $\deg(r_1) = 3$, $\deg(r_2) = 6$, and $\deg(r_3) = 3$, and $S = 3 + 6 + 3 = 12$ which is expected as there are six edges. The border for each region in Fig. 6-13$(b)$ is

$$r_1 = (A, B, C, A), \qquad r_2 = (A, B, E, D, E, A), \qquad r_3 = (A, C, B, E, A)$$

Thus $\deg(r_1) = 3$, $\deg(r_2) = 5$, and $\deg(r_3) = 4$, and $S = 3 + 5 + 4 = 12$, again twice the number of edges.

**6.21** Repeat Problem 6.20 for the two multigraphs shown in Fig. 6-14.

▍ The border for each region in Fig. 6-14$(a)$ is

$$r_1 = (B, B) \qquad r_3 = (C, E, C) \qquad r_5 = (A, D, E, B, B, A)$$
$$r_2 = (A, D, C, E, B, A) \qquad r_4 = (C, D, E, C)$$

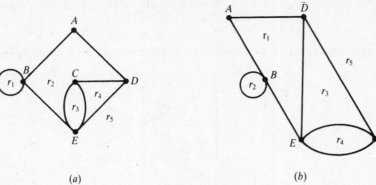

Fig. 6-14

Thus the degrees of the regions are 1, 5, 2, 3, and 5, respectively, and $S = 16$ which is expected as there are eight edges.

The border for each region in Fig. 6-14($b$) is

$$r_1 = (A, D, E, B, A) \qquad r_3 = (D, C, E, D) \qquad r_5 = (A, D, C, E, B, B, A)$$
$$r_2 = (B, B) \qquad\qquad r_4 = (E, C, E)$$

Thus the degrees of regions are 4, 1, 3, 2, and 6, respectively, and, as in ($a$), $S = 16$.

## 6.3  EULER'S FORMULA

The mathematician Euler gave a formula which relates the number of vertices, the number of edges, and the number of regions of any connected map.

**Theorem 6.2 (Euler):**   Let $M$ be a connected map with $V$ vertices, $E$ edges, and $R$ regions. Then

$$V - E + R = 2$$

**6.22**   Prove Theorem 6.2 (Euler's Formula).

▌ Suppose the connected map $M$ consists of a single vertex $P$ as in Fig. 6-15($a$). Then $V = 1$ and $E = 0$, and there is one region, i.e., $R = 1$. Thus in this case $V - E + R = 2$. Otherwise $M$ can be built up from a single vertex by the following two constructions:

(1)   Add a new vertex $Q_2$ and connect it to an existing vertex $Q_1$ by an edge which does not cross any existing edge, as in Fig. 6-15($b$).

(2)   Connect two existing vertices $Q_1$ and $Q_2$ by an edge $e$ which does not cross any existing edge, as in Fig. 6-15($c$).

The first operation does not change the value of $V - E + R$ since both $V$ and $E$ increased by 1, but the number $R$ of regions is not changed. The second operation also does not change the value of $V - E + R$ since $V$ does not change, $E$ is increased by 1, and it can be shown that the number $R$ of regions is also increased by 1. Accordingly, $M$ must have the same value of $V - E + R$ as the map consisting of a single vertex; that is, $V - E + R = 2$, and the theorem is proved.

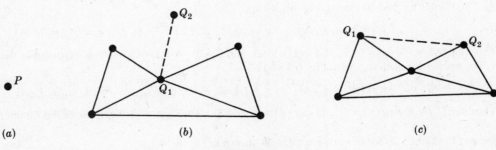

Fig. 6-15

**6.23**   Find the numbers $V$ of vertices, $E$ of edges, and $R$ of regions of each map in Fig. 6-16, and verify Euler's formula.

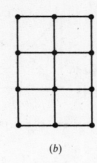
(a)

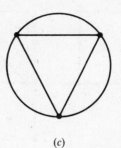
(b)

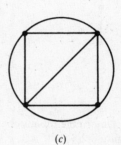
(c)

**Fig. 6-16**

▮ Euler's formula is $V - E + R = 2$. Thus
Figure 6-16(a): $V = 5$, $E = 8$, $R = 5$, and $5 - 8 + 5 = 2$.
Figure 6-16(b): $V = 12$, $E = 17$, $R = 7$, and $12 - 17 + 7 = 2$.
Figure 6-16(c): $V = 3$, $E = 6$, $R = 5$, and $3 - 6 + 5 = 2$.

**6.24**    Repeat Problem 6.23 for the maps in Fig. 6-17.

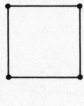
(a)

(b)

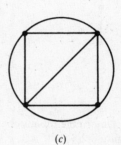
(c)

**Fig. 6-17**

▮ Euler's formula is $V - E + R = 2$. Thus
Figure 6-17(a): $V = 4$, $E = 4$, $R = 2$, and $4 - 4 + 2 = 2$.
Figure 6-17(b): $V = 5$, $E = 8$, $R = 5$, and $5 - 8 + 5 = 2$.
Figure 6-17(c): $V = 4$, $E = 9$, $R = 7$, and $4 - 9 + 7 = 2$.

**6.25**    Repeat Problem 6.23 for the maps in Fig. 6-18.

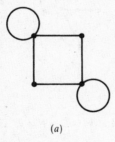
(a)

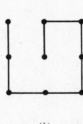
(b)

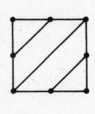
(c)

**Fig. 6-18**

▮ Euler's formula is $V - E + R = 2$. Thus
Figure 6-18(a): $V = 4$, $E = 6$, $R = 4$, and $4 - 6 + 4 = 2$.
Figure 6-18(b): $V = 9$, $E = 8$, $R = 1$, and $9 - 8 + 1 = 2$.
Figure 6-18(c): $V = 8$, $E = 11$, $R = 5$, and $8 - 11 + 5 = 2$.

**6.26**    Consider the sequence of connected maps shown in Fig. 6-19. Each map in the sequence is obtained from the preceding map by either (1) adding a vertex and connecting it to the map with an edge that does not cross any existing edge or (2) connecting two existing vertices with an edge that does not cross any existing edge. Verify Euler's formula for each map in the sequence.

▮ To verify Euler's formula, determine the number of vertices, edges, and regions of each map and check that $V - E + R = 2$. Thus
Figure 6-19(a): $V = 4$, $E = 4$, $R = 2$, and $4 - 4 + 2 = 2$.
Figure 6-19(b): $V = 5$, $E = 5$, $R = 2$, and $5 - 5 + 2 = 2$.
Figure 6-19(c): $V = 5$, $E = 6$, $R = 3$, and $5 - 6 + 3 = 2$.

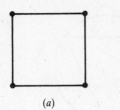 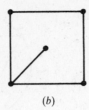 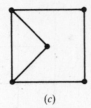 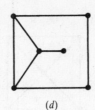 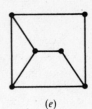

(a)          (b)          (c)          (d)          (e)

**Fig. 6-19**

Figure 6-19(d): $V = 6$, $E = 7$, $R = 3$, and $6 - 7 + 3 = 2$.
Figure 6-19(e): $V = 6$, $E = 8$, $R = 4$, and $6 - 8 + 4 = 2$.

**6.27** Repeat Problem 6.26 for the sequence of connected maps shown in Fig. 6-20.

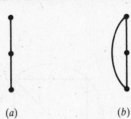 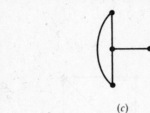  

(a)          (b)          (c)          (d)          (e)

**Fig. 6-20**

▌ Determine the number of vertices, edges, and regions of each map and check that $V - E + R = 2$. Thus
Figure 6-20(a): $V = 3$, $E = 2$, $R = 1$, and $3 - 2 + 1 = 2$.
Figure 6-20(b): $V = 3$, $E = 3$, $R = 2$, and $3 - 3 + 2 = 2$.
Figure 6-20(c): $V = 4$, $E = 4$, $R = 2$, and $4 - 4 + 2 = 2$.
Figure 6-20(d): $V = 4$, $E = 5$, $R = 3$, and $4 - 5 + 3 = 2$.
Figure 6-20(e): $V = 4$, $E = 6$, $R = 4$, and $4 - 6 + 4 = 2$.

**6.28** Repeat Problem 6.26 for the sequence of connected maps shown in Fig. 6-21.

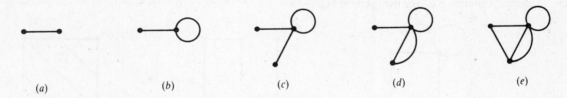

(a)          (b)          (c)          (d)          (e)

**Fig. 6-21**

▌ Determine the number of vertices, edges, and regions and check that $V - E + R = 2$. Thus
Figure 6-21(a): $V = 2$, $E = 1$, $R = 1$, and $2 - 1 + 1 = 2$.
Figure 6-21(b): $V = 2$, $E = 2$, $R = 2$, and $2 - 2 + 2 = 2$.
Figure 6-21(c): $V = 3$, $E = 3$, $R = 2$, and $3 - 3 + 2 = 2$.
Figure 6-21(d): $V = 3$, $E = 4$, $R = 3$, and $3 - 4 + 3 = 2$.
Figure 6-21(e): $V = 3$, $E = 5$, $R = 4$, and $3 - 5 + 4 = 2$.

**6.29** The number of vertices and the number of edges for four connected planar multigraphs are given below. Determine the number $R$ of regions each graph must have.
(a) $V = 10$, $E = 14$,    (c) $V = 25$, $E = 60$,
(b) $V = 6$, $E = 7$,    (d) $V = 14$, $E = 12$.

▌ Rearranging Euler's formula, we obtain $R = 2 - V + E$. Therefore
(a) $R = 2 - 10 + 14 = 6$,    (c) $R = 2 - 25 + 60 = 37$,
(b) $R = 2 - 6 + 7 = 3$,    (d) $R = 2 - 14 + 13 = 1$.

**6.30** The number of vertices and the number of regions for four connected planar multigraphs are given below. Determine the number $E$ of edges each graph must have.

(a)  $V = 5$, $R = 3$,     (c)  $V = 1$, $R = 8$,
(b)  $V = 2$, $R = 2$,     (d)  $V = 32$, $R = 14$.

❚ Rearranging Euler's formula, we obtain $E = V + R - 2$. Hence
(a)  $E = 5 + 3 - 2 = 6$,     (c)  $E = 1 + 8 - 2 = 7$,
(b)  $E = 2 + 2 - 2 = 2$,     (d)  $E = 32 + 14 - 2 = 54$.

**6.31**     The number of edges and the number of regions for four connected planar multigraphs are given below. Determine the number $V$ of vertices each graph must have.
(a)  $E = 6$, $R = 3$,     (c)  $E = 10$, $R = 8$,
(b)  $E = 4$, $R = 1$,     (d)  $E = 27$, $R = 11$.

❚ Rearranging Euler's formula, we obtain $V = E - R + 2$. Thus
(a)  $V = 6 - 3 + 2 = 5$,     (c)  $V = 10 - 8 + 2 = 4$,
(b)  $V = 4 - 1 + 2 = 5$,     (d)  $V = 27 - 11 + 2 = 18$.

**6.32**     Draw three connected maps of a graph with six edges and three regions.

❚ Three possible maps are shown in Fig. 6-22. Note that every map has $V = E - R + 2 = 6 - 3 + 2 = 5$ vertices as predicted by Euler's formula.

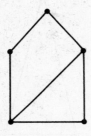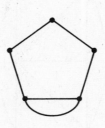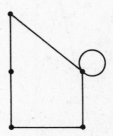

**Fig. 6-22**

**6.33**     Draw three connected maps of a graph with four vertices and five regions.

❚ Three possible maps are shown in Fig. 6-23. Note that every map has $E = V + R - 2 = 4 + 5 - 2 = 7$ edges as predicted by Euler's formula.

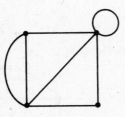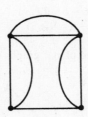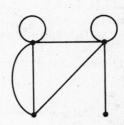

**Fig. 6-23**

**6.34**     Draw three connected maps of a graph with six vertices and seven edges.

❚ Three possible maps are shown in Fig. 6-24. Note that each map has $R = E - V + 2 = 7 - 6 + 2 = 3$ regions as predicted by Euler's formula.

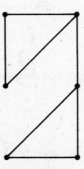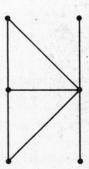

**Fig. 6-24**

**Theorem 6.3:**    Let $G$ be a connected planar graph (not multigraph) with $p$ vertices and $q$ edges, where $p \geq 3$. Then
$q \leq 3p - 6$.

6.35    Prove Theorem 6.3.

▮    Let $r$ be the number of regions in a planar representation of $G$. By Euler's formula,

$$p - q + r = 2$$

Now the sum of the degrees of the regions equals $2q$ by Theorem 6.1. But each region has degree 3 or more; hence

$$2q \geq 3r$$

Thus $r \leq 2q/3$. Substituting this in Euler's formula gives

$$2 = p - q + r \leq p - q + 2q/3 \quad \text{or} \quad 2 \leq p - q/3$$

Multiplying the inequality by 3 gives $6 \leq 3p - q$ which gives us our result.

6.36    Verify Theorem 6.3 for the connected planar graphs shown in Fig. 6-25.

   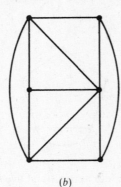   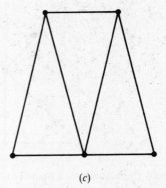

(a)                          (b)                          (c)                          **Fig. 6-25**

▮    Theorem 6.3 states that if the number of vertices, $p$, satisfies $p \geq 3$, then the number of edges, $q$, will satisfy $q \leq 3p - 6$. Therefore
Figure 6-25(a): $p = 3$, $q = 3$, and $3 \cdot 3 - 6 = 3 = 3$.
Figure 6-25(b): $p = 6$, $q = 11$, and $3 \cdot 6 - 6 = 12 \geq 11$.
Figure 6-25(c): $p = 5$, $q = 7$, and $3 \cdot 5 - 6 = 9 \geq 7$.

6.37    Repeat Problem 6.36 for the connected planar graphs shown in Fig. 6-26.

            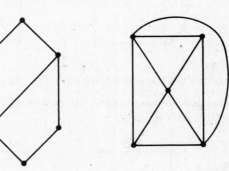

(a)                          (b)                          (c)                          **Fig. 6-26**

▮    Determine the number of vertices, $p$, and the number of edges, $q$, and then verify Theorem 6.3:
Figure 6-26(a); $p = 4$, $q = 5$, and $3 \cdot 4 - 6 = 6 \geq 5$.
Figure 6-26(b): $p = 6$, $q = 7$, and $3 \cdot 6 - 6 = 12 \geq 7$.
Figure 6-26(c): $p = 5$, $q = 9$, and $3 \cdot 5 - 6 = 9 = 9$.

6.38    What is the maximum number of edges possible in a planar graph with eight vertices? With four vertices?

▮ From Theorem 6.3, $q \le 3p - 6$. For a planar graph with eight vertices,

$$q \le 3 \cdot 8 - 6 = 18$$

Hence the maximum number of edges possible in a planar graph with eight vertices is 18. For a planar graph with four vertices,

$$q \le 3 \cdot 4 - 6 = 6$$

and so the maximum number of edges possible is six.

**6.39**  What is the minimum number of vertices necessary for a graph with six edges to be planar? With eleven edges?

▮ Rearranging the formula of Theorem 6.3 we obtain $p \ge (6 + q)/3$. For a planar graph with six edges,

$$p \ge (6 + 6)/3 = 4$$

Hence the minimum number of vertices required for a graph with six edges to be planar is four. For a graph with eleven edges,

$$p \ge (6 + 11)/3 = 17/3$$

Since the number of vertices must be a positive integer, the minimum number of vertices required would be six, the smallest integer greater than 17/3.

**6.40**  Let $G$ be a finite connected planar graph with at least three vertices. Show that $G$ has at least one vertex of degree five or less.

▮ Let $p$ be the number of vertices and $q$ the number of edges of $G$, and suppose $\deg(u) \ge 6$ for each vertex $u$ of $G$. But $2q$ equals the sum of the degrees of the vertices of $G$, i.e., $2q \ge 6p$. Therefore

$$q \ge 3p > 3p - 6$$

This contradicts Theorem 6.3. Thus some vertex of $G$ has degree five or less.

## 6.4 NONPLANAR GRAPHS

The following theorem, due to Kuratowski, gives a simple test for determining whether a given graph is or is not planar.

**Theorem 6.4:**  A graph is nonplanar if and only if it contains a subgraph homeomorphic to $K_{3,3}$ or $K_5$.

**Remark:**  Recall that graphs $G$ and $H$ are homeomorphic if they can be obtained, respectively, from isomorphic graphs $G'$ and $H'$ by dividing the edges of $G'$ and $H'$ with additional vertices.

**6.41**  Use Euler's formula and Theorem 6.1 to show that the graph $K_{3,3}$ is nonplanar.

▮ $K_{3,3}$ is a complete bipartite graph with $p = 6$ vertices and $q = 9$ edges and is shown in Fig. 6-27(a). Suppose the graph is planar. By Euler's formula a planar representation of this graph would have five regions. Observe that no three vertices are connected to each other; hence the degree of each region must be four or more and the sum of the degrees must be twenty or more. By Theorem 6.1, this graph must therefore have ten or more edges. Since this graph has only nine edges, our assumption of the graph being planar is false. Hence we have shown that $K_{3,3}$ is nonplanar.

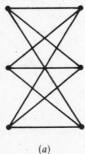   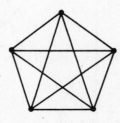

(a)                    (b)         **Fig. 6-27**

**6.42** Show that the graph $K_5$ is nonplanar using Theorem 6.3.

▌ The graph $K_5$ is the star graph shown in Fig. 6-27($b$). It is a complete graph with $p = 5$ vertices and $q = 10$ edges. Suppose the graph is planar. By Theorem 6.3,

$$10 = q \le 3p - 6 = 3 \cdot 5 - 6 = 15 - 6 = 9$$

which is false. Hence $K_5$ is nonplanar.

**6.43** The graph shown in Fig. 6-28($a$) has a subgraph isomorphic to $K_{3,3}$. Identify the subgraph.

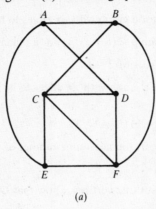
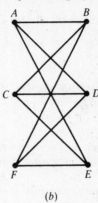

(a)                                    (b)                    **Fig. 6-28**

▌ By removing edge $\{C, F\}$, we obtain a graph isomorphic to $K_{3,3}$. To see this clearly, transpose the locations of vertices $E$ and $F$ and redraw the edges. The result is shown in Fig. 6-28($b$).

**6.44** The graph shown in Fig. 6-29($a$) has a subgraph isomorphic to $K_5$. Identify the subgraph.

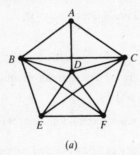
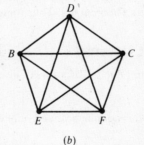

(a)                                    (b)                    **Fig. 6-29**

▌ By removing the vertex $A$ and the three edges $\{B, A\}$, $\{C, A\}$, and $\{D, A\}$ incident on $A$, we obtain a graph isomorphic to $K_5$. To see this clearly, move the vertex $D$ upwards above the edge connecting $B$ and $C$. The result is shown in Fig. 6-29($b$).

**6.45** The graph shown in Fig. 6-30($a$) has a subgraph homeomorphic to $K_{3,3}$. Identify the subgraph.

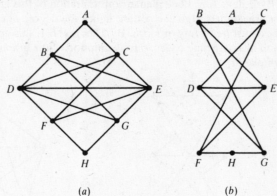

(a)                                    (b)                    **Fig. 6-30**

▌ By deleting edges $\{B, D\}$, $\{D, F\}$, $\{C, E\}$, and $\{E, G\}$, we obtain a graph homeomorphic to $K_{3,3}$. This subgraph is shown in Fig. 6-30($b$).

**6.46**    The graph shown in Fig. 6-31(a) has a subgraph homeomorphic to $K_5$. Identify the subgraph.

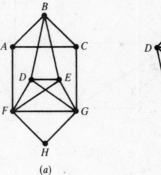

(a)                    (b)          **Fig. 6-31**

❚ By deleting vertex $H$, the edges, $\{F, H\}$ and $\{G, H\}$, incident on it, and the edge $\{A, C\}$, we obtain a graph homeomorphic to $K_5$. This subgraph can be easily identified by transposing the location of vertices $A$ and $D$, and $C$ and $E$. The subgraph is shown in Fig. 6-31(b).

**6.47**    Identify which of the graphs shown in Fig. 6-32 are nonplanar, i.e., identify which graphs have a subgraph homeomorphic to $K_{3,3}$ or $K_5$.

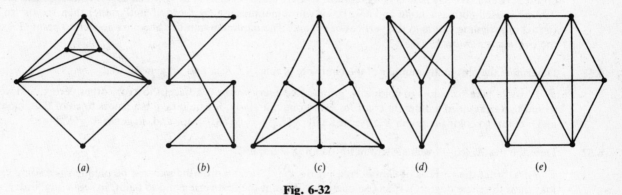

(a)              (b)              (c)              (d)              (e)

**Fig. 6-32**

❚ Graphs (a), (c), and (d) are nonplanar. Graph (a) has a subgraph isomorphic to $K_5$, graph (c) itself is homeomorphic to $K_{3,3}$, and graph (d) itself is isomorphic to $K_{3,3}$.

**6.48**    Identify which of the graphs shown in Fig. 6-33 are nonplanar.

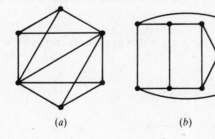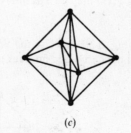

(a)              (b)              (c)              (d)

**Fig. 6-33**

❚ Graphs (b) and (c) are nonplanar. Graph (b) itself is homeomorphic to $K_{3,3}$, and graph (c) has a subgraph isomorphic to $K_{3,3}$.

**6.49**    Identify which of the graphs shown in Fig. 6-34 are nonplanar.

❚ Graphs (a), (c), and (e) are nonplanar. Graph (a) has a subgraph homeomorphic to $K_{3,3}$, graph (c) is $K_6$ and has subgraphs isomorphic to both $K_{3,3}$ and $K_5$, and graph (e) itself is homeomorphic to $K_5$.

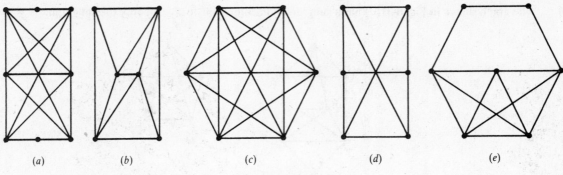

Fig. 6-34

## 6.5 COLORED GRAPHS

**6.50** Define a *vertex coloring*, or simply a *coloring*, of a graph $G$, and the chromatic number of $G$, denoted by $\chi(G)$. ($\chi$ is the Greek letter chi.)

▌ A *coloring* of a graph $G$ is an assignment of colors to the vertices of $G$ such that adjacent vertices have different colors. We say that $G$ is *n-colorable* if there exists a coloring of $G$ which uses $n$ colors. (Since the word "color" is used both as a noun and a verb, we will sometimes use the word "paint" rather than "color" to mean the act of assigning colors to the vertices of a map.) The minimum number of colors needed to paint $G$ is called the *chromatic number* of $G$.

**6.51** Determine the chromatic number of the complete graphs $K_6$, $K_{10}$, and, in general, $K_n$.

▌ It would take six colors to color a $K_6$ graph since every vertex is adjacent to every other vertex, and we would therefore need a different color for every one. Similarly, it would take ten colors to color the graph $K_{10}$ and $n$ colors to color the graph $K_n$. Accordingly, $\chi(K_6) = 6$, $\chi(K_{10}) = 10$, and, in general, $\chi(K_n) = n$.

**6.52** Describe the Welch–Powell algorithm for painting a graph $G$.

▌ First, order the vertices of $G$ in decreasing degree. (Such an ordering may not be unique since some vertices may have the same degree.) Then use one color to paint the first vertex and to paint, in sequential order, each vertex on the list that is not adjacent to a vertex previously painted with this color. Start again at the top of the list and repeat the process painting previously unpainted vertices using a second color. Continue repeating with additional colors until all the vertices have been painted.

**Remark:** The Welch–Powell algorithm is an efficient way to paint a graph $G$. We emphasize that the algorithm only gives an upper bound for $\chi(G)$, that is, that the algorithm does not always give the minimum number of colors which is needed to paint $G$. In fact, finding $\chi(G)$ may be extremely difficult except in simple cases as those illustrated in the following problems.

**6.53** Consider the graph $G$ in Fig. 6-35. (*a*) Use the Welch–Powell algorithm to paint $G$ (referring to colors simply as "*a*", "*b*", etc.). (*b*) Find the chromatic number of $G$.

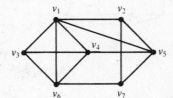

Fig. 6-35

▌ (*a*) List the vertices of $G$ in order of decreasing degrees as shown below. Assign color $a$ to the first vertex, $v_1$. The next vertex on the list not adjacent to $v_1$ is $v_7$: assign color $a$ to $v_7$. Now move to color $b$. Assign color $b$ to the first unpainted vertex, $v_4$. The next unpainted vertex not adjacent to $v_4$ is $v_2$: assign color $b$ to $v_2$. Since all remaining unpainted vertices are adjacent to $v_4$ or $v_2$, move to color $c$.

Repeat this process with additional colors until all vertices are painted. The completed assignment is listed as follows.

| Vertex | $v_1$ | $v_4$ | $v_5$ | $v_6$ | $v_2$ | $v_3$ | $v_7$ |
|--------|-------|-------|-------|-------|-------|-------|-------|
| Degree | 5 | 4 | 4 | 4 | 3 | 3 | 3 |
| Color | $a$ | $b$ | $c$ | $c$ | $b$ | $d$ | $a$ |

(b) The vertices $v_1$, $v_3$, $v_4$, and $v_6$ are connected to each other and hence must be painted different colors. Thus at least four colors are required to paint $G$. Since (a) uses only four colors to paint $G$, $\chi(G) = 4$.

**6.54** Repeat Problem 6.53 using the graph $H$ in Fig. 6-36.

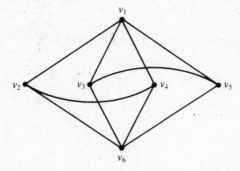

**Fig. 6-36**

▌ (a) Following the steps as in Problem 6.53 yields the following data:

| Vertex | $v_1$ | $v_3$ | $v_4$ | $v_6$ | $v_2$ | $v_5$ |
|--------|-------|-------|-------|-------|-------|-------|
| Degree | 4 | 4 | 4 | 4 | 3 | 3 |
| Color | $a$ | $b$ | $c$ | $a$ | $b$ | $c$ |

(b) The vertices $v_1$, $v_3$, and $v_4$ are connected to each other, so at least three colors are needed to color $H$. Since (a) uses three colors, $\chi(H) = 3$.

**6.55** Repeat Problem 6.53 using the graph $G$ in Fig. 6-37.

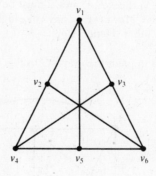

**Fig. 6-37**

▌ (a) Following the steps as in Problem 6.53, we have

| Vertex | $v_1$ | $v_2$ | $v_3$ | $v_4$ | $v_5$ | $v_6$ |
|--------|-------|-------|-------|-------|-------|-------|
| Degree | 3 | 3 | 3 | 3 | 2 | 3 |
| Color | $a$ | $b$ | $b$ | $a$ | $b$ | $a$ |

(b) The vertices $v_1$ and $v_2$ are connected to each other, so at least two colors are needed to color $G$. From (a), $\chi(G) = 2$.

**6.56** Repeat Problem 6.53 using the graph $H$ in Fig. 6-38.

▌ (a) Following the steps as in Problem 6.53, we have

| Vertex | $v_1$ | $v_5$ | $v_2$ | $v_6$ | $v_3$ | $v_4$ |
|--------|-------|-------|-------|-------|-------|-------|
| Degree | 4 | 4 | 3 | 3 | 2 | 2 |
| Color | $a$ | $b$ | $b$ | $c$ | $c$ | $a$ |

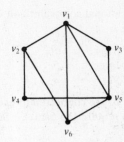

Fig. 6-38

**(b)** The vertices $v_1$, $v_3$, and $v_5$ are connected to each other, so at least three colors are needed to color $H$. From **(a)**, $\chi(H) = 3$.

**6.57** Use the Welch–Powell algorithm to paint the graph in Fig. 6-39, and find the chromatic number $n$ of the graph.

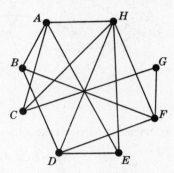

Fig. 6-39

❚ First order the vertices according to decreasing degrees to obtain the sequence

$$H, A, D, F, B, C, E, G$$

Proceeding sequentially, we use the first color to paint the vertices $H$, $B$ and then $G$. (We cannot paint $A$, $D$, or $F$ the first color since each is connected to $H$, and we cannot paint $C$ or $E$ the first color since each is connected to either $H$ or $B$.) Proceeding sequentially with the unpainted vertices, we use the second color to paint the vertices $A$ and $D$. The remaining vertices $F$, $C$ and $E$ must be painted with the third color. Thus the chromatic number $n$ cannot be greater than 3. However, in any coloring, $H$, $D$ and $E$ must be painted different colors since they are connected to each other. Hence $n = 3$.

**6.58** Use the Welch–Powell algorithm to paint the graph $G$ in Fig. 6-40, and find the chromatic number $n$ of the graph.

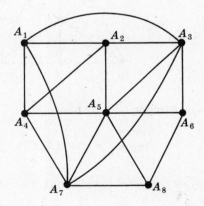

Fig. 6-40

❚ Ordering the vertices according to decreasing degrees we obtain the sequence

$$A_5, A_3, A_7, A_1, A_2, A_4, A_6, A_8$$

The first color is used to paint the vertices $A_5$ and $A_1$. The second color is used to paint the vertices $A_3$, $A_4$, and $A_8$. The third color is used to paint the vertices $A_7$, $A_2$, and $A_6$. Thus $G$ is 3-colorable. Note that $G$ is not 2-colorable since $A_1$, $A_2$, and $A_3$ must be painted different colors. Accordingly, $n = \chi(G) = 3$.

**6.59** Determine those connected graphs $G$, if any, which are one-colorable.

▌ If $G$ has an edge $e$ connecting vertices $v$ and $v'$, then $v$ and $v'$ must be painted different colors. Thus $G$ can only be the graph with one vertex and no edges.

## Bipartite Graphs and Colorings

**6.60** Find the chromatic number of the bipartite graphs $K_{3,4}$ and $K_{2,6}$.

▌ A bipartite graph is a graph whose vertices can be divided into two subsets where the vertices of each subset are connected to all the vertices of the other subset and not to any vertices in its own subset (see Problem 5.125). Since no vertex is connected to any other vertex in the same subset, all the vertices of a given subset can be assigned the same color. Since the two subsets are connected, then each subset must be painted different colors; thus two colors are required to color any bipartite graph. Accordingly, $\chi(K_{3,4}) = 2$ and $\chi(K_{2,6}) = 2$. This notion is formalized and extended in Theorem 6.5.

**Theorem 6.5:** The following are equivalent for a graph $G$:
    (i)   $G$ is 2-colorable
    (ii)  $G$ is bipartite
    (iii) Every cycle of $G$ has even length.

**6.61** Prove Theorem 6.5.

▌ (i) *implies* (ii). Suppose $G$ is 2-colorable. Let $M$ be the set of vertices painted the first color, and let $N$ be the set of vertices painted the second color. Then $M$ and $N$ form a bipartite partition of the vertices of $G$ since neither the vertices of $M$ nor the vertices of $N$ can be adjacent to each other since they are of the same color.

(ii) *implies* (iii). Suppose $G$ is bipartite and $M$ and $N$ form a bipartite partition of the vertices of $G$. If a cycle begins at a vertex $u$ of, say $M$, then it will go to a vertex of $N$, and then to a vertex of $M$, and then to $N$ and so on. Hence when the cycle returns to $u$ it must be of even length. That is, every cycle of $G$ will have even length.

(iii) *implies* (i). Lastly, suppose every cycle of $G$ has even length. We pick a vertex in each connected component and paint it the first color, say red. We then successively paint all the vertices as follows: If a vertex is painted red, then any vertex adjacent to it will be painted the second color, say blue. If a vertex is painted blue, then any vertex adjacent to it will be painted red. Since every cycle has even length, no adjacent vertices will be painted the same color. Hence $G$ is 2-colorable, and the theorem is proved.

**6.62** Graph $G$ of Problem 6.55 was determined to be 2-colorable. Thus, by Theorem 6.5, $G$ must be bipartite. Verify this by identifying the two subsets of vertices that generate $G$.

▌ By inspection we see that $G$ is $K_{3,3}$ where $m = \{v_1, v_4, v_6\}$ and $n = \{v_2, v_3, v_5\}$. However, since we know that all vertices of the same subset must have the same color, we can easily identify each subset by examining the assignment of colors.

**6.63** Consider the bipartite graph $K_{2,4}$ in Fig. 6-41. Find: (**a**) a 2-coloring of the graph, and (**b**) the six cycles that start with $v_1$ and show that they are even.

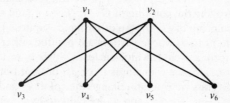

    **Fig. 6-41**

▌ (**a**) Here $m = \{v_1, v_2\}$ and $n_2 = \{v_3, v_4, v_5, v_6\}$ yield the bipartite graph. Thus paint $v_1$ and $v_2$ one color, and $v_3$, $v_4$, $v_5$, and $v_6$ a second color.

    (**b**) The six cycles that start with vertex $v_1$ are:

$$(v_1, v_3, v_2, v_4, v_1) \qquad (v_1, v_4, v_2, v_6, v_1) \qquad (v_1, v_4, v_2, v_5, v_1)$$
$$(v_1, v_3, v_2, v_6, v_1) \qquad (v_1, v_3, v_2, v_5, v_1) \qquad (v_1, v_5, v_2, v_6, v_1)$$

All these cycles have length 4, hence each length is even.

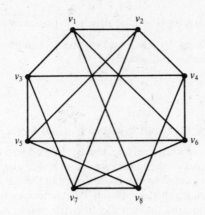

**Fig. 6-42**

**6.64**    The graph $G$ shown in Fig. 6-42 is bipartite. Assign colors to the vertices of $G$ with the Welch–Powell algorithm in order to identify the two subsets of vertices that generate $G$.

┃    Since every vertex is of degree 4, $G$ must be $K_{4,4}$. Using the Welch–Powell algorithm we can identify the two subsets as $m = \{v_1, v_4, v_5, v_7\}$ and $n = \{v_2, v_3, v_6, v_8\}$.

### Planar Graphs and Colorings

**Theorem 6.6:**    Any planar graph $G$ is five-colorable.

**6.65**    Prove Theorem 6.6.

┃    The proof is by induction on the number $p$ of vertices of $G$. If $p \le 5$, then the theorem obviously holds. Suppose $p > 5$, and the theorem holds for graphs with less than $p$ vertices. By Problem 6.40, $G$ has a vertex $v$ such that deg $(v) \le 5$. By induction, the subgraph $G - v$ is 5-colorable. Assume one such coloring. If the vertices adjacent to $v$ use less than the five colors, then we simply paint $v$ with one of the remaining colors and obtain a 5-coloring of $G$. We are still left with the case that $v$ is adjacent to five vertices which are painted different colors. Say the vertices, moving counterclockwise about $v$, are $v_1, \ldots, v_5$ and are painted respectively by the colors $c_1, \ldots, c_5$. (See Fig. 6-43.)

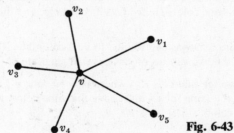

**Fig. 6-43**

Consider now the subgraph $H$ of $G$ generated by the vertices painted $c_1$ and $c_3$. Note $H$ includes $v_1$ and $v_3$. If $v_1$ and $v_3$ belong to different components of $H$, then we can interchange the colors $c_1$ and $c_3$ in the component containing $v_1$ without destroying the coloring of $G - v$. Then $v_1$ and $v_3$ are painted by $c_3$, $c_1$ can be chosen to paint $v$, and we have a 5-coloring of $G$. On the other hand, suppose $v_1$ and $v_3$ are in the same component of $H$. Then there is a path $P$ from $v_1$ to $v_3$ whose vertices are painted either $c_1$ or $c_3$. The path $P$ together with the edges $\{v, v_1\}$ and $\{v, v_3\}$ form a cycle $C$ which encloses either $v_2$ or $v_4$. Consider now the subgraph $K$ generated by the vertices painted $c_2$ or $c_4$. Since $C$ encloses $v_2$ or $v_4$, but not both, the vertices $v_2$ and $v_4$ belong to different components of $K$. Thus we can interchange the colors $c_2$ and $c_4$ in the component containing $v_2$ without destroying the coloring of $G - v$. Then $v_2$ and $v_4$ are painted by $c_4$, and we can choose $c_2$ to paint $v$ and obtain a 5-coloring of $G$. Thus $G$ is 5-colorable and the theorem is proved.

## 6.6    COLORS AND MAPS

**6.66**    Define adjacent regions of a map $M$.

┃    Two regions of a planar multigraph are said to be *adjacent* if they have an edge in common. Consider, for example, the map shown in Fig. 6-44. Regions $r_2$ and $r_3$ are adjacent but regions $r_2$ and $r_4$ are not.

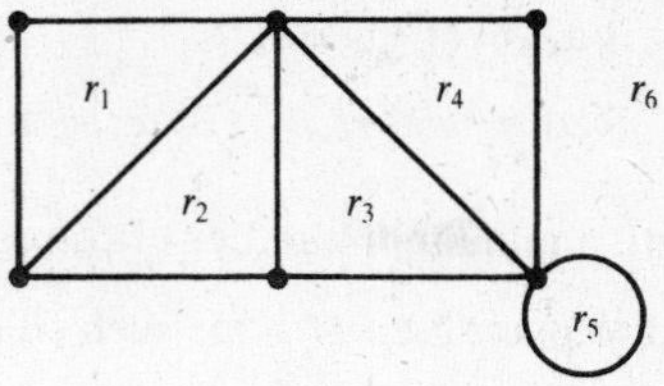

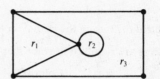

Fig. 6-44

**6.67** Consider the map $N$ in Fig. 6-45. Identify the regions of $N$ that are adjacent to the regions: **(a)** $r_7$, **(b)** $r_2$, and **(c)** $r_6$.

❚ Those regions which share an edge with $r_k$ are adjacent to $r_k$. Hence **(a)** $r_4$, $r_5$, and $r_8$; **(b)** $r_1$ and $r_4$; **(c)** only $r_4$ is adjacent to $r_6$.

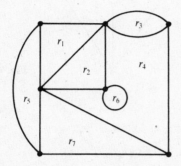

Fig. 6-45

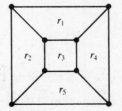

Fig. 6-46

**6.68** Find the number of regions adjacent to each region of the map $R$ shown in Fig. 6-46.

❚ The number of regions adjacent to a given region is found by counting the number of regions that share at least one edge with that region. Hence the four regions $r_1$, $r_2$, $r_3$, and $r_4$ of $R$ have 2, 1, 3, and 2 adjacent regions respectively.

**6.69** Explain what is meant by a coloring of a map $M$.

❚ By a *coloring* of a map $M$ we mean an assignment of colors to the regions of $M$ such that adjacent regions have different colors. A map is *n-colorable* if there exists a coloring of $M$ which uses $n$ colors. The map in Fig. 6-44 is 3-colorable since its regions could be painted as follows:

$r_1$ blue, $r_2$ white, $r_3$ blue, $r_4$ white, $r_5$ blue, $r_6$ green

**6.70** Consider the map $P$ in Fig. 6-47. **(a)** Find a 4-coloring of $P$. **(b)** Is $P$ 3-colorable?

❚ **(a)** A 4-coloring of map $P$ assigns four colors to the regions of $P$ such that adjacent regions are assigned different colors. One possible 4-coloring is as follows:

Red: $r_1$ and $r_3$, Blue: $r_2$ and $r_6$, Green: $r_5$ and $r_4$, Yellow: $r_7$

**(b)** No, we cannot paint $P$ with three colors. Note that regions $r_1$, $r_2$, $r_5$, and $r_7$ are all adjacent to each other and must therefore be painted different colors. Hence, at least four colors are needed to paint $P$.

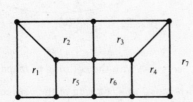

Fig. 6-47

Fig. 6-48

**6.71** Consider the map $Q$ in Fig. 6-48. **(a)** Find a 4-coloring of $Q$. **(b)** Is $Q$ 3-colorable?

❚ **(a)** One possible 4-coloring is as follows:

Red: $r_1$ and $r_5$, Blue: $r_3$, Green: $r_2$ and $r_4$, Yellow: $r_6$

**(b)**   Yes, e.g., the following is a 3-coloring of $Q$:

Red: $r_1$ and $r_5$,     Blue: $r_2$ and $r_4$,     Green: $r_3$ and $r_6$

**6.72**   Paint the map $M$ in Fig. 6-49 with a minimum number of colors. Name the colors simply as "$a$", "$b$", etc.

❙   Only two colors are required to paint map $M$. One such coloring is as follows:

Color $a$: $r_1$, $r_4$, $r_6$     Color $b$: $r_2$, $r_3$, $r_5$, $r_7$, $r_8$

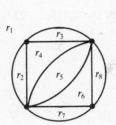

Fig. 6-49

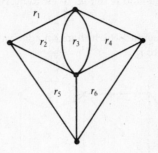

Fig. 6-50

**6.73**   Repeat Problem 6.72 using the map $N$ in Fig. 6-50.

❙   Three colors are required to color map $M$. One such coloring is as follows:

Color $a$: $r_1$, $r_3$,     Color $b$: $r_2$, $r_6$,     Color $c$: $r_4$, $r_5$

Three colors are needed since $r_1$, $r_2$, and $r_5$ are adjacent to each other.

## Dual Map

**6.74**   Define the (Whitney) dual of a map $M$ with an example.

❙   Consider a map $M$. In each region of $M$ choose a point. If two regions have an edge in common, then the corresponding points can be connected by a line through the common edge. These curves can be drawn so they are noncrossing. Thus we obtain a new map $M^*$, called the *dual* of $M$, such that each vertex of $M^*$ corresponds to exactly one region of $M$. Figure 6-51(b) shows the dual of the map in Fig. 6-51(a). We can prove that each region of $M^*$ will include exactly one vertex of $M$ and that each edge of $M^*$ will intersect exactly one edge of $M$ and vice versa. Thus $M$ will be the dual of the map $M^*$.

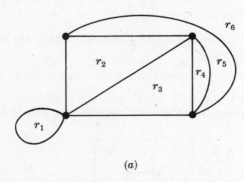

(a)

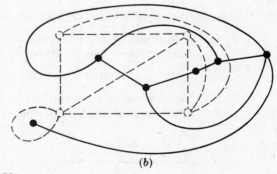

(b)

Fig. 6-51

**6.75**   Explain how the dual map relates the coloring of graphs (i.e., vertices) with the coloring of maps (i.e., regions).

❙   Observe that any coloring of the regions of map $M$ will correspond to a coloring of the vertices of the dual map $M^*$. In other words, a map $M$ is $n$-colorable if and only if the planar graph of the dual map $M^*$ is $n$-colorable. Theorem 6.6 can therefore be restated as follows.

**Theorem 6.6 (Alternate):**   Every planar map $M$ is 5-colorable.

**6.76**   Draw the map which is dual to each map in Fig. 6-52.

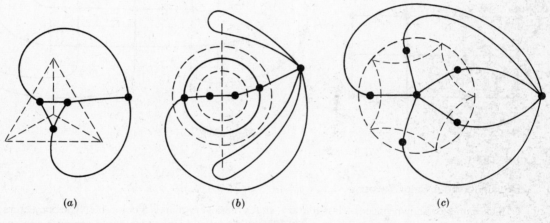

Fig. 6-52

▮ Choose a vertex (point) in each region, and connect two vertices if the corresponding regions have an edge in common. We emphasize that a map and its dual must have the same number of edges. The corresponding results are shown in Fig. 6-53. Observe that there are two loops in Fig. 6-53(b), which correspond to the two edges in the original map that are entirely contained in the "outside" region.

Fig. 6-53

**6.77**    Draw the map which is dual to each map in Fig. 6-54.

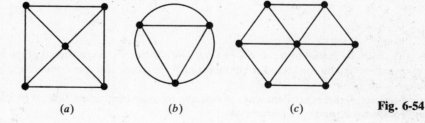

(a)            (b)            (c)            Fig. 6-54

▮ Start by placing a vertex (point) in each region of each map $M$, and then connect two vertices if the corresponding regions have an edge in common. In this manner, we obtain the corresponding dual maps $M^*$ in Fig. 6-55.

**6.78**    Consider the map $M$ in Fig. 6-56(a). (a) How many regions has $M$? (b) Draw the map $M^*$ which is dual to $M$. (c) Determine how many vertices are in $M^*$. (d) Draw the map which is dual to $M^*$.

▮   (a)    $M$ has six bounded regions and one unbounded region.
   (b)    The dual map $M^*$ appears in Fig. 6-56(b).
   (c)    $M^*$ has seven vertices, one for each region in $M$.
   (d)    The original map $M$ in Fig. 6-56(a) is the dual of the map $M^*$ in Fig. 6-56(b).

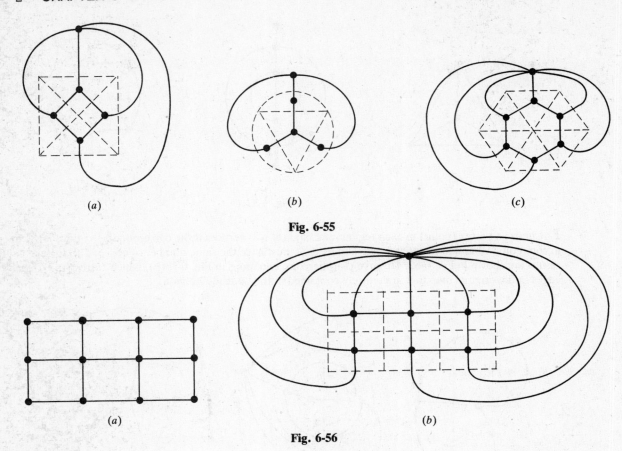

**Fig. 6-55**

**Fig. 6-56**

## Four Color Theorem

**6.79**    Explain the Four Color Theorem.

▮    Theorem 6.6, known since the last century, states that every map is 5-colorable. The conjecture, that only four colors are needed, was finally proven in 1976 by Appel and Haken who used computers to analyze almost 2000 graphs involving millions of cases. We now formally state this result, known as the Four Color Theorem.

**Four Color Theorem 6.7(*a*):**    If the regions of a map *M* are colored so that adjacent regions have different colors, then no more than four colors are required.

**Four Color Theorem 6.7(*b*):**    Every planar graph is (vertex) 4-colorable.

## 6.7    TREES

A graph *G* without cycles is said to be *acyclic* or *cycle-free*. A *tree T* is a connected graph without cycles. A *forest F* is a graph without cycles; hence the connected components of *F* are trees. The tree consisting of a single vertex with no edges is called the *degenerate tree*.

The following theorems give equivalent ways of defining trees and important related properties. (Theorems 6.8 and 6.9 are proved in Problems 6.90 and 6.91 respectively.)

**Theorem 6.8:**    Let *G* be a graph with more than one vertex. Then the following are equivalent:
    (i)    *G* is a tree.
    (ii)    Each pair of vertices is connected by exactly one simple path.
    (iii)    *G* is connected, but if any edge is deleted then the resulting graph is not connected.
    (iv)    *G* is cycle-free, but if any edge is added to the graph then the resulting graph has exactly one cycle.

**Theorem 6.9:**    Let *G* be a finite graph with $n > 1$ vertices. Then the following are equivalent:
    (i)    *G* is a tree.
    (ii)    *G* is cycle-free and has $n - 1$ edges.
    (iii)    *G* is connected and has $n - 1$ edges.

**Theorem 6.10:** Trees (and hence forests) are 2-colorable.

**6.80**  Suppose $T$ is a tree with six vertices. How many edges does $T$ have?

▌ By Theorem 6.9, $T$ will have $6 - 1 = 5$ edges.

**6.81**  Verify Theorem 6.8 for the graph $A$ in Fig. 6-57.

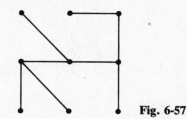

**Fig. 6-57**

▌ The following hold for the graph $A$:
 (i)   $A$ is a tree since it is connected and has no cycles.
 (ii)  Select any two vertices in $A$ and they will be connected by only one simple path.
 (iii) If any edge is removed, $A$ is no longer connected.
 (iv)  If any edge is added to $A$, then $A$ has exactly one cycle.
Hence Theorem 6.8 is verified for the graph $A$.

**6.82**  Verify Theorem 6.9 for the graph $A$ in Fig. 6-57.

▌ The following hold for the graph $A$:
 (i)   $A$ is a tree since it is connected and has no cycles.
 (ii)  $A$ is cycle-free and has nine vertices and eight edges.
 (iii) $A$ is connected and has nine vertices and eight edges.
Hence Theorem 6.9 is verified for the graph $A$.

**6.83**  Consider the tree $T$ in Fig. 6-58. (*a*) Which vertices, if any, are cut points of $T$? (*b*) Which edges, if any, are bridges of $T$?

▌ (*a*)   Each vertex of degree more than one is a cut point in a tree; hence $c$, $r$, $u$, $w$, and $y$ are cut points of $T$.
 (*b*)   Every edge in a tree is a bridge since the removal of any edge leaves a tree disconnected (Theorem 6.8).

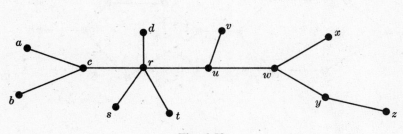

**Fig. 6-58**

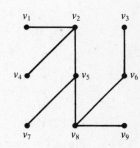

**Fig. 6-59**

**6.84**  Find a 2-coloring of the tree $T$ in Fig. 6-59.

▌ To find a 2-coloring of any tree, assign the first color to any vertex. Then assign the second color to all vertices adjacent to that first vertex. Next assign the first color to all vertices adjacent to the vertices that have been assigned the second color. Repeat this process until all vertices are colored. In tree $T$, for example, assign the color red to vertex $v_2$. Then assign the color green to vertices $v_1$, $v_4$, and $v_5$. Then assign red to vertices $v_7$ and $v_8$. Continuing in this fashion yields the assignment:

Red:  $v_2$, $v_3$, $v_7$, $v_8$,      Green:  $v_1$, $v_4$, $v_5$, $v_6$, $v_9$

**6.85** Find a 2-coloring of the tree $T$ in Fig. 6-60.

▮ Using colors red and green, assign red to $v_1$ and proceed as in Problem 6.84. The following coloring of $T$ obtains:

$$\text{Red:} \quad v_1, v_6, v_7, \qquad \text{Green:} \quad v_2, v_3, v_4, v_5, v_8$$

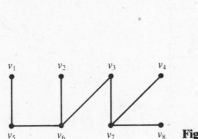

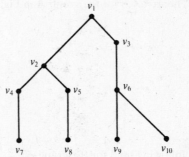

**Fig. 6-60**     **Fig. 6-61**

**6.86** Find a 2-coloring of the tree $T$ in Fig. 6-61.

▮ Proceeding as in Problem 6.85 yields the following coloring of $T$:

$$\text{Red:} \quad v_1, v_4, v_5, v_6, \qquad \text{Green:} \quad v_2, v_3, v_7, v_8, v_9, v_{10}$$

**6.87** Consider the complete bipartite graph $K_{m,n}$. Show that $K_{m,n}$ is not a tree when $m$ and $n$ exceed one.

▮ Let $u$ and $u'$ be vertices in the first set and $v$ and $v'$ vertices in the second set. Then $(u, v, u', v', u)$ is a cycle. Hence $K_{m,n}$ is not a tree for $m, n > 1$.

**6.88** Consider the complete graph $K_n$. Show that $K_n$ is not a tree when $n > 2$.

▮ Let $u$, $v$, and $w$ be vertices in $K_n$. Then $(u, v, w, u)$ is a cycle in $K_n$. Hence $K_n$ is not a tree for $n > 2$.

**6.89** Suppose there are two distinct simple paths, say $P_1$ and $P_2$, from a vertex $u$ to a vertex $v$ in a graph $G$. Prove that $G$ contains a cycle.

▮ Let $w$ be a vertex on $P_1$ and $P_2$ such that the next vertices on $P_1$ and $P_2$ are distinct. Let $w'$ be the first vertex following $w$ which lies on both $P_1$ and $P_2$. (See Fig. 6-62.) Then the subpaths of $P_1$ and $P_2$ between $w$ and $w'$ have no vertices in common except $w$ and $w'$; hence these two subpaths form a cycle.

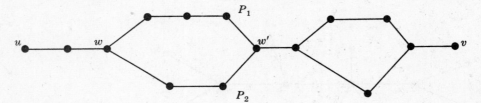

**Fig. 6-62**

**6.90** Prove Theorem 6.8.

▮ (i) *implies* (ii). Let $u$ and $v$ be two vertices in $G$. Since $G$ is a tree, $G$ is connected so there is at least one path between $u$ and $v$. Moreover, there can only be one path between $u$ and $v$, otherwise $G$ will contain a cycle (Problem 6.89).

(ii) *implies* (iii). Suppose we delete an edge $e = \{u, v\}$ from $G$. Note $e$ is a path from $u$ to $v$. Suppose the resulting graph $G - e$ has a path $P$ from $u$ to $v$. Then $P$ and $e$ are two distinct paths from $u$ to $v$, which contradicts the hypothesis. Thus there is no path between $u$ and $v$ in $G - e$, so $G - e$ is disconnected.

(iii) *implies* (iv). Suppose $G$ contains a cycle $C$ which contains an edge $e = \{u, v\}$. By hypothesis, $G$ is connected but $G' = G - e$ is disconnected, with $u$ and $v$ belonging to different components of $G'$ (Problem 5.32). This contradicts the fact that $u$ and $v$ are connected by the path $P = C - e$ which lies in $G'$. Hence $G$ is cycle-free. Now let $x$ and $y$ be vertices of $G$ and let $H$ be the graph obtained by adjoining the edge $e = \{x, y\}$ to $G$. Since $G$ is connected, there is a path $P$ from $x$ to $y$ in $G$; hence $C = Pe$ forms a cycle in $H$. Suppose $H$

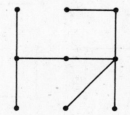

**Fig. 6-63**

contains another cycle $C'$. Since $G$ is cycle-free, $C'$ must contain the edge $e$, say $C' = P'e$. Then $P$ and $P'$ are two paths in $G$ from $x$ to $y$. (See Fig. 6-63.) Accordingly (Problem 6.89), $G$ contains a cycle, which contradicts the fact that $G$ is cycle-free. Hence $H$ contains only one cycle.

(iv) *implies* (i). Since adding any edge $e = \{x, y\}$ to $G$ produces a cycle, the vertices $x$ and $y$ must already be connected in $G$. Hence $G$ is connected and by hypothesis $G$ is cycle-free; that is, $G$ is a tree.

**6.91**    Prove Theorem 6.9.

▮ The proof is by induction on the number $n$ of vertices of $G$. Suppose $n = 1$, i.e., $G$ has only one vertex. Then $G$ has $0 = 1 - 1$ edges and so $G$ is connected and cycle-free. Thus the theorem holds for $n = 1$.

Suppose $n > 1$, i.e., $G$ has more than one vertex. We show that (i), (ii), and (iii) are equivalent for $G$ where we assume they are equivalent for all graphs with less than $n$ vertices.

(i) *implies* (ii). Suppose $G$ is a tree. Then $G$ is cycle-free, so we only need to show that $G$ has $n - 1$ edges. By Problem 5.137, $G$ has a vertex of degree 1. Deleting this vertex and its edge, we obtain a tree $T$ which has $n - 1$ vertices. The theorem holds for $T$, so $T$ has $n - 2$ edges. Hence $G$ has $n - 1$ edges.

(ii) *implies* (iii). Suppose $G$ is cycle-free and has $n - 1$ edges. We only need show that $G$ is connected. Suppose $G$ is disconnected and has $k$ components, $T_1, \ldots, T_k$, which are trees since each is connected and cycle-free. Say $T_i$ has $n_i$ vertices. Note $n_i < n$. Hence the theorem holds for $T_i$, so $T_i$ has $n_i - 1$ edges. Thus

$$n = n_1 + n_2 + \cdots + n_k$$

and

$$n - 1 = (n_1 - 1) + (n_2 - 1) + \cdots + (n_k - 1) = n_1 + n_2 + \cdots + n_k - k = n - k$$

Hence $k = 1$. But this contradicts the assumption that $G$ is disconnected and has $k > 1$ components. Hence $G$ is connected.

(iii) *implies* (i). Suppose $G$ is connected and has $n - 1$ edges. We only need to show that $G$ is cycle-free. Suppose $G$ has a cycle containing an edge $e$. Deleting $e$ we obtain the graph $H = G - e$ which is also connected. But $H$ has $n$ vertices and $n - 2$ edges, and must therefore be unconnected. Thus $G$ is cycle-free and hence it is a tree.

## Spanning Trees

**6.92**    Explain what is meant by a spanning tree.

▮ A subgraph $T$ of a graph $G$ is called a *spanning tree* of $G$ if $T$ is a tree and $T$ includes all the vertices of $G$.

**6.93**    Find two spanning trees for the graph $G$ shown in Fig. 6-64.

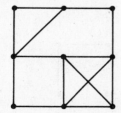

**Fig. 6-64**

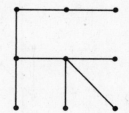

**Fig. 6-65**

▮ A spanning tree of $G$ is a subgraph of $G$ that is a tree and includes all the vertices of $G$. Two possible spanning trees are shown in Fig. 6-65.

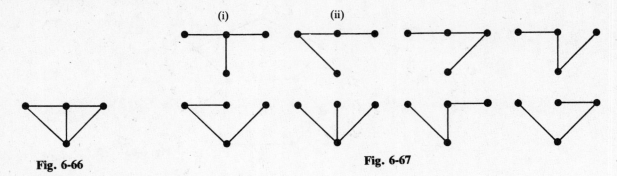

Fig. 6-66                                    Fig. 6-67

**6.94**    Find all spanning trees of the graph *G* shown in Fig. 6-66.

▌ See Fig. 6-67. Note that all are isomorphic to either (i) or (ii).

**6.95**    Find all spanning trees of the graph *H* shown in Fig. 6-68.

▌ See Fig. 6-69. Again all are isomorphic to either (i) or (ii) of Fig. 6-67.

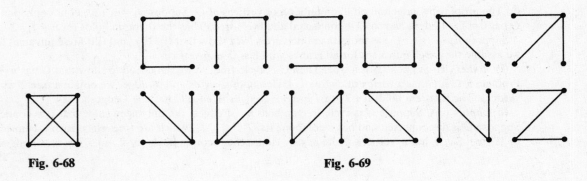

Fig. 6-68                                    Fig. 6-69

**6.96**    Consider a finite connected graph *G*. Must all the spanning trees *T* of *G* have the same number of edges?

▌ Yes. In fact, if *G* has *n* vertices, then any spanning tree *T* of *G* must have $n - 1$ edges.

## Minimal Spanning Trees

**6.97**    Suppose *G* is a graph whose edges are assigned lengths, that is, are labeled with positive numbers. Define a *minimal spanning tree T* of *G*.

▌ Among all spanning trees of *G*, *T* has the smallest length-sum.

**6.98**    The labeled graph *G* in Fig. 6-70 has three spanning trees. (*a*) Find the spanning trees of *G* and their lengths. (*b*) Which is the minimal spanning tree of *G*?

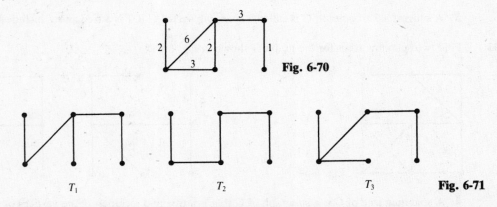

Fig. 6-70

$T_1$                    $T_2$                    $T_3$            **Fig. 6-71**

▌ (*a*)    The three spanning trees are shown in Fig. 6-71. The length of each spanning tree is the sum of the lengths of its edges. Thus the lengths of $T_1$, $T_2$, and $T_3$ are, respectively, 14, 11, and 15.

**(b)**  $T_2$ is the minimal spanning tree since it has the shortest length among the spanning trees.

**6.99**  Give two algorithms to find a minimal spanning tree of a finite connected labeled graph $G$.

▐ **Algorithm 6.1:**  The input is a graph $G$ with $m$ vertices.
*Step 1.*  Order the edges of $G$ by decreasing lengths.
*Step 2.*  Proceeding sequentially, delete each edge which does not disconnect the graph until $m - 1$ edges remain.
*Step 3.*  Output the remaining edges (as they form a minimal spanning tree $T$ of $G$).

**Algorithm 6.2:**  The input is a graph $G$ with $m$ vertices.
*Step 1.*  Order the edges of $G$ by increasing lengths.
*Step 2.*  Proceeding sequentially, add one edge at a time to the $m$ vertices of $G$ such that no cycle is formed until $m - 1$ edges are added.
*Step 3.*  Output the $m - 1$ edges that were added (as they form a minimal spanning tree $T$ of $G$).

**6.100**  Apply Algorithm 6.1 of Problem 6.99 to the labeled connected graph $Q$ in Fig. 6-72($a$) to find a minimal spanning tree of $Q$.

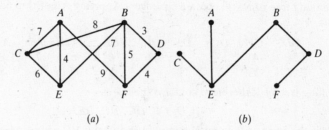

| | |
|---|---|
| ($a$) | ($b$) |

**Fig. 6-72**

▐ Graph $Q$ has six vertices; hence any spanning tree of $Q$ will have five edges. By Algorithm 6.1, the edges are ordered by decreasing lengths and are successively deleted (without disconnecting $Q$) until five edges remain. This yields the following data:

| Edges | AF | BC | AC | BE | CE | BF | AE | DF | BD |
|---|---|---|---|---|---|---|---|---|---|
| Length | 9 | 8 | 7 | 7 | 6 | 5 | 4 | 4 | 3 |
| Delete? | Y | Y | Y | N | N | Y | | | |

Thus the minimal spanning tree of $Q$ contains the edges

$$\{BE, CE, AE, DF, BD\}$$

This spanning tree has length 24 and it is shown in Fig. 6-72($b$).

**6.101**  Apply Algorithm 6.2 of Problem 6.99 to the graph $Q$ in Fig. 6-72($a$).

▐ Again, any spanning tree of $Q$ will have five edges. By Algorithm 6.2, the edges are ordered by increasing lengths and are successively added (without forming any cycles) until five edges are included. This yields the following data:

| Edges | BD | AE | DF | BF | CE | AC | BE | BC | AF |
|---|---|---|---|---|---|---|---|---|---|
| Length | 3 | 4 | 4 | 5 | 6 | 7 | 7 | 8 | 9 |
| Add? | Y | Y | Y | N | Y | N | Y | | |

The minimal spanning tree of $Q$ therefore contains the edges

$$\{BD, AE, DF, CE, BE\}$$

This spanning tree is the same as the one obtained in Problem 6.100 where Algorithm 6.1 was used.

**6.102**  Apply Algorithm 6.1 to the labeled connected graph $R$ in Fig. 6-73($a$) to find a minimal spanning tree of $R$.

▐ Graph $R$ has seven vertices; hence any spanning tree of $R$ will have six edges. Applying Algorithm 6.1 (as in Problem 6.100) yields the following data:

| Edges | AC | EG | AB | BD | DE | BC | BE | FG | DF | CD | CF | DG |
|---|---|---|---|---|---|---|---|---|---|---|---|---|
| Length | 9 | 9 | 8 | 8 | 7 | 6 | 6 | 6 | 5 | 4 | 4 | 4 |
| Delete? | Y | Y | N | Y | Y | N | N | Y | Y | | | |

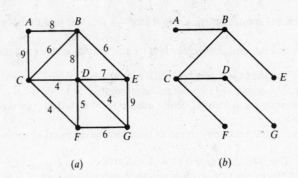

(a)                    (b)              Fig. 6-73

The minimal spanning tree of R therefore contains the edges

$$\{AB, BC, BE, CD, CF, DG\}$$

This spanning tree has length 32 and it is shown in Fig. 6-73(b).

**6.103** Apply Algorithm 6.2 to the graph R in Fig. 6-73(a).

❚ Again, any spanning tree of R will contain six edges. Applying Algorithm 6.2 (as in Problem 6.101) yields the following data:

| Edges | CD | CF | DG | DF | BC | BE | FG | DE | AB | BD | AC | EG |
|-------|----|----|----|----|----|----|----|----|----|----|----|----|
| Length | 4 | 4 | 4 | 5 | 6 | 6 | 6 | 7 | 8 | 8 | 9 | 9 |
| Add? | Y | Y | Y | N | Y | Y | N | N | Y | N | | |

The minimal spanning tree of R therefore contains the edges

$$\{CD, CF, DG, BC, BE, AB\}$$

This spanning tree is the same as the one obtained in Problem 6.102 where Algorithm 6.1 was used.

**6.104** Find two distinct minimal spanning trees of the labeled graph G in Fig. 6-74(a). (Thus minimal spanning trees need not be unique.)

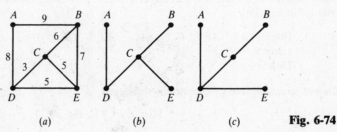

(a)              (b)              (c)              Fig. 6-74

❚ Applying Algorithm 6.1, we first delete edges AB and BE. Then we have the choice of deleting either edge CE or DE which have the same length. Deleting one or the other produces the two minimal spanning trees shown in Figs. 6-74(b) and (c).

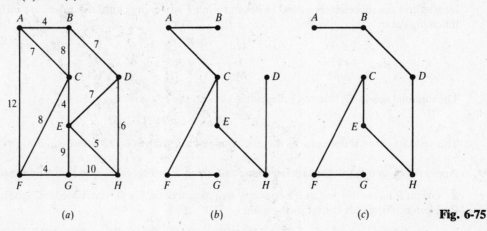

(a)                      (b)                      (c)              Fig. 6-75

**6.105** Find two distinct minimal spanning trees of the labeled graph in Fig. 6-75(a) using Algorithm 6.2.

Proceeding as outlined in Problem 6.100 yields the following data:

| Edges | AB | CE | FG | EH | DH | AC | BD | DE | BC | CF | EG | GH | AF |
|---|---|---|---|---|---|---|---|---|---|---|---|---|---|
| Length | 4 | 4 | 4 | 5 | 6 | 7 | 7 | 7 | 8 | 8 | 9 | 10 | 12 |
| Add? | Y | Y | Y | Y | Y | Y | N | N | N | Y | | | |

This produces the spanning tree shown in Fig. 6-75(b) with edges

$$\{AB, CE, FG, EH, DH, AC, CF\}$$

Note that either edge AC or BD could have been added since both have length 7 and neither would have produced a cycle. Thus a second minimal spanning tree, shown in Fig. 6-75(c), has edges

$$\{AB, CE, FG, EH, DH, BD, CF\}$$

# CHAPTER 7
# Directed Graphs and Binary Trees

## 7.1 DIRECTED GRAPHS

This chapter examines a particular type of graph called a *directed graph*. Rooted and binary trees, which may be viewed as special types of directed graphs, will also be discussed.

**7.1**  Define a directed graph.

▌ A *directed graph*, or *digraph*, $G$ consists of:
  (i)  a set $V = V(G)$ whose elements are called *vertices*, *points*, or *nodes*.
  (ii)  a collection $E = E(G)$ of ordered pairs of vertices called *arcs* or *directed edges* or, simply, *edges*.
We write $G(V, E)$ when we want to emphasize the two parts of $G$. The digraph $G$ is said to be *finite* if the set $V$ of vertices and the set $E$ of arcs are finite.

**7.2**  Describe the diagram of a digraph $G = G(V, E)$, and give an example.

▌ Each vertex $v$ in $V$ is represented by a dot (or small circle) and each arc (directed edge) $e = [u, v]$ is represented by an arrow, i.e., a directed curve, from its *initial point u* to its *terminal point v*. For example, Fig. 7-1 represents the digraph $G(V, E)$ where $V = \{A, B, C, D\}$ and $E$ consists of the eight arcs (directed edges)

$$e_1 = [A, D], \quad e_2 = [B, A], \quad e_3 = [B, A], \quad e_4 = [D, B], \quad e_5 = [B, C],$$
$$e_6 = [D, C], \quad e_7 = [B, B], \quad e_8 = [C, D]$$

We will usually denote a digraph, when possible, by drawing its diagram rather than explicitly listing its vertices and edges.

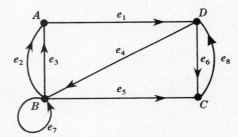

**Fig. 7-1**

**7.3**  Explain the terms loop and parallel arcs, with examples.

▌ A *loop* is an arc with the initial point the same as the terminal point, i.e., an arc which begins and terminates at the same point. Arcs with the same initial point and with the same terminal point are said to be *parallel*. For example, in Fig. 7-1, $e_7 = [B, B]$ is a loop and $e_2 = [B, A]$ and $e_3 = [B, A]$ are parallel arcs. (Although $e_6 = [D, C]$ and $e_8 = [C, D]$ have the same vertices, they are not parallel since they have different initial and terminal points.)

**7.4**  Describe formally the graph $G$ shown in Fig. 7-2.

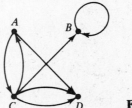

**Fig. 7-2**

▌ Figure 7-2 shows a digraph $G(V, E)$ where $V = \{A, B, C, D\}$ and $E$ consists of the seven directed edges

$$[A, C], [A, D], [B, B], [C, A], [C, B], [C, D], [C, D]$$

**7.5** Identify any loops or parallel arcs in the digraph of Problem 7.4.

▌ The arc $[B, B]$ is a loop, and the two arcs from $C$ to $D$ are parallel.

**7.6** Describe formally each of the digraphs $G$ shown in Fig. 7-3.

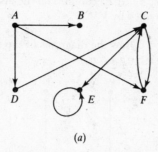
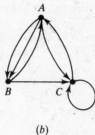

(a)          (b)          **Fig. 7-3**

▌ A formal description of $G$ is the list $V(G)$ of its vertices and the list $E(G)$ of its arcs. Thus in Fig. 7-3(a),

$$V(G) = \{A, B, C, D, E, F\}$$

$$E(G) = \{[A, B], [A, D], [A, F], [C, E], [C, F], [D, C], [E, E], [F, C]\}$$

In Fig. 7-3(b)

$$V(G) = \{A, B, C\}$$

$$E(G) = \{[A, B], [A, B], [A, C], [B, A], [B, C], [C, A], [C, C]\}$$

**7.7** Identify any loops or parallel arcs in the digraph in Fig. 7-3(a).

▌ The arc $[E, E]$ is a loop. The digraph has no parallel arcs.

**7.8** Identify any loops or parallel arcs in the digraph in Fig. 7-3(b).

▌ There is a loop $[C, C]$ and two parallel arcs from $A$ to $B$.

**7.9** Draw a diagram of each of the following directed graphs $G$ where $V(G) = \{A, B, C, D, E\}$ and

**(a)** $E(G) = \{[A, B], [A, C], [B, C], [B, D], [C, C], [D, B]\}$

**(b)** $E(G) = \{[A, D], [B, C], [C, E], [D, B], [D, D], [D, E], [E, A]\}$

▌ First draw the vertices and then connect them with arrows to represent the given arcs. The solutions are shown in Fig. 7-4. The vertex $E$ in Fig. 7-4(a) is *isolated* since no edge begins or ends at $E$.

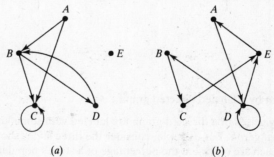

(a)          (b)          **Fig. 7-4**

**7.10** Identify any loops or parallel arcs in a digraph $G$ where

$$V(G) = \{a, b, c, d, e, f, g\}$$

$$E(G) = \{[a, a], [b, e], [a, e], [e, b], [g, c], [a, e], [d, f], [d, b], [g, g]\}$$

▌ By definition (Problem 7.3), any arc where the initial point is also the terminal point is a loop. Thus $[a, a]$ and $[g, g]$ are loops. Any two or more arcs where the corresponding initial terminal points are the same are parallel arcs. Thus $[a, e]$ and $[a, e]$ are parallel arcs.

## Subgraphs

**7.11**    Explain what is meant by a subgraph of a digraph $G(V, E)$.

▮ Let $V'$ be a subset of $V$ and let $E'$ be a subset of $E$ whose endpoints belong to $V'$. Then $H(V', E')$ is a directed graph and is called a *subgraph* of $G(V, E)$. If $E'$ contains *all* the arcs of $E$ whose endpoints belong to $V'$, then $H(V', E')$ is called the subgraph *generated* by $V'$.

**7.12**    Consider the digraph $G(V, E)$ shown in Fig. 7-5. Draw the diagrams of the subgraphs generated by
(**a**)    $V' = \{v_1, v_4, v_5, v_8\}$,    (**b**)    $V' = \{v_1, v_2, v_3, v_7, v_8\}$

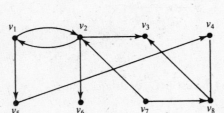  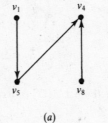  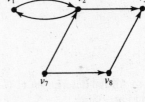

Fig. 7-5    (a)    (b)    Fig. 7-6

▮ The subgraph generated by $V'$ consists of $V'$ and all the arcs in $E$ whose endpoints lie in $V'$. Hence, the subgraphs are shown in Figs. 7-6(a) and (b) respectively.

**7.13**    Consider the digraph $G(V, E)$ where

$$V = \{v_1, v_2, v_3, v_4, v_5, v_6\}$$

$$E = \{[v_1, v_3], [v_2, v_1], [v_2, v_3], [v_2, v_4], [v_3, v_2], [v_3, v_4],$$

$$[v_3, v_5], [v_4, v_6], [v_5, v_5], [v_5, v_4], [v_6, v_2]\}$$

Draw the diagrams of the subgraphs of $G$ generated by
(**a**)    $V' = \{v_1, v_2, v_3, v_4\}$,    (**b**)    $V' = \{v_2, v_3, v_4, v_5\}$

▮ The subgraphs generated by these sets of vertices are shown in Fig. 7-7.

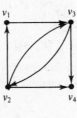  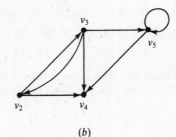

(a)    (b)    Fig. 7-7

## Labeled Directed Graphs

**7.14**    Describe what is meant by a labeled directed graph.

▮ If the arcs and/or vertices of a directed graph are labeled with some kind of data, then the directed graph is called a *labeled directed graph*. For example, consider the three states shown in the digraph in Fig. 7-8. The numbers assigned to each arc represent the percentage of a state's population that emigrates from the initial state to the terminal state each year. Thus, 10% of the New York population moves to California each year while 14% of the California population moves to New York.

**7.15**    Consider the labeled graph in Fig. 7-8. (**a**) What percent of the population of Michigan moves to New York each year? (**b**) What percent of the population of California moves to either New York or Michigan each year? (**c**) To which state does 10% of the population of New York move each year?

▮ Using the information contained in the labeled graph, we have
(**a**)    8% of the population of Michigan moves to New York each year.

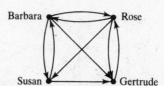

Fig. 7-8

Fig. 7-9

**(b)** Since 14% of the population of California moves to New York and 5% moves to Michigan, a total of 19% moves to either of these states each year.

**(c)** 10% of the population of New York moves to California each year.

**7.16** Draw a labeled digraph that represents the following situation. Three sisters, Barbara, Rose, and Susan, each regularly telephone their mother Gertrude, though Gertrude calls only Rose. Susan will not call Rose, though Rose continues to call Susan. Barbara and Susan will call each other, as will Barbara and Rose.

▌ The labeled digraph will have four vertices, each representing the three sisters and their mother. The arcs will represent the lines of communication. The resulting labeled digraph representing this situation is shown in Fig. 7-9.

**7.17** The map in Fig. 7-10(a) shows the location of three art galleries, A, B, and C, in a neighborhood with only one-way streets. Draw a labeled digraph that indicates the least number of blocks you must drive to get from one gallery to another.

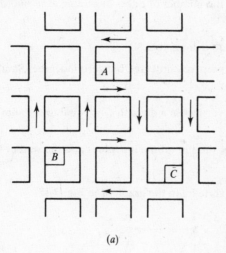

(a)

(b)

**Fig. 7-10**

▌ The labeled digraph will have three vertices representing the three galleries and the arcs will be labeled to reflect the distance, in number of blocks, between each gallery. The resulting digraph is shown in Fig. 7-10(b).

**7.18** Consider the three galleries in Problem 7.17. Beginning at any one gallery, say gallery A, there are only two possible circuits that would include all three galleries and return you to where you started: A to B to C to A, or A to C to B to A. Which circuit is the shortest?

▌ Referring to the labeled digraph in Fig. 7-10(b), add the numbers of blocks in each circuit. Thus the shortest circuit is A to C to B to A. Specifically, this circuit consists of only 10 blocks whereas the other circuit requires 14 blocks.

**7.19** Suppose Friendly Airways has nine daily flights with their corresponding flight numbers as follows:

| 103 | Atlanta to Houston | 203 | Boston to Denver | 305 | Chicago to Miami |
| 106 | Houston to Atlanta | 204 | Denver to Boston | 308 | Miami to Boston |
| 201 | Boston to Chicago | 301 | Denver to Reno | 401 | Reno to Chicago |

Describe the data by means of a labeled directed graph.

▌ The data are described by the graph in Fig. 7-11 (where the flight numbers have been omitted for notational convenience).

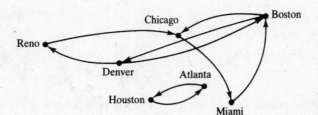

**Fig. 7-11**

**7.20** Consider the flight information in Problem 7.19. Identify other data that might also be assigned to the (*a*) edges and (*b*) vertices.

▌ (*a*) The flights (edges) usually contain the price, time, type of aircraft, etc.
(*b*) The cities (vertices) may contain the name of their airport, hotels at the airport, etc.

## 7.2 BASIC DEFINITIONS: DEGREES, PATHS, CONNECTIVITY

Let $G$ be a directed graph. A directed edge $e = [u, v]$ is said to *begin* at its initial point $u$ and *end* at its terminal point $v$, and $u$ and $v$ are said to be *adjacent*.

**7.21** Define the outdegree and indegree of a vertex $v$.

▌ The *outdegree of $v$*, written outdeg $(v)$, is the number of edges beginning at $v$, and the *indegree* of $v$, written indeg $(v)$, is the number of edges ending at $v$.

**7.22** Explain what is meant by a source and a sink in a digraph $G$.

▌ A vertex $v$ in $G$ is called a *source* if it has positive outdegree but zero indegree. Similarly, $v$ is called a *sink* if $v$ has positive indegree but zero outdegree.

**7.23** Show that the sum of all the indegrees of the vertices in a digraph $G$ is equal to the sum of all the outdegrees and are equal to the number $n$ of arcs in $G$.

▌ Since each arc begins and ends at a vertex, the sum of the indegrees and the sum of the outdegrees must equal $n$, the number of arcs in $G$.

**7.24** Find the indegree and the outdegree of each vertex $v$ in the graph $M$ in Fig. 7-12.

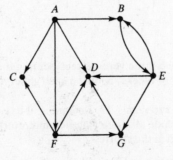

**Fig. 7-12**

▌ Count the number of arcs ending at $v$ to obtain indeg $(v)$ and count the number of arcs beginning at $v$ to obtain outdeg $(v)$. This yields the following data:

| Vertex | A | B | C | D | E | F | G |
|--------|---|---|---|---|---|---|---|
| Indegree | 0 | 2 | 2 | 4 | 1 | 1 | 2 |
| Outdegree | 4 | 1 | 0 | 0 | 3 | 3 | 1 |

Note that the sum of the indegrees and the sum of the outdegrees equal 12, the number of arcs.

**7.25** Refer to the graph $M$ of Fig. 7-12. Identify any sources or sinks.

**❙** The vertex $A$ is a source since edges begin at $A$ but do not end at $A$. Analogously, $C$ and $D$ are sinks since arcs end at $C$ and at $D$ but do not begin there.

**7.26** Find the indegree and the outdegree of each vertex $v$ in the graph $N$ in Fig. 7-13.

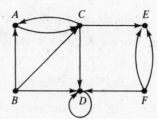

**Fig. 7-13**

**❙** Count the number of arcs ending at $v$ to obtain indeg $(v)$ and count the number of arcs beginning at $v$ to obtain outdeg $(v)$. This yields the following data:

| Vertex | A | B | C | D | E | F |
|---|---|---|---|---|---|---|
| Indegree | 2 | 0 | 2 | 4 | 3 | 0 |
| Outdegree | 1 | 3 | 3 | 1 | 0 | 3 |

Note that the sum of the indegrees and the sum of the outdegrees equal 11, the number of arcs.

**7.27** Refer to the graph $N$ of Problem 7.26. Identify any sources or sinks.

**❙** The vertex $B$ and $F$ are sources since arcs begin at $B$ and $F$ but do not end there. Analogously, $E$ is a sink since arcs end at $E$ but do not begin there.

## Paths and Cycles

**7.28** The concept of a path carries over from undirected graphs (Section 5.3) except that the directions of the arcs must now agree with the direction of the path or cycle. Rewrite the definition of a path in light of this difference.

**❙** A *path* $W$ in a directed graph $G$ is an alternating sequence of vertices and directed edges of the form

$$W = (v_0, e_1, v_1, e_2, v_2, \ldots, e_n, v_n)$$

such that each edge $e_i$ begins at $v_{i-1}$ and ends at $v_i$. If there is no ambiguity, we denote $W$ by its sequence of vertices or its sequence of arcs. Note that a path in a directed graph can also be closed, in which case the first and last vertices in the sequence will be the same.

**7.29** Give the definitions for a simple path and a cycle in a directed graph.

**❙** A *simple path* in a directed graph $G$ is a path in $G$ where every vertex is distinct. A *cycle* in a directed graph is a path in $G$ where all the vertices are distinct except the first and last. Note that the paths must satisfy the necessary condition on the direction of the arcs.

**7.30** Consider the graph $G$ in Fig. 7-14. Find two paths from $v_1$ to $v_6$.

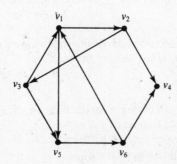

**Fig. 7-14**

▌ There are many paths from $v_1$ to $v_6$. Two such paths are

$$(v_1, v_5, v_6) \quad \text{and} \quad (v_1, v_2, v_3, v_1, v_5, v_6)$$

Note that the sequence of vertices $v_1$, $v_2$, $v_4$, $v_6$ is not a path from $v_1$ to $v_6$ since the arc joining $v_4$ to $v_6$ does not begin at $v_4$, i.e., the arc does not point in the same direction as the path.

**7.31**  Find two simple paths from $v_1$ to $v_6$ in the graph $G$ of Problem 7.30.

▌ A simple path is a path where all vertices are distinct. There are only two simple paths from $v_1$ to $v_6$ in Fig. 7-14:

$$(v_1, v_5, v_6) \quad \text{and} \quad (v_1, v_2, v_3, v_5, v_6)$$

**7.32**  Find a cycle in the graph $G$ of Problem 7.30 that includes vertex $v_3$.

▌ There are two cycles in $G$ that contain the vertex $v_3$:

$$(v_3, v_1, v_2, v_3) \quad \text{and} \quad (v_3, v_5, v_6, v_1, v_2, v_3)$$

Note that the sequences of vertices $v_3$, $v_1$, $v_5$, $v_3$ is not a path (and hence not a cycle) in $G$ since the arc joining $v_5$ to $v_3$ does not begin at $v_5$ and end at $v_3$.

**7.33**  Consider the graph $G$ in Fig. 7-15. Find: **(a)** two simple paths from $v_1$ to $v_4$; **(b)** a nonsimple path from $v_1$ to $v_4$; and **(c)** some cycles that include $v_4$.

▌ **(a)** Two simple paths from $v_1$ to $v_4$ are

$$(v_1, v_6, v_7, v_4) \quad \text{and} \quad (v_1, v_6, v_7, v_2, v_5, v_3, v_4)$$

**(b)** A nonsimple path must repeat at least one vertex. Thus a nonsimple path from $v_1$ to $v_4$ is

$$(v_1, v_6, v_7, v_2, v_6, v_7, v_4)$$

**(c)** Two such cycles are $(v_4, v_8, v_7, v_4)$ and $(v_4, v_8, v_7, v_2, v_5, v_3, v_4)$.

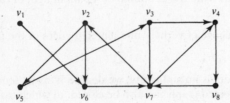 Fig. 7-15

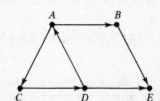 Fig. 7-16

**7.34**  Let $G$ be a directed graph. **(a)** Define a spanning path of $G$. **(b)** Explain what is meant by the statement that a vertex $v$ is reachable from a vertex $u$.

▌ **(a)** A *spanning* path of $G$ is a path which contains all the vertices of $G$. Not every diagram has a spanning path.

**(b)** The vertex $v$ is *reachable* from $u$ if there is a path from $u$ to $v$.

**7.35**  Find the shortest spanning path of the graph $M$ shown in Fig. 7-16.

▌ Any spanning path must end in the sink $E$. Working backwards, we find that $(C, D, A, B, E)$ is a *simple*, hence shortest, spanning path.

**7.36**  Consider graph $M$ of Problem 7.35. For each of the following pairs of vertices, determine whether the second vertex is reachable from the first. If so, identify the path.
**(a)** $A$ and $E$,      **(b)** $E$ and $A$,
**(c)** $C$ and $B$,      **(d)** $B$ and $D$

▌ **(a)** Vertex $E$ is reachable from vertex $A$ by the path $(A, B, E)$.
**(b)** Vertex $A$ is not reachable from vertex $E$.
**(c)** Vertex $B$ is reachable from vertex $C$ by the path $(C, D, A, B)$.
**(d)** Vertex $D$ is not reachable from vertex $B$.

## Connectivity

**7.37**    Define strongly connected and unilaterally connected for a directed graph $G$.

▌ A digraph $G$ is said to be *strongly connected* if, for any vertices $u$ and $v$ of $G$, $u$ is reachable from $v$ *and* $v$ is reachable from $u$, i.e., there is a path from $u$ to $v$ and a path from $v$ to $u$. If there is a path from $u$ to $v$ *or* from $v$ to $u$ (but not necessarily both), we say $D$ is *unilaterally connected*. Obviously, strongly connected implies unilaterally connected.

**7.38**    Identify whether or not each graph in Fig. 7-17 is strongly connected.

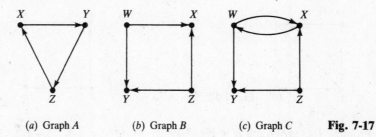

(*a*) Graph *A*          (*b*) Graph *B*          (*c*) Graph *C*          **Fig. 7-17**

▌ From Problem 7.37 we have
(***a***)    *A* is strongly connected.
(***b***)    *B* is not strongly connected since, for instance, there is no path from *X* to *W*.
(***c***)    *C* is not strongly connected since, for instance, there is no path from *X* to *Z*.

**7.39**    Identify whether or not each graph in Fig. 7-17 is unilaterally connected.

▌ From Problem 7.37 we have
(***a***)    *A* is strongly connected and so it is also unilaterally connected.
(***b***)    *B* is not unilaterally connected since there is no path from *W* to *Z* or from *Z* to *W*.
(***c***)    Although *C* is not strongly connected, it is still unilaterally connected.

**Theorem 7.1:**    Let $G$ be a finite directed graph. Then
(i)    $G$ is strongly connected if and only if $G$ has a closed spanning path.
(ii)    $G$ is unilaterally connected if and only if $G$ has a spanning path.

**7.40**    Prove Theorem 7.1(i).

▌ Suppose $G$ is strongly connected. Let $P = (u, v, \ldots, u)$ be a closed path which includes a maximum number of vertices in $G$. (Such a path $P$ exists since $G$ is finite.) Suppose $P$ is not a spanning path, say $P$ does not include vertex $w$. Since $G$ is strongly connected, there are paths $Q = (w, \ldots, u)$ and $Q' = (u, \ldots, w)$. Hence the path $QPQ'$ is a closed path including the vertices of $P$ and also $w$. This contradicts the maximality of $P$. Thus $P$ is a closed spanning path.

Conversely, suppose $G$ contains a closed spanning path $P$. Then every vertex of $G$ can be reached by any other vertex of $G$ along the path $P$. Thus $G$ is strongly connected.

**7.41**    Verify Theorem 7.1 for the graphs in Fig. 7-17.

▌ (***a***)    *A* is strongly connected. Note $(X, Y, Z, X)$ is a closed spanning path for *A*.
(***b***)    As found in Problems 7.38 and 7.39, *B* is neither strongly nor unilaterally connected. Hence *B* must not have a spanning path. Indeed, a spanning path would have to end in the sink *X* and in the sink *Y*, which is impossible.
(***c***)    As found in Problems 7.38 and 7.39, *C* is unilaterally connected but not strongly connected. Hence *C* must have a spanning path but not a closed spanning path. One spanning path is $(Z, X, W, Y)$.
   To see that no closed spanning paths are possible, note that every vertex in a closed path must have arcs both entering and leaving that vertex. Since vertex *Y* is a sink, no closed path can include *Y* and thus no closed spanning path is possible.

**Theorem 7.2:**    Suppose a finite directed graph $G$ contains no (directed) cycles. Then $G$ contains a source and a sink.

**7.42**    Prove Theorem 7.2.

▌ Let $P = (v_0, v_1, \ldots, v_n)$ be a simple path of maximum length. (Such a path exists since $G$ is finite.) Then the last vertex $v_n$ must be a sink; otherwise an arc $[v_n, u]$ will either extend $P$ or form a cycle if $u = v_i$ for some $i$. Similarly, the first vertex must be a source.

**7.43**    Graph $G$ in Fig. 7-18 contains no directed cycles. Find a simple path of maximum length and verify that the first vertex is a source and the last vertex is a sink.

▌ A simple path of maximum length is $(W, X, Y, Z)$. Note that vertex $W$ is a source and vertex $Z$ is a sink.

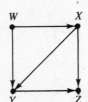

Fig. 7-18

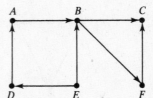

**Fig. 7-19**

**7.44**    Repeat Problem 7.43 for Graph $H$ in Fig. 7-19.

▌ A simple path of maximum length is $(E, D, A, B, F, C)$. Note that vertex $E$ is a source and vertex $C$ is a sink.

## 7.3    DIGRAPHS, RELATIONS, AND MATRICES

**7.45**    Describe how digraphs without parallel arcs and relations on a set are, in fact, identical concepts.

▌ Let $G(V, E)$ be a directed graph without parallel arcs. Then $E$ is simply a subset of $V \times V$ and hence $E$ is a relation on $V$. Conversely, if $R$ is a relation on a set $V$, then $G(V, R)$ is a directed graph without parallel arcs. Thus digraphs without parallel arcs and relations on a set are one and the same concept. (Recall that in Chapter 2 we discussed directed graphs corresponding to relations on a set.)

**7.46**    Describe how digraphs can be represented by a square matrices.

▌ Let $G$ be a directed graph with vertices $v_1, v_2, v_3, \ldots, v_m$. The matrix of $G$ is the $m \times m$ matrix $M_G = (m_{ij})$ where

$$m_{ij} = \text{number of arcs beginning at } v_i \text{ and ending at } v_j$$

If $D$ has no parallel arcs, then the entries of $M_G$ will be either zeros or ones; otherwise the entries will be nonnegative integers. Conversely, every $m \times m$ matrix $M$ with nonnegative integer entries uniquely defines a digraph with $m$ vertices. Figure 7-20 shows a digraph $G$ and its matrix $M$.

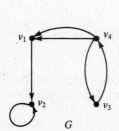

$$M = \begin{pmatrix} 0 & 1 & 0 & 0 \\ 0 & 1 & 0 & 0 \\ 0 & 0 & 0 & 1 \\ 2 & 0 & 1 & 0 \end{pmatrix}$$

$G$

**Fig. 7-20**

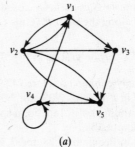

$(a)$                    $(b)$

**Fig. 7-21**

**7.47**    Find the matrix $M$ for each of the digraphs in Fig. 7-21.

▌ The matrix $M$ for a digraph with $m$ vertices is the $m \times m$ square matrix where $m_{ij}$ is equal to the number of arcs beginning at $v_i$ and ending at $v_j$; hence

$$\text{Fig. 7-21}(a): \quad M = \begin{pmatrix} 0 & 1 & 1 & 0 & 0 \\ 1 & 0 & 1 & 0 & 2 \\ 0 & 0 & 0 & 0 & 1 \\ 1 & 0 & 0 & 1 & 0 \\ 0 & 0 & 0 & 1 & 0 \end{pmatrix}, \qquad \text{Fig. 7-21}(b): \quad M = \begin{pmatrix} 1 & 1 & 2 & 0 \\ 0 & 0 & 0 & 0 \\ 0 & 1 & 0 & 2 \\ 0 & 1 & 0 & 1 \end{pmatrix}$$

**7.48**    Find the matrix $M$ for each of the digraphs in Fig. 7-22.

▌ Constructing the matrix $M$ as outlined in Problem 7.46 yields the following matrices:

$$\text{Fig. 7-22}(a): \quad M = \begin{pmatrix} 0 & 0 & 2 & 1 & 1 \\ 1 & 0 & 0 & 1 & 0 \\ 0 & 1 & 0 & 0 & 0 \\ 0 & 0 & 0 & 1 & 1 \\ 0 & 0 & 1 & 0 & 0 \end{pmatrix}, \qquad \text{Fig. 7-22}(b): \quad M = \begin{pmatrix} 0 & 1 & 2 & 0 \\ 1 & 0 & 0 & 0 \\ 0 & 0 & 2 & 1 \\ 0 & 1 & 0 & 0 \end{pmatrix}$$

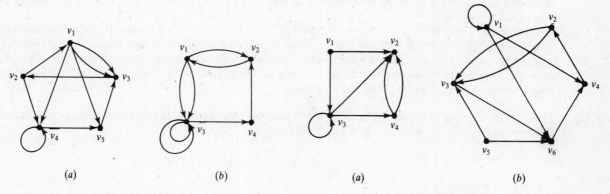

Fig. 7-22          Fig. 7-23

**7.49**    Draw the digraph $G$ corresponding to each of the following matrices:

$$(a) \quad M = \begin{pmatrix} 0 & 1 & 1 & 0 \\ 0 & 0 & 0 & 0 \\ 0 & 1 & 1 & 1 \\ 0 & 2 & 0 & 0 \end{pmatrix}, \qquad (b) \quad M = \begin{pmatrix} 1 & 0 & 0 & 1 & 0 & 1 \\ 0 & 0 & 2 & 0 & 0 & 0 \\ 0 & 0 & 0 & 0 & 0 & 1 \\ 0 & 1 & 0 & 0 & 0 & 0 \\ 0 & 0 & 1 & 0 & 0 & 1 \\ 0 & 0 & 0 & 1 & 0 & 0 \end{pmatrix}$$

▌ Each entry $m_{ij}$ of $M$ corresponds to the number of arcs originating at vertex $v_i$ and terminating at vertex $v_j$. Thus, to draw the digraph, first draw the appropriate number of vertices and then connect them with arcs as indicated by the entries in $M$. The resulting digraphs are shown in Fig. 7-23.

**7.50**    Repeat Problem 7.49 for each of the following matrices:

$$(a) \quad M = \begin{pmatrix} 0 & 1 & 0 & 1 & 0 \\ 0 & 0 & 1 & 0 & 1 \\ 0 & 0 & 1 & 1 & 0 \\ 0 & 0 & 0 & 0 & 0 \\ 0 & 1 & 1 & 0 & 0 \end{pmatrix}, \qquad (b) \quad M = \begin{pmatrix} 0 & 1 & 0 & 1 & 0 \\ 0 & 0 & 2 & 0 & 0 \\ 0 & 0 & 0 & 0 & 0 \\ 1 & 0 & 1 & 0 & 1 \\ 0 & 0 & 1 & 1 & 0 \end{pmatrix}$$

▌ Proceeding as in Problem 7.49, we obtain the digraphs shown in Fig. 7-24.

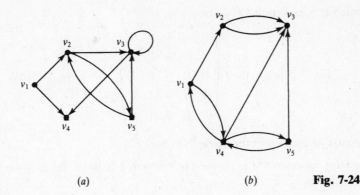

(a)                          (b)                    **Fig. 7-24**

**Theorem 7.3:**  Let $M$ be the matrix of a directed graph $G$. Then the $ij$ entry of the matrix $M^n$ gives the number of paths of length $n$ from vertex $v_i$ to vertex $v_j$.

**7.51**  Prove Theorem 7.3.

▌ The proof is by induction on $n$. Note first that a path of length 1 from $v_i$ to $v_j$ is precisely an arc $[v_i, v_j]$. Thus the theorem holds for $n = 1$ since the $ij$ entry of $M$ gives the number of arcs $[v_i, v_j]$ which is the number of paths of length 1 from $v_i$ to $v_j$.

Suppose $n > 1$ and $M^{n-1} = (a_{ik})$, $M = (b_{kj})$, and $M^n = (c_{ij})$ where $c_{ij} = \sum_{k=1}^{n} a_{ik}b_{kj}$. By induction $a_{ik}$ equals the number of paths of length $n - 1$ from $v_i$ to $v_k$. Also, $b_{kj}$ equals the number of arcs from $v_k$ to $v_j$. Thus $a_{ik}b_{kj}$ gives the number of paths of length $n$ from $v_i$ to $v_j$ where $v_k$ is the next-to-last vertex in the path. Thus all paths of length $n$ from $v_i$ to $v_j$ can be obtained by summing up the $a_{ik}b_{kj}$ for all $k$. That is, $c_{ij}$ is the number of paths of length $n$ from $v_i$ to $v_j$. Thus the theorem is proved.

**7.52**  Consider the digraph $G$ shown in Fig. 7-25. Use Theorem 7.3 to determine how many paths of length 3 exist in $G$ and which vertices are connected by a path of length 3.

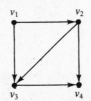

**Fig. 7-25**

▌ First construct the matrix $M$ representing $G$. Then calculate $M^3$. The results of these two steps are

$$M = \begin{pmatrix} 0 & 1 & 1 & 0 \\ 0 & 0 & 1 & 1 \\ 0 & 0 & 0 & 1 \\ 0 & 0 & 0 & 0 \end{pmatrix} \quad \text{and} \quad M^3 = \begin{pmatrix} 0 & 0 & 0 & 1 \\ 0 & 0 & 0 & 0 \\ 0 & 0 & 0 & 0 \\ 0 & 0 & 0 & 0 \end{pmatrix}$$

From this we can conclude that $G$ has only one path of length 3 and this path connects vertex $v_1$ to $v_4$.

**7.53**  Suppose a directed graph $G$ has $m$ vertices. Show that if there is a path $P$ from vertex $u$ to vertex $v$, then there is a (simple) path $P'$ of length $m - 1$ or less from $u$ to $v$.

▌ Suppose $P = (u, Q_1, w, Q_2, w, Q_3, v)$ where some vertex $w$ occurs twice in $P$ and $Q_1$, $Q_2$, and $Q_3$ are subpaths. Then $P_1 = (u, Q_1, w, Q_3, v)$ is also a path from $u$ to $v$ and has length shorter than $P$. Repeating this process we finally obtain a path $P'$ from $u$ to $v$ where no vertex is repeated, i.e., $P'$ is a simple path. Since $G$ has $m$ vertices, $P'$ cannot contain more than $m - 1$ arcs.

**Theorem 7.4:**  Let $M$ be the matrix of a digraph $G$ with $m$ vertices. Let

$$C = M + M^2 + M^3 + \cdots + M^{m-1}$$

Then $G$ is strongly connected if and only if $C$ has no zero entry off the main diagonal.

**7.54**  Prove Theorem 7.4.

■ The $ij$ entry of $C$ is zero if and only if the $ij$ entries of $M, M^2, \ldots, M^{m-1}$ are all zero. This means there is no path from $v_i$ to $v_j$ of length $m-1$ or less and hence (Problem 7.53) there is no path from $v_i$ to $v_j$. Thus $G$ is strongly connected if and only if the $ij$ entries of $C$, for $i \neq j$, are nonzero.

## 7.4  ROOTED TREES

Recall (Section 6.7) that a tree $T$ is a connected graph without cycles and that any pair of vertices in $T$ is connected by a unique simple path.

**7.55**    Define a rooted tree $T$, with an example, and show how such a tree may be viewed as a directed graph.

■ A rooted tree $T$ consists of a tree graph together with a designated vertex $R$ called the *root* of the tree. Figure 7-26 is the diagram of a rooted tree where, as is now common practice, the root $R$ appears on the top of the tree (that is, the tree grows downward). A direction may be imposed on $T$ as follows: An edge $e$ joining vertices $u$ and $v$ is directed from $u$ to $v$ or from $v$ to $u$ according as the unique simple path from $R$ to $v$ does or does not contain $u$.

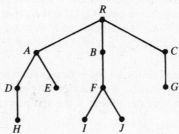

**Fig. 7-26**

**Remark:**    Throughout the rest of this section, the term tree shall mean rooted tree and the term path shall mean simple path, unless otherwise specified or implied.

**7.56**    Define the terms leaves and branches in a rooted tree $T$, and give examples.

■ Those vertices with degree one, other than the root $R$, are called the *leaves* of $T$. A directed (simple) path from any vertex to a leaf is called a *branch*. The tree $T$ in Fig. 7-26 has five leaves, $H, E, I, J,$ and $G$. The paths $(B, F, J)$, $(R, A, E)$, and $(A, D, H)$ are branches.

**7.57**    Let $v$ be a vertex in a rooted tree $T$ with root $R$. Define the level or depth of $v$.

■ Since there is a unique simple path $P$ from the root $R$ to the vertex $v$, we define the *level* or *depth of $v$* to be the length of $P$. Thus, for example, in Fig. 7-26 the level of $F$ is 2 and the level of $H$ is 3.

**7.58**    Consider the rooted tree $T$ in Fig. 7-27. Identify the path from the root $R$ to each of the following vertices: **(a)** $A$, **(b)** $H$, **(c)** $F$, **(d)** $M$.

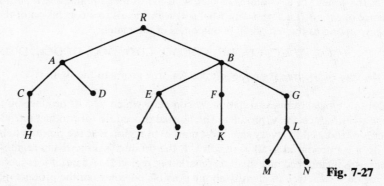

**Fig. 7-27**

■ List the vertices while proceeding from $R$ to the given vertex along the tree.
**(a)**  $R, A$;    **(b)**  $R, A, C, H$;    **(c)**  $R, B, F$;    **(d)**  $R, B, G, L, M$

**7.59**    Consider the rooted tree $T$ of Problem 7.58. Find the level of each of the following vertices: **(a)** $A$, **(b)** $H$, **(c)** $F$, **(d)** $M$.

▮ The level of a vertex in $T$ is the length of the path from the root $R$ to that vertex. Thus (*a*) 1, (*b*) 3, (*c*) 2, (*d*) 4.

**7.60**  Let $T$ be a rooted tree with root $R$. (*a*) Explain what it means for a vertex to precede or follow another vertex in $T$. (*b*) Define the notion of parent, children, and siblings in $T$.

▮ (*a*)  Since $T$ gives a direction to the edges, we say that a vertex $u$ *precedes* a vertex $v$ or that $v$ *follows* $u$ if the path from the root $R$ to $v$ includes $u$. In particular, we say $v$ *immediately follows* $u$ if there is no vertex between $u$ and $v$, i.e., if $v$ is adjacent to $u$.

(*b*)  Let $v$ be a vertex in $T$. Then $v$ is called the *parent* of all the vertices which immediately follow $v$, and such vertices are said to be *sons* or *children* of $v$. Moreover, the children of a given vertex are called *siblings*.

**7.61**  Consider the tree $T$ in Fig. 7-27. Identify: (*a*) all vertices which precede $L$; (*b*) all vertices which follow $A$; (*c*) the children of $B$; (*d*) the siblings of $C$.

▮ (*a*)  The path from the root $R$ to $L$ includes the vertices $R$, $B$, $G$, and $L$. Hence $R$, $B$, and $G$ precede $L$.

(*b*)  All paths from $A$ include the vertices $C$, $D$, and $H$, that is, $C$, $D$, and $H$ follow $A$.

(*c*)  The vertices $E$, $F$, and $G$ are the children of $B$ since they immediately follow $B$.

(*d*)  The parent of $C$ is $A$ and the children of $A$ are $C$ and $D$; hence $D$ is the only sibling of $C$.

**7.62**  A tree is a useful device for enumerating all the logical possibilities of a sequence of events where each event can occur in a finite number of ways. Use a tree to identify all the possible results of a tennis match between two players, Charles and Daphne, where the winner is the first player who wins two sets in a row or the first player who wins a total of three sets.

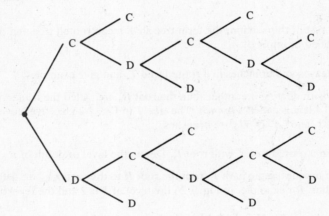

**Fig. 7-28**

▮ The rooted tree in Fig. 7-28 shows all the possible ways in which the match can proceed. Each branch indicates the winner of a set and is labeled with the winner's initial. Each path from the root to a leaf represents a sequence of events (i.e., who won what set) which leads to a conclusion of the match. There are ten leaves which correspond to the ten possible outcomes of the match:

CC, CDCC, CDCDC, CDCDD, CDD, DCC, DCDCC, DCDCD, DCDD, DD

(Here the root of the tree is on the left and the tree grows to the right.)

**7.63**  Consider this typical business situation. A company which sells its products in two major geographic regions is planning to introduce a new product. The normal procedure for product introduction is as follows. First, the product is introduced in a very small test market in region I. If the product fails, it is discontinued; if it succeeds, it is introduced in all of region I. If the product is a success in region I, it is introduced in all of region II; if not, it is introduced in a small test market in region II. Again, if it is successful, it is introduced to the entire region. Use a tree to identify all the possible outcomes of the product introduction procedure.

▮ The possible outcomes are described by the tree in Fig. 7-29. There are four possible outcomes as indicated by the four branches from the root to the leaves of the tree:

(1)  The product is not successful in the first small market test of region I and is discontinued.

(2)  The product is successful in the first small test market, is successful in region I, and is introduced in region II.

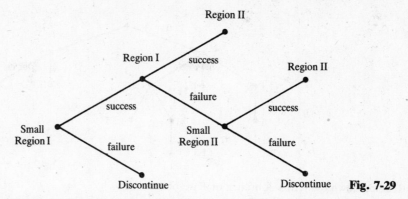

**Fig. 7-29**

(3) The product is successful in the first small test market but is not successful in region I. It is tested in the small test market in region II, is not successful, and is discontinued.

(4) The product is successful in the first small test market but is not successful in region I. It is tested in a small test market in region II, is successful, and is introduced to that region.

(Here, again, the root is on the left of the tree.)

## Ordered Rooted Trees

**7.64**  Define an ordered rooted tree.

▮  A rooted tree $T$ is called an *ordered* tree if the edges leaving each vertex are ordered or, equivalently, if the children of any parent are ordered. Such trees are pictured with the root $R$ at the top and the edges directed downward and the children are ordered from left to right.

**7.65**  Describe the universal address system for the vertices of an ordered rooted tree $T$, and give an example.

▮  The vertices of $T$ are labeled as follows: First assign 0 to the root $R$ and assign 1, 2, 3, . . . to the vertices immediately following $R$ according to the order of these vertices. Then the remaining vertices are labeled as follows: If $a$ is the label of a vertex $v$, then $a.1$, $a.2$, . . . are assigned to the vertices immediately following $v$ according to the order of the vertices. An example of this address system is shown in Fig. 7-30, where the vertices are ordered from left to right.

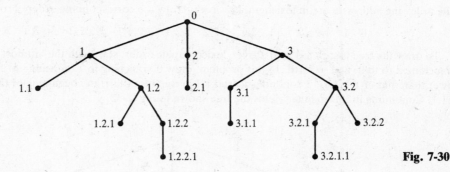

**Fig. 7-30**

**7.66**  Describe a lexicographical order for an ordered rooted tree.

▮  The universal address system provides an important way of linearly describing (or storing) an ordered rooted tree. Specifically, given addresses $a$ and $b$, we let $a < b$ whenever
 (i)  $a$ is an initial segment of $b$, i.e., if $b = a.c$ (e.g., $a = 2.4$ and $b = 2.4.1$) *or*
 (ii)  there exist positive integers $m$ and $n$ with $m < n$ such that

$$a = r.m.s \quad \text{and} \quad b = r.n.t$$

(e.g., $a = 1.4.1$ and $b = 1.5.1$).
This order is called a *lexicographic order* because it is similar to the way words are arranged in a dictionary.

**7.67**  Since an ordered rooted tree is usually drawn so that edges are ordered left to right, it is easy to obtain the lexicographic order; just read down the leftmost branch, then the second branch from the left, and so forth. Use this approach to find the lexicographic order of the addresses of the tree $T$ shown in Fig. 7-31.

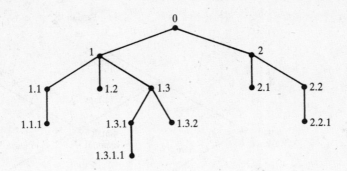

**Fig. 7-31**

▌ Reading down the leftmost branch of $T$ we obtain

$$0 \quad 1 \quad 1.1 \quad 1.1.1$$

The next branch is 1.2, so we add 1.2 to our list and obtain

$$0 \quad 1 \quad 1.1 \quad 1.1.1 \quad 1.2$$

Similarly, the next branch adds

$$1.3 \quad 1.3.1 \quad 1.3.1.1$$

to our list. Proceeding in this manner, we obtain

$$0 \quad 1 \quad 1.1 \quad 1.1.1 \quad 1.2 \quad 1.3 \quad 1.3.1 \quad 1.3.1.1 \quad 1.3.2 \quad 2 \quad 2.1 \quad 2.2 \quad 2.2.1$$

**7.68**   Give the lexicographic ordering of the addresses in Fig. 7-30.

▌ The addresses are linearly ordered as follows:

| | | | |
|---|---|---|---|
| 0 | 1.2.1 | 2.1 | 3.2 |
| 1 | 1.2.2 | 3 | 3.2.1 |
| 1.1 | 1.2.2.1 | 3.1 | 3.2.1.1 |
| 1.2 | 2 | 3.1.1 | 3.2.2 |

**7.69**   The following addresses are in lexicographic order. Draw the corresponding ordered rooted tree.

$$0 \quad 1 \quad 1.1 \quad 2 \quad 2.1 \quad 2.1.1 \quad 2.2 \quad 2.2.1 \quad 2.2.1.1 \quad 2.2.1.2 \quad 3 \quad 3.1 \quad 3.1.1 \quad 3.2$$

▌ To draw the tree associated with a given lexicographic order, start with the leftmost branch, then add the branch next to that, and so forth. In this problem, draw 0 branching to 1 branching to 1.1. Since the level of 2 is lower than that of 1.1, i.e., 2 does not succeed 1.1 in the tree, this is the beginning of the next branch 2, 2.1, 2.1.1. Continuing in this manner yields the tree shown in Fig. 7-32.

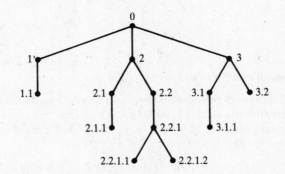

**Fig. 7-32**

**7.70**   Consider the following addresses which are in random order:

$$1 \quad 2.2.1 \quad 3.2 \quad 2.2.1.1 \quad 1.1.1 \quad 0 \quad 2.1 \quad 3.2.1.1$$
$$3 \quad 3.1 \quad 2.2 \quad 2.1.1 \quad 3.2.1 \quad 1.1 \quad 3.2.1.2 \quad 2 \quad 1.1.2$$

(**a**) Place the addresses in lexicographic order. (**b**) Draw the corresponding ordered rooted tree.

**▌** **(a)** The lexicographic order of these addresses is

$$0 \quad 1 \quad 1.1 \quad 1.1.1 \quad 1.1.2 \quad 2 \quad 2.1 \quad 2.1.1 \quad 2.2 \quad 2.2.1$$

$$2.2.1.1 \quad 3 \quad 3.1 \quad 3.2 \quad 3.2.1 \quad 3.2.1.1 \quad 3.2.1.2$$

**(b)** The required ordered rooted tree is shown in Fig. 7-33.

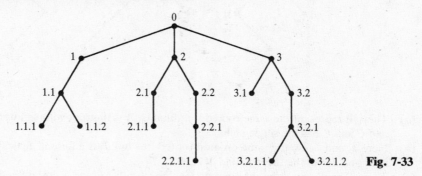

**Fig. 7-33**

## 7.5 BINARY TREES

The binary tree is a fundamental structure in mathematics and computer science. Some of the terminology of ordinary rooted trees, such as parent, child, edge, path, leaf, branch, depth, and level number, will also be used for the binary trees. However, the term node rather than vertex will be used here.

**7.71** Define a binary tree $T$ and give an example.

**▌** A *binary tree* $T$ is defined to be a finite set of elements, called *nodes*, such that:
**(a)** $T$ is empty (called the *null tree* or *empty tree*), or
**(b)** $T$ contains a distinguished node $R$, called the *root* of $T$, and the remaining nodes of $T$ form an ordered pair of disjoint binary trees $T_1$ and $T_2$.
If $T$ does contain a root $R$, then the two trees $T_1$ and $T_2$ are called, respectively, the *left* and *right subtrees* of $R$. If $T_1$ is nonempty, then its root is called the *left successor* of $R$; similarly, if $T_2$ is nonempty, then its root is called the *right successor* of $R$.

Figure 7-34 represents a binary tree $T$ as follows. (i) $T$ consists of 11 nodes, represented by the letters $A$ through $L$, excluding $I$. (ii) The root of $T$ is the node $A$ at the top of the diagram. (iii) A left-downward (right-downward) line from a node $N$ indicates a left (right) successor of $N$.

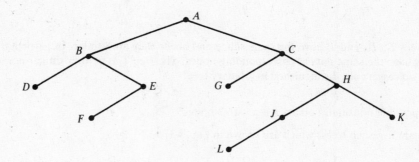

**Fig. 7-34**

**7.72** Consider the binary tree $T$ in Fig. 7-34. Identify: **(a)** the left and right successors of $A$, **(b)** the right and left subtrees of $A$.

**▌** **(a)** $B$ is the left successor and $C$ is the right successor of the node $A$.
**(b)** The left subtree of the root $A$ consists of the nodes $B$, $D$, $E$, and $F$, and the right subtree of $A$ consists of the nodes $C$, $G$, $H$, $J$, $K$, and $L$.

**7.73** Any node $N$ in a binary tree $T$ can have either 0, 1, or 2 successors. Nodes with no successors are called *terminal nodes*. Identify the number of successors of each node in Fig. 7-34.

**▌** The nodes $A$, $B$, $C$, and $H$ have two successors, the nodes $E$ and $J$ have only one successor, and the nodes $D$, $F$, $G$, $L$, and $K$ have no successors.

**7.74** Consider the three trees $T_1$, $T_2$, and $T_3$ in Fig. 7-35. Identify those which represent the same (**a**) rooted tree, (**b**) ordered rooted tree, (**c**) binary tree.

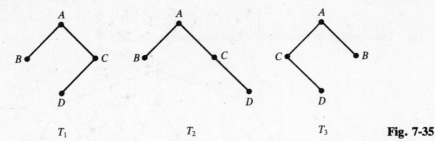

Fig. 7-35

▮ (**a**) They all represent the same rooted tree, that is, $A$ is the root with children (immediate successors) $B$ and $C$ and $C$ has the single child $D$.

(**b**) Here $T_1$ and $T_2$ are the same ordered rooted tree but $T_3$ is different. Specifically, $B$ is the first child of $A$ in $T_1$ and $T_2$ but the second child of $A$ in $T_3$.

(**c**) They all represent different binary trees. Specifically, $T_1$ and $T_2$ are different since we distinguish between left and right successors even when there is only one successor (which is not true for ordered rooted trees). That is, $D$ is a left successor of $C$ in $T_1$ but a right successor of $C$ in $T_2$.

**7.75** Explain the terms similar and copies with respect to binary trees.

▮ Binary trees $T$ and $T'$ are said to be *similar* if they have the same structure or, in other words, if they have the same shape. The trees are said to be *copies* if they are similar and if they have the same contents at corresponding nodes.

**7.76** Consider the four binary trees in Fig. 7-36. Identify the trees that are similar and those that are copies.

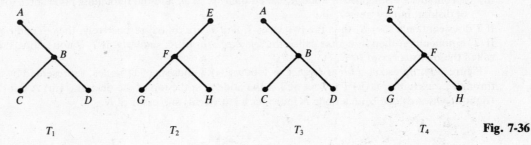

Fig. 7-36

▮ The trees $T_1$, $T_3$, and $T_4$ have the same shape and hence they are similar. In particular, $T_1$ and $T_3$ are copies since they have the same data at corresponding nodes. The tree $T_2$ is neither similar nor a copy of $T_4$ since left and right successors are distinguished in a binary tree.

**7.77** Draw all possible nonsimilar binary trees with 3 nodes

▮ There are five such trees, which are shown in Fig. 7-37.

**Fig. 7-37** Binary trees with 3 nodes.

**7.78** Consider the algebraic expression $E = (2x + y)(5a - b)^3$ involving only binary operations. (**a**) Draw the binary tree $T$ which corresponds to the expression $E$. (**b**) Find the *scope* of the exponential operator; i.e., find the subtree rooted at the exponential operator.

▮ (**a**) Use an arrow ($\uparrow$) for exponentiation and an asterisk ($*$) for multiplication to obtain the tree $T$ in Fig. 7-38. Note that each operation in $E$ appears as an "internal" node in $T$ and each variable or constant appears as a terminal node.

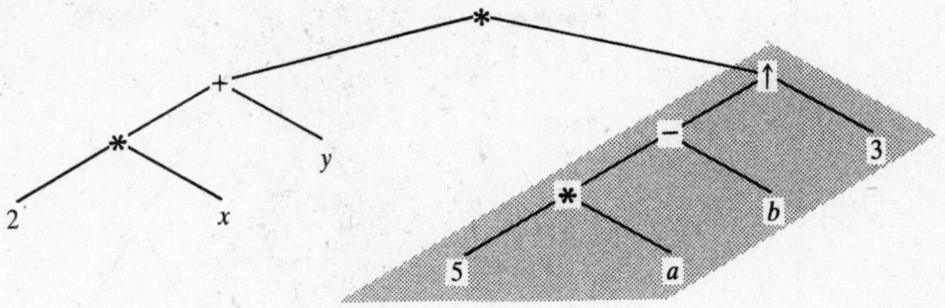

**Fig. 7-38**

(**b**) The scope of ↑ is the tree shaded in Fig. 7-38. It corresponds to the subexpression $(5a - b)^3$.

**7.79** A binary tree T is usually maintained in memory using three parallel linear arrays INFO, LEFT, and RIGHT and a pointer variable ROOT as follows. First of all, each node N of T will correspond to a location K such that
(1)  INFO[K] contains the data at the node N.
(2)  LEFT[K] contains the location of the left child of node N.
(3)  RIGHT[K] contains the location of the right child of node N.
Furthermore, ROOT will contain the location of the root R of T. If any subtree is empty, then the corresponding pointer will contain the null value; if the tree T itself is empty, then ROOT will contain the null value. Draw the tree T maintained in memory as in Fig. 7-39.

|    | INFO | LEFT | RIGHT |
|----|------|------|-------|
| 1  | 20   | 0    | 0     |
| 2  | 30   | 1    | 13    |
| 3  | 40   | 0    | 0     |
| 4  | 50   | 0    | 0     |
| 5  | 60   | 2    | 6     |
| 6  | 70   | 0    | 8     |
| 7  | 80   | 0    | 0     |
| 8  | 90   | 7    | 14    |
| 9  |      |      |       |
| 10 |      |      |       |
| 11 | 35   | 0    | 12    |
| 12 | 45   | 3    | 4     |
| 13 | 55   | 11   | 0     |
| 14 | 95   | 0    | 0     |

ROOT = 5          **Fig. 7-39**

▌ The tree T is drawn from its root R downward as follows:
(**a**)  The root R is obtained from the value of the pointer ROOT. Note that ROOT = 5. Hence INFO[5] = 60 is the root R of T.
(**b**)  The left child of R is obtained from the left pointer field of R. Note that LEFT[5] = 2. Hence INFO[2] = 30 is the left child of R.
(**c**)  The right child of R is obtained from the right pointer field of R. Note that RIGHT[5] = 6. Hence INFO[6] = 70 is the right child of R.
We can now draw the top part of the tree as shown in Fig. 7-40(a). Repeating the above process with each new node, we finally obtain the required tree T in Fig. 7-40(b).

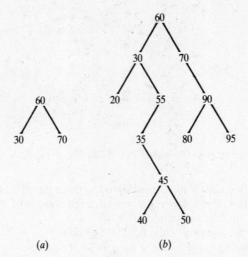

Fig. 7-40

*(a)*                          *(b)*

**7.80**    Draw the diagram of the binary tree T maintained in memory as in Fig. 7-41.

▮    Note ROOT = 14, hence INFO[14] = A is the root of T. Note LEFT[14] = 5, hence INFO[5] = B is the left child of A. Note RIGHT[14] = 9, hence INFO[9] = C is the right child of A. Continuing this process for each new node yields the required diagram of T shown in Fig. 7-42.

|    | INFO | LEFT | RIGHT |
|----|------|------|-------|
| 1  | H    | 4    | 11    |
| 2  | R    | 0    | 0     |
| 3  |      |      |       |
| 4  | P    | 0    | 0     |
| 5  | B    | 18   | 7     |
| 6  |      |      |       |
| 7  | E    | 1    | 0     |
| 8  |      |      |       |
| 9  | C    | 0    | 10    |
| 10 | F    | 15   | 16    |
| 11 | Q    | 0    | 12    |
| 12 | S    | 0    | 0     |
| 13 |      |      |       |
| 14 | A    | 5    | 9     |
| 15 | K    | 2    | 0     |
| 16 | L    | 0    | 0     |
| 17 |      |      |       |
| 18 | D    | 0    | 0     |

ROOT = 14            **Fig. 7-41**

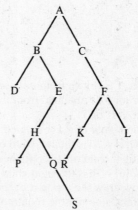

**Fig. 7-42**

## Traversing Binary Trees

**7.81** Identify the three standard algorithms to traverse a binary tree T with root R.

▮ These three algorithms, called *preorder, inorder,* and *postorder,* are as follows:

Preorder:    (1)  Process the root R.
                (2)  Traverse the left subtree of R in preorder.
                (3)  Traverse the right subtree of R in preorder.

Inorder:     (1)  Traverse the left subtree of R in inorder.
                (2)  Process the root R.
                (3)  Traverse the right subtree of R in inorder.

Postorder:   (1)  Traverse the left subtree of R in postorder.
                (2)  Traverse the right subtree of R in postorder.
                (3)  Process the root R.

Observe that each algorithm contains the same three steps, and that the left subtree of R is always traversed before the right subtree. The difference between the algorithms is the time at which the root R is processed. Specifically, in the "pre" algorithm, the root R is processed before the subtrees are traversed; in the "in" algorithm, the root R is processed between the traversals of the subtrees; and in the "post" algorithm, the root R is processed after the subtrees are traversed.

The three algorithms are sometimes called, respectively, the node-left-right (NLR) traversal, the left-node-right (LNR) traversal, and the left-right-node (LRN) traversal.

**7.82** Consider the binary tree T in Fig. 7-43. Observe that A is the root of T, that its left subtree $L_T$ consists of the nodes B, D, and E and that its right subtree $R_T$ consists of nodes C and F. Traverse T using the following algorithms: **(a)** preorder, **(b)** inorder, **(c)** postorder.

▮ **(a)** The preorder traversal of T processes A, traverses $L_T$, and traverses $R_T$. However, the preorder traversal of $L_T$ processes the root B and then D and E, and the preorder traversal of $R_T$ processes the root C and then F. Hence ABDECF is the preorder traversal of T.

    **(b)** The inorder traversal of T traverses $L_T$, processes A, and traverses $R_T$. However, the inorder traversal of $L_T$ processes D, B, and then E, and the inorder traversal of $R_T$ processes C and then F. Hence DBEACF is the inorder traversal of T.

    **(c)** The postorder traversal of T traverses $L_T$, traverses $R_T$, and processes A. However, the postorder traversal of $L_T$ processes D, E, and then B, and the postorder traversal of $R_T$ processes F and then C. Accordingly, DEBFCA is the postorder traversal of T.

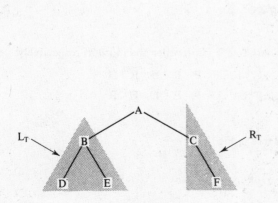

**Fig. 7-43**

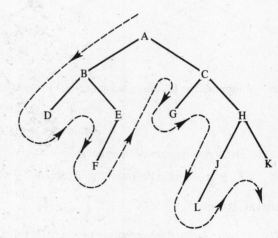

**Fig. 7-44**

**7.83** Traverse the binary tree T in Fig. 7-44 using the preorder traversal algorithm.

▮ The preorder traversal of T is ABDEFCGHJLK. This order is the same as the one obtained by scanning the tree from the left as indicated by the path in Fig. 7-44. That is, one "travels" down the leftmost branch until meeting a terminal node, then one backtracks to the next branch, and so on. In the preorder traversal, the rightmost terminal node, node K, is the last node scanned. Observe that the left subtree of the root A is traversed before the right subtree, and both are traversed after A.

**7.84**  Consider the binary tree T in Fig. 7-44. (**a**) Identify the inorder and postorder traversals of T. (**b**) Find a common property of the terminal nodes in all three traversals.

(**a**)  By inspection one can obtain the following traversals of T:

Inorder:  D B F E A G C L J  H K

Postorder:  D F E B G L J K H C A

(**b**)  The terminal nodes, D, F, G, L, and K, are traversed in the same order, from left to right, in all three traversals. We emphasize that this is true for any binary tree T.

**7.85**  A binary tree T has 9 nodes. The inorder and preorder traversals of T yield the following sequences of nodes:

Inorder:  E  A  C  K  F  H  D  B  G

Preorder:  F  A  E  K  C  D  H  G  B

Draw the tree T.

The tree T is drawn from its root downward as follows.

(**a**)  The root of T is obtained by choosing the first node in its preorder. Thus F is the root of T.

(**b**)  The left child of the node F is obtained as follows. First use the inorder of T to find the nodes in the left subtree $T_1$ of F. Thus $T_1$ consists of the nodes E, A, C, and K. Then the left child of F is obtained by choosing the first node in the preorder of $T_1$ (which appears in the preorder of T). Thus A is the left son of F.

(**c**)  Similarly, the right subtree $T_2$ of F consists of the nodes H, D, B, and G, and D is the root of $T_2$, that is, D is the right child of F.

Repeating the above process with each new node, we finally obtain the required tree in Fig. 7-45.

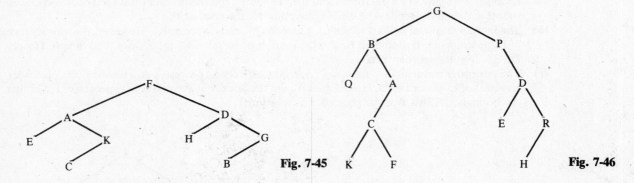

Fig. 7-45        Fig. 7-46

**7.86**  Suppose the following sequences list the nodes of a binary tree T in preorder and inorder, respectively:

Preorder:  G B Q A C K F P D E R H

Inorder:  Q B K C F A G P E D H R

Draw the diagram of the tree.

Proceed as in Problem 7.85 to obtain the required tree in Fig. 7-46.

## General Trees

**7.87**  Give a (recursive) definition of a general tree.

A *general tree* is defined to be a nonempty finite set T of elements, called *nodes*, such that:

(1)  T contains a distinguished element R, called the *root* of T.

(2)  The remaining elements of T form an ordered collection of zero or more disjoint trees $T_1, T_2, \ldots, T_m$. The trees $T_1, T_2, \ldots, T_m$ are called *subtrees* of the root R, and the roots of $T_1, T_2, \ldots, T_m$ are called *successors* of R.

Terminology from geneology, graph theory, and horticulture is used for general trees in the same way as for binary trees. In particular, if N is a node with successors $S_1, S_2, \ldots, S_m$, then N is called the *parent* of the $S_i$'s, the $S_i$'s are called *children* of N, and the $S_i$'s are called *siblings* of each other.

**Remark:** The above definition of a general tree is equivalent to the definition of an ordered rooted tree discussed in Section 7.4.

**7.88** Give an example of a general tree using a diagram.

▌ Figure 7-47 shows a general tree $T$ with 13 nodes,

$$A, B, C, D, E, F, G, H, J, K, L, M, N$$

Unless otherwise stated, the root of a tree $T$ is the node at the top of the diagram, and the children of a node are ordered from left to right. Accordingly, $A$ is the root of $T$, and $A$ has three children; the first child $B$, the second child $C$, and the third child $D$.

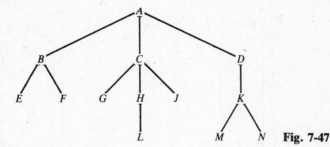

**Fig. 7-47**

**7.89** Consider the general tree in Fig. 7-47. Identify those nodes with **(a)** three children, **(b)** two children, **(c)** one child, and **(d)** no children.

▌ **(a)** $A$ and $C$, **(b)** $B$ and $K$, **(c)** $D$ and $H$, **(d)** $E, F, G, L, J, M$, and $N$. (These nodes are also called terminal nodes.)

**7.90** Is a binary tree a special case of a general tree?

▌ No. Binary trees and general trees are different objects. The two basic differences follow:
(1) A binary tree $T'$ may be empty, but a general tree $T$ is nonempty.
(2) Suppose a node $N$ has only one child. Then the child is distinguished as a left child or right child in a binary tree $T'$, but no such distinction exists in a general tree $T$.
The second difference is illustrated by the trees $T_1$ and $T_2$ in Fig. 7-35. Specifically, as binary trees, $T_1$ and $T_2$ are distinct trees, since $D$ is the left child of $C$ in the tree $T_1$ but $D$ is the right child of $C$ in the tree $T_2$. On the other hand, there is no difference between the trees $T_1$ and $T_2$ as general trees.

**7.91** Define a forest (in the context of general trees).

▌ A *forest* $F$ is defined to be an ordered collection of zero or more distinct trees. Clearly, if we delete the root $R$ from a general tree $T$, then we obtain the forest $F$ consisting of the subtrees of $R$ (which may be empty). Conversely, if $F$ is a forest, then we may adjoin a node $R$ to $F$ to form a general tree $T$ where $R$ is the root of $T$ and the subtrees of $R$ consist of the original trees in $F$.

**7.92** Suppose $T$ is a general tree. Describe how $T$ is usually maintained in the memory of a computer.

▌ $T$ is usually maintained in memory by means of three parallel arrays INFO, CHILD (or DOWN), and SIBL (or HORZ), and a pointer variable ROOT as follows. First of all, each node $N$ of $T$ will correspond to a location K such that:
(1) INFO[K] contains the data at node $N$.
(2) CHILD[K] contains the location of the first child of $N$. The condition CHILD[K] = NULL indicates that $N$ has no children.
(3) SIBL[K] contains the location of the next sibling of $N$. The condition SIBL[K] = NULL indicates that $N$ is the last child of its parent.
Furthermore, ROOT will contain the location of the root $R$ of $T$. Although this representation may seem artificial, it has the important advantage that each node $N$ of $T$, regardless of the number of children of $N$, will contain exactly three fields.

The above representation may easily be extended to represent a forest $F$ consisting of trees $T_1, T_2, \ldots, T_m$ by assuming the roots of the trees are siblings. In such a case, ROOT will contain the location of the root $R_1$ of the first tree $T_1$; or when $F$ is empty, ROOT will equal NULL.

**7.93**    Consider the general tree $T$ in Fig. 7-47. Suppose the data of the nodes of $T$ are stored in an array INFO as in Fig. 7-48. Let CHILD and SIBL be arrays parallel to INFO, and let ROOT be a pointer variable. Assign values to ROOT, CHILD, and SIBL to reflect the structural relationships in $T$.

❚    Values are assigned to ROOT, CHILD and SIBL as follows:

(*a*)    Since the root $A$ of $T$ is stored in INFO[2], set ROOT := 2.

(*b*)    Since the first child of $A$ is the node $B$, which is stored in INFO[3], set CHILD[2] := 3. Since $A$ has no sibling, set SIBL[2] := NULL.

(*c*)    Since the first child of $B$ is the node $E$, which is stored in INFO[15], set CHILD[3] := 15. Since node $C$ is the next sibling of $B$ and $C$ is stored in INFO[4], set SIBL[3] := 4.

And so on. Figure 7-49 gives the final values in CHILD and SIBL.

| INFO |  |
|---|---|
| 1 |  |
| 2 | A |
| 3 | B |
| 4 | C |
| 5 |  |
| 6 | G |
| 7 | H |
| 8 | J |
| 9 | N |
| 10 | M |
| 11 | L |
| 12 | K |
| 13 |  |
| 14 | F |
| 15 | E |
| 16 | D |

**Fig. 7-48**

|  | CHILD | SIBL |
|---|---|---|
| 1 |  |  |
| 2 | 3 | 0 |
| 3 | 15 | 4 |
| 4 | 6 | 16 |
| 5 |  |  |
| 6 | 0 | 7 |
| 7 | 11 | 8 |
| 8 | 0 | 0 |
| 9 | 0 | 0 |
| 10 | 0 | 9 |
| 11 | 0 | 0 |
| 12 | 10 | 0 |
| 13 |  |  |
| 14 | 0 | 0 |
| 15 | 0 | 14 |
| 16 | 12 | 0 |

**Fig. 7-49**

**7.94**    Suppose $T$ is a general tree. Show how a unique binary tree $T'$ is assigned to $T$ which essentially preserves the structure of $T$. Illustrate with the general tree in Fig. 7-47.

❚    The binary tree $T'$ is obtained from $T$ as follows. First of all, the nodes of the binary tree $T'$ will be the same as the nodes of the general tree $T$, and the root of $T'$ will be the root of $T$. Let $N$ be an arbitrary node of the binary tree $T'$. Then the left child of $N$ in $T'$ will be the first child of the node $N$ in the general tree $T$ and the right child of $N$ in $T'$ will be the next sibling of $N$ in the general tree $T$.

The reader can verify that the binary tree $T'$ in Fig. 7-50 corresponds to the general tree $T$ in Fig. 7-47 as described above. Observe that by rotating counterclockwise the picture of $T'$ in Fig. 7-50 until the edges pointing to right children are horizontal, we obtain a picture in which the nodes occupy the same relative position as the nodes in Fig. 7-47.

**7.95**    Describe the relationship, if any, between the computer representation of a general tree $T$ and the computer representation of the corresponding binary tree $T'$.

❚    The representations are exactly the same except that the names of the arrays CHILD and SIBL for the

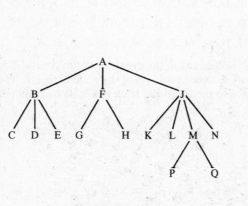

**Fig. 7-50** Binary tree $T'$.

general tree $T$ will correspond to the names of the arrays LEFT and RIGHT for the binary tree $T'$. The importance of this correspondence is that certain algorithms that applied to binary trees, such as the traversal algorithms, may now apply to general trees.

**7.96** Consider the general tree T in Fig. 7-51(*a*). Find the corresponding binary tree $T'$.

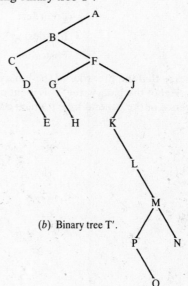

(*a*) General tree T.  (*b*) Binary tree T'.

**Fig. 7-51**

▌ The nodes of T' will be the same as the nodes of the general tree T, and in particular, the root of T' will be the same as the root of T. Furthermore, if N is a node in the binary tree T', then its left child is the first child of N in T and its right child is the next sibling of N in T. Constructing T' from the root down, we obtain the tree in Fig. 7-51(*b*).

**7.97** Suppose T is a general tree with root R and subtrees $T_1, T_2, \ldots, T_M$. The preorder traversal and the postorder traversal of T are defined as follows:

Preorder:  (1)  Process the root R.
          (2)  Traverse the subtrees $T_1, T_2, \ldots, T_M$ in preorder.
Postorder:  (1)  Traverse the subtrees $T_1, T_2, \ldots, T_M$ in postorder.
          (2)  Process the root R.

Let T be the general tree in Fig. 7-51(*a*). (***a***) Traverse T in preorder. (***b***) Traverse T in postorder.

▌ Note that T has the root A and subtrees $T_1, T_2$, and $T_3$ such that

        $T_1$ consists of nodes B, C, D, and E.

        $T_2$ consists of nodes F, G, and H.

        $T_3$ consists of nodes J, K, L, M, N, P, and Q.

**(a)** The preorder traversal of T consists of the following steps:
  (i)  Process root A.
  (ii)  Traverse $T_1$ in preorder:    Process nodes B, C, D, E.
  (iii)  Traverse $T_2$ in preorder:    Process nodes F, G, H.
  (iv)  Traverse $T_3$ in preorder:    Process nodes J, K, L, M, P, Q, N.
That is, the preorder traversal of T is as follows:

$$A, B, C, D, E, F, G, H, J, K, L, M, P, Q, N$$

**(b)** The postorder traversal of T consists of the following steps:
  (i)  Traverse $T_1$ in postorder:    Process nodes C, D, E, B.
  (ii)  Traverse $T_2$ in postorder:    Process nodes G, H, F.
  (iii)  Traverse $T_3$ in postorder:    Process nodes K, L, P, Q, M, N, J.
  (iv)  Process root A.
In other words, the postorder traversal of T is as follows:

$$C, D, E, B, G, H, F, K, L, P, Q, M, N, J, A$$

**7.98**   Consider the binary tree T′ in Fig. 7-51(*b*). Find the preorder, inorder, and postorder traversals of T′. Compare them with the preorder and postorder traversals obtained in Problem 7.97 for the corresponding general tree T in Fig. 7-51(*a*).

❚  Using the binary tree traversal algorithms in Problem 7.81, we obtain the following traversals of T′:

Preorder:   A, B, C, D, E, F, G, H, J, K, L, M, P, Q, N

Inorder:   C, D, E, B, G, H, F, K, L, P, Q, M, N, J, A

Postorder:   E, D, C, H, G, Q, P, N, M, L, K, J, F, B, A

Observe that the preorder of the binary tree T′ is identical to the preorder of the general T, and that the inorder traversal of the binary tree T′ is identical to the postorder traversal of the general tree T. There is no natural traversal of the general tree T which corresponds to the postorder traversal of its corresponding binary tree T′.

## 8.1 COUNTING PRINCIPLE, FACTORIAL NOTATION

The following basic principle of counting is applied throughout this chapter:

**Fundamental Principle of Counting:** If some event can occur in $n_1$ different ways, and if, following this event, a second event can occur in $n_2$ different ways, and, following this second event, a third event can occur in $n_3$ different ways, . . . , then the number of ways the events can occur in the order indicated is $n_1 \cdot n_2 \cdot n_3 \cdots$.

**8.1** Suppose a license plate contains two letters followed by three digits with the first digit not zero. How many different license plates can be printed?

▮ Each letter can be printed in twenty-six different ways, the first digit in nine ways and each of the other two digits in ten ways. Hence $26 \cdot 26 \cdot 9 \cdot 10 \cdot 10 = 608\,400$ different plates can be printed.

**8.2** Find the number $n$ of license plates that can be made where each plate contains two distinct letters followed by three different digits.

▮ Here $n = 26 \cdot 25 \cdot 10 \cdot 9 \cdot 8 = 468\,000$. That is, there are twenty-six choices for the first letter, but only twenty-five choices for the second letter which must be different from the first letter. Similarly, the choices for the digits are 10, 9, and 8 since the digits must be distinct.

**8.3** Solve Problem 8.2 if the first digit cannot be 0.

▮ Here $n = 26 \cdot 25 \cdot 9 \cdot 9 \cdot 8 = 421\,200$ which is the same as in Problem 8.2 except that now there are only nine choices for the first digit.

**8.4** Find the number $n$ of ways that an organization consisting of twenty-six members can elect a president, treasurer, and secretary (assuming no person is elected to more than one position).

▮ The president can be elected in twenty-six different ways; following this, the treasurer can be elected in twenty-five different ways (since the person chosen president is not eligible to be treasurer); and, following this, the secretary can be elected in twenty-four different ways. Thus, by the above principle of counting, there are $n = 26 \cdot 25 \cdot 24 = 15\,600$ different ways in which the organization can elect the officers.

**8.5** There are four bus lines between $A$ and $B$; and three bus lines between $B$ and $C$. Find the number of ways a person can travel: (**a**) by bus from $A$ to $C$ by way of $B$; (**b**) roundtrip by bus from $A$ to $C$ by way of $B$.

▮ (**a**) There are four ways to go from $A$ to $B$ and three ways to go from $B$ to $C$; hence there are $4 \cdot 3 = 12$ ways to go from $A$ to $C$ by way of $B$.

(**b**) There are twelve ways to go from $A$ to $C$ by way of $B$, and 12 ways to return. Hence there are $12 \cdot 12 = 144$ ways to travel roundtrip.

**8.6** Suppose the person in Problem 8.5 does not want to use a bus line more than once. In how many ways can the roundtrip by bus be taken from $A$ to $C$ by way of $B$?

▮ The person will travel from $A$ to $B$ to $C$ to $B$ to $A$. Enter these letters with connecting arrows as follows:

$$A \rightarrow B \rightarrow C \rightarrow B \rightarrow A$$

The person can travel four ways from $A$ to $B$ and three ways from $B$ to $C$, but only two ways from $C$ to $B$ and three ways from $B$ to $A$ since a bus line cannot be used more than once. Enter these numbers above the corresponding arrows as follows:

$$A \xrightarrow{4} B \xrightarrow{3} C \xrightarrow{2} B \xrightarrow{3} A$$

Thus there are $4 \cdot 3 \cdot 2 \cdot 3 = 72$ ways to travel roundtrip without using the same bus line more than once.

**8.7** A student can take one of four mathematics sections and one of five English sections. Find the number $n$ of ways he can register for the two courses.

▌ There are four choices for the mathematics course and five choices for the English course; hence $n = 4 \cdot 5 = 20$.

**8.8** Solve Problem 8.7 if one of the mathematics sections and one of the English sections meet at the same time.

▌ Subtract one of the twenty possibilities to obtain $n = 20 - 1 = 19$.

## Factorial Function

This subsection covers the factorial function $n!$ (read "$n$ factorial") where $n!$ is defined by

$$n! = 1 \cdot 2 \cdot 3 \cdot \cdots \cdot (n-2)(n-1)n$$

In other words, $n!$ is the product of the positive integers from 1 to $n$ inclusive. It is also convenient to define $0! = 1$.

**8.9** Give a recursive definition of the factorial function.

▌ We can define $n!$ recursively by

$$0! = 1 \quad \text{and} \quad n! = n \cdot (n-1)!$$

[This definition is recursive since $(n-1)!$ is used to define $n!$].

**8.10** Find 2!, 3!, and 4!

▌ Multiply the integers from 1 to $n$: $2! = 1 \cdot 2 = 2$, $3! = 1 \cdot 2 \cdot 3 = 6$, $4! = 1 \cdot 2 \cdot 3 \cdot 4 = 24$.

**8.11** Find 5!, 6!, 7!, and 8!

▌ For $n > 1$, we have $n! = n(n-1)!$ Hence

$5! = 5 \cdot 4! = 5 \cdot 24 = 120$;  $6! = 6 \cdot 5! = 6 \cdot 120 = 720$;  $7! = 7 \cdot 6! = 7 \cdot 720 = 5040$;  $8! = 8 \cdot 7! = 8 \cdot 5040 = 40\,320$

**8.12** Find: (**a**) 10!, and (**b**) $(-3)!$

▌ (**a**) First use Problem 8.11 to find: $9! = 9(8!) = 9(40\,320) = 362\,880$. Then

$$10! = (10)9! = (10)(362\,880) = 3\,628\,800$$

(**b**) $(-3)!$ is not defined.

**8.13** Write in terms of factorials: (**a**) $35 \cdot 34 \cdot 33$, and (**b**) $\dfrac{1}{16 \cdot 15}$.

▌ (**a**) $35 \cdot 34 \cdot 33 = \dfrac{35 \cdot 34 \cdot 33 \cdot 32!}{32!} = \dfrac{35!}{32!}$  (**b**) $\dfrac{1}{16 \cdot 15} = \dfrac{14!}{16 \cdot 15 \cdot 14!} = \dfrac{14!}{16!}$

**8.14** Write in terms of factorials: (**a**) $n(n-1) \cdots (n-r+1)$, (**b**) $\dfrac{n(n-1) \cdots (n-r+1)}{1 \cdot 2 \cdot 3 \cdots (r-1)r}$.

▌ (**a**) $n(n-1) \cdots (n-r+1) = \dfrac{n(n-1) \cdots (n-r+1)(n-r)(n-r-1) \cdots 3 \cdot 2 \cdot 1}{(n-r)(n-r-1) \cdots 3 \cdot 2 \cdot 1} = \dfrac{n!}{(n-r)!}$

(**b**) $\dfrac{n(n-1) \cdots (n-r+1)}{1 \cdot 2 \cdot 3 \cdots (r-1)r} = n(n-1) \cdots (n-r+1)\dfrac{1}{r!} = \dfrac{n!}{(n-r)!}\dfrac{1}{r!} = \dfrac{n!}{r!\,(n-r)!}$

**8.15** Simplify: (**a**) $\dfrac{(n+1)!}{n!}$, and (**b**) $\dfrac{n!}{(n-2)!}$.

▌ (**a**) $\dfrac{(n+1)!}{n!} = \dfrac{(n+1)n(n-1) \cdots 3 \cdot 2 \cdot 1}{n(n-1) \cdots 3 \cdot 2 \cdot 1} = n+1$ or, simply,

$$\frac{(n+1)!}{n!} = \frac{(n+1)n!}{n!} = n+1$$

(**b**) $\dfrac{n!}{(n-2)!} = \dfrac{n(n-1)(n-2) \cdots 3 \cdot 2 \cdot 1}{(n-2) \cdots 3 \cdot 2 \cdot 1} = n(n-1) = n^2 - n$ or, simply,

$$\frac{n!}{(n-2)!} = \frac{n(n-1)(n-2)!}{(n-2)!} = n(n-1) = n^2 - n$$

**8.16**   Simplify: **(a)** $\dfrac{(n+1)!}{(n-1)!}$, and **(b)** $\dfrac{(n-1)!}{(n+2)!}$.

▌ **(a)**   $\dfrac{(n+1)!}{(n-1)!} = \dfrac{(n+1)n(n-1)(n-2)\cdots 3\cdot 2\cdot 1}{(n-1)(n-2)\cdots 3\cdot 2\cdot 1} = (n+1)n = n^2 + n$ or, simply,

$$\frac{(n+1)!}{(n-1)!} = \frac{(n+1)n(n-1)!}{(n-1)!} = (n+1)\cdot n = n^2 + n$$

**(b)**   $\dfrac{(n-1)!}{(n+2)!} = \dfrac{(n-1)!}{(n+2)(n+1)n(n-1)!} = \dfrac{1}{(n+2)(n+1)n} = \dfrac{1}{n^3 + 3n^2 + 2n}$

**8.17**   Simplify $\dfrac{(n-r+1)!}{(n-r-1)!}$.

▌ We have   $\dfrac{(n-r+1)!}{(n-r-1)!} = \dfrac{(n-r+1)(n-r)(n-r-1)!}{(n-r-1)!} = (n-r+1)(n-r)$

**8.18**   Simplify $\dfrac{(n-r)!}{(n-r-2)!}$.

▌ We have   $\dfrac{(n-r)!}{(n-r-2)!} = \dfrac{(n-r)(n-r-1)(n-r-2)!}{(n-r-2)!} = (n-r)(n-r-1)$

## 8.2   BINOMIAL COEFFICIENTS

The symbol $\dbinom{n}{r}$ (read "$n\,C\,r$"), where $r$ and $n$ are positive integers with $r \le n$, is defined as

$$\binom{n}{r} = \frac{n(n-1)(n-2)\cdots(n-r+1)}{1\cdot 2\cdot 3\cdots(r-1)r}$$

Note that there are exactly $r$ factors in both the numerator and the denominator. These numbers are called the *binomial coefficients* in view of Theorem 8.2 below.

**8.19**   Compute: **(a)** $\dbinom{16}{3}$, and **(b)** $\dbinom{12}{4}$.

▌ Recall that there are as many factors in the numerator as in the denominator.

**(a)**   $\dbinom{16}{3} = \dfrac{16\cdot 15\cdot 14}{1\cdot 2\cdot 3} = 560$

**(b)**   $\dbinom{12}{4} = \dfrac{12\cdot 11\cdot 10\cdot 9}{1\cdot 2\cdot 3\cdot 4} = 495$

**8.20**   Compute: **(a)** $\dbinom{8}{2}$, **(b)** $\dbinom{9}{4}$, and **(c)** $\dbinom{10}{3}$.

▌ **(a)**   $\dbinom{8}{2} = \dfrac{8\cdot 7}{1\cdot 2} = 28$,   **(b)**   $\dbinom{9}{4} = \dfrac{9\cdot 8\cdot 7\cdot 6}{1\cdot 2\cdot 3\cdot 4} = 126$,   **(c)**   $\dbinom{10}{3} = \dfrac{10\cdot 9\cdot 8}{1\cdot 2\cdot 3} = 120$

**8.21**   Compute: **(a)** $\dbinom{12}{5}$, **(b)** $\dbinom{13}{1}$, and **(c)** $\dbinom{15}{4}$.

▌ **(a)**   $\dbinom{12}{5} = \dfrac{12\cdot 11\cdot 10\cdot 9\cdot 8}{1\cdot 2\cdot 3\cdot 4\cdot 5} = 792$,   **(b)**   $\dbinom{13}{1} = \dfrac{13}{1} = 13$,   **(c)**   $\dbinom{15}{4} = \dfrac{15\cdot 14\cdot 13\cdot 12}{1\cdot 2\cdot 3\cdot 4} = 1365$

**8.22**   Show that $\dbinom{n}{r} = \dfrac{n!}{r!\,(n-r)!}$.

▌ By Problem 8.14,   $\dbinom{n}{r} = \dfrac{n(n-1)\cdots(n-r+1)}{1\cdot 2\cdot 3\cdots(r-1)r} = \dfrac{n!}{r!\,(n-r)!}$

**Remark:** Using the above formula for $\binom{n}{r}$ and the fact that $0! = 1$, we can extend the definition of $\binom{n}{r}$ to the following cases:

$$\binom{n}{0} = \frac{n!}{0!\, n!} = 1 \qquad \text{and, in particular,} \qquad \binom{0}{0} = \frac{0!}{0!\, 0!} = 1$$

**8.23**  Prove: $\binom{n}{n-r} = \binom{n}{r}$ or, in other words, if $a + b = n$ then $\binom{n}{a} = \binom{n}{b}$.

▋ The proof follows from Problem 8.22 and the fact that $n - (n - r) = r$.

**8.24**  Compute $\binom{10}{7}$.

▋ By definition $\qquad \binom{10}{7} = \dfrac{10 \cdot 9 \cdot 8 \cdot 7 \cdot 6 \cdot 5 \cdot 4}{1 \cdot 2 \cdot 3 \cdot 4 \cdot 5 \cdot 6 \cdot 7} = 120$

On the other hand, $10 - 7 = 3$ and so we can also compute $\binom{10}{7}$ as follows:

$$\binom{10}{7} = \binom{10}{3} = \frac{10 \cdot 9 \cdot 8}{1 \cdot 2 \cdot 3} = 120$$

(Observe that the second method saves space and time.)

**8.25**  Compute $\binom{8}{5}$.

▋ By definition, $\qquad \binom{8}{5} = \dfrac{8 \cdot 7 \cdot 6 \cdot 5 \cdot 4}{1 \cdot 2 \cdot 3 \cdot 4 \cdot 5} = 56$

Note that $8 - 5 = 3$; hence we could also compute $\binom{8}{5}$ as follows:

$$\binom{8}{5} = \binom{8}{3} = \frac{8 \cdot 7 \cdot 6}{1 \cdot 2 \cdot 3} = 56$$

**8.26**  Compute: **(a)** $\binom{14}{12}$, and **(b)** $\binom{20}{17}$.

▋ **(a)** Now $14 - 12 = 2$; hence $\binom{14}{12} = \binom{14}{2} = \dfrac{14 \cdot 13}{1 \cdot 2} = 91$.

**(b)** Now $20 - 17 = 3$; hence $\binom{20}{17} = \binom{20}{3} = \dfrac{20 \cdot 19 \cdot 18}{1 \cdot 2 \cdot 3} = 1140$.

**8.27**  Compute: **(a)** $\binom{9}{7}$, and **(b)** $\binom{10}{6}$.

▋ **(a)** Now $9 - 7 = 2$; hence $\binom{9}{7} = \binom{9}{2} = \dfrac{9 \cdot 8}{1 \cdot 2} = 36$.

**(b)** Now $10 - 6 = 4$; hence $\binom{10}{6} = \binom{10}{4} = \dfrac{10 \cdot 9 \cdot 8 \cdot 7}{1 \cdot 2 \cdot 3 \cdot 4} = 210$.

**8.28**  Prove: $\binom{12}{7} = \binom{11}{6} + \binom{11}{7}$ (which is Theorem 8.1 when $n = 11$ and $r = 7$).

▋ Here $\binom{11}{6} + \binom{11}{7} = \dfrac{11!}{6!\, 5!} + \dfrac{11!}{7!\, 4!}$ . Multiply the first fraction by 7/7 and the second fraction by 5/5 to obtain the same denominator in both fractions; and then add:

$$\binom{11}{6} + \binom{11}{7} = \frac{7 \cdot 11!}{7 \cdot 6! \, 5!} + \frac{5 \cdot 11!}{7! \, 5 \cdot 4!} = \frac{7 \cdot 11!}{7! \, 5!} + \frac{5 \cdot 11!}{7! \, 5!}$$

$$= \frac{7 \cdot 11! + 5 \cdot 11!}{7! \, 5!} = \frac{(7+5) \cdot 11!}{7! \, 5!} = \frac{12 \cdot 11!}{7! \, 5!} = \frac{12!}{7! \, 5!} = \binom{12}{7}$$

**8.29**     Prove: $\binom{17}{6} = \binom{16}{5} + \binom{16}{6}$.

▌ Now $\binom{16}{5} + \binom{16}{6} = \frac{16!}{5! \, 11!} + \frac{16!}{6! \, 10!}$. Multiply the first fraction by 6/6 and the second by 11/11 to obtain the same denominator in both fractions; and then add:

$$\binom{16}{5} + \binom{16}{6} = \frac{6 \cdot 16!}{6 \cdot 5! \, 11!} + \frac{11 \cdot 16!}{6! \cdot 11 \cdot 10!} = \frac{6 \cdot 16!}{6! \, 11!} + \frac{11 \cdot 16!}{6! \, 11!}$$

$$= \frac{6 \cdot 16! + 11 \cdot 16!}{6! \, 11!} = \frac{(6+11)16!}{6! \, 11!} = \frac{17 \cdot 16!}{6! \, 11!} = \frac{17!}{6! \, 11!} = \binom{17}{6}$$

**Theorem 8.1:**     $\binom{n+1}{r} = \binom{n}{r-1} + \binom{n}{r}$.

**8.30**     Prove Theorem 8.1.

▌ (The technique in this proof is similar to that of Problems 8.28 and 8.29.)

Now $\binom{n}{r-1} + \binom{n}{r} = \frac{n!}{(r-1)! \, (n-r+1)!} + \frac{n!}{r! \, (n-r)!}$. To obtain the same denominator in both fractions,

multiply the first fraction by $\frac{r}{r}$ and the second fraction by $\frac{n-r+1}{n-r+1}$. Hence

$$\binom{n}{r-1} + \binom{n}{r} = \frac{r \cdot n!}{r(r-1)! \, (n-r+1)!} + \frac{(n-r+1)n!}{r! \, (n-r+1)(n-r)!}$$

$$= \frac{r \cdot n!}{r! \, (n-r+1)!} + \frac{(n-r+1)n!}{r! \, (n-r+1)!}$$

$$= \frac{r \cdot n! + (n-r+1)n!}{r! \, (n-r+1)!} = \frac{[r + (n-r+1)]n!}{r! \, (n-r+1)!}$$

$$= \frac{(n+1)n!}{r! \, (n-r+1)!} = \frac{(n+1)!}{r! \, (n+1-r)!} = \binom{n+1}{r}$$

## Binomial Theorem, Pascal's Triangle

This subsection uses the following binomial theorem (proved, using induction, in Problem 8.42) which gives the general expression for the expansion of $(a+b)^n$:

**Theorem 8.2 (Binomial Theorem):**

$$(a+b)^n = a^n + na^{n-1}b + \frac{n(n-1)}{1 \cdot 2} a^{n-2}b^2 + \frac{n(n-1)(n-2)}{1 \cdot 2 \cdot 3} a^{n-3}b^3 + \cdots$$

$$+ \frac{n(n-1)}{1 \cdot 2} a^2 b^{n-2} + nab^{n-1} + b^n$$

$$= a^n + \binom{n}{1}a^{n-1}b + \binom{n}{2}a^{n-2}b^2 + \binom{n}{3}a^{n-3}b^3 + \cdots$$

$$+ \binom{n}{2}a^2 b^{n-2} + \binom{n}{1}ab^{n-1} + b^n$$

$$= \sum_{r=0}^{n} \binom{n}{r}a^{n-r}b^r$$

**Remark:** The above expansion of $(a + b)^n$ has the following properties:
  (i) There are $n + 1$ terms.
 (ii) The sum of the exponents of $a$ and $b$ in every term is $n$.
(iii) The exponents of $a$ decrease term by term from $n$ to 0; the exponents of $b$ increase term by term from 0 to $n$.
 (iv) The coefficient of any term is $\binom{n}{k}$ where $k$ is the exponent of either $a$ or $b$.
  (v) The coefficients of terms equidistant from the ends are equal.

**8.31**   Expand: **(a)** $(a + b)^6$, and **(b)** $(a + b)^7$.

   ▌ Using the Binomial Theorem 8.2,

   **(a)**   $(a + b)^6 = a^6 + 6a^5b + \dfrac{6 \cdot 5}{1 \cdot 2} a^4b^2 + \dfrac{6 \cdot 5 \cdot 4}{1 \cdot 2 \cdot 3} a^3b^3 + \dfrac{6 \cdot 5}{1 \cdot 2} a^2b^4 + 6ab^5 + b^6$

   $\qquad = a^6 + 6a^5b + 15a^4b^2 + 20a^3b^3 + 15a^2b^4 + 6ab^5 + b^6$

   **(b)**   $(a + b)^7 = a^7 + 7a^6b + \dfrac{7 \cdot 6}{1 \cdot 2} a^5b^2 + \dfrac{7 \cdot 6 \cdot 5}{1 \cdot 2 \cdot 3} a^4b^3 + \dfrac{7 \cdot 6 \cdot 5}{1 \cdot 2 \cdot 3} a^3b^4 + \dfrac{7 \cdot 6}{1 \cdot 2} a^2b^5 + 7ab^6 + b^7$

   $\qquad = a^7 + 7a^6b + 21a^5b^2 + 35a^4b^3 + 35a^3b^4 + 21a^2b^5 + 7ab^6 + b^7$

**8.32**   Expand $(2x + 3y^2)^5$ and simplify.

   ▌ Here $2x$ and $3y^2$ correspond, respectively, to $a$ and $b$ in the binomial theorem. Thus

   $$(2x + 3y^2)^5 = (2x)^5 + 5(2x)^4(3y^2) + \frac{5 \cdot 4}{1 \cdot 2}(2x)^3(3y^2)^2 + \frac{5 \cdot 4}{1 \cdot 2}(2x)^2(3y^2)^3 + 5(2x)(3y^2)^4 + (3y^2)^5$$

   $$= 2^5x^5 + 5 \cdot 2^4x^4 \cdot 3y^2 + 10 \cdot 2^3x^3 \cdot 3^2y^4 + 10 \cdot 2^2x^2 \cdot 3^3y^6 + 5 \cdot 2x \cdot 3^4y^8 + 3^5y^{10}$$

   $$= 32x^5 + 240x^4y^2 + 720x^3y^4 + 1080x^2y^6 + 810xy^8 + 243y^{10}$$

**8.33**   Expand and simplify: $(x + 3y)^3$.

   ▌   $$(x + 3y)^3 = (x)^3 + \frac{3}{1}(x)^2(3y) + \frac{3}{1}(x)(3y)^2 + (3y)^3 = x^3 + 9x^2y + 27xy^2 + 27y^3$$

**8.34**   Expand and simplify: $(2x - y)^4$.

   ▌   $$(2x - y)^4 = (2x)^4 + \frac{4}{1}(2x)^3(-y) + \frac{4 \cdot 3}{1 \cdot 2}(2x)^2(-y)^2 + \frac{4}{1}(2x)(-y)^3 + (-y)^4$$

   $$= 16x^4 - 32x^3y + 24x^2y^2 - 8xy^3 + y^4$$

**8.35**   Expand and simplify: $(2x + y^2)^5$.

   ▌   $$(2x + y^2)^5 = (2x)^5 + \frac{5}{1}(2x)^4(y^2) + \frac{5 \cdot 4}{1 \cdot 2}(2x)^3(y^2)^2 + \frac{5 \cdot 4}{1 \cdot 2}(2x)^2(y^2)^3 + \frac{5}{1}(2x)(y^2)^4 + (y^2)^5$$

   $$= 32x^5 + 80x^4y^2 + 80x^3y^4 + 40x^2y^6 + 10xy^8 + y^{10}$$

**8.36**   **(a)** Describe how $(a - b)^n$ differs from $(a + b)^n$. **(b)** Obtain $(2x - y^2)^5$ using Problem 8.35.

   ▌ **(a)**   The expansion of $(a - b)^n$ will be identical to the expansion of $(a + b)^n$ except that the signs in $(a - b)^n$ will alternate beginning with plus, i.e., terms with even powers of $b$ will be plus and terms with odd powers of $b$ will be minus. This follows from the fact that $(-b)^r = b^r$ if $r$ is even and $(-b)^r = -b^r$ if $r$ is odd.
   **(b)**   By Problem 8.35,

   $$(2x + y^2)^5 = 32x^5 + 80x^4y^2 + 80x^3y^4 + 40x^2y^6 + 10xy^6 + y^{10}$$

   To obtain $(2x - y^2)^5$, just alternate the signs in $(2x + y^2)^5$:

   $$(2x - y^2)^5 = 32x^5 - 80x^4y^2 + 80x^3y^4 - 40x^2y^6 + 10xy^6 - y^{10}$$

**8.37**   Explain why the $k$ in the coefficient $\binom{n}{k}$ may come from either the exponent of $a$ or the exponent of $b$ in the binomial theorem.

▮ It follows from the fact that $\binom{n}{n-k} = \binom{n}{k}$ as proved in Problem 8.23.

**8.38** Define Pascal's triangle.

▮ The coefficients of the successive powers of $a + b$ can be arranged in a triangular array as indicated in Fig. 8-1; this triangular array of numbers is called Pascal's triangle. It has the following two basic properties:
 (i)  The first number and the last number in each row is 1.
 (ii) Every other number in the array can be obtained by adding the two numbers appearing obliquely above it. For example: $10 = 4 + 6$, $15 = 5 + 10$, $20 = 10 + 10$.
Property (ii) follows from Theorem 8.1.

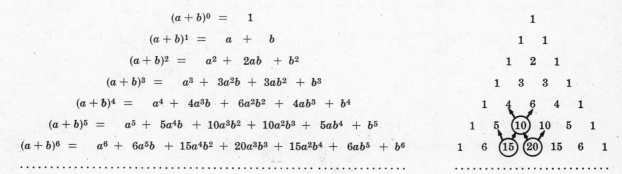

$$(a + b)^0 = 1$$
$$(a + b)^1 = a + b$$
$$(a + b)^2 = a^2 + 2ab + b^2$$
$$(a + b)^3 = a^3 + 3a^2b + 3ab^2 + b^3$$
$$(a + b)^4 = a^4 + 4a^3b + 6a^2b^2 + 4ab^3 + b^4$$
$$(a + b)^5 = a^5 + 5a^4b + 10a^3b^2 + 10a^2b^3 + 5ab^4 + b^5$$
$$(a + b)^6 = a^6 + 6a^5b + 15a^4b^2 + 20a^3b^3 + 15a^2b^4 + 6ab^5 + b^6$$

**Fig. 8-1**

**8.39** Given $(a + b)^6 = a^6 + 6a^5b + 15a^4b^2 + 20a^3b^3 + 15a^2b^4 + 6ab^5 + b^6$. Expand $(a + b)^7$ and $(a + b)^8$.

▮ We could expand $(a + b)^7$ and $(a + b)^8$ using the binomial theorem. However, given the expansion of $(a + b)^6$, it is simpler to use Pascal's triangle to obtain the coefficients of $(a + b)^7$ and $(a + b)^8$. First write down the coefficients of $(a + b)^6$ and then compute the next two rows of the triangle:

$$\begin{array}{ccccccccccccc}
 & & 1 & & 6 & & 15 & & 20 & & 15 & & 6 & & 1 \\
 & 1 & & 7 & & 21 & & 35 & & 35 & & 21 & & 7 & & 1 \\
1 & & 8 & & 28 & & 56 & & 70 & & 56 & & 28 & & 8 & & 1
\end{array}$$

Recall that each number is obtained by adding the two numbers above, e.g., $35 = 15 + 20$, $28 = 7 + 21$, $56 = 35 + 21$. From the above diagram we obtain

$$(a + b)^7 = a^7 + 7a^6b + 21a^5b^2 + 35a^4b^3 + 35a^3b^4 + 21a^2b^5 + 7ab^6 + b^7$$
$$(a + b)^8 = a^8 + 8a^7b + 28a^6b^2 + 56a^5b^3 + 70a^4b^4 + 56a^3b^5 + 28a^2b^6 + 8ab^7 + b^8$$

**8.40** Prove: $\binom{4}{0} + \binom{4}{1} + \binom{4}{2} + \binom{4}{3} + \binom{4}{4} = 2^4 = 16$.

▮ Expand $(1 + 1)^4$ using the binomial theorem:

$$2^4 = (1 + 1)^4 = \binom{4}{0}1^4 + \binom{4}{1}1^31^1 + \binom{4}{2}1^21^2 + \binom{4}{3}1^11^3 + \binom{4}{4}1^4$$

$$= \binom{4}{0} + \binom{4}{1} + \binom{4}{2} + \binom{4}{3} + \binom{4}{4}$$

**8.41** Prove: **(a)** $\binom{n}{0} + \binom{n}{1} + \binom{n}{2} + \binom{n}{3} + \cdots + \binom{n}{n} = 2^n$.

**(b)** $\binom{n}{0} - \binom{n}{1} + \binom{n}{2} - \binom{n}{3} + \cdots \pm \binom{n}{n} = 0$.

▮ **(a)** Expanding $(1 + 1)^n$ using the binomial theorem gives the identity (as in Problem 8.40).
 **(b)** Expanding $(1 - 1)^n$ using the binomial theorem gives the identity.

**8.42**    Prove the Binomial Theorem 8.2: $(a+b)^n = \sum_{r=0}^{n} \binom{n}{r} a^{n-r} b^r$.

$\blacksquare$ The theorem is true for $n = 1$, since

$$\sum_{r=0}^{1} \binom{1}{r} a^{1-r} b^r = \binom{1}{0} a^1 b^0 + \binom{1}{1} a^0 b^1 = a + b = (a+b)^1$$

We assume the theorem holds for $(a+b)^n$ and prove it is true for $(a+b)^{n+1}$.

$$(a+b)^{n+1} = (a+b)(a+b)^n = (a+b) \sum_{r=0}^{n} \binom{n}{r} a^{n-r} b^r$$

Now the term in the product which contains $b^r$ is obtained from

$$b\left[\binom{n}{r-1} a^{n-r+1} b^{r-1}\right] + a\left[\binom{n}{r} a^{n-r} b^r\right] = \binom{n}{r-1} a^{n-r+1} b^r + \binom{n}{r} a^{n-r+1} b^r$$

$$= \left[\binom{n}{r-1} + \binom{n}{r}\right] a^{n-r+1} b^r$$

By Theorem 8.1, $\binom{n}{r-1} + \binom{n}{r} = \binom{n+1}{r}$. Thus the term containing $b^r$ is $\binom{n+1}{r} a^{n-r+1} b^r$. Note that $(a+b)(a+b)^n$ is a polynomial of degree $n+1$ in $b$. Consequently,

$$(a+b)^{n+1} = (a+b)(a+b)^n = \sum_{r=0}^{n+1} \binom{n+1}{r} a^{n-r+1} b^r$$

which was to be proved.

## Multinomial Coefficients

Given nonnegative integers $n_1, n_2, \ldots, n_r$ such that $n_1 + n_2 + \cdots + n_r = n$, then the expression $\binom{n}{n_1, n_2, \ldots, n_r}$ is defined as follows:

$$\binom{n}{n_1, n_2, \ldots, n_r} = \frac{n!}{n_1! \, n_2! \cdots n_r!}$$

These numbers are called the *multinomial coefficients* in view of the following theorem which generalizes the binomial theorem.

**Theorem 8.3:**   $(a_1 + a_2 + \cdots + a_r)^n = \sum_{n_1+n_2+\cdots+n_r=n} \binom{n}{n_1, n_2, \ldots, n_r} a_1^{n_1} a_2^{n_2} \cdots a_r^{n_r}$

**8.43**    Compute: **(a)** $\binom{7}{2, 3, 2}$, and **(b)** $\binom{8}{4, 2, 2, 0}$.

$\blacksquare$ **(a)** $\binom{7}{2, 3, 2} = \frac{7!}{2! \, 3! \, 2!} = \frac{7 \cdot 6 \cdot 5 \cdot 4 \cdot 3 \cdot 2 \cdot 1}{2 \cdot 1 \cdot 3 \cdot 2 \cdot 1 \cdot 2 \cdot 1} = 210$

   **(b)** $\binom{8}{4, 2, 2, 0} = \frac{8!}{4! \, 2! \, 2! \, 0!} = \frac{8 \cdot 7 \cdot 6 \cdot 5 \cdot 4 \cdot 3 \cdot 2 \cdot 1}{4 \cdot 3 \cdot 2 \cdot 1 \cdot 2 \cdot 1 \cdot 2 \cdot 1 \cdot 1} = 420$

**8.44**    Compute: **(a)** $\binom{6}{3, 2, 1}$, and **(b)** $\binom{10}{5, 3, 2, 2}$.

$\blacksquare$ **(a)** $\binom{6}{3, 2, 1} = \frac{6!}{3! \, 2! \, 1!} = \frac{6 \cdot 5 \cdot 4 \cdot 3 \cdot 2 \cdot 1}{3 \cdot 2 \cdot 1 \cdot 2 \cdot 1 \cdot 1} = 60$

   **(b)** The expression $\binom{10}{5, 3, 2, 2}$ has no meaning since $5 + 3 + 2 + 2 \neq 10$.

**8.45**    Expand $(a + b + c)^3$.

▮ Consider all triplets of nonnegative integers $(n_1, n_2, n_3)$ for which $n_1 + n_2 + n_3 = 3$. Thus

$$(a + b + c)^3 = \binom{3}{3, 0, 0}a^3 b^0 b^0 + \binom{3}{2, 1, 0}a^2 b^1 c^0 + \binom{3}{2, 0, 1}a^2 b^0 c^1$$

$$+ \binom{3}{1, 1, 1}a^1 b^1 c^1 + \binom{3}{0, 3, 0}a^0 b^3 c^0 + \binom{3}{0, 2, 1}a^0 b^2 c^1$$

$$+ \binom{3}{1, 2, 0}a^1 b^2 c^0 + \binom{3}{0, 0, 3}a^0 b^0 c^3 + \binom{3}{1, 0, 2}a^1 b^0 c^2 + \binom{3}{0, 1, 2}a^0 b^1 c^2$$

$$= a^3 + 3a^2 b + 3a^2 c + 6abc + b^3 + 3b^2 c + 3ab^2 + c^3 + 3ac^2 + 3bc^2$$

**8.46** Show that $\binom{n}{n_1, n_2} = \binom{n}{n_1} = \binom{n}{n_2}$.

▮ Observe that the expression $\binom{n}{n_1, n_2}$ implicitly implies that $n_1 + n_2 = n$ or $n_2 = n - n_1$. Hence

$$\binom{n}{n_2} = \binom{n}{n_1} = \frac{n!}{n_1! \, (n - n_1)} = \frac{n!}{n_1! \, n_2!} = \binom{n}{n_1, n_2}$$

**8.47** Find the term in the expansion of $(2x^3 - 3xy^2 + z^2)^6$ which contains $x^{11}$ and $y^4$.

▮ The general term of the expansion is

$$\binom{6}{a, b, c}(2x^3)^a(-3xy^2)^b(z^2)^c = \binom{6}{a, b, c}2^a x^{3a}(-3)^b x^b y^{2b} z^{2c}$$

$$= \binom{6}{a, b, c}2^a(-3)^b x^{3a+b} y^{2b} z^{2c}$$

Thus the term containing $x^{11}$ and $y^4$ has $3a + b = 11$ and $2b = 4$ or $b = 2$ and $a = 3$. Also, since $a + b + c = 6$, we have $c = 1$. Substituting in the above gives

$$\binom{6}{3, 2, 1}2^3(-3)^2 x^{11} y^4 z^2 = -\frac{6!}{3! \, 2! \, 1!} 8 \cdot 9 x^{11} y^4 z^2 = -4320 x^{11} y^4 z^2$$

## 8.3 PERMUTATIONS

The number of permutations of $n$ objects taken $r$ at a time will be denoted by

$$P(n, r)$$

Some texts use the notation $_nP_r$, $P_{n,r}$, or $(n)_r$.

**8.48** Discuss permutations using the set $S = \{a, b, c, d\}$ as an example.

▮ Any arrangement of a set of $n$ objects in a given order is called a *permutation* of the objects (taken all at a time). Any arrangement of any $r \le n$ of these objects in a given order is called an *r-permutation* or a *permutation of the n objects taken r at a time*. Thus, for the given set $S$,
  (i) *bdca, dcba,* and *acdb* are permutations of the four letters (taken all at a time);
  (ii) *bad, adb, cbd,* and *bca* are permutations of the four letters taken three at a time;
  (iii) *ad, cb, da,* and *bd* are permutations of the four letters taken two at a time.

**8.49** Find the number of permutations of six objects, say $a, b, c, d, e, f$, taken three at a time. In other words, find the number of "three-letter words" using the given six letters without repeating any letter in a given word.

▮ Let the general three-letter word be represented by the following three boxes:

□□□

Now the first letter can be chosen in six different ways; following this, the second letter can be chosen in five different ways; and, following this, the last letter can be chosen in four different ways. Write each number in its appropriate box as follows:

$\boxed{6}\,\boxed{5}\,\boxed{4}$

Thus by the fundamental principle of counting there are $6 \cdot 5 \cdot 4 = 120$ possible three-letter words without repetitions from the six letters, or there are 120 permutations of six objects taken three at a time, or by our notation, $P(6, 3) = 120$.

**Theorem 8.4:** $P(n, r) = \dfrac{n!}{(n-r)!} = n(n-1)(n-2) \cdots (n-r+1)$.

**8.50** Prove Theorem 8.4.

▌ The derivation of the formula for the number of permutations of $n$ objects taken $r$ at a time, or the number of $r$-permutations of $n$ objects, $P(n, r)$, follows the procedure in Problem 8.49. The first element in an $r$-permutation of $n$ objects can be chosen in $n$ different ways; following this, the second element in the permutation can be chosen in $n - 1$ ways; and, following this, the third element in the permutation can be chosen in $n - 2$ ways. Continuing in this manner, we have that the $r$th (last) element in the $r$-permutation can be chosen in $n - (r - 1) = n - r + 1$ ways. Thus, by the fundamental principle of counting, we have

$$P(n, r) = n(n-1)(n-2) \cdots (n-r+1)$$

Thus, by Problem 8.14,

$$P(n, r) = n(n-1)(n-2) \cdots (n-r+1) = \frac{n(n-1)(n-2) \cdots (n-r+1)(n-r)!}{(n-r)!} = \frac{n!}{(n-r)!}$$

**Corollary 8.5:** There are $n!$ permutations of $n$ objects (taken all at a time).

**8.51** Prove Corollary 8.5.

▌ Using $r = n$ in Theorem 8.4 yields

$$P(n, n) = n(n-1)(n-2) \cdots 3 \cdot 2 \cdot 1 = n!$$

**8.52** Find all the permutations of the three letters $a$, $b$, and $c$.

▌ There are $3! = 1 \cdot 2 \cdot 3 = 6$ such permutations. These are *abc, acb, bac, bca, cab, cba*.

**8.53** Discuss sampling with and without replacement.

▌ Many problems in combinatorial analysis and, in particular, probability, are concerned with choosing a ball from an urn containing $n$ balls (or a card from a deck, or a person from a population). When we choose one ball after the other from the urn, say $r$ times, we call each choice an ordered sample of size $r$. There are two important cases:

(i) *Sampling with replacement.* Here the ball is replaced in the urn before the next ball is chosen. Now since there are $n$ different ways to choose each ball, by the fundamental principle of counting there are

$$\overbrace{n \cdot n \cdot n \cdots n}^{r \text{ times}} = n^r$$

different ordered samples with replacement of size $r$.

(ii) *Sampling without replacement.* Here the ball is not replaced in the urn after it is chosen. Thus there are no repetitions in the ordered sample. In other words, an ordered sample of size $r$ without replacement is simply an $r$-permutation of the objects in the urn. Accordingly, there are

$$P(n, r) = n(n-1)(n-2) \cdots (n-r+1) = \frac{n!}{(n-r)!}$$

different ordered samples of size $r$ without replacement from a population of $n$ objects.

**8.54** Suppose repetitions are not permitted. (*a*) How many three-digit numbers can be formed from the six digits 2, 3, 4, 5, 7, and 9? (*b*) How many of these numbers are less that 400? (*c*) How many are even? (*d*) How many are odd? (*e*) How many are multiples of 5?

▌ In each case draw three boxes ☐☐☐ to represent an arbitrary number, and then write in each box the number of digits that can be placed there.

(*a*) The box on the left can be filled in six ways; following this, the middle box can be filled in five ways; and, lastly, the box on the right can be filled in four ways: ⑥⑤④. Thus there are $6 \cdot 5 \cdot 4 = 120$ numbers.

**(b)** The box on the left can be filled in only two ways, by 2 or 3, since each number must be less than 400; the middle box can be filled in five ways; and, lastly, the box on the right can be filled in four ways: ☐2☐5☐4☐. Thus there are $2 \cdot 5 \cdot 4 = 40$ numbers.

**(c)** The box on the right can be filled in only two ways, by 2 or 6, since the numbers must be even; the box on the left can then be filled in five ways; and, lastly, the middle box can be filled in four ways: ☐5☐4☐2☐. Thus there are $5 \cdot 4 \cdot 2 = 40$ numbers.

**(d)** The box on the right can be filled in only four ways, by 3, 5, 7, or 9, since the numbers must be odd; the box on the left can then be filled in five ways; and, lastly, the box in the middle can be filled in four ways: ☐5☐4☐4☐. Thus there are $5 \cdot 4 \cdot 4 = 80$ numbers.

**(e)** The box on the right can be filled in only one way, by 5, since the numbers must be multiples of 5; the box on the left can then be filled in five ways; and, lastly, the box in the middle can be filled in four ways: ☐5☐4☐1☐. Thus there are $5 \cdot 4 \cdot 1 = 20$ numbers.

**8.55** Solve Problem 8.54 if repetitions are permitted.

▮ **(a)** Each box can be filled in six ways: ☐6☐6☐6☐. Thus there are $6 \cdot 6 \cdot 6 = 216$ numbers.

▮ **(b)** The box on the left can still be filled in only two ways, by 2 or 3, and each of the others in six ways: ☐2☐6☐6☐. Thus there are $2 \cdot 6 \cdot 6 = 72$ numbers.

▮ **(c)** The box on the right can still be filled in only two ways, by 2 or 6, and each of the others in six ways: ☐6☐6☐2☐. Thus there are $6 \cdot 6 \cdot 2 = 72$ numbers.

▮ **(d)** The box on the right can still be filled in only four ways, by 3, 5, 7, or 9, and each of the other boxes in six ways: ☐6☐6☐4☐. Thus there are $6 \cdot 6 \cdot 4 = 144$ numbers.

▮ **(e)** The box on the left can still be filled in only one way, by 5, and each of the other boxes in six ways: ☐6☐6☐1☐. Thus there are $6 \cdot 6 \cdot 1 = 36$ numbers.

**8.56** Find the number of ways that a party of seven persons can arrange themselves in a row of seven chairs.

▮ The seven persons can arrange themselves in a row in $7 \cdot 6 \cdot 5 \cdot 4 \cdot 3 \cdot 2 \cdot 1 = 7!$ ways.

**8.57** Solve Problem 8.56 if they sit around a circular table.

▮ One person can sit at any place in the circular table. The other six persons can then arrange themselves in $6 \cdot 5 \cdot 4 \cdot 3 \cdot 2 \cdot 1 = 6!$ ways around the table.

**8.58** What is a circular permutation of $n$ objects and how many are there?

▮ A circular permutation of $n$ objects is an arrangement of the objects around a circle. There are $(n-1)!$ such permutations as illustrated in Problem 8.57 for $n = 7$.

**8.59** Find the number $n$ of ways that a judge can award first, second, and third places in a contest with eighteen contestants.

▮ There are 18 choices for first place, 17 for second place, and 16 for third place. Thus $n = 18 \cdot 17 \cdot 16 = 4896$. Note that $n = P(18, 3)$.

**8.60** A box contains 10 light bulbs. Find the number $n$ of ordered samples of: **(a)** size 3 with replacement, and **(b)** size 3 without replacement.

▮ **(a)** $n = 10^3 = 10 \cdot 10 \cdot 10 = 1000$,   and   **(b)** $n = P(10, 3) = 10 \cdot 9 \cdot 8 = 720$.

**8.61** Solve Problem 8.60 for: **(a)** size 4 with replacement, and **(b)** size 5 without replacement.

▮ **(a)** $n = 10^4 = 10\,000$,   and   **(b)** $n = P(10, 5) = 10 \cdot 9 \cdot 8 \cdot 7 \cdot 6 = 5824$.

**8.62** A poker hand consists of five cards from an ordinary playing deck with 52 cards. In closed poker, a player is dealt five cards down (only the player can see them) and then the bidding begins. In 5-card stud poker, a player is dealt one card down and then four cards open (which all the players can see). Bidding occurs after each card. Which, if any, of the poker hands is considered a permutation and which, if any, is considered a combination? (See Section 8.4 for the definition of combination.)

▮ The hand in closed poker is a combination since the order in which the five cards are dealt does not matter. The hand in 5-card stud poker is a permutation since the order does make a difference.

**8.63**    Find the number $n$ of poker hands in 5-card stud poker.

▮    Since the deck has 52 cards, $n = P(52, 5) = 52 \cdot 51 \cdot 50 \cdot 49 \cdot 48 = 311\ 875\ 200$.

**8.64**    Find the number $n$ of poker hands in 5-card stud poker if the closed card is an ace.

▮    There are four choices for the closed card, and then 51, 50, 49, and 48 choices for the other four cards, respectively. Thus $n = 4 \cdot 51 \cdot 50 \cdot 49 \cdot 48 = 23\ 990\ 400$.

**8.65**    Solve Problem 8.64 if the closed card is a diamond.

▮    Here there are 13 choices for the closed card; hence $n = 13 \cdot 51 \cdot 50 \cdot 49 \cdot 48 = 77\ 968\ 800$.

**8.66**    Find the number $n$ of ways that six people can ride a toboggan. Note that anyone can drive it.

▮    Here $n = 6! = 6 \cdot 5 \cdot 4 \cdot 3 \cdot 2 \cdot 1 = 720$ ways they can ride the toboggan.

**8.67**    Solve Problem 8.66 if only half of the people can drive the toboggan.

▮    Here there are only three choices for the first (driving) position. Thus $n = 3 \cdot 5 \cdot 4 \cdot 3 \cdot 2 \cdot 1 = 360$.

**8.68**    A debating team consists of three boys and two girls. Find the number $n$ of ways they can sit in a row.

▮    Since there are five persons, $n = 5 \cdot 4 \cdot 3 \cdot 2 \cdot 1 = 5! = 120$.

**8.69**    A debating team consists of three boys and two girls. Find the number $n$ of ways they can sit in a row if: **(a)** the boys and girls are each to sit together, **(b)** just the girls are to sit together.

▮    **(a)**    There are two ways to distribute them according to sex: BBBGG or GGBBB. In each case the boys can sit in $3 \cdot 2 \cdot 1 = 3! = 6$ ways, and the girls can sit in $2 \cdot 1 = 2! = 2$ ways. Thus $n = 2 \cdot 3!\ 2! = 2 \cdot 6 \cdot 2 = 24$.

   **(b)**    There are four ways to distribute them according to sex: GGBBB, BGGBB, BBGGB, BBBGG. Note that each way corresponds to the number, 0, 1, 2, or 3, of boys sitting to the left of the girls. In each case, the boys can sit in 3! ways, and the girls in 2! ways. Thus, altogether, $n = 4 \cdot 3!\ 2! = 4 \cdot 6 \cdot 2 = 48$.

**8.70**    Solve Problem 8.69 in the case of $r$ boys and $s$ girls. (Answers are to be left in terms of factorials.)

▮    **(a)**    There are still two ways to distribute them according to sex, the boys on the left or the girls on the left. In each case the boys can sit in $r!$ ways and the girls in $s!$ ways. Thus, altogether, there are $2r!\ s!$ ways.

   **(b)**    There are $r + 1$ ways to distribute them according to sex, each way corresponding to the number, $0, 1, \ldots, r$, of boys sitting to the left of the girls. In each case the boys can sit in $r!$ ways and the girls in $s!$ ways. Thus, altogether, there are $(r + 1)r!\ s!$ ways.

**8.71**    Find the number of ways that four mathematics books, three history books, three chemistry books, and two sociology books can be arranged on a shelf so that all books of the same subject are together.

▮    First the books must be arranged on the shelf in four units according to subject matter: ☐☐☐☐. The box on the left can be filled by any of the four subjects; the next by any three subjects remaining; the next by any two subjects remaining; and the box on the right by the last subject: ④③②①. Thus there are $4 \cdot 3 \cdot 2 \cdot 1 = 4!$ ways to arrange the books on the shelf according to subject matter.

   In each of the above cases, the mathematics books can be arranged in 4! ways, the history books in 3! ways, the chemistry books in 3! ways, and the sociology books in 2! ways. Thus, altogether, there are $4!\ 4!\ 3!\ 3!\ 2! = 41\ 472$ arrangements.

**8.72**    Solve Problem 8.71 if there are $r$ subjects, $A_1, A_2, \ldots, A_r$, covered in $s_1, s_2, \ldots, s_r$ books, respectively.

▮    Since there are $r$ subjects, the books can be arranged on the shelf in $r!$ ways according to subject matter. In each case, the books in subject $A_1$ can be arranged in $s_1!$ ways, the books in subject $A_2$ in $s_2!$ ways, . . . , the books in subject $A_r$ in $s_r!$ ways. Thus, altogether, there are $r!\ s_1!\ s_2! \cdots s_r!$ arrangements.

**8.73**    Find the number of ways that three Americans, four Frenchmen, four Danes, and two Italians can be seated in a row so that those of the same nationality sit together.

▮    The four nationalities can be arranged in a row in 4! ways. In each case, the three Americans can be seated in 3! ways, the four Frenchmen in 4! ways, the four Danes in 4! ways, and the two Italians in 2! ways. Thus, altogether, there are $4!\ 3!\ 4!\ 4!\ 2! = 165\ 888$ arrangements.

**8.74**    Solve Problem 8.73 if they sit at a round table.

    ❚  The four nationalities can be arranged in a circle in 3! ways (see Problem 8.58 on circular permutations). In each case, the three Americans can be seated in 3! ways, the four Frenchmen in 4! ways, the four Danes in 4! ways, and the two Italians in 2! ways. Thus, altogether, there are 3! 3! 4! 4! 2! = 41 472 arrangements.

**8.75**    Find the total number of positive integers that can be formed from the digits 1, 2, 3, and 4 if no digit is repeated in any one integer.

    ❚  Note that no integer can contain more than four digits. Let $s_1$, $s_2$, $s_3$, and $s_4$ denote the number of integers containing one, two, three, and four digits respectively. We compute each $s_i$ separately.

    Since there are four digits, there are four integers containing exactly one digit, i.e., $s_1 = 4$. Also, since there are four digits, there are $4 \cdot 3 = 12$ integers containing two digits, i.e., $s_2 = 12$. Similarly, there are $4 \cdot 3 \cdot 2 = 24$ integers containing three digits and $4 \cdot 3 \cdot 2 \cdot 1 = 24$ integers containing four digits, i.e., $s_3 = 24$ and $s_4 = 24$. Thus, altogether, there are $s_1 + s_2 + s_3 + s_4 = 4 + 12 + 24 + 24 = 64$ integers.

**8.76**    Find the number $n$ of four-letter words that can be formed from the word NUMERICAL. [A word need not make sense.]

    ❚  Since there are nine letters, $n = P(9, 4) = 9 \cdot 8 \cdot 7 \cdot 6 = 3024$.

**8.77**    Solve Problem 8.76 if the words are to begin and end in a consonant.

    ❚  There are only five consonants. Thus there are five choices for the first letter, four choices for the last letter, and then seven and six choices for the second and third letters, respectively. Thus $n = 5 \cdot 7 \cdot 6 \cdot 4 = 840$.

**8.78**    Solve Problem 8.76 if the words must contain the letter R.

    ❚  There are four places to put R in the word. The other three places can be chosen in eight, seven, and six ways respectively. Thus $n = 4 \cdot 8 \cdot 7 \cdot 6 = 1344$.

**8.79**    Solve Problem 8.76 if the words must contain the letter M and end in a vowel.

    ❚  There are four vowels, and so there are four choices for the last letter. There are three places to put the letter M in the word. The remaining two places can be chosen in seven and six ways, respectively. Thus $n = 4 \cdot 3 \cdot 7 \cdot 6 = 504$.

**8.80**    Find the number $n$ of ways that five large books, four medium-sized books, and three small books can be placed on a shelf so that all books of the same size are together.

    ❚  The three blocks of books can be arranged on the shelf in 3! ways. In each case, the large books can be arranged in 5! ways, the medium-sized books in 4! ways, and the small books in 3! ways. Thus $n = 3! \, 5! \, 4! \, 3! = 103 680$.

**8.81**    Find: (**a**) $P(7, 3)$, and (**b**) $P(12, 2)$.

    ❚  Note $P(n, r) = n(n - 1)(n - 2) \cdots (n - r + 1)$ contains $r$ factors.
(**a**)  $P(7, 3) = 7 \cdot 6 \cdot 5 = 210$.
(**b**)  $P(12, 2) = 12 \cdot 11 = 132$.

**8.82**    Find: (**a**) $P(5, 7)$, and (**b**) $P(8, 3)$.

    ❚  (**a**)  $P(5, 7)$ is not defined since the second integer cannot exceed the first integer.
      (**b**)  $P(8, 3) = 8 \cdot 7 \cdot 6 = 336$.

**8.83**    Find: (**a**) $P(19, 1)$, and (**b**) $P(6, -2)$.

    ❚  (**a**)  $P(19, 1) = 19$.
      (**b**)  $P(6, -2)$ is not defined since $P(n, r)$ is not defined for negative integers.

**8.84**    Find $n$ if (**a**) $P(n, 2) = 72$, and (**b**) $P(n, 4) = 42P(n, 2)$.

    ❚  (**a**)  $P(n, 2) = n(n - 1) = n^2 - n$; hence $n^2 - n = 72$ or $n^2 - n - 72 = 0$ or $(n - 9)(n + 8) = 0$. Since $n$ must be positive, the only answer is $n = 9$.

**(b)** $P(n, 4) = n(n-1)(n-2)(n-3)$ and $P(n, 2) = n(n-1)$. Hence

$$n(n-1)(n-2)(n-3) = 42n(n-1) \quad \text{or,} \quad \text{if } n \neq 0, \ n \neq 1, \ (n-2)(n-3) = 42$$

$$\text{or} \quad n^2 - 5n + 6 = 42 \quad \text{or} \quad n^2 - 5n - 36 = 0 \quad \text{or} \quad (n-9)(n+4) = 0$$

Since $n$ must be positive, the only answer is $n = 9$.

**8.85**   Find $n$ if $2P(n, 2) + 50 = P(2n, 2)$.

▌ $P(n, 2) = n(n-1) = n^2 - n$ and $P(2n, 2) = 2n(2n-1) = 4n^2 - 2n$. Hence

$$2(n^2 - n) + 50 = 4n^2 - 2n \quad \text{or} \quad 2n^2 - 2n + 50 = 4n^2 - 2n \quad \text{or} \quad 50 = 2n^2 \quad \text{or} \quad n^2 = 25$$

Since $n$ must be positive, the only answer is $n = 5$.

**8.86**   Show that $P(n, r) = r! \binom{n}{r}$.

▌ Recall that $\binom{n}{r} = \dfrac{n!}{r!\,(n-r)!}$ and $P(n, r) = \dfrac{n!}{(n-r)!}$. Multiply $P(n, r)$ by $\dfrac{r!}{r!}$ to obtain

$$P(n, r) = \frac{n!}{(n-r)!} = \frac{r!}{r!} \frac{n!}{(n-r)!} = r! \frac{n!}{r!\,(n-r)!} = r! \binom{n}{r}$$

## Permutations with Repetitions

**8.87**   Find the number $m$ of all possible five-letter "words" using the letters from the word "DADDY".

▌ Note first that there are $5! = 120$ permutations of the objects $D_1, A, D_2, D_3, Y$, where the three D's are distinguished. Furthermore, the following six permutations

$$D_1 D_2 D_3 AY, \ D_2 D_1 D_3 AY, \ D_3 D_1 D_2 AY, \ D_1 D_3 D_2 AY, \ D_2 D_3 D_1 AY, \ \text{and} \ D_3 D_2 D_1 AY$$

produce the same word when the subscripts are removed. The 6 comes from the fact that there are $3! = 3 \cdot 2 \cdot 1 = 6$ different ways of placing the three D's in the first three positions in the permutation. This is true for each set of three positions in which the D's can appear. Accordingly,

$$m = \frac{5!}{3!} = \frac{120}{6} = 20$$

**Theorem 8.6:**   The number of permutations of $n$ objects of which $n_1$ are alike, $n_2$ are alike, . . . , $n_r$ are alike is

$$\frac{n!}{n_1!\, n_2! \cdots n_r!}$$

**8.88**   Prove Theorem 8.6.

▌ The derivation of the formula follows the procedure in Problem 8.87. That is, there are $n!$ permutations when all the $n$ objects are distinguished. We must then divide the $n!$ by $n_1!$ to account for the fact that the $n_1$ objects which are alike will identify $n_1!$ of these permutations for any given set of positions of the $n_1$ objects in the permutation. Similarly, we must divide $n!$ by $n_2!, \ldots, n_r!$, which are the number of permutations of the corresponding alike objects. Thus the theorem is proved.

**8.89**   Find the number $m$ of seven-letter "words" that can be formed using the letters of the word "BENZENE".

▌ We seek the number of permutations of seven objects of which three are alike (the three E's) and two are alike (the two N's). By Theorem 8.6,

$$m = \frac{7!}{3!\, 2!} = \frac{7 \cdot 6 \cdot 5 \cdot 4 \cdot 3 \cdot 2 \cdot 1}{3 \cdot 2 \cdot 1 \cdot 2 \cdot 1} = 420$$

**8.90**   How many different signals, each consisting of eight flags hung in a vertical line, can be formed from a set of four indistinguishable red flags, three indistinguishable white flags, and a blue flag?

▮ We seek the number of permutations of eight objects of which four are alike and three are alike. There are

$$\frac{8!}{4!\,3!}=\frac{8\cdot 7\cdot 6\cdot 5\cdot 4\cdot 3\cdot 2\cdot 1}{4\cdot 3\cdot 2\cdot 1\cdot 3\cdot 2\cdot 1}=280$$

different signals.

**8.91** Find the number of distinct permutations that can be formed from all the letters of each word: (*a*) THEM, and (*b*) THAT.

▮ (*a*) $4!=24$, since there are four letters and no repetitions.

(*b*) $\dfrac{4!}{2!}=12$, since there are four letters of which two are T.

**8.92** Find the number of distinct permutations that can be formed from all the letters of each word: (*a*) RADAR, and (*b*) UNUSUAL.

▮ (*a*) $\dfrac{5!}{2!\,2!}=30$, since there are five letters of which two are R and two are A.

(*b*) $\dfrac{7!}{3!}=840$, since there are seven letters of which three are U.

**8.93** How many different signals, each consisting of six flags hung in a vertical line, can be formed from four identical red flags and two identical blue flags?

▮ This problem concerns permutations with repetitions. There are $\dfrac{6!}{4!\,2!}=15$ signals since there are six flags of which four are red and two are blue.

**8.94** Find the number $m$ of permutations that can be formed from all the letters of the word MISSISSIPPI.

▮ There are eleven letters of which four are I, four are S, and two are P; hence $m=\dfrac{11!}{4!\,4!\,2!}=34\,650$.

**8.95** Solve Problem 8.94 if the words are to begin with an I.

▮ Now there are ten positions left to fill where three are I, four are S, and two are P. Thus $m=\dfrac{10!}{3!\,4!\,2!}=12\,600$.

**8.96** Solve Problem 8.94 if the words are to begin and end in S.

▮ Now there are nine positions left to fill where four are I, two are S, and two are P. Hence $m=\dfrac{9!}{4!\,2!\,2!}=7560$.

**8.97** Solve Problem 8.94 if the two P's are to be next to each other.

▮ There are ten ways to place the two P's, the first and second letter, or the second and third letters, . . . , or the tenth and eleventh letters. In each case, there are nine positions left to fill where four are I and four are S. Thus $m=10\,\dfrac{9!}{4!\,4!}=6300$.

**8.98** Solve Problem 8.94 if the four S's are to be next to each other.

▮ Consider the four S's as one letter. Then there are eight letters of which four are I and two are P. Thus $m=\dfrac{8!}{4!\,2!}=840$. Alternatively, there are eight ways to place the four S's and, in each case, there are seven positions left to fill where four are I and two are P. Then $m=8\,\dfrac{7!}{4!\,2!}=840$.

**8.99** Find the number $m$ of permutations that can be formed from all the letters of the word ELEVEN.

*I* There are six letters of which three are E; hence $m = \dfrac{6!}{3!} = 120$.

**8.100** Solve Problem 8.99 if the words are to begin with L.

*I* Now there are five positions left to fill where three are E. Thus $m = \dfrac{5!}{3!} = 20$.

**8.101** Solve Problem 8.99 if the words are to begin and end in E.

*I* Now there are only four positions to fill with four distinct letters; hence $m = 4! = 24$.

**8.102** Solve Problem 8.99 if the words are to begin with E and end in N.

*I* Now there are four positions left to fill where two are E. Hence $m = \dfrac{4!}{2!} = 12$.

**8.103** Find the number $m$ of permutations that can be formed from all the letters of the word BASEBALL.

*I* There are eight letters of which two are B, two are A, and two are L. Thus $m = \dfrac{8!}{2!\,2!\,2!} = 5040$.

**8.104** Solve Problem 8.103 if the two B's are to be next to each other.

*I* Consider the two B's as one letter. Then there are seven letters of which two are A and two are L. Hence $m = \dfrac{7!}{2!\,2!} = 1260$.

**8.105** Solve Problem 8.103 if the words are to begin and end in a vowel.

*I* There are three possibilities, the words begin and end in A, the words begin in A and end in E, or the words begin in E and end in A. In each case there are six positions left to fill where two are B and two are L. Hence $m = 3\,\dfrac{6!}{2!\,2!} = 540$.

## 8.4 COMBINATIONS

Given a set of $n$ objects, a *combination* of these $n$ objects taken $r$ at a time is any selection of $r$ of the objects where order does not count. In other words, an $r$-combination of a set of $n$ objects is any subset of $r$ elements. Thus the following are combinations of the set $S$ of Problem 8.48 taken three at a time:

$$\{a, b, c\}, \{a, b, d\}, \{a, c, d\}, \{b, c, d\} \qquad \text{or simply} \qquad abc, abd, acd, bcd$$

Observe that the following combinations are equal:

$$abc, acb, bac, bca, cab \quad \text{and} \quad cba$$

That is, each denotes the same set $\{a, b, c\}$.

The number of combinations of $n$ objects taken $r$ at a time or, in other words, the number of $r$-element subsets of a set with $n$ elements will be denoted by

$$C(n, r)$$

Some texts use the notation $_nC_r$ or $C_{n,r}$.

**8.106** Find the number of combinations of four objects, say, $a$, $b$, $c$, $d$, taken three at a time, that is, find $C(4, 3)$.

*I* *Method 1.* List all possible subsets of $S = \{a, b, c, d\}$ with three elements obtaining:

$$\{a, b, c\}, \{a, b, d\}, \{a, c, d\}, \{b, c, d\} \qquad \text{or simply} \qquad abc, abd, acd, bcd$$

Thus $C(4, 3) = 4$.

*Method 2.* Each combination consisting of three objects determines $3! = 6$ permutations of the objects in the combination as indicated in Fig. 8-2. Thus the number $C(4, 3)$ of combinations multiplied by $3!$ equals the

| Combination | Permutations |
|:-----------:|:------------:|
| abc | abc, acb, bac, bca, cab, cba |
| abd | abd, adb, bad, bda, dab, dba |
| acd | acd, adc, cad, cda, dac, dca |
| bcd | bcd, bdc, cbd, cdb, dbc, dcb |

**Fig. 8-2**

number $P(4, 3)$ of permutations, that is,

$$C(4, 3) \cdot 3! = P(4, 3) \quad \text{or} \quad C(4, 3) = \frac{P(4, 3)}{3!}$$

But $P(4, 3) = 4 \cdot 3 \cdot 2 = 24$ and $3! = 6$; hence $C(4, 3) = 4$ as noted above.

**Theorem 8.7:** $\quad C(n, r) = \dfrac{P(n, r)}{r!} = \dfrac{n!}{r! \, (n - r)!}$.

**Remark:** Recall that the binomial coefficient $\binom{n}{r}$ was defined to be $\dfrac{n!}{r! \, (n - r)!}$; hence

$$C(n, r) = \binom{n}{r}$$

Accordingly, we shall use $C(n, r)$ and $\binom{n}{r}$ interchangeably.

**8.107** Prove Theorem 8.7.

▮ Any combination of $n$ objects taken $r$ at a time determines $r!$ permutations of the objects in the combination as illustrated in Fig. 8-2 for $r = 3$. Accordingly,

$$P(n, r) = r! \, C(n, r)$$

Dividing by $r!$ gives us our result.

**8.108** Find the number $m$ of committees of three that can be formed from eight people.

▮ Each committee is, essentially, a combination of the eight people taken three at a time. Thus

$$m = C(8, 3) = \binom{8}{3} = \frac{8 \cdot 7 \cdot 6}{1 \cdot 2 \cdot 3} = 56$$

**8.109** A farmer buys three cows, two pigs, and four hens from a man who has six cows, five pigs, and eight hens. How many choices does the farmer have?

▮ The farmer can choose the cows in $\binom{6}{3}$ ways, the pigs in $\binom{5}{2}$ ways, and the hens in $\binom{8}{4}$ ways. Hence altogether the farmer can choose the animals in

$$\binom{6}{3}\binom{5}{2}\binom{8}{4} = \frac{6 \cdot 5 \cdot 4}{1 \cdot 2 \cdot 3} \frac{5 \cdot 4}{1 \cdot 2} \frac{8 \cdot 7 \cdot 6 \cdot 5}{1 \cdot 2 \cdot 3 \cdot 4} = 20 \cdot 10 \cdot 70 = 14\,000 \text{ ways}$$

**8.110** A class consists of seven men and five women. Find the number $m$ of committees of five that can be selected from the class.

▮ Each committee is a combination of the twelve people taken five at a time. Thus

$$m = C(12, 5) = \binom{12}{5} = \frac{12 \cdot 11 \cdot 10 \cdot 9 \cdot 8}{5 \cdot 4 \cdot 3 \cdot 2 \cdot 1} = 5544$$

**8.111** Solve Problem 8.110 if the committee is to consist of three men and two women.

▮ The three men can be chosen from the seven men in $\binom{7}{3}$ ways, and the two women can be chosen from the five women in $\binom{5}{2}$ ways. Hence

$$m = \binom{7}{3}\binom{5}{2} = \frac{7 \cdot 6 \cdot 5}{1 \cdot 2 \cdot 3}\frac{5 \cdot 4}{1 \cdot 2} = 350$$

**8.112**   Solve Problem 8.110 if the committee is to consist of at least one man and at least one woman.

▮ By Problem 8.110, there are $C(12, 5) = 5544$ possible committees. Among these possible committees, there is $C(5, 5) = 1$ committee consisting of the five women, and $C(7, 5) = 21$ consisting of five men. Eliminating these from all possible committees yields $m = 5544 - 21 - 1 = 5522$.

**8.113**   A bag contains five red marbles and six white marbles. Find the number $m$ of ways that four marbles can be drawn from the bag.

▮ The four marbles (of any color) can be chosen from the eleven marbles in

$$m = \binom{11}{4} = \frac{11 \cdot 10 \cdot 9 \cdot 8}{1 \cdot 2 \cdot 3 \cdot 4} = 330 \text{ ways}$$

**8.114**   Solve Problem 8.113 if two of the marbles must be red and two of the marbles must be white.

▮ The two red marbles may be chosen in $\binom{5}{2}$ ways and the two white marbles may be chosen in $\binom{6}{2}$ ways. Thus

$$m = \binom{5}{2}\binom{6}{2} = \frac{5 \cdot 4}{2 \cdot 1}\frac{6 \cdot 5}{2 \cdot 1} = 150$$

**8.115**   Solve Problem 8.113 if the four marbles must be of the same color.

▮ There are $\binom{6}{4} = 15$ ways of drawing four white marbles, and $\binom{5}{4} = 5$ ways of drawing four red marbles. Thus there are $15 + 5 = 20$ ways of drawing four marbles of the same color.

**8.116**   There are twelve students who are eligible to attend the National Student Association annual meeting. Find the number $m$ of ways a delegation of four students can be selected from the twelve eligible students.

▮ The four students can be chosen from the twelve students in $m = \binom{12}{4} = \frac{12 \cdot 11 \cdot 10 \cdot 9}{1 \cdot 2 \cdot 3 \cdot 4} = 495$ ways.

**8.117**   Solve Problem 8.116 if two of the eligible students will not attend the meeting together.

▮ Let $A$ and $B$ denote the students who will not attend the meeting together.

*Method 1.*  If neither $A$ nor $B$ is included, then the delegation can be chosen in $\binom{10}{4} = \frac{10 \cdot 9 \cdot 8 \cdot 7}{1 \cdot 2 \cdot 3 \cdot 4} = 210$

ways. If either $A$ or $B$, but not both, is included, then the delegation can be chosen in $2 \cdot \binom{10}{3} =$

$2 \cdot \frac{10 \cdot 9 \cdot 8}{1 \cdot 2 \cdot 3} = 240$ ways. Altogether, the delegation can be chosen in $m = 210 + 240 = 450$ ways.

*Method 2.*  If $A$ and $B$ are both included, then the other two members of the delegation can be chosen in $\binom{10}{2} = 45$ ways. Thus there are $m = 495 - 45 = 450$ ways the delegation can be chosen if $A$ and $B$ are not both included

**8.118**   Solve Problem 8.116 if two of the eligible students are married and will only attend the meeting together.

▮ Let $C$ and $D$ denote the married students. If $C$ and $D$ do not go, then the delegation can be chosen in

$\binom{10}{4} = 210$ ways. If both $C$ and $D$ go, then the delegation can be chosen in $\binom{10}{2} = 45$ ways. Altogether, the delegation can be chosen in $m = 210 + 45 = 255$ ways.

**8.119**  A student is to answer eight out of ten questions on an exam. Find the number $m$ of ways that the student can choose the eight questions.

▮  The eight questions can be selected in $m = \binom{10}{8} = \binom{10}{2} = \dfrac{10 \cdot 9}{1 \cdot 2} = 45$ ways.

**8.120**  Solve Problem 8.119 if the student must answer the first three questions.

▮  If the first three questions are answered, then the student can choose the other five questions from the last seven questions in $m = \binom{7}{5} = \binom{7}{2} = \dfrac{7 \cdot 6}{1 \cdot 2} = 21$ ways.

**8.121**  Solve Problem 8.119 if the student must answer at least four out of the first five questions.

▮  If the student answers all the first five questions, then the other three questions can be chosen from the last five in $\binom{5}{3} = 10$ ways. On the other hand, if the student answers only four of the first five questions, then these four can be chosen in $\binom{5}{4} = \binom{5}{1} = 5$ ways, and the other four questions from the last five in $\binom{5}{4} = \binom{5}{1} = 5$ ways; hence the student can choose the eight questions in $5 \cdot 5 = 25$ ways. Thus there will be a total of $m = 10 + 25 = 35$ choices.

**8.122**  There are twelve points $A, B, \ldots$ in a given plane, no three on the same line. (**a**) How many lines are determined by the points? (**b**) How many lines pass through the point $A$?

▮  (**a**)  Since two points determine a line, there are $\binom{12}{2} = \dfrac{12 \cdot 11}{1 \cdot 2} = 66$ lines.

  (**b**)  To determine a line through $A$, one other point must be chosen; hence there are eleven lines through $A$.

**8.123**  There are twelve points $A, B, \ldots$ in a given plane, no three on the same line. (**a**) How many triangles are determined by the points? (**b**) How many of these triangles contain the point $A$ as a vertex?

▮  (**a**)  Since three points determine a triangle, there are $\binom{12}{3} = \dfrac{12 \cdot 11 \cdot 10}{1 \cdot 2 \cdot 3} = 220$ triangles.

  (**b**)  *Method 1.*  To determine a triangle with vertex $A$, two other points must be chosen; hence there are $\binom{11}{2} = \dfrac{11 \cdot 10}{1 \cdot 2} = 55$ triangles with $A$ as a vertex.

  *Method 2.*  There are $\binom{11}{3} = \dfrac{11 \cdot 10 \cdot 9}{1 \cdot 2 \cdot 3} = 165$ triangles without $A$ as a vertex. Thus $220 - 165 = 55$ of the triangles do have $A$ as a vertex.

**8.124**  How many committees of five with a given chairperson can be selected from twelve persons?

▮  The chairperson can be chosen in twelve ways and, following this, the other four on the committee can be chosen from the eleven remaining in $\binom{11}{4}$ ways. Thus there are $12 \cdot \binom{11}{4} = 12 \cdot 330 = 3960$ such committees.

**8.125**  Find the number of subsets of a set $X$ containing $n$ elements.

▮  *Method 1.*  The number of subsets of $X$ with $r \le n$ elements is given by $\binom{n}{r}$. Hence, altogether there are

$$\binom{n}{0} + \binom{n}{1} + \binom{n}{2} + \cdots + \binom{n}{n-1} + \binom{n}{n}$$

subsets of $X$. The above sum is equal to $2^n$ (Problem 8.41), and so there are $2^n$ subsets of $X$.

*Method 2.* There are two possibilities for each element of $X$: either it belongs to the subset or it doesn't; hence there are

$$\overbrace{2 \cdot 2 \cdot \cdots \cdot 2}^{n \text{ times}} = 2^n$$

ways to form a subset of $X$, i.e., there are $2^n$ different subsets of $X$.

**8.126**  In how many ways can a teacher choose one or more students from six eligible students?

▌ *Method 1.* By Problem 8.125, there are $2^6 = 64$ subsets of the set consisting of the six students. However, the empty set must be deleted since one or more students are chosen. Accordingly, there are $2^6 - 1 = 64 - 1 = 63$ ways to choose the students.

*Method 2.* Either one, two, three, four, five, or six students are chosen. Hence the number of choices is

$$\binom{6}{1} + \binom{6}{2} + \binom{6}{3} + \binom{6}{4} + \binom{6}{5} + \binom{6}{6} = 6 + 15 + 20 + 15 + 6 + 1 = 63$$

**8.127**  In how many ways can three or more persons be selected from twelve persons?

▌ There are $2^{12} - 1 = 4096 - 1 = 4095$ ways of choosing one or more of the twelve persons. Now there are $\binom{12}{1} + \binom{12}{2} = 12 + 66 = 78$ ways of choosing one or two of the twelve persons. Hence there are $4095 - 78 = 4017$ ways of choosing three or more.

**8.128**  How many diagonals has an octagon?

▌ An octagon has eight sides and eight vertices. Any two vertices determine either a side or a diagonal. Thus there are $\binom{8}{2} = \frac{8 \cdot 7}{1 \cdot 2} = 28$ sides plus diagonals. But there are eight sides; hence there are $28 - 8 = 20$ diagonals.

**8.129**  How many diagonals has a regular polygon with $n$ sides?

▌ The regular polygon with $n$ sides has, also, $n$ vertices. Any two vertices determine either a side or a diagonal. Thus there are $\binom{n}{2} = \frac{n(n-1)}{1 \cdot 2} = \frac{n(n-1)}{2}$ sides plus diagonals. But there are $n$ sides; hence there are

$$\frac{n(n-1)}{2} - n = \frac{n^2 - n}{2} - \frac{2n}{2} = \frac{n^2 - 3n}{2} = \frac{n(n-3)}{2} \quad \text{diagonals}$$

**8.130**  Which regular polygon has the same number of diagonals as sides?

▌ The regular polygon with $n$ sides has, by Problem 8.129, $\frac{n^2 - 3n}{2}$ diagonals. Thus we seek the polygon of $n$ sides for which

$$\frac{n^2 - 3n}{2} = n \quad \text{or} \quad n^2 - 3n = 2n \quad \text{or} \quad n^2 - 5n = 0 \quad \text{or} \quad n(n-5) = 0$$

Since $n$ must be a positive integer, the only answer is $n = 5$. In other words, the pentagon is the only regular polygon with the same number of diagonals as sides.

**8.131**  A card player is dealt a poker hand (five cards) from an ordinary playing deck with 52 cards. Find the number $m$ of ways the player could be dealt a spade flush (five spades).

▌ The five spades can be dealt from the thirteen spades in $\binom{13}{5} = \frac{13 \cdot 12 \cdot 11 \cdot 10 \cdot 9}{1 \cdot 2 \cdot 3 \cdot 4 \cdot 5} = 1287$ ways.

**8.132**  Solve Problem 8.131 if the player is dealt an ace-high spade flush (five spades with the ace).

▌ If the spade ace is dealt, then the player can be dealt the other four spades from the remaining twelve spades in $m = \binom{12}{4} = \frac{12 \cdot 11 \cdot 10 \cdot 9}{1 \cdot 2 \cdot 3 \cdot 4} = 495$ ways.

**8.133**    Solve Problem 8.131 if the player is dealt a flush (five of the same suit).

❚   There are four suits, and a flush from each suit can be dealt in $\binom{13}{5}$ ways; hence

$$m = 4 \cdot \binom{13}{5} = 5148 \text{ ways}$$

**8.134**    Solve Problem 8.131 if the player is dealt an ace-high full house (three aces with another pair).

❚   The three aces can be dealt from the four aces in $\binom{4}{3} = \binom{4}{1} = 4$ ways. The pair can be selected in twelve ways, and the two cards of this pair can be dealt in $\binom{4}{2}$ ways. Thus

$$m = 4 \cdot 12 \cdot \binom{4}{2} = 4 \cdot 12 \cdot \frac{4 \cdot 3}{1 \cdot 2} = 288 \text{ ways}$$

**8.135**    Solve Problem 8.131 if a full house (three of a kind with another pair) is dealt.

❚   One kind can be selected in thirteen ways and three of this kind can be dealt in $\binom{4}{3}$ ways; another kind can be selected in twelve ways and two of this kind can be dealt in $\binom{4}{2}$ ways. Thus

$$m = 13 \cdot \binom{4}{3} \cdot 12 \cdot \binom{4}{2} = 3744 \text{ ways}$$

**8.136**    Solve Problem 8.131 if the player is dealt three aces (without the fourth ace or another pair).

❚   The three aces can be selected from four aces in $\binom{4}{3}$ ways. The two other cards can be selected from the remaining twelve kinds in $\binom{12}{2}$ ways; and one card in each kind can be dealt in four ways. Thus a poker hand of three aces can be dealt in

$$m = \binom{4}{3}\binom{12}{2} \cdot 4 \cdot 4 = 4224 \text{ ways}$$

**8.137**    Solve Problem 8.131 if the player is dealt three of a kind (without another pair).

❚   One kind can be selected in thirteen ways; and three of this kind can be dealt in $\binom{4}{3}$ ways. The two other kinds can be selected from the remaining twelve kinds in $\binom{12}{2}$ ways; and one card in each kind can be dealt in four ways. Thus a poker hand of three of a kind can be dealt in

$$m = 13 \cdot \binom{4}{3}\binom{12}{2} \cdot 4 \cdot 4 = 54\,912 \text{ ways}$$

**8.138**    Solve Problem 8.131 if two pairs are dealt.

❚   Two kinds (for the pairs) can be selected from the thirteen kinds in $\binom{13}{2}$ ways; and two of each kind can be dealt in $\binom{4}{2}$ ways. Another kind can be selected in eleven ways; and one of this kind in four ways. Thus a poker hand of two pair can be dealt in

$$m = \binom{13}{2}\binom{4}{2}\binom{4}{2} \cdot 11 \cdot 4 = 123\,552 \text{ ways}$$

**8.139**    Consider four vowels (including $A$) and eight consonants (including $B$). Find the number $m$ of five-letter "words" containing two different vowels and three different consonants that can be formed from the given letters.

▌ The two vowels can be selected from the four vowels in $\binom{4}{2}$ ways, and the three consonants can be selected from the eight consonants in $\binom{8}{3}$ ways. Furthermore, each five letters can be arranged in a row (as a "word") in 5! ways. Thus we can form

$$m = \binom{4}{2}\binom{8}{3} \cdot 5! = 6 \cdot 56 \cdot 120 = 40\,320 \text{ words}$$

**8.140**   Solve Problem 8.139 if the words must contain the letter $B$.

▌ The two vowels can still be selected in $\binom{4}{2}$ ways. However, since $B$ is one of the consonants, the other two consonants can be selected from the remaining seven consonants in $\binom{7}{2}$ ways. Again each five letters can be arranged as a word in 5! ways. Thus

$$m = \binom{4}{2}\binom{7}{2} \cdot 5! = 6 \cdot 21 \cdot 120 = 15\,120$$

**8.141**   Solve Problem 8.139 if the words must begin with $B$.

▌ The two vowels can be selected in $\binom{4}{2}$ ways, and the other two consonants can be selected in $\binom{7}{2}$ ways. The four letters can be arranged, following $B$, in 4! ways. Thus $m = \binom{4}{2}\binom{7}{2} \cdot 4! = 6 \cdot 21 \cdot 24 = 3024$.

**8.142**   Solve Problem 8.139 if the words must begin with $A$.

▌ The other vowel can be chosen in three ways, and the three consonants can be chosen in $\binom{8}{3}$ ways. The four letters can be arranged, following $A$, in 4! ways. Thus $m = 3 \cdot \binom{8}{3} \cdot 4! = 3 \cdot 56 \cdot 24 = 4032$.

**8.143**   Solve Problem 8.139 if the words must begin with $A$ and contain $B$.

▌ The other vowel can be chosen in three ways, and the two other consonants can be chosen in $\binom{7}{2}$ ways. The four letters can be arranged, following $A$, in 4! ways. Thus $m = 3 \cdot \binom{7}{2} \cdot 4! = 3 \cdot 21 \cdot 24 = 1512$.

**8.144**   The English alphabet has 26 letters of which five are vowels. (Thus 21 letters are consonants.) Find the number $m$ of five-letter words which contain three different consonants and two different vowels.

▌ The three consonants can be chosen in $\binom{21}{3}$ ways, and the two vowels can be chosen in $\binom{5}{2}$ ways. Also, the five letters can be arranged in 5! ways. Thus $m = \binom{21}{3}\binom{5}{2} \cdot 5! = 1\,596\,000$ words.

**8.145**   Solve Problem 8.144 if the words must contain the letter $B$.

▌ Here the remaining two consonants can be chosen in $\binom{20}{2}$ ways. Thus $m = \binom{20}{2}\binom{5}{2} \cdot 5! = 228\,000$.

**8.146**   Solve Problem 8.144 if the words must contain the letters $B$ and $C$.

▌ Here the third consonant can be chosen in 19 ways. Thus $m = 19 \cdot \binom{5}{2} \cdot 5! = 22\,800$.

**8.147**   Solve Problem 8.144 if the words must begin with $B$ and end with $C$.

▮ This is the same as Problem 8.146 except now only the middle three letters can change positions, i.e., can be arranged in 3! ways. Thus $m = 19 \cdot \binom{5}{2} \cdot 3! = 1140$.

**8.148** Solve Problem 8.144 if the words must contain the letters $A$ and $B$.

▮ The second vowel can be chosen in four ways, and the remaining two consonants can be chosen in $\binom{20}{2}$ ways. Thus $m = 4 \cdot \binom{20}{2} \cdot 5! = 91\,200$.

**8.149** Solve Problem 8.144 if the words must begin with $A$ and end with $B$.

▮ This is the same as Problem 8.148 except now only the middle three letters can change positions, i.e., can be arranged in 3! ways. Thus $m = 4 \cdot \binom{20}{2} \cdot 3! = 4456$.

**8.150** Solve Problem 8.144 if the words must contain the letters $A$, $B$, and $C$.

▮ There are four ways to choose the second vowel and 19 ways to choose the third consonant. Thus $m = 4 \cdot 19 \cdot 5! = 9120$.

**8.151** Solve Problem 8.144 if the words must contain the letters $A$, $B$, $C$, $D$, and $E$.

▮ No other letters can be chosen. Thus $m = 5! = 120$.

**8.152** Solve Problem 8.144 if the words must contain the letters $A$, $E$, and $I$.

▮ No words can contain $A$, $E$, and $I$ since the words can only contain two vowels. Thus $m = 0$.

**8.153** Find the regular polygon which has twice as many diagonals as sides.

▮ The regular polygon with $n$ sides has $(n^2 - 3n)/2$ diagonals (Problem 8.129). Set
$$(n^2 - 3n)/2 = 2n \quad \text{or} \quad n^2 - 3n = 4n \quad \text{or} \quad n(n - 7) = 0$$

Since $n$ must be a positive integer, the only answer is $n = 7$ sides.

**8.154** Find the regular polygon which has three times as many diagonals as sides.

▮ Now set $(n^2 - 3n)/2 = 3n$ or $n^2 - 3n = 6n$ or $n(n - 9) = 0$. Thus $n = 9$ sides.

**8.155** Find the number $m$ of triangles that can be formed by the vertices of an octagon.

▮ We can choose any three vertices from the eight vertices of the octagon; hence $m = \binom{8}{3} = 56$ triangles.

**8.156** Solve Problem 8.155 if the sides of the octagon are not to be sides of any triangle.

▮ First we find the number $n_1$ of triangles with exactly one side on the octagon. This side can be chosen in eight ways. The remaining vertex of the triangle can be chosen in $8 - 4$ ways since this vertex cannot be one of the two consecutive vertices already chosen or one of the two adjacent vertices. Thus $n_1 = 8 \cdot 4 = 32$. The number $n_2$ of triangles with two sides on the octagon corresponds to the number of ways to choose three consecutive vertices which corresponds to the number of ways to choose the first vertex. Thus $n_2 = 8$. Hence $m = 56 - 32 - 8 = 16$ triangles.

**8.157** Find the number $m$ of triangles that can be formed by the vertices of a regular polygon with $n$ sides (and hence $n$ vertices).

▮ We can choose any three vertices of the $n$ vertices; hence
$$m = \binom{n}{3} = \frac{n(n - 1)(n - 2)}{6}$$

**8.158** Solve Problem 8.157 if the sides of the polygon are not to be sides of any triangle.

▌ As in Problem 8.156, there are $n(n-4)$ triangles with one side on the polygon, and $n$ triangles with two sides on the polygon. Thus

$$m = n(n-1)(n-2)/6 - n(n-4) - n = n(n-5)(n-4)/6$$

and $n > 5$.

## 8.5  ORDERED AND UNORDERED PARTITIONS

**8.159**  Explain the difference between an ordered and an unordered partition of a finite set $S$, and give an example.

▌ An *unordered* partition of $S$ is simply a collection $[A_1, A_2, \ldots, A_k]$ of disjoint (nonempty) subsets of $S$ (called *cells*) whose union is $S$. The partition is *ordered* if the order of the cells in the list counts. For example, the two collections.

$$P_1 = [\{1, 2\}, \{3, 4, 5\}, \{6, 7\}] \quad \text{and} \quad P_2 = [\{6, 7\}, \{3, 4, 5\}, \{1, 2\}]$$

determine the same partition of $S = \{1, 2, \ldots, 7\}$ but are distinct ordered partitions.

**8.160**  Suppose a box $B$ contains seven marbles numbered 1 through 7. Find the number $m$ of ways of drawing from $B$ the first two marbles, then three marbles, and lastly the remaining two marbles. That is, find the number $m$ of ordered partitions $[A_1, A_2, A_3]$ of the set of seven marbles into cell $A_1$ containing two marbles, $A_2$ containing three marbles, and $A_3$ containing two marbles.

▌ First there are seven marbles in the box $B$; hence there are $\binom{7}{2}$ ways of drawing the first two marbles, i.e., of determining $A_1$. Following this, there are five marbles left in $B$ and so there are $\binom{5}{3}$ ways of drawing the three marbles, i.e., of determining $A_2$. Finally, there are two marbles left in $B$ and so there are $\binom{2}{2}$ ways of determining the cell $A_3$. Thus

$$m = \binom{7}{2}\binom{5}{3}\binom{2}{2} = \frac{7 \cdot 6}{1 \cdot 2}\frac{5 \cdot 4 \cdot 3}{1 \cdot 2 \cdot 3}\frac{2 \cdot 1}{1 \cdot 2} = 210$$

Observe that

$$\binom{7}{2}\binom{5}{3}\binom{2}{2} = \frac{7!}{2!\,5!}\frac{5!}{3!\,2!}\frac{2!}{2!\,0!} = \frac{7!}{2!\,3!\,2!}$$

since each numerator after the first factor is canceled by the second term in the denominator of the previous factor.

**Theorem 8.8:**  Let $S$ contain $n$ elements and let $n_1, n_2, \ldots, n_r$ be positive integers with $n_1 + n_2 + \cdots + n_r = n$. Then there exist

$$\frac{n!}{n_1!\,n_2!\,n_3!\cdots n_r!}$$

different ordered partitions of $S$ of the form $[A_1, A_2, \ldots, A_r]$ where $A_1$ contains $n_1$ elements, $A_2$ contains $n_2$ elements, $\ldots$, and $A_r$ contains $n_r$ elements.

**8.161**  Prove Theorem 8.8.

▌ There are $\binom{n}{n_1}$ ways of determining the cell $A_1$, then $\binom{n-n_1}{n_2}$ ways of determining the cell $A_2$, then $\binom{n-n_1-n_2}{n_3}$ ways of determining the cell $A_3$, and so on. Thus there are

$$\binom{n}{n_1}\binom{n-n_1}{n_2}\binom{n-n_1-n_2}{n_3}\cdots\binom{n_r}{n_r} = \frac{n!}{n_1!\,(n-n_1)!}\frac{(n-n_1)!}{n_2!\,(n-n_1-n_2)!}\frac{(n-n_1-n_2)!}{n_3!\,(n-n_1-n_2-n_3)!}\cdots\frac{n_r!}{n_r!}$$

$$= \frac{n!}{n_1!\,n_2!\,n_3!\cdots n_r!}$$

partitions of $S$ of the form $[A_1, A_2, \ldots, A_r]$. The last equality follows from the fact that each numerator after the first factor is canceled by the second term in the denominator of the previous factor as in Problem 8.160.

**8.162**  Find the number $m$ of ways that nine toys can be divided among four children if the youngest child is to receive three toys and each of the others two toys.

▌ We wish to find the number $m$ of ordered partitions of the nine toys into four cells containing three, two, two, and two toys, respectively. By Theorem 8.8, $m = \dfrac{9!}{3!\,2!\,2!\,2!} = 2520$.

**8.163**  There are twelve students in a class. Find the number of ways that the twelve students take three different tests if four students are to take each test.

▌ *Method 1.* We seek the number of ordered partitions of the twelve students into cells containing four students each. By Theorem 8.8, there are $\dfrac{12!}{4!\,4!\,4!} = 34\,650$ such partitions.

*Method 2.* There are $\binom{12}{4}$ ways to choose four students to take the first test; following this, there are $\binom{8}{4}$ ways to choose four students to take the second test. The remaining students take the third test. Thus, altogether, there are $\binom{12}{4}\binom{8}{4} = 495 \cdot 70 = 34\,650$ ways for the students to take the tests.

**8.164**  Find the number $m$ of ways that twelve students can be partitioned into three teams, $A_1$, $A_2$, and $A_3$, so that each team contains four students.

▌ *Method 1.* Observe that each partition $\{A_1, A_2, A_3\}$ of the students can be arranged in $3! = 6$ ways as an ordered partition. Since (see Problem 8.163) there are $\dfrac{12!}{4!\,4!\,4!} = 34\,650$ such ordered partitions, there are $m = 34\,650/6 = 5775$ (unordered) partitions.

*Method 2.* Let $A$ denote one of the students. Then there are $\binom{11}{3}$ ways to choose three other students to be on the same team as $A$. Now let $B$ denote a student who is not on the same team as $A$; then there are $\binom{7}{3}$ ways to choose three students of the remaining students to be on the same team as $B$. The remaining four students constitute the third team. Thus, $m = \binom{11}{3}\binom{7}{3} = 165 \cdot 35 = 5775$.

**8.165**  Solve Problem 8.164 if the students must be divided into three teams containing five, four, and three students, respectively.

▌ Since all the cells contain different numbers of students, the number of unordered partitions equals the number of ordered partitions. Thus $m = \dfrac{12!}{5!\,4!\,3!} = 46\,530$.

**8.166**  Find the number $m$ of ways that nine toys can be divided evenly among three children.

▌ We seek the number $m$ of ordered partitions of nine toys into three cells containing three toys each. Thus $m = \dfrac{9!}{3!\,3!\,3!} = 1680$.

**8.167**  Find the number $m$ of ways that nine students can be divided evenly into three teams.

▌ Divide the number $\dfrac{9!}{3!\,3!\,3!} = 1680$ of ordered partitions by $3! = 6$ to obtain the number $m = 1680/6 = 280$ unordered partitions.

**8.168**  Solve Problem 8.167 if the students must be divided into three teams containing four, three, and two students, respectively.

▮ Since all the cells contain different numbers of students, the number of unordered partitions equals the number of ordered partitions, $\dfrac{9!}{4!\,3!\,2!} = 1260$.

**8.169** Find the number of ways that six students can be partitioned into two teams containing three students each.

▮ *Method 1.* There are $\dfrac{6!}{3!\,3!} = 20$ ordered partitions into two cells containing three students each. Since each unordered partition determines $2! = 2$ ordered partitions, there are $20/2 = 10$ unordered partitions.

*Method 2.* Let $A$ denote one of the students; then there are $\binom{5}{2} = 10$ ways to choose two other students to be on the same team as $A$. The other three students constitute the other team. In other words, there are ten ways to partition the students.

**8.170** Solve Problem 8.169 if the students must be partitioned into three teams containing two students each.

▮ There are $\dfrac{6!}{2!\,2!\,2!} = 90$ ordered partitions into three cells containing two students each. Since each unordered partition determines $3! = 6$ ordered partitions, there are $90/6 = 15$ unordered partitions.

**8.171** Find the number $m$ of ways that a class $X$ with ten students can be partitioned into four teams $A_1$, $A_2$, $B_1$, and $B_2$ where $A_1$ and $A_2$ contain two students each and $B_1$ and $B_2$ contain three students each.

▮ There are $\dfrac{10!}{2!\,2!\,3!\,3!} = 25\,200$ ordered partitions of $X$ into four cells containing two, two, three, and three students, respectively. However, each unordered partition $[A_1, A_2, B_1, B_2]$ of $X$ determines $2!\,2! = 4$ ordered partitions of $X$. Thus, $m = 25\,000/4 = 6300$.

**8.172** Find the number $m$ of ways that a set $X$ containing ten elements can be partitioned into two cells.

▮ *Method 1.* Each subset $A$ of $X$ divides $X$ into two disjoint sets $A$ and $A^c$, where $A^c$ is the complement of $A$. Thus there are $2^{10} = 1024$ such divisions of $X$. However, we must exclude the possibility that $A = \emptyset$ or $A = X$ since a partition consists of nonempty sets. Thus there are $1024 - 2 = 1022$ ordered partitions $[A, A^c]$ of $X$. Each unordered partition determines two ordered partitions, hence $m = 1022/2 = 511$.

*Method 2.* Let $x$ denote one of the elements in $X$. Now $X \backslash \{x\}$ has nine elements, and so there are $2^9 = 512$ ways of choosing a subset of $X \backslash \{x\}$ to be in the same cell as $x$. In other words, there are 512 such partitions including $\{X, \emptyset\}$. Thus there are $m = 512 - 1 = 511$ partitions of $X$ into two nonempty disjoint cells.

**8.173** Find the number $m$ of ways that $n$ students can be divided into two teams where each team contains at least one student.

▮ Let $x$ denote one of the students. Then there are $2^{n-1}$ ways of choosing a subset of the remaining $n - 1$ students. However, we must exclude the possibility that all the remaining students are on the same team as $x$. Thus $m = 2^{n-1} - 1$. (Compare with Method 2 of Problem 8.172.)

**8.174** Find the number $m$ of ways that fourteen people can be partitioned into six committees where two of the committees contain three people each and the remaining four committees contain two people each.

▮ Each unordered partition determines $2!\,4!$ ordered partitions. Thus

$$m = \frac{14!}{3!\,3!\,2!\,2!\,2!\,2!} \, \frac{1}{2!\,4!} = 3\,153\,150$$

**8.175** Assuming a cell can be empty, find the number $m$ of ways that a set with three elements can be partitioned into: (a) three ordered cells, and (b) three unordered cells.

▮ (a) Each of the three elements can be placed in any of the three cells; hence $m = 3^3 = 27$.
(b) The numbers of elements in the three cells can be as follows: $[3, 0, 0]$, $[2, 1, 0]$, or $[1, 1, 1]$. Thus

$$m = \binom{3}{3} + \binom{3}{1} + 1 = 1 + 3 + 1 = 5.$$

**8.176** Solve Problem 8.175 using a set with 4 elements.

▮ (a) Each of the four elements can be placed in any of the three cells; hence $m = 3^4 = 81$.

(b) The numbers of elements in the three cells can be as follows: [4, 0, 0], [3, 1, 0], [2, 2, 0], or [2, 1, 1]. Thus

$$m = \binom{4}{4} + \binom{4}{1} + \frac{1}{2}\binom{4}{2} + \binom{4}{2} = 1 + 4 + 3 + 6 = 14$$

**8.177** There are four players in the game of bridge who are called North, South, East, and West. Each player is dealt 13 cards and the distribution of the cards is called a bridge hand. Find the number $m$ of possible bridge hands. (Leave answer in factorial notation.)

▮ We seek the number $m$ of ordered partitions of the 52 cards into four cells with 13 cards each. Thus $m = \dfrac{52!}{13!\,13!\,13!\,13!}$.

**8.178** Solve Problem 8.177 if one player is to be dealt all four aces.

▮ There are four ways to distribute the four aces. Then the remaining 48 cards are to be partitioned into ordered cells with 9, 13, 13, and 13 cards respectively. Thus $m = 4\,\dfrac{48!}{9!\,13!\,13!\,13!}$.

**8.179** Solve Problem 8.177 if each player is to be dealt an ace.

▮ There are 4! ways to distribute the four aces. Then the remaining 48 cards are to be partitioned into ordered cells with 12 cards in each cell. Thus $m = 4!\,\dfrac{48!}{12!\,12!\,12!\,12!}$.

**8.180** Solve Problem 8.177 if North is to be dealt eight spades and South the other five spades.

▮ There are $\binom{13}{8}$ ways to choose the eight spades for North and the remaining five spades go to South. Then the remaining 39 cards are to be partitioned into ordered cells with 5, 8, 13, and 13 cards, respectively. Thus $m = \binom{13}{8}\dfrac{39!}{5!\,8!\,13!\,13!}$.

**8.181** Solve Problem 8.177 if one player is to be dealt all 13 spades.

▮ There are four ways to distribute the 13 spades. Then the remaining 39 cards are to be partitioned into three cells with 13 cards each. Thus $m = 4\,\dfrac{39!}{13!\,13!\,13!}$.

**8.182** Solve Problem 8.177 if North and South have, together, all four aces.

▮ There are three cases for the distribution of the aces. First, North or South has all four aces and this can occur in two ways. Second, North or South has only one ace and this can occur in $2 \cdot 4$ ways. Lastly, each has two aces and this can occur in $_4C_2 = 6$ ways. Thus

$$m = 2\,\frac{48!}{9!\,13!\,13!\,13!} + 2 \cdot 4\,\frac{48!}{10!\,12!\,13!\,13!} + 6\,\frac{48!}{11!\,11!\,13!\,13!} = 2300\,\frac{48!}{11!\,13!\,13!\,13!}$$

## 8.6 TREE DIAGRAMS

A (rooted) tree diagram is a useful device to enumerate all the logical possibilities of a sequence of events where each event can occur in a finite number of ways.

**8.183** Find the product set $A \times B \times C$ where $A = \{1, 2\}$, $B = \{a, b, c\}$, and $C = \{3, 4\}$.

▮ Construct the appropriate tree diagram as shown in Fig. 8-3. Note that the tree is constructed from left to right and that the number of branches at each point corresponds to the number of ways the next event can occur. There are 12 endpoints corresponding to the 12 elements in $A \times B \times C$. Specifically, each path from the beginning of the tree to the endpoint designates an element of $A \times B \times C$ which is listed to the right of the tree. That is,

$$A \times B \times C = \{(1, a, 3), (1, a, 4), (1, b, 3), (1, b, 4), (1, c, 3), (1, c, 4),$$

$$(2, a, 3), (2, a, 4), (2, b, 3), (2, b, 4), (2, c, 3), (2, c, 4)\}$$

**8.184** A man has time to play roulette at most five times. At each play he wins or loses a dollar. The man begins with

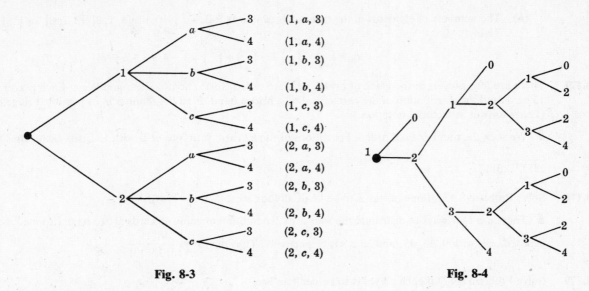

Fig. 8-3                                          Fig. 8-4

one dollar and will stop playing before the five times if he loses all his money or if he wins three dollars, i.e., if he has four dollars. (*a*) Find the number of possible ways that the playing can occur. (*b*) Determine the number of times the betting will stop before he has played five times.

▌ (*a*)  Construct the appropriate tree diagram, as shown in Fig. 8-4. There are 11 endpoints; hence the betting can occur in 11 different ways.

(*b*)  As indicated in Fig. 8-4, the betting will stop before the five times are up in only three of the ways.

**8.185**  Find the permutations of $\{a, b, c\}$.

▌ Theorem 8.7 tells us that there are $3! = 3 \cdot 2 \cdot 1 = 6$ such permutations. However, one can find the six permutations by constructing the appropriate tree diagram, as shown in Fig. 8-5. The six permutations are listed on the right of the diagram.

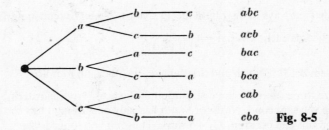

abc

acb

bac

bca

cab

cba     **Fig. 8-5**

**6.186**  Teams A and B play in a basketball tournament. The team that first wins three games wins the tournament. Find the number of possible ways in which the tournament can occur.

▌ Construct the appropriate tree diagram, as shown in Fig. 8-6. The tournament can occur in twenty ways:

AAA, AABA, AABBA, AABBB, ABAA, ABABA, ABABB, ABBAA, ABBAB, ABBB,

BAAA, BAABA, BAABB, BABAA, BABAB, BABB, BBAAA, BBAAB, BBAB, BBB

**8.187**  Find the product set $\{1, 2, 3\} \times \{2, 4\} \times \{2, 3, 4\}$ by constructing the appropriate tree diagram.

▌ The required diagram is shown in Fig. 8-7. Note that there are $n = 3 \cdot 2 \cdot 3 = 18$ elements in the product set which are listed to the right of the tree diagram.

**8.188**  A woman is at the origin on the $x$ axis and takes a one unit step either to the left or to the right. She stops if she reaches 3 or $-3$, or if she occupies any position, other than the origin, more than once. Find the number of different paths the woman can travel.

▌ Construct the appropriate tree diagram, as shown in Fig. 8-8. There are 14 different paths, each path corresponding to an end point of the tree diagram.

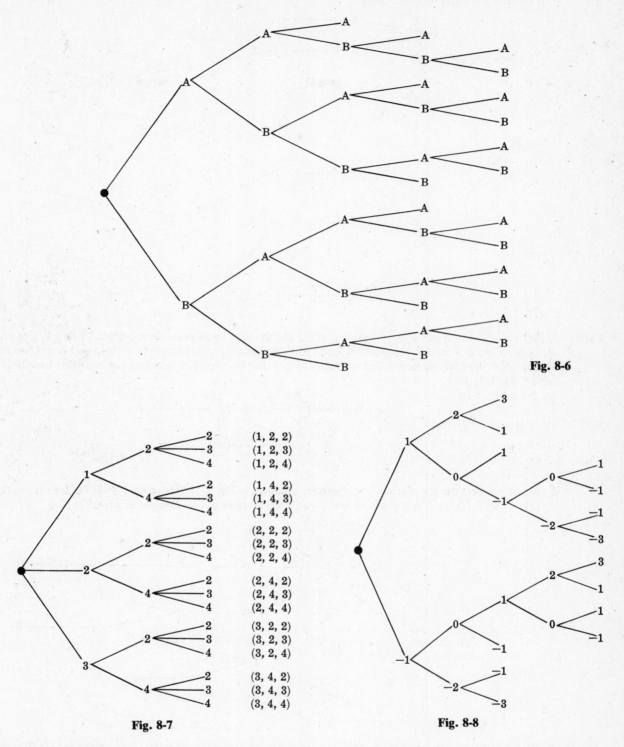

Fig. 8-6

Fig. 8-7

Fig. 8-8

**8.189** Teams A and B play in baseball's world series. Here, the team that first wins four games wins the series. Find the number of ways the series can occur given that A wins the first game and that the team that wins the second game also wins the fourth game.

▌ Construct the appropriate tree diagram, as shown in Fig. 8-9. Note that there is only one choice in the fourth game, the winner of the second game. Also, the tree begins with A, the winner of the first game. The diagram shows that the series can occur in the following 15 ways:

AAAA, AABAA, AABABA, AABABBA, AABABBB, ABABAA, ABABABA, ABABABB,

ABABBAA, ABABBAB, ABABBB, ABBBAAA, ABBBAAB, ABBBAB, ABBBB

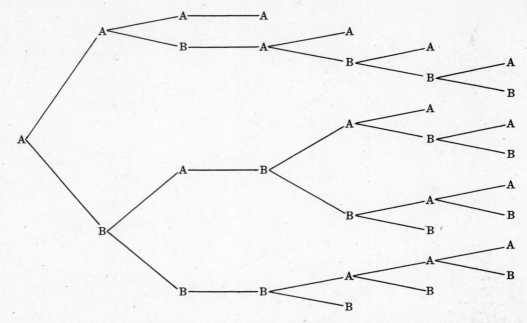

**Fig. 8-9**

**8.190** Suppose $A, B, \ldots, F$ in Fig. 8-10 denote islands, and the lines connecting them bridges. A man begins at $A$ and walks from island to island. He stops for lunch when he cannot continue to walk without crossing the same bridge twice. (**a**) Find the number of ways that he can take his walk before eating lunch. (**b**) At which islands can he eat his lunch?

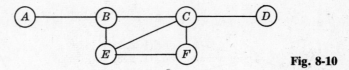

**Fig. 8-10**

 (**a**) Construct the appropriate tree diagram, as shown in Fig. 8-11. There are 11 ways to take his walk.
 (**b**) Only $B, D$, or $E$ appears at an end point. Thus he must eat his lunch at either $B, D$ or $E$.

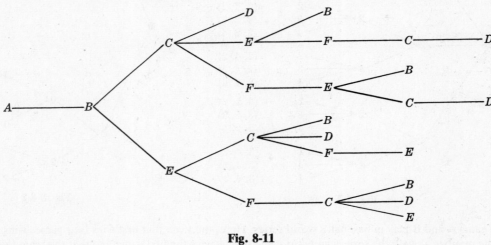

**Fig. 8-11**

**8.191** Solve Problem 8.190 if the man begins at the island $E$.

 (**a**) Construct the appropriate tree diagram as shown in Fig. 8-12. There are 13 ways to take his walk.
 (**b**) Only $A$ and $D$ appear as end points of the tree diagram; hence he must eat his lunch at either $A$ or $D$.

**8.192** Solve Problem 8.190 if the man begins at the island $F$.

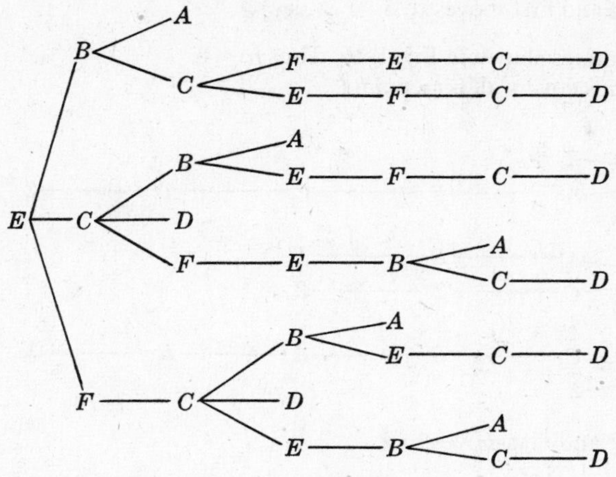

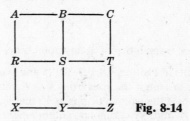

**Fig. 8-12** 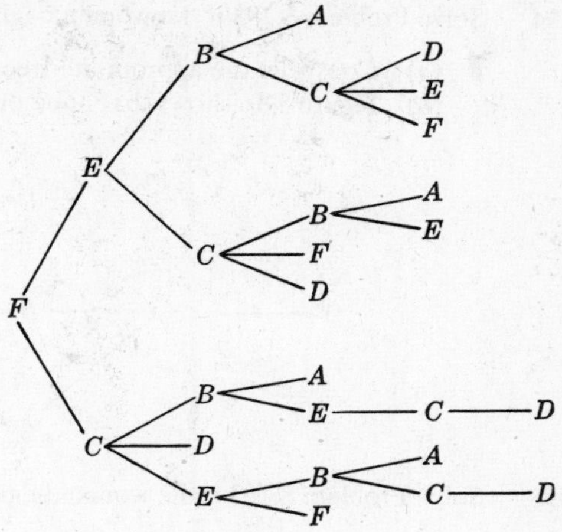          **Fig. 8-13**

(*a*)  Construct the appropriate tree diagram, as shown in Fig. 8-13. There are only 14 ways he can take his walk.

(*b*)  As shown by Fig. 8-13, the man must eat his lunch at either *A*, *D*, *E*, or *F*.

**8.193**  There are nine points *A, B, C, R, S, T, X, Y,* and *Z* in Fig. 8-14. Suppose a woman begins at *X* and is allowed to move horizontally or vertically, one step at a time. She stops when she cannot continue to walk without reaching the same point more than once. (**a**) Find the number *m* of ways she can take her walk, if she first moves from *X* to *R*. (**b**) Find the number of such trips which cover all nine points.

**Fig. 8-14**

❚  (*a*)  Construct the appropriate tree diagram, as shown in Fig. 8-15. Thus *m* = 10.

(*b*)  Figure 8-15 shows that only four of the trips cover all nine points.

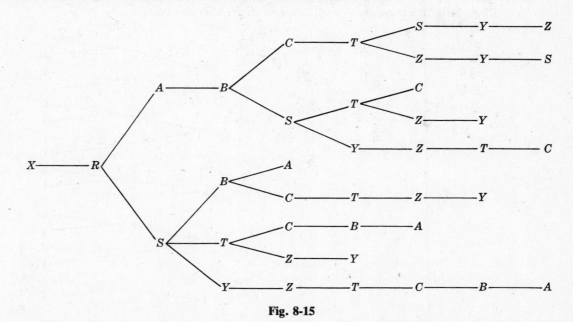

**Fig. 8-15**

**8.194** Solve Problem 8.193 if the woman begins at $Y$ and first moves to $S$.

▌ (a) Construct the appropriate tree diagram, as shown in Fig. 8-16. Thus $m = 6$.
(b) Figure 8-16 shows that none of the trips covers all nine points.

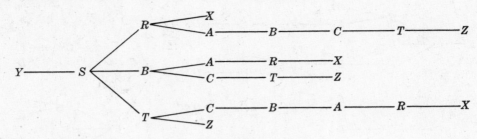

Fig. 8-16

**8.195** Solve Problem 8.193 if the woman begins at $Y$ and first moves to $Z$.

▌ (a) Construct the appropriate tree diagram, as shown in Fig. 8-17. Thus $m = 8$.
(b) Figure 8-17 shows that none of the trips covers all nine points.

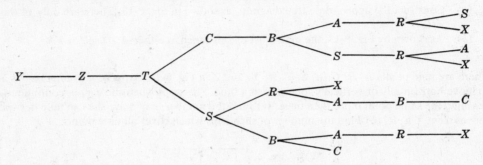

Fig. 8-17

**8.196** Solve Problem 8.193 if the woman begins at any point other than the middle point $S$.

▌ (a) We use the results in Problems 8.193–8.195 and symmetry. There are 20 trips if the woman begins at $X$; that is, there are ten if she goes from $X$ to $R$ and, by symmetry, another ten if she goes from $X$ to $Y$. There are 22 trips if the woman begins at $Y$; that is, there are six if she goes from $Y$ to $S$, eight if she goes from $Y$ to $Z$, and, by symmetry, another eight if she goes from $Y$ to $X$. Similarly, by symmetry, there are 20 trips if she begins at $A$, $C$, or $Z$, and there are 22 trips if she begins at $B$, $R$, or $T$. Thus, altogether, $m = 4 \cdot 20 + 4 \cdot 22 = 164$.
(b) There are $2 \cdot 4 = 8$ trips that cover all nine points if the woman begins at $X$ and none if she begins at $Y$. Thus, altogether there are $4 \cdot 8 = 32$ trips which cover all nine points.

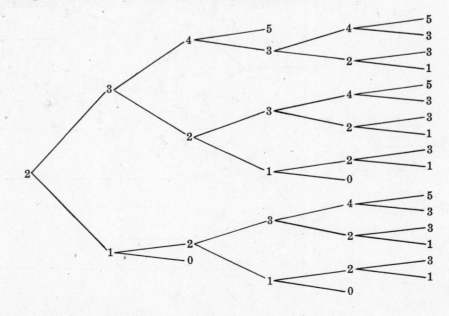

Fig. 8-18

**8.197**    A woman has time to play roulette at most five times. She wins or loses a dollar at each play. The woman begins with two dollars and will stop playing before the five times if she loses all her money or wins three dollars, i.e., if she has five dollars. (*a*) Find the number of ways the playing can occur. (*b*) In how many of these ways will she lose all her money?

    ▌  **(a)**  Construct the appropriate diagram, as shown in Fig. 8-18. There are only 20 ways the betting can occur.

        **(b)**  As shown by Fig. 8-18, the woman loses all her money in only three of the ways.

**8.198**    A man is at the origin on the $x$ axis and takes a unit step either to the left or to the right. He stops after five steps or if he reaches 3 or $-2$. Find the number $m$ of paths the man can travel.

    ▌  The tree diagram for this problem is the same as in Fig. 8-18 (for Problem 8.197) except that we must replace each number $n$ by $n - 2$. Thus $m = 20$.

**8.199**    Teams A and B play in baseball's world series and the team that first wins four games wins the series. Find the number of ways the series can occur if the team that wins the first game also wins the third game, and the team that wins the second game also wins the fourth game.

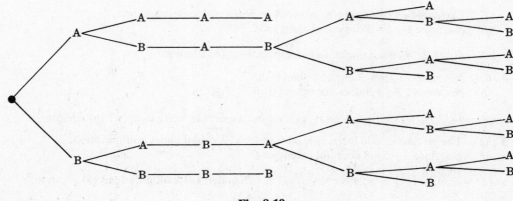

**Fig. 8-19**

    ▌  Construct the appropriate tree diagram, as shown in Fig. 8-19. Thus the series can occur in 14 ways.

# CHAPTER 9
# Algebraic Systems

## 9.1 OPERATIONS AND SEMIGROUPS

A (*binary*) *operation* on a nonempty set $S$ is a function $*$ from $S \times S$ into $S$. In such a case, we write

$$a * b \quad \text{or simply} \quad ab \quad \text{instead of} \quad *(a, b)$$

If $S$ is a finite set, then the operation can be given by its operation table where the entry in the row labeled $a$ and the column labeled $b$ is $a * b$. If $A$ is a subset of $S$, then $A$ is said to be *closed under* $*$ if $a * b$ belongs to $A$ for any elements $a$ and $b$ in $A$.

**9.1** Let $A = \{0, 1\}$. Is $A$ closed under: (*a*) multiplication? (*b*) addition?

    (*a*)  Compute each possible product:

$$0 \cdot 0 = 0, \quad 0 \cdot 1 = 0, \quad 1 \cdot 0 = 0, \quad \text{and} \quad 1 \cdot 1 = 1$$

        Each product belongs to $A$; hence $A$ is closed under multiplication.

    (*b*)  No, since $1 + 1 = 2$ does not belong to $A$.

**9.2** Let $B = \{1, 2\}$. Is $B$ closed under: (*a*) multiplication? (*b*) addition?

    (*a*)  No, since $2 \cdot 2 = 4$ does not belong to $B$.
    (*b*)  No, since $1 + 2 = 3$ does not belong to $B$.

**9.3** Let $C = \{1, 3, 5, \ldots\} = \{n: n \text{ is odd}\}$. Is $C$ closed under: (*a*) multiplication? (*b*) addition?

    (*a*)  The product of odd integers is odd; hence $C$ is closed under multiplication.
    (*b*)  No, since $3 + 5 = 8$ does not belong to $C$.

**9.4** Let $D = \{2, 4, 6, \ldots\} = \{n: n \text{ is even}\}$. Is $D$ closed under: (*a*) multiplication? (*b*) addition?

    (*a*)  Yes, since the product of even integers is even.
    (*b*)  Yes, since the sum of even integers is even.

**9.5** Let $F = \{2, 4, 8, \ldots\} = \{x: x = 2^n, n \in \mathbf{N}\}$. Is $F$ closed under: (*a*) multiplication? (*b*) addition?

    (*a*)  Since $2^r \cdot 2^s = 2^{r+s}$, $F$ is closed under multiplication.
    (*b*)  No, since $2 + 4 = 6$ does not belong to $F$.

**9.6** Define an associative operation.

    An operation $*$ on a set $S$ is associative if, for any $a$, $b$, $c$ in $S$, we have $(a * b) * c = a * (b * c)$.

**9.7** Consider the set $\mathbf{Z} = \{\ldots, -1, 0, 1, 2, \ldots\}$ of integers. Determine whether or not the following operations in $\mathbf{Z}$ are associative: (*a*) addition, (*b*) subtraction, and (*c*) multiplication.

    (*a*)  Yes, since $(a + b) + c = a + (b + c)$ for any integers $a$, $b$, and $c$.
    (*b*)  No. For example, $(12 - 6) - 2 = 6 - 2 = 4$ but $12 - (6 - 2) = 12 - 4 = 8$, and hence $(12 - 6) - 2 \neq 12 - (6 - 2)$.
    (*c*)  Yes, since $(ab)c = a(bc)$ for any integers $a$, $b$, and $c$.

**9.8** Determine whether or not the following operations on the integers $\mathbf{Z}$ are associative: (*a*) division, and (*b*) exponentiation.

    (*a*)  Division is not a (complete) operation on $\mathbf{Z}$ since, for example, $7/3$ and $-4/5$ are not defined (as elements in $\mathbf{Z}$). However, even when division is defined, it is not associative. For example, $(12/6)/2 = 6/2 = 3$ but $12/(6/2) = 12/3 = 4$.
    (*b*)  No. For example, if we let $a \circ b = a^b$, then

$$(2 \circ 2) \circ 3 = (2^2)^3 = 4^3 = 64 \quad \text{but} \quad 2 \circ (2 \circ 3) = 2^{2^3} = 2^8 = 256$$

        and hence $(2 \circ 2) \circ 3 \neq 2 \circ (2 \circ 3)$.

**9.9**   Suppose an operation $*$ on a set $S$ is not associative. How many ways can the product $a * b * c * d$ of the four elements be formed?

▌ There are five ways to insert parentheses: $((ab)c)d$, $(ab)(cd)$, $(a(bc))d$, $a((bc)d)$, and $a(b(cd))$.

**Theorem 9.1:**   Suppose $*$ is an associative operation on a set $S$. Then any product $a_1 * a_2 * \cdots * a_n$ requires no parentheses, i.e., all possible products are equal.

**9.10**   Prove Theorem 9.1.

▌ The proof is by induction on $n$. Since $n$ is associative, the theorem holds for $n = 1$, $2$, and $3$. Suppose $n \geq 4$. We use the notation:

$$(a_1 a_2 \cdots a_n) = (\cdots((a_1 a_2)a_3) \cdots)a_n \quad \text{and} \quad [a_1 a_2 \cdots a_n] = \text{any product}$$

We show $[a_1 a_2 \cdots a_n] = (a_1 a_2 \cdots a_n)$ and so all such products will be equal. Since $[a_1 a_2 \cdots a_n]$ denotes some product, there exists an $r < n$ such that $[a_1 a_2 \cdots a_n] = [a_1 a_2 \cdots a_r][a_{r+1} \cdots a_n]$. Therefore, by induction,

$$\begin{aligned}
[a_1 a_2 \cdots a_n] &= [a_1 a_2 \cdots a_r][a_{r+1} \cdots a_n] = [a_1 a_2 \cdots a_r](a_{r+1} \cdots a_n) \\
&= [a_1 \cdots a_r]((a_{r+1} \cdots a_{n-1})a_n) = ([a_1 \cdots a_r](a_{r-1} \cdots a_{n-1}))a_n \\
&= [a_1 \cdots a_{n-1}]a_n = (a_1 \cdots a_{n-1})a_n = (a_1 a_2 \cdots a_n).
\end{aligned}$$

Thus the theorem is proved.

**9.11**   Define an identity element for an operation $*$ on a set $S$.

▌ An element $e$ in $S$ is called an *identity element* for $*$ if $a * e = e * a = a$ for any element $a$ in $S$. More generally, $e$ is called a *right identity* if $a * e = a$ for any $a$ in $S$, and a *left identity* if $e * a = a$ for any $a$ in $S$.

**9.12**   Suppose $e$ is a left identity and $f$ is a right identity for an operation. Show that $e = f$.

▌ The proof is very simple. Since $e$ is a left identity, $ef = f$; but since $f$ is a right identity, $ef = e$. Hence $e = f$. This result tells us, in particular, that an identity element is unique, and that if an operation has more than one left identity then it has no right identity and vice versa.

**9.13**   Suppose an operation $*$ on a set $S$ has an identity element $e$. Define the inverse of an element $a$ in $S$.

▌ The *inverse* of $a$, usually denoted by $a^{-1}$, is an element with the property that

$$a * a^{-1} = a^{-1} * a = e$$

**9.14**   Define: **(a)** semigroup, and **(b)** monoid.

▌ **(a)**   A set $S$ together with an associative operation $*$ is called a *semigroup*. We denote the semigroup by $(S, *)$ or simply $S$ when the operation is understood.

   **(b)**   A set $M$ together with an associative operation $*$ with an identity element $e$ is called a *monoid*. In other words, a semigroup with an identity element is a monoid.

(Some authors define a semigroup to include an identity element.)

**9.15**   Let $S$ be a semigroup with an identity element $e$, and suppose $b$ and $b'$ are inverses of an element $a$ in $S$. Show that $b = b'$, that is, that inverses are unique if they exist. We note that this result need not be true if the operation is nonassociative.

▌ We have

$$b * (a * b') = b * e = b \quad \text{and} \quad (b * a) * b' = e * b' = b'$$

Since $S$ is associative, $(b * a) * b' = b * (a * b')$; hence $b = b'$.

**9.16**   Define the left and right cancellation laws for an operation $*$ on a set $S$.

▌ The operation $*$ on $S$ satisfies the *left cancellation law* if $a * b = a * c$ implies $b = c$, and the *right cancellation law* if $b * a = c * a$ implies $b = c$.

**9.17**   Define a commutative operation.

▐ An operation * on a set $S$ is said to be *commutative* (or, to satisfy the *commutative law*) if $a * b = b * a$ for all $a, b$ in $S$.

**9.18**  Consider the set **N** of positive integers, and let * be the operation of least common multiple (l.c.m.) on **N**. (*a*) Find $4 * 6$, $3 * 5$, $9 * 18$, and $1 * 6$. (*b*) Is (**N**, *) a semigroup? Is it commutative? (*c*) Find the identity element of *.

▐ (*a*)  Since $x * y$ means the least common multiple of $x$ and $y$, we have:

$$4 * 6 = 12, \quad 3 * 5 = 15, \quad 9 * 18 = 18, \quad 1 * 6 = 6$$

(*b*)  One proves in number theory that $(a * b) * c = a * (b * c)$, i.e., that the operation of l.c.m. is associative, and that $a * b = b * a$, i.e., that the operation of l.c.m. is commutative. Hence (**N**, *) is a commutative semigroup.

(*c*)  The integer 1 is the identity element since the l.c.m. of 1 and any positive integer $a$ is $a$, i.e., $1 * a = a * 1 = a$ for any $a \in$ **N**.

**9.19**  Which elements in Problem 9.18, if any, have inverses and what are they?

▐ Since l.c.m. $(a, b) = 1$ if and only if $a = 1$ and $b = 1$, the only number which has an inverse is 1 and it is its own inverse.

**9.20**  Consider the set **Q** of rational numbers, and let * be the operation on **Q** defined by

$$a * b = a + b - ab \tag{1}$$

(*a*) Find $3 * 4$, $2 * (-5)$, and $7 * 1/2$. (*b*) Is (**Q**, *) a semigroup? Is it commutative? (*c*) Find the identity element for *.

▐ (*a*)  Using (*1*), we have

$$3 * 4 = 3 + 4 - 3 \cdot 4 = 3 + 4 - 12 = -5$$
$$2 * (-5) = 2 + (-5) - 2 \cdot (-5) = 2 - 5 + 10 = 7$$
$$7 * 1/2 = 7 + 1/2 - 7(1/2) = 4$$

(*b*)  Determine whether or not * is associative:

$$(a * b) * c = (a + b - ab) * c$$
$$= (a + b - ab) + c - (a + b - ab)c$$
$$= a + b - ab + c - ac - bc + abc$$
$$= a + b + c - ab - ac - bc + abc$$

$$a * (b * c) = a * (b + c - bc)$$
$$= a + (b + c - bc) - a(b + c - bc)$$
$$= a + b + c - bc - ab - ac + abc$$

Hence * is associative and (**Q**, *) is a semigroup. Also,

$$a * b = a + b - ab = b + a - ba = b * a$$

Hence (**Q**, *) is a commutative semigroup.

(*c*)  An element $e$ is an identity element if $a * e = a$ for every $a \in$ **Q**. Compute as follows:

$$a * e = a, \quad a + e - ae = a, \quad e - ea = 0, \quad e(1 - a) = 0, \quad e = 0$$

Accordingly, 0 is the identity element.

**9.21**  Which elements in Problem 9.20, if any, have inverses and what are they?

▐ In order for $a$ to have an inverse $x$, we must have $a * x = 0$ since 0 is the identity element by (*c*) of Problem 9.20. Compute as follows:

$$a * x = 0, \quad a + x - ax = 0, \quad a = ax - x, \quad a = x(a - 1), \quad x = a/(a - 1)$$

Thus if $a \neq 1$, then $a$ has an inverse and it is $a/(a - 1)$.

**9.22**  Let $S$ be any nonempty set with the operation $a * b = a$. Is the operation (*a*) associative? (*b*) commutative?

**(a)** Yes. In fact, $(a*b)*c = a*c = a$ and $a*(b*c) = a*b = a$.

**(b)** If $S$ has more than one element, then $*$ is not commutative. Specifically, for $a \neq b$ we have $a*b = a$ but $b*a = b$, and so $a*b \neq b*a$.

**9.23** Show that the right cancellation law holds in Problem 9.22. Does the left cancellation law hold?

Suppose $a*c = b*c$. We have $a*c = a$ and $b*c = b$. Hence $a = b$. Thus the right cancellation law holds. The left cancellation law does not hold. For example, suppose $b \neq c$. Then $a*b = a*c = a$, but $b \neq c$.

**9.24** Let $S$ be a set of symbols. Define the free semigroup on $S$.

A *word* on $S$ is a finite sequence of its elements. For example, $U = ababb$ and $V = accba$ are words on $S = \{a, b, c\}$. When discussing words on $S$, we frequently call $S$ the *alphabet* and its elements *letters*. For convenience, the empty sequence, denoted by $\varepsilon$ or $1$, is also considered a word on $S$. We shall also abbreviate our notation by writing $a^2$ for $aa$, $a^3$ for $aaa$, and so on. The set of all words on $S$ is usually denoted by $S^*$.

Now consider two words $U$ and $V$ on $S$. We can form the word $UV$ obtained by writing the letters of $V$ after the letters of $U$. For example, if $U$ and $V$ are the words above, then

$$UV = ababbaccba = abab^2ac^2ba$$

This operation is called *concatenation*. Clearly the operation is associative. Thus the set of words on $S$ is a semigroup under the concatenation operation. This semigroup is called the *free semigroup* on $S$ (or, generated by $S$). Clearly the empty word $\varepsilon$ is an identity element for the semigroup, and the semigroup satisfies both right and left cancellation laws.

## 9.2 GROUPS AND SUBGROUPS

**9.25** Define a group.

Let $G$ be a nonempty set with a binary operation (denoted by juxtaposition). Then $G$ is called a *group* if the following axioms hold:

[$G_1$] *Associative law*, i.e., for any $a$, $b$, $c$ in $G$, we have $(ab)c = a(bc)$.
[$G_2$] *Identity element*, i.e., there exists an element $e$ in $G$ such that $ae = ea = a$ for any element $a$ in $G$.
[$G_3$] *Inverses*, i.e., for each $a$ in $G$, there exists an element $a^{-1}$ (the *inverse* of $a$) in $G$ such that $aa^{-1} = a^{-1}a = e$.

([$G_2$] and [$G_3$] make a semigroup into a group.)

**9.26** Define an abelian group.

A group $G$ is said to be *abelian* [or *commutative*] if the commutative law holds; i.e., if $ab = ba$ for every $a, b \in G$.

When the binary operation is denoted by juxtaposition as above, the group $G$ is said to be written *multiplicatively*. When $G$ is abelian, the binary operation is frequently denoted by $+$ and $G$ is said to be written *additively*. In such a case the identity element is denoted by $0$ and is called the *zero* element, and the inverse is denoted by $-a$ and is called the *negative* of $a$. If $A$ and $B$ are subsets of $G$, then we write

$$AB = \{ab : a \in A, b \in B\} \quad \text{or} \quad A + B = \{a + b : a \in A, b \in B\}$$

**9.27** Define: **(a)** order of a group, and **(b)** finite group.

**(a)** The number of elements in a group $G$, denoted by $|G|$, is called the *order* of $G$.
**(b)** $G$ is a *finite group* if its order is finite.

**9.28** Which of the following are groups under addition: $\mathbf{N}$, $\mathbf{Z}$, $\mathbf{Q}$, $\mathbf{R}$, $\mathbf{C}$?

The integers $\mathbf{Z}$, the rationals $\mathbf{Q}$, the reals $\mathbf{R}$, and the complex numbers $\mathbf{C}$ are each a (abelian) group under addition. The positive integers $\mathbf{N}$ do not form a group under addition, e.g., $0 \notin \mathbf{N}$.

**9.29** The nonzero rational numbers $\mathbf{Q} \setminus \{0\}$ form an abelian group under multiplication. What is the identity element, and what are the inverses?

The rational number $1$ is the identity element and $q/p$ is the multiplicative inverse of the rational number $p/q$.

**9.30**  Let $S$ be the set of $n \times n$ matrices with rational entries, under the operation of matrix multiplication. Is $S$ a group?

▌ No. Although matrix multiplication is associative and matrix multiplication has an identity element $I$ (with rational entries), $S$ is not a group since inverses do not always exist.

**9.31**  The set $G$ of nonsingular $n \times n$ matrices does form a group under matrix multiplication. What is the identity element, and what are inverses?

▌ The identity element is the identity matrix $I$, and the inverse of $A$ is its inverse matrix $A^{-1}$. This is an example of a nonabelian group, since matrix multiplication is noncommutative. In particular, when $n = 2$ we have $I = \begin{pmatrix} 1 & 0 \\ 0 & 1 \end{pmatrix}$ and the inverse of $A = \begin{pmatrix} a & b \\ c & d \end{pmatrix}$ is $A^{-1} = \begin{pmatrix} d/|A| & -b/|A| \\ -c/|A| & a/|A| \end{pmatrix}$ where $|A| = ad - bc$ is the determinant of $A$.

**9.32**  Define the symmetric group of degree $n$, denoted by $S_n$.

▌ A one-to-one mapping $\sigma$ of the set $\{1, 2, \ldots, n\}$ onto itself is called a *permutation*. Such a permutation is frequently denoted by $\sigma = \begin{pmatrix} 1 & 2 & \cdots & n \\ j_1 & j_2 & \cdots & j_n \end{pmatrix}$ where $j_i = \sigma(i)$. The set of such permutations is denoted by $S_n$, and there are $n! = 1 \cdot 2 \cdots \cdots n$ of them. The composition of permutations in $S_n$ belongs to $S_n$, the identity mapping $\varepsilon$ belongs to $S_n$, and the inverses of permutations in $S_n$ belong to $S_n$. Thus $S_n$ forms a group under composition of mappings. This is the *symmetric group of degree n*.

**9.33**  Find the elements and the multiplication table of the symmetric group $S_3$.

▌ $S_3$ has $3! = 6$ elements, as follows:

$$\varepsilon = \begin{pmatrix} 1 & 2 & 3 \\ 1 & 2 & 3 \end{pmatrix} \qquad \sigma_2 = \begin{pmatrix} 1 & 2 & 3 \\ 3 & 2 & 1 \end{pmatrix} \qquad \phi_1 = \begin{pmatrix} 1 & 2 & 3 \\ 2 & 3 & 1 \end{pmatrix}$$

$$\sigma_1 = \begin{pmatrix} 1 & 2 & 3 \\ 1 & 3 & 2 \end{pmatrix} \qquad \sigma_3 = \begin{pmatrix} 1 & 2 & 3 \\ 2 & 1 & 3 \end{pmatrix} \qquad \phi_2 = \begin{pmatrix} 1 & 2 & 3 \\ 3 & 1 & 2 \end{pmatrix}$$

The multiplication table of $S_3$ is shown in Fig. 9-1.

|  | $\epsilon$ | $\sigma_1$ | $\sigma_2$ | $\sigma_3$ | $\phi_1$ | $\phi_2$ |
|---|---|---|---|---|---|---|
| $\epsilon$ | $\epsilon$ | $\sigma_1$ | $\sigma_2$ | $\sigma_3$ | $\phi_1$ | $\phi_2$ |
| $\sigma_1$ | $\sigma_1$ | $\epsilon$ | $\phi_1$ | $\phi_2$ | $\sigma_2$ | $\sigma_3$ |
| $\sigma_2$ | $\sigma_2$ | $\phi_2$ | $\epsilon$ | $\phi_1$ | $\sigma_3$ | $\sigma_1$ |
| $\sigma_3$ | $\sigma_3$ | $\phi_1$ | $\phi_2$ | $\epsilon$ | $\sigma_1$ | $\sigma_2$ |
| $\phi_1$ | $\phi_1$ | $\sigma_3$ | $\sigma_1$ | $\sigma_2$ | $\phi_2$ | $\epsilon$ |
| $\phi_2$ | $\phi_2$ | $\sigma_2$ | $\sigma_3$ | $\sigma_1$ | $\epsilon$ | $\phi_1$ |

**Fig. 9-1**

**9.34**  Show that the identity element in a group $G$ is unique.

▌ Suppose $e$ and $e'$ are identity elements in $G$. Then $ee' = e$ since $e'$ is an identity element and $ee' = e'$ since $e$ is an identity element. Hence $e = e'$.

**9.35**  Show that the inverse $a^{-1}$ of any element $a$ of $G$ is unique.

▌ Follows from Problem 9.15 and the fact that $G$ is associative.

**9.36**  Show that the left and right cancellation laws hold in $G$.

▌ If $ab = ac$, then $b = eb = (a^{-1}a)b = a^{-1}(ab) = a^{-1}(ac) = (a^{-1}a)c = ec = c$. Similarly, if $ba = ca$, then $b = c$.

**9.37**  Show that $(a^{-1})^{-1} = a$ for any element $a$ in $G$.

▌ Since $a^{-1}$ is the inverse of $a$, we have $aa^{-1} = a^{-1}a = e$. Hence $a$ is the inverse of $a^{-1}$; that is, $a = (a^{-1})^{-1}$.

**9.38**   Show that $(ab)^{-1} = b^{-1}a^{-1}$.

▮ Here $(b^{-1}a^{-1})(ab) = b^{-1}(a^{-1}a)b = b^{-1}eb = b^{-1}b = e$. Similarly, $(ab)(b^{-1}a^{-1}) = e$. Therefore, $b^{-1}a^{-1}$ is the inverse of $ab$, that is, $b^{-1}a^{-1} = (ab)^{-1}$.

**9.39**   Consider the group $G = \{1, 2, 3, 4, 5, 6\}$ under multiplication modulo 7. Find the multiplication table of $G$.

▮ To find $a * b$ in $G$, find the remainder when the product $ab$ is divided by 7. For example, $5 \cdot 6 = 30$ which yields a remainder of 2 when divided by 7; hence $5 * 6 = 2$ in $G$. The multiplication table of $G$ appears in Fig. 9-2.

| * | 1 | 2 | 3 | 4 | 5 | 6 |
|---|---|---|---|---|---|---|
| 1 | 1 | 2 | 3 | 4 | 5 | 6 |
| 2 | 2 | 4 | 6 | 1 | 3 | 5 |
| 3 | 3 | 6 | 2 | 5 | 1 | 4 |
| 4 | 4 | 1 | 5 | 2 | 6 | 3 |
| 5 | 5 | 3 | 1 | 6 | 4 | 2 |
| 6 | 6 | 5 | 4 | 3 | 2 | 1 |

**Fig. 9-2**

**9.40**   Find $2^{-1}$, $3^{-1}$, and $6^{-1}$ for the group $G$ in Fig. 9-2.

▮ Note first that 1 is the identity element of $G$. Recall that $a^{-1}$ is that element of $G$ such that $aa^{-1} = 1$. Hence $2^{-1} = 4$, $3^{-1} = 5$, and $6^{-1} = 6$.

## Subgroups

**9.41**   Define a subgroup of a group.

▮ A subset $H$ of a group $G$ is called a *subgroup* of $G$ if $H$ itself forms a group under the operation of $G$.

**9.42**   Suppose $H$ is a subset of a group $G$. Show that $H$ is a subgroup of $G$ if $H$ has the following three properties: (i) The identity element $e$ belongs to $H$. (ii) $H$ is closed under the operation of $G$, i.e., if $a$, $b \in H$ then $ab \in H$. (iii) $H$ is closed under inverses, i.e., if $a \in H$ then $a^{-1} \in H$.

▮ $H$ is nonempty and has an identity element by (i). The operation is well-defined in $H$ by (ii). Inverses exist in $H$ by (iii). Lastly, the associative law holds in $H$ since it holds in $G$. Thus $H$ is a subgroup of $G$.

**9.43**   Consider the group $\mathbf{Z}$ of integers under addition. Let $H$ be the subset of $\mathbf{Z}$ consisting of all multiples of a positive integer $m$; that is, $H = \{\ldots, -3m, -2m, -m, 0, m, 2m, 3m, \ldots\}$. Show that $H$ is a subgroup of $\mathbf{Z}$.

▮ (i) $H$ contains the identity element 0 of $\mathbf{Z}$. (ii) If $rm$ and $sm$ are any elements of $H$, then the sum $rm + sm = (r + s)m$ is also an element of $H$. (iii) If $rm$ is any element of $H$, then its negative $-rm$ also belongs to $H$.

**9.44**   Let $G$ be any group and let $a$ be any element of $G$. Define the *cyclic group generated* by $a$, denoted by $gp(a)$.

▮ As usual, we define $a^0 = e$ and $a^{n+1} = a^n \cdot a$. Clearly, $a^m \cdot a^n = a^{m+n}$ and $(a^m)^n = a^{mn}$, for any integers $m$ and $n$. Let $gp(a)$ denote the set of all powers of $a$:

$$gp(a) = \{\cdots, a^{-2}, a^{-1}, e, a, a^2, a^3, \ldots\}$$

Then $gp(a)$ contains $e$, is closed under the group operation, and contains inverses. Thus $gp(a)$ is a subgroup of $G$, and it is called the *cyclic group generated* by $a$.

**9.45**   Let $a$ be any element in a group $G$. Describe the cyclic group $gp(a)$ when $gp(a)$ is finite, and define the order of $a$.

▮ If $gp(a)$ is finite, then some of the powers of $a$ are not distinct; say $a^r = a^s$ with, say, $r > s$. Then $a^{r-s} = e$ where $r - s > 0$. The smallest positive integer $m$ such that $a^m = e$ is called the *order* of $a$ and will be denoted by

$|a|$. If $|a| = m$, then its cyclic subgroup $gp(a)$ has $m$ elements given by

$$gp(a) = \{e, a, a^2, a^3, \ldots, a^{m-1}\}$$

If $gp(a)$ is not finite, then we define $|a| = 0$.

**9.46** Consider the group $G$ of Problem 9.39. (*a*) Find the orders and subgroups generated by 2 and 3. (*b*) Is $G$ cyclic?

▌ (*a*) We have $2^1 = 2$, $2^2 = 4$, but $2^3 = 1$. Hence $|2| = 3$ and $gp(2) = \{1, 2, 4\}$. We have $3^1 = 3$, $3^2 = 2$, $3^3 = 6$, $3^4 = 4$, $3^5 = 5$, $3^6 = 1$. Hence $|3| = 6$ and $gp(3) = G$.

(*b*) $G$ is cyclic since $G = gp(3)$.

**9.47** Let $H$ be a subgroup of a group $G$. Define a right (left) coset of $H$.

▌ Let $a$ be any element of $G$. Then the set $Ha = \{ha: h \in H\}$ is called a *right coset* of $H$. Analogously, $aH$ is called a *left coset* of $H$.

**Theorem 9.2:** Let $H$ be a subgroup of a group $G$. Then the right cosets $Ha$ form a partition of $G$.

**9.48** Prove Theorem 9.2.

▌ Since $e \in H$, $a = ea \in Ha$; hence every element belongs to a coset. In fact, $a \in Ha$. Now suppose $Ha$ and $Hb$ are not disjoint. Say $c \in Ha \cap Hb$. The proof is complete if we show that $Ha = Hb$.

Since $c$ belongs to both $Ha$ and $Hb$, we have $c = h_1 a$ and $c = h_2 b$ where $h_1, h_2 \in H$. Then $h_1 a = h_2 b$, and so $a = h_1^{-1} h_2 b$. Let $x \in Ha$. Then

$$x = h_3 a = h_3 h_1^{-1} h_2 b$$

where $h_3 \in H$. Since $H$ is a subgroup, $h_3 h_1^{-1} h_2 \in H$; hence $x \in Hb$. Since $x$ was any element of $Ha$, we have $Ha \subseteq Hb$. Similarly, $Hb \subseteq Ha$. Both inclusions imply $Ha = Hb$, and the theorem is proved.

**9.49** Let $H$ be a finite subgroup of $G$. Show that $H$ and any coset $Ha$ have the same number of elements.

▌ Let $H = \{h_1, h_2, \ldots, h_k\}$, where $H$ has $k$ elements. Then $Ha = \{h_1 a, h_2 a, \ldots, h_k a\}$. However, $h_i a = h_j a$ implies $h_i = h_j$; hence the $k$ elements listed in $Ha$ are distinct.

**Theorem 9.3 (Lagrange):** Let $H$ be a subgroup of a finite group $G$. Then the order of $H$ divides the order of $G$.

**9.50** Prove Theorem 9.3.

▌ Suppose $H$ has $r$ elements and there are $s$ distinct right cosets. By Theorem 9.2, the cosets partition $G$ and, by Problem 9.49, each coset has $r$ elements. Therefore $G$ has $rs$ elements, and so the order of $H$ divides the order of $G$.

**9.51** Let $H$ be a subgroup of a group $G$. Define the index of $H$ in $G$, denoted by $[G:H]$.

▌ The *index* of $H$ in $G$ is equal to the number of right (or left) cosets of $H$ in $G$. If $G$ and $H$ are finite, then $[G:H] = |G|/|H|$.

**9.52** Let $H$ be a subgroup of a group $G$. Define a coset representative system for $H$ in $G$.

▌ A subset $C$ of $G$ is a *coset representative system* of $H$ if $C$ contains exactly one element from each coset. Such an element is called a *representative* of the coset. Thus the number of elements in $C$ or, in other words, the number of coset representatives, is equal to $[G:H]$, the index of $H$ in $G$.

**9.53** Let $H$ be a subgroup of a finite group $G$. How many coset representative systems exist for the cosets of $H$?

▌ There are $|H|$ ways of choosing an element from any coset [see Problem 9.49], and there are $[G:H]$ distinct cosets. Hence the desired number is $|H|^{[G:H]}$.

**9.54** Consider the group $\mathbf{Z}$ of integers under addition and the subgroup $H = \{\ldots, -10, -5, 0, 5, 10, \ldots\}$ consisting of the multiples of 5. Find: (*a*) the cosets of $H$ in $\mathbf{Z}$, and (*b*) the index of $H$ in $\mathbf{Z}$.

▌ **(a)** There are five distinct [left] cosets of $H$ in $\mathbf{Z}$, as follows:

$$0 + H = H = \{\ldots, -10, -5, 0, 5, 10, \ldots\}$$
$$1 + H = \{\ldots, -9, -4, 1, 6, 11, \ldots\}$$
$$2 + H = \{\ldots, -8, -3, 2, 7, 12, \ldots\}$$
$$3 + H = \{\ldots, -7, -2, 3, 8, 13, \ldots\}$$
$$4 + H = \{\ldots, -6, -1, 4, 9, 14, \ldots\}$$

Any other coset $n + H$ coincides with one of the above cosets.

**(b)** Although $\mathbf{Z}$ and $H$ are both infinite, the index of $H$ in $\mathbf{Z}$ is finite. Specifically, $[\mathbf{Z}: H] = 5$, the number of cosets.

**9.55** Find coset representatives for the subgroup $H$ of $\mathbf{Z}$ in Problem 9.54.

▌ Choose exactly one element from each coset; e.g., $\{0, 1, 2, 3, 4\}$ or $\{-1, 0, 1, 2, 3\}$. (We usually choose the smallest nonnegative integers or the smallest integers as coset representatives for a subgroup $H$ of $\mathbf{Z}$. In general, we choose the identity element for the representative of $H$.)

**9.56** Consider the symmetric group $S_3$ of Problem 9.33. Find the order of, and the subgroup generated by, each element of $S_3$.

▌ $\varepsilon^1 = \varepsilon$, so $|\varepsilon| = 1$ and $gp(\varepsilon) = \{\varepsilon\}$. $\sigma_1^1 = \sigma_1$, $\sigma_1^2 = \varepsilon$; so $|\sigma_1| = 2$ and $gp(\sigma_1) = \{\sigma_1, \varepsilon\}$. Similarly, $|\sigma_2| = 2$, $gp(\sigma_2) = \{\sigma_2, \varepsilon\}$; and $|\sigma_3| = 2$, $gp(\sigma_3) = \{\sigma_3, \varepsilon\}$. We have

$$\phi_1^1 = \phi_1, \qquad \phi_1^2 = \phi_2, \qquad \phi_1^3 = \phi_2 \cdot \phi_1 = \varepsilon$$

Hence $|\phi_1| = 3$ and $gp(\phi_1) = \{\varepsilon, \phi_1, \phi_2\}$. Also, $\phi_2^1 = \phi_2$, $\phi_2^2 = \phi_1$, $\phi_2^3 = \phi_1 \cdot \phi_2 = \varepsilon$; hence $|\phi_2| = 3$ and $gp(\phi_2) = \{\varepsilon, \phi_2, \phi_1\}$.

**9.57** Is $S_3$ cyclic?

▌ $S_3$ is not cyclic, since $S_3$ is not generated by any of its elements.

**9.58** Find a subgroup $H$ of order four for the symmetric group $S_3$.

▌ The order of $S_3$ is six. By Lagrange's theorem, the order of $H$ must divide the order of $S_3$. Hence there is no subgroup of order four.

**9.59** Consider the symmetric group $S_3$ in Fig. 9-1. Let $A = \{\sigma_1, \sigma_2\}$ and $B = \{\phi_1, \phi_2\}$. Find **(a)** $AB$, **(b)** $\sigma_3 A$, and **(c)** $A\sigma_3$.

▌ **(a)** Multiply each element of $A$ by each element of $B$: $\sigma_1\phi_1 = \sigma_2$, $\sigma_1\phi_2 = \sigma_3$, $\sigma_2\phi_1 = 3$, $\sigma_2\phi_2 = \sigma_1$. Hence $AB = \{\sigma_1, \sigma_2, \sigma_3\}$.

**(b)** Multiply $\sigma_3$ by each element of $A$: $\sigma_3\sigma_1 = \phi_1$, $\sigma_3\sigma_2 = \phi_2$. Hence $\sigma_3 A = \{\phi_1, \phi_2\}$.

**(c)** Multiply each element of $A$ by $\sigma_3$: $\sigma_1\sigma_3 = \phi_2$, $\sigma_2\sigma_3 = \phi_1$. Hence $A\sigma_3 = \{\phi_1, \phi_2\}$.

**9.60** Consider the subgroups $H = gp(\sigma_1)$ and $K = gp(\sigma_2)$ of $S_3$ in Fig. 9-1. Show that $HK$ is not a subgroup of $S_3$.

▌ $H = \{\varepsilon, \sigma_1\}$, $K = \{\varepsilon, \sigma_2\}$ and then $HK = \{\varepsilon, \sigma_1, \sigma_2, \phi_1\}$, which is not a subgroup of $S_3$ since $HK$ has four elements.

**9.61** If $H$ is a subgroup of $G$, show that $HH = H$.

▌ Since $H$ is closed under the operation of $G$, we have $HH \subseteq H$. On the other hand, suppose $h \in H$. Since $H$ is a subgroup, the identity element $e$ belongs to $H$. Hence $eh = h \in HH$, and so $H \subseteq HH$. The two inclusions give $HH = H$.

**9.62** Exhibit all subgroups of the cyclic group of order $p$ where $p$ is a prime.

▌ $\{\varepsilon\}$ is the only subgroup, by Lagrange's theorem.

**9.63** Find a subset $S$ of the group $\mathbf{Z}$ of integers under addition such that $S + S \neq S$ and $a \notin a + S$ for some element $a \in \mathbf{Z}$.

■ Let $S = \{1, 2, 3, \ldots\}$. Then $S + S = \{2, 3, 4, \ldots\} \neq S$, and $2 + S = \{3, 4, 5, \ldots\}$ does not contain 2.

**9.64** If $H$ is a subgroup of $G$, show that $Ha = Hb$ if and only if $ab^{-1} \in H$.

■ If $Ha = Hb$, then $a \in Ha = Hb$. Hence there exists $h \in H$ such that $a = hb$, and $ab^{-1} = h$ belongs to $H$. On the other hand, suppose $h \equiv ab^{-1} \in H$. Then $a = hb \in Hb$. But $a \in Ha$. Thus $Ha = Hb$, since the cosets form a partition of $G$.

**9.65** Let $G$ be a finite group of order $n$. Show that $a^n = e$ for any $a \in G$.

■ If $|gp(a)| = m$, then $a^m = e$. By Lagrange's theorem, $m$ divides $n$; say, $n = mr$. Then $a^n = a^{mr} = (a^m)^r = e^r = e$.

## 9.3 NORMAL SUBGROUPS, FACTOR GROUPS, GROUP HOMOMORPHISMS

**9.66** Define a normal subgroup of a group $G$.

■ A subgroup $H$ of $G$ is called a *normal* subgroup if $a^{-1}Ha \subseteq H$ for every $a \in G$. Equivalently, $H$ is normal if $aH = Ha$ for every $a \in G$, i.e., if the right and left cosets of $H$ coincide.

**9.67** Let $G$ be the group of nonsingular $2 \times 2$ matrices under matrix multiplication. Let $H$ be the subset of $G$ consisting of the lower triangular matrices; i.e., matrices of the form $\begin{pmatrix} a & 0 \\ c & d \end{pmatrix}$ where $ad \neq 0$. Show that $H$ is a subgroup of $G$, but not a normal subgroup.

■ $H$ is closed under matrix multiplication and inverses, and the identity matrix $I$ belongs to $H$. Hence $H$ is a subgroup of $G$. However, $H$ is not a normal subgroup since, for example,

$$\begin{pmatrix} 1 & 2 \\ 1 & 3 \end{pmatrix}^{-1} \begin{pmatrix} 1 & 0 \\ 1 & 1 \end{pmatrix} \begin{pmatrix} 1 & 2 \\ 1 & 3 \end{pmatrix} = \begin{pmatrix} 3 & -2 \\ -1 & 1 \end{pmatrix} \begin{pmatrix} 1 & 0 \\ 1 & 1 \end{pmatrix} \begin{pmatrix} 1 & 2 \\ 1 & 3 \end{pmatrix} = \begin{pmatrix} -1 & -4 \\ 1 & 3 \end{pmatrix}$$

does not belong to $H$.

**9.68** Let $G$ be the group of matrices in Problem 9.67. Let $K$ be the subset of $G$ consisting of matrices with determinant 1. Show that $K$ is a normal subgroup of $G$.

■ Since $\det(I) = 1$, $I$ belongs to $K$. If $A$ and $B$ belong to $K$, then $\det(AB) = \det(A) \cdot \det(B) = (1)(1) = 1$ and so $AB$ belongs to $K$. Also, $\det(A^{-1}) = 1/\det(A) = 1$ and so $A^{-1}$ belongs to $K$. Thus $K$ is a subgroup. Moreover, for any matrix $X$ in $G$ and any matrix $A$ in $K$, $\det(X^{-1}AX) = 1$. Hence $X^{-1}AX$ belongs to $K$. So $K$ is a normal subgroup of $G$.

**9.69** Consider the permutation group $S_3$, whose multiplication table appears in Fig. 9-1. Is the subgroup $H = \{\varepsilon, \sigma_1\}$ normal?

■ The right and left cosets of $H$ are as follows:

| Right Cosets | Left Cosets |
|---|---|
| $H = \{\varepsilon, \sigma_1\}$ | $H = \{\varepsilon, \sigma_1\}$ |
| $H\phi_1 = \{\phi_1, \sigma_2\}$ | $\phi_1 H = \{\phi_1, \sigma_3\}$ |
| $H\phi_2 = \{\phi_2, \sigma_3\}$ | $\phi_2 H = \{\phi_2, \sigma_2\}$ |

Since $H\phi_1 \neq \phi_1 H$, $H$ is not a normal subgroup of $S_3$.

**9.70** Show that any subgroup $H$ of an abelian group $G$ is normal.

■ Let $h$ be any element of $H$ and let $g$ be any element of $G$. Then $g^{-1}hg = hg^{-1}g = h$ belongs to $H$. Hence $H$ is a normal subgroup.

**9.71** Let $H$ be a subgroup, and let $K$ be a normal subgroup, of a group $G$. Prove that $HK$ is a subgroup of $G$. [Compare with Problem 9.60.]

■ We must show that $e \in HK$ and that $HK$ is closed under multiplication and inverses. Since $H$ and $K$ are subgroups, $e \in H$ and $e \in K$. Hence $e = ee$ belongs to $HK$. Suppose $x, y \in HK$. Then $x = h_1 k_1$ and $y = h_2 k_2$ where $h_1, h_2 \in H$ and $k_1, k_2 \in K$. Then

$$xy = h_1 k_1 h_2 k_2 = h_1 h_2 (h_2^{-1} k_1 h_2) k_2$$

Since $K$ is normal, $h_2^{-1} k_1 h_2 \in K$; and since $H$ and $K$ are subgroups, $h_1 h_2 \in H$ and $(h_2^{-1} k_2 h_2) k_2 \in K$. Thus $xy \in HK$, and so $HK$ is closed under multiplication. We also have that

$$x^{-1} = (h_1 k_1)^{-1} = k_1^{-1} h_1^{-1} = h_1^{-1} (h_1 k_1^{-1} h_1^{-1})$$

Since $K$ is a normal subgroup, $h_1 k_1^{-1} h_1^{-1}$ belongs to $K$. Also $h_1^{-1}$ belongs to $H$. Therefore $x^{-1} \in HK$, and hence $HK$ is closed under inverses. Consequently, $HK$ is a subgroup.

The following theorem defines the *quotient group, $G/H$,* corresponding to a normal subgroup $H$ of $G$.

**Theorem 9.4:** Let $H$ be a normal subgroup of a group $G$. Then the cosets of $H$ in $G$ form a group under *coset multiplication*, as defined by $(aH)(bH) = abH$.

**9.72** Prove Theorem 9.4.

▌ Coset multiplication is well-defined, since

$$(aH)(bH) = a(Hb)H = a(bH)H = ab(HH) = abH$$

(Here we used the fact that $H$ is normal, so $Hb = bH$, and, from Problem 9.61, that $HH = H$.) Associativity of coset multiplication follows from the fact that associativity holds in $G$. $H$ is the identity element of $G/H$, since

$$(aH)H = a(HH) = aH \qquad \text{and} \qquad H(aH) = (Ha)H = (aH)H = aH$$

Lastly, $a^{-1}H$ is the inverse of $aH$ since

$$(a^{-1}H)(aH) = a^{-1}aH = eH = H \qquad \text{and} \qquad (aH)(a^{-1}H) = aa^{-1}H = eH = H$$

Thus $G/H$ is a group under coset multiplication.

**9.73** Let $\mathbf{Z}$ be the group of integers under addition, and let $H$ be the subgroup of $\mathbf{Z}$ consisting of the multiples of 5. Show that $H$ is a normal subgroup of $\mathbf{Z}$, and find the quotient group $\mathbf{Z}/H$.

▌ Since $\mathbf{Z}$ is abelian, $H$ is automatically a normal subgroup. Let $\bar{0}, \bar{1}, \bar{2}, \bar{3}$, and $\bar{4}$ denote, respectively, the five cosets $H$, $1 + H$, $2 + H$, $3 + H$, and $4 + H$, which are listed in Problem 9.54. The addition table for the quotient group $\mathbf{Z}/H = \{\bar{0}, \bar{1}, \bar{2}, 3, \bar{4}\}$ is given in Fig. 9-3. [This group is usually called *the integers modulo 5* and is frequently denoted $\mathbf{Z}_5$. Analogously, for any positive integer $m$, there exists the quotient group $\mathbf{Z}_m$ called *the integers modulo m.*]

| + | $\bar{0}$ | $\bar{1}$ | $\bar{2}$ | $\bar{3}$ | $\bar{4}$ |
|---|---|---|---|---|---|
| $\bar{0}$ | $\bar{0}$ | $\bar{1}$ | $\bar{2}$ | $\bar{3}$ | $\bar{4}$ |
| $\bar{1}$ | $\bar{1}$ | $\bar{2}$ | $\bar{3}$ | $\bar{4}$ | $\bar{0}$ |
| $\bar{2}$ | $\bar{2}$ | $\bar{3}$ | $\bar{4}$ | $\bar{0}$ | $\bar{1}$ |
| $\bar{3}$ | $\bar{3}$ | $\bar{4}$ | $\bar{0}$ | $\bar{1}$ | $\bar{2}$ |
| $\bar{4}$ | $\bar{4}$ | $\bar{0}$ | $\bar{1}$ | $\bar{2}$ | $\bar{3}$ |

**Fig. 9-3**

## Homomorphisms

**9.74** Define a group homomorphism. Also, define a group isomorphism.

▌ A mapping $f$ from a group $G$ (with operation $*$) into a group $G'$ [with operation $*'$] is a *homomorphism* if $f(a * b) = f(a) *' f(b)$ for every $a$, $b$ in $G$. In addition, if $f$ is one-to-one and onto, then $f$ is an *isomorphism* and $G$ and $G'$ are said to be *isomorphic*, written $G \simeq G'$.

**9.75** Let $G$ be the group of real numbers under addition, and let $G'$ be the group of positive real numbers under multiplication. Show that the mapping $f: G \to G'$, defined by $f(a) = 2^a$, is a homomorphism. Is it an isomorphism?

▮ The mapping $f$ is a homomorphism since $f(a + b) = 2^{a+b} = 2^a 2^b = f(a)f(b)$. Moreover, since $f$ is one-to-one and onto, $f$ is an isomorphism.

**9.76** Let $G$ be the group of real, nonsingular, $n$-square matrices under multiplication. Show that the determinant function is a homomorphism of $G$ into the group $G'$ of nonzero real numbers under multiplication.

▮ Let $A$ and $B$ be matrices in $G$. Then $\det(AB) = \det(A) \cdot \det(B)$. Hence the determinant function is a homomorphism.

**9.77** Given a homomorphism $f: G \to G'$, show that $f(e) = e'$ where $e$ and $e'$ are the identity elements of $G$ and $G'$, respectively.

▮ Since $e = e * e$ and $f$ is a homomorphism, $f(e) = f(e * e) = f(e) *' f(e)$. Hence

$$e' = f(e)^{-1} *' f(e) = [f(e)^{-1} *' f(e)] *' f(e) = e' *' f(e) = f(e).$$

**9.78** Given a homomorphism $f: G \to G'$, show that $f(a^{-1}) = f(a)^{-1}$, for any element $a$ in $G$.

▮ Using Problem 9.77, we have

$$f(a) *' f(a^{-1}) = f(a * a^{-1}) = f(e) = e' = f(e) = f(a^{-1} * a) = f(a^{-1}) *' f(a)$$

Thus $f(a)^{-1} = f(a^{-1})$.

**9.79** Define the kernel and the image of a group homomorphism $f: G \to G'$.

▮ The *kernel* of $f$, written $\operatorname{Ker} f$, is the set of elements of $G$ whose image is the identity element $e'$ of $G'$:

$$\operatorname{Ker} f = \{a \in G : f(a) = e'\}.$$

The *image* of $f$, written $f(G)$ or $\operatorname{Im} f$, consists of the images of elements of $G$ under $f$:

$$\operatorname{Im} f = \{b \in G' : b = f(a) \text{ for some } a \in G\}$$

The term *range* is also used for image.

**Theorem 9.5:** Let $f: G \to G'$ be a homomorphism with kernel $K$. Then (i) $K$ is a normal subgroup of $G$, and (ii) the quotient group $G/K$ is isomorphic to the image of $f$.

**9.80** Prove Theorem 9.5(i).

▮ By Problem 9.77, $f(e) = e'$ and so $e \in K$. Now suppose $a, b \in K$ and $g \in G$. Then $f(a) = e'$ and $f(b) = e'$. Hence (using juxtaposition to indicate either group operation),

$$f(ab) = f(a)f(b) = e'e' = e'$$
$$f(a^{-1}) = f(a)^{-1} = e'^{-1} = e'$$
$$f(gag^{-1}) = f(g)f(a)f(g^{-1}) = f(g)e'f(g)^{-1} = e'$$

Hence $ab$, $a^{-1}$, and $gag^{-1}$ belong to $K$, and so $K$ is a normal subgroup.

**9.81** Prove Theorem 9.5(ii).

▮ Let $H \subseteq G'$ be the image of $f$, and define a mapping $\phi: G/K \to H$ by $\phi(Ka) = f(a)$. We show that $\phi$ is well-defined; i.e., if $Ka = Kb$ then $\phi(Ka) = \phi(Kb)$. Suppose $Ka = Kb$. Then $ab^{-1} \in K$ (Problem 9.64). Then $f(ab^{-1}) = e'$, and so

$$f(a)f(b)^{-1} = f(a)f(b^{-1}) = f(ab^{-1}) = e'$$

Hence $f(a) = f(b)$, and so $\phi(Ka) = \phi(Kb)$. Thus $\phi$ is well-defined. We next show that $\phi$ is a homomorphism:

$$\phi(KaKb) = \phi(Kab) = f(ab) = f(a)f(b) = \phi(Ka)\phi(Kb)$$

Thus $\phi$ is a homomorphism. We next show that $\phi$ is one-to-one. Suppose $\phi(Ka) = \phi(Kb)$. Then

$$f(a) = f(b) \quad \text{or} \quad f(a)f(b)^{-1} = e' \quad \text{or} \quad f(a)f(b^{-1}) = e' \quad \text{or} \quad f(ab^{-1}) = e'$$

Thus $ab^{-1} \in K$ and, again by Problem 9.64, $Ka = Kb$. Thus $\phi$ is one-to-one. Finally, we show that $\phi$ is onto. Let $h \in H$. Since $H$ is the image of $f$, there exists $a \in G$ such that $f(a) = h$. Thus $\phi(Ka) = f(a) = h$, and so $\phi$ is onto. Consequently $G/K \simeq H$ and Theorem 9.5(ii) is proved.

**9.82**  Let $f: G \to G'$ be defined by $f(z) = |z|$ where $G$ = group of nonzero complex numbers under multiplication, and $G'$ = group of nonzero real numbers under multiplication. (*a*) Show that $f$ is a group homomorphism, and (*b*) describe geometrically the kernel $K$ of the homomorphism $f$.

▌ (*a*)  $f(z_1 z_2) = |z_1 z_2| = |z_1| \, |z_2| = f(z_1)f(z_2)$.

▌ (*b*)  $K$ consists of those complex numbers $z$ such that $|z| = 1$; i.e., $K$ is the unit circle.

**9.83**  Describe the quotient group $G/K$ in Problem 9.82.

▌ $G/K$ is isomorphic to the image of $f$, which is the group of positive real numbers under multiplication.

**9.84**  Show that any cyclic group is isomorphic either to the integers $\mathbf{Z}$ under addition, or to $\mathbf{Z}_m$, the integers under addition modulo $m$.

▌ Let $a$ be any element in a group $G$. The function $f: \mathbf{Z} \to G$ defined by $f(n) = a^n$ is a homomorphism since $f(m + n) = a^{m+n} = a^m \cdot a^n = f(m)f(n)$. The image of $f$ is $gp(a)$, the cyclic subgroup generated by $a$. Thus, $gp(a) \simeq \mathbf{Z}/K$, where $K$ is the kernel of $f$. If $K = \{0\}$, then $gp(a) \simeq \mathbf{Z}$. On the other hand, if $m$ is the order of $a$, then $K = \{$multiples of $m\}$, and so $gp(a) \simeq \mathbf{Z}_m$.

## 9.4  RINGS AND IDEALS

**9.85**  Define a ring.

▌ Let $R$ be a nonempty set with two binary operations, an operation of addition (denoted by $+$) and an operation of multiplication (denoted by juxtaposition). Then $R$ is called a *ring* if the following axioms are satisfied:

[$\mathbf{R}_1$]  For any $a, b, c \in R$, we have $(a + b) + c = a + (b + c)$.
[$\mathbf{R}_2$]  There exists an element $0 \in R$, called the *zero* element, such that $a + 0 = 0 + a = a$ for every $a \in R$.
[$\mathbf{R}_3$]  For each $a \in R$ there exists an element $-a \in R$, called the *negative* of $a$, such that $a + (-a) = (-a) + a = 0$.
[$\mathbf{R}_4$]  For any $a, b \in R$, we have $a + b = b + a$.
[$\mathbf{R}_5$]  For any $a, b, c \in R$, we have $(ab)c = a(bc)$.
[$\mathbf{R}_6$]  For any $a, b, c \in R$, we have: (i) $a(b + c) = ab + ac$, and (ii) $(b + c)a = ba + ca$.

Axioms [$\mathbf{R}_1$] through [$\mathbf{R}_4$] make $R$ an abelian group under addition.

**9.86**  How is subtraction defined in a ring $R$?

▌ $a - b \equiv a + (-b)$

**9.87**  Define a commutative ring.

▌ A ring $R$ is *commutative* if $ab = ba$ for every $a, b \in R$.

**9.88**  Define a unity element in a ring $R$.

▌ A nonzero element $1 \in R$ is called a *unity element* if $a \cdot 1 = 1 \cdot a = a$ for every element $a \in R$.

**9.89**  Let $R$ be a ring with unity element 1. Define a unit in $R$.

▌ An element $a \in R$ is a *unit* if $a$ has a multiplicative inverse, $a^{-1} \in R$, such that $aa^{-1} = a^{-1}a = 1$.

**9.90**  Consider the ring $\mathbf{Z}$ of integers. (*a*) Is $\mathbf{Z}$ commutative? (*b*) Does $\mathbf{Z}$ have a unity element? (*c*) What are the units in $\mathbf{Z}$?

▌ (*a*) $\mathbf{Z}$ is a commutative ring since $ab = ba$ for any integers $a, b \in \mathbf{Z}$. (*b*) The number 1 is a unity element in $\mathbf{Z}$. (*c*) The only units in $\mathbf{Z}$ are 1 and $-1$.

**9.91**  Find the units of $\mathbf{Z}_m$, the ring of integers modulo $m$.

▌ If $a$ is a unit in $\mathbf{Z}_m$, then $a^{-1}a \equiv 1 \pmod{m}$, or, in $\mathbf{Z}$,

$$a^{-1}a = 1 + rm \qquad \text{or} \qquad a^{-1}a - rm = 1$$

This shows that any common divisor of $a$ and $m$ must divide 1; i.e., that $a$ and $m$ are relatively prime.

Conversely, if $a$ and $m$ are relatively prime in $\mathbf{Z}$, then (using g.c.d. for greatest common divisor)

$$1 = \text{g.c.d. } (a, m) = pa + qm \qquad \text{or} \qquad pa \equiv 1 \pmod{m}$$

which shows that $a$ is a unit of $\mathbf{Z}_m$ (with inverse $p$). Thus the units of $\mathbf{Z}_m$ are precisely those integers which are relatively prime to $m$.

**9.92** In $\mathbf{Z}_{10}$ find $-3$, $-8$, and $3^{-1}$.

▮ By $-a$ in a ring $R$ we mean that element such that $a + (-a) = (-a) + a = 0$. Hence $-3 = 7$ since $3 + 7 = 7 + 3 = 0$ in $\mathbf{Z}_{10}$. Similarly $-8 = 2$. By $a^{-1}$ in a ring $R$ we mean that element such that $a \cdot a^{-1} = a^{-1} \cdot a = 1$. Hence $3^{-1} = 7$ since $3 \cdot 7 = 7 \cdot 3 = 1$ in $\mathbf{Z}_{10}$.

**9.93** Let $f(x) = 2x^2 + 4x + 4$. Find the roots of $f(x)$ over $\mathbf{Z}_{10}$.

▮ Substitute each of the ten elements of $\mathbf{Z}_{10}$ into $f(x)$ to see which elements yield 0. We have:

$$f(0) = 4, \qquad f(1) = 0, \qquad f(2) = 0, \qquad f(3) = 4, \qquad f(4) = 2,$$
$$f(5) = 4, \qquad f(6) = 0, \qquad f(7) = 0, \qquad f(8) = 4, \qquad f(9) = 2$$

Thus the roots are 1, 2, 6, and 7. This example shows that a polynomial of degree $n$ can have more than $n$ roots over an arbitrary ring. This cannot happen if the ring is a field.

**9.94** Let $R$ be the ring of $n$-square matrices. (*a*) Is $R$ commutative? (*b*) Does $R$ have a unity element? (*c*) Find the units in $R$.

▮ (*a*) No; matrix multiplication is not commutative. (*b*) Yes; the identity matrix $I$. (*c*) The nonsingular or invertible matrices are the units in $R$.

**9.95** Prove that $a \cdot 0 = 0 \cdot a = 0$ in a ring $R$.

▮ Since $0 = 0 + 0$, we have $a \cdot 0 = a(0 + 0) = a \cdot 0 + a \cdot 0$. Adding $-(a \cdot 0)$ to both sides yields $0 = a \cdot 0$. Similarly, $0 \cdot a = 0$.

**9.96** Show that negatives are unique in any ring.

▮ Given an element $a$, suppose element $x$ has the property that $a + x = 0$ (which automatically makes $x + a = 0$). We have
$$-a = -a + 0 = -a + (a + x) = (-a + a) + x = 0 + x = x$$

**9.97** Show that $a(-b) = (-a)b = -ab$ in a ring $R$.

▮ $ab + a(-b) = a(b + (-b)) = a \cdot 0 = 0$; hence (Problem 9.96) $a(-b) = -ab$. Similarly, $(-a)b = -ab$.

**9.98** Show that $(-1)a = -a$ in a ring $R$ with a unity element 1.

▮ $a + (-1)a = 1 \cdot a + (-1)a = (1 + (-1))a = 0 \cdot a = 0$; hence (Problem 9.96) $(-1)a = -a$.

**9.99** Let $R$ be a ring with a unity element 1. Show that the set $R^*$ of units in $R$ is a group under multiplication.

▮ If $a$ and $b$ are units in $R$, then $ab$ is a unit, since $b^{-1}a^{-1}$ is the inverse of $ab$. Thus $R^*$ is closed under multiplication. Also, $R^*$ is nonempty, since $1 \in R^*$; and $R^*$ is associative, since $R$ is associative. Finally, if $a$ is a unit in $R$, so is $a^{-1}$ (since it has the inverse $a$); consequently, $R^*$ is closed under inverses. Thus $R^*$ is a group under multiplication.

**9.100** Define a subring of a ring $R$.

▮ A nonempty subset $S$ of $R$ is a *subring* of $R$ if $S$ itself forms a ring under the operations of $R$. It is clear that $S$ is a subring of $R$ if and only if $a, b \in S$ implies $a - b \in S$ and $ab \in S$. (Closure under subtraction implies inclusion of 0, inclusion of negatives, and hence closure under addition.)

## Ideals

**9.101** Define an ideal in a ring $R$.

▮ A subset $J$ of $R$ is an *ideal* in $R$ if
(i) $0 \in J$.

(ii) $J$ is closed under subtraction; i.e., $a - b \in J$ for any $a, b \in J$.

(iii) $J$ is closed under multiples from $R$; i.e., $ra, ar \in J$ for $a \in J, r \in R$.

With respect to (iii), $J$ is called a *left ideal* if only $ra \in J$, and a *right ideal* if only $ar \in J$. Thus the term *ideal* shall mean two-sided ideal, as above. In a commutative ring, any left or right ideal is an ideal.

**9.102** Show that $\{0\}$ is an ideal in any ring $R$.

▮ Follows from the fact that $0 - 0 = 0$ belongs to $\{0\}$, and, for any $r \in R$, $r \cdot 0 = 0 \cdot r = 0$ belongs to $\{0\}$.

**9.103** Let **Z** be the ring of integers and let $J_m$ consist of the multiples of $m \geq 2$. Show that $J_m$ is an ideal in **Z**.

▮ Clearly $0 \in J_m$. Suppose $ma$ and $mb$ are arbitrary elements in $J_m$. Then $ma - mb = m(a - b)$ also belongs to $J_m$. Also, for any $r \in \mathbf{Z}$, we have $r(ma) = (ma)r = m(ar)$ as an element of $J_m$. Thus $J_m$ is an ideal in **Z**.

**9.104** Let $M$ be the ring of real $2 \times 2$ matrices. Give an example of a left ideal, $J$, which is not a right ideal, and an example of a right ideal, $K$, which is not a left ideal.

▮
$$J = \left\{ \begin{pmatrix} 0 & a \\ 0 & b \end{pmatrix} \right\}, \qquad K = \left\{ \begin{pmatrix} a & b \\ 0 & 0 \end{pmatrix} \right\}$$

**9.105** Suppose $J$ and $K$ are ideals in a ring $R$. Prove that $J \cap K$ is an ideal in $R$.

▮ Since $J$ and $K$ are ideal, $0 \in J$ and $0 \in K$. Hence $0 \in J \cap K$. Now let $a, b \in J \cap K$ and let $r \in R$. Then $a, b \in J$ and $a, b \in K$. Since $J$ and $K$ are ideals,

$$a - b, ra, ae \in J \qquad \text{and} \qquad a - b, ra, ar \in K$$

Hence $a - b, ra, ar \in J \cap K$. Therefore $J \cap K$ is an ideal.

**9.106** Let $J$ be an ideal in a ring $R$ with an identity element 1. Prove: (*a*) If $1 \in J$, then $J = R$. (*b*) If any unit $u \in J$, then $J = R$.

▮ (*a*) If $1 \in J$, then for any $r \in R$ we have $r \cdot 1 \in J$, or $r \in J$. Hence $J = R$. (*b*) If $u \in J$, then $u^{-1} \cdot u \in J$, or $1 \in J$. Hence $J = R$, by (*a*).

The following theorem uses the fact that an ideal $J$ in a ring $R$ is a subgroup (necessarily normal) of the additive group of $R$. Thus the collection of cosets $\{a + J : a \in R\}$ forms a partition of $R$.

**Theorem 9.6:** Let $J$ be an ideal in a ring $R$. Then the cosets $\{a + J : a \in R\}$ form a ring under the coset operations

$$(a + J) + (b + J) = (a + b) + J \qquad \text{and} \qquad (a + J)(b + J) = ab + J$$

**9.107** Prove Theorem 9.6. The ring of cosets is denoted by $R/J$ and is called the *quotient ring*.

▮ The analogous Theorem 9.4 for groups shows that $R/J$ is a commutative group under addition, with $J$ as the zero element. Coset multiplication is well-defined, since

$$(a + J)(b + J) = ab + aJ + Jb + JJ = ab + J + J + J = ab + J$$

Associativity and the distributive laws hold in $R/J$, since they hold in $R$. Thus $R/J$ is a ring.

**9.108** Suppose $J$ is an ideal in a commutative ring $R$. Show that $R/J$ is commutative.

▮
$$(a + J)(b + J) = ab + J = ba + J = (b + J)(a + J)$$

**9.109** Suppose that $J$ is an ideal in a ring $R$ with unity element 1, and suppose that $1 \notin J$. Show that $1 + J$ is a unity element for $R/J$.

▮ For any coset $a + J$, we have $(a + J)(1 + J) = a \cdot 1 + J = a + J$ and $(1 + J)(a + J) = 1 \cdot a + J = a + J$. Thus $1 + J$ is a unity element in $R/J$.

## Ring Homomorphisms

**9.110** Define ring homomorphism, ring isomorphism.

▮ A mapping $f$ from a ring $R$ into a ring $R'$ is called a *homomorphism* if $f(a + b) = f(a) + f(b)$ and $f(ab) = f(a)f(b)$, for every $a, b \in R$. (Though here notated as if they are the same, the ring operations in $R'$

will generally differ from those in $R$.) In addition, if $f$ is one-to-one and onto, then $f$ is called an *isomorphism* and $R$ and $R'$ are said to be *isomorphic*, written $R \simeq R'$.

**9.111**  Discuss the relation between ring homomorphisms and group homomorphisms (see Section 9.3). Following the discussion, state the ring analog to Theorem 9.5.

▌  A ring homomorphism $f: R \to R'$ is automatically a group homomorphism on the additive structures of $R$ and $R'$. Thus $f(0) = 0'$. If $R$ and $R'$ have unity elements 1 and 1', respectively, then we also require that $f(1) = 1'$ in order for $f$ to be a ring homomorphism. We also define the kernel of $f$ by $\operatorname{Ker} f = \{a \in R : f(a) = 0'\}$.

The fundamental theorem on ring homomorphisms follows.

**Theorem 9.7:**  Let $f: R \to R'$ be a ring homomorphism with kernel $J$. Then $J$ is an ideal in $R$, and $R/J$ is isomorphic to the image of $f$.

**9.112**  Consider the rings $R = 2\mathbf{Z}$ and $R' = 3\mathbf{Z}$, that is, $R$ consists of all multiples of 2, and $R'$ consists of all multiples of 3. Show that $R$ is not isomorphic to $R'$.

▌  If $f: R \to R'$ is a ring homomorphism, then $f(2) = 3k$ for some integer $k$. Since $f$ is a homomorphism, $f(4) = f(2+2) = f(2) + f(2) = 3k + 3k = 6k$; further, $f(4) = f(2 \cdot 2) = f(2) \cdot f(2) = (3k) \cdot (3k) = 9k^2$. Thus $9k^2 = 6k$ and, since $k$ is integral, $k = 0$. Hence $f(2) = 0$. But $f(0) = 0$. Thus $f$ is not an isomorphism.

**9.113**  Let $J$ be an ideal in a ring $R$. Consider the (canonical) map $f: R \to R/J$ defined by $f(a) = a + J$. (Recall Theorem 9.6.) Show that $f$ is (a) a ring homomorphism, and (b) an onto mapping.

▌  (a)  Using Theorem 9.6, we obtain

$$f(a+b) = (a+b) + J = (a+J) + (b+J) = f(a) + f(b)$$
$$f(ab) = ab + J = (a+J)(b+J) = f(a)f(b)$$

(b)  Any coset $a + J$ in $R/J$ is the image of $a \in R$.

**9.114**  Find the kernel $K$ of the (canonical) map $f$ in Problem 9.113.

▌  The zero element of $R/J$ is $J$. Thus $K$ consists of those $a \in R$ such that $f(a) = J$, or $a + J = J$. But $a + J = J$ if and only if $a \in J$. Thus $J$ is the kernel of $f$.

## 9.5 INTEGRAL DOMAINS, PID, UFD

All rings $R$ in this section are assumed to be commutative and to have a unity element 1, unless otherwise specified.

**9.115**  Define a zero divisor in a ring $R$.

▌  A nonzero element $a \in R$ is a *zero divisor* if there exists a nonzero element $b$ such that $ab = 0$.

**9.116**  Define integral domain.

▌  A commutative ring $D$ with a unity element 1 is an *integral domain* if $D$ has no zero divisors.

**9.117**  Show that the ring $\mathbf{Z}_{105}$ of the integers modulo 105 is not an integral domain.

▌  Any $\mathbf{Z}_m$ with $m$ composite has divisors of zero; for $m = ab$ $(1 < a, b < m)$ implies $ab = 0$ in $\mathbf{Z}_m$.

**9.118**  Show that the ring $\mathbf{Z}_{29}$ of integers modulo 29 is an integral domain.

▌  Conversely to Problem 9.117, if $p$ is prime then $\mathbf{Z}_p$ has no zero divisors. In fact, for $1 < a, b < p$,

$$ab = 0 + kp \quad \text{implies} \quad p \mid a \text{ or } p \mid b \quad \text{implies} \quad a = 0 \text{ or } b = 0$$

**9.119**  Suppose $D$ is an integral domain. Show that if $ab = ac$, with $a \neq 0$, then $b = c$.

▌  If $ab = ac$, then $ab - ac = 0$ and so $a(b - c) = 0$. Since $a \neq 0$ and $D$ has no zero divisors, we must have $b - c = 0$, or $b = c$, as claimed. Thus, multiplication in $D$ obeys the *cancellation law*.

**9.120**  Define a principal ideal in a commutative ring $R$ with an identity element 1.

▮ Let $a$ be any element in $R$. Then the set $(a) = \{ra: r \in R\}$ is an ideal; it is called the *principal ideal generated by a.*

**9.121** What is a PID?

▮ PID abbreviates a *Principal Ideal Domain.* A ring is a PID if $R$ is an integral domain and if every ideal in $R$ is principal.

**9.122** Show that **Z** is a PID.

▮ **Z** is an integral domain, since **Z** has no zero divisors. Suppose $J$ is an ideal in **Z**. If $J = \{0\}$, then $J = (0)$, the ideal generated by 0. Suppose that $J \neq \{0\}$ and that $x \neq 0$ belongs to $J$. Then $-x = (-1)x$ belongs to $J$; hence $J$ contains at least one positive integer. Let $a$ be the smallest positive integer in $J$. We claim that $J = (a)$; i.e., that $J$ consists of all the multiples of $a$. Suppose $x \in J$. By the division algorithm, $x = qa + r$ where $0 \leq r \leq a$. Since $J$ is an ideal and $a, x \in J$, we have $r = x - qa$ belongs to $J$. Since $a$ is the smallest positive integer in $J$ and $r < a$, we must have $r = 0$, making $x$ a multiple of $a$. Thus $J = (a)$ and hence **Z** is a PID.

**9.123** Define associates in a ring $R$.

▮ An element $b \in R$ is called an *associate* of $a \in R$ if $b = ua$ for some unit $u \in R$.

**9.124** Find the associates of 4 in $\mathbf{Z}_{10}$ (the integers modulo 10).

▮ The units in $\mathbf{Z}_{10}$ are 1, 3, 7, and 9 [see Problem 9.91]. Multiply 4 by each of the units to obtain $1 \cdot 4 = 4$, $3 \cdot 4 = 2$, $7 \cdot 4 = 8$, and $9 \cdot 4 = 6$. (The multiplication is done modulo 10.) Thus 2, 4, 6, and 8 are the associates of 4 in $\mathbf{Z}_{10}$.

**9.125** Find the associates of 5 in $\mathbf{Z}_{10}$.

▮ Multiply 5 by each of the units to obtain $1 \cdot 5 = 5$, $3 \cdot 5 = 5$, $7 \cdot 5 = 5$, and $9 \cdot 5 = 5$. Thus only 5 is an associate of 5 in $\mathbf{Z}_{10}$.

**9.126** Show that the relation of being associates is an equivalence relation in a ring $R$.

▮ Any element $a$ is an associate of itself, since $a = 1 \cdot a$ (*reflexive law*). Suppose $b$ is an associate of $a$. Then $b = ua$, where $u$ is a unit. Then $a = u^{-1}b$, where $u^{-1}$ is a unit; hence $a$ is an associate of $b$ (*symmetric law*). Lastly, suppose $a$ is an associate of $b$ and $b$ is an associate of $c$: $a = u_1 b$ and $b = u_2 c$, where $u_1$ and $u_2$ are units. Then $a = u_1(u_2 c) = (u_1 u_2)c$, where the product $u_1 u_2$ is also a unit. Hence $a$ is an associate of $c$ (*transitive law*).

**9.127** Define an irreducible element in an integral domain $D$.

▮ A nonunit $p \in D$ is *irreducible* if $p = ab$ implies $a$ or $b$ is a unit. (This is obviously an extension of the notion of "prime" in **Z**.)

**9.128** Define a *unique factorization domain* (*UFD*).

▮ An integral domain $D$ is a UFD if every nonunit $a \in D$ can be written uniquely (up to associates and order) as a product of irreducible elements.

**9.129** Find the associates of $n \in \mathbf{Z}$.

▮ The only units in **Z** are 1 and $-1$ (Problem 9.90). Hence $n$ and $-n$ are the only associates of $n$.

**9.130** What are the irreducible elements in **Z**?

▮ The prime numbers (and their negatives) are the irreducible elements in **Z**.

**9.131** Express 12 in **Z** as a product of irreducible elements.

▮ There are twelve such products:

$$12 = 2 \cdot 2 \cdot 3 = (-2) \cdot (-2) \cdot 3 = (-2) \cdot 2 \cdot (-3) = 2 \cdot (-2) \cdot (-3)$$
$$= 2 \cdot 3 \cdot 2 = (-2) \cdot (-3) \cdot 2 = (-2) \cdot 3 \cdot (-2) = 2 \cdot (-3) \cdot (-2)$$
$$= 3 \cdot 2 \cdot 2 = (-3) \cdot (-2) \cdot 2 = (-3) \cdot 2 \cdot (-2) = 3 \cdot (-2) \cdot (-2)$$

**9.132**   Is **Z** a UFD?

▮ Yes. Although 12, etc., can be written in many ways as a product of irreducible elements, all such products differ only with respect to order or associates.

**9.133**   The set $D = \{a + b\sqrt{13}: a, b$ integers$\}$ is an integral domain. The units of $D$ are $\pm 1$, $18 \pm 5\sqrt{13}$. and $-18 \pm 5\sqrt{13}$. The elements 2, $3 - \sqrt{13}$, and $-3 - \sqrt{13}$ are irreducible in $D$. Show that $D$ is not a UFD.

▮ $4 = 2 \cdot 2$ and $4 = (3 - \sqrt{13})(-3 - \sqrt{13})$.

## 9.6   FIELDS

All rings $R$ in this section are assumed to be commutative and have a unity element 1 unless otherwise specified.

**9.134**   Define a field.

▮ A commutative ring $F$ with a unity element 1 is called a *field* if every nonzero $a \in F$ has a multiplicative inverse, i.e., there exists an element $a^{-1} \in F$ such that $aa^{-1} = a^{-1}a = 1$. Alternatively, $F$ is a field if its nonzero elements form a group under multiplication.

**9.135**   Show that a field $F$ is an integral domain; i.e., has no zero divisors.

▮ If $ab = 0$ and $a \neq 0$, then $b = 1 \cdot b = a^{-1}ab = a^{-1} \cdot 0 = 0$.

**9.136**   Which of the following are fields with respect to the usual operations of addition and multiplication: the integers **Z**, the rational numbers **Q**, the real numbers **R**, the complex numbers **C**?

▮ **Z** is the classical example of an integral domain which is not a field (only 1 and $-1$ are units). **Q**, **R**, and **C** are fields.

**9.137**   Let $S$ be the set of real numbers of the form $a + b\sqrt{3}$, where $a$ and $b$ are rational numbers. Show that $S$ is a field.

▮ A set $S$ of real or complex numbers is a field if $S$ contains 0 and 1 and $S$ is closed under addition, subtraction, multiplication, and division (except by zero). Since $0 = 0 + 0\sqrt{3}$ and $1 = 1 + 0\sqrt{3}$, both 0 and 1 belong to $S$. Also,

$$(a + b\sqrt{3}) + (c + d\sqrt{3}) = (a + c) + (b + d)\sqrt{3}$$
$$(a + b\sqrt{3}) - (c + d\sqrt{3}) = (a - c) + (b - d)\sqrt{3}$$
$$(a + b\sqrt{3})(c + d\sqrt{3}) = (ac + 3bd) + (ad + bc)\sqrt{3}$$

Hence $S$ is closed under addition, subtraction, and multiplication. We show that $S$ is closed under division (making every nonzero element a unit) as follows:

$$\frac{(a + b\sqrt{3})}{(c + d\sqrt{3})} = \frac{(a + b\sqrt{3})(c - d\sqrt{3})}{(c + d\sqrt{3})(c - d\sqrt{3})} = \frac{ac - 3bd}{c^2 - 3d^2} + \frac{bc - ad}{c^2 - 3d^2}\sqrt{3}$$

Thus $S$ is a field.

**9.138**   Let $D$ be the ring of real $2 \times 2$ matrices of the form $\begin{pmatrix} a & -b \\ b & a \end{pmatrix}$. Show that $D$ is isomorphic to the complex numbers **C**, whence $D$ is a field.

▮ Let $f: \mathbf{C} \to D$ be defined by $f(a + bi) = \begin{pmatrix} a & -b \\ b & a \end{pmatrix}$. Clearly $f$ is one-to-one and onto. Suppose $z_1 = a + bi$ and $z_2 = c + di$; then

$$z_1 + z_2 = (a + c) + (b + d)i \quad \text{and} \quad z_1 z_2 = (ac - bd) + (ad + bc)i$$

Therefore

$$f(z_1) + f(z_2) = \begin{pmatrix} a & -b \\ b & a \end{pmatrix} + \begin{pmatrix} c & -d \\ d & c \end{pmatrix} = \begin{pmatrix} a + c & -(b + d) \\ b + d & a + c \end{pmatrix} = f(z_1 + z_2)$$

$$f(z_1)f(z_2) = \begin{pmatrix} a & -b \\ b & a \end{pmatrix}\begin{pmatrix} c & -d \\ d & c \end{pmatrix} = \begin{pmatrix} ac - bd & -(ad + bc) \\ ad + bc & ac - bd \end{pmatrix} = f(z_1 z_2)$$

Lastly, $f(1) = f(1 + 0i) = I$, the identity matrix. Thus $f$ is an isomorphism.

**Theorem 9.8:**    A finite integral domain $D$ is a field.

**9.139**    Prove Theorem 9.8.

▌ Suppose $D$ has $n$ elements, say $D = \{a_1, a_2, \ldots, a_n\}$. Let $a$ be any nonzero element of $D$, and consider the $n$ elements $aa_1, aa_2, \ldots, aa_n$. Since $a \neq 0$, we have $aa_i = aa_j$ implies $a_i = a_j$ (see Problem 9.119). Thus the $n$ elements above are distinct, and so they must be a rearrangement of the elements $D$. One of them, say $aa_k$, must equal the identity element 1 of $D$; that is, $aa_k = 1$. Thus $a_k$ is the inverse of $a$. Since $a$ was any nonzero element of $D$, we have that $D$ is a field.

**9.140**    Show that $\mathbf{Z}_p$ is a field where $p$ is a prime number.

▌ $\mathbf{Z}_p$ is an integral domain (see Problem 9.118) and finite; hence $\mathbf{Z}_p$ is a field by Theorem 9.8.

**9.141**    Show that the only ideal $J$ in a field $F$ is $\{0\}$ or $F$ itself.

▌ If $J \neq \{0\}$, then $J$ contains a nonzero element $a$. Since $F$ is a field, $a$ is a unit. By Problem 9.106, $J = F$.

**9.142**    Suppose $f : K \to K'$ is a homomorphism from a field $K$ to a field $K'$. Show that $f$ is an *embedding*; that is, that $f$ is one-to-one.

▌ Let $J = \operatorname{Ker} f$, which is an ideal in $K$, by Theorem 9.7. If $J = K$, then $f(1) = 0'$. But, since $f$ is a homomorphism, we require $f(1) = 1'$. Hence $J \neq K$ and so $J = \{0\}$ by Problem 9.141. Suppose $f(a) = f(b)$. Then $f(a - b) = f(a) - f(b) = 0$. Hence $a - b$ belongs to $J$, and so $a - b = 0$, or $a = b$. Accordingly, $f$ is one-to-one.

**9.143**    Let $D$ be an integral domain. Define the field of quotients of $D$.

▌ Let $S$ consist of all ordered pairs [quotients] $a/b$, where $a, b \in D$ and $b \neq 0$. Define $a/b = c/d$ if $ad = bc$. (This is an equivalence relation.) Let $F(D)$ be the set of equivalence class $[a/b]$, with the operations of addition and multiplication defined by

$$[a/b] + [c/d] = [(ad + bc)/(bd)] \quad \text{and} \quad [a/b] \cdot [c/d] = [(ac)/(bd)]$$

Then $F(D)$ is the desired field, defined as the *field of quotients* of $D$.

**9.144**    What is the field of quotients of the integral domain $\mathbf{Z}$ of integers?

▌ $F(\mathbf{Z}) = \mathbf{Q}$, the field of rational numbers.

**9.145**    Let $K = D[x]$, the integral domain of polynomials in $x$ with real coefficients. What is the field of quotients of $K$?

▌ $F(K)$ is the field of rational functions of the form $f(x)/g(x)$, where $f(x)$ and $g(x) \neq 0$ are polynomials.

**9.146**    Let $D$ be an integral domain. Show how $D$ is embedded in its field of quotients $F(D)$.

▌ Let $f : D \to F(D)$ be defined by $f(a) = [a/1]$. Then $f$ is an embedding; i.e., $f$ is a homomorphism and $f$ is one-to-one. For example, we identify an integer $n$ in $\mathbf{Z}$ with the fraction $n/1$ in $\mathbf{Q}$.

**9.147**    Define a *maximal* ideal $K$ in a ring $R$.

▌ $K$ is a maximal ideal in $R$ if $K \neq R$ and if no ideal $J$ lies strictly between $K$ and $R$; that is, if $K \subseteq J \subseteq R$, then $K = J$ or $J = R$.

**9.148**    Suppose $K$ is a maximal ideal in a commutative ring $R$ with identity element 1. Prove that the quotient ring $R/K$ is a field.

▌ Since $K \neq R$, we have $1 \notin K$ (Problem 9.106). Furthermore, by Problem 9.109, the coset $1 + K$ is a unity element for $R/K$, and, by Problem 9.108, $R/K$ is commutative. It remains to show that any coset other than $K$ has a multiplicative inverse in $R/K$. Suppose $a + K \neq K$. Then $a \notin K$. Let

$$J = \{ra + sk : r, s \in R, k \in K\}$$

Then $J$ is an ideal containing both $a$ and $K$. Since $a \notin K$, we have $K \neq J$. Since $K$ is maximal, $J = R$. Thus $1 \in J$.

Therefore there exist $r_0, s_0 \in R$ and $k_0 \in K$ such that $1 = r_0 a + s_0 k_0$. Therefore

$$1 + K = r_0 a + s_0 k_0 + K = r_0 a + K = (r_0 + K)(a + K)$$

Hence $r_0 + K$ is the multiplicative inverse of $a + K$. Thus $R/K$ is a field.

## 9.7  POLYNOMIALS OVER A FIELD

This section investigates the ring $K[t]$ of polynomials over a field $K$ and shows that $K[t]$ has many properties which are analogous to properties of the ring $\mathbf{Z}$ of integers.

**9.149**    Define a polynomial over a field $K$ and its degree.

❚ Let $K$ be a field. Formally, a *polynomial $f$* over $K$ is an infinite sequence of elements from $K$ in which all except a finite number of them are 0; that is,

$$f = (\ldots, 0, a_n, \ldots, a_1, a_0) \quad \text{or, equivalently,} \quad f(t) = a_n t^n + \cdots + a_1 t + a_0$$

where the symbol $t$ is used as an indeterminate. The entry $a_k$ is called the $k$th coefficient of $f$. If $n$ is the largest integer for which $a_n \neq 0$, then we say that the *degree* of $f$ is $n$, written $\deg f = n$. We also call $a_n$ the *leading coefficient* of $f$, and, if $a_n = 1$, we call $f$ a *monic polynomial*. On the other hand, if every coefficient of $f$ is 0 then $f$ is called the *zero polynomial*, written $f \equiv 0$. The degree of the zero polynomial is not defined.

**9.150**    Define the ring of polynomials over the field $K$.

❚ Let $K[t]$ be the collection of all polynomials $f(t)$. Addition and multiplication is defined in $K[t]$ as follows. Suppose

$$f(t) = a_n t^n + \cdots + a_1 t + a_0 \quad \text{and} \quad g(t) = b_m t^m + \cdots + b_1 t + b_0$$

Then the *sum $f + g$* is the polynomial obtained by adding corresponding coefficients. that is, if $m \leq n$, then

$$f(t) + g(t) = a_n t^n + \cdots + (a_m + b_m)t^m + \cdots + (a_1 + b_1)t + (a_0 + b_0)$$

Furthermore, the product of $f$ and $g$ is the polynomial $f(t)g(t) = a_n b_m t^{n+m} + \cdots + (a_1 b_0 + a_0 b_1)t + a_0 b_0$. That is,

$$f(t)g(t) = c_{n+m} t^{n+m} + \cdots + c_1 t + c_0 \quad \text{where} \quad c_k = \sum_{i=0}^{k} a_i b_{k-i} = a_0 b_k + a_1 b_{k-1} + \cdots + a_k b_0$$

Theorem 9.9 applies.

**Theorem 9.9:**    $K[t]$ under the operations of addition and multiplication of Problem 9.150 is a commutative ring with a unity element and with no zero divisors. (That is, $K[t]$ is an integral domain.)

**9.151**    Show how $K$ may be viewed as a subset of $K[t]$.

❚ We identify the scalar $a_0 \in K$ with the polynomial $f(t) = a_0$ or $a_0 = (\ldots, 0, a_0)$. Then the operations of addition and multiplication of elements of $K$ are preserved under this identification:

$$(\ldots, 0, a_0) + (\ldots, 0, b_0) = (\ldots, 0, a_0 + b_0) \quad \text{and} \quad (\ldots, 0, a_0) \cdot (\ldots, 0, b_0) = (\ldots, 0, a_0 b_0)$$

**Theorem 9.10:**    Suppose $f$ and $g$ are polynomials in $K[t]$. Then $\deg(fg) = \deg f + \deg g$.

**9.152**    Prove Theorem 9.10.

❚ Suppose $f(t) = a_n t^n + \cdots + a_0$ and $g(t) = b_m t^m + \cdots + b_0$ and $a_n \neq 0$ and $b_m \neq 0$. Then $f(t)g(t) = a_n b_m t^{n+m} +$ terms of lower degree. Also, since the field $K$ has no zero divisors, $a_n b_m \neq 0$. Thus $\deg(fg) = n + m = \deg f + \deg g$.

**9.153**    Show that the nonzero elements of $K$ are the units of $K[t]$.

❚ Suppose $f(t)g(t) = 1$. Then $0 = \deg(1) = \deg(fg) = \deg f + \deg g$. Hence $\deg f = 0$ and $\deg g = 0$ and $f$ and $g$ are scalars in $K$. On the other hand, if $a \in K$ and $a \neq 0$, then $a \cdot a^{-1} = 1$ and $a$ is a unit of $K[t]$.

**Remark:**    A polynomial $g$ is said to divide a polynomial $f$ if there exists a polynomial $h$ such that $f(t) = g(t)h(t)$.

**9.154**    Suppose $g(t)$ divides $f(t)$. Show that $\deg g \leq \deg f$.

❚ If $g$ divides $f$, then there exists $h$ such that $f(t) = g(t)h(t)$. Then, by Theorem 9.10, $\deg f = \deg g + \deg h \geq \deg g$.

**9.155**  Suppose $f$ and $g$ are polynomials such that $f$ divides $g$ and $g$ divides $f$. Show that (*a*) $\deg f = \deg g$ and (*b*) $f$ and $g$ are associates, i.e., $f(t) = kg(t)$ where $k \in K$.

▮  (*a*)  By Problem 9.154 (or Theorem 9.10), $\deg f \le \deg g$ and $\deg g \le \deg f$. Hence $\deg f = \deg g$.
   (*b*)  Since $g$ divides $f$, there exist $h$ such that $f(t) = h(t)g(t)$. Since $\deg f = \deg g$, we have $\deg h = 0$. In other words, $h(t) = k$, an element of $K$.

**9.156**  Suppose $d$ and $d'$ are monic polynomials such that $d$ divides $d'$ and $d'$ divides $d$. Prove $d = d'$.

▮  By Problem 9.155, $d(t) = kd'(t)$ where $k \in K$. The leading coefficient of $d$ is 1 since $d$ is monic and the leading coefficient of $kd'$ is $k$ since $d'$ is monic. Hence $k = 1$ and $d = d'$.

## Euclidean Algorithm, Roots of Polynomials

This subsection uses the following three theorems whose proofs appear in Problems 9.160–9.162.

**Theorem 9.11  (Euclidean Division Algorithm):**  Let $f(t)$ and $g(t)$ be polynomials over a field $K$ with $g(t) \ne 0$. Then there exist polynomials $q(t)$ and $r(t)$ such that $f(t) = q(t)g(t) + r(t)$ where either $r(t) \equiv 0$ or $\deg r < \deg g$.

The above theorem formalizes the process known as "long division."

**Theorem 9.12:**  Suppose $a \in K$ is a root of a polynomial $f(t)$ over $K$ with $\deg f = n$. Then there exists a polynomial $q(t)$ with $\deg q = n - 1$ such that $f(t) = (t - a)q(t)$. [That is, $t - a$ divides $f(t)$.]

**Theorem 9.13:**  Suppose a rational number $p/q$ (reduced to lowest terms) is a root of the polynomial $f(t) = a_n t^n + \cdots + a_1 t + a_0$ where $a_n, \ldots, a_1, a_0 \in \mathbf{Z}$. Then $p$ divides the constant term $a_0$ and $q$ divides the leading coefficient $a_n$. [In particular, if $c = p/q$ is an integer, then $c$ divides $a_0$.]

**9.157**  Suppose $f(t) = t^3 + t^2 - 8t + 4$. Assuming $f(t)$ has a rational root, find all the roots of $f(t)$.

▮  Since the leading coefficient is 1, the rational roots of $f(t)$ must be integers from among $\pm 1$, $\pm 2$, $\pm 4$. Note $f(1) \ne 0$ and $f(-1) \ne 0$. By synthetic division, or dividing by $t - 2$, we get

$$
\begin{array}{r|l}
2 & 1 + 1 - 8 + 4 \\
  & \phantom{1 + }2 + 6 - 4 \\
\hline
  & 1 + 3 - 2 + 0
\end{array}
$$

Therefore $t = 2$ is a root and $f(t) = (t - 2)(t^2 + 3t - 2)$. Using the quadratic formula for $t^2 + 3t - 2 = 0$, we obtain the following roots of $f(t)$: $t = 2$, $t = (-3 + \sqrt{17})/2$, $t = (-3 - \sqrt{17})/2$.

**9.158**  Suppose $g(t) = t^3 - 2t^2 - 6t - 3$. Find the roots of $g(t)$ assuming $g(t)$ has an integer root.

▮  The integer roots of $g(t)$ must be among $\pm 1$, $\pm 3$. Note $f(1) \ne 0$. Using synthetic division, or dividing by $t + 1$, we get

$$
\begin{array}{r|l}
-1 & 1 - 2 - 6 - 3 \\
   & \phantom{1}-1 + 3 + 3 \\
\hline
   & 1 - 3 - 3 + 0
\end{array}
$$

Therefore $t = -1$ is a root and $g(t) = (t + 1)(t^2 - 3t - 3)$. We can now use the quadratic formula on $t^2 - 3t - 3$ to obtain the following three roots of $g(t)$: $t = -1$, $t = (3 + \sqrt{21})/2$, $t = (3 - \sqrt{21})/2$.

**9.159**  Suppose $h(t) = t^4 - 2t^3 + 11t - 10$. Find all the real roots of $h(t)$ assuming there are two integer roots.

▮  The integer roots must be among $\pm 1$, $\pm 2$, $\pm 5$, $\pm 10$. By synthetic division [or dividing by $t - 1$ and then $t + 2$] we get

$$
\begin{array}{r|l}
1 & 1 - 2 + 0 + 11 - 10 \\
  & \phantom{1}1 - 1 - \phantom{1}1 + 10 \\
-2 & 1 - 1 - 1 + 10 + \phantom{1}0 \\
  & \phantom{1}-2 + 6 - 10 \\
\hline
  & 1 - 3 + 5 + \phantom{1}0
\end{array}
$$

Thus $t = 1$ and $t = -2$ are roots and $h(t) = (t - 1)(t + 2)(t^2 - 3t + 5)$. The quadratic formula with $t^2 - 3t + 5$ tells us that there are no other real roots. That is, $t = 1$ and $t = -2$ are the only real roots of $h(t)$.

**9.160** Suppose $f(t) = 2t^3 - 3t^2 - 6t - 2$. Find all the roots of $f(t)$ knowing that there is a rational root.

$\blacksquare$ The rational roots must be among $\pm 1$, $\pm 2$, $\pm 1/2$. Testing each possible root, we get, by synthetic division (or dividing by $2t + 1$),

$$
\begin{array}{r|l}
-1/2 & 2 - 3 - 6 - 2 \\
& \underline{-1 + 2 + 2} \\
& 2 - 4 - 4 + 0
\end{array}
$$

Thus $t = -1/2$ is a root and $f(t) = (t + 1/2)(2t^2 - 4t - 4) = (2t + 1)(t^2 - 2t - 2)$. We can now use the quadratic formula on $t^2 - 2t - 2$ to obtain the following three roots of $f(t)$: $t = -1/2$, $t = 1 + \sqrt{3}$, $t = 1 - \sqrt{3}$.

**9.161** Prove Theorem 9.11.

$\blacksquare$ If $f(t) \equiv 0$ or if $\deg f < \deg g$, then we have the required representation $f(t) = 0g(t) + f(t)$. Now suppose $\deg f \geq \deg g$, say $f(t) = a_n t^n + \cdots + a_1 t + a_0$ and $g(t) = b_m t^m + \cdots + b_1 t + b_0$ where $a_n$, $b_m \neq 0$ and $n \geq m$. We form the polynomial

$$
f_1(t) = f(t) - \frac{a_n}{b_m} t^{n-m} g(t) \tag{1}
$$

[This is the first subtraction step in "long division."] Then $\deg f_1 < \deg f$. By induction, there exist polynomials $q_1(t)$ and $r(t)$ such that $f_1(t) = q_1(t)g(t) + r(t)$ where either $r(t) \equiv 0$ or $\deg r < \deg g$. Substituting this into $(1)$ and solving for $f(t)$, we get

$$
f(t) = \left[ q_1(t) + \frac{a_n}{b_m} t^{n-m} \right] g(t) + r(t)
$$

which is the desired representation.

**9.162** Prove Theorem 9.12.

$\blacksquare$ By Theorem 9.11, there exist $q(t)$ and $r(t)$ such that

$$
f(t) = (t - a)g(t) + r(t) \tag{1}
$$

with $r(t) \equiv 0$ or $\deg r < \deg (t - a) = 1$. Thus $r(t) = k$, a constant. Substituting $t = a$ and $r(t) = k$ into $(1)$ yields $f(a) = (a - a)q(a) + k$. Since $f(a) = 0$ and $a - a = 0$, we get $k = r(t) = 0$. Thus $f(t) = (t - a)q(t)$. Also $n = \deg f = \deg (t - a) + \deg q = 1 + \deg q$. Hence $\deg q = n - 1$.

**9.163** Prove Theorem 9.13.

$\blacksquare$ Substitute $t = p/q$ into $f(t) = 0$ to obtain $a_n(p/q)^n + \cdots + a_1(p/q) + a_0 = 0$. Multiply both sides of the equation by $q^n$ to obtain

$$
a_n p^n + a_{n-1} p^{n-1} q + a_{n-2} p^{n-2} q^2 + \cdots + a_1 p q^{n-1} + a_0 q^n = 0 \tag{1}
$$

Since $p$ divides all of the first $n$ terms of $(1)$, $p$ must divide the last term $a_0 q^n$. Assuming $p$ and $q$ are relatively prime, $p$ divides $a_0$. Similarly, $q$ divides the last $n$ terms of $(1)$, hence $q$ divides the first term $a_n p^n$. Since $p$ and $q$ are relatively prime, $q$ divides $a_n$.

**Theorem 9.14:** Suppose $f(t)$ is a polynomial over a field $K$ and $\deg f = n$. Then $f(t)$ has at most $n$ roots in $K$.

**9.164** Prove Theorem 9.14.

$\blacksquare$ The proof is by induction on $n$. If $n = 1$, then $f(t) = at + b$ and $f(t)$ has the unique root $t = -b/a$. Suppose $n > 1$. If $f(t)$ has no roots, then the theorem is true. Suppose $a \in K$ is a root of $f(t)$. Then

$$
f(t) = (t - a)g(t) \tag{1}
$$

where $\deg g = n - 1$. We claim that any other root of $f(t)$ must also be a root of $g(t)$. Suppose $b \neq a$ is another root of $f(t)$. Substituting $t = b$ in $(1)$ yields $0 = f(b) = (b - a)g(b)$. Since $K$ has no zero divisors, and $b - a \neq 0$, we must have $g(b) = 0$. By induction, $g(t)$ has at most $n - 1$ roots. Thus $f(t)$ has at most $n - 1$ roots other than $a$. Thus $f(t)$ has at most $n$ roots.

**Theorem 9.15:** Suppose $f(t)$ is a polynomial over the real field **R**, and suppose the complex number $z = a + bi$, $b \neq 0$, is a root of $f(t)$. Then the complex conjugate $\bar{z} = a - bi$ is also a root of $f(t)$ and hence $c(t) = (t - z)(t - \bar{z}) = t^2 - 2at + a^2 + b^2$ is a factor of $f(t)$.

**9.165** Prove Theorem 9.15.

▮ Since $\deg c = 2$, there exist $q(t)$ and $M, N \in \mathbf{R}$ such that

$$f(t) = c(t)q(t) + Mt + N \tag{1}$$

Since $z = a + bi$ is a root of $f(t)$ and $c(t)$, we have by substituting $t = a + bi$ in (1)

$$f(z) = c(z)q(z) + M(z) + N \quad \text{or} \quad 0 = 0q(z) + M(z) + N \quad \text{or} \quad M(a + bi) + N = 0$$

Thus $Ma + N = 0$ and $Mb = 0$. Since $b \neq 0$, we must have $M = 0$. Then $0 + N = 0$ or $N = 0$. Accordingly, $f(t) = c(t)q(t)$ and $\bar{z} = a - bi$ is a root of $f(t)$.

**9.166** Suppose $f(t) = t^4 - 3t^3 + 6t^2 + 25t - 39$. Find all the roots of $f(t)$ given that $t = 2 + 3i$ is a root.

▮ Since $2 + 3i$ is a root, then $2 - 3i$ is a root and $c(t) = t^2 - 4t + 13$ is a factor of $f(t)$. Dividing $f(t)$ by $c(t)$ we get $f(t) = (t^2 - 4t + 13)(t^2 + t - 3)$. The quadratic formula with $t^2 + t - 3$ gives us the other roots of $f(t)$. That is, the four roots of $f(t)$ follow: $2 + 3i$, $2 - 3i$, $(-1 + \sqrt{13})/2$, $(-1 - \sqrt{13})/2$.

**9.167** Suppose $f(t)$ is a real polynomial with odd degree. Show that $f(t)$ must have a real root.

▮ The complex roots of $f(t)$ come in pairs by Theorem 9.15. The Fundamental Theorem of Algebra (Problem 9.175) implies that $f(t)$ has an odd number of roots. Hence at least one root of $f(t)$ must be real.

**9.168** Prove geometrically that a real polynomial $f(t)$ of odd degree has a real root.

▮ Suppose the leading coefficient of $f(t)$ is positive [otherwise, multiply $f(t)$ by $-1$]. Since $\deg f = n$ where $n$ is odd, we have

$$\lim_{t \to \infty} f(t) = +\infty \quad \text{and} \quad \lim_{t \to -\infty} f(t) = -\infty$$

Thus the graph of $f(t)$ must cross the $t$ axis in at least one point as shown in Fig. 9-4.

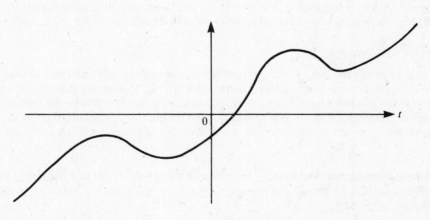

**Fig. 9-4**

## $K[t]$ as a PID and UFD

This subsection proves that the ring $K[t]$ of polynomials over a field $K$ is a principal ideal domain and a unique factorization domain. (The reader is referred to Section 9.5 for the relevant definitions.)

**Theorem 9.16:** The ring $K[t]$ of polynomials over a field $K$ is a principal ideal domain. If $J$ is an ideal in $K[t]$, then there exists a unique monic polynomial $d$ which generates $J$, i.e., divides every polynomial $f \in J$.

**9.169** Prove Theorem 9.16.

▮ Let $d$ be a polynomial of lowest degree in $J$. Since we can multiply $d$ by a nonzero scalar and still remain in

$J$, we can assume without loss in generality that $d$ is a monic polynomial. Now suppose $f \in J$. By the division algorithm there exist polynomials $q$ and $r$ such that $f = qd + r$ where either $r = 0$ or $\deg r < \deg d$. Now $f, d \in J$ implies $qd \in J$ and hence $r = f - qd \in J$. But $d$ is a polynomial of lowest degree in $J$. Accordingly, $r = 0$ and $f = qd$, that is, $d$ divides $f$. It remains to show that $d$ is unique. If $d'$ is another monic polynomial which generates $J$, then $d$ divides $d'$ and $d'$ divides $d$. This implies that $d = d'$, because $d$ and $d'$ are monic. Thus the theorem is proved.

**Theorem 9.17:**  Let $f$ and $g$ be nonzero polynomials in $K[t]$. Then there exists a unique monic polynomial $d$ such that (i) $d$ divides $f$ and $g$ and (ii) if $d'$ divides $f$ and $g$, then $d'$ divides $d$.

**9.170**  Prove Theorem 9.17.

▌  The set $I = \{mf + ng: m, n \in K[t]\}$ is an ideal. Let $d$ be the monic polynomial which generates $I$. Note $f, g \in I$; hence $d$ divides $f$ and $g$. Now suppose $d'$ divides $f$ and $g$. Let $J$ be the ideal generated by $d'$. Then $f, g \in J$ and hence $I \subseteq J$. Accordingly, $d \in J$ and so $d'$ divides $d$ as claimed. It remains to show that $d$ is unique. If $d_1$ is another [monic] greatest common divisor of $f$ and $g$, then $d$ divides $d_1$ and $d_1$ divides $d$. This implies that $d = d_1$ because $d$ and $d_1$ are monic. Thus the theorem is proved.

**Remark:**  The polynomial $d$ in Theorem 9.17 is called the *greatest common divisor* of $f$ and $g$. If $d = 1$, then $f$ and $g$ are said to be *relatively prime*.

**Corollary 9.18:**  Let $d$ be the greatest common divisor of the polynomials $f$ and $g$. Then there exist polynomials $m$ and $n$ such that $d = mf + ng$. In particular, if $f$ and $g$ are relatively prime, then there exist polynomials $m$ and $n$ such that $mf + ng = 1$.

**9.171**  Prove Corollary 9.18.

▌  From the proof of Theorem 9.17, $d$ generates the ideal $I = \{mf + ng: m, n \in K[t]\}$. Thus there exists $m, n \in K[t]$ such that $d = mf + ng$.

**9.172**  Define an irreducible polynomial.

▌  A polynomial $p \in K[t]$ is said to be *irreducible* if $p$ has positive degree, i.e., $p$ is not a constant, and if $p = fg$ implies $f$ or $g$ is a scalar.

**Lemma 9.19:**  Suppose $p \in K[t]$ is irreducible. If $p$ divides the product $fg$ of polynomials $f, g \in K[t]$, then $p$ divides $f$ or $p$ divides $g$. More generally, if $p$ divides the product of $n$ polynomials $f_1 f_2 \cdots f_n$, then $p$ divides one of them.

**9.173**  Prove Lemma 9.19.

▌  Suppose $p$ divides $fg$ but not $f$. Since $p$ is irreducible, the polynomials $f$ and $p$ must then be relatively prime. Thus there exist polynomials $m, n \in K[t]$ such that $mf + np = 1$. Multiplying this equation by $g$, we obtain $mfg + npg = g$. But $p$ divides $fg$ and so $mfg$, and $p$ divides $npg$; hence $p$ divides the sum $g = mfg + npg$.

Now suppose $p$ divides $f_1 f_2 \cdots f_n$. If $p$ divides $f_1$, then we are through. If not, then by the above result $p$ divides the product $f_2 \cdots f_n$. By induction on $n$, $p$ divides one of the polynomials $f_2, \ldots, f_n$. Thus the lemma is proved.

**Theorem 9.20  (Unique Factorization Theorem):**  Let $f$ be a nonzero polynomial in $K[t]$. Then $f$ can be written uniquely (except for order) as a product $f = kp_1 p_2 \cdots p_n$ where $k \in K$ and the $p_i$ are monic irreducible polynomials in $K[t]$.

**9.174**  Prove Theorem 9.20.

▌  We prove the existence of such a product first. If $f$ is irreducible or if $f \in K$, then such a product clearly exists. On the other hand, suppose $f = gh$ where $f$ and $g$ are nonscalars. Then $g$ and $h$ have degrees less than that of $f$. By induction, we can assume $g = k_1 g_1 g_2 \cdots g_r$ and $h = k_2 h_1 h_2 \cdots h_s$ where $k_1, k_2 \in K$ and the $g_i$ and $h_j$ are monic irreducible polynomials. Accordingly, $f = (k_1 k_2) g_1 g_2 \cdots g_r h_1 h_2 \cdots h_s$ is our desired representation.

We next prove uniqueness (except for order) of such a product for $f$. Suppose $f = kp_1 p_1 \cdots p_n = k' q_1 q_2 \cdots q_m$ where $k, k' \in K$ and the $p_1, \ldots, p_n, q_1, \ldots, q_m$ are monic irreducible polynomials. Now $p_1$ divides $k' q_1 \cdots q_m$. Since $p_1$ is irreducible it must divide one of the $q_i$ by Lemma 9.19. Say $p_1$ divides $q_1$. Since $p_1$ and $q_1$ are both irreducible and monic, $p_1 = q_1$. Accordingly, $kp_2 \cdots p_n = k' q_2 \cdots q_m$. By induction, we have that $n = m$ and $p_2 = q_2, \ldots, p_n = q_m$ for some rearrangement of the $q_i$. We also have that $k = k'$. Thus the theorem is proved.

**9.175**  State without proof the Fundamental Theorem of Algebra.

▌ **Fundamental Theorem of Algebra:**  The complex field **C** is closed. That is, any nonzero polynomial $f(t)$ over **C** has a root in **C** and therefore $f(t)$ can be written uniquely (except for order) as a product $f(t) = k(t - r_1)(t - r_2) \cdots (t - r_n)$ where $k$, $r_i \in$ **C**, and $n = \deg f$.

**Theorem 9.21:**  Let $f(t)$ be a nonzero polynomial over the real field **R**. Then $f(t)$ can be written uniquely (except for order) as a product $f(t) = kp_1(t)p_2(t) \cdots p_m(t)$ where $k \in$ **R** and the $p_i(t)$ are monic irreducible polynomials of degree one or two.

**9.176**  Prove Theorem 9.21.

▌ By the fundamental theorem of algebra, $f(t) = k(t - r_1)(t - r_2) \cdots (t - r_n)$ where $k$, $r_i \in$ **C**. Since $k$ is the leading coefficient of $f(t)$ we have $k \in$ **R**. Also, if $r_i = a + bi$ is a nonreal root, then there exists a root $r_j = a - bi$. Furthermore, $p(t) = (t - r_i)(t - r_j) = t^2 - 2at + a^2 + b^2$ is a polynomial over **R**, $p(t)$ is monic, and $p(t)$ is irreducible over **R** since its roots are nonreal. The theorem follows.

# CHAPTER 10
# Languages, Grammars, Automata

## 10.1 WORDS

**10.1** Define a word or string from a set $A$, and give an example.

▌ Let $A$ be an *alphabet*, that is, a set whose elements are called *letters*. A word (string) $w$ from $A$ (or: over $A$ or on $A$) is a finite sequence of letters. For example,

$$u = ababb \qquad \text{and} \qquad v = accbaa$$

are words from the alphabet $A = \{a, b, c\}$. The empty sequence, denoted by $\lambda$ (Greek letter lambda) or 1, is also defined to be a word from $A$. We shall usually abbreviate our notation by writing $a^2$ for $aa$, $a^3$ for $aaa$, and so on. Thus, for the above words, $u = abab^2$ and $v = ac^2ba^2$. The set of all words on $A$ is denoted by $A^*$.

**Remark:** Unless otherwise stated or implied, the alphabet $A$ will be finite, the symbols $u$, $v$, $w$ will be reserved for words from $A$, and the elements of $A$ will come from the letters $a$, $b$, $c$.

**10.2** Define the operation of concatenation, and give an example.

▌ Consider two words $u$ and $v$ from an alphabet $A$. The *concatenation* of $u$ and $v$ written $uv$, is the word from $A$ obtained by writing the letters of $u$ followed by the letters of $v$. For example, from Problem 10.1, for the words $u = abab^2$ and $v = ac^2ba^2$,

$$uv = abab^2ac^2ba^2 \qquad \text{and} \qquad vu = accbaaababb$$

Thus concatenation is not commutative. We also define $u^2 = uu$, $u^3 = u^2u$ and, in general, $u^{n+1} = u^nu$.

**10.3** Consider the words $u = a^2ba^3b^2$ and $v = bab^2$. Find: **(a)** $uv$, **(b)** $vu$, and **(c)** $v^2$.

▌ Write the letters of the first word followed by the letters of the second word:

**(a)** $\qquad\qquad uv = (a^2ba^3b^2)(bab^2) = a^2ba^3b^3ab^2$

**(b)** $\qquad\qquad vu = (bab^2)(a^2ba^3b^2) = bab^2a^2ba^3b^2$

**(c)** $\qquad\qquad v^2 = vv = (bab^2)(bab^2) = bab^3ab^2$

**10.4** Suppose $u = a^2b$ and $v = b^3ab$. Find: **(a)** $uvu$, and **(b)** $\lambda u$, $u\lambda$, $u\lambda v$.

▌ **(a)** Write down the letters in $u$, then $v$, and finally $u$ to obtain $uvu = a^2b^4aba^2b$.

**(b)** Since $\lambda$ is the empty word, $\lambda u = u\lambda = u = a^2b$ and $u\lambda v = uv = a^2b^4ab$.

**10.5** Define a subword and an initial segment of a word $w$.

▌ A word $u$ is called a *subword* of $w$ if $w = v_1uv_2$. If $v_1 = \lambda$, the empty word, then $u$ is an *initial segment* of $w$. Note $\lambda$ is a subword of $w$ since $w = \lambda\lambda w$. Also, $w$ is a subword of $w$ since $w = \lambda w\lambda$.

**10.6** Let $w = abcd$. Find all subwords of $w$. Which of them are initial segments of $w$?

▌ The subwords are: $\lambda$, $a$, $b$, $c$, $d$, $ab$, $bc$, $cd$, $abc$, $bcd$, and $w = abcd$. The initial segments are $\lambda$, $a$, $ab$, $abc$, and $abcd$. We emphasize that $v = acd$ is not a subword of $w$ although its letters all belong to $w$.

**10.7** Define the length of a word $u$, written $\|u\|$ or $\ell(u)$.

▌ The *length* of $u$ is equal to the number of elements in its sequence of letters. That is, if $u = a_1a_2 \cdots a_n$ then $\|u\| = n$, and if $u = \lambda$ then $\|u\| = 0$.

**10.8** Find $\|u\|$, $\|v\|$, $\|uv\|$, $\|vu\|$, and $\|v^2\|$ for the words $u$ and $v$ in Problem 10.3.

▌ Count the number of letters in each word to obtain $\|u\| = 8$, $\|v\| = 4$, $\|uv\| = 12$, $\|vu\| = 12$, $\|v^2\| = 8$.

**10.9** For any words $u$ and $v$ on $A$, show that: **(a)** $\|uv\| = \|u\| + \|v\|$, and **(b)** $\|uv\| = \|vu\|$.

**(a)** Suppose $\|u\| = r$ and $\|v\| = s$. Then $uv$ will contain the $r$ letters of $u$ followed by the $s$ letters of $v$; hence $\|uv\| = r + s = \|u\| + \|v\|$.

**(b)** Using **(a)** yields $\|uv\| = \|u\| + \|v\| = \|v\| + \|u\| = \|uv\|$.

**10.10** Define the free semigroup.

Let $F$ be the set of all words from an alphabet $A$ with the operation of concatenation. Clearly, the operation is associative and the empty word $\lambda$ is an identity element. Thus $F$ is a semigroup, called the *free semigroup* over $A$. Note that $F$ satisfies both the right and left cancellation laws.

## 10.2 LANGUAGES

**10.11** Define a language over a set $A$.

Any collection $L$ of words from an alphabet $A$, that is, any subset $L$ of $A^*$, is called a *language* over $A$.

**10.12** Describe in words the following languages over $A = \{a, b\}$:

**(a)** $L_1 = \{a, ab, ab^2, \ldots\}$   **(c)** $L_3 = \{a^m b^m : m > 0\}$

**(b)** $L_2 = \{a^m b^n : m > 0, n > 0\}$   **(d)** $L_4 = \{b^m a b^n : m > 0, n > 0\}$

**(a)** $L_1$ consists of all words which begin with an $a$ followed by one or more $b$'s.

**(b)** $L_2$ consists of all words beginning with one or more $a$'s followed by one or more $b$'s.

**(c)** $L_3$ consists of all words beginning with one or more $a$'s followed by the same number of $b$'s.

**(d)** $L_4$ consists of all words with exactly one $a$ which is neither the first nor last letter of the word, i.e., there is one or more $b$'s before and after $a$.

**10.13** Let $K$ and $L$ be languages over an alphabet $A$. Define the language $KL$ over $A$.

$KL$ consists of all words over $A$ formed by concatenating words in $K$ with words in $L$. That is, $KL = \{w : w = uv \text{ where } u \in K \text{ and } v \in L\}$.

**10.14** Let $K = \{a, ab, a^2\}$ and $L = \{b^2, aba\}$ be languages over $A = \{a, b\}$. Find: **(a)** $KL$, and **(b)** $LL$.

**(a)** Concatenate words in $K$ with words in $L$ to obtain $KL = \{ab^2, a^2ba, ab^3, ababa, a^2b^2, a^3ba\}$.

**(b)** Concatenate words in $L$ with words in $L$ to obtain $LL = \{b^4, b^2aba, abab^2, aba^2ba\}$.

**10.15** Let $L$ be a language over $A$. Define: **(a)** $L^n$ for $n \geq 0$, and **(b)** $L^*$.

**(a)** $L^0 = \{\lambda\}$, $L^1 = L$, and $L^{n+1} = L^n L$ for $n > 0$.

**(b)** $L^*$ consists of all words whose letters are of words in $L$, that is,

$$L^* = \bigcup_{k=0}^{\infty} L^k$$

Note that $L^*$ includes the empty word $\lambda$ and that this definition agrees with the definition of $A^*$ (Problem 10.1).

**10.16** Consider the language $L = \{ab, c\}$ over $A = \{a, b, c\}$. Find: **(a)** $L^0$, **(b)** $L^3$, and **(c)** $L^{-2}$.

**(a)** $L^0 = \{\lambda\}$, by definition.

**(b)** Form all three-word sequences from $L$ to obtain

$$L = \{ababab, ababc, abcab, abc^2, cabab, cabc, c^2ab, c^3\}$$

**(c)** The negative power of a language is not defined.

**10.17** Let $A = \{a, b, c\}$. Find $L^*$ where: **(a)** $L = \{b^2\}$, **(b)** $L = \{a, b\}$, and **(c)** $L = \{a, b, c^3\}$.

**(a)** $L^*$ consists of all words $b^n$ where $n$ is even (including the empty word $\lambda$).

**(b)** $L^*$ consists of words in $a$ and $b$.

**(c)** $L^*$ consists of all words from $A$ with the property that the length of each *maximal* subword composed entirely of $c$'s is divisible by 3.

**10.18** Consider a countable alphabet $A = \{a_1, a_2, \ldots\}$. Let $L_k$ be the language over $A$ consisting of those words $w$ such that the sum of the subscripts of the letters in $w$ is equal to $k$. For example, $a_2 a_3 a_3 a_6 a_4$ belongs to $L_{18}$. Find $L_4$.

▮ No letter $a_n$ with $n > 4$ can be used in a word in $L_4$. Also, no word in $L_4$ can have more than four letters. Thus we obtain the following list:

$$a_1a_1a_1a_1, \quad a_1a_1a_2, \quad a_1a_2a_1, \quad a_2a_1a_1, \quad a_1a_3, \quad a_3a_1, \quad a_2a_2, \quad a_4$$

**10.19**  Consider the languages $L_k$ over $A = \{a_1, a_2, \ldots\}$ in Problem 10.18. Show that $L_k$ is finite.

▮ Only a finite number of the $a$'s, that is, $a_1, a_2, \ldots, a_k$, can be used as letters in words in $L_k$ and no word in $L_k$ can have more than $k$ letters. Accordingly, $L_k$ is finite.

**10.20**  Consider a countable alphabet $A = \{a_1, a_2, \ldots\}$. Show that: **(a)** $A^*$ is countable, and **(b)** any language $L$ over $A$ is countable.

▮ **(a)** $A^*$ is the countable union of the finite sets $L_k$ defined in Problem 10.18. Hence $A^*$ is countable.
  **(b)** $L$ is a subset of the countable set $A^*$; hence $L$ is also countable.

## 10.3  REGULAR EXPRESSIONS, REGULAR LANGUAGES

**10.21**  Define a regular expression $r$ over an alphabet $A$ and the language $L(r)$ over $A$ which is defined by $r$.

▮ A *regular expression r over A* is a special type of string coming from $A$ with five new elements:

$$\text{``(",   ``)",   ``*",   ``}\vee\text{",   ``}\lambda\text{"}$$

Here "$\vee$" is read as "or" and "$*$" is read as "star". The expression $r$ and the language $L(r)$ over $A$ are defined inductively on the length of $r$ as follows:

*Base Criteria*:
  (i)   There is no regular expression of length 0.
  (ii)  The regular expressions of length 1 are $\lambda$ and every $a \in A$. $L(\lambda) = \{\lambda\}$ and $L(a) = \{a\}$.
  (iii) The only regular expression of length 2 is ( ), and the language it defines is the empty set, the language with no elements.

*Inductive Step*:
  (i)   Suppose $r$ is a regular expression defining a language $L$. Then $(r)$ is a regular expression and $L((r)) = L(r)$ and $(r^*)$ is a regular expression defining the language $L^*$.
  (ii)  Suppose $r_1$ and $r_2$ are regular expressions defining the languages $L_1$ and $L_2$, respectively. Then $(r_1 \vee r_2)$ is a regular expression defining the language $L_1 \cup L_2$ and $(r_1r_2)$ is a regular expression defining the language $L_1L_2$.

All regular expressions are formed in this way.

**Remark:**  We usually omit parentheses from regular expressions when possible. Since concatenation of languages and union of languages are associative, many parentheses can be omitted. Also, by adopting the convention that "$*$" takes precedence over concatenation, and concatenation takes precedence over "$\vee$", other parentheses can be omitted.

**10.22**  Define a *regular set* or *regular language* $L$ over an alphabet $A$.

▮ $L$ is regular if $L$ is a language defined by a regular expression $r$ over $A$; that is, if there is a regular expression $r$ such that $L = L(r)$.

**10.23**  Let $A = \{a, b\}$ and $r = (a \vee b)^*bb$. **(a)** Show that $r$ is a regular expression over $A$. **(b)** Describe $L(r)$, the language over $A$ defined by $r$.

▮ **(a)** Here $a$ and $b$ are regular since they belong to $A$. Hence $(a \vee b)$ and $(bb)$ are regular. Thus $(a \vee b)^*$ is regular and so $r = (a \vee b)^*bb$ is regular.
  **(b)** Note $(a \vee b)^* = A^*$ consists of all words in $a$ and $b$; hence $L(r)$ consists of all words ending in $b^2 = bb$.

**10.24**  Let $A = \{a, b\}$. Determine whether or not each $r$ is a regular expression over $A$ and, if it is, describe $L(r)$:
**(a)** $r = a^*$ and **(b)** $r = aa^*$.

▮ **(a)** Note $a^*$ is an abbreviation for $(a^*)$; hence $r = a^*$ is a regular expression since $a \in A$ is regular. $L(r)$ consists of all words in $a$ (including the empty word $\lambda$).
  **(b)** Here $r = aa^*$ is regular since $a$ and $a^*$ are regular. Also, $L(r)$ consists of all words in $a$ excluding the empty word.

**10.25** Repeat Problem 10.24 for: **(a)** $r = ab^*$, **(b)** $r = a \vee b^*$, and **(c)** $r = a \wedge b^*$.

▌ **(a)** Since $a$ and $b^*$ are regular, so is $r = ab^*$. $L(r)$ consists of all words beginning with $a$ and followed by zero or more $b$'s.

**(b)** Since $a$ and $b^*$ are regular, so is $r = a \vee b^*$. $L(r)$ consists of the word $w = a$ and any word in $b$.

**(c)** Since $\wedge$ is not one of the five elements adjoined to $A$, $r$ is not a regular expression.

**10.26** Let $A = \{a, b, c\}$ and let $w = ac$. State whether or not $w$ belongs to $L(r)$ where: **(a)** $r = ab^*c^*$, and **(b)** $r = (a^*b \vee c)^*$.

▌ **(a)** Yes, since $w = a\lambda c$ and $\lambda \in L(b^*)$ and $c \in L(c^*)$.

**(b)** No. Note $L(a^*b)$ consists of the words $w = a^n b$. Thus, if $a$ appears in any word in $L(r)$, then the $a$ can only be followed by an $a$ or $b$, not $c$.

**10.27** Let $A = \{a, b, c\}$ and $w = abc$. State whether or not $w$ belongs to $L(r)$ where: **(a)** $r = a^* \vee (b \vee c)^*$, and **(b)** $r = a^*(b \vee c)^*$.

▌ **(a)** No. Here $L(r)$ consists of words in $a$ or words in $b$ and $c$.

**(b)** Yes, since $a \in L(a^*)$ and $bc \in L((b \vee c)^*)$.

**10.28** Find $L(r)$ for the regular expression $r = abb^*a$ over $A = \{a, b\}$.

▌ $L(r)$ will consist of all words beginning and ending in $a$ and enclosing one or more $b$'s.

**10.29** Find $L(r)$ for the regular expression $r = b^*ab^*ab^*$ over $A = \{a, b\}$.

▌ $L(r)$ will consist of all words with exactly two $a$'s.

**10.30** Find a regular expression $r$ over $A = \{a, b\}$ such that $L(r) = \{a^m b^m, m > 0, n > 0\}$. [See Problem 10.12(b).]

▌ Note $L(r)$ consists of those words beginning with one or more $a$'s followed by one or more $b$'s. Hence we can set $r = aa^*bb^*$. (Note $r$ is not unique; for example, $r = a^*ab^*b$ is also a solution.)

**10.31** Find a regular expression $r$ over $A = \{a, b\}$ such that $L(r) = \{b^m ab^n: m > 0, n > 0\}$. [See Problem 10.12(d).]

▌ Note $L(r)$ consists of those words $w$ whose letters are all $b$ except for one $a$ that is not the first or last letter of $w$. Thus $r = bb^*abb^*$ is a solution.

**10.32** Find a regular expression $r$ over $A = \{a, b\}$ such that $L(r) = \{a^m b^m: m > 0\}$. [See Problem 10.12(c).]

▌ No such $r$ exists, that is, the language is not regular. The proof is given in Problem 10.46.

## 10.4 FINITE STATE AUTOMATA

**10.33** Define a finite state automaton (FSA).

▌ A *finite state automaton* or, simply, an *automaton M* consists of five parts:
(1) A finite set (alphabet) $A$ of inputs.
(2) A finite set $S$ of internal states.
(3) A subset $Y$ of $S$ (whose elements are called accepting or "yes" states).
(4) An initial state $s_0$ in $S$.
(5) A next-state function $F$ from $S \times A$ into $S$.
Such an automaton $M$ is denoted by $M = \langle A, S, Y, s_0, F \rangle$ when we want to indicate its five parts.

Some texts define the next-state function $F: S \times A \to S$ in (5) by means of a collection of functions $f_a: S \to S$, one for each $a \in A$; that is, each input $a$ may be viewed as causing a change in the state of the automaton $M$. Setting $F(s, a) = f_a(s)$ shows that both definitions are equivalent.

**10.34** Give an example of a finite state automaton $M$.

▌ Define the five parts of $M$ as follows:
(1) $A = \{a, b\}$, input symbols.
(2) $S = \{s_0, s_1, s_2\}$, internal states.
(3) $Y = \{s_0, s_1\}$, accepting states.
(4) $s_0$, initial state.

(5)  Next-state function $F: S \times A \to S$ defined by

$$F(s_0, a) = s_0 \qquad F(s_1, a) = s_0 \qquad F(s_2, a) = s_2$$
$$F(s_0, b) = s_1 \qquad F(s_1, b) = s_2 \qquad F(s_2, b) = s_2$$

Then $M$ is an automaton. The next-state function $F$ is frequently given by means of a table as in Fig. 10-1.

| $F$ | $a$ | $b$ |
|-----|-----|-----|
| $s_0$ | $s_0$ | $s_1$ |
| $s_1$ | $s_0$ | $s_2$ |
| $s_2$ | $s_2$ | $s_2$ |

**Fig. 10-1**

**10.35**  Define the state diagram $D = D(M)$ of a finite state automaton $M$, and give an example. Usually, an automaton $M$ is defined by means of its state diagram rather than by listing its five parts.

▌ $D(M)$ is a labeled directed graph as follows. The vertices of $D(M)$ are the states of $S$ and an accepting state is labeled by means of a double circle. There is an arrow (directed edge) in $D(M)$ from state $s_j$ to state $s_k$ labeled by an input $a$ if $F(s_j, a) = s_k$ or, equivalently, if $f_a(s_j) = s_k$. (For notational convenience, we label a single arrow by all the inputs which cause a given change of state rather than having an arrow for each such input.) Furthermore, initial state $s_0$ is labeled by means of a special arrow which terminates at the vertex $s_0$ but has no initial vertex.

The state diagram $D$ of the automaton $M$ in Problem 10.32 is shown in Fig. 10-2. Note that both $a$ and $b$ label the arrow from $s_2$ to $s_2$ since $F(s_2, a) = s_2$ and also $F(s_2, b) = s_2$.

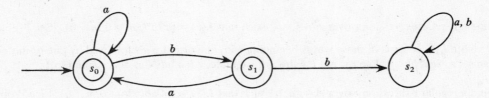

**Fig. 10-2**

**10.36**  Let $M$ be an automaton with input $A$. Define the language $L(M)$ over $A$ determined by $M$.

▌ Each word $w = a_1 a_2 \cdots a_n$ from $A$ determines a sequence of changes of state

$$s_0 \to s_1 \to s_2 \to \cdots \to s_n$$

where $s_0$ is the initial state and $s_i = F(s_{i-1}, a_i)$ for $i > 0$. Equivalently, the word $w$ determines a path $P$ in the graph $D(M)$ which begins at $s_0$ and goes from vertex to vertex using the sequence of arrows labeled by the letters in $w$.

We say that $M$ *recognizes* or *accepts* $w$ if the final state $s_n$ is an accepting state in $Y$. The language $L(M)$ of $M$ is the collection of all words from $A$ which are accepted by $M$.

**10.37**  Consider the automaton $M$ in Fig. 10-2. Determine whether or not $M$ accepts the word $w$ where:
**(a)** $w = ababba$, **(b)** $w = baab$, and **(c)** $w = \lambda$.

▌ **(a)**  Use Fig. 10-2 and the word $w = ababba$ to obtain the path

$$P = s_0 \xrightarrow{a} s_0 \xrightarrow{b} s_1 \xrightarrow{a} s_0 \xrightarrow{b} s_1 \xrightarrow{b} s_2 \xrightarrow{a} s_2$$

The final state $s_2$ is not in $Y$; hence $w$ is not accepted by $M$.
  **(b)**  The word $w = baab$ determines the path

$$P = s_0 \xrightarrow{b} s_1 \xrightarrow{a} s_0 \xrightarrow{a} s_0 \xrightarrow{b} s_1$$

The final state $s_1$ is in $Y$; hence $w$ is accepted by $M$.
  **(c)**  Here the final state is the initial state $s_0$ since $w$ is the empty word. Since $s_0$ belongs to $Y$, $\lambda$ is accepted by $M$.

**10.38**  Describe the language $L(M)$ of the automaton $M$ in Fig. 10-2.

▐ $L(M)$ will consist of all words $w$ over $A$ which do not have two successive $b$'s since (1) we can enter the state $s_2$ only after two successive $b$'s, (2) we never leave $s_2$, and (3) the state $s_2$ is the only rejecting state.

The fundamental relationship between regular languages and automata is contained in the following theorem.

**Theorem 10.1:** A language $L$ over an alphabet $A$ is regular if and only if there is a finite state automaton $M$ such that $L = L(M)$.

**10.39** Let $A = \{a, b\}$. Construct an automaton $M$ which will accept precisely those words from $A$ which have an even number of $a$'s. For example, *aababbab, aa, bbb, ababaa* will be accepted by $M$, but *ababa, aaa, bbabb* will be rejected by $M$.

▐ We need only two states, $s_0$ and $s_1$. We assume that $M$ is in state $s_0$ or $s_1$ according as the number of $a$'s up to the given step is even or odd. (Thus $s_0$ is an accepting state, but $s_1$ is a rejecting state.) Then only $a$ will change the state. Also, $s_0$ is the initial state. The state diagram of $M$ is shown in Fig. 10-3.

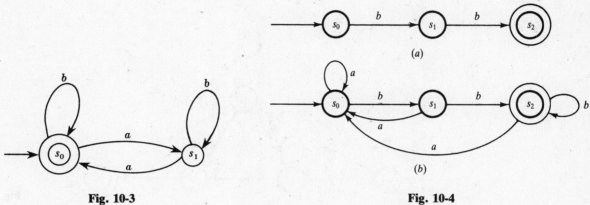

(a)

(b)

**Fig. 10-3**          **Fig. 10-4**

**10.40** Let $A = \{a, b\}$. Construct an automaton $M$ which will accept precisely those words from $A$ which end in two $b$'s.

▐ Since $b^2$ is accepted, but not $\lambda$ or $b$, we need three states, $s_0$, the initial state, and $s_1$ and $s_2$ with an arrow labeled $b$ going from $s_0$ to $s_1$ and one from $s_1$ to $s_2$. Also, $s_2$ is an accepting state, but not $s_0$ and $s_1$. This gives the graph in Fig. 10-4(a). On the other hand, if there is an $a$, then we want to go back to $s_0$, and if we are in $s_2$ and there is a $b$, then we want to stay in $s_2$. These additional conditions give the required automaton $M$ which is shown in Fig. 10-4(b).

**10.41** Let $A = \{a, b\}$. Construct an automaton $M$ which will accept those words from $A$ where the number of $b$'s is divisible by three.

▐ We need three states, $s_0$, the initial state, $s_1$ and $s_2$. We need arrows labeled $b$ going from $s_0$ to $s_1$, from $s_1$ to $s_2$, and from $s_2$ back to $s_0$. The states count the number of $b$'s modulo 3, so $s_0$ is an accepting state but not $s_1$ or $s_2$. The arrows labeled $a$ do not change the state. The required automaton is shown in Fig. 10-5.

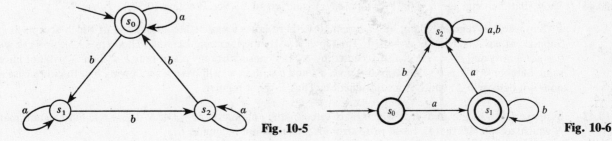

**Fig. 10-5**          **Fig. 10-6**

**10.42** Let $A = \{a, b\}$. Construct an automaton $M$ which will accept the language $L_1$ of Problem 10.12.

▐ See Fig. 10-6.

**10.43**  Let $A = \{a, b\}$. Construct an automaton $M$ which will accept the language $L = \{a^m b^n : m$ and $n$ positive$\}$. [See Problem 10.12($b$).]

▮  See Fig. 10-7.

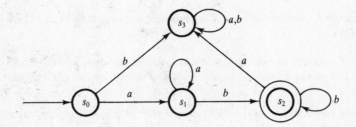

**Fig. 10-7**

**10.44**  Let $A = \{a, b\}$. Construct an automaton $M$ which will accept the language $L = \{b^m a b^n : m$ and $n$ positive$\}$. [See Problem 10.12($d$).]

▮  See Fig. 10-8.

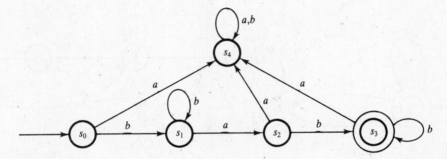

**Fig. 10-8**

**Theorem 10.2 (Pumping Lemma):**  Suppose (i) an automaton $M$ over $A$ has $k$ states; (ii) $w$ is a word from $A$ which is accepted by $M$; and (iii) $\|w\| > k$. Then $w = xyz$ where, for every positive $m$, $w_m = xy^m z$ is accepted by $M$.

**10.45**  Prove Theorem 10.2.

▮  Suppose $w = a_1 a_2 \cdots a_n$ and let $P = (s_0, s_1, \ldots, s_n)$ be the corresponding sequence of states determined by $w$. By assumption, $n > k$, the number of states. Hence two of the states in $P$ must be equal, say $s_i = s_j$ where $i < j$. Let $x = a_1 a_2 \cdots a_i$, $y = a_{i+1} \cdots a_j$, and $z = a_{j+1} \cdots a_n$. As shown in Fig. 10-9, $xy$ ends in $s_i = s_j$ and $xy^m$ also ends in $s_i$. Thus $w_m = xy^m z$ ends in $s_n$, which is an accepting state. Thus the theorem is proved.

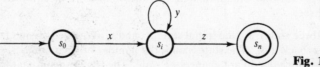

**Fig. 10-9**

**10.46**  Show that the language $L = \{a^m b^m : m$ positive$\}$ is not regular. (See Problem 10.32.)

▮  Suppose $L$ is regular. Then, by Theorem 10.1, there exists a finite state automaton $M$ which accepts $L$. Suppose $M$ has $k$ states. Let $w = a^k b^k$. Then $\|w\| > k$. By the Pumping Lemma (Theorem 10.2), $w = xyz$ where $y$ is not empty and $w_2 = xy^2 z$ is also accepted by $M$. If $y$ consists of only $a$'s or only $b$'s, then $w_2$ will not have the same number of $a$'s as $b$'s. If $y$ contains both $a$'s and $b$'s, then $w_2$ will have $a$'s following $b$'s. In either case $w_2$ does not belong to $L$, which is a contradiction. Thus $L$ is not regular.

**10.47**  Suppose $L$ is a language over $A$ which is accepted by the automaton $M = \langle A, S, Y, s_0, F \rangle$. Find an automaton $N$ which accepts $L^c$, that is, those words from $A$ which do not belong to $L$.

▮  Simply interchange the accepting and rejecting states in $M$ to obtain $N$. Then $w$ will be accepted in the new machine $N$ if and only if $w$ is rejected in $M$, i.e., if and only if $w$ belongs to $L^c$. Formally, $N = \langle A, S, S \backslash Y, s_0, F \rangle$.

**10.48** Let $M = \langle A, S, Y, s_0, F \rangle$ and $M' = \langle A, S', Y', s'_0, F' \rangle$ be automaton over the same alphabet $A$ which accept the languages $L(M)$ and $L(M')$ over $A$, respectively. Construct an automaton $N$ over $A$ which accepts precisely $L(M) \cap L(M')$.

▌ Let $S \times S'$ be the set of states of $N$. Let $(s, s')$ be an accepting state of $N$ if $s$ and $s'$ are accepting states in $M$ and $M'$, respectively; and let $(s_0, s'_0)$ be the initial state of $N$. The next-state function of $N$, $G: (S \times S') \times A \to (S \times S')$, is defined as

$$G((s, s'), a) = (F(s, a), F'(s', a))$$

Then $N$ will accept precisely those words in $L(M) \cap L(M')$.

**10.49** Repeat Problem 10.48 except now construct an automaton $N$ over $A$ which accepts precisely $L(M) \cup L(M')$.

▌ Again, let $S \times S'$ be the set of states of $N$ and let $(s_0, s'_0)$ be the initial state of $N$. Now let $(S \times Y') \cup (Y \times S')$ be the accepting states in $N$. The next-state function $G$ is again defined by

$$G((s, s'), a) = (F(s, a), F'(s', a))$$

Then $N$ will accept precisely those words in $L(M) \cup L(M')$.

**10.50** Construct an automaton $M$ over $A = \{a, b\}$ which accepts those words from $A$ such that the number of $a$'s is even and the number of $b$'s is divisible by three.

▌ Use Problems 10.39, 10.41, and 10.48 to obtain the automaton $M$ in Fig. 10-10.

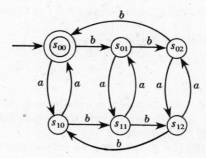

**Fig. 10-10**

**10.51** Construct an automaton $M$ over $A = \{a, b\}$ which accepts those words from $A$ such that the number of $a$'s is even or the number of $b$'s is divisible by three.

▌ By Problems 10.49 and 10.50, Fig. 10-10 is the diagram of such an automaton $M$ providing we let $s_{00}$, $s_{01}$, $s_{02}$, and $s_{10}$ be the accepting states.

**10.52** Construct an automaton $M$ over $A = \{a, b\}$ which will accept those words over $A$ where the number of $b$'s is not divisible by three.

▌ Figure 10-5 gives an automaton which accepts words where the number of $b$'s is divisible by three. Thus simply change the diagram so that $s_0$ is a rejecting state and $s_1$ and $s_2$ are accepting states to obtain the required automaton $M$.

**10.53** Find the language $L(M)$ accepted by the automaton $M$ in Fig. 10-11.

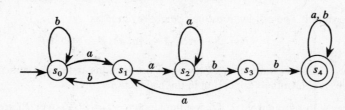

**Fig. 10-11**

▌ A word $w$ will reach the accepting state $s_4$ and stay in the accepting state if and only if $w$ contains $aabb$ as a subword. $L(M)$ consists of all such words.

**10.54**    Describe the words $w$ in the language $L$ accepted by the automaton in Fig. 10-12.

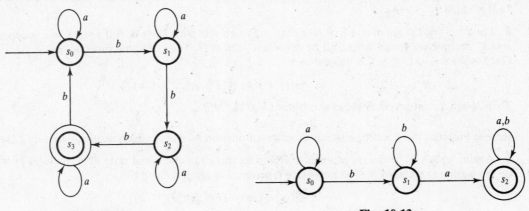

**Fig. 10-12**                    **Fig. 10-13**

▌ Each $a$ in $w$ does not change the state of the system, whereas each $b$ in $w$ changes the state of the system from $s_i$ to $s_{i+1}$ (modulo 4). Thus $w$ is accepted by $M$ if the number $n$ of $b$'s in $w$ is congruent to 3 modulo 4, i.e., where $n = 3, 7, 11, \ldots$ .

**10.55**    Describe the words $w$ in the language $L$ accepted by the automaton $M$ in Fig. 10-13.

▌ The system can reach the accepting state $s_2$ only when there exists an $a$ in $w$ which follows a $b$.

## 10.5  GRAMMARS AND LANGUAGES

**10.56**    Define a grammar.

▌ A *grammar* $G$ consists of four parts:
(1)    A finite set $V$ of elements called *variables* or *nonterminals*.
(2)    A finite set $T$ of elements called *terminals* (which is disjoint from $V$).
(3)    An element $S$ in $V$ called the *start symbol*.
(4)    A finite set $P$ of productions. A *production* is an ordered pair $(\alpha, \beta)$ usually written $\alpha \rightarrow \beta$ where $\alpha$ and $\beta$ are words in $V \cup T$. At least one of the $\alpha$'s must contain a variable.
Such a grammar $G$ is denoted by $G(V, T, S, P)$ when we want to indicate its four parts.

The following notation, unless otherwise stated or implied, will be used for our grammars. Terminals will be denoted by italic lowercase Latin letters, $a, b, c, \ldots$ , and variables will be denoted by italic capital Latin letters, $A, B, C, \ldots$ , with $S$ denoting the start variable. Also Greek letters, $\alpha, \beta, \ldots$ , will denote words in both variables and terminals. Furthermore, we will write

$$\alpha \rightarrow (\beta_1, \ldots, \beta_k)$$

for the productions $\alpha \rightarrow \beta_1, \ldots, \alpha \rightarrow \beta_k$ .

**10.57**    Give an example of a grammar $G$.

▌ Define the four parts of $G$ as follows:

$$V = \{A, B, S\}, \qquad T = \{a, b\}, \qquad \overset{1}{P = \{S \rightarrow AB}, \overset{2}{A \rightarrow Aa}, \overset{3}{B \rightarrow Bb}, \overset{4}{A \rightarrow a}, \overset{5}{B \rightarrow b}\}$$

with $S$ as the start symbol. The productions may be abbreviated as

$$P = \{S \rightarrow AB, A \rightarrow Aa, a), B \rightarrow (Bb, b)\}$$

**Remark:**   Frequently we will define a grammar $G$ by giving its productions assuming implicitly that $S$ is the start symbol and $V$ and $T$ are the variables and terminals appearing in the productions.

**10.58**    Let $G$ be a grammar with terminal set $T$. Define the language $L = L(G)$ over $T$ determined by $G$.

▌ Let $\omega$ and $\omega'$ be words in $V \cup T$. We write

$$\omega \Rightarrow \omega'$$

if $w'$ can be obtained from $w$ using one of the productions; i.e., if there exists words $\mu$ and $v$ such that $w = \mu\alpha v$ and $w' = \mu\beta v$, where $\alpha \to \beta$ is a producton. We write

$$w \Rightarrow^* w'$$

if $w'$ can be obtained from $w$ using a finite sequence of productions. The language of $G$, denoted by $L(G)$, consists of all words in the terminals that can be obtained from the start symbol $S$ by the above process, i.e.,

$$L(G) = \{w : S \Rightarrow^* w\}$$

**10.59** Consider the grammar $G$ in Problem 10.57. Show that $w = a^2 b^4$ belongs to $L(G)$, the language determined by $G$.

▌ Starting with $S$ we obtain the following sequence of substitutions:

$$S \Rightarrow AB \Rightarrow AaB \Rightarrow aaB \Rightarrow aaBb \Rightarrow aaBbb \Rightarrow aaBbbb \Rightarrow aabbbb = a^2 b^4$$

Here we used the productions 1, 2, 4, 3, 3, 3, and 5 respectively. Thus we can write $S \Rightarrow^* a^2 b^4$. Accordingly, $w = a^2 b^4$ belongs to $L(G)$.

**10.60** Describe the language $L(G)$ of the grammar $G$ in Problem 10.57.

▌ The production sequence 1, 2 ($r$ times), 4, 3 ($s$ times), 5 will yield the word $w = a^r ab^s b$ where $r$ and $s$ are nonnegative integers. On the other hand, no sequence of productions can produce an $a$ after a $b$. Accordingly,

$$L(G) = \{a^m b^n : m \text{ and } n \text{ positive}\}$$

i.e., words which begin with a string of $a$'s followed by a string of $b$'s.

**10.61** Find the language $L(G)$ generated by the grammar $G$ with variables $S$, $A$, $B$, terminals $a$, $b$ and productions $S \to aB$, $B \to b$, $B \to bA$, $A \to aB$.

▌ Observe that we can only use the first production once since the start symbol $S$ does not appear anywhere else. Also, we can only obtain a terminal word by finally using the second production. Otherwise we alternately add $a$'s and $b$'s using the third and fourth productions. In other words,

$$L(G) = \{(ab)^n = ababab \cdots ab : n \in \mathbf{N}\}$$

**10.62** Find the language $L(G)$ over $\{a, b, c\}$ generated by the grammar $G$ with productions: $S \to aSb$, $aS \to Aa$, $Aab \mapsto c$.

▌ First we must apply the first production one or more times to obtain the word $w = a^n S b^n$ where $n > 0$. To eliminate $S$, we must apply the second production to obtain the word $w' = a^m Aabb^m$ where $m = n - 1 \geq 0$. Now we can only apply the third production to finally obtain the word $w'' = a^m c b^m$ where $m \geq 0$. Accordingly,

$$L(G) = \{a^m c b^m : m \text{ nonnegative}\}$$

i.e., the same nonnegative number of $a$'s and $b$'s separated by $c$.

**10.63** Let $L$ be the set of all words in $a$ and $b$ with an even number of $a$'s. Find a grammar $G$ which will generate $L$.

▌ We claim that the grammar $G$ with the following productions will generate $L$:

$$S \to aA, \quad S \to bB, \quad B \to bB, \quad B \to aA, \quad A \to aB, \quad A \to bA, \quad A \to a, \quad B \to b$$

Observe that the sum of the $a$'s and $A$'s in any word $\alpha$ either remains the same or is increased by 2 when any production is applied to $\alpha$. Thus any word $w$ in the terminals $a$ and $b$ which is derived from $S$ must contain an even number of $a$'s. In other words $L(G) \subseteq L$. On the other hand, it is clear which productions should be used to print any word $v$ in $L$; that is, we use $S \to aA$ or $S \to bB$ according as $v$ begins with $a$ or $b$, and we use $A \to aB$ or $B \to aA$ if any subsequent letter is an $a$, and we use $A \to bA$ or $B \to bB$ if any subsequent letter is a $b$. For the last letter of $v$ we use $A \to a$ or $B \to b$. Thus $L(G) = L$.

## Types of Grammars and Languages

**10.64** Define the grammars and languages of Types 1, 2, and 3. (Otherwise, a grammar (language) is of Type 0.)

▌ These grammars are defined by the kinds of productions which are permitted (with the exception noted

below):
(1) A grammar $G$ is said to be of Type 1 if every production $\alpha \rightarrow \beta$ has the property that $\|\alpha\| \leq \|\beta\|$.
(2) A grammar $G$ is said to be of Type 2 if every production is of the form $A \rightarrow \beta$, i.e., the left side is a variable and the right side is a word in one or more symbols.
(3) A grammar $G$ is said to be of Type 3, or regular, if all the productions are of the form $A \rightarrow a$ or $A \rightarrow aB$, i.e., the left side is a single variable and the right side is either a single terminal or a terminal followed by a variable.

The above three types of grammars each allow the "trivial" production $S \rightarrow \lambda$ (where $\lambda$ is the empty sequence).

A language $L$ is said to be of Type 1, 2, or 3 according as it can be generated by a grammar of Type 1, 2 or 3, respectively. (The production $S \rightarrow \lambda$ is permitted so that the empty sequence can belong to the language.)

**10.65** Determine the type of the grammar $G$ which consists of the productions:

    (a)   $S \rightarrow aA, \ A \rightarrow aAB, \ B \rightarrow b, \ A \rightarrow a,$     (b)   $S \rightarrow aAB, \ AB \rightarrow bB, \ B \rightarrow b, \ A \rightarrow aB$

    **(a)** Since each production is of the form $A \rightarrow \alpha$, i.e., a variable is on the left, $G$ is a Type 2 grammar.
    **(b)** The length of the left side of each production does not exceed the length of the right side; hence $G$ is a Type 1 grammar.

**10.66** Determine the type of the grammar $G$ which consists of the productions:

    (a)   $S \rightarrow aAB, \ AB \rightarrow c, \ A \rightarrow b, \ B \rightarrow AB,$     (b)   $S \rightarrow aB, \ B \rightarrow bA, \ B \rightarrow b, \ B \rightarrow a, \ A \rightarrow aB, \ A \rightarrow a$

    **(a)** The production $AB \rightarrow c$ means that $G$ is a Type 0 grammar.
    **(b)** $G$ is a Type 3, or regular, grammar since each production is of the form $A \rightarrow a$ or $A \rightarrow aB$.

**10.67** Determine the type of the grammar $G$ which consists of the productions:

    (a)   $S \rightarrow aSb, \ S \rightarrow AB, \ A \rightarrow a, \ B \rightarrow b,$     (b)   $S \rightarrow aB, \ B \rightarrow AB, \ aA \rightarrow b, \ A \rightarrow b, \ B \rightarrow Aa$

    **(a)** $G$ is of Type 2 since each production has a single variable on the left.
    **(b)** The production $aA \rightarrow b$ shows that $G$ is a Type 0 grammar.

**10.68** Explain the terms: (a) context-sensitive grammar, and (b) context-free grammar.

    **(a)** A grammar $G$ is said to be *context-sensitive* if the productions are of the form

$$\alpha A \alpha' \rightarrow \alpha \beta \alpha'$$

The name "context-sensitive" comes from the fact that we can replace the variable $A$ by $\beta$ in a word only when $A$ lies between $\alpha$ and $\alpha'$.

    **(b)** A grammar $G$ is said to be *context-free* if the productions are of the form

$$A \rightarrow \beta$$

The name "context-free" comes from the fact that we can now replace the variable $A$ by $\beta$ regardless of where $A$ appears.

Note that a context-free grammar is the same as a Type 2 grammar.

A fundamental relationship between regular grammars and finite automata follows:

**Theorem 10.3:** A language $L$ can be generated by a Type 3 grammar, i.e., $L$ is regular, if and only if there exists a finite automaton $M$ which accepts $L$.

**10.69** Consider the language $L = \{a^n b^n : n > 0\}$ over $\{a, b\}$. (a) Find a context-free grammar $G$ which will generate $L$. (b) Can we find a Type 3 (regular) grammar which will generate $L$?

    **(a)** Clearly the grammar $G$ with the following productions will generate $L$:

$$S \rightarrow ab, \qquad S \rightarrow aSb$$

Note that $G$ is a context-free grammar.

    **(b)** No. By Problem 10.46, there is no finite automaton $M$ which accepts $L$ and therefore, by Theorem 10.3, $L$ cannot be generated by a Type 3 grammar.

**10.70** Find a regular grammar $G$ which generates the language $L$ which consists of all words on $a$ and $b$ with exactly one $b$, i.e.,

$$L = \{b,\ a^r b,\ ba^s,\ a^r ba^s : r > 0,\ s > 0\}$$

▮ We claim that the grammar $G$ with the following productions will generate $L$:

$$S \to (b, aA), \qquad A \to (b, aA, bB), \qquad B \to (a, aB)$$

That is, the letter $b$ can only appear once in any word $w$ derived from $S$. $G$ is regular since every production has the required form.

**10.71**  Find a regular grammar $G$ which generates the language $L$ which consists of all the words on $a$ and $b$ such that no two $a$'s appear next to each other.

▮ The grammar $G$ with the following productions will generate $G$:

$$S \to (a, b, aB, bA), \qquad A \to (bA, ab, a, b), \qquad B \to (b, bA)$$

Note $G$ is regular.

**10.72**  Find a context-free grammar $G$ which generates the language $L$ which consists of all words of the form $a^r b^s c^t$, $r, s, t > 0$, i.e., $a$'s followed by $b$'s followed by $c$'s.

▮ The context-free grammar $G$ with the following productions will generate $L$:

$$S \to ABC, \qquad A \to (a, aA), \qquad B \to (b, bB), \qquad C \to (c, cC)$$

**10.73**  Is the language $L$ in Problem 10.72 regular?

▮ Yes, since the regular grammar $G$ with the following productions also generates $L$:

$$S \to aA, \qquad A \to (aA, bB), \qquad B \to (bB, c, cC), \qquad C \to (c, cC)$$

**10.74**  Find a context-free grammar $G$ which generates the language $L$ which consists of all words on $a$ and $b$ with twice as many $a$'s as $b$'s.

▮ The context-free grammar $G$ with the following productions will generate $L$:

$$S \to (AAB, ABA, BAA), \qquad A \to (a, BAAA, ABAA, AABA, AAAB),$$
$$B \to (b, BBAA, BABA, BAAB, ABAB, AABB)$$

## Derivation Trees

**10.75**  Consider a context-free grammar $G$ with the following productions:

$$S \to aAB, \qquad A \to Bba, \qquad B \to bB, \qquad B \to c$$

The word $w = acbabc$ can be derived from $S$ as follows:

$$S \Rightarrow aAB \to a(Bba)B \Rightarrow acbaB \Rightarrow acba(bB) \Rightarrow acbabc$$

Draw the *derivation tree* $T$ of $w$.

▮ Figure 10-14 shows the steps in the construction of the derivation tree $T$. Specifically, we begin with $S$ as the root and then add branches to the tree according to the production used in the derivation of $w$. This yields the completed tree $T$ which is shown in Fig. 10-14($e$). The sequence of leaves from left to right in $T$ is the derived word $w$. Also, any nonleaf in $T$ is a variable, say $A$, and the immediate successors (children) of $A$ form a word $\alpha$ where $A \to \alpha$ is the production of $G$ used in the derivation of $w$.

**10.76**  Consider the context-free grammar $G$ with productions $S \to (a, aAS)$ and $A \to bS$. Find the derivation tree of the word $w = abaabaa$.

▮ Note first that $w$ can be derived from $S$ as follows:

$$S \Rightarrow aAS \Rightarrow a(bS)S \Rightarrow abaS \Rightarrow aba(aAS) \Rightarrow abaa(bS)S \Rightarrow abaabaS \Rightarrow abaabaa$$

Figure 10-15 shows the corresponding derivation tree.

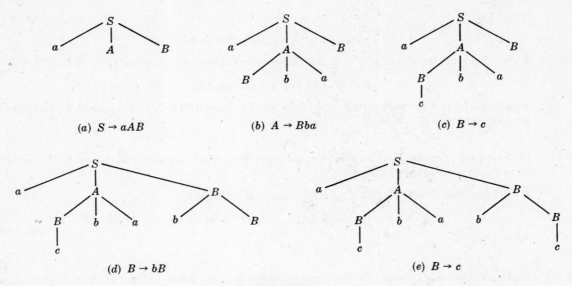

(a) $S \to aAB$

(b) $A \to Bba$

(c) $B \to c$

(d) $B \to bB$

(e) $B \to c$

**Fig. 10-14**

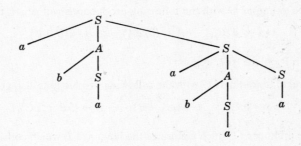

**Fig. 10-15**

**10.77** Consider the regular grammar $G$ with productions

$$S \to aA, \quad A \to aB, \quad B \to bB, \quad B \to a$$

(a) Find the derivation tree of the word $w = aaba$. (b) Describe all words $w$ in the language $L$ generated by $G$.

▌ (a) Note first that $w$ can be derived from $S$ as follows:

$$S \Rightarrow aA \Rightarrow a(aB) \Rightarrow aa(bB) \Rightarrow aaba$$

Figure 10-16 shows the corresponding derivation tree.

(b) Using the productions 1, 2, 3 ($r$ times), and 4 will derive the word $w = aab^ra$ where $r \geq 0$. No other words $w$ can be derived from $S$.

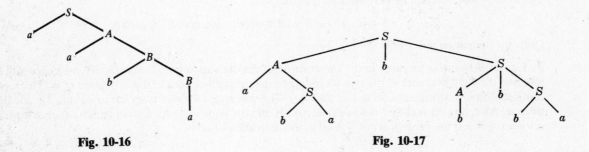

**Fig. 10-16**          **Fig. 10-17**

**10.78** Figure 10-17 is the derivation tree of a word $w$ in the language $L$ of a context-free grammar $G$. (a) Find $w$. (b) Which terminals, variables, and productions must lie in $G$?

▌ (a) The sequence of leaves from left to right yields the word $w = ababbba$.

(b) The leaves show that $a$ and $b$ must be terminals, and the internal vertices show that $S$ and $A$ must be variables with $S$ the starting variable. The children of each variable show that $S \rightarrow AbS$, $A \rightarrow aS$, $S \rightarrow ba$, and $A \rightarrow b$ must be productions.

**10.79** Figure 10-18 is the derivation tree of a word $w$ in the language $L$ of a context-free grammar $G$. (a) Find $w$. (b) Which terminals, variables, and productions must lie in $G$?

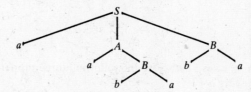

**Fig. 10-18**

▌ (a) Reading the leaves from left to right yields $w = aababa$.

(b) $G$ must contain terminals $a$ and $b$, variables $S$, $A$, and $B$, and productions $S \rightarrow aAB$, $A \rightarrow aB$, and $B \rightarrow ba$.

**10.80** Does a derivation tree exist for any word $w$ derived from the start symbol $S$ in a grammar $G$?

▌ No. Derivation trees only exist for Type 2 and 3 grammars, that is, for context-free and regular grammars.

# CHAPTER 11
# Ordered Sets and Lattices

## 11.1 ORDERED SETS

**11.1**   Define a partially ordered set.

   ❚ Suppose $R$ is a relation on a set $S$ satisfying the following three properties:
   [$O_1$]   Reflexive: $a\,R\,a$ for every $a \in S$.
   [$O_2$]   Antisymmetric: If $a\,R\,b$ and $b\,R\,a$, then $a = b$.
   [$O_3$]   Transitive: If $a\,R\,b$ and $b\,R\,c$, then $a\,R\,c$.
   Then $R$ is called a *partial order* or an *order relation,* and $S$ together with the partial order is called a *partially ordered set* or, simply, an *ordered set* or *poset.*

**11.2**   Define the usual order on the positive integers $\mathbf{N}$, and describe the usual notation for a partially ordered set.

   ❚ The most familiar order relation, called the *usual order,* is the relation $\leq$ ("less than or equal") on $\mathbf{N}$ or, more generally, on any subset of $\mathbf{R}$. For this reason, a partial order relation is usually denoted by $\preceq$; and $a \preceq b$ is read "$a$ precedes $b$". In this case, we also write:

   $$a \prec b \text{ (read "}a\text{ strictly precedes }b\text{") if } a \preceq b \text{ but } a \neq b$$

   $$a \succeq b \text{ (read "}a\text{ succeeds }b\text{") if } b \preceq a$$

   $$a \succ b \text{ (read "}a\text{ strictly succeeds }b\text{") if } b \prec a$$

   When there is no ambiguity, the symbols $\leq$, $<$, $>$, and $\geq$ are frequently used instead of $\preceq$, $\prec$, $\succ$, and $\succeq$, respectively.

**11.3**   Let $\mathscr{S}$ be any collection of sets. Is the relation of set inclusion $\subseteq$ a partial order on $\mathscr{S}$?

   ❚ Yes, since set inclusion is reflexive, antisymmetric, and transitive. That is, for any sets $A$, $B$, $C$ in $\mathscr{S}$, we have: (i) $A \subseteq A$. (ii) If $A \subseteq B$ and $B \subseteq A$, then $A = B$. (iii) If $A \subseteq B$ and $B \subseteq C$, then $A \subseteq C$.

**11.4**   Consider the positive integers $\mathbf{N}$. We say "$a$ divides $b$", written $a \mid b$, if there is a $c \in \mathbf{N}$ such that $ac = b$. For example, $2 \mid 4$, $3 \mid 12$, $7 \mid 21$, and so on. Show that divisibility is a partial ordering of $\mathbf{N}$, that is, show that:
   **(a)** $a \mid a$; **(b)** if $a \mid b$ and $b \mid a$, then $a = b$; and **(c)** if $a \mid b$ and $b \mid c$, then $a \mid c$.

   ❚ **(a)**   Since $a \cdot 1 = a$, we have $a \mid a$.
   **(b)**   Suppose $a \mid b$ and $b \mid a$, say $b = ra$ and $a = sb$. Then $b = rsb$ and hence $rs = 1$. Since $r$ and $s$ are positive integers, $r = 1$ and $s = 1$. Accordingly, $a = b$.
   **(c)**   Suppose $a \mid b$ and $b \mid c$, say $b = ra$ and $c = sb$. Then $c = sra$ and hence $a \mid c$.

**11.5**   Consider the relation of divisibility on the set $\mathbf{Z}$ of integers. **(a)** Is this relation a partial ordering of $\mathbf{Z}$? **(b)** If not, why doesn't the proof in Problem 11.4 carry over to $\mathbf{Z}$?

   ❚ **(a)**   No, for example, $2 \mid -2$ and $-2 \mid 2$ but $2 \neq -2$, that is the relation is not antisymmetric.
   **(b)**   If $rs = 1$, then $r$ and $s$ as integers need not be 1; they could both be $-1$.

**11.6**   Consider the set $\mathbf{Z}$ of integers. Define $a\,R\,b$ by $b = a^r$ for some positive integer $r$. Show that $R$ is a partial order on $\mathbf{Z}$, that is, show that $R$ is: **(a)** reflexive, **(b)** antisymmetric, and **(c)** transitive.

   ❚ **(a)**   $R$ is reflexive since $a = a^1$.
   **(b)**   Suppose $a\,R\,b$ and $b\,R\,a$, say $b = a^r$ and $a = b^s$. Then $a = (a^r)^s = a^{rs}$. There are three possibilities: (i) $rs = 1$, (ii) $a = 1$, and (iii) $a = -1$. If $rs = 1$, then $r = 1$ and $s = 1$ and so $a = b$. If $a = 1$, then $b = 1^r = 1 = a$, and, similarly, if $b = 1$, then $a = 1$. Lastly, if $a = -1$, then $b = -1$ (since $b \neq 1$) and so $a = b$. In all three cases, $a = b$. Thus $R$ is antisymmetric.
   **(c)**   Suppose $a\,R\,b$ and $b\,R\,c$, say $b = a^r$ and $c = b^s$. Then $c = (a^r)^s = a^{rs}$ and hence $a\,R\,c$. Hence $R$ is transitive.

**11.7**   Let $\preceq$ be a partial ordering of a set $S$. Define the dual order on $S$. How is the dual order related to the inverse of the relation $\preceq$?

▮ The relation $\succeq$, i.e., $a$ succeeds $b$, is also a partial ordering of $S$, called the *dual order*. Note $a \succeq b$ if and only if $b \preceq a$; hence $\succeq$ is the inverse of the relation $\preceq$, that is, $\succeq = \preceq^{-1}$.

**11.8** Describe the dual (inverse) order of the following relations: (*a*) set inclusion $\subseteq$, (*b*) divisibility on **N**.

▮ (*a*) $A \supseteq B$ if and only if $B \subseteq A$, that is, "$B$ contains $A$" is the dual of "$A$ is a subset of $B$".
   (*b*) Note $a$ divides $b$ if and only if $b$ is a multiple of $a$. Thus "is a multiple of" is the inverse of "divides".

**11.9** Let $A$ be a subset of an ordered set $S$. What is meant by the induced order on $A$? What is an ordered subset of $S$?

▮ Suppose $a, b \in A$. Let $a \preceq b$ as elements of $A$ whenever $a \preceq b$ as elements of $S$. This defines a partial order on $A$, called the *induced order* on $A$. The subset $A$ with the induced order is called an *ordered subset* of $S$. Unless otherwise stated or implied, any subset of $S$ will be treated as an ordered subset of $S$.

**11.10** Suppose **N** is ordered by divisibility. Determine whether or not $A$ is an ordered subset of **N** where: (*a*) $A = \{2, 3, 4, 5, 6\}$ with the usual order, and (*b*) $A = \{2, 4, 8, 32\}$ with the usual order.

▮ (*a*) No, since the orderings are different, e.g., 2 precedes 3 under the usual order but not under divisibility.
   (*b*) Yes. Here the usual order and divisibility coincide on $A$, that is, for elements $a, b \in A$, $a \leq b$ if and only if $a \mid b$.

**11.11** Some texts define a partial order on a set $S$ to be a relation $R$ which satisfies the following three properties:
[$\mathbf{O_1^*}$]  Irreflexive: $a \not{R} a$ for every $a \in S$.
[$\mathbf{O_2^*}$]  Asymmetric: If $a R b$, then $b \not{R} a$.
[$\mathbf{O_3^*}$]  Transitive: If $a R b$ and $b R c$, then $a R c$.
Why the different definition from that given in Problem 11.1?

▮ Let $\Delta$ denote the diagonal or equality relation on $S$, that is, $\Delta = \{(a, a): a \in S\}$. If $R$ satisfies [$\mathbf{O_1^*}$], [$\mathbf{O_2^*}$], and [$\mathbf{O_3^*}$], then $R \cup \Delta$ satisfies the original axioms [$\mathbf{O_1}$], [$\mathbf{O_2}$], and [$\mathbf{O_3}$] of a partial order. Conversely, if $R'$ satisfies [$\mathbf{O_1}$], [$\mathbf{O_2}$], and [$\mathbf{O_3}$], then $R' \backslash \Delta$ satisfies [$\mathbf{O_1^*}$], [$\mathbf{O_2^*}$], and [$\mathbf{O_3^*}$]. Thus both definitions are essentially the same.
  In other words, $\leq$ satisfies [$\mathbf{O_1}$], [$\mathbf{O_2}$], and [$\mathbf{O_3}$] if and only if $<$ satisfies [$\mathbf{O_1^*}$], [$\mathbf{O_2^*}$], and [$\mathbf{O_3^*}$]. Thus we will frequently define a partial order by means of $<$ rather than $\leq$.

**11.12** Give examples of relations which satisfy [$\mathbf{O_1^*}$], [$\mathbf{O_2^*}$], and [$\mathbf{O_3^*}$].

▮ One such familiar relation is $>$ ("greater than") on **N** or any subset of **R**. Another such relation is $\subset$ ("proper subset") on any collection of sets.

## Comparability, Linearly Ordered Sets

**11.13** What is meant when elements $a$ and $b$ in an ordered set $S$ are said to be comparable? noncomparable? Give examples.

▮ The elements $a$ and $b$ are *comparable* if one of them precedes the other, that is, if $a \preceq b$ or $b \preceq a$. Thus $a$ and $b$ are *noncomparable* if neither $a \preceq b$ nor $b \preceq a$. For example, suppose **N** is ordered by divisibility. Then 21 and 7 are comparable since $7 \mid 21$, but 3 and 5 are noncomparable since neither $3 \mid 5$ nor $5 \mid 3$.

**11.14** Define a linearly ordered set, and give an example.

▮ An ordered set $S$ is said to be *linearly* or *totally* ordered, and $S$ is called a *chain*, if every pair of elements in $S$ are comparable. For example, the positive integers **N** with the usual order $\leq$ is linearly ordered.

**11.15** Suppose $\mathbf{N} = \{1, 2, 3, \ldots\}$ is ordered by divisibility. State whether each of the following subsets of **N** are linearly (totally) ordered.

|   |   |   |   |   |   |
|---|---|---|---|---|---|
| (*a*) | $\{24, 2, 6\}$ | (*c*) | $\mathbf{N} = \{1, 2, 3, \ldots\}$ | (*e*) | $\{7\}$ |
| (*b*) | $\{3, 15, 5\}$ | (*d*) | $\{2, 8, 32, 4\}$ | (*f*) | $\{15, 5, 30\}$ |

▮ (*a*) Since 2 divides 6 which divides 24, the set is linearly ordered.
   (*b*) Since 3 and 5 are not comparable, the set is not linearly ordered.
   (*c*) Since 2 and 3 are not comparable, the set is not linearly ordered.
   (*d*) This set is linearly ordered since $2 < 4 < 8 < 32$.
   (*e*) Any set consisting of one element is linearly ordered.
   (*f*) Since 5 divides 15 which divides 30, the set is linearly ordered.

**11.16**  Consider **N** with the usual order ≤. Find all the linearly ordered subsets of **N**.

▌  Since **N** itself is linearly ordered under ≤, every subset of **N** will also be linearly ordered.

**11.17**  Suppose $A = \{2, 3, 6, 8, 9, 18\}$ is ordered by divisibility. Identify the noncomparable pairs of elements of $A$.

▌  The noncomparable pairs are those in which one element does not precede or succeed the other. Thus

$$\{2, 3\}, \quad \{2, 9\}, \quad \{3, 8\}, \quad \{6, 8\}, \quad \{6, 9\}, \quad \{8, 9\}, \quad \{8, 18\}$$

are the noncomparable pairs of elements since, for instance, neither $2 \mid 3$ nor $3 \mid 2$.

**11.18**  Consider the ordered set $A$ in Problem 11.17. Identify the linearly ordered subsets of $A$ with three or more elements.

▌  A linearly ordered subset is one in which every pair of elements is comparable. Of course, any set with one element is linearly ordered and any pair of comparable elements is linearly ordered. The linearly ordered subsets of $A$ with three or more elements are $\{2, 6, 18\}, \{3, 6, 18\}, \{3, 9, 18\}$. Note that the set $\{2, 6, 8\}$ is not linearly ordered since the elements 6 and 8 are not comparable.

**11.19**  Consider the set **Z** of integers under the partial order of Problem 11.6. Is each of the following subsets linearly ordered?

$$(a) \quad A = \{2, 4, 64\}, \quad (b) \quad B = \{3, 9, 18\}, \quad (c) \quad \{8\}$$

▌  A linearly ordered set is one in which every pair of elements are comparable.
(a)  Yes, since $4 = 2^2$, $64 = 4^3$, and $64 = 2^6$.
(b)  No, since the elements 9 and 18 are not comparable.
(c)  Yes, any set with one element is linearly ordered.

**11.20**  Repeat Problem 11.19 for the subsets

$$(a) \quad D = \{1, 5, 25\}, \quad (b) \quad E = \{3, 27, 729\}, \quad (c) \quad F = \{2, 8, 32\}$$

▌  (a)  No. The elements 1 and 5 are noncomparable.
(b)  Yes, since $27 = 3^3$, $729 = 27^2$, and $729 = 3^6$.
(c)  No. The elements 8 and 32 are not comparable.

## Product Sets and Order

**11.21**  Suppose $S$ and $T$ are ordered sets. Let $R$ be the relation on the product set $S \times T$ defined by $(a, b) \, R \, (a', b')$ whenever $a \leq a'$ and $b \leq b'$. Show that $R$ is a partial order on $S \times T$, that is, show that $R$ is: (a) reflexive, (b) antisymmetric, and (c) transitive. This ordering of $S \times T$ is called the *product order*.

▌  (a)  Since $a \leq a$ and $b \leq b$, we have $(a, b) \, R \, (a, b)$. Hence $R$ is reflexive.
(b)  Suppose $(a, b) \, R \, (a', b')$ and $(a', b') \, R \, (a, b)$. Then $a \leq a'$, $a' \leq a$, $b \leq b'$, and $b' \leq b$. Hence $a = a'$ and $b = b'$, and so $(a, b) = (a', b')$. Thus $R$ is antisymmetric.
(c)  Suppose $(a, b) \, R \, (a', b')$ and $(a', b') \, R \, (a'', b'')$. Then $a \leq a'$ and $a' \leq a''$ and so $a \leq a''$. Similarly, $b \leq b''$. Thus $(a, b) \, R \, (a'', b'')$. Hence $R$ is transitive.

**11.22**  Suppose $\mathbf{N} \times \mathbf{N}$ is given the product order (Problem 11.21) where **N** has usual order ≤. Insert the correct symbol, $<$, $>$, or ∥ (not comparable), between each of the following pairs of elements of $\mathbf{N} \times \mathbf{N}$:

$$(a) \quad (5, 7) \underline{\quad} (7, 1) \qquad (c) \quad (5, 5) \underline{\quad} (4, 8) \qquad (e) \quad (7, 9) \underline{\quad} (4, 1)$$
$$(b) \quad (4, 6) \underline{\quad} (4, 2) \qquad (d) \quad (1, 3) \underline{\quad} (1, 7) \qquad (f) \quad (7, 9) \underline{\quad} (8, 2)$$

▌  Here $(a, b) \leq (a', b')$ provided $a \leq a'$ and $b \leq b'$. Hence $(a, b) < (a', b')$ if $a < a'$ and $b \leq b'$ or if $a \leq a'$ and $b < b'$.
(a)  ∥ since $5 < 7$ but $7 > 1$ .
(b)  $>$ since $4 \geq 4$ and $6 > 2$.
(c)  ∥ since $5 > 4$ and $5 < 8$.
(d)  $<$ since $1 \leq 1$ and $3 < 7$.
(e)  $>$ since $7 > 4$ and $9 > 1$.
(f)  ∥ since $7 < 8$ and $9 > 2$.

**11.23**  Suppose the English alphabet $A = \{a, b, c, \ldots, y, z\}$ is given the *usual* (alphabetical) *order,* and suppose $A \times A = A^2$ is given the product order (Problem 11.21). Insert the correct symbol, $<$, $>$, or ∥ (not comparable), between each of the following two-letter words (viewed as elements in $A^2$):

$$(a)\quad cx \_\_ at \qquad (c)\quad cx \_\_ cz \qquad (e)\quad cx \_\_ dx$$
$$(b)\quad cx \_\_ by \qquad (d)\quad cx \_\_ rs \qquad (f)\quad cx \_\_ cs$$

▌ (a) $>$ since $c > a$ and $x > t$.     (c) $<$ since $c \le c$ and $x < z$.     (e) $<$ since $c < d$ and $x \le x$.

   (b) $\parallel$ since $c > b$ but $x < y$.     (d) $\parallel$ since $c < r$ but $x > s$.     (f) $>$ since $c \ge c$ and $x > s$.

**11.24** Suppose $S$ and $T$ are linearly ordered. Define the *lexicographical*, or *dictionary*, order on $S \times T$ and, in particular (for $T = S^{n-1}$), on $S^n$.

▌ Here $S \times T$ is ordered as follows:

$$(a, b) < (a', b') \text{ if } a < a' \text{ or if } a = a' \text{ and } b < b' \qquad (1)$$

For $S \times S \times \cdots \times S$, $n =$ fold application of (1) yields

$$(a_1, \ldots, a_n) < (a_1', \ldots, a_n') \text{ if } a_i = a_i' \text{ for } i = 1, 2, \ldots, k - 1 \text{ and } a_k < a_k' \qquad (2)$$

Note that the lexicographical order is linear.

**11.25** Repeat Problem 11.23 using the lexicographical ordering of $A \times A = A^2$.

▌ (a) $>$ since $c > a$.     (c) $<$ since $c = c$ and $x < z$.     (e) $<$ since $c < d$.

   (b) $>$ since $c > b$.     (d) $<$ since $c < r$.     (f) $>$ since $c = c$ and $x > s$.

**11.26** Let $A$ be a nonempty set and let $A^*$ denote all the words (finite sequences) $w = a_1 a_2 \cdots a_n$ over $A$. The length of $w$, written $|w|$, is the number $n$ of elements in $w$. Suppose $A$ is linearly ordered. Define the free semigroup order on $A^*$.

▌ Let $w$ and $w'$ be words over $A$. Then $w < w'$ if $|w| < |w'|$ or if $|w| = |w'|$ but $w$ precedes $w'$ lexicographically. This defines the *free semigroup* order on $A^*$. Note this is also a linear ordering of $A^*$.

**11.27** Suppose the English alphabet $A = \{a, b, c, \ldots, y, z\}$ is given the usual (alphabetical) order and suppose $A^*$ is given the free semigroup order (Problem 11.26). Place the following elements of $A^*$ in their appropriate order, that is, sort the following elements:

went, forget, to, medicine, me, toast, melt, for, we, arm

▌ First order the elements by length and then order them lexicographically:

me, to, we, arm, for, melt, went, toast, forget, medicine

**11.28** Repeat Problem 11.27 using the usual (alphabetical) ordering of $A^*$.

▌ The usual ordering yields:

arm, for, forget, me, medicine, melt, to, toast, we, went

**11.29** Suppose $\mathbf{N} = \{1, 2, 3, \ldots\}$ and $A = \{a, b, c, \ldots, z\}$ are ordered with the usual orders. Consider the following subset of $\mathbf{N} \times A$:

$$S = \{(2, a), (1, c), (2, c), (4, b), (4, z), (3, b)\}$$

Assuming $\mathbf{N} \times A$ is ordered lexicographically, place the elements of $S$ in the appropriate order.

▌ In a lexicographic order, we order by the first element unless there is a tie, in which case we order by the second element. Thus the appropriate order for these elements is

$$(1, c), \quad (2, a), \quad (2, c), \quad (3, b), \quad (4, b), \quad (4, z)$$

**11.30** Repeat Problem 11.29 using the product order (Problem 11.21) on $\mathbf{N} \times A$.

▌ Although $\mathbf{N}$ and $A$ are linearly ordered, the product set $\mathbf{N} \times A$ and the set $S$ are not linearly ordered. Two maximal linearly ordered subsets of $S$ follow:

$$\{(1, c), (2, c), (4, z)\} \quad \text{and} \quad \{(2, a), (3, b), (4, b), (4, z)\}$$

## 11.2 DIAGRAMS OF PARTIALLY ORDERED SETS

**11.31**   Define the terms "immediate predecessor" and "immediate successor".

▮   Let $S$ be a partially ordered set. We say $a$ is an *immediate predecessor* of $b$ in $S$, or $b$ is an *immediate successor* of $a$ in $S$, written

$$a \ll b$$

if $a < b$ but no element of $S$ lies between $a$ and $b$, i.e., there exists no element $c$ in $S$ such that $a < c < b$.

**11.32**   Let $S = \{2, 3, 4, 5, 12, 16, 24, 36, 48\}$ be ordered by divisibility. Find: (*a*) the predecessors and immediate predecessors of 12, and (*b*) the successors and immediate successors of 12.

▮   (*a*)   The numbers 2, 3, and 4 all precede 12. Note 2 is not an immediate predecessor of 12 since $2 \mid 4 \mid 12$. However 3 and 4 are immediate predecessors of 12 since no elements in $S$ lie between 3 and 12 or between 4 and 12.

   (*b*)   The numbers 24, 36, and 48 succeed 12 but only 24 and 36 are immediate successors of 12. (Recall that 16 does not succeed 12 since 12 does not divide 16.) Note that for partially ordered sets immediate predecessors and immediate successors need not be unique.

**11.33**   Show why each element of a linearly ordered set can have at most one immediate predecessor.

▮   Consider elements $a$, $b$, and $c$ of a linearly ordered set $S$. Let $a$ and $b$ both precede $c$. Suppose that $a$ and $b$ are both immediate predecessors of $c$. Since $S$ is linearly ordered, any pair of elements of $S$ are comparable. Thus, either $a < b$ or $b < a$. Without loss of generality, assume $a < b$. Then the element $b$ lies between $a$ and $c$ and so we arrive at a contradiction. Hence $a$ and $b$ cannot both be immediate predecessors of $c$.

**11.34**   Describe the diagram of a partially ordered set $S$.

▮   The diagram of a partially ordered set $S$ is the directed graph whose vertices are the elements of $S$ and there is an edge from $a$ to $b$ whenever $a \ll b$ in $S$. (Instead of drawing an arrow from $a$ to $b$, we sometimes place $b$ higher than $a$ and draw a line between them. It is then understood that movement upwards indicates succession.) In the diagram thus created, there is a directed path from a vertex $x$ to a vertex $y$ if and only if $x < y$. Also, there can be no (directed) cycles in the diagram of $S$ since the order relation is antisymmetric. Observe that the diagram need not be connected.

**11.35**   Let $A = \{1, 2, 3, 4, 6, 8, 9, 12, 18, 24\}$ be ordered by divisibility. Draw the diagram of $A$.

▮   The diagram of $A$ is shown in Fig. 11-1. In contrast to a rooted tree, the direction of a line in a diagram of a poset is always upward.

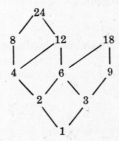

**Fig. 11-1**

**11.36**   Consider the set $B = \{a, b, c\}$ and the set $P$ which is the set of all subsets (the power set) of $B$. Draw the diagram for the elements of $P$ under the partial order of set inclusion.

▮   The elements of $P$ are

$$\varnothing, \{a\}, \{b\}, \{c\}, \{a, b\}, \{a, c\} \ \{b, c\}, \{a, b, c\}$$

and the diagram for this partially ordered set is shown in Fig. 11-2.

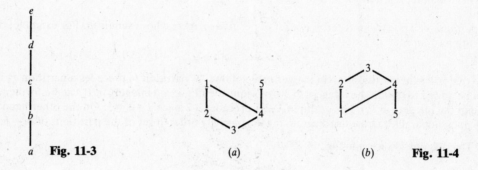

**Fig. 11-2**

**11.37** Let $B = \{a, b, c, d, e\}$ be ordered in the usual way (alphabetically) for letters. Draw the diagram of $B$. What do you notice about this diagram?

▮ The diagram of $B$ is given in Fig. 11-3. This diagram turns out to be a single path from $a$ to $e$ since $B$ is linearly ordered by the given relation.

**Fig. 11-3**

(a)

(b) **Fig. 11-4**

**11.38** Consider the partially ordered set $D = \{1, 2, 3, 4, 5\}$ which is ordered as shown in Fig. 11-4(a). Draw the diagram for the inverse order on $D$.

▮ The diagram of the inverse order is simply the original diagram with the direction of the edges reversed. The inverse order is shown in Fig. 11-4(b).

**11.39** Prerequisites in college courses are a familiar partial ordering of available classes. We say that $A \preceq B$ if successful completion of course $A$ is required for the successful completion of course $B$. (This particular phrasing allows the relation to be reflexive.) Consider the prerequisites given below for Mathematics classes and draw the diagram for the partial ordering of these classes.

| Class | Prerequisites |
|---|---|
| Math 101 | None |
| Math 201 | Math 101 |
| Math 250 | Math 101 |
| Math 251 | Math 250 |
| Math 340 | Math 201 |
| Math 341 | Math 340 |
| Math 450 | Math 201, Math 250 |
| Math 500 | Math 450, Math 251 |

▮ The diagram for the partial order of classes is shown in Fig. 11-5.

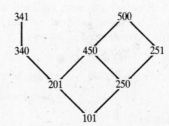

**Fig. 11-5**

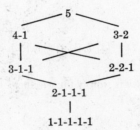

**Fig. 11-6**

**11.40** Let $V = \{a, b, c, d, e\}$ be ordered by the diagram in Fig. 11-6. Insert the correct symbol, $<$, $>$, or $\|$ (not comparable), between each of the following pairs of elements:

$$(a)\quad a\_e, \qquad (b)\quad c\_b, \qquad (c)\quad b\_d, \qquad (d)\quad a\_d$$

   (a) There is a path from $a$ to $e$ (either $a, b, e$ or $a, c, e$); hence $a < e$.
   (b) There is no path from $c$ to $b$ or $b$ to $c$ (recall that all edges point upwards); hence $c \| b$.
   (c) There is a path from $d$ to $b$; hence $b > d$.
   (d) Neither $a < d$ nor $d > a$; hence $a \| b$.

**11.41** A *partition* of a positive integer $m$ is a set of positive integers whose sum is $m$. For example, there are 7 partitions of $m = 5$:

$$5, \quad 3\text{-}2, \quad 2\text{-}2\text{-}1, \quad 1\text{-}1\text{-}1\text{-}1\text{-}1, \quad 4\text{-}1, \quad 3\text{-}1\text{-}1, \quad 2\text{-}1\text{-}1\text{-}1$$

We can order the partitions of an integer $m$ as follows. A partition $P_1$ precedes a partition $P_2$ if any integers in $P_1$ can be added to obtain the integers in $P_2$ (or, equivalently, if the integers in $P_2$ can be further subdivided to obtain the integers in $P_1$). For example, 2-2-1 precedes 3-2 since $2 + 1 = 3$. On the other hand, 3-1-1 and 2-2-1 are not comparable. Draw the diagram for the partially ordered set of the partitions of $m = 5$.

   The diagram is shown in Fig. 11-7.

```
                5
        4-1           3-2
         |    ✕        |
       3-1-1         2-2-1
              2-1-1-1
                 |
             1-1-1-1-1         Fig. 11-7
```

### Consistent Enumerations

**11.42** Define a consistent enumeration of a finite partially ordered set $S$.

   Frequently positive integers are assigned to the elements of a finite partially ordered set $S$ in such a way that the order in $S$ is preserved in the usual order on the integers. That is, we seek a one-to-one function $f: S \to \mathbf{N}$, or frequently $f: S \to \{1, 2, \ldots, n\}$ when $S$ has $n$ elements, such that if $a < b$ then $f(a) < f(b)$. Such a function is called a *consistent enumeration* of $S$. (That such an enumeration can always be found is the content of the following theorem.)

**Theorem 11.1:** There exists a consistent enumeration for any finite poset $S$.

**11.43** Prove Theorem 11.1.

   The proof is by induction on the number of elements in $S$. If $S = \{s\}$ has only one element, then obviously $f: S \to \mathbf{N}$, defined by $f(s) = 1$, is a consistent enumeration of $S$. Now suppose $S$ has $n > 1$ elements and the theorem holds for posets with less than $n$ elements. Suppose $b \in S$, and consider the subset $T = S \backslash \{b\}$ of $S$. Then $T$ has $n - 1$ elements and hence, by induction, $T$ admits a consistent enumeration; say, $g: T \to \mathbf{N}$. Then $h: T \to \mathbf{N}$, defined by $h(x) = 2g(x)$, is also a consistent enumeration. (Prove!) Note that the image of $h$ only contains even numbers. Let $f: S \to \mathbf{N}$ be defined as follows:

$$f(x) = \begin{cases} h(x) & x \neq b \\ h(a) + 1 & x = b \text{ and } a \ll b \\ 1 & x = b \text{ and no element precedes } b \end{cases}$$

Then $f$ is a consistent enumeration of $S$.

**11.44**  Find two consistent enumerations for the partially ordered set $S$ in Fig. 11-8.

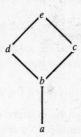

**Fig. 11-8**

▌ A consistent enumeration assigns integers to each element in the poset such that the order of the poset is preserved in the order of the integers. Two possibilities follow:

$$f(a) = 1, \qquad f(b) = 2, \qquad f(c) = 3, \qquad f(d) = 4, \qquad f(e) = 5$$
$$f(a) = 1, \qquad f(b) = 2, \qquad f(c) = 4, \qquad f(d) = 3, \qquad f(e) = 5$$

We emphasize that we usually cannot recreate the original partial order from a given consistent enumeration.

**11.45**  Let $S = \{a, b, c, d, e\}$ be ordered as in Fig. 11-9. Find all consistent enumerations of $S$ into $\{1, 2, 3, 4, 5\}$.

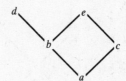

**Fig. 11-9**

▌ There are five possible enumerations. These are

| $a$ | $b$ | $c$ | $d$ | $e$ |
|-----|-----|-----|-----|-----|
| 1 | 2 | 3 | 4 | 5 |
| 1 | 3 | 2 | 4 | 5 |
| 1 | 2 | 3 | 5 | 4 |
| 1 | 3 | 2 | 5 | 4 |
| 1 | 2 | 4 | 3 | 5 |

**11.46**  Suppose the following are three consistent enumerations of an ordered set $A = \{a, b, c, d\}$:

| $a$ | $b$ | $c$ | $d$ |
|-----|-----|-----|-----|
| 1 | 2 | 3 | 4 |
| 1 | 3 | 2 | 4 |
| 1 | 4 | 2 | 3 |

Assuming the diagram $D$ of $A$ is connected, draw $D$.

▌ The partial order defined by these enumerations is shown in Fig. 11-10.

**Fig. 11-10**

## Maximal and Minimal Elements

**11.47**  Define the maximal and minimal elements of a partially ordered set $S$.

▌ An element $a$ in $S$ is said to be *maximal* if no other element succeeds $a$, i.e., if $a \leq x$ implies $a = x$.

Analogously, an element $b$ in a poset $S$ is said to be *minimal* if no other element precedes $b$, i.e., if $y \leq b$ implies $y = b$. There can be more than one maximal or more than one minimal element.

**11.48**    Let $S = \{2, 4, 6, 12, 20\}$ be ordered by divisibility. Find the maximal and minimal elements of $S$.

▮    Maximal elements are those which have no succeeding elements. Hence 12 and 20 are the maximal elements of $S$. Minimal elements are those which have no preceding elements. Hence the only minimal element is 2.

**11.49**    Let $T = \{2, 3, 4, 16\}$ be ordered by divisibility. Find the maximal and minimal elements of $T$.

▮    The maximal elements are 3 and 16, and the minimal elements are 2 and 3. Notice that 3 is both a maximal and minimal element. This is because 3 is not comparable with any other element in $T$.

**11.50**    Find the maximal and minimal elements of the set $P = \{2, 3, 5, 7, 11, 13, \ldots\}$ of prime numbers ordered by divisibility.

▮    Since each prime number is divisible only by itself and 1 and since 1 does not belong to $P$, any two numbers in the infinite set $P$ are noncomparable. Hence, every element of $P$ is both a maximal and minimal element.

**11.51**    Find the maximal and minimal elements of the partially ordered set $B$ diagrammed in Fig. 11-11.

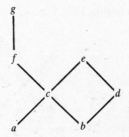

**Fig. 11-11**

▮    No element strictly precedes $a$ or $b$; hence $a$ and $b$ are the minimal elements of $B$. No element strictly succeeds $e$ and $g$; hence $e$ and $g$ are the maximal elements of $B$.

**11.52**    Suppose $S$ is a linearly ordered set. Show that $S$ has at most one maximal element.

▮    Assume that $a$ and $b$ are distinct maximal elements of $S$. Since all elements of $S$ are comparable, either $a < b$ or $b < a$. But this implies that $a = b$ by the definition of a maximal element; hence we contradict the assumption that $a$ and $b$ are distinct.

**11.53**    Suppose $F = \{a, b, c, d, e\}$ is ordered as in Fig. 11-12. Find all the subsets of $F$ in which the element $c$ is a minimal element.

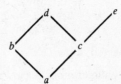

**Fig. 11-12**

▮    The subsets of $F$ which contain $c$ but do not contain any elements which precede $c$ are those subsets which do not contain the element $a$. Hence

$$\{c\}, \quad \{c, b\}, \quad \{c, d\}, \quad \{c, e\}, \quad \{c, b, d\}, \quad \{c, b, e\}, \quad \{c, d, e\}, \quad \{c, b, d, e\}$$

are the subsets of $F$ in which $c$ is a minimal element.

**11.54**    Repeat Problem 11.53 with $c$ a maximal element.

▮    The subsets of $F$ which contain $c$ but do not contain any elements which succeed $c$ are those subsets which do not contain the elements $d$ and $e$. Hence $\{c\}, \{c, a\}, \{c, b\}, \{c, a, b\}$ are the subsets of $F$ in which $c$ is a maximal element.

**11.55** How are minimal and maximal elements related to consistent enumerations?

   ❚ Suppose $S$ has $n$ elements and $f: S \rightarrow \{1, 2, \ldots, n\}$ is a consistent enumeration. If $f(a) = 1$, then $a$ must be a minimal element of $S$ and, if $f(b) = n$, then $b$ must be a maximal element of $S$.

**11.56** Suppose a student wants to take all eight mathematics courses in Problem 11.39, but only one per semester.
   **(a)** Which choice or choices does she have for her first and for her last (eighth) semester?
   **(b)** Suppose she wants to take Math 250 in her first year (first or second semester) and Math 340 in her senior year (seventh or eighth semester). Find all the ways that she can take the eight courses.

   ❚ **(a)** By Fig. 11-5, Math 101 is the only minimal element and hence must be taken in the first semester, and Math 341 and 500 are the maximal elements and hence one of them must be taken in the last semester.
   **(b)** Math 250 is not a minimal element and hence must be taken in the second semester, and Math 340 is not a maximal element so it must be taken in the seventh semester and Math 341 in the eighth semester. Also Math 500 must be taken in the sixth semester. The following give the three possible ways to take the eight courses:

$$[101, 250, 251, 201, 450, 500, 340, 341]$$
$$[101, 250, 201, 251, 450, 500, 340, 341]$$
$$[101, 250, 201, 450, 251, 500, 340, 341]$$

## 11.3 SUPREMUM AND INFIMUM

**11.57** Let $A$ be a subset of a partially ordered set $S$. Define: **(a)** an upper bound and the supremum of $A$, and **(b)** a lower bound and the infimum of $A$. **(c)** What does it mean to say that $A$ is bounded?

   ❚ **(a)** An element $M$ in $S$ is called an *upper bound* of $A$ if $M$ succeeds every element of $A$, i.e., $M$ is an upper bound of $A$ if, for every $x$ in $A$, we have

$$x \leq M$$

If an upper bound of $A$ precedes every other upper bound of $A$, then it is called the *least upper bound* or *supremum* of $A$ and is denoted by

$$\sup{(A)}$$

   **(b)** Similarly, an element $m$ in $S$ is called a *lower bound of* $A$ if $m$ precedes every element of $A$, i.e., $m$ is a lower bound of $A$ if, for every $x$ in $A$, we have

$$m \leq x$$

If a lower bound of $A$ succeeds every other lower bound of $A$, then it is called the *greatest lower bound* or *infimum* of $A$ and is denoted by

$$\inf{(A)}$$

     The sup $(A)$ and the inf $(A)$ are each unique if they exist.
   **(c)** If $A$ has an upper bound we say $A$ is *bounded above,* and if $A$ has a lower bound, we say $A$ is *bounded below.* In particular, $A$ is *bounded* if it has an upper and lower bound.

**11.58** Let $V = \{a, b, c, d, e, f, g\}$ be ordered as shown in Fig. 11-13 and let $X = \{c, d, e\}$. Find the upper and lower bounds of $X$.

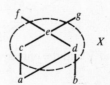

**Fig. 11-13**

   ❚ The elements $e$, $f$, and $g$ succeed every element of $X$; hence $e$, $f$, and $g$ are the upper bounds of $X$. The element $a$ precedes every element of $X$; hence it is the lower bound of $X$. Note that $b$ is not a lower bound since $b$ does not precede $c$; $b$ and $c$ are not comparable.

**11.59**  Find the supremum and infimum of $X$ in Problem 11.58.

▌ Since $e$ precedes both $f$ and $g$, we have $e = \sup(X)$. Likewise, since $a$ precedes (trivially) every lower bound of $X$, we have $a = \inf(X)$. Note that $\sup(X)$ belongs to $X$ but $\inf(X)$ does not belong to $X$.

**11.60**  Let $W = \{a, b, c, d, e, f\}$ be ordered as shown in Fig. 11-14 and let $Y = \{b, c, d\}$. Find the upper and lower bounds of $Y$.

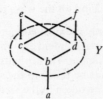

**Fig. 11-14**

▌ The elements $e$ and $f$ succeed every element in $Y$; hence $e$ and $f$ are the upper bounds of $Y$. The elements $a$ and $b$ precede every element in $Y$; hence $a$ and $b$ are the lower bounds of $Y$.

**11.61**  Find the supremum and infimum of $Y$ in Problem 11.60.

▌ Since the two upper bounds of $Y$, $e$ and $f$, are not comparable, the $\sup(X)$ does not exist. Recall that the supremum must precede *every* upper bound. Since the element $b$ succeeds $a$, we have $b = \inf(Y)$.

**11.62**  Let **N**, the natural numbers, be ordered by divisibility and let $A = \{a_1, a_2, a_3, \ldots, a_w\}$ be a finite subset of **N**. Show that $\sup(A)$ and $\inf(A)$ exist.

▌ The least common multiple of the $a_i$, written l.c.m. $(A)$, will be the $\sup(A)$ and the greatest common divisor of the $a_i$ written g.c.d. $(A)$, will be the $\inf(A)$. Since the least common multiple and greatest common divisor are both elements of **N**, both $\inf(A)$ and $\sup(A)$ always exist.

**11.63**  Consider **Q**, the set of rational numbers, with its usual order, and the subset $D$ where

$$D = \{x : x \in \mathbf{Q} \text{ and } 8 < x^3 < 15\}$$

*(a)* Is $D$ bounded above or below? *(b)* Do $\sup(D)$ and $\inf(D)$ exist?

▌ *(a)* The subset $D$ is bounded both above and below. For example, 1 is a lower bound and 100 an upper bound.

*(b)* $\sup(D)$ does not exist. Suppose, on the contrary, $\sup(D) = x$. Since $\sqrt[3]{15}$ is irrational, $x > \sqrt[3]{15}$. However, there exists a rational number $y$ such that $\sqrt[3]{15} < y < x$. Thus $y$ is also an upper bound for $D$. This contradicts the assumption that $x = \sup(D)$. On the other hand, $\inf(D)$ does exist. Specifically, $\inf(D) = 2$.

**11.64**  Let $S = \{1, 2, 3, \ldots, 8\}$ be ordered as shown in Fig. 11-15 and let $L = \{4, 5, 7\}$. *(a)* Find the upper and lower bounds of $L$. *(b)* Identify $\sup(L)$ and $\inf(L)$ if either exists.

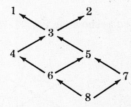

**Fig. 11-15**

▌ *(a)* The upper bounds are 1, 2, and 3, and the only lower bound is 8. Note 7 is not a lower bound since 7 does not precede 4.

*(b)* Here $\sup(L) = 3$ and $\inf(L) = 8$.

**11.65**  Repeat Problem 11.64 for the subset $M = \{2, 3, 6\}$ of $S$.

▌ *(a)* The upper bound is 2 and the lower bounds are 6 and 8.

*(b)* Here $\sup(M) = 2$ and $\inf(M) = 6$.

**11.66** Repeat Problem 11.64 for $K = \{1, 2, 4, 7\}$ of $S$.

    **▮** **(a)** There are no upper bounds for $K$ since no element of $S$ succeeds every element of $K$. The lower bound of $K$ is 8.

        **(b)** Here sup $(K)$ does not exist, but inf $(K) = 8$.

**11.67** Let the set $S = \{3, 6, 9, 12, 18\}$ be ordered by divisibility. For what subsets of $S$ is $\{6, 12, 18\}$ the set of upper bounds?

    **▮** The sets $\{6\}$ and $\{6, 3\}$ have 6, 12, and 18 as upper bounds.

**11.68** For what subsets of $S$ in Problem 11.67 is $\{3, 6\}$ the set of lower bounds?

    **▮** The subsets $\{6\}$, $\{6, 12\}$, $\{6, 18\}$, $\{12, 18\}$, and $\{6, 12, 18\}$ have 3 and 6 as lower bounds.

## 11.4 SIMILAR SETS AND WELL-ORDERED SETS

**11.69** Define similar ordered sets.

    **▮** Two ordered sets are said to be *similar* if there exists a one-to-one correspondence between the elements of each set which preserves the order relation. Specifically, an ordered set $A$ is similar to an ordered set $B$, denoted by

$$A \simeq B$$

if there exists a function $f: A \to B$ which is one-to-one and onto and which has the property that, for any elements $a$ and $a'$ in $A$, we have

$$a < a' \qquad \text{if and only if} \qquad f(a) < f(a')$$

Such a function $f$ is called a *similarity mapping* from $A$ into $B$.

**11.70** Let $V = \{1, 2, 6, 8, 12\}$ be ordered by divisibility and let $W = \{a, b, c, d, e\}$. Draw the diagram for $W$ if the following is a similarity mapping from $V$ into $W$:

$$f = \{(1, e), (2, d), (6, b), (8, c), (12, a)\}$$

    **▮** The similarity mapping preserves exactly the order of the initial set and is one-to-one and onto. Thus the mapping can be viewed simply as a relabeling of the vertices in the diagram of the initial set. The diagrams for both $V$ and $W$ appear in Fig. 11-16.

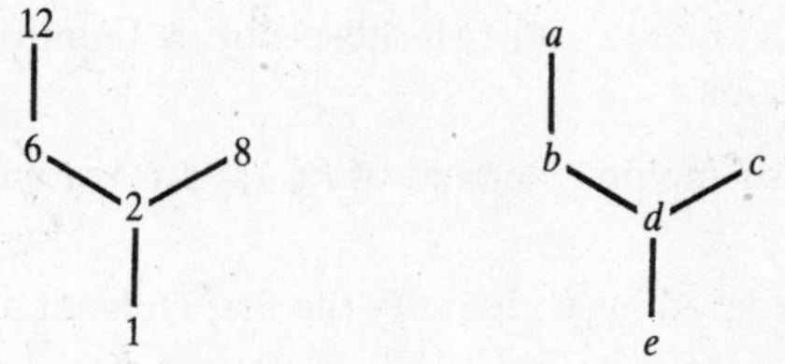

Fig. 11-16

**11.71** Let $X = \{3, 9, 18, 27\}$ and $Y = \{a, b, c, d\}$ be ordered as shown in Fig. 11-17. Identify all the possible similarity mappings of $X$ onto $Y$.

Fig. 11-17

    **▮** There are only two possible similarity mappings from $X$ onto $Y$ as follows:

$$f = \{(3, a), (9, b), (27, c), (18, d)\}$$
$$g = \{(3, a), (9, b), (27, d), (18, c)\}$$

**11.72** Let $A = \{2, 4, 8, 16\}$ be ordered by divisibility and let $B = \{u, v, w, x\}$ be ordered alphabetically. Find all possible similarity mappings of $A$ onto $B$.

▮ Since $A$ and $B$ are linearly ordered, there is only one possible similarity mapping from $A$ onto $B$: $\{(2, u), (4, v), (8, w), (16, x)\}$.

## First and Last Elements

**11.73** Let $A$ be an ordered set. Define a first element and a last element of $A$.

▮ The element $a$ in $A$ is called a *first element* of $A$ if, for every element $x$ in $A$,

$$a \lesssim x$$

In other words, $a$ precedes every element in $A$. Analogously, an element $b$ in $a$ is called a *last element* if, for every element $x$ in $A$,

$$x \lesssim b$$

That is, if $b$ succeeds every element of $A$. An ordered set can have at most one first element and one last element.

**11.74** Let $S = \{a, b, c, d, e\}$ be ordered as shown in Fig. 11-18. Identify the first element and last element of $S$ if either exists.

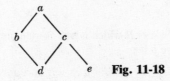

**Fig. 11-18**

▮ Since $a$ succeeds every element of $S$, $a$ is the last element of $S$. The ordered set $S$ does not have a first element. Note that the element $d$ does not precede the element $e$.

**11.75** Consider $\mathbf{N}$, the natural numbers under their usual order. Identify the first element and last element of $\mathbf{N}$ if either exists.

▮ The first element of $\mathbf{N}$ is the number 1. There is no last element.

**11.76** Let $A$ be any set and let $P(A)$ be the set of all subsets of $A$. Identify the first element and last element of $P(A)$ if $P(A)$ is ordered by set inclusion.

▮ The empty set $\varnothing$ would be the first element of $P(A)$ and $A$ would be the last element of $P(A)$.

**11.77** Let $A = \{x : 0 < x < 1\}$ be ordered by $\leq$. Identify the first element and last element of $A$ if either exists.

▮ The set $A$, which is linearly ordered, has neither a first nor a last element. [Note that if $A$ is viewed as a subset of $[0, 1]$ then $\inf(A) = 0$ and $\sup(A) = 1$.]

## Well-ordered Sets

**11.78** Define a well-ordered set and give an example.

▮ An ordered set $A$ is *well-ordered* if every subset of $A$ contains a first element. The classical example of a well-ordered set is the set $\mathbf{N}$ of positive integers with the usual order.

**11.79** Show that a well-ordered set $A$ must be linearly ordered.

▮ Given any pair of elements $a$ and $b$ in $A$, the subset $\{a, b\}$ of $A$ must contain a first element. Thus one element must precede the other; hence any two elements of $A$ are comparable.

**11.80** Suppose the set $E = \{2, 4, 6, 8, \ldots\}$ of positive even integers is ordered by divisibility. Is $E$ a well-ordered set?

▮ The set $E$ is not well-ordered since not every subset has a first element. For example, the subset $\{4, 6\}$ has no first element. Of course, every subset containing the element 2 has a first element, namely 2 itself.

**11.81** Suppose $S$ is a finite linearly ordered set. Is $S$ well-ordered?

▮ Yes. Any subset $A$ of $S$ is finite and linearly ordered and hence it has a first element.

**11.87** Suppose the following collection of sets is ordered by set inclusion:

$$B = [\{a\}, \{a, b\}, \{a, b, c, d\}, \{a, b, c, d, e, f\}]$$

Is $B$ well-ordered?

▮ Since $B$ is finite and linearly ordered, it is also well-ordered.

**11.83** Consider $\mathbf{N}$ and its subset $E = \{2, 4, 6, 8, \ldots\}$. (*a*) Find a similarity function $f: \mathbf{N} \to E$. (*b*) Show that $x \leq f(x)$ for every $x$ in $\mathbf{N}$.

▮ (*a*) The function $f: \mathbf{N} \to E$ defined by $f(x) = 2x$ is a similarity mapping of $\mathbf{N}$ into its subset $E$.
(*b*) Since $x$ is positive, $x \leq 2x = f(x)$.

**Theorem 11.2:** Let $A$ be a well-ordered set and $B$ a subset of $A$, and let the function $f: A \to B$ be a similarity mapping from $A$ into $B$. Then, for every $a$ in $A$, we have $a \leq f(a)$.

**11.84** Prove Theorem 11.2.

▮ Let $D = \{x: f(x) < x\}$. If $D$ is empty the theorem is true. Suppose $D \neq \emptyset$. Then, since $A$ is well-ordered, $D$ has a first element $d_0$. Note $d_0 \in D$ implies $f(d_0) < d_0$. Since $f$ is a similarity mapping,

$$f(d_0) < d_0 \quad \text{implies} \quad f(f(d_0)) < f(d_0)$$

Consequently, $f(d_0)$ also belongs to $D$. But $f(d_0) < d_0$ and $f(d_0) \in D$ contradicts the fact that $d_0$ is the first element of $D$. Hence the original assumption that $D \neq \emptyset$ leads to a contradiction. Therefore $D$ is empty and the theorem is true.

**11.85** Find a similarity mapping from $\mathbf{N}$ into its subset $A = \{1, 3, 5, 7, \ldots\}$.

▮ For each element $x$ in $\mathbf{N}$ define $f(x) = 2x - 1$. This mapping preserves the order of the positive integers $\mathbf{N}$.

**Theorem 11.3:** Let $A$ and $B$ be similar well-ordered sets. Then there exists only one similarity mapping from $A$ into $B$.

**11.86** Prove Theorem 11.3.

▮ Let $f: A \to B$ and $g: A \to B$ be similarity mappings. Suppose $f \neq g$. Then there exists an element $x \in A$ such that $f(x) \neq g(x)$. Consequently, by Problem 11.79, either $f(x) < g(x)$ or $g(x) < f(x)$. Say $f(x) < g(x)$.
Since $g: A \to B$ is a similarity mapping, $g^{-1}: B \to A$ is also a similarity mapping. Furthermore, $g^{-1} \circ f: A \to A$, the product of two similarity mappings, is a similarity mapping. But

$$f(x) < g(x) \quad \text{implies} \quad (g^{-1} \circ f)(x) < (g^{-1} \circ g)(x) = x$$

We have $g^{-1} \circ f$ is a similarity mapping and $(g^{-1} \circ f)(x) < x$. These facts contradict Theorem 11.2. Hence the assumption that $f \neq g$ leads to a contradiction. Accordingly, there can be only one similarity mapping of $A$ into $B$.

## 11.5 LATTICES

**11.87** Define the term lattice.

▮ Let $L$ be a nonempty set closed under two binary operations called *meet* and *join*, denoted respectively by $\wedge$ and $\vee$. Then $L$ is a *lattice* if for any elements $a$, $b$, and $c$ of $L$ the following axioms hold.
  (i) Commutative Laws:
    **(1a)** $a \wedge b = b \wedge a$         **(1b)** $a \vee b = b \vee a$
  (ii) Associative Laws:
    **(2a)** $(a \wedge b) \wedge c = a \wedge (b \wedge c)$     **(2b)** $(a \vee b) \vee c = a \vee (b \vee c)$
  (iii) Absorption Laws:
    **3(a)** $a \wedge (a \vee b) = a$        **(3b)** $a \vee (a \wedge b) = a$
A lattice is often denoted by $(L, \wedge, \vee)$ to emphasize the operations involved.

**11.88** Let $C$ be a collection of sets which are closed under intersection and union. Verify that $(C, \cap, \cup)$ is a lattice.

❚ The operations of intersection and union satisfy the three axioms that define a lattice. Specifically, for any three sets $X$, $Y$, and $Z$:
 (i) $X \cap Y = Y \cap X$ $\qquad\qquad$ $X \cup Y = Y \cup X$
 (ii) $(X \cap Y) \cap Z = X \cap (Y \cap Z)$ $\qquad$ $(X \cup Y) \cup Z = X \cup (Y \cup Z)$
 (iii) $X \cap (X \cup Y) = X$ $\qquad\qquad$ $X \cup (X \cap Y) = X$

**11.89** Show that the positive integers $\mathbf{N}$ is a lattice with respect to the operations

$$a \vee b = \text{l.c.m. } (a, b) \qquad \text{and} \qquad a \wedge b = \text{g.c.d. } (a, b) \tag{1}$$

where l.c.m. means least common multiple and g.c.d. means greatest common divisor.

❚ We must show that $\mathbf{N}$ with the two operations ($1$) satisfy the three axioms that define a lattice. However, number theory shows that:
 (i) g.c.d. $(a, b) =$ g.c.d. $(b, a)$, $\qquad$ l.c.m. $(a, b) =$ l.c.m. $(b, a)$
 (ii) g.c.d. (g.c.d. $(a, b), c) =$ g.c.d. $(a,$ g.c.d. $(b, c))$
 $\qquad$ l.c.m. (l.c.m. $(a, b), c) =$ l.c.m. $(a,$ l.c.m. $(b, c))$
 (iii) g.c.d. $(a,$ l.c.m. $(a, b)) = a,$ $\qquad$ l.c.m. $(a,$ g.c.d. $(a, b)) = b$
Thus $\mathbf{N}$ is a lattice with respect to l.c.m. and g.c.d..

**11.90** Define the dual of a statement in a lattice $L$. Why does the principle of duality apply to $L$?

❚ The *dual* of any statement in a lattice $(L, \wedge, \vee)$ is defined to be the statement obtained by interchanging $\wedge$ and $\vee$. Since the dual of an axiom of $L$ is again an axiom of $L$, the principle of duality says that the dual of any theorem in $L$ is also a theorem.

**11.91** Write the dual of each statement:

$$\textbf{(a)} \quad (a \wedge b) \vee c = (b \vee c) \wedge (c \vee a), \qquad \textbf{(b)} \quad (a \wedge b) \vee a = a \wedge (b \vee a)$$

❚ Replace $\vee$ by $\wedge$ and $\wedge$ by $\vee$ in each statement to obtain the dual statements

$$\textbf{(a)} \quad (a \vee b) \wedge c = (b \wedge c) \vee (c \wedge a), \qquad \textbf{(b)} \quad (a \vee b) \wedge a = a \vee (b \wedge a)$$

**11.92** Prove the *idempotent laws* for elements of a lattice: (i) $a \wedge a = a$, and (ii) $a \vee a = a$.

❚ The proof of (i) requires only two applications of the absorption law (Problem 11.87(iii)):

$$a \wedge a = a \wedge (a \vee (a \wedge b)) = a$$

The proof of (ii) follows by duality.

**Theorem 11.4:** Let $L$ be a lattice. Then $a \wedge b = a$ if and only if $a \vee b = b$.

**11.93** Prove Theorem 11.4.

❚ Suppose $a \wedge b = a$. Using the absorption law in the first step we have

$$b = b \vee (b \wedge a) = b \vee (a \wedge b) = b \vee a = a \vee b$$

Now suppose $a \vee b = b$. Again using the absorption law in the first step we have

$$a = a \wedge (a \vee b) = a \wedge b$$

Thus $a \wedge b = a$ if and only if $a \vee b = b$.

## 11.6 LATTICES AS ORDERED SETS

The following three theorems are used below.

**Theorem 11.5:** Let $L$ be a lattice. Then the relation $a \preceq b$ defined by either $a \wedge b = a$ or $a \vee b = b$ is a partial ordering on $L$.

(We refer to the above partial ordering of $L$ as the partial order *induced by the lattice*.)

**Theorem 11.6:** Let $L$ be any lattice. Then inf $(x, y)$ and sup $(x, y)$ exist for every pair $\{x, y\}$ in the partial ordering induced by $L$.

**Theorem 11.7:** Let $P$ be a partially ordered set such that inf $(x, y)$ and sup $(x, y)$ exist for any pair $\{x, y\}$ in $P$. Then the following define a lattice on $P$:

$$x \wedge y = \inf (x, y) \qquad \text{and} \qquad x \vee y = \sup (x, y)$$

The partial ordering of $P$ induced by this lattice is the same as the original partial ordering of $P$.

From Theorems 11.6 and 11.7 the following alternative definition for a lattice obtains:

**Alternate Definition:** A lattice is a partially ordered set in which

$$a \wedge b = \inf (a, b) \qquad \text{and} \qquad a \vee b = \sup (a, b)$$

exist for any pair of elements $a$ and $b$.

**11.94** Prove Theorem 11.5.

❚ For any $a$ in $L$, we have $a \wedge a = a$ by idempotency. Hence $a \preceq a$, and so $\preceq$ is reflexive.
Suppose $a \preceq b$ and $b \preceq a$. Then $a \wedge b = a$ and $b \wedge a = b$. Therefore, $a = a \wedge b = b \wedge a = b$, and so $\preceq$ is antisymmetric.
Lastly, suppose $a \preceq b$ and $b \preceq c$. Then $a \wedge b = a$ and $b \wedge c = b$. Thus

$$a \wedge c = (a \wedge b) \wedge c = a \wedge (b \wedge c) = a \wedge b = a$$

Therefore $a \preceq c$, and so $\preceq$ is transitive. Accordingly, $\preceq$ is a partial order on $L$.

**11.95** Let $P$ be the power set of $\{a, b, c\}$. Draw the diagram of the partial order induced on $P$ by the lattice $(P, \cap, \cup)$.

❚ Under the partial ordering induced by a lattice, $a \preceq b$ whenever $a \wedge b = a$. Thus, in this case,

$$a \preceq b \qquad \text{whenever} \qquad a \cap b = a.$$

Thus the set $\{a\}$ precedes the set $\{a, b\}$ since $\{a\} \cap \{a, b\} = \{a\}$. Proceeding in this manner we obtain the diagram shown in Fig. 11-19. Note that this is the same diagram (Fig. 11-2) obtained under the partial ordering of set inclusion (Problem 11.36).

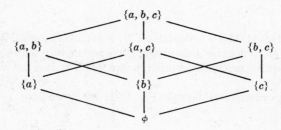

**Fig. 11-19**

**11.96** Consider the lattice $L$ on the set $D_m$ of divisors of a positive integer $m$ where

$$a \vee b = \text{l.c.m.} (a, b) \qquad \text{and} \qquad a \wedge b = \text{g.c.d.} (a, b)$$

Draw the diagram of the partial order induced by $L$ for $m = 36$.

❚ Here the partial ordering induced by $L$ is: $a \preceq b$ whenever g.c.d. $(a, b) = a$. The diagram of this partial ordering of $D_{36}$ is shown in Fig. 11-20.

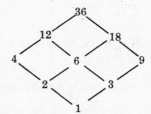

**Fig. 11-20**

**11.97** Explain briefly why any linearly ordered set is a lattice.

▮ Consider any two elements $a$ and $b$ of a linearly ordered set where $a \leq b$. Then inf $(a, b) = a$ and sup $(a, b) = b$. Since inf $(a, b)$ and sup $(a, b)$ exist for any pair of elements, a linearly ordered set is a lattice.

**11.98** Identify which of the partially ordered sets shown in Fig. 11-21 are lattices.

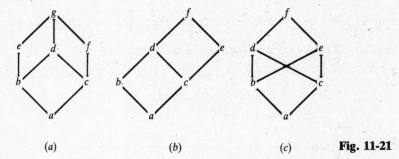

(a)          (b)          (c)          **Fig. 11-21**

▮ An ordered set $S$ is a lattice if and only if sup $(x, y)$ and inf $(x, y)$ exist for each pair $\{x, y\}$ in $S$. Posets $(a)$ and $(b)$ of Fig. 11-21 are lattices. Poset $(c)$ is not a lattice since $\{b, c\}$ has three upper bounds, $d$, $e$, and $f$, and no one of them precedes the other two; hence sup $(b, c)$ does not exist.

**11.99** Which of the partially ordered sets shown in Fig. 11-22 are lattices?

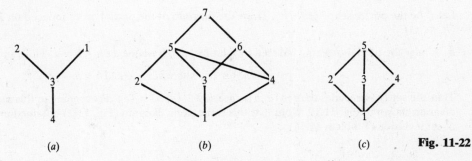

(a)          (b)          (c)          **Fig. 11-22**

▮ Only poset $(c)$ of Fig. 11-22 is a lattice. Poset $(a)$ is not a lattice since the elements 1 and 2 have no upper bound and hence sup $(1, 2)$ does not exist. Poset $(b)$ is not a lattice since the elements 5 and 6 have two lower bounds 3 and 4, but neither precedes the other; hence inf $(5, 6)$ does not exist.

**11.100** Which of the partially ordered sets shown in Fig. 11-23 are lattices?

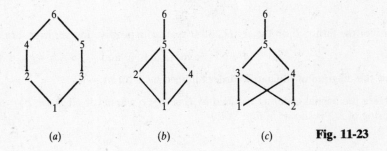

(a)          (b)          (c)          **Fig. 11-23**

▮ Posets $(a)$ and $(b)$ of Fig. 11-23 are lattices. Poset $(c)$ is not a lattice since the elements 1 and 2 have no lower bound, hence inf $(1, 2)$ does not exist.

**11.101** Let $A$ be any subset of the real number system $\mathbf{R}$ with the usual order. Under what conditions is $A$ a lattice?

▮ As long as $A$ is not empty, $A$ is a lattice since it is linearly ordered.

**11.102** Determine whether or not each of the following sets is a lattice with respect to divisibility: $A = \{2, 3, 4, 12\}$ and $B = \{1, 2, 3, 9, 18\}$.

*I* Neither of the sets is a lattice since sup $(a, b)$ and inf $(a, b)$ do not always exist. For example, in set $A$, we have g.c.d. $(2, 3) = 1$ but 1 does not belong to $A$ and so inf $(2, 3)$ does not exist. Also, in set $B$, l.c.m. $(4, 3) = 12$ but 12 does not belong to $B$.

**11.103** Determine whether or not each of the following sets is a lattice with respect to divisibility: $C = \{1, 3, 4, 9\}$ and $D = \{1, 2, 3, 9, 18\}$.

*I* Only $C$ is a lattice since the infimum and supremum exist for every pair of elements in $C$. In set $D$, l.c.m. $(2, 3) = 6$ but 6 does not belong to $D$.

**11.104** Consider the partially ordered set $P = \{a, b, c, d, e\}$ shown in Fig. 11-24. Find two subsets of $P$ that are lattices with respect to the operation on $P$.

**Fig. 11-24**

*I* We must identify two subsets where the infimum and supremum exist for every pair of elements in that subset. Any linearly ordered subset is a lattice. Two subsets which are lattices are

$$\{a, b, c, d\} \qquad \text{and} \qquad \{a, b, c, e\}$$

Note that the whole set $P$ is not a lattice since sup $(d, e)$ does not exist.

## Sublattices

**11.105** Define the term sublattice.

*I* Suppose $M$ is a nonempty subset of a lattice $L$. We say $M$ is a *sublattice* of $L$ if $M$ itself is a lattice with respect to the operations of $L$. Note that $M$ is a sublattice of $L$ if and only if $M$ is closed under the operations $\wedge$ and $\vee$ of $L$. Thus the infimum and supremum of any pair of elements in $M$ must also be an element of $M$. For example, consider the positive integers $\mathbf{N}$ under the operation of divisibility. The set $D_m$ consisting of all divisors of $m > 1$ is a sublattice of $\mathbf{N}$ while the set $C = \{2, 3, 6\}$ is not a sublattice of $\mathbf{N}$ since inf $(2, 3) = 1$ does not belong to $C$.

**11.106** Consider the lattice $L$ in Fig. 11-25. Determine whether or not each of the following is a sublattice of $L$:

$$L_1 = \{x, a, b, y\}, \quad L_2 = \{x, a, e, y\}, \quad L_3 = \{a, c, d, y\}, \quad L_4 = \{x, c, d, y\}$$

**Fig. 11-25**

*I* A subset $L'$ is a sublattice if it is closed under $\wedge$ and $\vee$. Then $L_1$ is not a sublattice since $a \vee b = c$, which does not belong to $L_1$. The set $L_4$ is not a sublattice since $c \wedge d = a$ does not belong to $L_4$. The other two sets, $L_2$ and $L_3$, are sublattices.

**11.107** Consider the lattice $D = \{v, w, x, y, z\}$ shown in Fig. 11-26. Find all sublattices with three or more elements.

**Fig. 11-26**

*I* We must identify all subsets with three or more elements where the supremum and infimum exist (and are elements of the subset) for every pair of elements in the subset. These are

$$\{v, w, x\}, \{v, y, z\}, \{v, x, z\}, \{v, w, z\}, \{w, x, z\}, \{v, w, y, z\}, \{v, x, y, z\}, \{v, w, x, z\}, \{v, w, x, y, z\}$$

### Isomorphic Lattices

**11.108**  Define isomorphic lattices.

▮ Two lattices $L$ and $L'$ are said to be *isomorphic* if there is a bijective function $f: L \to L'$ such that

$$f(a \wedge b) = f(a) \wedge f(b) \qquad \text{and} \qquad f(a \vee b) = f(a) \vee f(b)$$

for any elements $a$, $b$ in $L$.

**11.109**  Are the two lattices shown in Fig. 11-27 isomorphic?

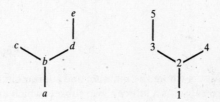

**Fig. 11-27**

▮ Yes. Consider the mapping $f = \{(a, 1), (b, 2), (c, 4), (d, 3), (e, 5)\}$. This mapping preserves, in effect, the structure of the original set. For example, $f(c \wedge d) = f(b) = 2$ and $f(c) \wedge f(d) = 3 \wedge 4 = 2$.

**11.110**  Are the lattices $L$ and $L'$ in Fig. 11-28 isomorphic?

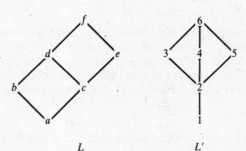

$L$          $L'$          **Fig. 11-28**

▮ No. To see this, first notice that $a$ must map to 1 and $f$ to 6 for obvious reasons. Then inf $(2, x) = 2$ for $x \neq 1$ in $L'$. This is not true for $b$, $c$, $d$, or $e$ in $L$. Thus $L$ and $L'$ are not isomorphic.

**11.111**  Are the two lattices in Fig. 11-29 isomorphic?

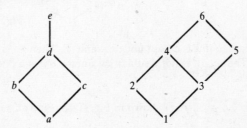

**Fig. 11-29**

▮ No, since two lattices do not have the same number of elements. Hence, trivially, no one-to-one and onto mapping exists that satisfies the given conditions.

## 11.7  BOUNDED LATTICES

**11.112**  Let $L$ be a lattice. Define the lower bound and upper bound of $L$ and determine when $L$ is bounded.

▮ $L$ is said to have a *lower bound*, denoted 0, if for any element $x$ in $L$ we have $0 \leq x$. Analogously, $L$ is said to have an *upper bound*, denoted $I$, if, for any $x$ in $L$, we have $x \le I$. We say that $L$ is *bounded* if $L$ has both a lower bound and an upper bound. In such a lattice we have the identities

$$a \vee I = I, \qquad a \wedge I = I, \qquad a \vee 0 = a, \qquad a \wedge 0 = 0$$

for any element $a$ in $L$.

**11.113**   Identify the lower bound and upper bound, if they exist, of the positive integers **N** with the usual ordering.

▮ **N** has a lower bound 1 but has no upper bound.

**11.114**   Identify the lower and upper bound, if they exist, of the set $A = \{x : 1 < x < 2\}$ and $A$ is ordered by the usual order.

▮ The set $A$ has neither lower nor upper bound.

**11.115**   Identify the lower and upper bound, if they exist, of the power set $P(A)$ of a set $A$ under the operations of intersection and union.

▮ The empty set $\emptyset$ is the lower bound of $P(A)$ and the set $A$ is the upper bound.

**11.116**   Show that every finite lattice is bounded.

▮ Suppose $L = \{a_1, a_2, a_3, \ldots, a_n\}$ is a finite lattice. Then $a_1 \vee a_2 \vee \cdots \vee a_n$ and $a_1 \wedge a_2 \wedge \cdots \wedge a_n$ are the upper bound and lower bound for $L$, respectively.

## 11.8  DISTRIBUTIVE LATTICES, DECOMPOSITIONS

**11.117**   Define a distributive lattice.

▮ A lattice $L$ is said to be *distributive* if for any elements $a$, $b$, and $c$ of $L$ we have the following Distributive Laws:
**(4a)**   $a \wedge (b \vee c) = (a \wedge b) \vee (a \wedge c)$        **(4b)**   $a \vee (b \wedge c) = (a \vee b) \wedge (a \vee c)$
Otherwise, $L$ is said to be *nondistributive*. Note that by the principle of duality (see Problem 11.90) **(4a)** holds if and only if **(4b)** holds.

**11.118**   The power set $P$ of a set $A$ is a lattice under the operations $\cap$ and $\cup$. Is $P$ a distributive lattice?

▮ $P$ is a distributive lattice since

$$a \cap (b \cup c) = (a \cap b) \cup (a \cap c) \quad \text{and} \quad a \cup (b \cap c) = (a \cup b) \cap (a \cup c)$$

for any sets $a$, $b$, and $c$ in $P$.

**11.119**   Define the term join irreducible in a lattice $L$ with a lower bound 0.

▮ An element $a$ in $L$ is said to be *join irreducible* if $a = x \vee y$ implies $a = x$ or $a = y$. Clearly 0 has this property. (Note that prime numbers under multiplication have this property, i.e., if $p$ is prime and $p = ab$, then $p = a$ or $p = b$.)

**11.120**   Suppose $a \ne 0$ in a lattice $L$. Show that $a$ is join irreducible if and only if it has a unique immediate predecessor.

▮ Suppose $a$ has at least two immediate predecessors, say $b_1$ and $b_2$ as in Fig. 11-30(a). Then $a = b_1 \vee b_2$ and thus $a$ is not join irreducible. On the other hand, if $a$ has a unique immediate predecessor $c$, then, for any $b_1$

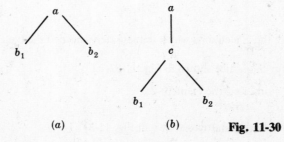

(a)                          (b)            **Fig. 11-30**

and $b_2$ preceding $a$, we cannot have

$$a = b_1 \vee b_2 = \sup(b_1, b_2)$$

because $c$ would then lie between them as in Fig. 11-30($b$).

**11.121** Find the join-irreducible elements of the lattice $K$ shown in Fig. 11-31($a$).

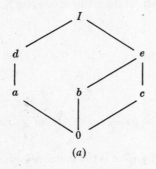 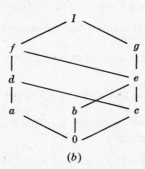

($a$)        ($b$)        **Fig. 11-31**

❚ The join-irreducible elements are those with a unique predecessor. Hence the elements $a$, $b$, $c$, and $d$ are join irreducible.

**11.122** Find the join-irreducible elements of the lattice $L$ shown in Fig. 11-31($b$).

❚ The join-irreducible elements are $a$, $b$, $c$, and $g$.

**11.123** Let $L$ be a lattice with an upper bound $I$. An element $a$ in the lattice $L$ is said to be *meet irreducible* if $a = x \wedge y$ implies $a = x$ or $a = y$, and, similarly, $a \neq I$ is meet irreducible if and only if $a$ has only one immediate successor. Find all meet-irreducible elements of the lattice shown in Fig. 11-31($a$).

❚ The meet-irreducible elements are those that have only one immediate successor. Hence, $a$, $b$, $c$, $d$, and $e$ are meet irreducible.

**11.124** Find all meet-irreducible elements of the lattice shown in Fig. 11-31($b$).

❚ The meet-irreducible elements are $a$, $b$, $d$, $f$, and $g$.

**11.125** Let $L$ be a lattice with lower bound 0. Define the term atom.

❚ Those elements which immediately succeed 0 are join irreducible and are called *atoms*. [We emphasize that not all join-irreducible elements need be atoms.]

**11.126** Find the atoms for the lattice shown in Fig. 11-32($a$). (Here 1 is the lower bound, i.e., the 0 element.)

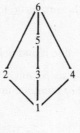 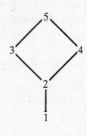

($a$)        ($b$)        **Fig. 11-32**

❚ The atoms are those elements which immediately succeed the 0 element. Hence, the atoms are 2, 3, and 4.

**11.127** Find the atoms for the lattice shown in Fig. 11-32($b$).

❚ There is one atom, i.e., the element 2.

**11.128** Find the atoms for the two lattices shown in Fig. 11-31.

▮ In both lattices, the elements which immediately succeed 0 are $a$, $b$, and $c$; hence these are the atoms.

**11.129** Consider the lattice **N** of positive integers ordered by divisibility. (Here 1 is the lower bound.) **(a)** Which elements of **N** are atoms? **(b)** Which are join irreducible?

▮ **(a)** The prime numbers are the atoms.
**(b)** All powers of prime numbers and 1 are join irreducible.

**11.130** The power set $P(A)$ of any nonempty set $A$ is a lattice with respect to set inclusion. **(a)** Which elements of $P(A)$ are atoms? **(b)** Which are join irreducible?

▮ **(a)** The singleton sets $\{a\}$ are the atoms of $P(A)$.
**(b)** The singleton sets $\{a\}$ are the only join-irreducible elements other than the lower bound $\varnothing$.

### Decompositions

**11.131** Suppose an element $a$ in a lattice $L$ can be expressed in the form $a = d_1 \vee d_2 \vee \cdots \vee d_n$ where the $d_i$ are join irreducible. What is meant by saying that the $d_i$'s are *irredundant*?

▮ If $d_j \leq d_k$, that is, if $d_j \vee d_k = d_k$, then we can delete $d_j$ from the expression for $a$. Thus the expression is *irredundant* if no $d_j$ precedes $d_k$.

**11.132** Suppose $L$ is a finite lattice. Show that an element $a$ in $L$ can be expressed as the join of irredundant join-irreducible elements.

▮ If $a$ is not join irreducible, then we write

$$a = b_1 \vee b_2$$

Furthermore if either $b_1$ or $b_2$ is not join irreducible, then it can be replaced by the join of two elements; and so on. This process can be repeated until $a$ is expressed as the join of irreducible elements. Thus

$$a = d_1 \vee d_2 \vee \cdots \vee d_n$$

where the $d$'s are join irreducible. If $d_i$ precedes $d_j$, then we can delete $d_i$ from the expression. Continuing this process gives us the required decomposition.

**11.133** Is the decomposition of an element $a$ of a lattice $L$ into irredundant and join-irreducible elements unique?

▮ No, there can be many decompositions of $a$. Consider the element $f$ in Fig. 11-33. There are four decompositions, $d \vee e$, $d \vee c$, $b \vee e$, and $b \vee c$.

**Fig. 11-33**

**11.134** Find an irredundant and join-irreducible decomposition for the element $h$ in Fig. 11-34.

**Fig. 11-34**

▮ We begin by expressing $h$ as the join of two elements $h = e \vee g$. Then, since $e = b \vee c$ and $g = c \vee d$, we substitute to obtain $h = b \vee c \vee c \vee d$. Finally, since $c \leq c$, we delete one $c$ from our expression to obtain the solution

$$h = b \vee c \vee d$$

where $b$, $c$, and $d$ are irredundant and join irreducible. Note that we could have expressed $h$ as $h = e \vee f$ or $h = f \vee g$. However, in this last case we would have arrived at the same solution.

**11.135**    Find an irredundant and join-irreducible decomposition for the element $g$ in Fig. 11-35.

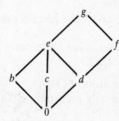

**Fig. 11-35**

▮ We begin by expressing $g$ as the join of two elements $g = e \vee f$. Then, since $e = c \vee d$, we substitute to obtain

$$g = c \vee d \vee f$$

Since $c$, $d$, and $f$, are irredundant and join irreducible, this is our solution. Had we expressed $e$ as $e = b \vee c$ or $e = b \vee d$, we would have arrived at the alternative solutions $g = b \vee c \vee f$ and $g = b \vee d \vee f$.

**11.136**    Consider the lattice $K$ shown in Fig. 11-31($a$). Express the elements which are not join irreducible as the join of irredundant join-irreducible elements.

▮ The elements that are not join irreducible are $I$ and $e$. The decompositions are

$$I = d \vee b \vee c \qquad \text{and} \qquad e = b \vee c$$

**11.137**    Repeat Problem 11.136 for the lattice $L$ shown in Fig. 11-31($b$).

▮ The elements that are not join-irreducible are $I$, $f$, $d$, and $e$. The decompositions are

$$I = a \vee g, \qquad f = a \vee b \vee c, \qquad d = a \vee c, \qquad e = b \vee c$$

Note that to arrive at $I = a \vee g$, we first express $I$ as $I = f \vee g$, then we replace $f$ by $a \vee b \vee c$ to obtain $I = a \vee b \vee c \vee g$. But, since $b$ and $c$ precede $g$, they can be eliminated.

**11.138**    Consider the lattice $D_{60} = \{1, 2, 3, 4, 5, 6, 10, 12, 15, 30, 60\}$, the divisors of 60, ordered by divisibility. (See Fig. 11-36.) Express each number that is not join irreducible as the join of a minimum number of irredundant join-irreducible elements.

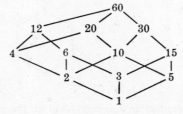

**Fig. 11-36**

▮ The results are $60 = 4 \vee 3 \vee 5$, $30 = 2 \vee 3 \vee 5$, $20 = 4 \vee 5$, $15 = 3 \vee 5$, $12 = 3 \vee 4$, $10 = 2 \vee 5$, $6 = 2 \vee 3$.

**11.139**    Consider the lattice $D_m$ consisting of all divisors of $m > 1$ under divisibility. Express $a \neq 1$ as the join of a minimum number of irredundant join-irreducible elements.

▮ The join-irreducible elements in $D_m$ are powers of primes. Let $a = p_1^{n_1} p_2^{n_2} \cdots p_k^{n_k}$ be the decomposition of $a$ into a product of primes. Then

$$a = p_1^{n_1} \vee p_2^{n_2} \vee \cdots \vee p_k^{n_k}$$

is the required decomposition.

**11.140**    Let $P(A)$ be the power set of a nonempty finite set $A$. Consider $P(A)$ as a lattice under set inclusion. Express $B \neq \emptyset$ as the join of irredundant join-irreducible elements.

▌ The join-irreducible elements in $P(A)$ are the singleton sets $\{a\}$. Thus

$$B = \{a_1\} \vee \{a_2\} \vee \cdots \vee \{a_k\}$$

is the required decomposition of $B$ where $a_1, a_2, \ldots, a_k$ are the distinct elements in $B$.

**Theorem 11.8:**   Let $L$ be a finite distributive lattice. Then every $a$ in $L$ can be written uniquely (except for order) as the join of irredundant join-irreducible elements.

**11.141**   Prove Theorem 11.8.

▌ Since $L$ is finite we can write $a$ as the join of irredundant join-irreducible elements. Thus we need to prove uniqueness. Suppose

$$a = b_1 \vee b_2 \vee \cdots \vee b_r = c_1 \vee c_2 \vee \cdots \vee c_s$$

where the $b$'s are irredundant and join irreducible and the $c$'s are irredundant and join irreducible. For any given $i$ we have

$$b_i \leq (b_1 \vee b_2 \vee \cdots \vee b_r) = (c_1 \vee c_2 \vee \cdots \vee c_s)$$

Hence

$$b_i = b_i \wedge (c_1 \vee c_2 \vee \cdots \vee c_s) = (b_i \wedge c_1) \vee (b_i \wedge c_2) \vee \cdots \vee (b_i \wedge c_s)$$

Since $b_i$ is join irreducible, there exists a $j$ such that $b_i = b_i \wedge c_j$, and so $b_i \leq c_j$. By a similar argument, for $c_j$ there exists a $b_k$ such that $c_j \leq b_k$. Therefore

$$b_i \leq c_j \leq b_k$$

which gives $b_i = c_j = b_k$ since the $b$'s are irredundant. Accordingly, the $b$'s and $c$'s may be paired off. Thus the representation for $a$ is unique except for order.

**11.142**   Theorem 11.8 can be generalized to lattices of *finite length*. (*a*) Define a lattice of finite length. (*b*) Give an example of an infinite lattice $L$ with finite length.

▌ (*a*) A lattice $L$ has finite length if every linearly ordered subset of $L$ is finite.
(*b*) Let $L = \{0, I, a_1, a_2, \ldots\}$ be ordered as in Fig. 11-37. That is, for every $n$ in $\mathbf{N}$, we have $0 < a_n < I$. Then $L$ has finite length since $L$ has no infinite linearly ordered subset.

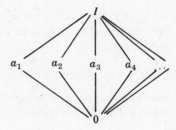

**Fig. 11-37**

The proof of the following theorem lies beyond the scope of this book.

**Theorem 11.9:**   A lattice $L$ is nondistributive if and only if it contains a sublattice isomorphic to the lattices (*a*) or (*b*) in Fig. 11-38.

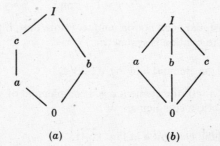

(*a*)                    (*b*)          **Fig. 11-38**

**11.143** Determine which of the lattices in Fig. 11-39 are nondistributive.

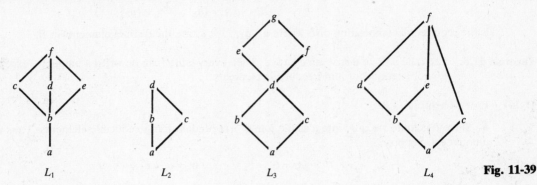

**Fig. 11-39**

▌ Use Theorem 11.9. Lattices $L_2$ and $L_3$ are distributive. However, $L_1$ is nondistributive since its sublattice $\{b, c, d, e, f\}$ is isomorphic to the lattice in Fig. 11-38(b), and $L_4$ is nondistributive since its sublattice $\{a, b, c, d, f\}$ is isomorphic to the lattice in Fig. 11-38(a).

**11.144** Consider the lattice $M$ in Fig. 11-40. **(a)** Find the nonzero join-irreducible elements and the atoms of $M$. **(b)** Is $M$ distributive?

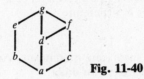

**Fig. 11-40**

▌ **(a)** Note first that $a$ is the zero element. The elements $b$, $c$, $d$, and $e$ are join irreducible since they have unique immediate predecessors, and $b$, $c$, and $d$ are the atoms since they immediately succeed the zero element $a$.

**(b)** No, since $\{a, b, d, e, g\}$ is a sublattice isomorphic to the lattice in Fig. 11-38(a).

**11.145** Suppose $L'$ is a sublattice of a distributive lattice $L$. Show that $L'$ is distributive.

▌ The distributive laws (see Problem 11.117) $a \wedge (b \vee c) = (a \wedge b) \vee (a \wedge c)$ and $a \vee (b \wedge c) = (a \vee b) \wedge (a \vee c)$ hold for every $a$, $b$, and $c$ in $L$. Since each element of $L'$ is also in $L$, the distributive laws hold for every $a'$, $b'$, and $c'$ in $L'$. Hence $L'$ is a distributive lattice.

**11.146** Show that every linearly ordered set $L$ is a distributive lattice.

▌ Both lattices in Fig. 11-38 contain noncomparable elements. Thus $L$, which is linearly ordered, cannot contain a sublattice isomorphic to either diagram in Fig. 11-38. Accordingly, by Theorem 11.9, $L$ is distributive.

## 11.9 COMPLEMENTED LATTICES

**11.147** Let $L$ be a bounded lattice with lower bound 0 and upper bound $I$. Define a complement of an element $x$ in $L$.

▌ An element $y$ in $L$ is a *complement* of $x$ if

$$x \vee y = I \quad \text{and} \quad x \wedge y = 0$$

Complements need not exist and need not be unique. (Note that, if $y$ is a complement of $x$, then $x$ is a complement of $y$, that is, the relation is symmetric.)

**11.148** Find the complement(s) of the element $b$ in Fig. 11-38(a).

▌ Since $b \vee a = I$ and $b \wedge a = 0$, the element $a$ is a complement of $b$. Furthermore, since $b \vee c = I$ and $b \wedge c = 0$, the element $c$ is also a complement of $b$.

**11.149** Find the complement(s) of the element $a$ in Fig. 11-41.

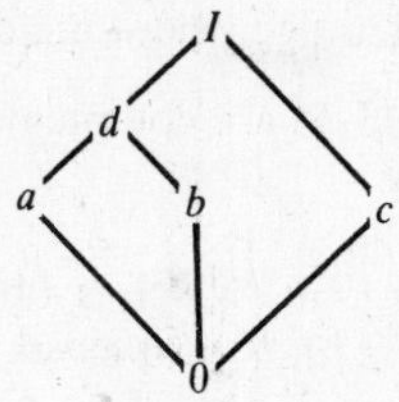

Fig. 11-41

▌ Since $a \vee c = I$ and $a \wedge c = 0$, the element $c$ is a complement of $a$. Note that $b$ is not a complement of $a$ since $a \vee b = d \neq I$.

**Theorem 11.10:** Let $L$ be a bounded distributive lattice. Then complements are unique if they exist.

**11.150** Prove Theorem 11.10.

▌ Suppose $x$ and $y$ are complements of any element $a$ in $L$. Then

$$a \vee x = I, \qquad a \vee y = I, \qquad a \wedge x = 0, \qquad a \wedge y = 0$$

Using distributivity,

$$x = x \vee 0 = x \vee (a \wedge y) = (x \vee a) \wedge (x \vee y) = I \wedge (x \vee y) = x \vee y$$

Similarly,

$$y = y \vee 0 = y \vee (a \wedge x) = (y \vee a) \wedge (y \vee x) = I \wedge (y \vee x) = y \vee x$$

Thus $x = x \vee y = y \vee x = y$ and the theorem is proved.

**11.151** The lattice shown in Fig. 11-42 is distributive. Verify that every complement is unique if it exists.

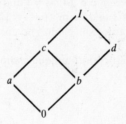

Fig. 11-42

▌ The element $a$ is a complement of $d$ and vice versa. No complements exist for the other elements. Thus all complements which exist are unique.

**11.152** Use Theorem 11.10 to show that the lattice $L$ in Fig. 11-43 is not distributive.

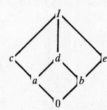

Fig. 11-43

▌ The element $c$ has two complements, $b$ and $e$. Thus, by Theorem 11.10, $L$ cannot be distributive (otherwise complements would be unique.).

**11.153** Suppose $L$ is a bounded lattice with lower bound 0 and upper bound $I$. Show that 0 and $I$ are complements of each other.

▌ We have $0 \vee I = I \vee 0 = I$ and $0 \wedge I = I \wedge 0 = 0$. Thus 0 and $I$ are complements of each other.

**11.154** Define a complemented lattice.

▌ A lattice $L$ is *complemented* if $L$ is bounded and every element in $L$ has a complement.

**11.155** Give two examples of a complemented lattice where the complements are not unique.

▮ The nondistributive lattices in Fig. 11-38 are complemented lattices where some of the complements are not unique.

**11.156** Consider the power set $P(A)$ of $A = \{a, b, c\}$ which is a bounded lattice under the operations of intersection and union. Find the complement of $X = \{a, b\}$ if it exists.

▮ Consider $X^c = A \backslash X = \{c\}$. Then

$$\{a, b\} \cap \{c\} = \emptyset \quad \text{and} \quad \{a, b\} \cup \{c\} = A$$

Thus $X^c$ is a (lattice) complement of $X$. Also it is the only complement of $X$.

**11.157** Generalize the result in Problem 11.156.

▮ The lattice $P(U)$ of all subsets of any nonempty set $U$ is complemented and each subset $X$ of $U$ has the unique complement $X^c = U \backslash X$.

**11.158** Consider the lattice $D_{12} = \{1, 2, 3, 4, 6, 12\}$, the divisors of 12 ordered by divisibility (whose diagram is shown in Fig. 11-44). Find **(a)** the lower bound and upper bound of $D_{12}$, and **(b)** the complement(s) of 4 and 6. **(c)** Is $D_{12}$ a complemented lattice?

**Fig. 11-44**

▮ **(a)** The lower bound is 1 and upper bound is 12.
  **(b)** The complement of 4 is 3 since g.c.d. $(4, 3) = 1$ and l.c.m. $(4, 3) = 12$. However 6 has no complement since g.c.d. $(6, x) \neq 1$ for $x \neq 1$ and l.c.m. $(6, 1) \neq 12$.
  **(c)** $D_{12}$ is not a complemented lattice since 6 has no complement.

**Theorem 11.11:** Let $L$ be a complemented lattice with unique complements. Then the join-irreducible elements of $L$, other than 0, are its atoms.

**11.159** Prove Theorem 11.11.

▮ Suppose $a$ is join irreducible and is not an atom. Then $a$ has a unique immediate predecessor $b \neq 0$. Let $b'$ be the complement of $b$. Since $b \neq 0$, we have $b' \neq I$. If $a$ precedes $b'$, then $b \leq a \leq b'$, and so $b \wedge b' = b'$, which is impossible since $b \wedge b' = I$. Thus $a$ does not precede $b'$, and so $a \wedge b'$ must strictly precede $a$. Since $b$ is the unique immediate predecessor of $a$, we also have that $a \wedge b'$ precedes $b$ as in Fig. 11-45. But $a \wedge b'$ precedes $b'$. Hence

$$a \wedge b' \leq \inf (b, b') = b \wedge b' = 0$$

**Fig. 11-45**

Thus $a \wedge b' = 0$. Since $a \vee b = a$, we also have that

$$a \vee b' = (a \vee b) \vee b' = a \vee (b \vee b') = a \vee I = I$$

Therefore $b'$ is a complement of $a$. Since complements are unique, $a = b$. This contradicts the assumption that $b$ is an immediate predecessor of $a$. Thus the only join-irreducible elements of $L$ are its atoms.

# CHAPTER 12
# Propositional Calculus

## 12.1 STATEMENTS, BASIC OPERATIONS

The following notation will be used:

$p \wedge q$   *conjunction* of $p$ and $q$, read "$p$ and $q$"
$p \vee q$   *disjunction* of $p$ and $q$, read "$p$ or $q$"
$\sim p$   *negation* of $p$, read "not $p$"

Also, T and F will be used for true and false, respectively.

*Note*: Some texts use

$$p \,\&\, q, p \cdot q, \text{ or } pq \quad \text{for} \quad p \wedge q; \qquad p + q \quad \text{for} \quad p \vee q; \qquad p', \bar{p}, \text{ or } \neg p \quad \text{for} \quad \sim p$$

and 1 and 0 for T and F, respectively.

**12.1**   Define a statement, and give examples.

▎ A *statement* (or *verbal assertion*) is any collection of symbols (or sounds) which is either *true* or *false*, but not both. The truth or falsity of a statement is called its *truth value*. For example, consider the following expressions:
(*a*)   Paris is in England.      (*c*)   Where are you going?
(*b*)   $2 + 2 = 4$              (*d*)   Put the homework on the blackboard.

The expressions (*a*) and (*b*) are statements; the first is false and the second is true. The expressions (*c*) and (*d*) are not statements since neither is true or false.

**12.2**   Define a compound statement, and give examples.

▎ Some statements are composed of substatements and various logical connectives. Such composite statements are called *compound statements*. For example
(*a*)   "Roses are red and violets are blue" is a compound statement with substatements "Roses are red" and "Violets are blue".
(*b*)   "He is intelligent or studies every night" is, implicitly, a compound statement with substatements "He is intelligent" and "He studies every night".

**12.3**   Let $p$ be "It is cold" and let $q$ be "It is raining." Give a simple verbal sentence which describes each of the following statements: (*a*) $\sim p$, (*b*) $p \wedge q$, (*c*) $p \vee q$, (*d*) $q \vee -p$.

▎ In each case, translate $\wedge$, $\vee$, and $\sim$ to read "and", "or", and "It is false that" or "not", respectively, and then simplify the English sentence.
(*a*)   It is not cold.          (*c*)   It is cold or it is raining.
(*b*)   It is cold and raining.  (*d*)   It is raining or it is not cold.

**12.4**   Repeat Problem 12.3 for: (*a*) $\sim p \wedge \sim q$, and (*b*) $\sim(\sim q)$.

▎ (*a*)   "It is not cold and it is not raining," or, in other words, "It is neither cold nor raining."
(*b*)   "It is not true that it is not raining," or, in other words, "It is false that it is not raining."

**12.5**   Let $p$ be "He is tall" and let $q$ be "He is handsome." Write each of the following statements in symbolic form using $p$ and $q$: (Assume that "He is short" means "He is not tall", i.e., $\sim p$.)
(*a*)   He is tall and handsome.        (*c*)   It is false that he is short or handsome.
(*b*)   He is tall but not handsome.    (*d*)   He is neither tall nor handsome.

▎ (*a*)   $p \wedge q$, (*b*) $p \wedge \sim q$, (*c*) $\sim(\sim p \vee q)$, and (*d*) $\sim p \wedge \sim q$.

**12.6**   Repeat Problem 12.5 for each of the following statements.
(*a*)   He is tall, or he is short and handsome.
(*b*)   It is not true that he is short or not handsome.

▎ (*a*)   $p \vee (\sim p \wedge q)$, and (*b*) $\sim(\sim p \vee \sim q)$.

341

**12.7**    Let $p$ be "Erik reads *Newsweek*", let $q$ be "Erik reads *The New Yorker*", and let $r$ be "Erik reads *Time*". Write each of the following in symbolic form:

    **(a)**   Erik reads *Newsweek* or *The New Yorker*, but not *Time*.

    **(b)**   Erik reads *Newsweek* and *The New Yorker*, or he does not read *Newsweek* and *Time*.

    **(c)**   It is not true that Erik reads *Newsweek* but not *Time*.

    **(d)**   It is not true that Erik reads *Time* or *The New Yorker* but not *Newsweek*.

    ▮   **(a)** $(p \vee q) \wedge \sim r$, **(b)** $(p \wedge q) \vee \sim (p \wedge r)$, **(c)** $\sim (p \wedge \sim r)$, and **(d)** $\sim [(r \vee q) \wedge \sim p]$.

**12.8**    Let $p$ be "Audrey speaks French" and let $q$ be "Audrey speaks Danish". Give a simple verbal sentence which describes each of the following: **(a)** $p \vee q$, **(b)** $p \wedge q$, **(c)** $p \wedge \sim q$, and **(d)** $\sim p \vee \sim q$.

    In each case, translate $\wedge$, $\vee$, and $\sim$ to read "and", "or", and "It is false that" or "not", respectively, and then simplify the English sentence.

    ▮   **(a)**   Audrey speaks French or Danish.

    **(b)**   Audrey speaks French and Danish.

    **(c)**   Audrey speaks French but not Danish.

    **(d)**   Audrey does not speak French or she does not speak Danish.

**12.9**    Repeat Problem 12.8 for: **(a)** $\sim \sim p$, and **(b)** $\sim (\sim p \wedge \sim q)$.

    ▮   **(a)**   It is not true that Audrey does not speak French.

    **(b)**   It is not true that Audrey speaks neither French nor Danish.

**12.10**    Let $p$ be "Sam is rich" and let $q$ be "Sam is happy". Write each of the following in symbolic form. (Assume "Sam is poor" means "Sam is not rich", i.e., $\sim p$.)

    **(a)**   Sam is poor but happy.          **(c)**   Sam is either rich or unhappy.

    **(b)**   Sam is neither rich nor happy.    **(d)**   Sam is poor or else he is both rich and unhappy.

    ▮   **(a)** $\sim p \wedge q$, **(b)** $\sim p \wedge \sim q$, **(c)** $p \vee \sim q$, and **(d)** $\sim p \vee (p \wedge \sim q)$.

## Polish Notation

Polish (prefix) notation refers to the placing of an operational symbol before its arguments rather than between them. This subsection will use the notation

$$Apq \quad \text{for} \quad p \wedge q \quad \text{and} \quad Np \quad \text{for} \quad \sim p$$

Such notation, named after the Polish mathematician Lukasiewicz, makes parentheses unnecessary.

**12.11**    Rewrite each of the following expressions using $A$ and $N$ instead of $\wedge$ and $\sim$:

    **(a)** $p \wedge \sim q$, **(b)** $\sim (\sim p \wedge q)$, and **(c)** $\sim p \wedge (\sim q \wedge r)$

    ▮   **(a)**   $p \wedge \sim q = p \wedge Nq = ApNq$

    **(b)**   $\sim (\sim p \wedge q) = \sim (Np \wedge q) = \sim (ANpq) = NANpq$

    **(c)**   $\sim p \wedge (\sim q \wedge r) = Np \wedge (Nq \wedge r) = Np \wedge (ANqr) = ANpANqr$

**12.12**    Rewrite each of the following expressions using $A$ and $N$ instead of $\wedge$ and $\sim$, respectively:

    **(a)** $(\sim p \wedge q) \wedge (p \wedge \sim r)$, and **(b)** $\sim (p \wedge \sim q) \wedge (\sim q \wedge \sim r)$

    ▮   **(a)**   $(\sim p \wedge q) \wedge (p \wedge \sim r) = (Np \wedge q) \wedge (p \wedge Nr) = (ANpq) \wedge (ApNr) = AANpqApNr$

    **(b)**   $\sim (p \wedge \sim q) \wedge (\sim q \wedge \sim r) = \sim (ApNq) \wedge (ANqNr) = (NApNq) \wedge (ANqNr) = ANApNqANqNr$

Note that no parentheses are needed in the final statements.

**12.13**    Rewrite the following using $\wedge$ and $\sim$ instead of $A$ and $N$: **(a)** $NApq$, **(b)** $ANpq$.

    ▮   **(a)**   $NApq = N(p \wedge q) = \sim (p \wedge q)$,    **(b)**   $ANpq = A(\sim p)q = \sim p \wedge q$

**12.14**    Rewrite the following using $\wedge$ and $\sim$ instead of $A$ and $N$: **(a)** $ApNq$ and **(b)** $ApAqr$.

    ▮   **(a)**   $ApNq = Ap(\sim q) = p \wedge \sim q$,    **(b)**   $ApAqr = Ap(q \wedge r) = p \wedge (q \wedge r)$

**12.15**    Rewrite the following using $\wedge$ and $\sim$ instead of $A$ and $N$: **(a)** $NAANpqr$ and **(b)** $ANpAqNr$

▌ (a)  $NAANpqr = NAA(\sim p)qr = NA(\sim p \wedge q)r = N[(\sim p \wedge q) \wedge r] = \sim[(\sim p \wedge q) \wedge r]$
▌ (b)  $ANpAqNr = ANpAq(\sim r) = ANp(q \wedge \sim r) = A(\sim p)(q \wedge \sim r) = \sim p \wedge (q \wedge \sim r)$

Note that the expressions involving $A$ and $N$ are unraveled from right to left.

## 12.2  TRUTH VALUE OF COMPOUND STATEMENTS

The fundamental property of a compound statement is that its truth value is completely determined by the truth values of its substatements together with the way in which they are connected to form the compound statement.

**12.16**  Define the truth value of the compound statement $p \wedge q$; that is, "$p$ and $q$".

▌ The statement $p \wedge q$ is true whenever both $p$ is true and $q$ is true; otherwise $p \wedge q$ is false. A convenient way to state this property is by the "truth" table in Fig. 12-1(a). That is, the first line is a short way of saying that if $p$ is true and $q$ is true then $p \wedge q$ is true. The other lines have analogous meaning. We regard this table as defining precisely the truth value of the compound statement $p \wedge q$ as a function of the truth values of $p$ and of $q$.

| $p$ | $q$ | $p \wedge q$ |
|---|---|---|
| T | T | T |
| T | F | F |
| F | T | F |
| F | F | F |

(a)

| $p$ | $q$ | $p \vee q$ |
|---|---|---|
| T | T | T |
| T | F | T |
| F | T | T |
| F | F | F |

(b)

| $p$ | $\sim p$ |
|---|---|
| T | F |
| F | T |

(c)

Fig. 12-1

**12.17**  Referring to Fig. 12-1(a), determine the truth value of each of the following statements:
(a)  Paris is in France and $2 + 2 = 4$.        (c)  Paris is in England and $2 + 2 = 4$.
(b)  Paris is in France and $2 + 2 = 5$.        (d)  Paris is in England and $2 + 2 = 5$.

▌ By Fig. 12-1(a), the statement $p \wedge q$, that is, "$p$ and $q$", is true, only when both statements are true. Thus only (a) is true.

**12.18**  Determine the truth value of each of the following statements:
(a)  $4 + 2 = 5$ and $6 + 3 = 9$        (c)  $4 + 5 = 9$ and $1 + 2 = 4$
(b)  $3 + 2 = 5$ and $6 + 1 = 7$        (d)  $3 + 2 = 5$ and $4 + 7 = 11$

▌ The statement "$p$ and $q$" is true only when both substatements are true. Thus: (a) false, (b) true, (c) false, and (d) true.

**12.19**  Define the truth value of the compound statement $p \vee q$; that is, "$p$ or $q$".

▌ The statement $p \vee q$ is true whenever $p$ is true or $q$ is true or both $p$ and $q$ are true; otherwise $p \vee q$ is false. This property is also stated by the truth table in Fig. 12-1(b) which we regard as defining $p \vee q$.

**Remark:**  The English word "or" is commonly used in two distinct ways. Sometimes it is used in the sense of "$p$ or $q$ or both", i.e., at least one of the two alternates occurs, as in Problem 12.19, and sometimes it is used in the sense of "$p$ or $q$ but not both", i.e., exactly one of the two alternatives occurs. For example, the sentence "He will go to Harvard or to Yale" uses "or" in the latter sense, called the *exclusive disjunction*. Unless otherwise stated, "or" shall be used in the former sense. This discussion points out the precision we gain from our symbolic language: $p \vee q$ is defined by its truth table and *always* means "$p$ and/or $q$".

**12.20**  Referring to Fig. 12-1(b), repeat Problem 12.17.

▌ By Fig. 12-1(b), the statement $p \vee q$, that is, "$p$ or $q$", is false, only when both substatements are false. Thus only (d) is false, the other statements are true.

**12.21**  Determine the truth value of each of the following statements:
(a)  $1 + 1 = 5$ or $2 + 2 = 4$        (c)  $2 + 5 = 9$ or $3 + 7 = 8$
(b)  $1 + 1 = 5$ or $3 + 3 = 4$        (d)  $2 + 5 = 9$ or $1 + 7 = 8$

▌ The statement "$p$ or $q$" is false only when both substatements are false. Thus: (a) true, (b) false, (c) false, (d) true.

**12.22**  Define the truth value of $\sim p$, (that is, "not $p$" or "It is false that $p$"), called the negation of $p$.

▋ The statement $\sim p$ is true whenever $p$ is false, and $\sim p$ is false whenever $p$ is true. That is, the truth value of negation of any statement is always the opposite of the truth value of the original statement. This defining property of $\sim p$ is shown in the truth table in Fig. 12-1($c$).

**12.23** Find the truth value of each statement: (**a**) Paris is in France. (**b**) It is false that Paris is in France. (**c**) Paris is not in France.

▋ The statement (**a**) is true. The statements (**b**) and (**c**) are false since each is the negation of (**a**).

**12.24** Find the truth value of each statement: (**a**) $3 + 3 = 7$. (**b**) It is false that $3 + 3 = 7$. (**c**) $3 + 3 \neq 7$.

▋ The statement (**a**) is false. Then (**b**) and (**c**) are true since each is the negation of (**a**), (**b**) and (**c**) are true statements.

**12.25** Determine the truth value of each of the following statements: (**a**) It is false that $2 + 2 = 4$ and $1 + 1 = 5$. (**b**) It is false that $2 + 2 = 4$ or London is in France.

 (**a**) The statement "$2 + 2 = 4$ and $1 + 1 = 5$" is false since one of its substatements, "$1 + 1 = 5$", is false. Accordingly its negation, the given statement, is true.
 (**b**) The statement "$2 + 2 = 4$ or London is in France" is true since one of its substatements, "$2 + 2 = 4$", is true. Accordingly its negation, the given statement, is false.

**12.26** Determine the truth value of each of the following statements: (**a**) Copenhagen is in Denmark, and $1 + 1 = 5$ or $2 + 2 = 4$. (**b**) Paris is in England, or $1 + 1 = 2$ and $3 + 3 = 7$.

 (**a**) The statement "$1 + 1 = 5$ or $2 + 2 = 4$" is true since one of its substatements, "$2 + 2 = 4$", is true. Hence the given statement is true since it is the conjunction of two true statements, "Copenhagen is in Denmark" and "$1 + 1 = 5$ or $2 + 2 = 4$".
 (**b**) The statement "$1 + 1 = 2$ and $3 + 3 = 7$" is false since one of its substatements, "$3 + 3 = 7$", is false. Thus the given statement is false since it is the disjunction of two false statements.

**12.27** Determine the truth value of each of the following statements: (**a**) Copenhagen is in Denmark, or $1 + 5 = 8$ and $3 + 3 = 6$. (**b**) Paris is in England, and $3 + 4 = 7$ or $2 + 6 = 8$.

 (**a**) Since "Copenhagen is in Denmark" is true, the given statement, of the form "$p$ or $q$", is true.
 (**b**) Since "Paris is in England" is false, the given statement, of the form "$p$ and $q$", is false.

## 12.3 PROPOSITIONS AND TRUTH TABLES

**12.28** Define a proposition and its truth table.

▋ A proposition, also called a well-formed formula (wff), is either a logical variable $p, q, r, \ldots$ or an expression constructed from such variables and the logical connectives ($\wedge$, $\vee$, $\sim$ and others discussed subsequently). We sometimes denote such a proposition by $P(p, q, \ldots)$.

 Now the truth value of a proposition depends exclusively upon the truth values of its variables, that is, the truth value of a proposition is known once the truth values of its variables are known. A simple concise way to show this relationship is through a *truth table* as illustrated in Problem 12.29.

**12.29** Give two methods to find the truth table of the proposition $\sim(p \wedge \sim q)$.

▋ *Method 1.* The truth table for $\sim(p \wedge \sim q)$ is constructed as in Fig. 12-2($a$). Observe that the first columns of the table are for the variables $p, q, \ldots$ and that there are enough rows in the table to allow for all possible combinations of T and F for these variables. (For 2 variables, as here, 4 rows are necessary; for 3 variables, 8 rows are necessary; and, in general, for $n$ variables, $2^n$ rows are required.) There is then a column for each "elementary" stage of the construction of the proposition, the truth value at each step being determined from the previous stages by the definitions of the connectives $\wedge$, $\vee$, $\sim$. Finally we obtain the truth value of the proposition, which appears in the last column.

| $p$ | $q$ | $\sim q$ | $p \wedge \sim q$ | $\sim(p \wedge \sim q)$ | $p$ | $q$ | $\sim(p \wedge \sim q)$ |
|-----|-----|----------|-------------------|--------------------------|-----|-----|--------------------------|
| T | T | F | F | T | T | T | T |
| T | F | T | T | F | T | F | F |
| F | T | F | F | T | F | T | T |
| F | F | T | F | T | F | F | T |

| | | | | | | | |
|---|---|---|---|---|---|---|---|
| | | ($a$) | | | | ($b$) | **Fig. 12-2** |

*Remark*:   The truth table of the proposition consists precisely of the columns under the variables and the column under the proposition, as shown in Fig. 12-2(*b*).

| p | q | ~ | (p | ∧ | ~ | q) |
|---|---|---|----|---|---|-----|
| T | T |   |    |   |   |     |
| T | F |   |    |   |   |     |
| F | T |   |    |   |   |     |
| F | F |   |    |   |   |     |
| Step |   |   |   |   |   |    |

**Fig. 12-3**

*Method 2.* Here we first construct the table as in Fig. 12-3. Observe that the proposition is written on the top row to the right of its variables, and that there is a column under each variable or connective in the proposition. Truth values are then entered into the truth table in various steps as shown in Fig. 12-4. The truth table of the proposition then consists of the original columns under the variables and the last column entered into the table, i.e., Step 4.

| p | q | ~ | (p | ∧ | ~ | q) |
|---|---|---|----|---|---|-----|
| T | T |   | T  |   |   | T   |
| T | F |   | T  |   |   | F   |
| F | T |   | F  |   |   | T   |
| F | F |   | F  |   |   | F   |
| Step |   |   | 1 |   |   | 1  |

| p | q | ~ | (p | ∧ | ~ | q) |
|---|---|---|----|---|---|-----|
| T | T |   | T  |   | F | T   |
| T | F |   | T  |   | T | F   |
| F | T |   | F  |   | F | T   |
| F | F |   | F  |   | T | F   |
| Step |   |   | 1 |   | 2 | 1  |

| p | q | ~ | (p | ∧ | ~ | q) |
|---|---|---|----|---|---|-----|
| T | T |   | T  | F | F | T   |
| T | F |   | T  | T | T | F   |
| F | T |   | F  | F | F | T   |
| F | F |   | F  | F | T | F   |
| Step |   |   | 1 | 3 | 2 | 1  |

| p | q | ~ | (p | ∧ | ~ | q) |
|---|---|---|----|---|---|-----|
| T | T | T | T  | F | F | T   |
| T | F | F | T  | T | T | F   |
| F | T | T | F  | F | F | T   |
| F | F | T | F  | F | T | F   |
| Step |   | 4 | 1 | 3 | 2 | 1  |

**Fig. 12-4**

**12.30**   Find the truth table of ~p ∧ q.

❚ See Fig. 12-5, which gives both methods introduced in Problem 12.29 for constructing the truth table.

| p | q | ~p | ~p ∧ q |
|---|---|----|--------|
| T | T | F  | F      |
| T | F | F  | F      |
| F | T | T  | T      |
| F | F | T  | F      |

**Method 1**

| p | q | ~ | p | ∧ | q |
|---|---|---|---|---|---|
| T | T | F | T | F | T |
| T | F | F | T | F | F |
| F | T | T | F | T | T |
| F | F | T | F | F | F |
| Step |   | 2 | 1 | 3 | 1 |

**Method 2**          **Fig. 12-5**

**12.31**   Find the truth table of ~(p ∨ q).

❚ See Fig. 12-6.

**12.32**   Find the truth table of ~(p ∨ ~q)

❚ See Fig. 12-7.

| p | q | p∨q | ~(p∨q) |
|---|---|-----|--------|
| T | T | T | F |
| T | F | T | F |
| F | T | T | F |
| F | F | F | T |

**Method 1**

| p | q | ~ | (p | ∨ | q) |
|---|---|---|----|---|---|
| T | T | F | T | T | T |
| T | F | F | T | T | F |
| F | T | F | F | T | T |
| F | F | T | F | F | F |
| Step | | 3 | 1 | 2 | 1 |

**Method 2**

**Fig. 12-6**

| p | q | ~q | p∨~q | ~(p∨~q) |
|---|---|----|------|---------|
| T | T | F | T | F |
| T | F | T | T | F |
| F | T | F | F | T |
| F | F | T | T | F |

**Method 1**

| p | q | ~ | (p | ∨ | ~ | q) |
|---|---|---|----|---|---|---|
| T | T | F | T | T | F | T |
| T | F | F | T | T | T | F |
| F | T | T | F | F | F | T |
| F | F | F | F | T | T | F |
| Step | | 4 | 1 | 3 | 2 | 1 |

**Method 2**

**Fig. 12-7**

**12.33** Find the truth tables of the following: **(a)** $p \wedge (q \vee r)$ and **(b)** $(p \wedge q) \vee (p \wedge r)$.

▮ Since there are three variables, the truth tables will require $2^3 = 8$ rows (see Problem 12.29). The truth tables are constructed in Fig. 12-8. Observe that both propositions have the same truth table.

| p | q | r | q∨r | p∧(q∨r) |
|---|---|---|-----|---------|
| T | T | T | T | T |
| T | T | F | T | T |
| T | F | T | T | T |
| T | F | F | F | F |
| F | T | T | T | F |
| F | T | F | T | F |
| F | F | T | T | F |
| F | F | F | F | F |

(a)

| p | q | r | p∧q | p∧r | (p∧q)∨(p∧r) |
|---|---|---|-----|-----|-------------|
| T | T | T | T | T | T |
| T | T | F | T | F | T |
| T | F | T | F | T | T |
| T | F | F | F | F | F |
| F | T | T | F | F | F |
| F | T | F | F | F | F |
| F | F | T | F | F | F |
| F | F | F | F | F | F |

(b)

**Fig. 12-8**

**12.34** Find the truth tables for: **(a)** $p \vee \sim q$, and **(b)** $\sim p \wedge \sim q$.

▮ See Fig. 12-9.

| p | q | ~q | p∨~q |
|---|---|----|------|
| T | T | F | T |
| T | F | T | T |
| F | T | F | F |
| F | F | T | T |

(a)

| p | q | ~p | ~q | ~p∧~q |
|---|---|----|----|-------|
| T | T | F | F | F |
| T | F | F | T | F |
| F | T | T | F | F |
| F | F | T | T | T |

(b)

**Fig. 12-9**

## 12.4 TAUTOLOGIES AND CONTRADICTIONS

**12.35** Define a tautology and a contradiction, and give examples.

▮ A proposition $P(p, q, \ldots)$ is a tautology if it contains only T in the last column of its truth table, i.e., if P is true for any truth values of its variables. Analogously, a proposition $P(p, q, \dots)$ is a contradiction if it contains only F in the last column of its truth table, i.e., if $P$ is false for any truth values of its variables.

For example, the proposition "$p$ or not $p$", i.e., $p \vee \sim p$, is a tautology; and the proposition "$p$ and not $p$", i.e., $p \wedge \sim p$, is a contradiction. This is verified by constructing their truth tables as in Fig. 12-10.

| $p$ | $\sim p$ | $p \vee \sim p$ | | $p$ | $\sim p$ | $p \wedge \sim p$ | |
|---|---|---|---|---|---|---|---|
| T | F | T | | T | F | F | |
| F | T | T | | F | T | F | **Fig. 12-10** |

**12.36**  Verify that the proposition $p \vee \sim(p \wedge q)$ is a tautology.

❚  Construct the truth table of $p \vee \sim(p \wedge q)$ as shown in Fig. 12-11. Since the truth value of $p \vee \sim(p \wedge q)$ is T for all values of $p$ and $q$, the proposition is a tautology.

| $p$ | $q$ | $p \wedge q$ | $\sim(p \wedge q)$ | $p \vee \sim(p \wedge q)$ | |
|---|---|---|---|---|---|
| T | T | T | F | T | |
| T | F | F | T | T | |
| F | T | F | T | T | |
| F | F | F | T | T | **Fig. 12-11** |

**12.37**  Verify that the proposition $(p \wedge q) \wedge \sim(p \vee q)$ is a contradiction.

❚  Construct the truth table of $(p \wedge q) \wedge \sim(p \vee q)$ as shown in Fig. 12-12. Since the truth value of $(p \wedge q) \wedge \sim(p \vee q)$ is F for all values of $p$ and $q$, the proposition is a contradiction.

| $p$ | $q$ | $p \wedge q$ | $p \vee q$ | $\sim(p \vee q)$ | $(p \wedge q) \wedge \sim(p \vee q)$ | |
|---|---|---|---|---|---|---|
| T | T | T | T | F | F | |
| T | F | F | T | F | F | |
| F | T | F | T | F | F | |
| F | F | F | F | T | F | **Fig. 12-12** |

**Theorem 12.1:**  If $P(p, q, \dots)$ is a tautology, then $\sim P(p, q, \dots)$ is a contradiction, and conversely.

**12.38**  Prove Theorem 12.1.

❚  Since a tautology is always true, the negation of a tautology is always false, i.e., is a contradiction, and vice versa.

**Theorem 12.2 (Principle of Substitution):**  Suppose $P(p, q, \dots)$ is a tautology. Then $P(P_1, P_2, \dots)$ is a tautology for any propositions $P_1, P_2, \dots$.

**12.39**  Prove Theorem 12.2.

❚  Since $P(p, q, \dots)$ does not depend upon the particular truth values of its variables $p, q, \dots$, we can substitute $P_1$ for $p$, $P_2$ for $q$, $\dots$ in the tautology $P(p, q, \dots)$ and still have a tautology.

**12.40**  Verify that the proposition $(p \wedge \sim q) \vee \sim(p \wedge \sim q)$ is a tautology.

❚  This proposition has the form $P \vee \sim P$ where $P = p \wedge \sim q$. By Fig. 12-10(a), $P \vee \sim P$ is a tautology. Thus, by the principle of substitution (Theorem 12.2), $(p \wedge \sim q) \vee \sim(p \wedge \sim q)$ is also a tautology.

## 12.5  LOGICAL EQUIVALENCE

**12.41**  Define logically equivalent propositions.

❚  Two propositions $P(p, q, \dots)$ and $Q(p, q, \dots)$ are said to be *logically equivalent,* or simply *equivalent* or *equal,* denoted by

$$P(p, q), \ldots) \equiv Q(p, q, \ldots)$$

if they have identical truth tables.

**12.42**   Show that the propositions $\sim(p \wedge q)$ and $\sim p \vee \sim q$ are logically equivalent.

❚ Construct the truth tables of $\sim(p \wedge q)$ and $\sim p \vee \sim q$ as in Fig. 12-13. Since the truth tables are the same, i.e., both propositions are false in the first case and true in the other three cases, the propositions $\sim(p \wedge q)$ and $\sim p \vee \sim q$ are logically equivalent and we can write

$$\sim(p \wedge q) \equiv \sim p \vee \sim q$$

| $p$ | $q$ | $p \wedge q$ | $\sim(p \wedge q)$ | $p$ | $q$ | $\sim p$ | $\sim q$ | $\sim p \vee \sim q$ |
|---|---|---|---|---|---|---|---|---|
| T | T | T | F | T | T | F | F | F |
| T | F | F | T | T | F | F | T | T |
| F | T | F | T | F | T | T | F | T |
| F | F | F | T | F | F | T | T | T |

**Fig. 12-13**

**12.43**   Prove the associative law [see Table 12-1(2*b*)]: $(p \wedge q) \wedge r \equiv p \wedge (q \wedge r)$.

❚ Construct the required truth tables as in Fig. 12-14. Since the truth tables are identical, the propositions are equivalent.

| $p$ | $q$ | $r$ | $p \wedge q$ | $(p \wedge q) \wedge r$ | $q \wedge r$ | $p \wedge (q \wedge r)$ |
|---|---|---|---|---|---|---|
| T | T | T | T | T | T | T |
| T | T | F | T | F | F | F |
| T | F | T | F | F | F | F |
| T | F | F | F | F | F | F |
| F | T | T | F | F | T | F |
| F | T | F | F | F | F | F |
| F | F | T | F | F | F | F |
| F | F | F | F | F | F | F |

**Fig. 12-14**

**12.44**   Prove that disjunction distributes over conjunction; that is, prove the distributive law [see Table 12-1(4*a*)]: $p \vee (q \wedge r) \equiv (p \vee q) \wedge (p \vee r)$.

❚ Construct the required truth tables as in Fig. 12-15. Since the truth tables are identical, the propositions are equivalent.

| $p$ | $q$ | $r$ | $q \wedge r$ | $p \vee (q \wedge r)$ | $p \vee q$ | $p \vee r$ | $(p \vee q) \wedge (p \vee r)$ |
|---|---|---|---|---|---|---|---|
| T | T | T | T | T | T | T | T |
| T | T | F | F | T | T | T | T |
| T | F | T | F | T | T | T | T |
| T | F | F | F | T | T | T | T |
| F | T | T | T | T | T | T | T |
| F | T | F | F | F | T | F | F |
| F | F | T | F | F | F | T | F |
| F | F | F | F | F | F | F | F |

**Fig. 12-15**

**12.45**   Prove that the operation of disjunction can be written in terms of the operations of conjunction and negation. Specifically, $p \vee q \equiv \sim(\sim p \wedge \sim q)$.

❚ Construct the required truth tables as in Fig. 12-16.
Since the truth tables are identical, the propositions are equivalent.

| $p$ | $q$ | $p \vee q$ | $\sim p$ | $\sim q$ | $\sim p \wedge \sim q$ | $\sim(\sim p \wedge \sim q)$ |
|---|---|---|---|---|---|---|
| T | T | T | F | F | F | T |
| T | F | T | F | T | F | T |
| F | T | T | T | F | F | T |
| F | F | F | T | T | T | F |

**Fig. 12-16**

**12.46** Let $P(p)$ be a proposition in one variable $p$. **(a)** Find the number $m$ of nonequivalent propositions $P(p)$. **(b)** Give an example of each proposition in **(a)**.

▮ **(a)** The truth table of $P(p)$ will contain two rows or lines (since $p$ can be either T or F). In each of the lines T or F can appear as in Fig. 12-17(a); hence $m = 4$.

**(b)** Consider the truth table in Fig. 12-17(b). Thus

$$P_1(p) \equiv p \vee \sim p, \qquad P_2(p) \equiv p, \qquad P_3(p) \equiv \sim p, \qquad P_4(p) \equiv p \wedge \sim p$$

| $p$ | $P_1(p)$ | $P_2(p)$ | $P_3(p)$ | $P_4(p)$ |
|---|---|---|---|---|
| T | T | T | F | F |
| F | T | F | T | F |

(a)

| $p$ | $\sim p$ | $p \vee \sim p$ | $p \wedge \sim p$ |
|---|---|---|---|
| T | F | T | F |
| F | T | T | F |

(b)

**Fig. 12-17**

**12.47** Determine the number $m$ of nonequivalent propositions $P(p, q)$ in two variables $p$ and $q$.

▮ The truth table of $P(p, q)$ will contain $2^2 = 4$ lines. In each line, T or F can appear as shown in Fig. 12-18. Thus $m = 2^4 = 16$.

| $p$ | $q$ | $P_1$ | $P_2$ | $P_3$ | $P_4$ | $P_5$ | $P_6$ | $P_7$ | $P_8$ | $P_9$ | $P_{10}$ | $P_{11}$ | $P_{12}$ | $P_{13}$ | $P_{14}$ | $P_{15}$ | $P_{16}$ |
|---|---|---|---|---|---|---|---|---|---|---|---|---|---|---|---|---|---|
| T | T | T | T | T | T | T | T | T | T | F | F | F | F | F | F | F | F |
| T | F | T | T | T | T | F | F | F | F | T | T | T | T | F | F | F | F |
| F | T | T | T | F | F | T | T | F | F | T | T | F | F | T | T | F | F |
| F | F | T | F | T | F | T | F | T | F | T | F | T | F | T | F | T | F |

**Fig. 12-18**

**12.48** Determine the number $m$ of nonequivalent propositions in: **(a)** three variables $p$, $q$, and $r$; **(b)** $n$ variables $p_1, p_2, \ldots, p_n$.

▮ **(a)** The truth table of $P(p, q, r)$ will contain $2^3 = 8$ lines. In each line, either T or F can appear; hence $m = 2^8 = 256$.

**(b)** The truth table of $P(p_1, p_2, \ldots, p_n)$ will contain $2^n$ lines; hence, as above, $m = 2^{2^n}$.

## Exclusive Disjunction, Joint Denial

**12.49** The propositional connective $\veebar$ is called the *exclusive disjunction*; $p \veebar q$ is read "$p$ or $q$ but not both". Construct a truth table for $p \veebar q$.

▮ Now $p \veebar q$ is true if $p$ is true or if $q$ is true but not if both are true; the truth table of $p \veebar q$ is shown in Fig. 12-19(a).

| $p$ | $q$ | $p \veebar q$ |
|---|---|---|
| T | T | F |
| T | F | T |
| F | T | T |
| F | F | F |

(a)

| $p$ | $q$ | $(p$ | $\vee$ | $q)$ | $\wedge$ | $\sim$ | $(p$ | $\wedge$ | $q)$ |
|---|---|---|---|---|---|---|---|---|---|
| T | T | T | T | T | F | F | T | T | T |
| T | F | T | T | F | T | T | T | F | F |
| F | T | F | T | T | T | T | F | F | T |
| F | F | F | F | F | F | T | F | F | F |
| Step | | 1 | 2 | 1 | 4 | 3 | 1 | 2 | 1 |

(b)

**Fig. 12-19**

**12.50**    Prove: $p \veebar q \equiv (p \vee q) \wedge \sim(p \wedge q)$. Accordingly $\veebar$ can be written in terms of the original three connectives $\wedge$, $\vee$, and $\sim$.

▮  Construct the truth table of $(p \vee q) \wedge \sim(p \wedge q)$, say by the second method used in Problem 12.29, as in Fig. 12-19(b). Figures 12-19(a) and (b) show that the truth tables of $p \veebar q$ and $(p \vee q) \wedge \sim(p \wedge q)$ are identical: hence $p \veebar q \equiv (p \vee q) \wedge \sim(p \wedge q)$.

**12.51**    The propositional connective $\downarrow$ is called the *joint denial*; $p \downarrow q$ is read "Neither $p$ nor $q$". Construct a truth table for $p \downarrow q$.

▮  Now $p \downarrow q$ is true only in the case that $p$ is not true and $q$ is not true; the truth table of $p \downarrow q$ is shown in Fig. 12-20.

| $p$ | $q$ | $p \downarrow q$ |
|-----|-----|------|
| T | T | F |
| T | F | F |
| F | T | F |
| F | F | T |

**Fig. 12-20**

**Proposition 12.3:**    The three connectives $\vee$, $\wedge$, and $\sim$ may be expressed in terms of the connective $\downarrow$ as follows:

$$\text{(i)} \quad \sim p \equiv p \downarrow p, \quad \text{(ii)} \quad p \wedge q \equiv (p \downarrow p) \downarrow (q \downarrow q), \quad \text{(iii)} \quad p \vee q \equiv (p \downarrow q) \downarrow (p \downarrow q)$$

**12.52**    Prove Proposition 12.3(i).

▮  Construct the truth tables for $\sim p$ and $p \downarrow p$ as in Fig. 12-21. Since the two propositions have the same truth tables, $\sim p \equiv p \downarrow p$.

| $p$ | $\sim p$ | $p \downarrow p$ |
|-----|-----|------|
| T | F | F |
| F | T | T |

**Fig. 12-21**

**12.53**    Prove Proposition 12.3(ii).

▮  Construct the appropriate truth tables as in Fig. 12-22. Since the propositions have the same truth tables, $p \wedge q \equiv (p \downarrow p) \downarrow (q \downarrow q)$.

| $p$ | $q$ | $p \wedge q$ | $p \downarrow p$ | $q \downarrow q$ | $(p \downarrow p) \downarrow (q \downarrow q)$ |
|-----|-----|-----|-----|-----|-----|
| T | T | T | F | F | T |
| T | F | F | F | T | F |
| F | T | F | T | F | F |
| F | F | F | T | T | F |

**Fig. 12-22**

**12.54**    Prove Proposition 12.3(iii).

▮  Construct the appropriate truth tables as in Fig. 12-23. Since the truth tables are the same, $p \vee q \equiv (p \downarrow q) \downarrow (p \downarrow q)$.

| $p$ | $q$ | $p \vee q$ | $p \downarrow q$ | $(p \downarrow q) \downarrow (p \downarrow q)$ |
|-----|-----|-----|-----|-----|
| T | T | T | F | T |
| T | F | T | F | T |
| F | T | T | F | T |
| F | F | F | T | F |

**Fig. 12-23**

## 12.6  NEGATION, DeMORGAN'S LAWS

**12.55**  Prove DeMorgan's laws (see Table 12-1): **(a)** $\sim(p \wedge q) \equiv \sim p \vee \sim q$; **(b)** $\sim(p \vee q) \equiv p \wedge \sim q$.

▌ Construct the appropriate truth tables as in Figs. 12-24(a) and (b).

| $p$ | $q$ | $p \wedge q$ | $\sim(p \wedge q)$ | $\sim p$ | $\sim q$ | $\sim p \vee \sim q$ |
|---|---|---|---|---|---|---|
| T | T | T | F | F | F | F |
| T | F | F | T | F | T | T |
| F | T | F | T | T | F | T |
| F | F | F | T | T | T | T |

(a)

| $p$ | $q$ | $p \vee q$ | $\sim(p \vee q)$ | $\sim p$ | $\sim q$ | $\sim p \wedge \sim q$ |
|---|---|---|---|---|---|---|
| T | T | T | F | F | F | F |
| T | F | T | F | F | T | F |
| F | T | T | F | T | F | F |
| F | F | F | T | T | T | T |

(b)

**Fig. 12-24**

**12.56**  Verify: $\sim \sim p \equiv p$ [see Table 12-1(8a)].

▌ Construct the appropriate truth tables as in Fig. 12-25.

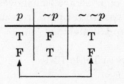

| $p$ | $\sim p$ | $\sim \sim p$ |
|---|---|---|
| T | F | T |
| F | T | F |

**Fig. 12-25**

**12.57**  Use the results of Problems 12.55 and 12.56 to simplify each of the following propositions: **(a)** $\sim(p \vee \sim q)$, and **(b)** $\sim(\sim p \wedge q)$.

▌ **(a)**  $\sim(p \vee \sim q) \equiv \sim p \wedge \sim \sim q \equiv \sim p \wedge q$,     **(b)**  $\sim(\sim p \wedge q) \equiv \sim \sim p \vee \sim q \equiv p \vee \sim q$

**12.58**  Use the results of Problems 12.55 and 12.56 to simplify each of the following propositions: **(a)** $\sim(p \wedge \sim q)$, and **(b)** $\sim(\sim p \vee \sim q)$.

▌ **(a)**  $\sim(p \wedge \sim q) \equiv \sim p \vee \sim \sim q \equiv \sim p \vee q$,     **(b)**  $\sim(\sim p \vee \sim q) \equiv \sim \sim p \wedge \sim \sim q \equiv p \wedge q$

**12.59**  Simplify each of the following propositions: **(a)** $\sim(\sim p \vee q)$, and **(b)** $\sim(\sim p \wedge \sim q)$.

▌ **(a)**  $\sim(\sim p \vee q) \equiv \sim \sim p \wedge \sim q \equiv p \wedge \sim q$,     **(b)**  $\sim(\sim p \wedge \sim q) \equiv \sim \sim p \vee \sim \sim q \equiv p \vee q$

**12.60**  Use the results of the preceding problems to simplify each of the following statements: **(a)** It is not true that his mother is English or his father is French. **(b)** It is not true that he studies physics but not mathematics.

▌ **(a)**  Let $p$ denote "His mother is English" and let $q$ denote "His father is French". Then the given statement is $\sim(p \vee q)$. But $\sim(p \vee q) \equiv \sim p \wedge \sim q$. Hence the given statement is logically equivalent to the statement "His mother is not English and his father is not French".

**(b)**  Let $p$ denote "He studies physics" and let $q$ denote "He studies mathematics". Then the given statement is $\sim(p \wedge \sim q)$. But $\sim(p \wedge \sim q) \equiv \sim p \vee \sim \sim q \equiv \sim p \vee q$. Hence the given statement is logically equivalent to the statement "He does not study physics or he studies mathematics".

**12.61**  Simplify each of the following statements: **(a)** It is not true that sales are decreasing and prices are rising. **(b)** It is not true that it is not cold or it is raining.

▌ **(a)**  Since $\sim(p \wedge q) \equiv \sim p \vee \sim q$, the given statement is logically equivalent to the statement "Sales are increasing or prices are falling".

**(b)** Since $\sim(\sim p \vee q) \equiv p \wedge \sim q$, the given statement is logically equivalent to the statement "It is cold and it is not raining".

**12.62** Write the negation of each of the following statements as simply as possible.
**(a)** He is tall but handsome.    **(b)** He has blond hair or blue eyes.

▌ **(a)** Use $\sim(p \wedge q) \equiv \sim p \vee \sim q$ to obtain: "He is not tall or not handsome".
**(b)** Use $\sim(p \vee q) \equiv \sim p \wedge \sim q$ to obtain: "He has neither blond hair nor blue eyes".

**12.63** Write the negation of each of the following statements as simply as possible.
**(a)** He is neither rich nor happy.    **(b)** He has lost his job or he did not go to work today.

▌ **(a)** Use $\sim(\sim p \wedge \sim q) \equiv p \vee q$ to obtain: "He is rich or happy".
**(b)** Use $\sim(p \vee \sim q) \equiv \sim p \wedge q$ to obtain: "He has not lost his job and he did go to work today."

**12.64** Write the negation of each of the following propositions as simply as possible. **(a)** $(\sim p \vee q) \wedge r$, **(b)** $p \vee (q \wedge \sim r)$.

▌ **(a)** $\sim[(\sim p \vee q) \wedge r] \equiv \sim(\sim p \vee q) \vee \sim r \equiv (p \wedge \sim q) \vee \sim r$
**(b)** $\sim[p \vee (q \wedge \sim r)] \equiv \sim p \wedge \sim(q \wedge r) \equiv \sim p \wedge (\sim q \vee r)$

**12.65** Express $\wedge$ in terms of $\vee$ and $\sim$ by showing $p \wedge q \equiv \sim(\sim p \vee \sim q)$. (Compare with Problem 12.45.)

▌ Use DeMorgan's laws to obtain

$$\sim(\sim p \vee \sim q) \equiv \sim \sim p \wedge \sim \sim q \equiv p \wedge q$$

## 12.7 ALGEBRA OF PROPOSITIONS

Propositions, under the relation of logical equivalence, satisfy various laws (identities) which are listed in Table 12-1 (where $t$ and $f$ denote variables restricted to the truth values true and false, respectively). Some of the laws were already proven previously. For completeness, we formally state:

**Theorem 12.4:** Propositions satisfy the laws in Table 12-1.

**TABLE 12-1**

| LAWS OF THE ALGEGBRA OF PROPOSITIONS | |
|---|---|
| **Idempotent Laws** | |
| 1a.  $p \vee p \equiv p$ | 1b.  $p \wedge p \equiv p$ |
| **Associative Laws** | |
| 2a.  $(p \vee q) \vee r \equiv p \vee (q \vee r)$ | 2b.  $(p \wedge q) \wedge r \equiv p \wedge (q \wedge r)$ |
| **Commutative Laws** | |
| 3a.  $p \vee q \equiv q \vee p$ | 3b.  $p \wedge q \equiv q \wedge p$ |
| **Distributive Laws** | |
| 4a.  $p \vee (q \wedge r) \equiv (p \vee q) \wedge (p \vee r)$ | 4b.  $p \wedge (q \vee r) \equiv (p \wedge q) \vee (p \wedge r)$ |
| **Identity Laws** | |
| 5a.  $p \vee f \equiv p$ | 5b.  $p \wedge t \equiv p$ |
| 6a.  $p \vee t \equiv t$ | 6b.  $p \wedge f \equiv f$ |
| **Complement Laws** | |
| 7a.  $p \vee \sim p \equiv t$ | 7b.  $p \wedge \sim p \equiv f$ |
| 8a.  $\sim \sim p \equiv p$ | 8b.  $\sim t \equiv f, \sim f \equiv t$ |
| **DeMorgan's Laws** | |
| 9a.  $\sim p(\vee q) \equiv \sim p \wedge \sim q$ | 9b.  $\sim(p \wedge q) \equiv \sim p \vee \sim q$ |

**12.66**   Show that the logical equivalence $(p \vee q) \wedge \sim p \equiv \sim p \wedge q$ follows from the laws in Table 12-1.

▮

| | Statement | | Reason |
|---|---|---|---|
| (1) | $(p \vee q) \wedge \sim p \equiv \sim p \wedge (p \vee q)$ | (1) | Commutative law |
| (2) | $\equiv (\sim p \wedge p) \vee (\sim p \wedge q)$ | (2) | Distributive law |
| (3) | $\equiv f \vee (\sim p \wedge q)$ | (3) | Complement law |
| (4) | $\equiv \sim p \wedge q$ | (4) | Identity law |

**12.67**   Show that $p \vee (p \wedge q) \equiv p$ follows from the laws in Table 12-1.

▮

| | Statement | | Reason |
|---|---|---|---|
| (1) | $p \vee (p \wedge q) \equiv (p \wedge t) \vee (p \wedge q)$ | (1) | Identity law |
| (2) | $\equiv p \wedge (t \vee q)$ | (2) | Distributive law |
| (3) | $\equiv p \wedge t$ | (3) | Identity law |
| (4) | $\equiv p$ | (4) | Identity law |

**12.68**   Use the laws in Table 12-1 to show that $\sim(p \vee q) \vee (\sim p \wedge q) \equiv \sim p$.

▮

| | Statement | | Reason |
|---|---|---|---|
| (1) | $\sim(p \vee q) \vee (\sim p \wedge q) \equiv (\sim p \wedge \sim q) \vee (\sim p \wedge q)$ | (1) | DeMorgan's law |
| (2) | $\equiv \sim p \wedge (\sim q \vee q)$ | (2) | Distributive law |
| (3) | $\equiv \sim p \wedge t$ | (3) | Complement law |
| (4) | $\equiv \sim p$ | (4) | Identity law |

**12.69**   Use the laws in Table 12-1 to show that $p \wedge (p \vee q) \equiv p$.

▮   $$p \wedge (p \vee q) \equiv (p \vee f) \wedge (p \vee q) \equiv p \vee (f \wedge q) \equiv p \vee f \equiv p$$

**12.70**   Use the laws in Table 12-1 to show that $p \wedge (\sim p \vee q) \equiv p \wedge q$.

▮   $$p \wedge (\sim p \vee q) \equiv (p \wedge \sim p) \vee (p \wedge q) \equiv f \vee (p \wedge q) \equiv p \wedge q$$

**12.71**   Use the laws in Table 12-1 to show that $(p \wedge q) \vee \sim p \equiv \sim p \vee q$.

▮   $$(p \wedge q) \vee \sim p \equiv \sim p \vee (p \wedge q) \equiv (\sim p \vee p) \wedge (\sim p \vee q)$$
$$\equiv (p \vee \sim p) \wedge (\sim p \vee q) \equiv t \wedge (\sim p \vee q)$$
$$\equiv (\sim p \vee q) \wedge t \equiv \sim p \vee q$$

## 12.8   CONDITIONAL, $p \rightarrow q$

Many statements, particularly in mathematics, are of the form "If $p$ then $q$". Such statements are called *conditional* statements and are denoted by

$$p \rightarrow q$$

The conditional $p \rightarrow q$ is sometimes read: (1) $p$ implies $q$, (2) $p$ only if $q$, (3) $p$ is sufficient for $q$, (4) $q$ is necessary for $p$.

**12.72**   Let $p$ denote "It is cold" and let $q$ denote "It rains". Write the following statements in symbolic form.
   (*a*)   It rains only if it is cold.
   (*b*)   A necessary condition for it to be cold is that it rain.
   (*c*)   A sufficient condition for it to be cold is that it rain.

   ▮   Recall that $p \rightarrow q$ can be read "$p$ only if $q$", "$p$ is sufficient for $q$", or "$q$ is necessary for $p$". Then
   (*a*) $q \rightarrow p$, (*b*) $p \rightarrow q$, and (*c*) $q \rightarrow p$.

**12.73**   Repeat Problem 12.72 for the following statements: (*a*) Whenever it rains it is cold. (*b*) It never rains when it is cold.

   ▮   (*a*)   Now the statement "Whenever it rains it is cold" is equivalent to "If it rains then it is cold". That is, $q \rightarrow p$.
   (*b*)   The statement "It never rains when it is cold" is equivalent to "If it is cold then it does not rain". That is, $p \rightarrow \sim q$.

**12.74**   Define the truth value of the compound statement $p \rightarrow q$, that is, "If $p$ then $q$".

▮ The statement $p \rightarrow q$ is true except in the case that $p$ is true and $q$ is false. This property is also stated by the truth table in Fig. 12-26(a)

| $p$ | $q$ | $p \rightarrow q$ |
|---|---|---|
| T | T | T |
| T | F | F |
| F | T | T |
| F | F | T |

(a)

| $p$ | $q$ | $\sim p$ | $\sim p \vee q$ |
|---|---|---|---|
| T | T | F | T |
| T | F | F | F |
| F | T | T | T |
| F | F | T | T |

(b)

**Fig. 12-26**

**12.75**  Show that $p \rightarrow q$ is logically equivalent to $\sim p \vee q$, that is,

$$p \rightarrow q \equiv \sim p \vee q$$

In other words, the conditional statement "If $p$ then $q$" is logically equivalent to the statement "Not $p$ or $q$" which only involves the connectives $\vee$ and $\sim$ and thus was already a part of our language. We may regard $p \rightarrow q$ as an abbreviation for an oft-recurring statement.

▮ Construct the truth table for $\sim p \vee q$ as in Fig. 12-26(b). It is the same as the truth table for $p \rightarrow q$ in Fig. 12-26(a). Accordingly, $p \rightarrow q \equiv \sim p \vee q$.

**12.76**  Determine the truth value of each of the following statements:
(a)  If Paris is in France, then $2 + 2 = 4$.  (c)  If Paris is in England, then $2 + 2 = 4$.
(b)  If Paris is in France, then $2 + 2 = 5$.  (d)  If Paris is in England, then $2 + 2 = 5$.

▮ By Fig. 12-26(a), the statement "If $p$ then $q$" is false only when $p$ is true and $q$ is false. Thus only (b) is false.

**12.77**  Rewrite the following statements without using the conditional.
(a)  If it is cold, he wears a hat.
(b)  If productivity increases, then wages rise.

▮ Recall that "If $p$ then $q$" is equivalent to "Not $p$ or $q$"; that is, $p \rightarrow q \equiv \sim p \vee q$.
(a)  It is not cold or he wears a hat.
(b)  Productivity does not increase or wages rise.

**12.78**  Construct the truth table of $(p \rightarrow q) \rightarrow (p \wedge q)$.

▮ See Fig. 12-27.

| $p$ | $q$ | $p \rightarrow q$ | $p \wedge q$ | $(p \rightarrow q) \rightarrow (p \wedge q)$ |
|---|---|---|---|---|
| T | T | T | T | T |
| T | F | F | F | T |
| F | T | T | F | F |
| F | F | T | F | F |

**Fig. 12-27**

**12.79**  Construct the truth table of $\sim p \rightarrow (q \rightarrow p)$.

▮ See Fig. 12-28.

| $p$ | $q$ | $\sim p$ | $q \rightarrow p$ | $\sim p \rightarrow (q \rightarrow p)$ |
|---|---|---|---|---|
| T | T | F | T | T |
| T | F | F | T | T |
| F | T | T | F | F |
| F | F | T | T | T |

**Fig. 12-28**

**12.80**  Verify that $(p \wedge q) \rightarrow (p \vee q)$ is a tautology.

▮ Construct the truth table for $(p \wedge q) \rightarrow (p \vee q)$ as in Fig. 12-29. Since the truth value of $(p \wedge q) \rightarrow (p \vee q)$ is T for all values of $p$ and $q$, it is a tautology.

| $p$ | $q$ | $p \wedge q$ | $p \vee q$ | $(p \wedge q) \rightarrow (p \vee q)$ |
|---|---|---|---|---|
| T | T | T | T | T |
| T | F | F | T | T |
| F | T | F | T | T |
| F | F | F | F | T |

**Fig. 12-29**

**12.81**  Prove that the conditional operation distributes over conjunction; that is,

$$p \rightarrow (q \wedge r) \equiv (p \rightarrow q) \wedge (p \rightarrow r)$$

▮ Since we have three variables, the truth tables will need $2^3 = 8$ rows. The required truth tables are shown in Fig. 12-30. Observe that both propositions have the same truth table.

| $p$ | $q$ | $r$ | $q \wedge r$ | $p \rightarrow (q \wedge r)$ | $p \rightarrow q$ | $p \rightarrow r$ | $(p \rightarrow q) \wedge (p \rightarrow r)$ |
|---|---|---|---|---|---|---|---|
| T | T | T | T | T | T | T | T |
| T | T | F | F | F | T | F | F |
| T | F | T | F | F | F | T | F |
| T | F | F | F | F | F | F | F |
| F | T | T | T | T | T | T | T |
| F | T | F | F | T | T | T | T |
| F | F | T | F | T | T | T | T |
| F | F | F | F | T | T | T | T |

**Fig. 12-30**

### Conditional Statements and Variations

This subsection considers the conditional $p \rightarrow q$ and the following other simple propositions containing $p$ and $q$:

$$q \rightarrow p, \quad \sim p \rightarrow \sim q, \quad \text{and} \quad \sim q \rightarrow \sim p$$

These are called respectively the *converse, inverse,* and *contrapositive* of the original conditional proposition $p \rightarrow q$.

**12.82**  Which, if any, of the above propositions are logically equivalent to $p \rightarrow q$?

▮ Construct their truth tables as in Fig. 12-31. Only the contrapositive $\sim q \rightarrow \sim p$ is logically equivalent to the original conditional proposition $p \rightarrow q$.

| $p$ | $q$ | $\sim p$ | $\sim q$ | Conditional $p \rightarrow q$ | Converse $q \rightarrow p$ | Inverse $\sim p \rightarrow \sim q$ | Contrapositive $\sim q \rightarrow \sim p$ |
|---|---|---|---|---|---|---|---|
| T | T | F | F | T | T | T | T |
| T | F | F | T | F | T | T | F |
| F | T | T | F | T | F | F | T |
| F | F | T | T | T | T | T | T |

**Fig. 12-31**

We formally state the important result of Problem 12.82 in the following theorem:

**Theorem 12.5:**  A conditional statement $p \rightarrow q$ and its contrapositive $\sim q \rightarrow \sim p$ are logically equivalent.

**12.83**  Determine the contrapositive of each statement: (*a*) If John is a poet, then he is poor. (*b*) Only if Marc studies will he pass the test.

▮ (*a*)  The contrapositive of $p \rightarrow q$ is $\sim q \rightarrow \sim p$. Hence the contrapositive of the given statement is

If John is not poor, then he is not a poet.

(*b*)  The given statement is equivalent to "If Marc passes the test, then he studied". Hence its contrapositive is

If Marc does not study, then he will not pass the test.

**12.84**   Determine the contrapositive of each statement: (*a*) It is necessary to have snow in order for Eric to ski. (*b*) If $x$ is less than zero, then $x$ is not positive.

▮ (*a*)   The given statement is equivalent to "If Eric skis, then it snowed". Hence its contrapositive is

If it did not snow, then Eric will not ski.

(*b*)   The contrapositive of $p \to \sim q$ is $\sim \sim q \to \sim p \equiv q \to \sim p$. Hence the contrapositive of the given statement is

If $x$ is positive, then $x$ is not less than zero.

**12.85**   Find and simplify: (*a*) Contrapositive of the contrapositive of $p \to q$. (*b*) Contrapositive of the converse of $p \to q$. (*c*) Contrapositive of the inverse of $p \to q$.

▮ (*a*)   The contrapositive of $p \to q$ is $\sim q \to \sim p$. The contrapositive of $\sim q \to \sim p$ is $\sim \sim p \to \sim \sim q \equiv p \to q$, which is the original conditional proposition.

(*b*)   The converse of $p \to q$ is $q \to p$. The contrapositive of $q \to p$ is $\sim p \to \sim q$, which is the inverse of $p \to q$.

(*c*)   The inverse of $p \to q$ is $\sim p \to \sim q$. The contrapositive of $\sim p \to \sim q$ is $\sim \sim q \to \sim \sim p \equiv q \to p$, which is the converse of $p \to q$.

In other words, the inverse and converse are contrapositives of each other, and the conditional and contrapositive are contrapositives of each other!

**12.86**   Determine the contrapositive of each statement:
(*a*)   If he has courage he will win.
(*b*)   It is necessary to be strong in order to be a sailor.
(*c*)   Only if he does not tire will he win.
(*d*)   It is sufficient for it to be a square in order to be a rectangle.

▮ (*a*)   If he does not win, then he does not have courage.
(*b*)   If he is not strong, then he is not a sailor.
(*c*)   If he tires, then he will not win.
(*d*)   If it is not a rectangle, then it is not a square.

**12.87**   Prove: $(p \to q)$ If $x$ is an integer and $x^2$ is odd, then $x$ is odd.

▮ We show that the contrapositive $\sim q \to \sim p$, "If $x$ is even, then $x^2$ is even", is true. Let $x$ be even; then $x = 2n$ where $n$ is an integer. Hence $x^2 = (2n)(2n) = 2(2n^2)$ is also even. Since the contrapositive statement $\sim q \to \sim p$ is true, the original conditional statement $p \to q$ is also true.

## 12.9   BICONDITIONAL, $p \leftrightarrow q$

Another common statement, especially in mathematics, is of the form "$p$ if and only if $q$" or, simply, "$p$ iff $q$". Such statements, denoted by

$$p \leftrightarrow q$$

are called *biconditional* statements.

**12.88**   Define the truth table of the biconditional $p \leftrightarrow q$, that is, "$p$ if and only if $q$".

▮ The statement $p \leftrightarrow q$ is true whenever $p$ and $q$ have the same truth values; otherwise $p \leftrightarrow q$ is false. This property is also stated by the truth table in Fig. 12-32.

| $p$ | $q$ | $p \leftrightarrow q$ |
|:---:|:---:|:---:|
| T | T | T |
| T | F | F |
| F | T | F |
| F | F | T |

**Fig. 12-32**

**12.89** Determine the truth value of each of the following statements:
(*a*) Paris is in France if and only if $2 + 2 = 4$.
(*b*) Paris is in France if and only if $2 + 2 = 5$.
(*c*) Paris is in England if and only if $2 + 2 = 4$.
(*d*) Paris is in England if and only if $2 + 2 = 5$.

▮ By Fig. 12-32, (*a*) and (*d*) are true since the substatements are both true in (*a*) and both false in (*d*). On the other hand, (*c*) and (*d*) are false since the substatements have different truth values.

**Theorem 12.6:** The propositions $P(p, q, \ldots)$ and $Q(p, q, \ldots)$ are logically equivalent if and only if the proposition

$$P(p, q, \ldots) \leftrightarrow Q(p, q, \ldots)$$

is a tautology.

**12.90** Prove Theorem 12.6.

▮ Suppose $P(p, q, \ldots) \equiv Q(p, q, \ldots)$. Then they have the same truth table. Hence $P(p, q, \ldots) \leftrightarrow Q(p, q, \ldots)$ is true for any values of the variables $p, q, \ldots$; that is, the proposition is a tautology. The converse follows from the fact that each step is reversible.

**12.91** Show that "$p$ implies $q$ and $q$ implies $p$" is logically equivalent to the biconditional "$p$ if and only if $q$"; that is, $(p \rightarrow q) \wedge (q \rightarrow p) \equiv p \leftrightarrow q$.

▮ Find the truth tables for $p \leftrightarrow q$ and $(p \rightarrow q) \wedge (q \rightarrow p)$ as in Fig. 12-33. Since the truth tables are the same, they are logically equivalent.

| $p$ | $q$ | $p \leftrightarrow q$ | $p \rightarrow q$ | $q \rightarrow p$ | $(p \rightarrow q) \wedge (q \rightarrow p)$ |
|---|---|---|---|---|---|
| T | T | T | T | T | T |
| T | F | F | F | T | F |
| F | T | F | T | F | F |
| F | F | T | T | T | T |

Fig. 12-33

**12.92** Show that the biconditional $p \leftrightarrow q$ can be written in terms of the original three connectives $\vee$, $\wedge$, and $\sim$.

▮ Now $p \rightarrow q \equiv \sim p \vee q$ and $q \rightarrow p \equiv \sim q \vee p$; hence, by Problem 12.91,

$$p \leftrightarrow q \equiv (p \rightarrow q) \wedge (q \rightarrow p) \equiv (\sim p \vee q) \wedge (\sim q \vee p)$$

**12.93** Determine the truth value of each statement.
(*a*) $2 + 2 = 4$ iff $3 + 6 = 9$.　　(*c*) $1 + 1 = 2$ iff $3 + 2 = 8$.
(*b*) $2 + 2 = 7$ if and only if $5 + 1 = 2$.　　(*d*) $1 + 2 = 5$ if and only if $3 + 1 = 4$.

▮ Now $p \leftrightarrow q$ is true whenever $p$ and $q$ have the same truth value; hence (*a*) and (*b*) are true statements, but (*c*) and (*d*) are false. Observe that (*b*) is a true statement by definition of the conditional, even though both substatements $2 + 2 = 7$ and $5 + 1 = 2$ are false.

**12.94** Find the truth table for $(p \rightarrow q) \vee \sim (p \leftrightarrow \sim q)$.

▮ See Fig. 12-34.

| $p$ | $q$ | ($p$ | $\rightarrow$ | $q$) | $\vee$ | $\sim$ | ($p$ | $\leftrightarrow$ | $\sim$ | $q$) |
|---|---|---|---|---|---|---|---|---|---|---|
| T | T | T | T | T | T | T | T | F | F | T |
| T | F | T | F | F | F | F | T | T | T | F |
| F | T | F | T | T | T | F | F | T | F | T |
| F | F | F | T | F | T | T | F | F | T | F |
| | Step | 1 | 2 | 1 | 5 | 4 | 1 | 3 | 2 | 1 |

Fig. 12-34

**12.95** Find the truth table for $(p \leftrightarrow \sim q) \leftrightarrow (q \rightarrow p)$.

▌ See Fig. 12-35.

| $p$ | $q$ | $\sim q$ | $p \leftrightarrow \sim q$ | $q \rightarrow p$ | $(p \leftrightarrow \sim q) \leftrightarrow (q \rightarrow p)$ |
|---|---|---|---|---|---|
| T | T | F | F | T | F |
| T | F | T | T | T | T |
| F | T | F | T | F | F |
| F | F | T | F | T | F |

**Fig. 12-35**

## Conditional Statements and Their Negatives

This subsection considers both the conditional $p \rightarrow q$ and the biconditional $p \leftrightarrow q$ and their negatives.

**12.96** Let $p$ denote "He is rich" and let $q$ denote "He is happy". Write each statement in symbolic form using $p$ and $q$. (*Note.* Assume "He is poor" is equivalent to $\sim p$.)
   (a) If he is rich, then he is unhappy.
   (b) He is neither rich nor happy.
   (c) It is necessary to be poor in order to be happy.
   (d) To be poor is to be unhappy.

▌ Translate "If $p$ then $q$" or its equivalent by $p \rightarrow q$ and "$p$ if and only if $q$" by $p \leftrightarrow q$. Then

   (a) $p \rightarrow \sim q$,   (b) $\sim p \wedge \sim q$,   (c) $q \rightarrow \sim p$,   and   (d) $\sim p \leftrightarrow \sim q$

**12.97** Repeat Problem 12.96 for the following statements:
   (a) Being rich is a necessary condition to being happy.
   (b) One is never happy when one is rich.
   (c) He is poor only if he is happy
   (d) To be rich means the same as to be happy.

▌ (a) $q \rightarrow p$,   (b) $p \rightarrow \sim q$,   (c) $\sim p \rightarrow q$,   and   (d) $p \leftrightarrow q$

**12.98** Determine the truth value of each of the following statements:
   (a) If $7 < 2$, then $-2 < -7$.   (c) If $1 + 1 = 2$, then $2 + 3 = 6$.
   (b) $2 + 2 = 5$ iff $4 + 4 = 10$.   (d) $1 + 1 = 2$ iff $4 + 4 = 10$.

▌ (a) True, since both statements are false.
   (b) True, since both statements are false.
   (c) False, since the first statement is true but the second is false.
   (d) False, since the statements have different truth values.

**12.99** Determine the truth value of each of the following statements:
   (a) If $2 + 2 = 4$, then $3 + 3 = 5$ and $1 + 1 = 2$.
   (b) If $2 + 2 = 4$, then $3 + 3 = 7$ iff $1 + 1 = 4$.

▌ (a) False, since the "if" statement is true but the "then" statement is false.
   (b) True, since the "if" statement is true, and the "then" statement is also true.

**12.100** Verify by truth tables that the negations of the conditional and biconditional are as follows:
   (a) $\sim(p \rightarrow q) \equiv p \wedge \sim q$, and (b) $\sim(p \leftrightarrow q) \equiv p \leftrightarrow \sim q \equiv \sim p \leftrightarrow q$.

▌ See Figs. 12-36(a) and (b).
   *Remark:* Since $p \rightarrow q \equiv \sim p \wedge q$, we could have used DeMorgan's law to verify statement (a) as follows

$$\sim(p \rightarrow q) \equiv \sim(\sim p \vee q) \equiv \sim \sim p \wedge \sim q \equiv p \wedge \sim q$$

**12.101** Simplify: (a) $\sim(p \leftrightarrow \sim q)$, and (b) $\sim(\sim p \leftrightarrow q)$.

▌ (a) $\sim(p \leftrightarrow \sim q) \equiv p \leftrightarrow \sim \sim q \equiv p \leftrightarrow q$,   (b) $\sim(\sim p \leftrightarrow q) \equiv \sim \sim p \leftrightarrow q \equiv p \leftrightarrow q$

**12.102** Simplify: (a) $\sim(p \rightarrow \sim q)$, and (b) $\sim(\sim p \rightarrow \sim q)$.

(a)

| $p$ | $q$ | $p \to q$ | $\sim(p \to q)$ | $\sim q$ | $p \wedge \sim q$ |
|-----|-----|-----------|-----------------|----------|-------------------|
| T | T | T | F | F | F |
| T | F | F | T | T | T |
| F | T | T | F | F | F |
| F | F | T | F | T | F |

(b)

| $p$ | $q$ | $p \leftrightarrow q$ | $\sim(p \leftrightarrow q)$ | $\sim p$ | $\sim p \leftrightarrow q$ | $\sim q$ | $p \leftrightarrow \sim q$ |
|-----|-----|------------------------|------------------------------|----------|----------------------------|----------|-----------------------------|
| T | T | T | F | F | F | F | F |
| T | F | F | T | F | T | T | T |
| F | T | F | T | T | T | F | T |
| F | F | T | F | T | F | T | F |

**Fig. 12-36**

▌ **(a)** $\sim(p \to \sim q) \equiv p \wedge \sim \sim q \equiv p \wedge q$,   **(b)** $\sim(\sim p \to \sim q) \equiv \sim p \wedge \sim \sim q \equiv \sim p \wedge q$

**12.103** Write the negation of each statement as simply as possible.
(a) If he studies, he will pass the exam.
(b) He swims if and only if the water is warm.
(c) If it snows, then he does not drive the car.

▌ **(a)** Note that $\sim(p \to q) \equiv p \wedge \sim q$; hence the negation of the statement is

He studies and he will not pass the exam.

**(b)** Note that $\sim(p \leftrightarrow q) \equiv p \leftrightarrow \sim q \equiv \sim p \leftrightarrow q$; hence the negation of the statement is either of the following:

He swims if and only if the water is not warm.

He does not swim if and only if the water is warm.

**(c)** Note that $\sim(p \to \sim q) \equiv p \wedge \sim \sim q \equiv p \wedge q$. Hence the negation of the statement is

It snows and he drives the car.

**12.104** Write the negation of each statement in as simple a sentence as possible.
(a) If it is cold, then he wears a coat but no sweater.
(b) If he studies, then he will go to college or to art school.

▌ **(a)** Let $p$ be "It is cold", $q$ be "He wears a coat", and $r$ be "He wears a sweater". Then the given statement can be written as $p \to (q \wedge \sim r)$. Now

$$\sim[p \to (q \wedge \sim r)] \equiv p \wedge \sim(q \wedge \sim r) \equiv p \wedge (\sim q \vee r)$$

Hence the negation of the statement is

It is cold, and he wears a sweater or no coat.

**(b)** The given statement is of the form $p \to (q \vee r)$. But

$$\sim[p \to (q \vee r)] \equiv p \wedge \sim(q \vee r) \equiv p \wedge \sim q \wedge \sim r$$

Thus the negation of the statement is

He studies, and he will go neither to college nor to art school.

## 12.10 ARGUMENTS

**12.105** Define an argument. When is an argument valid?

▌ An *argument* is an assertion that a given set of propositions $P_1, P_2, \ldots, P_n$, called *premises*, yields (has as a consequence) another proposition $Q$, called the *conclusion*. Such an argument is denoted by

$$P_1, P_2, \ldots, P_n \vdash Q$$

The notion of a "logical argument" or "valid argument" is formalized as follows:

[T] An argument $P_1, P_2, \ldots, P_n \vdash Q$ is said to be *valid* if $Q$ is true whenever all the premises $P_1, P_2, \ldots, P_n$ are true.

An argument which is not valid is called a *fallacy*.

**12.106**  Show that the following argument is valid:

$$p, p \rightarrow q \vdash q \qquad \text{(Law of Detachment)}$$

    ❚  The proof of this rule follows from the truth table in Fig. 12-37. For $p$ is true in Cases (lines) 1 and 2, and $p \rightarrow q$ is true in Cases 1, 3, and 4; hence $p$ and $p \rightarrow q$ are true simultaneously in Case 1. Since in this Case $q$ is true, the argument is valid.

| $p$ | $q$ | $p \rightarrow q$ |
|-----|-----|-------------------|
| T | T | T |
| T | F | F |
| F | T | T |
| F | F | T |

**Fig. 12-37**

**12.107**  Show that the following argument is a fallacy: $p \rightarrow q, q \vdash p$.

    ❚  The required result follows from the truth table in Fig. 12-37; that is, both $p \rightarrow q$ and $q$ are true in Case (line) 3 in the table, but in this case the conclusion $p$ is false.

**Theorem 12.7:**  The argument $P_1, P_2, \ldots, P_n \vdash Q$ is valid if and only if the proposition $(P_1 \wedge P_2 \wedge \cdots \wedge P_n) \rightarrow Q$ is a tautology.

**12.108**  Prove Theorem 12.7.

    ❚  The propositions $P_1, P_2, \ldots, P_n$ are true simultaneously if and only if the proposition $P_1 \wedge P_2 \wedge \cdots \wedge P_n$ is true. Thus the argument $P_1, P_2, \ldots, P_n \vdash Q$ is valid if and only if $Q$ is true whenever $P_1 \wedge P_2 \wedge \cdots \wedge P_n$ is true or, equivalently, if the proposition $(P_1 \wedge P_2 \wedge \cdots \wedge P_n) \rightarrow Q$ is a tautology. Thus the theorem is proved.

**12.109**  A fundamental principle of logical reasoning states:

"If $p$ implies $q$ and $q$ implies $r$, then $p$ implies $r$"

that is, the following argument is valid:

$$p \rightarrow q, q \rightarrow r \vdash p \rightarrow r \quad \text{(Law of Syllogism)}$$

Verify that this principle is valid.

    ❚  Construct the truth table for $[(p \rightarrow q) \wedge (q \rightarrow r)] \rightarrow (p \rightarrow r)$ as in Fig. 12-38. It is a tautology (only contains T's in Step 4); hence the original argument is valid. Equivalently, the argument is valid since the premises $p \rightarrow q$ and $q \rightarrow r$ are true simultaneously only in cases (lines) 1, 5, 7, and 8, and in these cases the conclusion $p \rightarrow r$ is also true. (Observe that the truth table required $2^3 = 8$ lines since there are three variables $p$, $q$, and $r$.)

| $p$ | $q$ | $r$ | [($p$ | $\rightarrow$ | $q$) | $\wedge$ | ($q$ | $\rightarrow$ | $r$)] | $\rightarrow$ | ($p$ | $\rightarrow$ | $r$) |
|-----|-----|-----|-------|---------------|------|----------|------|---------------|-------|---------------|------|---------------|------|
| T | T | T | T | T | T | T | T | T | T | T | T | T | T |
| T | T | F | T | T | T | F | T | F | F | T | T | F | F |
| T | F | T | T | F | F | F | F | T | T | T | T | T | T |
| T | F | F | T | F | F | F | F | T | F | T | T | F | F |
| F | T | T | F | T | T | T | T | T | T | T | F | T | T |
| F | T | F | F | T | T | F | T | F | F | T | F | T | F |
| F | F | T | F | T | F | T | F | T | T | T | F | T | T |
| F | F | F | F | T | F | T | F | T | F | T | F | T | F |
| Step |  |  | 1 | 2 | 1 | 3 | 1 | 2 | 1 | 4 | 1 | 2 | 1 |

**Fig. 12-38**

**12.110** Show that the following argument is a fallacy: $p \to q$, $\sim p \vdash \sim q$.

▌ Construct the truth table for $[(p \to q) \wedge \sim p] \to \sim q$ as in Fig. 12-39. Since the proposition $[(p \to q) \wedge \sim p] \to \sim q$ is not a tautology, the argument is a fallacy. Equivalently, the argument is a fallacy since in Case (line) 3 of the truth table $p \to q$ and $\sim p$ are true but $\sim q$ is false.

| $p$ | $q$ | $p \to q$ | $\sim p$ | $(p \to q) \wedge \sim p$ | $\sim q$ | $[(p \to q) \wedge \sim p] \to \sim q$ |
|---|---|---|---|---|---|---|
| T | T | T | F | F | F | T |
| T | F | F | F | F | T | T |
| F | T | T | T | T | F | F |
| F | F | T | T | T | T | T |

**Fig. 12-39**

**12.111** Prove that the argument $p \to \sim q$, $q \vdash \sim p$ is valid using previous results.

▌

| Statement | Reason |
|---|---|
| (1)  $q$ is true. | (1)  Given |
| (2)  $p \to \sim q$ is true. | (2)  Given |
| (3)  $q \to \sim p$ is true. | (3)  Contrapositive of (2) |
| (4)  $\sim p$ is true. | (4)  Law of detachment, using (1) and (3) |

**12.112** Show that the following argument is valid: $p \leftrightarrow q$, $q \vdash p$.

▌ *Method 1.* Construct the truth table as in Fig. 12-40(*a*). Now $p \leftrightarrow q$ is true in Cases (lines) 1 and 4, and $q$ in Cases 1 and 3; hence $p \leftrightarrow q$ and $q$ are true simultaneously only in Case 1 where $p$ is also true. Thus the argument $p \leftrightarrow q$, $q \vdash p$ is valid.

*Method 2.* Construct the truth table of $[(p \leftrightarrow q) \wedge q] \to p$ as in Fig. 12-40(*b*). Since $[(p \leftrightarrow q) \wedge q] \to p$ is a tautology, the argument is valid.

| $p$ | $q$ | $p \leftrightarrow q$ |
|---|---|---|
| T | T | T |
| T | F | F |
| F | T | F |
| F | F | T |

(*a*)

| $p$ | $q$ | $p \leftrightarrow q$ | $(p \leftrightarrow q) \wedge q$ | $[(p \leftrightarrow q) \wedge q] \to p$ |
|---|---|---|---|---|
| T | T | T | T | T |
| T | F | F | F | T |
| F | T | F | F | T |
| F | F | T | F | T |

(*b*)

**Fig. 12-40**

**12.113** Determine the validity of the argument $p \to q$, $\sim q \vdash \sim p$.

▌ Construct the truth table of $[(p \to q) \wedge \sim q] \to \sim p$ as in Fig. 12-41. Since the proposition $[(p \to q) \wedge \sim q] \to \sim p$ is a tautology, the given argument is valid.

| $p$ | $q$ | [($p$ | $\to$ | $q$) | $\wedge$ | $\sim$ | $q$] | $\to$ | $\sim$ | $p$ |
|---|---|---|---|---|---|---|---|---|---|---|
| T | T | T | T | T | F | F | T | T | F | T |
| T | F | T | F | F | F | T | F | T | F | T |
| F | T | F | T | T | F | F | T | T | T | F |
| F | F | F | T | F | T | T | F | T | T | F |
| Step | | 1 | 2 | 1 | 3 | 2 | 1 | 4 | 2 | 1 |

**Fig. 12-41**

**12.114** Determine the validity of the argument $\sim p \to q$, $p \vdash \sim q$.

▌ Construct the truth table of $[(\sim p \to q) \wedge p] \to \sim q$ as in Fig. 12-42. Since the proposition $[(\sim p \to q) \wedge p] \to \sim q$ is not a tautology, the argument $\sim p \to q$, $p \vdash \sim q$ is a fallacy. Observe that $\sim p \to q$ and $p$ are both true in Case (line) 1 but in this case $\sim q$ is false.

| $p$ | $q$ | $\sim p$ | $\sim p \to q$ | $(\sim p \to q) \wedge p$ | $\sim q$ | $[(\sim p \to q) \wedge p] \to \sim q$ |
|---|---|---|---|---|---|---|
| T | T | F | T | T | F | F |
| T | F | F | T | T | T | T |
| F | T | T | T | F | F | T |
| F | F | T | F | F | T | T |

**Fig. 12-42**

**12.115** Prove that the following argument is valid: $p \rightarrow \sim q$, $r \rightarrow q$, $r \vdash \sim p$.

▌ Construct the truth tables of the premises and conclusion as in Fig. 12-43. Now $p \rightarrow \sim q$, $r \rightarrow q$, and $r$ are true simultaneously only in Case (line) 5, where $\sim p$ is also true; hence the given argument is valid.

| | $p$ | $q$ | $r$ | $p \rightarrow \sim q$ | $r \rightarrow q$ | $\sim p$ |
|---|---|---|---|---|---|---|
| 1 | T | T | T | F | T | F |
| 2 | T | T | F | F | T | F |
| 3 | T | F | T | T | F | F |
| 4 | T | F | F | T | T | F |
| 5 | F | T | T | T | T | T |
| 6 | F | T | F | T | T | T |
| 7 | F | F | T | T | F | T |
| 8 | F | F | F | T | T | T |

**Fig. 12-43**

**12.116** Repeat Problem 12.115 using previous results.

▌

| Statement | Reason |
|---|---|
| (1) $p \rightarrow \sim q$ is true. | (1) Given |
| (2) $r \rightarrow q$ is true. | (2) Given |
| (3) $\sim q \rightarrow \sim r$ is true. | (3) Contrapositive of (2) |
| (4) $p \rightarrow \sim r$ is true. | (4) Law of syllogism, using (1) and (3) |
| (5) $r \rightarrow \sim p$ is true. | (5) Contrapositive of (4) |
| (6) $r$ is true. | (6) Given |
| (7) $\sim p$ is true. | (7) Law of detachment, using (5) and (6) |

**12.117** Determine whether or not the proposition $P(p, q, r) = [(p \rightarrow \sim q) \wedge (r \rightarrow q) \wedge r] \rightarrow \sim p$ is a tautology.

▌ By Problem 12.115 (or Problem 12.116) the argument $p \rightarrow \sim q$, $r \rightarrow q$, $r \vdash \sim p$ is valid. Thus the given proposition $P(p, q, r)$ is a tautology (Theorem 12.6).

## Arguments and Statements

This subsection applies the above theory to arguments involving specific statements. We emphasize that the validity of an argument does not depend upon the truth values or the content of the statements appearing in the argument, but upon the particular form of the argument.

**12.118** Determine the validity of the following argument:

$S_1$: If a man is a bachelor, he is unhappy.
$S_2$: If a man is unhappy, he dies young.
................................
$S$: Bachelors die young.

Here the statement $S$ below the line denotes the conclusion of the argument, and the statements $S_1$ and $S_2$ above the line denote the premises.

▌ Translate the argument $S_1$, $S_2 \vdash S$ into the symbolic form

$$p \rightarrow q, q \rightarrow r \vdash p \rightarrow r$$

where $p$ is "He is a bachelor", $q$ is "He is unhappy", and $r$ is "He dies young". This argument is valid by the Law of Syllogism (see Problem 12.109); hence the given argument is valid.

**12.119** Test the validity of the following argument:

$S_1$: If two sides of a triangle are equal, then the opposite angles are equal.
$S_2$: Two sides of a triangle are not equal.
................................................
$S$: The opposite angles are not equal.

▮ First translate the argument into the symbolic form $p \to q$, $\sim p \vdash \sim q$, where $p$ is "Two sides of a triangle are equal" and $q$ is "The opposite angles are equal". By Problem 12.115, this argument is a fallacy.

Although the conclusion $S$ does follow from $S_2$ and axioms of Euclidean geometry, the above argument does not constitute such a proof since the argument is a fallacy.

**12.120** Determine the validity of the following argument:

$S_1$: If 7 is less than 4, then 7 is not a prime number.
$S_2$: 7 is not less than 4.
...............................................
$S$: 7 is a prime number.

▮ First translate the argument into symbolic form. Let $p$ be "7 is less than 4" and $q$ be "7 is a prime number". Then the argument is of the form

$$p \to \sim q, \ \sim p \vdash q$$

The argument is a fallacy since in Case (line) 4 of the truth table in Fig. 12-44, the premises $p \to \sim q$ and $\sim p$ are true, but the conclusion $q$ is false.

The fact that the conclusion of the argument happens to be a true statement is irrelevant to the fact that the argument is a fallacy.

| $p$ | $q$ | $\sim q$ | $p \to \sim q$ | $\sim p$ |
|---|---|---|---|---|
| T | T | F | F | F |
| T | F | T | T | F |
| F | T | F | T | T |
| F | F | T | T | T |

**Fig. 12-44**

**12.121** Test the validity of the following argument:

$S_1$: If 5 is a prime number, then 5 does not divide 15.
$S_2$: 5 divides 15.
...............................................
$S$: 5 is not a prime number.

▮ First translate the argument into symbolic form $p \to \sim q$, $q \vdash \sim p$, where $p$ is "5 is a prime number" and $q$ is "5 divides 15". By Problem 12.111, the argument is valid.

Although the conclusion here is obviously a false statement, the argument as given is still valid. It is because of the false premise $S_1$ that we can logically arrive at the false conclusion.

**12.122** Test the validity of each argument:
**(a)** If it rains, Erik will be sick.      **(b)** If it rains, Erik will be sick.
    It did not rain.                             Erik was not sick.
...........................              ...........................
    Erik was not sick.                           It did not rain.

▮ First translate the arguments into symbolic form:

**(a)** $p \to q$, $\sim p \vdash \sim q$,      **(b)** $p \to q$, $\sim q \vdash \sim p$

where $p$ is "It rains" and $q$ is "Erik is sick". By Problem 12.110, the argument **(a)** is a fallacy but, by Problem 12.113, the argument **(b)** is valid.

**12.123** Test the validity of the following argument:

If I like mathematics, then I will study.
Either I study or I fail.
.............................
If I fail, then I do not like mathematics.

▮ First translate the argument into symbolic form. Let $p$ be "I like mathematics", $q$ be "I study", and $r$ be "I fail". Then the given argument is of the form

$$p \to q, \ q \vee r \vdash r \to \sim p$$

| $p$ | $q$ | $r$ | $p \to q$ | $q \lor r$ | $\sim p$ | $r \to \sim p$ |
|---|---|---|---|---|---|---|
| T | T | T | T | T | F | F |
| T | T | F | T | T | F | T |
| T | F | T | F | T | F | F |
| T | F | F | F | F | F | T |
| F | T | T | T | T | T | T |
| F | T | F | T | T | T | T |
| F | F | T | T | T | T | T |
| F | F | F | T | F | T | T |

**Fig. 12-45**

To test the validity of the argument, construct the truth tables of the propositions $p \to q$, $q \lor r$ and $r \to \sim p$ as in Fig. 12-45.

Recall that an argument is valid if the conclusion is true whenever the premises are true. Now in Case (line) 1 of the above truth table, the premises $p \to q$ and $q \lor r$ are both true but the conclusion $r \to \sim p$ is false; hence the argument is a fallacy.

**12.124** Test the validity of the following argument:

> If I study, then I will not fail mathematics.
> If I do not play basketball, then I will study.
> But I failed mathematics.
> ...........................................
> Therefore I played basketball.

❙ First translate the argument into symbolic form. Let $p$ be "I study", $q$ be "I fail mathematics", and $r$ be "I play basketball". Then the given argument is as follows:

$$p \to \sim q, \ \sim r \to p, \ q \vdash r$$

To test the validity of the argument, construct the truth tables of the given propositions $p \to \sim q$, $\sim r \to p$, $q$, and $r$ as in Fig. 12-46.

Now the premises $p \to \sim q$, $\sim r \to p$, and $q$ are true simultaneously only in Case (line) 5, and in that case the conclusion $r$ is also true; hence the argument is valid.

| $p$ | $q$ | $r$ | $\sim q$ | $p \to \sim q$ | $\sim r$ | $\sim r \to p$ |
|---|---|---|---|---|---|---|
| T | T | T | F | F | F | T |
| T | T | F | F | F | T | T |
| T | F | T | T | T | F | T |
| T | F | F | T | T | T | T |
| F | T | T | F | T | F | T |
| F | T | F | F | T | T | F |
| F | F | T | T | T | F | T |
| F | F | F | T | T | T | F |

**Fig. 12-46**

## 12.11 LOGICAL IMPLICATION

**12.125** Define the relation of logical implication.

❙ A proposition $P(p, q, \dots)$ is said to *logically imply* a proposition $Q(p, q, \dots)$, written

$$P(p, q, \dots) \Rightarrow Q(p, q, \dots)$$

if $Q(p, q, \dots)$ is true whenever $P(p, q, \dots)$ is true.

**12.126** Show that $p \leftrightarrow q$ logically implies $p \to q$.

❙ Consider the truth tables of $p \leftrightarrow q$ and $p \to q$ as in Fig. 12-47. Now $p \leftrightarrow q$ is true in lines 1 and 4, and in these cases $p \to q$ is also true. Hence $p \leftrightarrow q$ logically implies $p \to q$.

| $p$ | $q$ | $p \leftrightarrow q$ | $p \rightarrow q$ |
|---|---|---|---|
| T | T | T | T |
| T | F | F | F |
| F | T | F | T |
| F | F | T | T |

Fig. 12-47

**12.127**  Show that $p$ logically implies $p \vee q$.

▌ Consider the truth tables for $p$ and $p \vee q$ as in Fig. 12-48. Now $p$ is true in Cases (lines) 1 and 2, and in these cases the proposition $p \vee q$ is also true. Hence $p$ logically implies $p \vee q$.

| $p$ | $q$ | $p \vee q$ |
|---|---|---|
| T | T | T |
| T | F | T |
| F | T | T |
| F | F | F |

Fig. 12-48

**12.128**  Show that $p \wedge q$ logically implies $p \leftrightarrow q$.

▌ Consider the truth tables of $p \wedge q$ and $p \leftrightarrow q$ as in Fig. 12-49. Now $p \wedge q$ is true only in Case (line) 1 and in this case, the proposition $p \leftrightarrow q$ is also true. Thus $p \wedge q$ logically implies $p \leftrightarrow q$.

| $p$ | $q$ | $p \wedge q$ | $p \leftrightarrow q$ |
|---|---|---|---|
| T | T | T | T |
| T | F | F | F |
| F | T | F | F |
| F | F | F | T |

Fig. 12-49

**12.129**  Determine the number of nonequivalent propositions $P(p, q)$ which logically imply the proposition $p \leftrightarrow q$.

▌ Consider the truth table of $p \leftrightarrow q$ in Fig. 12-50($a$). Now $P(p, q)$ logically implies $p \leftrightarrow q$ if $p \leftrightarrow q$ is true whenever $P(p, q)$ is true. But $p \leftrightarrow q$ is true only in Cases (lines) 1 and 4; hence $P(p, q)$ cannot be true in Cases 2 and 3. There are four such propositions that are listed in the truth table in Fig. 12-50($b$).

| $p$ | $q$ | $p \leftrightarrow q$ |
|---|---|---|
| T | T | T |
| T | F | F |
| F | T | F |
| F | F | T |

($a$)

| $P_1$ | $P_2$ | $P_3$ | $P_4$ | $p \leftrightarrow q$ |
|---|---|---|---|---|
| F | T | F | T | T |
| F | F | F | F | F |
| F | F | F | F | F |
| F | F | T | T | T |

($b$)

Fig. 12-50

**Theorem 12.8:**  For any propositions $P(p, q, \dots)$ and $Q(p, q, \dots)$, the following three statements are equivalent:
  (i)   $P(p, q, \dots)$ logically implies $Q(p, q, \dots)$.
  (ii)  The argument $P(p, q, \dots) \vdash Q(p, q, \dots)$ is valid.
  (iii) The proposition $P(p, q, \dots) \rightarrow Q(p, q, \dots)$ is a tautology.

**Remark:**  Some logicians and many texts use the word "implies" in the same sense as we use "logically implies", and so they distinguish between "implies" and "if . . . then". These two distinct concepts are, of course, intimately related as seen in the above theorem.

**12.130**  Prove Theorem 12.8.

▌ If $Q(p, q, \dots)$ is true whenever $P(p, q, \dots)$ is true, then the argument

$$P(p, q, \dots) \vdash Q(p, q, \dots)$$

is valid; and conversely. Furthermore, the argument $P \vdash Q$ is valid if and only if the conditional statement $P \rightarrow Q$ is always true, i.e., a tautology. Thus the theorem is proved.

**12.131** Prove: Let $P(p, q, \dots)$ logically imply $Q(p, q, \dots)$. Then for any propositions $P_1, P_2, \dots$, the proposition $P(P_1, P_2, \dots)$ logically implies $Q(P_1, P_2, \dots)$.

▌ By Theorem 12.8, if $P(p, q, \dots) \Rightarrow Q(p, q, \dots)$, then $P(p, q, \dots) \rightarrow Q(p, q, \dots)$ is a tautology. By the principle of substitution (Theorem 12.2), the proposition $P(P_1, P_2, \dots) \rightarrow Q(P_1, P_2, \dots)$ is also a tautology. Accordingly, $P(P_1, P_2, \dots) \Rightarrow Q(P_1, P_2, \dots)$.

**12.132** Show that $p \leftrightarrow {\sim}q$ does not logically imply $p \rightarrow q$.

▌ *Method 1.* Construct the truth tables of $p \leftrightarrow {\sim}q$ and $p \rightarrow q$ as in Fig. 12-51. Recall that $p \leftrightarrow {\sim}q$ logically implies $p \rightarrow q$ if $p \rightarrow q$ is true whenever $p \leftrightarrow {\sim}q$ is true. But $p \leftrightarrow {\sim}q$ is true in Case (line) 2 in the table, and in that case $p \rightarrow q$ is false. Hence $p \leftrightarrow {\sim}q$ does not logically imply $p \rightarrow q$.

*Method 2.* Construct the truth table of the proposition $(p \leftrightarrow {\sim}q) \rightarrow (p \rightarrow q)$. It will not be a tautology; hence, by Theorem 12.8, $p \leftrightarrow {\sim}q$ does not logically imply $p \rightarrow q$.

| $p$ | $q$ | ${\sim}q$ | $p \leftrightarrow {\sim}q$ | $p \rightarrow q$ |
|-----|-----|-----------|------------------------------|--------------------|
| T | T | F | F | T |
| T | F | T | T | F |
| F | T | F | T | T |
| F | F | T | F | T |

**Fig. 12-51**

**12.133** Suppose $P(p, q, \dots) \Rightarrow Q(p, q, \dots)$ and $Q(p, q, \dots) \Rightarrow R(p, q, \dots)$. Show that $P(p, q, \dots) \Rightarrow R(p, q, \dots)$.

▌ Since $P \Rightarrow Q$ and $Q \Rightarrow R$, we have $Q$ is true whenever $P$ is true and $R$ is true whenever $Q$ is true. Hence $R$ is true whenever $P$ is true, that is, $P \Rightarrow R$, as required.

**12.134** Suppose $P(p, q, \dots) \Rightarrow Q(p, q, \dots)$ and $Q(p, q, \dots) \Rightarrow P(p, q, \dots)$. Show that $P(p, q, \dots) \equiv Q(p, q, \dots)$.

▌ Since $P \Rightarrow Q$ and $Q \Rightarrow P$, we have $Q$ is true whenever $P$ is true and $P$ is true whenever $Q$ is true. Thus $P$ and $Q$ are true for the same values of the variables, that is, $P \equiv Q$.

## 12.12  QUANTIFIERS

The following notation and theorem involving the universal quantifier ∀ and the existential quantifier ∃ will be used throughout this section:

$$(\forall x \in A)p(x) \quad \text{or} \quad \forall x, p(x), \qquad \text{for every } x \in A, \ p(x) \text{ is true.}$$
$$(\exists x \in A)p(x) \quad \text{or} \quad \exists x, p(x), \qquad \text{there exists } x \in A \text{ such that } p(x) \text{ is true.}$$

Here $p(x)$ is a propositional function (or open-sentence or condition) on $A$, that is, $p(a)$ is true or false for every $a$ in $A$.

**Theorem 12.9 (DeMorgan):**   Let $p(x)$ be a propositional function on $A$. Then
  (i)   ${\sim}(\forall x \in A)p(x) \equiv (\exists x \in A){\sim}p(x)$
  (ii)   ${\sim}(\exists x \in A)p(x) \equiv (\forall x \in A){\sim}p(x)$

**Remark:**   Theorem 12.9 says, in words, that the following two statements are equivalent:
  (i)   "It is not true that, for every $a \in A$, $p(a)$ is true".
  (ii)   "There exists an $a \in A$ such that $p(a)$ is false".

and, similarly, the following two statements are equivalent:

  (i)   "It is not true that there exists an $a \in A$ such that $p(a)$ is true".
  (ii)   "For all $a \in A$, $p(a)$ is false".

**12.135** Let $p(x)$ denote the sentence "$x + 2 > 5$". State whether or not $p(x)$ is a propositional function on each of the following sets: **(a)** **N**, the set of positive integers; **(b)** $M = \{-1, -2, -3, \dots\}$; and **(c)** **C**, the set of complex numbers.

**(a)** Yes.
**(b)** Although $p(x)$ is false for every element in $M$, $p(x)$ is still a propositional function on $M$.
**(c)** No. Note that $2i + 2 > 5$ does not have any meaning. In other words, inequalities are not defined for complex numbers.

**12.136** Determine the truth value of each of the following statements. (Here **R** is the universal set.)
(a) $\forall x, |x| = x$;  (b) $\exists x, x^2 = x$;  (c) $\forall x, x + 1 > x$;  (d) $\exists x, x + 2 = x$

**(a)** False. Note that if $x_0 = -3$ then $|x_0| \neq x_0$.
**(b)** True. For if $x_0 = 1$ then $x_0^2 = x_0$.
**(c)** True. For every real number is a solution to $x + 1 > x$.
**(d)** False. There is no solution to $x + 2 = x$.

**12.137** Negate each of the statements in Problem 12.136.

**(a)** $\sim\forall x, |x| = x \equiv \exists x \sim (|x| = x) \equiv \exists x, |x| \neq x$
**(b)** $\sim\exists x, x^2 = x \equiv \forall x \sim (x^2 = x) \equiv \forall x, x^2 \neq x$
**(c)** $\sim\forall x, x + 1 > x \equiv \exists x \sim (x + 1 > x) \equiv \exists x, x + 1 \leq x$
**(d)** $\sim\exists x, x + 2 = x \equiv \forall x \sim (x + 2 = x) \equiv \forall x, x + 2 \neq x$

**12.138** Let $A = \{1, 2, 3, 4, 5\}$. Determine the truth value of each of the following statements:
(a) $(\exists x \in A)(x + 3 = 10)$,  (b) $(\forall x \in A)(x + 3 < 10)$,
(c) $(\exists x \in A)(x + 3 < 5)$,  (d) $(\forall x \in A)(x + 3 \leq 7)$

**(a)** False. For no number in $A$ is a solution to $x + 3 = 10$.
**(b)** True. For every number in $A$ satisfies $x + 3 < 10$.
**(c)** True. For if $x_0 = 1$, then $x_0 + 3 < 5$, i.e., 1 is a solution.
**(d)** False. For if $x_0 = 5$, then $x_0 + 3 \nleq 7$. In other words, 5 is not a solution to the given condition.

**12.139** Negate each of the statements in Problem 12.138.

**(a)** $\sim(\exists x \in A)(x + 3 = 10) \equiv (\forall x \in A) \sim (x + 3 = 10) \equiv (\forall x \in A)(x + 3 \neq 10)$
**(b)** $\sim(\forall x \in A)(x + 3 < 10) \equiv (\exists x \in A) \sim (x + 3 < 10) \equiv (\exists x \in A)(x + 3 \geq 10)$
**(c)** $\sim(\exists x \in A)(x + 3 < 5) \equiv (\forall x \in A) \sim (x + 3 < 5) \equiv (\forall x \in A)(x + 3 \geq 5)$
**(d)** $\sim(\forall x \in A)(x + 3 \leq 7) \equiv (\exists x \in A) \sim (x + 3 \leq 7) \equiv (\exists x \in A)(x + 3 > 7)$

**12.140** Determine the truth value of each of the following statements (where **R** is the universal set):
(a) $\forall x, x^2 = x$;  (b) $\exists x, 2x = x$;  (c) $\forall x, x - 3 < x$;  (d) $\exists x, x^2 - 2x + 5 = 0$

**(a)** False, for $x = 2$ does not satisfy $x^2 = x$.
**(b)** True, for $x = 0$ satisfies $2x = x$.
**(c)** True, since every real number satisfies $x - 3 < x$.
**(d)** False, since $x^2 - 2x + 5 = 0$ has no real roots.

**12.141** Let $A = \{1, 2, 3, 4\}$ be the universal set. Determine the truth value of each statement:
(a) $\forall x, x + 3 < 6$;  (b) $\exists x, x + 3 < 6$;  (c) $\exists x, 2x^2 + x = 15$

**(a)** False, since $x = 4$ does not satisfy $x + 3 < 6$.
**(b)** True, since $x = 1$ satisfies $x + 3 < 6$.
**(c)** False, since no number in $A$ satisfies $2x^2 + x = 15$.

**12.142** Negate each of the following statements: (a) All students live in the dormitories. (b) All mathematics majors are males. (c) Some students are 25 (years) or older.

Use Theorem 12.9 to negate the quantifiers.
**(a)** Some students do not live in the dormitories.
**(b)** Some mathematics majors are females.
**(c)** None of the students are 25 or older or, in other words, all the students are under 25.

**12.143** Negate each of the statements: (a) $\forall x\, p(x) \land \exists y\, q(y)$, (b) $\exists x\, p(x) \lor \forall y\, q(y)$.

**(a)** Note that $\sim(p \land q) \equiv \sim p \lor \sim q$; hence

$$\sim(\forall x\, p(x) \land \exists y\, q(y)) \equiv \sim\forall x\, p(x) \lor \sim\exists y\, q(y) \equiv \exists x \sim p(x) \lor \forall y \sim q(y)$$

**(b)** Note that $\sim(p \vee q) \equiv \sim p \wedge \sim q$; hence

$$\sim(\exists x\, p(x) \vee \forall y\, q(y)) \equiv \sim \exists x\, p(x) \wedge \sim \forall y\, q(y) \equiv \forall x \sim p(x) \wedge \exists y \sim q(y)$$

**12.144** Negate each of the following statements: **(a)** If there is a riot then someone is killed. **(b)** It is daylight and all the people have arisen.

▌ **(a)** Note that $\sim(p \to q) \equiv p \wedge \sim q$. Hence

> "It is false that, if there is a riot, then someone is killed"
>
> ≡ "There is a riot and it is false that someone is killed"
>
> ≡ "There is a riot and everyone is alive".

**(b)** Note that $\sim(p \wedge q) \equiv \sim p \vee \sim q$. Hence

> "It is false that it is daylight and all the people have arisen"
>
> ≡ "It is not daylight or it is false that all the people have arisen"
>
> ≡ "It is night or someone has not arisen".

**12.145** Negate each of the following statements:
 **(a)** If the teacher is absent, then some students do not complete their homework.
 **(b)** All the students completed their homework and the teacher is present.
 **(c)** Some of the students did not complete their homework or the teacher is absent.

▌ **(a)** The teacher is absent and all the students completed their homework.
 **(b)** Some of the students did not complete their homework or the teacher is absent.
 **(c)** All the students completed their homework and the teacher is present.

**12.146** Find a counterexample for each of the following statements. Here $B = \{2, 3, \ldots, 8, 9\}$.
 **(a)** $\forall x \in B,\ x + 5 < 12$;    **(b)** $\forall x \in B,\ x$ is prime;    **(c)** $\forall x \in B,\ x^2 > 1$;    **(d)** $\forall x \in B,\ x$ is even

▌ **(a)** If $x = 7, 8,$ or $9$, then $x + 5 < 12$ is not true; hence either 7, 8, or 9 is a counterexample.
 **(b)** Note that 4 is not a prime; hence 4 is a counterexample. (Also 6, 8, and 9 are counterexamples.)
 **(c)** The statement is true; hence there is no counterexample.
 **(d)** Note that 3 is odd; hence 3 is a counterexample. (Also 5, 7, and 9 are counterexamples.)

**12.147** Find a counterexample for each statement where $\{3, 5, 7, 9\}$ is the universal set: **(a)** $\forall x,\ x + 3 \geq 7$, **(b)** $\forall x,\ x$ is odd, **(c)** $\forall x,\ x$ is prime, **(d)** $\forall x,\ |x| = x$.

▌ **(a)** Here 5, 7, and 9 are counterexamples.
 **(b)** The statement is true; hence no counterexample exists.
 **(c)** Here 9 is the only counterexample.
 **(d)** The statement is true; hence there is no counterexample.

## Propositional Functions with Multiple Variables

This subsection considers propositional functions $p(x, y, \ldots)$ with more than one variable. If such an expression is preceded by a quantifier for each variable, for example,

$$\forall x\, \exists y\, p(x, y) \qquad \text{or} \qquad \exists x\, \forall z\, \forall y\, p(x, y, z)$$

then the quantified expression is a statement and has a truth value; otherwise, it is an open statement (in the variables without quantifiers) and has a *truth set*.

**12.148** Determine the truth value of each of the following statements where $\{1, 2, 3\}$ is the universal set:
 **(a)** $\exists x\, \forall y,\ x^2 < y + 1$; **(b)** $\forall x\, \exists y,\ x^2 + y^2 < 12$; **(c)** $\forall x\, \forall y,\ x^2 + y^2 < 12$.

▌ **(a)** True. For if $x = 1$, then $1 < y + 1$ has as solutions each of the numbers 1, 2, and 3.
 **(b)** True. For each $x_0$, let $y = 1$; then $x_0^2 + 1 < 12$ is a true statement.
 **(c)** False. For if $x_0 = 2$ and $y_0 = 3$, then $x_0^2 + y_0^2 < 12$ is not a true statement.

**12.149** Repeat Problem 12.148 for: **(a)** $\exists x\, \forall y\, \exists z,\ x^2 + y^2 < 2z^2$; **(b)** $\exists x\, \exists y\, \forall z,\ x^2 + y^2 < 2z^2$.

▌ (a) True. For if $x_0 = 1$ and $z_0 = 3$, then the truth set of $x_0^2 + y^2 < 2z_0^2$, i.e., $1 + y^2 < 18$, is the universal set 1, 2, 3.

  (b) False. For if $z_0 = 1$, then $x^2 + y^2 < 2z_0^2$ has no solution.

**12.150** Let $A = \{1, 2, \ldots, 9, 10\}$. Consider each of the following sentences. If it is a statement, then determine its truth value. If it is a propositional function, determine its truth set.

  (a) $(\forall x \in A)(\exists y \in A)(x + y < 14)$     (c) $(\forall x \in A)(\forall y \in A)(x + y < 14)$

  (b) $(\forall y \in A)(x + y < 14)$              (d) $(\exists y \in A)(x + y < 14)$

▌ (a) The open sentence in two variables is preceded by two quantifiers; hence it is a statement. Moreover, the statement is true.

  (b) The open sentence is preceded by one quantifier; hence it is a propositional function of the other variable. Note that for every $y \in A$, $x_0 + y < 14$ if and only if $x_0 = 1$, 2, or 3. Hence the truth set is $\{1, 2, 3\}$.

  (c) It is a statement and it is false. For if $x_0 = 8$ and $y_0 = 9$, then $x_0 + y_0 < 14$ is not true.

  (d) It is an open sentence in $x$. The truth set is $A$ itself.

**12.151** Negate each of the following statements: (a) $\exists x \forall y, p(x, y)$; (b) $\forall x \forall y, p(x, y)$; (c) $\exists y \exists x \forall z, p(x, y, z)$.

▌ (a) $\sim(\exists x \forall y, p(x, y)) \equiv \forall x \exists y \sim p(x, y)$

  (b) $\sim(\forall x \forall y, p(x, y)) \equiv \exists x \exists y \sim p(x, y)$

  (c) $\sim(\exists y \exists x \forall z, p(x, y, z)) \equiv \forall y \forall x \exists z \sim p(x, y, z)$

**12.152** Negate $\forall x \exists y \, (p(x) \lor q(y))$.

▌        $\sim[(\forall x \exists y \, (p(x) \lor q(y))] \equiv \exists x \forall y \sim (p(x) \lor q(y)) \equiv \exists x \forall y \, (\sim p(x) \land \sim q(y))$

**12.153** Negate $\exists x \forall y \, (p(x, y) \to q(x, y))$.

▌        $\sim[\exists x \forall y \, (p(x, y) \to q(x, y))] \equiv \forall x \exists y \sim (p(x, y) \to q(x, y)) \equiv \forall x \exists y \, (p(x, y) \land \sim q(x, y))$

**12.154** Negate $\exists y \exists x \, (p(x) \land \sim q(y))$.

       $\sim[\exists y \exists x \, (p(x) \land \sim q(y))] \equiv \forall y \forall x \sim (p(x) \land \sim q(y)) \equiv \forall y \forall x \, (\sim p(x) \lor q(y))$

# CHAPTER 13
# Boolean Algebra, Logic Gates

## 13.1 BASIC DEFINITIONS AND THEOREMS

Both sets (Chapter 1) and propositions (Chapter 12) have similar properties, as may be seen by comparing Tables 1-1 and 12-1. These properties are used to define a mathematical structure called *Boolean algebra,* after George Boole (1813–1864).

**13.1** Define a Boolean algebra.

▌ Let $B$ be a set on which are defined two binary operations, $+$ and $*$, and a unary operation, denoted $'$; let 0 and 1 denote two distinct elements of $B$. Then the sextuplet

$$\langle B, +, *, ', 0, 1 \rangle$$

is called a *Boolean algebra* if the following axioms hold for any elements $a, b, c$ of the set $B$:

[$B_1$] Commutative Laws:
    **(1a)** $a + b = b + a$         **(1b)** $a * b = b * a$

[$B_2$] Distributive Laws:
    **(2a)** $a + (b * c) = (a + b) * (a + c)$     **(2b)** $a * (b + c) = (a * b) + (a * c)$

[$B_3$] Identity Laws:
    **(3a)** $a + 0 = a$         **(3b)** $a * 1 = a$

[$B_4$] Complement Laws:
    **(4a)** $a + a' = 1$        **(4b)** $a * a' = 0$

The above Boolean algebra is usually denoted by $B$ alone when the operations are understood.

The element 0 is called the *zero* element, the element 1 is called the *unit* element, and $a'$ is called the *complement* of $a$. The results of the operations $+$ and $*$ are called the *sum* and the *product,* respectively. We will frequently drop the symbol $*$ and use juxtaposition instead. Then **(2b)** and **(2a)** are written:

    **(2b)** $a(b + c) = ab + ac$     **(2a)** $a + bc = (a + b)(a + c)$

The first is a familiar identity, but the second is not an identity in ordinary algebra.

We adopt the usual convention that, unless we are guided by parentheses, $'$ has precedence over $*$, and $*$ has precedence over $+$. For example,

$$a + b * c \text{ means } a + (b * c) \text{ and not } (a + b) * c$$

$$a * b' \text{ means } a * (b') \text{ and not } (a * b)'$$

Of course, when $a + b * c$ is written $a + bc$, then the meaning is clear.

**13.2** Describe the Boolean algebra $B$ with two elements, 0 and 1 (called *bits*).

▌ Let $+$ and $*$ be the operations in $B$ defined in Fig. 13-1. Suppose that complements are defined by $1' = 0$ and $0' = 1$. Then $B$ is a Boolean algebra.

| + | 1 | 0 | | * | 1 | 0 |
|---|---|---|---|---|---|---|
| 1 | 1 | 1 | | 1 | 1 | 0 |
| 0 | 1 | 0 | | 0 | 0 | 0 |

          (a)                 (b)     **Fig. 13-1**

**13.3** Let $B_n$ denote the set of $n$-bit sequences. Explain how $B_n$ is made into a Boolean algebra.

▌ Let $a$ and $b$ be $n$-bit sequences in $B_n$. Define the sum, product, and complement of these sequences bit by bit as in Problem 13.2. That is, in a given position, $a + b$ contains 1 if $a$ or $b$ contains 1; $a * b$ contains 1 if $a$ and $b$ contain 1; and $a'$ contains 1 if $a$ does not contain 1, i.e., if $a$ contains 0. Then $B_n$ is a Boolean algebra.

**13.4** Let $a = 1101010$ and $b = 1011011$ in $B_7$ (Problem 13.3). Find $a + b$, $a * b$, and $a'$.

❚ Calculate bit by bit using Fig. 13-1 and $1' = 0$ and $' = 1$ to obtain

$$a + b = 1111011, \qquad a * b = 1001010, \qquad a' = 0010101$$

**13.5** Describe a Boolean algebra of sets.

❚ Let $\mathscr{C}$ be a collection of sets closed under union, intersection, and complement. Then $\mathscr{C}$ is a Boolean algebra, with the empty set $\varnothing$ as the zero element and the universal set **U** as the unit element.

**13.6** Let $\Pi$ be the set of propositions. Explain how $\Pi$ is a Boolean algebra.

❚ $\Pi$ is a Boolean algebra under the operations $\vee$ and $\wedge$, with negation $\sim$ being the complement. (Propositions in $\Pi$ that are logically equivalent, i.e., have the same truth table, are taken to be identical.)

**13.7** What is the zero element and the unit element in the Boolean algebra $\Pi$ of propositions in Problem 13.6?

❚ As seen from Table 12-1, a contradiction $f$ is the zero element, and a tautology $t$ is the unit element.

**13.8** Let $D_{70} = \{1, 2, 5, 7, 10, 14, 35, 70\}$, the divisors of 70. Show how $D_{70}$ is made into a Boolean algebra.

❚ Let $+$, $*$, and $'$ be defined on $D_{70}$ as follows:

$$a + b \equiv \text{l.c.m. } (a, b) = \text{least common multiple of } a \text{ and } b$$
$$a * b \equiv \text{g.c.d. } (a, b) = \text{greatest common divisor of } a \text{ and } b$$
$$a' = 70/a$$

Then $D_{70}$ is a Boolean algebra, with 1 as the zero element and 70 as the unit element.

**13.9** Consider the Boolean algebra $D_{70}$ in Problem 13.8. Find $10 + 14$, $10 * 14$, and $10'$.

❚ Use the definitions of $+$, $*$, and $'$ to obtain

$$10 + 14 = \text{l.c.m. } (10, 14) = 70, \qquad 10 * 14 = \text{g.c.d. } (10, 14) = 2, \qquad 10' = 70/10 = 7$$

**13.10** Consider the Boolean algebra $D_{70}$ in Problem 13.8. Find the value of:
**(a)** $x = 35 * (2 + 7')$, **(b)** $y = (35 * 10) + 14'$, **(c)** $z = (2 + 7) * (14 * 10)'$.

❚ Calculate each expression step by step, using the definitions of $a + b$, $a * b$, and $a'$.
**(a)** $7' = 10$, $2 + 10 = 10$; hence, $x = 35 * 10 = 5$.
**(b)** $35 * 10 = 5$, $14' = 5$; hence, $y = 5 + 5 = 5$.
**(c)** $2 + 7 = 14$, $14 * 10 = 2$, $2' = 35$; hence, $z = 14 * 35 = 7$.

**13.11** Define a subalgebra.

❚ Suppose $C$ is a nonempty subset of a Boolean algebra $B$. We say $C$ is a *subalgebra* of $B$ if $C$ itself is a Boolean algebra (with respect to the operations of $B$). We note that $C$ is a subalgebra of $B$ if and only if $C$ is closed under the three operations of $B$, i.e., $+$, $*$, and $'$.

**13.12** Determine whether or not each of the following is a subalgebra of $D_{70}$:
**(a)** $X = \{1, 5, 10, 70\}$, **(b)** $Y = \{1, 2, 35, 70\}$.

❚ **(a)** No. Although $X$ is closed under $+$ and $*$, $5' = 14$ does not belong to $X$.
**(b)** Yes, since $Y$ is closed under $+$, $*$, and $'$.

**13.13** Define isomorphic Boolean algebras.

❚ Two Boolean algebras $B$ and $\bar{B}'$ are said to be *isomorphic* if there is a one-to-one correspondence $f : B \to \bar{B}'$ which preserves the three operations, i.e., such that

$$f(a + b) = f(a) + f(b), \qquad f(a * b) = f(a) * f(b), \qquad \text{and} \qquad f(a') = f(a)'$$

for any elements $a$, $b$ in $B$.

## Duality, Theorems

**13.14**   Define the dual of any statement $S$ in a Boolean algebra $B$.

▎ The dual of $S$ is the statement obtained by interchanging the operations $+$ and $*$, and interchanging the corresponding identity elements 0 and 1, in the original statement $S$.

**13.15**   Write the dual of each Boolean equation: **(a)** $(a*1)*(0+a')=0$, **(b)** $a+a'b=a+b$.

▎ **(a)**   To obtain the dual equation, interchange $+$ and $*$, and interchange 0 and 1. Thus
$$(a+0)+(1*a')=1$$

**(b)**   First write the equation using $*$: $a+(a'*b)=a+b$. Then the dual is $a*(a'+b)=a*b$, which can be written as $a(a'+b)=ab$.

**13.16**   Write the dual of each Boolean equation:
**(a)** $a(a'+b)=ab$,   **(b)** $(a+1)(a+0)=a$,   **(c)** $(a+b)(b+c)=ac+b$

▎ Write each equation using $*$; then interchange $+$ and $*$, and interchange 0 and 1. This yields
**(a)** $a+a'b=a+b$,   **(b)** $a*0+a*1=a$,   **(c)** $ab+bc=(a+c)b$

**Theorem 13.1   (Principle of Duality):**   The dual of any theorem in a Boolean algebra $B$ is also a theorem.

**13.17**   Prove Theorem 13.1.

▎ The dual of the set of axioms of $B$ is the same as the original set of axioms. Accordingly, if any statement is a consequence of the axioms of a Boolean algebra, then the dual is also a consequence of those axioms since the dual statement can be proven by using the dual of each step of the proof of the original statement.

**Theorem 13.2:**   Let $a$, $b$, $c$ be any elements in a Boolean algebra $B$.
    (i)   Idempotent Laws:
        **(5a)** $a+a=a$         **(5b)** $a*a=a$
    (ii)   Boundedness Laws
        **(6a)** $a+1=1$         **(6b)** $a*0=0$
    (iii)   Absorption Laws:
        **(7a)** $a+(a*b)=a$     **(7b)** $a*(a+b)=a$
    (iv)   Associative Laws:
        **(8a)** $(a+b)+c=a+(b+c)$   **(8b)** $(a*b)*c=a*(b*c)$

**13.18**   Prove Theorem 13.2(i).

▎ **(5b)** $a=a*1=a*(a+a')=(a*a)+(a*a')=(a*a)+0=a*a$
**(5a)**   Follows from **(5b)** and duality.

**13.19**   Prove Theorem 13.2(ii).

▎ **(6b)** $a*0=(a*0)+0=(a*0)+(a*a')=a*(0+a')=a*(a'+0)=a*a'=0$
**(6a)**   Follows from **(6b)** and duality.

**13.20**   Prove Theorem 13.2(iii).

▎ **(7b)** $a*(a+b)=(a+0)*(a+b)=a+(0*b)=a+(b*0)=a+0=a$, where the boundedness law was used in the next-to-last step.
**(7a)**   Follows from **(7b)** and duality.

**13.21**   Prove Theorem 13.2(iv).

▎ **(8b)**   Let $L=(a*b)*c$ and $R=a*(b*c)$. We need to prove that $L=R$. We first prove that $a+L=a+R$. Using the absorption laws in the last two steps,
$$a+L=a+((a*b)*c)=(a+(a*b))*(a+c)=a*(a+c)=a$$

Also, using the absorption law in the last step and the idempotent law in the next-to-last step,
$$a+R=a+(a*(b*c))=(a+a)*(a+(b*c))=a*(a+(b*c))=a$$

BOOLEAN ALGEBRA, LOGIC GATES □ 373

Thus $a + L = a + R$. Next we show that $a' + L = a' + R$. We have,

$$a' + L = a' + ((a * b) * c) = (a' + (a * b)) * (a' + c) = ((a' + a) * (a' + b)) * (a' + c)$$
$$= (1 * (a' + b)) * (a' + c) = (a' + b) * (a' + c) = a' + (b * c)$$

Also,

$$a' + R = a' + (a * (b * c)) = (a' + a) * (a' + (b * c)) = 1 * (a' + (b * c)) = a' + (b * c)$$

Thus $a' + L = a' + R$. Consequently,

$$L = L + 0 = L + (a * a') = (L + a) * (L + a') = (a + L) * (a' + L) = (a + R) * (a' + R) = R$$

**(8a)** Follows from **(8b)** and duality.

**Theorem 13.3:** Let $a$ be any element in a Boolean algebra $B$.
    (i) (Uniqueness of Complement)
        If $a + x = 1$ and $a * x = 0$, then $x = a'$.
    (ii) (Involution Law) $(a')' = a$
    (iii) **(9a)** $0' = 1$     **(9b)** $1' = 0$

**13.22** Prove Theorem 13.3(i).

    ▌ We have

$$a' = a' + 0 = a' + (a * x) = (a' + a) * (a' + x) = 1 * (a' + x) = a' + x$$

Also,

$$x = x + 0 = x + (a * a') = (x + a) * (x + a') = 1 * (x + a') = x + a'$$

Hence $x = x + a' = a' + x = a'$.

**13.23** Prove Theorem 13.3(ii).

    ▌ By definition of complement, $a + a' = 1$ and $a * a' = 0$. By commutativity, $a' + a = 1$ and $a' * a = 0$. By uniqueness of complement, $a$ is the complement of $a'$, that is, $a = (a')'$.

**13.24** Prove Theorem 13.3(iii).

    ▌ By boundedness law (6a), $0 + 1 = 1$, and by identity axiom (3b), $0 * 1 = 0$. By uniqueness of complement, 1 is the complement of 0, that is, $1 = 0'$. By duality, $0 = 1'$.

**Theorem 13.4 (DeMorgan's laws):** **(10a)** $(a + b)' = a' * b'$,     **(10b)** $(a * b)' = a' + b'$.

**13.25** Prove Theorem 13.4.

    ▌ **(10a)** We need to show that $(a + b) + (a' * b') = 1$ and $(a + b) * (a' * b') = 0$; then by uniqueness of complement, $a' * b' = (a + b)'$. We have

$$(a + b) + (a' * b') = b + a + (a' * b') = b + (a + a') * (a + b')$$
$$= b + 1 * (a + b') = b + a + b' = b + b' + a = 1 + a = 1$$

Also,

$$(a + b) * (a' * b') = ((a + b) * a') * b' = ((a * a') + (b * a')) * b' = (0 + (b * a')) * b'$$
$$= (b * a') * b' = (b * b') * a' = 0 * a' = 0$$

Thus $a' * b' = (a + b)'$.

    **(10b)** Follows from **(10a)** and duality.

**Theorem 13.5:** The following are equivalent in a Boolean algebra:
    (1) $a + b = b$,    (2) $a * b = a$,    (3) $a' + b = 1$,    (4) $a * b' = 0$.

**13.26** Prove the equivalence of (1) and (2) in Theorem 13.5.

❚ Suppose $a*b = a$. Using the absorption law in the first step, we have

$$b = b + (b*a) = b + (a*b) = b + a = a + b$$

Conversely, suppose $a + b = b$. Again using the absorption law in the first step, we have

$$a = a*(a+b) = a*b$$

Thus $a*b = a$ if and only if $a + b = b$, that is, (1) and (2) are equivalent.

**13.27**   Prove the equivalence of (1) and (3) in Theorem 13.5.

❚ Suppose (1) holds. Then

$$a' + b = a' + (a + b) = (a' + a) + b = 1 + b = 1$$

Now suppose (3) holds. Then

$$a + b = 1*(a+b) = (a'+b)*(a+b) = (a'*a) + b = 0 + b = b$$

Thus (1) and (3) are equivalent.

**13.28**   Prove the equivalence of (3) and (4) in Theorem 13.5.

❚ Suppose (3) holds. By DeMorgan's law and involution,

$$0 = 1' = (a'+b)' = a''*b' = a*b'$$

Conversely, if (4) holds, then

$$1 = 0' = (a*b')' = a' + b'' = a' + b$$

Thus (3) and (4) are equivalent. Accordingly, all four are equivalent.
This proof, together with those of Problems 13.26 and 13.27, completes the proof of Theorem 13.5.

## 13.2   ORDER AND BOOLEAN ALGEBRAS

For convenience, the following definitions and notations are repeated from Chapter 11. A relation $\preceq$ on a set $S$ is called a *partial ordering* on $S$ if it has the following three properties:

    (1)   $a \preceq a$ for every $a$ in $S$.    (2)   If $a \preceq b$ and $b \preceq a$, then $a = b$.    (3)   If $a \preceq b$ and $b \preceq c$, then $a \preceq c$.

A set $S$ together with a partial ordering is called a *partially ordered set*, or *poset*. In such a case, $a \preceq b$ is read "$a$ precedes $b$." We also write

$$a < b \text{ (read "} a \text{ strictly precedes } b \text{") if } a \preceq b \text{ but } a \neq b$$

$$a \succeq b \text{ (read "} a \text{ succeeds } b \text{") if } b \preceq a$$

$$a > b \text{ (read "} a \text{ strictly succeeds } b \text{") if } b < a$$

Elements $a$ and $b$ in $S$ are *noncomparable* if neither $a \preceq b$ nor $b \preceq a$.

An element $b$ of $S$ is said to be an *immediate successor* of an element $a$, written $a \ll b$, if $a < b$ but there is no element $x$ of $S$ such that $a < x < b$.

A *finite partially ordered set* $S$ can be illustrated by a diagram similar to the diagram of Problem 11.34. Thus in the diagram of $S$ the elements are joined by lines slanting upward, each line going from an element $a$ to an element $b$ whenever $a \ll b$.

The notion of a partially ordered set comes up in the context of Boolean algebras because of the following theorem:

**Theorem 13.6:**   Let $B$ be a Boolean algebra. Then $B$ is a partially ordered set, where $a \preceq b$ is defined by $a + b = b$.

**13.29**   Describe the order relation in the Boolean algebra $\mathscr{C}$ of sets (Problem 13.5).

❚ Set $A$ precedes set $B$ if $A$ is a subset of $B$. This follows from the fact that $A \cup B = B$ if and only if $A \subseteq B$.

**13.30**   Describe the order relation in the Boolean algebra $\Pi$ of propositions (Problem 13.6).

❚ Proposition $P(p, q, \ldots)$ precedes proposition $Q(p, q, \ldots)$ if $P$ logically implies $Q$.

**13.31**  Show that, for any element $a$ in a Boolean algebra $B$, $0 \leq a \leq 1$. (Thus 0 is the *lower bound* and 1 is the *upper bound* of $B$ and, in a diagram $D$ of $B$, 0 is on the bottom of $D$ and 1 is on the top of $D$.)

▐  Follows from the fact that $0 + a = a$ and $1 + a = 1$.

**13.32**  Define an atom in a Boolean algebra $B$.

▐  An element $a$ in $B$ is an *atom* if $a$ is an immediate successor of 0.

**13.33**  Consider the Boolean algebra $D_{70}$ (divisors of 70) in Problem 13.8. How are the elements of $D_{70}$ ordered? Draw the diagram of $D_{70}$.

▐  Note that $a + b = $ l.c.m. $(a, b) = b$ if and only if $b$ is a multiple of $a$. In other words, $D_{70}$ is ordered by divisibility. Figure 13-2 is the diagram of $D_{70}$. Observe that the "zero" element 1 is on the bottom of the diagram and the "unit" element 70 is on top of the diagram.

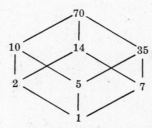

**Fig. 13-2**

**13.34**  Find the atoms of $D_{70}$.

▐  The atoms of $D_{70}$ are the immediate successors of 1; these are 2, 5, and 7 (the primes in $D_{70}$).

**13.35**  Let $P(A)$ be the Boolean algebra of all subsets of $A = \{a, b, c\}$. Note that

$$P(A) = [A, \{a, b\}, \{a, c\}, \{b, c\}, \{a\}, \{b\}, \{c\}, \emptyset]$$

Draw a diagram of $P(A)$.

▐  Here set $X$ precedes set $Y$ if $X \subseteq Y$. The diagram of $P(A)$ is shown in Fig. 13-3. Observe that $\emptyset$ is at the bottom and $A$ is at the top of the diagram.

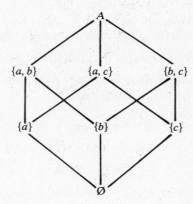

**Fig. 13-3**

**13.36**  Find the atoms in the Boolean algebra $P(A)$ in Problem 13.35.

▐  The atoms are the immediate successors of $\emptyset$ and, as shown in Fig. 13-3, they are the three single-element sets $\{a\}$, $\{b\}$, and $\{c\}$.

**Theorem 13.7:**  Let $B$ be a finite Boolean algebra having $n$ atoms. Then $B$ has $2^n$ elements, and every nonzero element of $B$ is the sum of a unique set of atoms.

**13.37**  Suppose $B$ is a Boolean algebra with less than 100 elements. How many elements can $B$ have?

**▌** By Theorem 13.7, $B$ has $2^n$ elements where $n$ is the number of atoms. Thus $B$ can have, 2, 4, 8, 16, 32, or 64 elements.

**13.38**    Consider the Boolean algebra $D_{210}$, the divisors of 210. Draw the diagram of $D_{210}$.

**▌** The divisors of 210 are 1, 2, 3, 5, 6, 7, 10, 14, 15, 21, 30, 35, 42, 70, 105, and 210. The diagram of $D_{210}$ is given in Fig. 13-4.

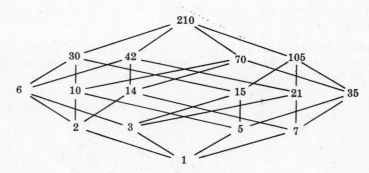

**Fig. 13-4**

**13.39**    Find the set $A$ of atoms of $D_{210}$.

**▌** $A = \{2, 3, 5, 7\}$, the set of prime divisors of 210.

**13.40**    Find two subalgebras of $D_{210}$ with eight elements.

**▌** $B = \{1, 2, 3, 35, 6, 70, 105, 210\}$ and $C = \{1, 5, 6, 7, 30, 35, 42, 210\}$ are subalgebras of $D_{210}$.

**13.41**    Find the number of subalgebras of $D_{210}$.

**▌** A subalgebra of $D_{210}$ must contain two, four, eight, or sixteen elements.
   (i)    There can be only one 2-element subalgebra, which consists of the upper and lower bounds, i.e., $\{1, 210\}$.
   (ii)   Since $D_{210}$ contains sixteen elements, the only 16-element subalgebra is $D_{210}$ itself.
   (iii)  Any 4-element subalgebra is of the form $\{1, x, x', 210\}$, i.e., consists of the upper and lower bounds and a nonbound element and its complement. There are fourteen nonbound elements in $D_{210}$ and so there are $14/2 = 7$ pairs $\{x, x'\}$. Thus $D_{210}$ has seven 4-element subalgebras.
   (iv)   Any 8-element subalgebra $S$ will itself contain three atoms $s_1$, $s_2$, $s_3$. We can choose $s_1$ and $s_2$ to be any two of the four atoms of $D_{210}$ and then $s_3$ must be the product of the other two atoms, e.g., we can let $s_1 = 2$, $s_2 = 3$, $s_3 = 5 \cdot 7 = 35$ (which determines the subalgebra $B$ in Problem 13.40), or we can let $s_1 = 5$, $s_2 = 7$, $s_3 = 2 \cdot 3 = 6$ (which determines the subalgebra $C$ in Problem 13.40). There are $\binom{4}{2} = 6$ ways to choose $s_1$ and $s_2$ from the four atoms of $D_{210}$ and so $D_{210}$ has six 8-element subalgebras.
Accordingly, $D_{210}$ has $1 + 1 + 7 + 6 = 15$ subalgebras.

**13.42**    Show that, in a Boolean algebra $B$, $a \leq b$ if and only if $b' \leq a'$.

**▌** Suppose $a \leq b$, that is, $a + b = b$. Then, using DeMorgan's law,

$$b' = (a + b)' = a' * b' = b' * a'$$

By Theorem 13.5, $b' + a' = a'$. Thus $b' \leq a'$. Conversely, suppose $b' \leq a'$. Then $(a')' \leq (b')'$ and hence $a \leq b$.

**13.43**    An element $M$ in a Boolean algebra $B$ is called a *maxiterm* if it is an immediate predecessor of the unit element 1. Show that the complements of atoms are maxiterms, and vice versa.

**▌** By Problem 13.42, $0 \leq x \leq a$ if and only if $a' \leq x' \leq 1$. Thus $a$ is an immediate successor of 0 if and only if $a'$ is an immediate predecessor of 1 or, in other words, $a$ is an atom if and only if $a'$ is a maxterm.

**13.44**    Find the maxiterms of the Boolean algebra of $D_{210}$.

**▌** By Fig. 13-4, the immediate predecessors of 210 are 30, 42, 70, and 105 and hence they are the maxiterms of $D_{210}$.

**13.45** Find the maxiterms of the Boolean algebra $P(A)$ consisting of the subsets of $A = \{a, b, c\}$.

$\blacksquare$ By Fig. 13-3, the immediate predecessors of $A$ are the sets $\{a, b\}$, $\{a, c\}$, and $\{b, c\}$ and hence they are the maxiterms of $P(A)$.

**Remark:** A Boolean algebra $B$ was defined (Problem 13.1) in terms of the operations of sum, product, and complements and then an order relation was introduced in $B$. Alternatively, we can define a Boolean algebra using an order relation (Chapter 11) as follows:

**Alternate Definition:** A Boolean algebra $B$ is a bounded, distributive, and complemented lattice.

## 13.3 BOOLEAN EXPRESSIONS; SUM-OF-PRODUCTS FORM

**13.46** Define a Boolean expression and give examples.

$\blacksquare$ Consider a set of variables (or letters or symbols), say $x_1, x_2, \ldots, x_n$. By a *Boolean expression* $E$ in these variables, sometimes written $E(x_1, \ldots, x_n)$, we mean any variable or any expression built up from the variables using the Boolean operations $+$, $*$, and $'$. For example,

$$E = (x + y'z)' + (xyz' + x'y)' \qquad \text{and} \qquad F = ((xy'z' + y)' + x'z)'$$

are Boolean expressions in $x$, $y$, and $z$.

**13.47** Define a literal and a fundamental product and give examples.

$\blacksquare$ A *literal* is a variable or complemented variable, e.g., $x$, $x'$, $y$, $y'$. By a *fundamental product* we mean a literal or a product of two or more literals in which no two literals involve the same variable. For example, $xz'$, $xy'z$, $x$, $y'$, $yz'$, $x'yz$ are fundamental products. However, $xyx'z$ and $xyzy$ are not fundamental products; the first contains $x$ and $x'$, and the second contains $y$ in two places.

**13.48** Reduce the following Boolean products to either 0, or a fundamental product:
(**a**) $xyx'z$ and $xyzy$, (**b**) $xyz'xyx$ and $xyz'xy'z'$.

$\blacksquare$ (**a**) Use commutativity, the complement law $x * x' = 0$ and the idempotent law $y * y = y$ to obtain

$$xyx'z = xx'yz = 0yz = 0 \qquad \text{and} \qquad xyzy = xyyz = xyz$$

(**b**) We have

$$xyz'xyx = xxxyyz' = xyz' \qquad \text{and} \qquad xyz'xy'z' = yy'xxz'z' = 0xxz'z' = 0$$

**13.49** Show that any Boolean product $P$ can be reduced to either 0 or a fundamental product.

$\blacksquare$ Suppose $P$ contains a variable and its complement, say $P = P_1 x P_2 x' P_3$. Then $P = xx'P_1P_2P_3 = 0P_1P_2P_3 = 0$. Suppose $P$ contains a literal in two places, say $P = P_1 x P_2 x P_3$. Then $P = xxP_1P_2P_3 = xP_1P_2P_3 = P'$ where $P'$ is a shorter notation for $P$. Continuing this process, $P$ is reduced to either 0 or a fundamental product.

**13.50** Suppose $P_1$ and $P_2$ are fundamental products. What do we mean by saying that $P_1$ is included in $P_2$? Give an example.

$\blacksquare$ $P_1$ is said to be included in or contained in $P_2$ if the literals of $P_1$ are also literals of $P_2$. For example, $x'z$ is included in $x'yz$, since $x'$ and $z$ are literals in $x'yz$. However, $x'z$ is not contained in $xy'z$, since $x'$ is not a literal in $xy'z$.

**13.51** Suppose $P_1$ and $P_2$ are fundamental products such that $P_1$ is contained in $P_2$. Show that $P_1 + P_2 = P_1$ and give an example.

$\blacksquare$ Since $P_1$ is contained in $P_2$, we have $P_2 = P_1 * Q$. Then, by the absorption law,

$$P_1 + P_2 = P_1 + P_1 * Q = P_1$$

For example, $x'z + x'yz = x'z$.

**13.52** Define a sum-of-products form for a Boolean expression $E$ and give examples.

$\blacksquare$ $E$ is said to be in a *sum-of-products* form or a *minterm* form if $E$ is a fundamental product or the sum of two or more fundamental products none of which is included in another. For example, consider the expressions

$$E_1 = xz' + y'z + xyz' \quad \text{and} \quad E_2 = xz' + x'yz' + xy'z$$

Although the first expression, $E_1$, is a sum of products, it is not in a sum-of-products form, since $xz'$ is contained in $xyz'$. However, by the absorption law, $E_1$ can be expressed as

$$E_1 = xz' + y'z - xyz' = xz' + xyz' + y'z = xz' + y'z$$

which is a sum-of-products form. The second expression, $E_2$, is already in a sum-of-products form.

**13.53** Give an algorithm which transforms any nonzero Boolean expression $E$ into a sum-of-products form.

▮ **Algorithm 13.53:** The input is a Boolean expression $E$.
*Step 1:* Use DeMorgan's laws and involution to move the complement operation into any parentheses until finally it applies only to variables. Then $E$ will consist only of sums and products of literals.
*Step 2:* Use the distributive law to next transform $E$ into a sum of products.
*Step 3:* Use the commutative, idempotent, and complement laws to transform each product in $E$ into 0 or a fundamental product. Finally, use the absorption law to put $E$ into a sum-of-products form.

**13.54** Transform $E = ((ab)'c)'((a' + c)(b' + c'))'$ into a sum-of-products form.

▮ Apply Algorithm 13.53 as follows:
*Step 1:* $E = ((ab)'' + c')((a' + c)' + (b' + c')') = (ab + c')(ac' + bc)$
*Step 2:* $E = abac' + abbc + ac'c' + bcc'$
*Step 3:* $E = abc' + abc + ac' + 0 = ac' + abc$

**13.55** Define a complete sum-of-products form for a Boolean expression.

▮ A (nonzero) Boolean expression $E(x_1, x_2, \ldots, x_n)$ is said to be in *complete sum-of-products form* if $E$ is in a sum-of-products form and each product involves all the variables (we note that there are a maximum of $2^n$ such products).

**Theorem 13.8:** Every nonzero Boolean expression $E(x_1, x_2, \ldots, x_n)$ can be put into complete sum-of-products form, and such a representation is unique.

**13.56** Give an algorithm which transforms a sum-of-products form of a Boolean expression into a complete sum-of-products form.

▮ **Algorithm 13.56:** The input is a Boolean expression $E(x_1, x_2, \ldots, x_n)$ in a sum-of-products form.
*Step 1:* Find a fundamental product $P$ of $E$ which does not involve the variable $x_i$ and then multiply $P$ by $x_i + x_i'$. (This is possible since $x_i + x_i' = 1$.)
*Step 2:* Repeat Step 1 until all the products in $E$ involve all the variables.

**13.57** Express $E(x, y, z) = x(y'z)'$ in complete sum-of-products form.

▮ Apply first Algorithm 13.53 and then Algorithm 13.56. First we have

$$E = x(y'z)' = x(y + z') = xy + xz'$$

and $E$ is in a sum-of-products form. Next we have

$$E = xy + xz' = xy(z + z') + x(y + y')z' = xyz + xyz' + xyz' + xy'z' = xyz + xyz' + xy'z'$$

which is in the complete sum-of-products form.

**13.58** Express $E = z(x' + y) + y'$ in complete sum-of-products form.

▮ First we have

$$E = z(x' + y) + y' = x'z + yz + y'$$

Then,

$$E = x'z + yz + y' = x'z(y + y') + yz(x + x') + y'(x + x')(z + z')$$
$$= x'yz + x'y'z + xyz + x'yz + xy'z + xy'z' + x'y'z + x'y'z'$$
$$= xyz + xy'z + xy'z' + x'yz + x'y'z + x'y'z'$$

**13.59** Express $E(x, y, z) = (x' + y)' + x'y$ in complete sum-of-products form.

▌ We have $E = (x' + y)' + x'y = xy' + x'y$, which would be the complete sum-of-products form of $E$ if $E$ were a Boolean expression in $x$ and $y$. However, it is specified that $E$ is a Boolean expression in the three variables $x$, $y$, and $z$. Hence,

$$E = xy' + x'y = xy'(z + z') + x'y(z + z') = xy'z + xy'z' + x'yz + x'yz'$$

is the complete sum of products form for $E$.

**13.60** Consider the Venn diagram of sets $A$, $B$, and $C$ given in Fig. 13-5. Observe that the universal set **U** (the rectangle) is partitioned into $2^3 = 8$ sets, which are labeled $(1)$ to $(8)$.
  **(a)** Express each of the sets in terms of $A$, $B$, and $C$.
  **(b)** Let $E(A, B, C)$ be any Boolean expression involving the sets $A$, $B$, and $C$. Give a geometrical interpretation of the complete sum-of-products form for $E$.

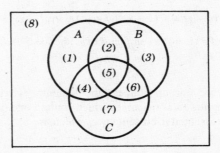

**Fig. 13-5**

▌ **(a)** Using the Boolean notations $AB$ for $A \cap B$ and $A'$ for $A^c$, each of the eight sets is a fundamental product involving $A$, $B$, and $C$:

$$
\begin{array}{llll}
(1) = AB'C' & (3) = A'BC' & (5) = ABC & (7) = A'B'C \\
(2) = ABC' & (4) = AB'C & (6) = A'BC & (8) = A'B'C'
\end{array}
$$

  **(b)** The Boolean expression $E$ is represented by the union of one or more of the areas $(1)$ through $(8)$ in Fig. 13-5. This union (sum) is unique, and yields the complete sum-of-products form for $E$.

**13.61** Write each of the following Boolean expressions $E(x, y, z)$ first as a sum of products, and then in complete sum-of-products form:
  **(a)** $E = x(xy' + x'y + y'z)$,  **(b)** $E = (x + y)'(xy')'$.

▌ **(a)** First we have $E = xxy' + xx'y + xy'z = xy' + xy'z$. Then

$$E = xy'(z + z') + xy'z = xy'z + xy'z' + xy'z = xy'z + xy'z'$$

  **(b)** First we have $E = x'y'(x' + y) = x'y'x' + x'y'y = x'y'$. Then

$$E = x'y'(z + z') = x'y'z + x'y'z'$$

**13.62** Repeat Problem 13.61 for the following:
  **(a)** $E = y(x + yz)'$  **(b)** $E = x(xy + y' + x'y)$.

▌ **(a)** $E = y(x'(yz)') = yx'(y' + z') = yx'y' + x'yz' = x'yz'$ which already is in complete sum-of-products form.
  **(b)** First we have $E = xxy + xy' + xx'y = xy + xy'$. Then

$$E = xy(z + z') + xy'(z + z') = xyz + xyz' + xy'z + xy'z'$$

**13.63** Write each set expression $E(A, B, C)$ involving sets $A$, $B$, and $C$ as a union of intersections:
  **(a)** $E = (A \cup B)^c \cap (C^c \cup B)$,  **(b)** $E = (B \cap C)^c \cap (A^c \cup C)^c$.

▌ Use the Boolean notation (as in Problem 13.46) and write $E$ as a sum of products:
  **(a)** $E = (A + B)'(C' + B) = A'B'(C' + B) = A'B'C' + A'B'B = A'B'C'$ or $E = A^c \cap B^c \cap C^c$
  **(b)** $E = (BC)'(A' + C)' = (B' + C')(AC') = AB'C' + AC'$ or $E = (A \cap B^c \cap C^c) \cup (A \cap C^c)$

**13.64** Let $E = xy' + xyz' + x'yz'$. Prove that: (a) $xz' + E = E$, (b) $x + E \neq E$, (c) $z' + E \neq E$.

▌ Since the complete sum-of-products form is unique, $A + E = E$, where $A \neq 0$, if and only if the summands in the complete sum-of-products form for $A$ are among the summands in the complete sum-of-products form for $E$. Hence, first find the complete sum-of-products form for $E$:

$$E = xy'(z + z') + xyz' + x'yz' = xy'z + xy'z' + xyz' + x'yz'$$

(a) Express $xz'$ in complete sum-of-products form:

$$xz' = xz'(y + y') = xyz' + xy'z'$$

Since the summands of $xz'$ are among those of $E$, we have $xz' + E = E$.

(b) Express $x$ in complete sum-of-products form:

$$x = x(y + y')(z + z') = xyz + xyz' + xy'z + xy'z'$$

The summand $xyz$ of $x$ is not a summand of $E$; hence $x + E \neq E$.

(c) Express $z'$ in complete sum-of-products form:

$$z' = z'(x + x')(y + y') = xyz' + xy'z' + x'yz' + x'y'z'$$

The summand $x'y'z'$ of $z'$ is not a summand of $E$; hence $z' + E \neq E$.

## 13.4 LOGIC GATES

Logic circuits are structures which are built up from certain elementary circuits called *logic gates*, some which are defined below. These circuits may be viewed as machines which contain one or more imput devices and exactly one output device. The input devices are assigned $n$-bit sequences which are processed by the circuit one bit at a time to produce an output $n$-bit sequence.

### OR Gate

**13.65** Describe the operation of an OR gate with two input devices, and also give its equivalent electrical circuit.

▌ Figure 13-6($a$) shows an OR gate with inputs $A$ and $B$ and output $Y$. The output of such an OR gate is denoted by $Y = A + B$ where "addition" is defined by Fig. 13-1($a$) or, equivalently, by the truth table in Fig. 13-6($b$). That is, $Y = 1$ if $A = 1$ or $B = 1$, and $Y = 0$ only if both $A = 0$ and $B = 0$. Figure 13-6($c$) shows an electrical circuit which contains, besides some source of energy (say, a battery) and an output device (say, a lamp), two switches $A$ and $B$ connected in parallel. Clearly, the lamp will light only when switch $A$ is closed or when switch $B$ is closed or when both switches are closed. This is precisely the property described by the truth table for the OR gate, where 1 denotes that a switch is on (closed) or that the lamp is on (lit) and 0 denotes that the switch is off (open) or that the lamp is off.

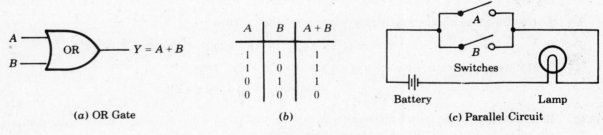

| $A$ | $B$ | $A + B$ |
|---|---|---|
| 1 | 1 | 1 |
| 1 | 0 | 1 |
| 0 | 1 | 1 |
| 0 | 0 | 0 |

(a) OR Gate      (b)      (c) Parallel Circuit

**Fig. 13-6**

**13.66** Determine how each of the following pairs of sequences of bits is processed by an OR gate:

      (a) 110001      (b) 10001111     (c) 101100111000
          101101          00111100         000111001101

▌ Recall that a 0 occurs as an output of an OR gate only where both inputs are 0. In ($a$), this occurs only in the 5th position; in ($b$), only in the 2nd position; in ($c$), only in the 2nd and 11th positions. Hence the outputs are

      (a) 111101,     (b) 10111111,    (c) 101111111101

**13.67** Determine the output of each gate in Fig. 13-7.

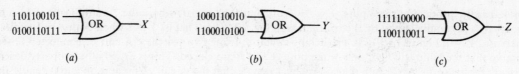

Fig. 13-7

▮ An OR gate yields a 0 only when both inputs are 0. Thus

$$X = 1101110111, \qquad Y = 1100110110, \qquad Z = 1111110011$$

**13.68** Find $Y = A + B$ when: (a) $A = 11000110$, $B = 10010101$, and (b) $A = 00001100$, $B = 11000000$.

▮ Addition yields a 0 only when both inputs are 0; hence (a) $Y = 11010111$, (b) $Y = 11001100$.

**13.69** Describe the operation of an OR gate with more than two, say four, input devices, and also give its electrical equivalent.

▮ Figure 13-8(a) shows an OR gate with four inputs, $A$, $B$, $C$, and $D$, and output $Y = A + B + C + D$. The output is 0 if and only if all inputs are 0. The analogous switching circuit appears in Fig. 13-8(b), consisting of four switches connected in parallel. Clearly, the lamp will be off only when all four switches are off (open).

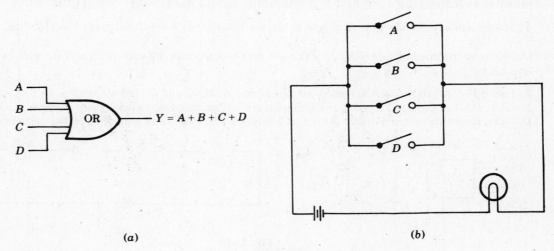

(a)

(b)

Fig. 13-8

**13.70** Find the output $Y$ of the OR gate in Fig. 13-8(a) if the input data are

$$A = 10000101, \qquad B = 10100001, \qquad C = 00100100, \qquad D = 10010101$$

▮ An OR gate yields a 0 only when all inputs are 0. This occurs only in the 2nd, 5th, and 7th positions; hence $Y = 10110101$.

## AND Gate

**13.71** Describe the operation of an AND gate with two input devices, and also give its equivalent electrical circuit.

▮ Figure 13-9(a) shows an AND gate with inputs $A$ and $B$ and output $Y$. The output of such an AND gate is

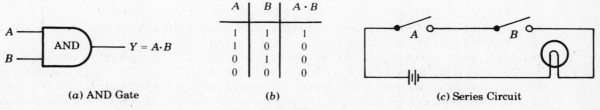

| A | B | $A \cdot B$ |
|---|---|---|
| 1 | 1 | 1 |
| 1 | 0 | 0 |
| 0 | 1 | 0 |
| 0 | 0 | 0 |

(a) AND Gate

(b)

(c) Series Circuit

Fig. 13-9

denoted as the product of the inputs, $Y = A \cdot B$ or, simply, $Y = AB$, where the "multiplication" is defined by Fig. 13-1($b$) or, equivalently, by the truth table in Fig. 13-9($b$). That is, $Y = 1$ when both $A = 1$ and $B = 1$; otherwise, $Y = 0$. Figure 13-9($c$) is a switching circuit showing two switches, $A$ and $B$, connected in series. Observe that the lamp will light only when both $A$ and $B$ are closed. This is exactly the property described by the truth table for the AND gate if again we let 1 denote that the circuit element is on and 0 denote that it is off.

**13.72**    Determine how each of the following pairs of sequences of bits is processed by an AND gate:

($a$)   110001        ($b$)   10001111        ($c$)   101100111000
        101101               00111100                000111001101

▮  Recall that a 1 occurs as an output of an AND gate only where both inputs are 1. In ($a$) this occurs only in the first and last positions; on ($b$) only in the 5th and 6th positions; in ($c$) only in the 4th and 9th positions. Hence the outputs are

($a$)   100001,        ($b$)   00001100,        ($c$)   000100001000

**13.73**    Suppose the OR gates in Fig. 13-7 are changed to AND gates. What would be the output of each gate?

▮  An AND gate yields a 1 only when both inputs are 1. Hence

$$X = 0100100101, \qquad Y = 1000010000, \qquad Z = 1100100000$$

**13.74**    Find $Y = A \cdot B$ when: ($a$) $A = 11100011$, $B = 10101010$, and ($b$) $A = 11011011$, $B = 11100111$.

▮  Multiplication yields a 1 only when both inputs are 1; hence ($a$) $Y = 10100010$, ($b$) $Y = 11000011$.

**13.75**    Describe the operation of an AND gate with more than two, say four, input devices, and also give its electrical equivalent.

▮  Figure 13-10($a$) shows an AND gate with four inputs, $A$, $B$, $C$, and $D$, and output $Y = A \cdot B \cdot C \cdot D$ or $Y = ABCD$. The output is 1 if and only if all inputs are 1. The analogous switching circuit appears in Fig. 13-10($b$), consisting of four switches in series. Clearly, the lamp will be on only when all the switches are on.

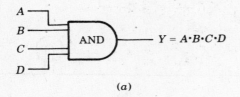
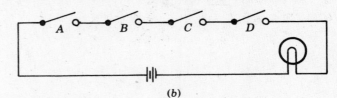

($a$)                                        ($b$)

**Fig. 13-10**

**13.76**    Find the output $Y$ of the AND gate in Fig. 13-10($a$) if the input data are

$$A = 11100111, \qquad B = 01111011, \qquad C = 01110011, \qquad D = 11101110$$

▮  An AND gate yields a 1 only when all inputs are 1. This occurs only in the 2nd, 3rd, and 7th positions; hence $Y = 01100010$.

## NOT Gate

**13.77**    Describe the operation of a NOT gate. Also, describe its equivalent electrical circuit.

▮  Figure 13-11($a$) shows a NOT gate, also called an *inverter*, with input $A$ and output $Y$. The NOT gate can have only one input, and its output is denoted by putting a bar over the input; that is,

$$Y = \bar{A}$$

The value of the output $Y$ is the opposite of the value of the input $A$; that is, $Y = 1$ when $A = 0$, and $Y = 0$ when $A = 1$. The truth table for the NOT gate appears in Fig. 13-11($b$).

Switching circuits also contain the analog of the NOT gate. Specifically, along with any switch $A$ we can include a switch $\bar{A}$ that is open when $A$ is closed and is closed when $A$ is open. This switch $\bar{A}$, pictured in Fig. 13-11($c$), is called the *complement* of the switch $A$. (We could also realize $\bar{A}$ as a lamp in parallel with switch $A$, the combination being in series with a battery. With the switch closed, the lamp would be shorted out (off); with the switch open, the lamp would be on.)

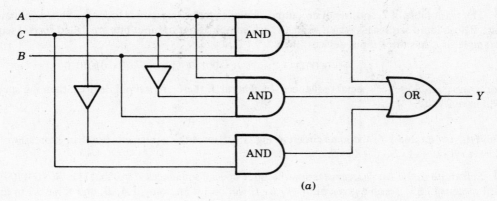

(a) NOT Gate     (b)     (c) Complement Switch     **Fig. 13-11**

**13.78** How would a NOT gate process each of the following sequences?

        (**a**) 110001,     (**b**) 10001111,     (**c**) 101100111000

    ▌A NOT gate changes 0 to 1 and 1 to 0. Hence the outputs are

        (**a**) 001110,     (**b**) 01110000,     (**c**) 010011000111

**13.79** Find $Y = \bar{A}$ when: (**a**) $A = 10101010$, (**b**) $A = 11100111$, and (**c**) $A = 00111100$.

    ▌Change 1 to 0 and 0 to 1 to obtain: (**a**) $Y = 01010101$, (**b**) $Y = 00011000$, and (**c**) $Y = 11000011$.

## 13.5 LOGIC CIRCUITS

The main content of this section is the following theorem.

**Theorem 13.9:** Logic circuits form a Boolean algebra.

**13.80** Prove Theorem 13.9.

    ▌The truth tables for the OR, AND, and NOT gates are respectively identical to those for the propositions $p \vee q$ (disjunction, "$p$ or $q$"), $p \wedge q$ (conjunction, "$p$ and $q$"), and $\sim p$ (negation, "not $p$"), which appear in Chapter 12. The only difference is that 1 and 0 are used here instead of T and F. Thus logic circuits, of which these gates are the circuit elements, satisfy the same laws as do propositions and hence they form a Boolean algebra.

**13.81** Describe an AND-OR circuit and give an example.

    ▌An AND-OR circuit, which corresponds to a Boolean sum-of-products expression, has several inputs, with some of the inputs or their complements fed into each AND gate. The outputs of all the AND gates are fed into a single OR gate which gives the output for the circuit. Figure 13-12 is a typical AND-OR circuit, with three inputs, $A$, $B$, and $C$. (Frequently, for economy of space, we omit the word from the interior of the gate symbol.)

(a)

**Fig. 13-12**

**13.82** Consider the logic circuit in Fig. 13-12. Express the output $Y$ as a Boolean expression in the inputs $A$, $B$, and $C$.

    ▌Label the first AND gate with inputs $A$, $B$, and $C$, and output $A \cdot B \cdot C$; the second AND gate with inputs $A$, $\bar{B}$, and $C$, and output $A \cdot \bar{B} \cdot C$; and the third AND gate with inputs $\bar{A}$ and $B$, and output $\bar{A} \cdot B$. See Fig. 13-13. Then the output of the OR gate, which is the output of the circuit, is the Boolean expression

$$Y = A \cdot B \cdot C + A \cdot \bar{B} \cdot C + \bar{A} \cdot B$$

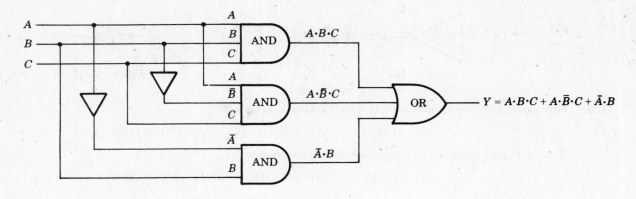

**Fig. 13-13**

**13.83**  Suppose $A = 1100110110$, $B = 1110000111$, and $C = 1010010110$. Find: **(a)** $A + B + C$, and **(b)** $A \cdot B \cdot C$.

▌ **(a)**  A 0 occurs in a sum, representing an OR gate, only where all the inputs are 0s. Note that there are three 0s only in the 4th and 7th positions. Hence

$$A + B + C = 1110110111$$

**(b)**  A 1 occurs in a product, representing an AND gate, only where all the inputs are 1s. This happens only in the 1st, 8th, and 9th positions. Hence

$$A \cdot B \cdot C = 1000000110$$

**13.84**  Given the sequences $A$, $B$, and $C$ in Problem 13.83, find: **(a)** $C(\bar{A} + B)$, **(b)** $A(\overline{B + C})$.

▌ **(a)**  Calculate step by step:

$$\bar{A} = 0011001001, \qquad \bar{A} + B = 1111001111, \qquad C(\bar{A} + B) = 1010000110$$

**(b)**  Calculate step by step:

$$B + C = 1110010111, \qquad \overline{B + C} = 0001101000, \qquad A(\overline{B + C}) = 0000100000$$

**13.85**  Define the truth table of a logic circuit $L$.

▌ The truth table of $L$ consists of an output sequence that corresponds to all possible combinations of input bits. Those input sequences which yield all such combinations of input bits are called *special* sequences. For example, if $L$ has three input devices, then

$$A = 00001111, \qquad B = 00110011, \qquad C = 01010101$$

form one possible set of special sequences. In general, if there are $n$ input devices, then the special sequences will have $2^n$ bits.

**13.86**  Find the truth table $T$ of the logic circuit in Fig. 13-13 or of the equivalent Boolean expression
$Y = A \cdot B \cdot C + A \cdot \bar{B} \cdot C + \bar{A} \cdot B$.

▌ Substitute in the Boolean expression the three special sequences $A = 00001111$, $B = 00110011$, $C = 01010101$ of Problem 13.85. Recall a given bit in $A \cdot B \cdot C$ will be 1 if and only if $A$, $B$, and $C$ have 1 in that position. Thus

$$A \cdot B \cdot C = 00000001$$

Similarly, $A \cdot \bar{B} \cdot C = 00000100$ and $\bar{A} \cdot B = 00110000$. Hence $Y = 00110101$ is the output. The truth table consists of the input sequences together with the output sequence; that is,

$$T = [A = 00001111, \ B = 00110011, \ C = 01010101, \ Y = 00110101]$$

**13.87**  Given five inputs, $A$, $B$, $C$, $D$, and $E$, find special sequences which give all the different possible combinations of input bits.

▌ Each sequence will contain $2^5 = 32$ bits. One assignment scheme is as follows:
  (i)   Let $A$ be assigned $2^4 = 16$ bits which are 0s, followed by $2^4 = 16$ bits which are 1s.
 (ii)   Let $B$ be assigned $2^3 = 8$ bits which are 0s, followed by $2^3 = 8$ bits which are 1s; and then repeat once.
(iii)   Let $C$ be assigned $2^2 = 4$ bits which are 0s, followed by $2^2 = 4$ bits which are 1s; and then repeat three times.
 (iv)   Let $D$ be assigned $2^1 = 2$ bits which are 0s, followed by $2^1 = 2$ bits which are 1s; and then repeat seven times.
  (v)   Let $E$ be assigned $2^0 = 1$ bit which is 0, followed by $2^0 = 1$ bit which is 1; and then repeat fifteen times.
The resulting special sequences are

$$A = 00000000000000001111111111111111$$
$$B = 00000000111111110000000011111111$$
$$C = 00001111000011110000111100001111$$
$$D = 00110011001100110011001100110011$$
$$E = 01010101010101010101010101010101$$

(Noting that the columns of the above array are, from left to right, the first 32 binary integers in increasing order, we have another, and perhaps simpler, assignment scheme.)

**13.88**  Given four inputs, $A$, $B$, $C$, and $D$, find special sequences which give all the different possible combinations of inputs.

▌ Each sequence will contain $2^4 = 16$ bits. Follow the pattern in Problem 13.87 to obtain

$$A = 0000000011111111$$
$$B = 0000111100001111$$
$$C = 0011001100110011$$
$$D = 0101010101010101$$

**13.89**  Given three inputs, $A$, $B$, and $C$. (**a**) find the truth tables of the eight fundamental products:

$$A \cdot B \cdot C, \quad A \cdot B \cdot \bar{C}, \quad A \cdot \bar{B} \cdot C, \quad A \cdot \bar{B} \cdot \bar{C}, \quad \bar{A} \cdot B \cdot C, \quad \bar{A} \cdot B \cdot \bar{C}, \quad \bar{A} \cdot \bar{B} \cdot C, \quad \bar{A} \cdot \bar{B} \cdot \bar{C}$$

(**b**) Use (**a**) to obtain the truth table $T$ for $Y = AB\bar{C} + \bar{A}BC$.

▌ (**a**)  Note first that the special sequences for $A$, $B$, and $C$ each contain $2^3 = 8$ bits. We have

$$A = 00001111$$
$$B = 00110011$$
$$C = 01010101$$

Then

$$\bar{A} = 11110000$$
$$\bar{B} = 11001100$$
$$\bar{C} = 10101010$$

and

$$A \cdot B \cdot C = 00000001$$
$$A \cdot B \cdot \bar{C} = 00000010$$
$$A \cdot \bar{B} \cdot C = 00000100$$
$$A \cdot \bar{B} \cdot \bar{C} = 00001000$$
$$\bar{A} \cdot B \cdot C = 00010000$$
$$\bar{A} \cdot B \cdot \bar{C} = 00100000$$
$$\bar{A} \cdot \bar{B} \cdot C = 01000000$$
$$\bar{A} \cdot \bar{B} \cdot \bar{C} = 10000000$$

It is seen that for each combination of inputs, exactly one of the eight fundamental products assumes the value 1. Thus, for $A = 0$, $B = 1$, $C = 1$ (i.e., $\bar{A} = B = C = 1$), only the product $\bar{A} \cdot B \cdot C$ equals 1. Furthermore, a given product takes on the value 1 for just one combination of inputs; that is, its truth table has 1 in exactly one position and 0s elsewhere.

**(b)** Here $Y = 1$ when $AB\bar{C} = 1$ or $\bar{A}BC = 1$, i.e., when $A = 1$, $B = 1$, $C = 0$ or when $A = 0$, $B = 1$, $C = 1$; otherwise $Y = 0$. Thus the truth table $T$ follows:

$$T = [A = 10\ldots, B = 11\ldots, C = 01\ldots, Y = 11000000]$$

(Here "…" represents the other possible combinations of bits for $A$, $B$, and $C$, for which $Y = 0$.)

**13.90**   Find a Boolean expression $Y = E(A, B, C)$ for the logic circuit in Fig. 13-14(a).

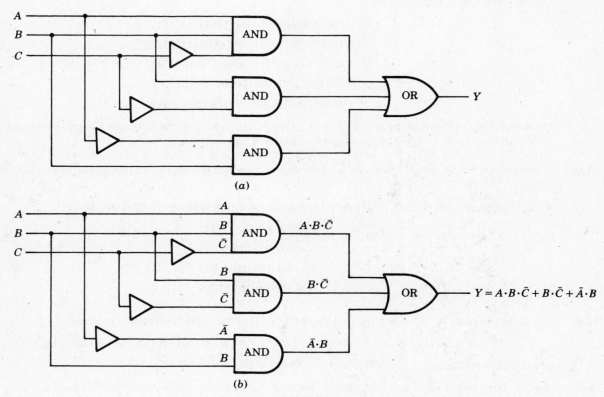

**Fig. 13-14**

▮   This is an AND-OR circuit. The inputs into the first AND gate are $A$, $B$, and $\bar{C}$; into the second AND gate are $B$ and $\bar{C}$, and into the third AND gate are $\bar{A}$ and $C$. Hence, as shown in Fig. 13-14(b),

$$Y = AB\bar{C} + B\bar{C} + \bar{A}B$$

**13.91**   Find the truth table $T$ for the logic circuit in Fig. 13-14(a) or for the equivalent Boolean expression $Y = AB\bar{C} + B\bar{C} + \bar{A}B$.

▮   Since there are three inputs, the truth table of the circuit will consist of 8-bit sequences. We calculate as follows:

$$A = 00001111 \qquad C = 01010101 \qquad \bar{C} = 10101010 \qquad B\bar{C} = 00100010$$
$$B = 00110011 \qquad \bar{A} = 11110000 \qquad AB\bar{C} = 00000010 \qquad \bar{A}B = 00110000$$

Thus $Y = 00110010$. Accordingly, the required truth table is

$$T = [A = 00001111, B = 00110011, C = 01010101, Y = 00110010]$$

**13.92**   Consider the Boolean expression $Y = AB\bar{C} + B\bar{C} + \bar{A}B$ which represents the logic circuit in Fig. 13-14. **(a)** Find the complete sum-of-products form for $Y$. **(b)** Use this form to obtain the truth table $T$ for the circuit.

▮   **(a)**   $Y = AB\bar{C} + B\bar{C}(A + \bar{A}) + \bar{A}B(C + \bar{C}) = AB\bar{C} + \bar{A}B\bar{C} + \bar{A}BC$
  **(b)**   By inspecting the complete sum-of-products form for $Y$ we see that $Y = 1$ when:

(i)   $A = 1$, $B = 1$, $C = 0$;     (ii)   $A = 0$, $B = 1$, $C = 0$;     (iii)   $A = 0$, $B = 1$, $C = 1$

Accordingly,

$$T = [A = 100\ldots, B = 111\ldots, C = 001\ldots, Y = 1110000]$$

This is the same, except for order, as the truth table in Problem 13.91.

**13.93** Express the output $Y$ as a Boolean expression in the inputs $A$, $B$, and $C$ for the logic circuit in (*a*) Fig. 13-15(*a*), and (*b*) Fig. 13-15(*b*).

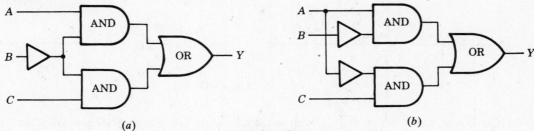

(*a*)                                                                                  (*b*)

**Fig. 13-15**

▌ (*a*)  The inputs to the first AND gate are $A$ and $\bar{B}$ and to the second AND gate are $\bar{B}$ and $C$. Hence $Y = A\bar{B} + \bar{B}C$.

    (*b*)  The inputs to the first AND gate are $A$ and $\bar{B}$ and to the second AND gate are $\bar{A}$ and $C$. Thus $Y = A\bar{B} + \bar{A}C$.

**13.94** Find the truth table $T$ for the logic circuit in (*a*) Fig. 13-15(*a*) and (*b*) Fig. 13-15(*b*).

▌ (*a*)  First write $Y = A\bar{B} + \bar{B}C$ in complete sum-of-products form:

$$Y = A\bar{B}(C + \bar{C}) + (A + \bar{A})\bar{B}C = A\bar{B}C + A\bar{B}\bar{C} + A\bar{B}C + \bar{A}\bar{B}C$$

By inspection,

$$T = [A = 1110\ldots, B = 0000\ldots, C = 1011, Y = 11110000]$$

    (*b*)  First write $Y = A\bar{B} + \bar{A}C$ in complete sum-of-products form:

$$Y = A\bar{B}(C + \bar{C}) + \bar{A}(B + \bar{B})C = A\bar{B}C + A\bar{B}\bar{C} + \bar{A}BC + \bar{A}\bar{B}C$$

By inspection,

$$T = [A = 1100\ldots, B = 0010\ldots, C = 1011, Y = 11110000]$$

**13.95** Determine a Boolean expression for each switching circuit in Fig. 13-16.

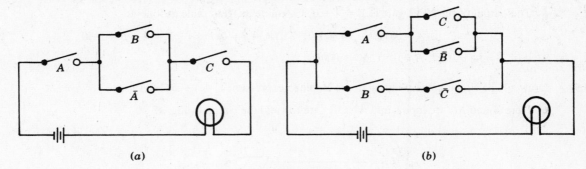

(*a*)                                                                                  (*b*)

**Fig. 13-16**

▌ Recall that we use a sum for a parallel circuit, and a product for a series circuit. Thus

      (*a*)  $A \cdot (B + \bar{A}) \cdot C$,        (*b*)  $A \cdot (C + \bar{B}) + B \cdot \bar{C}$

**13.96** Find the Boolean expression corresponding to each switching circuit in Fig. 13-17.

▌ Use a sum for a parallel circuit and a product for a series circuit to obtain (*a*) $A(D + B\bar{C})$, (*b*) $A(\bar{B} + C) + \bar{D}$.

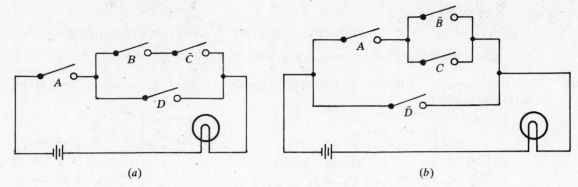

Fig. 13-17

**13.97** A NAND gate, shown in Fig. 13-18(a) with two inputs, is equivalent to an AND gate followed by a NOT gate, as shown in Fig. 13-18(b). Find the truth table $T$ for the NAND gate with inputs $A$ and $B$.

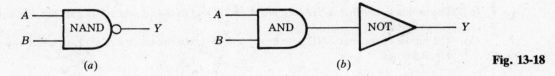

(a)                            (b)                            Fig. 13-18

❚ The output of the NAND gate is $Y = \overline{A \cdot B}$. Calculate the truth table as follows:

$$A = 0011, \quad B = 0101, \quad A \cdot B = 0001, \quad Y = \overline{A \cdot B} = 1110$$

That is, $T = [A = 0011, B = 0101, Y = 1110]$.

**13.98** A NOR gate, shown in Fig. 13-19(a) with two inputs, is equivalent to an OR gate followed by a NOT gate, as shown in Fig. 13-19(b). Find the truth table $T$ for the NOR gate with inputs $A$ and $B$.

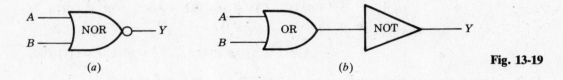

(a)                            (b)                            Fig. 13-19

❚ The output of the NOR gate is $Y = \overline{A + B}$. Calculate its truth table as follows:

$$A = 0011, \quad B = 0101, \quad A + B = 0111, \quad Y = \overline{A + B} = 1000$$

That is, $T = [A = 0011, B = 0101, Y = 1000]$.

**13.99** Draw a logic circuit corresponding to the Boolean expression $Y = \overline{A + BC} + B$.

❚ Here $A$ and $BC$ are inputs into a NOR gate to yield the circuit in Fig. 13-20.

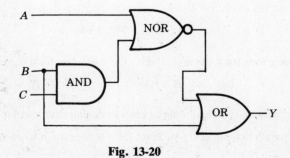

Fig. 13-20

**13.100** Draw a logic circuit corresponding to the Boolean expression $Y = \overline{AB} + \overline{A + C}$.

▮ Here $\bar{A}$ and $B$ are inputs into a NAND gate and $A$ and $C$ are inputs into a NOR gate to yield the circuit in Fig. 13-21.

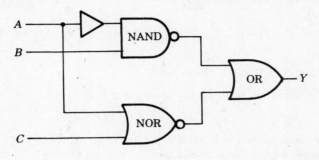

**Fig. 13-21**

## 13.6 MINIMAL BOOLEAN EXPRESSIONS, PRIME IMPLICANTS

This section defines and investigates minimal sum-of-products forms for a Boolean expression $E$, and uses the following theorem, given without proof:

**Theorem 13.10:** If a Boolean expression $E$ is in a minimal sum-of-products form, then each summand in $E$ is a prime implicant of $E$.

**13.101** For any sum-of-products Boolean expression $E$, let $E_L$ denote the number of literals in $E$ (counted according to multiplicity), and let $E_S$ denote the number of summands in $E$. Find $E_L$ and $E_S$ for each of the following:
   (**a**)  $E = xy'z + x'z' + yz' + x$          (**c**)  $E = xyt' + x'y'zt + xz't$
   (**b**)  $E = x'y'z + xyz + y + yz' + x'z$     (**d**)  $E = (xy' + z)' + xy'$

▮ Simply add up the number of literals and the number of summands in each expression:
   (**a**)                         $E_L = 3 + 2 + 2 + 1 = 8$          $E_S = 4$
   (**b**)                         $E_L = 3 + 3 + 1 + 2 + 2 = 11$     $E_S = 5$
   (**c**)                         $E_L = 3 + 4 + 3 = 10$             $E_S = 3$
   (**d**)  Because $E$ is not written as a sum of products, $E_L$ and $E_S$ are not defined.

**13.102** Given that $E$ and $F$ are each in a sum-of-products form and are equivalent Boolean expressions, define: (**a**) $E$ is simpler than $F$, (**b**) $E$ is minimal.

▮ (**a**)  $E$ is simpler than $F$ if $E_L < F_L$ and $E_S \le F_S$, or if $E_L \le F_L$ and $E_S < F_S$.
   (**b**)  $E$ is minimal if there is no equivalent sum-of-products expression which is simpler than $E$.

**13.103** Define the consensus of fundamental products.

▮ Let $P_1$ and $P_2$ be fundamental products such that exactly one variable, say $x_k$, appears complemented in one of $P_1$ and $P_2$ and uncomplemented in the other. Then the *consensus* of $P_1$ and $P_2$ is the product (without repetition) of the literals of $P_1$ and the literals of $P_2$ after $x_k$ and $x_k'$ are deleted. (We do not define a consensus of $P_1 = x$ and $P_2 = x'$.)

**13.104** Find the consensus $Q$ of $P_1$ and $P_2$ where:
   (**a**)  $P_1 = xyz's$ and $P_2 = xy't$     (**c**)  $P_1 = x'yz$ and $P_2 = x'yt$
   (**b**)  $P_1 = xy'$ and $P_2 = y$          (**d**)  $P_1 = x'yz$ and $P_2 = xyz'$

▮ (**a**)  Delete $y$ and $y'$ and then multiply the literals of $P_1$ and $P_2$ (without repetition) to obtain $Q = xz'st$.
   (**b**)  Deleting $y'$ and $y$ yields $Q = x$.
   (**c**)  They have no consensus, since no variable appears uncomplemented in one of the products and complemented in the other.
   (**d**)  They have no consensus, since *both* $x$ and $z$ appear complemented in one of the products and uncomplemented in the other.

**13.105** Suppose $Q$ is the consensus of $P_1$ and $P_2$. Prove that $P_1 + P_2 + Q = P_1 + P_2$.

▮ Since the literals commute, we can assume without loss of generality that

$$P_1 = a_1 a_2 \cdots a_r t, \qquad P_2 = b_1 b_2 \cdots b_s t', \qquad Q = a_1 a_2 \cdots a_r b_1 b_2 \cdots b_s$$

Now, $Q = Q(t + t') = Qt + Qt'$. Because $Qt$ contains $P_1$, $P_1 + Qt = P_1$; and because $Qt'$ contains $P_2$, $P_2 + Qt' = P_2$. Hence

$$P_1 + P_2 + Q = P_1 + P_2 + Qt + Qt' = (P_1 + Qt) + (P_2 + Qt') = P_1 + P_2$$

**13.106** Define prime implicants of a Boolean expression $E$.

▮ A fundamental product $P$ is called a *prime implicant of $E$* if

$$P + E = E$$

but no other fundamental product included in $P$ has this property. (Note that, in the Boolean algebra of propositions, the condition $P + E = E$ translates as "$P$ logically implies $E$"; hence the term "implicant.")

**13.107** Is $P = xz'$ a prime implicant of $E = xy' + xyz' + x'yz'$?

▮ From Problem 13.64 we have that $P + E = E$, but $x + E \neq E$ and $z' + E \neq E$. Accordingly, $P$ is a prime implicant of $E$.

**13.108** State the consensus-method algorithm. [*Remark*: A fundamental theorem in Boolean algebra states that the consensus method, applied to any Boolean sum of products $E$, will eventually stop, and then $E$ will be the sum of all its prime implicants.]

▮ **Algorithm 13.108 (Consensus Method):**  The input is a Boolean expression $E = P_1 + P_2 + \cdots + P_n$ where the $P$'s are fundamental products.
*Step 1:*  Delete any fundamental product $P_i$ which includes any other fundamental product $P_j$. (Permissible by the absorption law.)
*Step 2:*  Add the consensus $Q$ of any $P_i$ and $P_j$ providing $Q$ does not include any of the $P$'s. [Permissible by Problem 13.105.]
*Step 3:*  Repeat Step 1 and/or Step 2 until neither can be applied.

**13.109** Find the prime implicants of $E = xyz + x'z' + xyz' + x'y'z + x'yz'$.

▮ Apply the consensus method (Algorithm 13.108) to $E$:

$$
\begin{aligned}
E &= xyz + x'z' + xyz' + x'y'z & &(x'yz' \text{ includes } x'z')\\
&= xyz + x'y' + xyz' + x'y'z + xy & &(\text{Consensus of } xyz \text{ and } xyz')\\
&= x'z' + x'y'z + xy & &(xyz \text{ and } xyz' \text{ include } xy)\\
&= x'z' + x'y'z + xy + x'y' & &(\text{Consensus of } x'z' \text{ and } x'y'z)\\
&= x'z' + xy + x'y' & &(x'y'z \text{ includes } x'y')\\
&= x'z' + xy + x'y' + yz' & &(\text{Consensus of } x'z' \text{ and } xy)
\end{aligned}
$$

Observe that neither step in the consensus method can now be applied. (The consensus of the first two products includes—in fact, equals—the last product; the consensus of the last two products equals the first product.) Hence $E$ is now expressed as the sum of its prime implicants $x'z'$, $xy$, $x'y'$, and $yz'$.

**13.110** Suppose $E$ is expressed as the sum of all its prime implicants. State an algorithm that finds a minimal form for $E$.

▮ **Algorithm 13.110:**  The input is a Boolean expression $E = P_1 + P_2 + \cdots + P_n$ where the $P$'s are all the prime implicants of $E$.
*Step 1:*  Express each prime implicant in complete sum-of-products form.
*Step 2:*  Delete one by one those prime implicants whose summands appear among the summands of the remaining prime implicants.

**13.111** $E = x'z' + xy + x'y' + yz'$ is expressed as the sum of all its prime implicants. (See Problem 13.109.) Find a minimal sum for $E$.

❚ Apply Algorithm 13.4. We have

$$x'z' = x'z'(y + y') = x'yz' + x'y'z'$$

$$xy = xy(z + z') = xyz + xyz'$$

$$x'y' = x'y'(z + z') = x'y'z + x'y'z'$$

$$yz' = yz'(x + x') = xyz' + x'yz'$$

Now $x'z'$ can be deleted, since its summands, $x'yz'$ and $x'y'z'$, appear among the others. Thus

$$E = xy + x'y' + yz'$$

and this is a minimal-sum form for $E$ since none of the prime implicants is *superfluous*, i.e., can be deleted without changing $E$. Observe that, instead of $x'z'$, we might have eliminated $yz'$—which shows that the minimal sum for a Boolean expression is not necessarily unique.

**13.112**  Let $E = xy' + xyz' + x'yz'$. Find: **(a)** the prime implicants of $E$, and **(b)** a minimal sum for $E$.

❚ **(a)**  Apply Algorithm 13.108 (consensus method) to $E$ as follows:

$$
\begin{array}{ll}
E = xy' + xyz' + x'yz' + xz' & \text{(Consensus of } xy' \text{ and } xyz') \\
= xy' + x'yz' + xz' & (xyz' \text{ includes } xz') \\
= xy' + x'yz' + xz' + yz' & \text{(Consensus of } x'yz' \text{ and } xz') \\
= xy' + xz' + yz' & (x'yz' \text{ includes } yz')
\end{array}
$$

Neither step in the consensus method can now be applied. Hence $xy'$, $xz'$, and $yz'$ are the prime implicants of $E$.

**(b)**  Apply Algorithm 13.110. Write the prime implicants in complete sum-of-products form obtaining

$$xy' = xy'(z + z') = xy'z + xy'z'$$

$$xz' = xz'(y + y') = xyz' + xy'z'$$

$$yz' = yz'(x + x') = xyz' + x'yz'$$

Only the summands $xyz'$ and $xy'z'$ of $xz'$ appear among the other summands and hence $xz'$ can be eliminated as superfluous. Thus $E = xy' + yz'$ is a minimal sum for $E$.

**13.113**  Repeat Problem 13.112 for $E = xy + y't + x'yz' + xy'zt'$.

❚ **(a)**  Apply Algorithm 13.108 (consensus method) to $E$ as follows:

$$
\begin{array}{ll}
E = xy + y't + x'yz' + xy'zt' + xzt' & \text{(Consensus of } xy \text{ and } xy'zt') \\
= xy + y't + x'yz' + xzt' & (xy'zt' \text{ includes } xzt') \\
= xy + y't + x'yz' + xzt' + yz' & \text{(Consensus of } xy \text{ and } x'yz') \\
= xy + y't + xzt' + yz' & (x'yz' \text{ includes } yz') \\
= xy + y't + xzt' + yz' + xt & \text{(Consensus of } xy \text{ and } y't) \\
= xy + y't + xzt' + yz' + xt + xz & \text{(Consensus of } xzt' \text{ and } xt) \\
= xy + y't + yz' + xt + xz & (xzt' \text{ includes } xz) \\
= xy + y't + yz' + xt + xz + z't & \text{(Consensus of } y't \text{ and } yz')
\end{array}
$$

Neither step in the consensus method can now be applied. Hence the prime implicants of $E$ are $xy$, $y't$, $yz'$, $xt$, $xz$, and $z't$.

**(b)**  Apply Algorithm 13.110, that is, write each prime implicant in complete sum-of-products form and then delete one by one those which are superfluous. Finally, obtain $E = y't + xz + yz'$ as a minimal sum for $E$.

## 13.7  KARNAUGH MAPS

Karnaugh maps, where fundamental products in the same variables are represented by squares, are pictorial devices for finding prime implicants and minimal forms for Boolean expressions involving at most six variables. We will only treat the cases of two, three, and four variables. In the context of Karnaugh maps, we will sometimes use the terms "squares" and "fundamental products" interchangeably.

**13.114**  Define adjacent fundamental products.

▮  Two fundamental products $P_1$ and $P_2$ are said to be *adjacent* if $P_1$ and $P_2$ have the same variables and if they differ in exactly one literal, which must be a complemented variable in one product and uncomplemented in the other.

**13.115**  Show that the sum of two adjacent products (squares) $P_1$ and $P_2$ is a fundamental product with one less literal.

▮  Suppose $P_1 = a_1 \cdots a_r t b_1 \cdots b_s$ and $P_2 = a_1 \cdots a_r t' b_1 \cdots b_s$ where the $a$'s and $b$'s are literals and $t$ is a variable. Then

$$P_1 + P_2 = a_1 \cdots a_r (t + t') b_1 \cdots b_s = a_1 \cdots a_r (1) b_1 \cdots b_s = a_1 \cdots a_r b_1 \cdots b_s$$

which has one less literal than $P_1$ or $P_2$.

**13.116**  Find the sum of adjacent products $P_1$ and $P_2$ where:
(**a**)   $P_1 = xyz'$ and $P_2 = xy'z'$       (**c**)   $P_1 = x'yzt$ and $P_2 = xyz't$
(**b**)   $P_1 = x'yzt$ and $P_2 = x'yz't$     (**d**)   $P_1 = xyz'$ and $P_2 = xyzt$

▮  (**a**)   $P_1 + P_2 = xyz' + xy'z' = xz'(y + y') = xz'(1) = xz'$
   (**b**)   $P_1 + P_2 = x'yzt + x'yz't = x'yt(z + z') = x'yt(1) = x'yt$
   (**c**)   $P_1$ and $P_2$ are not adjacent. In particular,

$$P_1 + P_2 = x'yzt + xyz't = (x' + x)y(z + z')t = (1)y(1)t = yt$$

which has two less literals than $P_1$ or $P_2$.

   (**d**)   $P_1$ and $P_2$ are not adjacent since they have different variables. Thus, in particular, they will not appear as squares in the same Karnaugh map.

## Case of Two Variables

**13.117**  Describe the Karnaugh map for two variables.

▮  The Karnaugh map corresponding to Boolean expressions $E(x, y)$ is shown in Fig. 13-22(a). The Karnaugh map may be viewed as a Venn diagram where $x$ is represented by the points in the upper half of the map, shaded in Fig. 13-22(b), and $y$ is represented by points in the left half of the map, shaded in Fig. 13-22(c). Hence $x'$ is represented by the points in the lower half of the map, and $y'$ is represented by the points in the right half of the map. Accordingly, the four possible fundamental products with two literals,

$$xy, \qquad xy', \qquad x'y, \qquad x'y'$$

are represented by the four squares in the map, as labeled in Fig. 13-22(d). Note that two such squares are adjacent as defined above if and only if they are geometrically adjacent (have a side in common).

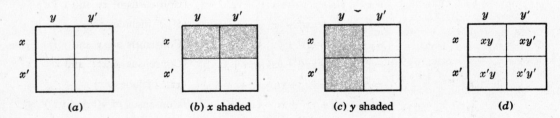

(*a*)           (*b*) *x* shaded           (*c*) *y* shaded           (*d*)

**Fig. 13-22**

**13.118**  Describe geometrically the prime implicants in a Karnaugh map with two variables.

▮  Any complete sum-of-products Boolean expression $E(x, y)$ is represented in a Karnaugh map by placing checks in the appropriate squares. A prime implicant of $E(x, y)$ will be either a pair of adjacent squares or an *isolated square*, i.e., a square which is not adjacent to any other square of $E(x, y)$.

**13.119**  Use Karnaugh maps to find the prime implicants and minimal form for each of the following complete sum-of-products Boolean expressions:

(**a**)   $E_1 = xy + xy'$,       (**b**)   $E_2 = xy + x'y + x'y'$,       (**c**)   $E_3 = xy + x'y'$

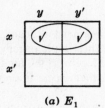
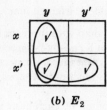
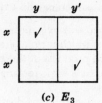

(a) $E_1$  (b) $E_2$  (c) $E_3$  **Fig. 13-23**

**▮ (a)** Check the squares corresponding to $xy$ and $xy'$ as in Fig. 13-23($a$). Note $E_1$ consists of one prime implicant, the two adjacent squares designated by the loop in Fig. 13-23($a$). This pair of adjacent squares represents the variable $x$, so $x$ is a (the only) prime implicant of $E_1$. Consequently, $E_1 = x$ is its minimal sum.

**(b)** Check the squares corresponding to $xy$, $x'y$, and $x'y'$ as in Fig. 13-23($b$). Note $E_2$ contains two pairs of adjacent squares (designated by the two loops) which include all the squares of $E_2$. The vertical pair represents $y$ and the horizontal pair represents $x'$; hence $y$ and $x'$ are the prime implicants of $E_2$. Thus $E_2 = x' + y$ is its minimal sum.

**(c)** Check the squares corresponding to $xy$ and $x'y'$ as in Fig. 13-23($c$). Note $E_3$ consists of two isolated squares which represent $xy$ and $x'y'$; hence $xy$ and $x'y'$ are the prime implicants of $E_3$ and $E_3 = xy + x'y'$ is its minimal sum.

## Case of Three Variables

**13.120** Describe the Karnaugh map for three variables.

▮ The Karnaugh map corresponding to Boolean expressions $E(x, y, z)$ is shown in Fig. 13-24($a$). Note that there are exactly eight fundamental products with three literals,

$$xyz, \quad xyz', \quad xy'z, \quad xy'z', \quad x'yz, \quad x'yz', \quad x'y'z, \quad x'y'z'$$

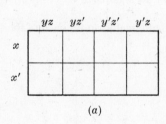
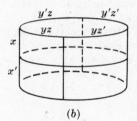

(a)  (b)  **Fig. 13-24**

and these eight fundamental products correspond to the eight squares in the Karnaugh map in the obvious way.

Furthermore, in order that every pair of adjacent products in Fig. 13-23($a$) are geometrically adjacent, the left and right edges of the map must be identified. This is equivalent to cutting out, bending, and glueing the map along the identified edges to obtain the cylinder pictured in Fig. 13-24($b$) where adjacent products are now represented by squares with one edge in common.

**13.121** Viewing the Karnaugh map with three variables, Fig. 13-24($a$), as a Venn diagram, determine the area represented by the variables $x$, $y$, and $z$.

▮ The variable $x$ is still represented by the points in the upper half of the map, as shaded in Fig. 13-25($a$), and the variable $y$ is still represented by the points in the left half of the map, as shaded in Fig. 13-25($b$). The new variable $z$ is represented by the points in the left and right quarters of the map, as shaded in Fig. 13-25($c$). Thus $x'$ is represented by points in the lower half of the map, $y'$ by the points in the right half of the map, and $z'$ by the points in the middle two quarters of the map.

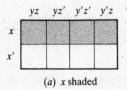
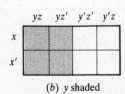
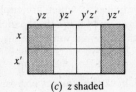

(a) $x$ shaded  (b) $y$ shaded  (c) $z$ shaded  **Fig. 13-25**

**13.122** Define a basic rectangle in a three-variable Karnaugh map.

▮ By a *basic rectangle* in the Karnaugh map with three variables, we mean a square, two adjacent squares, or four squares which form a one-by-four or a two-by-two rectangle. These basic rectangles correspond to fundamental products of three, two, and one literal, respectively. Moreover, the fundamental product represented by a basic rectangle is the product of just those literals that appear in every square of the rectangle.

**13.123** Find the fundamental product $P$ represented by each basic rectangle in the Karnaugh maps shown in Fig. 13-26.

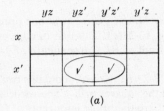 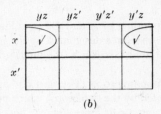 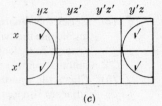

(a)          (b)          (c)

**Fig. 13-26**

▮ In each case, find those literals which appear in all the squares of the basic rectangle; $P$ is the product of such literals.

(a) $x'$ and $z'$ appear in both squares; hence $P = x'z'$.

(b) $x$ and $z$ appear in both squares; hence $P = xz$.

(c) Only $z$ appears in all four squares; hence $P = z$.

**13.124** Suppose a Boolean expression $E(x, y, z)$ is represented in a Karnaugh map, say, by checking the appropriate squares. How does one find the prime implicants of $E$ and a minimal sum for $E$?

▮ A prime implicant of $E$ will be a *maximal basic rectangle* of $E$, i.e., a basic rectangle which is not contained in any larger basic rectangle. A minimal sum for $E$ will consist of a *minimal cover* of $E$, i.e., a minimal number of maximal basic rectangles which together include all the squares of $E$.

**13.125** Use Karnaugh maps to find the prime implicants and minimal form for each of the following complete sum-of-products Boolean expressions:

(a) $E_1 = xyz + xyz' + x'yz' + x'y'z$

(b) $E_2 = xyz + xyz' + xy'z + x'yz + x'y'z$

(c) $E_3 = xyz + xyz' + x'yz' + x'y'z' + x'y'z$

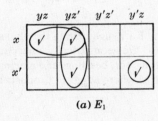 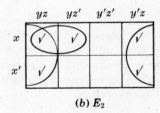 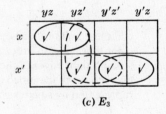

(a) $E_1$          (b) $E_2$          (c) $E_3$

**Fig. 13-27**

▮ (a) Check the squares corresponding to the four summands as in Fig. 13-27(a). Observe that $E_1$ has three prime implicants (maximal basic rectangles), which are circled; these are $xy$, $yz'$, and $x'y'z$. All three are needed to cover $E_1$; hence the minimal sum for $E_1$ is

$$E_1 = xy + yz' + x'y'z$$

(b) Check the squares corresponding to the five summands as in Fig. 13-27(b). Note that $E_2$ has two prime implicants, which are circled. One is the two adjacent squares which represents $xy$, and the other is the two-by-two square (spanning the identified edges) which represents $z$. Both are needed to cover $E_2$, so the minimal sum for $E_2$ is

$$E_2 = xy + z$$

(c) Check the squares corresponding to the five summands as in Fig. 13-27(c). As indicated by the loops,

$E_3$ has four prime implicants, $xy$, $yz'$, $x'z'$, and $x'y'$. However, only one of the two dashed ones, i.e., one of $yz'$ or $x'z'$, is needed in a minimal cover of $E_3$. Thus $E_3$ has two minimal sums:

$$E_3 = xy + yz' + x'y' = xy + x'z' + x'y'$$

## Case of Four Variables

**13.126** Describe the Karnaugh map for four variables.

❚ The Karnaugh map corresponding to Boolean expressions $E(x, y, z, t)$ is shown in Fig. 13-28. Each of the sixteen squares in the map corresponds to one of the following sixteen fundamental products,

$$xyzt, \quad xyzt', \quad xyz't', \quad xyz't, \quad xy'zt, \quad \ldots, \quad x'yz't$$

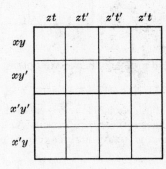

Fig. 13-28

as indicated by the labels of the row and column of the square. Observe that the top line and the left side are labeled so that adjacent products differ in precisely one literal. Again we must identify the left edge with the right edge (as we did with three variables) but we must also identify the top edge with the bottom edge. (These identifications give rise to a donut-shaped surface called a *torus*, and we may view our map as really being a torus.)

**13.127** Define a basic rectangle in a four-variable Karnaugh map. How are the basic rectangles related to the prime implicants and a minimal form for a Boolean expression?

❚ A basic rectangle is a square, two adjacent squares, four squares which form a one-by-four or two-by-two rectangle, or eight squares which form a two-by-four rectangle. These rectangles correspond to fundamental products with four, three, two, and one literal respectively. Again, maximal basic rectangles are the prime implicants. The minimization technique for a Boolean expression $E(x, y, z, t)$ is the same as before.

**13.128** Find the fundamental product $P$ represented by each basic rectangle in the Karnaugh maps shown in Fig. 13-29.

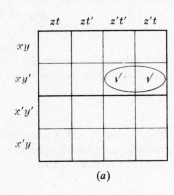 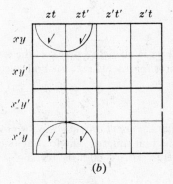 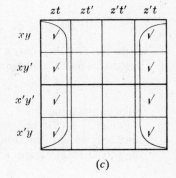

$(a)$ $\qquad\qquad\qquad\qquad$ $(b)$ $\qquad\qquad\qquad\qquad$ $(c)$

Fig. 13-29

❚ In each case, find those literals which appear in all the squares of the basic rectangle; $P$ is the product of such literals.

**(a)** $x$, $y'$, and $z'$ appear in both squares; hence $P = xy'z'$.

**(b)** Only $y$ and $z$ appear in all four squares; hence $P = yz$.

**(c)** Only $t$ appears in all eight squares; hence $P = t$.

**13.129**  Let $E$ be the Boolean expression given in the Karnaugh map in Fig. 13-30. **(a)** Write $E$ in its complete sum-of-products form. **(b)** Find a minimal form for $E$.

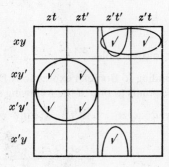

**Fig. 13-30**

▮  **(a)**  List the seven fundamental products checked to obtain

$$E = xyz't' + xyz't + xy'zt + xy'zt' + x'y'zt + x'y'zt' + x'yz't'$$

**(b)**  The two-by-two maximal basic rectangle represents $y'z$ since only $y'$ and $z$ appear in all four squares. The horizontal pair of adjacent squares represents $xyz'$, and the adjacent squares overlapping the top and bottom edges represent $yz't'$. As all three rectangles are needed for a minimal cover,

$$E = y'z + xyz' + yz't'$$

is the minimal sum for $E$.

**13.130**  Find minimal sums for the Boolean expressions $E_1$ and $E_2$ in variables $x$, $y$, $z$, $t$ which are given by the Karnaugh maps in Fig. 13-31.

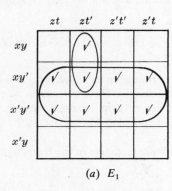  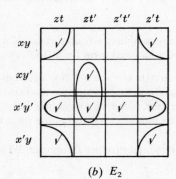

(a) $E_1$              (b) $E_2$              **Fig. 13-31**

▮  In Fig. 13-31(a), only $y'$ appears in all eight squares of the two-by-four maximal basic rectangle, and the designated pair of adjacent squares represents $xzt'$. As both rectangles are needed for a minimal cover,

$$E_1 = y' + xzt'$$

is the minimal sum for $E_1$.

   In Fig. 13-31(b), the four corner squares form a two-by-two maximal basic rectangle which represents $yt$, since only $y$ and $t$ appear in all the four squares. The four-by-one maximal basic rectangle represents $x'y'$, and the two adjacent squares represent $y'zt'$. As all three rectangles are needed for a minimal cover,

$$E_2 = yt + x'y' + y'zt'$$

is the minimal sum for $E_2$.

**13.131**  Use a Karnaugh map to find a minimal sum for $E = xy' + xyz + x'y'z' + x'yzt'$.

▮  Check all the squares representing each fundamental product. That is, check all four squares representing $xy'$, the two squares representing $xyz$, the two squares representing $x'y'z'$, and the one square representing $x'yzt'$, as in Fig. 13-32. A minimal cover of the map consists of the three designated maximal basic rectangles.

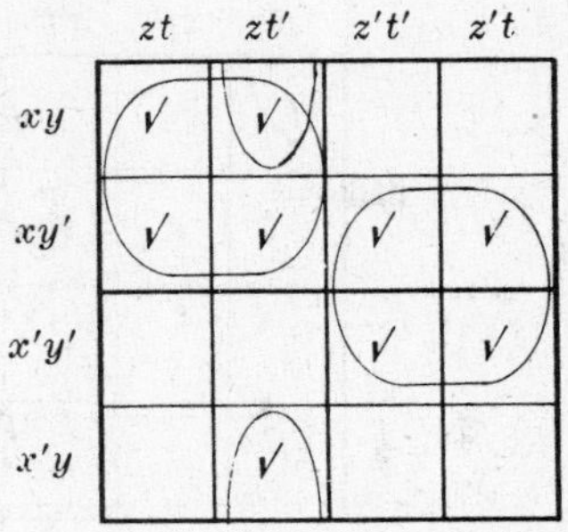

Fig. 13-32

Hence

$$E = xz + y'z' + yzt'$$

is a minimal sum for $E$.

**13.132** Use a Karnaugh map to find a minimal sum for $E = y't' + y'z' + yzt' + x'y'zt$.

▌ Check the four squares corresponding to the fundamental product $y't'$, the four squares corresponding to $y'z'$, the two squares corresponding to $yzt'$, and the one square corresponding to $x'y'zt$. This gives the Karnaugh map in Fig. 13-33. A minimal cover consists of the three designated maximal basic rectangles. Thus $E = zt' + y'z' + x'y'$ is a minimal sum for $E$.

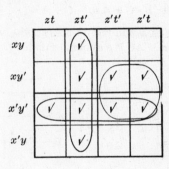

Fig. 13-33

**13.133** Find a minimal sum for the expression $E$ represented by the Karnaugh map in Fig. 13-34.

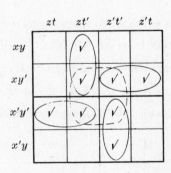

Fig. 13-34

▌ There are five prime implicants, designated by the four loops and the dashed circle. However, the dashed circle is not needed to cover all the squares, whereas the four loops are required.

Thus the four loops give the minimal sum for $E$; that is, $E = xzt' + xy'z' + x'y'z + x'z't'$.

**13.134** Find a minimal sum for the expression $E$ represented by the Karnaugh map in Fig. 13-35.

▌ There are five prime implicants, designated by the five loops of which two are dashed. Only one of the two dashed loops is needed to cover the $x'y'z't'$ square. Thus

$$E = x'y + yt + xy't' + y'z't' = x'y + yt + xy't' + x'z't'$$

are two minimal sums for $E$.

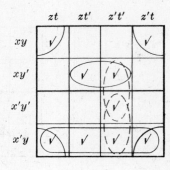

**Fig. 13-35**

## 13.8 MINIMAL AND-OR CIRCUITS

**13.135** What is a minimal AND-OR circuit?

▮ An AND-OR circuit is said to be *minimal* if the corresponding Boolean expression is a minimal sum.

**13.136** Design a three-input minimal AND-OR circuit $L$ that will have the following truth table:

$$T = [A = 00001111, \ B = 00110011, \ C = 01010101, \ L = 11001101]$$

▮ From the truth table we can read off the complete sum-of-products form for $L$:

$$L = \bar{A} \cdot \bar{B} \cdot \bar{C} + \bar{A} \cdot \bar{B} \cdot C + A \cdot \bar{B} \cdot \bar{C} + A \cdot \bar{B} \cdot C + A \cdot B \cdot C$$

The associated Karnaugh map is shown in Fig. 13-36(a). Observe that $L$ has two prime implicants, $\bar{B}$ and $AC$, in its minimal cover; hence $L = \bar{B} + AC$ is a minimal sum for $L$. Figure 13-36(b) gives the corresponding minimal AND-OR circuit for $L$.

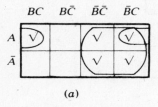

(a)

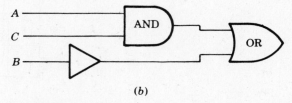

(b)

**Fig. 13-36**

**13.137** Design a minimal AND-OR circuit which yields the following truth table:

$$T = [A = 00001111, \ B = 00110011, \ C = 01010101, \ L = 10101001]$$

▮ From the truth table we have the complete sum-of-products representation

$$L = \bar{A} \cdot \bar{B} \cdot \bar{C} + \bar{A} \cdot B \cdot \bar{C} + A \cdot \bar{B} \cdot \bar{C} + A \cdot B \cdot C$$

The Karnaugh map of $L$ is shown in Fig. 13-37(a). There are three prime implicants, as indicated by the three

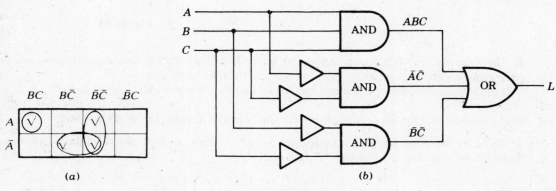

(a)

(b)

**Fig. 13-37**

loops. Hence $L = ABC + \bar{A}\bar{C} + \bar{B}\bar{C}$ is a minimal sum for $L$; the corresponding minimal AND-OR circuit is shown in Fig. 13-37($b$).

**13.138** Redesign the circuit $L$ in Fig. 13-38($a$) so that it becomes a minimal AND-OR circuit.

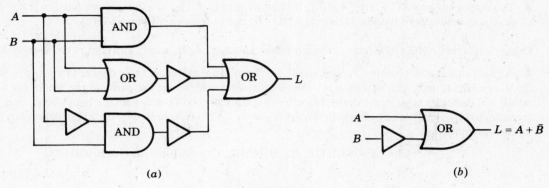

**Fig. 13-38**

▮ First, find the output of the circuit by successively labeling the input(s) and output of each gate until reaching the output $L = AB + \overline{(A + B)} + \bar{A}B$. Applying DeMorgan's laws and the absorption laws yields

$$L = AB + \bar{A}\bar{B} + A + \bar{B} = A + \bar{B}$$

The final expression is obviously a minimal sum for $L$. Figure 13-38($b$) shows the corresponding minimal AND-OR circuit.

**13.139** Redesign the circuit $L$ in Fig. 13-39($a$) so that it becomes a minimal AND-OR circuit.

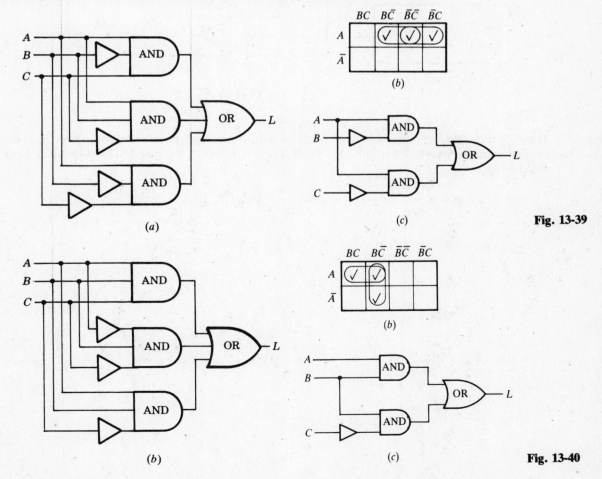

**❚** The output is $L = A\bar{B}C + AB\bar{C} + A\bar{B}\bar{C}$. Its Karnaugh map in Fig. 13-39(b) shows that $L = A\bar{B} + A\bar{C}$ is a minimal sum whose corresponding minimal AND-OR circuit is shown in Fig. 13-39(c).

**13.140** Redesign the circuit $L$ in Fig. 13-40(a) so that it becomes a minimal AND-OR circuit.

**❚** The output is $L = ABC + ABC + ABC$. Its Karnaugh map in Fig. 13-40(b) shows that $L = AB + B\bar{C}$ is a minimal sum whose corresponding minimal AND-OR circuit is shown in Fig. 13-40(c).

**13.141** Design a minimal AND-OR circuit $L$ whereby three switches, $A$, $B$, and $C$, can control the same hall light.

**❚** A given switch may be either "up" (closed) or "down" (open), respectively denoted by 1 and 0. Whatever the state of the three switches, a change in any single switch will change the parity of the number of 1s. The circuit will therefore achieve the desired function if it associates odd parity with the light's being "on" (represented by 1) and even parity with the lights's being "off" (represented by 0). These conditions yield the following truth table:

$$T = [A = 00001111, \quad B = 00110011, \quad C = 01010101, \quad L = 01101001]$$

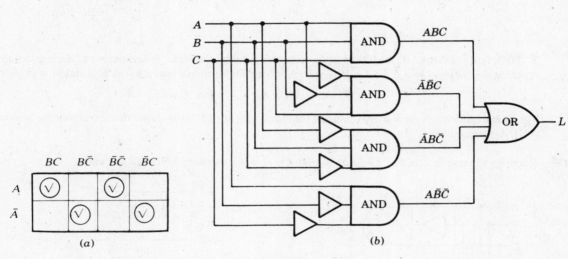

**Fig. 13-41**

From the truth table we obtain $L = \bar{A}\bar{B}C + \bar{A}B\bar{C} + A\bar{B}\bar{C} + ABC$ and this is a minimal sum for $L$, as may be verified from the Karnaugh map in Fig. 13-41(a). The corresponding minimal AND-OR circuit is shown in Fig. 13-41(b).

# Index

*Items are indexed by problem numbers.*